Global Issues

2 0 1 0   E D I T I O N

Global Issues

CQ PRESS

A Division of SAGE
Washington, D.C.

SELECTIONS FROM CQ RESEARCHER

CQ Press
2300 N Street, NW, Suite 800
Washington, DC 20037

Phone: 202-729-1900; toll-free, 1-866-4CQ-PRESS (1-866-427-7737)

Web: www.cqpress.com

Cover design: RichDesign Studio
Cover photo: Corbis/Paul Souders

⊗ The paper used in this publication exceeds the requirements of the American National Standard for Information Sciences—Permanence of Paper for Printed Library Materials, ANSI Z39.48-1992.

Printed and bound in the United States of America

14   13   12   11   10   1   2   3   4   5

A CQ Press College Division Publication

Executive director	Brenda Carter
Editorial director	Charisse Kiino
Acquisitions editor	Elise Frasier
Development editor	Dwain Smith
Marketing manager	Christopher O'Brien
Composition	C&M Digitals (P) Ltd.
Managing editor	Stephen Pazdan
Production editor	Belinda Josey
Production manager	Paul Pressau

ISBN: 978-1-60426-518-7
ISSN: 1559-8047

Contents

Annotated Contents

The 16 *CQ Researcher* reports reprinted in this book have been reproduced essentially as they appeared when first published. In the few cases in which important developments have since occurred, updates are provided in the overviews highlighting the principal issues examined.

CONFLICT, SECURITY AND TERRORISM

Afghanistan Dilemma

More than eight years ago, U.S. forces first entered Afghanistan to pursue the al-Qaida terrorists who plotted the September 11 terror attacks. American troops are still there today, along with thousands of NATO troops. Under a new strategy crafted by the Obama administration, military leaders are trying to deny terrorists a permanent foothold in the impoverished Central Asian country and in neighboring, nuclear-armed Pakistan, whose western border region has become a sanctuary for Taliban and al-Qaida forces. The Afghanistan-Pakistan conflict—"Af-Pak" in diplomatic parlance—poses huge challenges ranging from rampant corruption within Afghanistan's police force to a multibillion-dollar opium economy that funds the insurgency. But those problems pale in comparison with the ultimate nightmare scenario: Pakistan's nuclear weapons falling into the hands of terrorists, which foreign-policy experts say has become a real possibility.

U.S. Policy on Iran

The George W. Bush administration turned up the heat on Iran in October 2007. President Bush said Iran's nuclear program raised the specter of World War III. Vice President Cheney warned of "serious consequences" if Iran stayed on course as a "terror-supporting state." The heated rhetoric is widely seen as having been calculated to raise the specter of military action against Iran. Indeed, President Mahmoud Ahmadinejad calls the United States an international bully that's keeping Iraq violent to justify continued occupation. He also vows to maintain Iran's nuclear development program, which he says is not for creating weapons. But many observers—Israelis in particular—see the effort as a grave threat, prompting some U.S. hawks to advocate a preemptive strike on Iran's nuclear facilities. Other Iran-watchers say military action could further endanger U.S. forces fighting next door in Iraq. They urge the administration in the United States to aid dissidents rather than counter Iran by military force.

Prosecuting Terrorists

President Barack Obama is under fierce political attack for the administration's decision to try Khalid Sheikh Mohammed, the alleged mastermind of the September 11 attacks, and Umar Farouk Abdulmutallab, the so-called Christmas Day bomber, in civilian courts instead of military tribunals. Republican lawmakers argue the defendants in both cases should be treated as "enemy combatants" and tried in the military commissions established during the George W. Bush administration. Administration officials and Democratic lawmakers say criminal prosecutions are more effective, having produced hundreds of convictions since 9/11 compared to only three in the military system. And they insist that Abdulmutallab is providing useful information under interrogation by FBI agents. But the administration is reconsidering Attorney General Eric Holder's original decision to hold Mohammed's trial in New York City and considering making greater use of military commissions with other terrorism cases.

Terrorism and the Internet

A decade ago, terrorist organizations operated or controlled only about a dozen Web sites. Today there are more than 7,000. Terrorist groups use the Internet for many activities, ranging from raising funds to explaining how to build a suicide bomb. They find the Internet appealing for the same reasons everyone else does: it's cheap, easily accessible, unregulated and reaches a potentially enormous audience. As terrorist content spreads to chat rooms, blogs, user groups, social networking sites and virtual worlds, many experts, politicians and law enforcement officials are debating how government and industry should respond. Some want Internet companies to stop terrorists from using the Web; others say that is not the role of Internet service providers. As governments enact laws based on the belief that the Internet plays a significant role in promoting terrorism, critics say the new measures often overstep free-speech and privacy rights.

Nuclear Disarmament

Peace activists have sought to eliminate nuclear weapons for decades, but now they have a new ally. President Barack Obama has pledged to negotiate new U.S.-Russian arms reductions, end U.S. nuclear testing and reduce the role of nuclear weapons in national defense policy. Obama argues that these steps, plus new measures to combat nuclear smuggling and theft, will make the United States safer. But critics say further nuclear cuts will embolden rogue countries like North Korea and Iran, which are widely thought to be seeking nuclear capabilities. Although the United States and Russia have drastically shrunk their Cold War arsenals, the United States still spends at least $52 billion annually on nuclear-related programs. Liberals and conservatives sharply disagree about addressing post–Cold War security threats with nuclear arms. Some experts warn that new, regional nuclear arms races could break out if the United States fails to rebuild global support for nuclear reductions.

Attacking Piracy

After centuries of inactivity, piracy has returned with a vengeance. Maritime marauders now operate across the globe from Peru to the Philippines, but they pose the biggest threat off the coast of Somalia—a failed state in the Horn of Africa. In the first six months of 2009, attacks by Somali pirates jumped sixfold over the same period in the previous year. Piracy costs global shippers $10 billion to $50 billion a year in ransoms, lost cargoes, higher insurance premiums and disrupted shipping schedules—costs that are passed on to consumers. The world's largest navies have sent warships to the Horn of Africa in recent months and have captured more than 100 pirates. But it may be too costly to maintain the naval patrols over the long term. In addition, murky anti-piracy laws and jurisdictional issues are hampering prosecutions. Moreover, some security experts fear pirates may be exposing vulnerabilities that terrorists could exploit to disrupt global trade, raising the stakes in the fight to solve a growing international problem.

The Troubled Horn of Africa

Plagued by conflict, poverty and poor governance, the Horn of Africa is arguably the most troubled corner of the world's poorest continent. In desperately poor Somalia, a 19-year civil war has forced more than a million people from their homes, leaving behind a safe haven for pirates and, possibly, Islamic terrorists. In Ethiopia, an increasingly authoritarian, Western-backed government has jailed opposition leaders and clamped down on the press and human rights activists. In tiny Eritrea, a government that once won the admiration of legions of Western diplomats and journalists for its self-sufficiency and discipline has become an isolated dictatorship. The early 2009 withdrawal of Ethiopian troops from Somalia and the election of a moderate leader to the country's transitional government have raised international hopes that the lawlessness there will be brought under control. But Somalia's new government faces an insurgency from radical Islamists and worldwide pressure to stop the increasingly aggressive pirates who terrorize cargo ship crews off Somalia's coast and find refuge in its seaside villages.

Middle East Peace Prospects

Three major events reshaped the political landscape of the Middle East during a seven-week period beginning in late 2008. Israel launched a devastating 22-day assault on Gaza to halt ongoing Palestinian rocket and mortar fire, Israeli parliamentary elections displayed growing disenchantment with the peace process and President Barack Obama moved into the White House promising to try to help resolve the Arab-Israeli conflict after more than six decades of violence. Obama's pledge raised hopes in some quarters for a revival of peace talks that have been in limbo since the controversial Gaza war began in December 2008. But Israel's political shift to the right and deep, continuing Palestinian divisions raise the prospect of continued stalemate. Years of talks and several interim agreements have failed to encourage either side that it can eventually get what it wants. Israelis, pursuing

security, remain the target of militant attacks, while impoverished Palestinians—seeking a state of their own—effectively remain under Israeli control.

INTERNATIONAL POLITICAL ECONOMY

Evaluating Microfinance

Since the 1980s, millions of impoverished people around the world without access to banks have been able to take out tiny loans to start businesses. Nobel Prize–winning economist Muhammad Yunus, who established the first microfinance bank in Bangladesh and launched the modern microlending movement, claims microloans have lifted millions—especially women—out of poverty and spurred economic growth. But recent studies cast doubt on microcredit's effectiveness. Borrowers have been saddled with multiple loans at exorbitant interest rates, often having to borrow from loan sharks to make their microcredit payments. Economists fear overindebtedness could make borrowers even poorer and that a possible credit bubble could burst. Others worry that in recent years, for-profit investors have swarmed into the field, attracted by high returns on investment. Some governments have capped microlenders' interest rates, but the industry hopes to forestall regulation by adopting voluntary consumer protection measures.

Fixing Capitalism

Signs of life in stock markets around the globe stirred hopes that the world may have dodged a catastrophic financial bullet. But a long, hard road to recovery lies ahead, experts say, and the casualties of the meltdown are still being counted. Chief among them is the version of laissez-faire, self-policing market capitalism that held sway for a quarter-century. That model crashed in 2008 after raging global speculation in volatile, debt-financed securities raced through the poorly regulated "shadow" banking system that links financial centers in the United States, Europe and Asia. "Freewheeling capitalism" is dead, concluded British Finance Minister Alistair Darling. But a debate has just begun over what might take its place. World leaders have assembled for summit meetings. Studies have flown off presses. But there is only limited agreement on goals for financial and banking reforms, and as yet no prospect for binding international market rules.

Future of Globalization

Global trade has plummeted in recent months by rates not seen since the Great Depression. The World Trade Organization announced that trade tumbled by 12 percent in 2009 alone, the biggest contraction since World War II. While countries so far have avoided the kind of disastrous trade wars that marked the 1930s, protectionist measures and nationalist sentiments are rising across the globe, reflected in the original "Buy American" provision of the U.S. government's economic stimulus package. Clearly, globalization, so recently hailed in books like Thomas Friedman's best-selling *The World Is Flat,* has stalled. Some economic historians even believe the world is entering an era of "deglobalization," with nations turning inward economically and culturally, which could lead to a dangerous increase in international tensions. Other analysts say the economic, technological and social ties that bind nations to each other have grown so strong that globalization is an irreversible phenomenon that will help the global economy recover.

U.S.-China Relations

Disputes that have bedeviled relations between the United States and China for decades flared up again following President Barack Obama's decision to sell weapons to Taiwan and receive Tibet's revered Dalai Lama. From the U.S. perspective, China's refusal to raise the value of its currency is undermining U.S.—and European—economic recovery. Beijing also rebuffed Obama's proposal of "a partnership on the big global issues of our time." In addition, the Chinese insist on tackling their pollution problems in their own way and have been reluctant to support U.S. diplomatic efforts to impose tough sanctions on nuclear-minded Iran. With the central bank of China holding more than $800 billion of the U.S. national debt in the form of Treasury notes, and the country's economy speeding along at a 9 percent growth rate, the Chinese are in no mood to be accommodating.

INTERNATIONAL ISSUES

Women's Rights

Women around the world have made significant gains in the past decade, but tens of millions still face significant and often appalling hardship. Most governments now have gender-equality commissions, electoral gender quotas and laws to protect women against violence. But progress has been mixed. A record number of women now serve in parliaments, but only 14 of the world's 193 countries currently have elected female leaders. Globalization has produced more jobs for women, but they still constitute 70 percent of the world's poorest inhabitants and 64 percent of the world's illiterate. Spousal abuse, female infanticide, genital mutilation, forced abortions, bride-burnings, acid attacks and sexual slavery remain pervasive in some countries, and rape and sexual mutilation have reached epic proportions in the war-torn Democratic Republic of the Congo. Experts say that without greater economic, political and educational equality, the plight of women will not improve, and society will continue suffering the consequences.

Aiding Refugees

Some 42 million people worldwide have been uprooted by warfare or other violence, including 16 million refugees who are legally protected because they left their home countries. Most live in refugee camps and receive aid from the United Nations or other agencies but cannot work or leave the camps without special permission. Another 26 million people who fled violence are not protected by international treaties because they remained in their home countries. The number of such "internally displaced persons" (IDPs) has risen in the last decade, largely due to wars in Africa, Iraq, Afghanistan and Colombia. Millions of IDPs live in harsh conditions, and many receive no aid. Some critics say the U.N. High Commissioner for Refugees should do much more for IDPs, but the agency already faces severe budget shortfalls and bleak prospects for more donations from wealthy nations. Meanwhile, scientists warn that the number of people displaced by natural disasters—now about 50 million a year—could rise dramatically in coming years due to climate change.

Rewriting History

Every nation argues about its own history, seeking to find glory and a sense of identity by celebrating its heroes while downplaying the dark side of the past. Nations also argue with each other about the past, with one side's glorious victory still rankling as the other's ignominious defeat. Frequently, a neighboring country that has been harmed by another's actions complains that the guilty nation is whitewashing the worst incidents. A current attempt to normalize relations between Turkey and Armenia is proving a tough sell due to arguments about a mass slaughter that occurred more than 90 years ago. Russia and its neighbors are engaged in heated debates about revealing the crimes of the Stalinist era. Like individuals, nations need to confront their own ghosts, but finding the balance between acknowledging past wrongdoing and learning to get along in the present can be a difficult feat. Such conflicts raise a fundamental philosophical question: Is historical accountability a human right?

Climate Change

Delegates from around the globe arrived in Copenhagen, Denmark, for the U.N. Climate Change Conference in December 2009 hoping to forge a significant agreement to reduce greenhouse gas emissions and temper climate change. But despite years of diplomatic preparation, two weeks of intense negotiations and a clamor for action from thousands of protesters outside the meeting, the conferees adopted no official treaty. Instead, a three-page accord—cobbled together on the final night by President Barack Obama and the leaders of China, India, Brazil and South Africa—established only broad, nonbinding goals and postponed tough decisions. Yet defenders of the accord praised it for requiring greater accountability from emerging economies such as China, protecting forests and committing billions in aid to help poorer nations. But the key question remains: Will the accord help U.N. efforts to forge a legally binding climate change treaty for the world's nations?

Preface

In this pivotal era of international policymaking, scholars, students, practitioners and journalists seek answers to such critical questions as: Is the recession triggering deglobalization? Should Web sites that promote terrorism be shut down? Will the Copenhagen Accord slow global warming? Students must first understand the facts and contexts of these and other global issues if they are to analyze and articulate well-reasoned positions.

The 2010 edition of *Global Issues* provides comprehensive and unbiased coverage of today's most pressing global problems. This edition is a compilation of 16 recent reports from *CQ Researcher,* a weekly policy brief that unpacks difficult concepts and provides balanced coverage of competing perspectives. Each article analyzes past, present and possible future political maneuvering; is designed to promote in-depth discussion and further research; and helps readers formulate their own positions on crucial international issues.

This collection is organized into three subject areas that span a range of important international policy concerns: conflict, security and terrorism; international political economy; and international issues. Fourteen of these reports are new to this edition.

Global Issues is a valuable supplement for courses on world affairs in political science, geography, economics and sociology. Citizens, journalists and business and government leaders also turn to it to become better informed on key issues, actors and policy positions.

CQ RESEARCHER

CQ Researcher was founded in 1923 as *Editorial Research Reports* and was sold primarily to newspapers as a research tool. The magazine was renamed and redesigned in 1991 as *CQ Researcher*. Today, students are its primary audience. While still used by hundreds of journalists and newspapers, many of which reprint portions of the reports, *Researcher's* main subscribers are now high school, college and public libraries. In 2002, *Researcher* won the American Bar Association's coveted Silver Gavel Award for magazine excellence for a series of nine reports on civil liberties and other legal issues.

Researcher staff writers—all highly experienced journalists—sometimes compare the experience of writing a *Researcher* report to drafting a college term paper. Indeed, there are many similarities. Each report is as long as many term papers—about 11,000 words—and is written by one person without any significant outside help. One of the key differences is that the writers interview leading experts, scholars and government officials for each issue.

Like students, staff writers begin the creative process by choosing a topic. Working with *Researcher's* editors, the writer identifies a controversial subject that has important public policy implications. After a topic is selected, the writer embarks on one to two weeks of intense research. Newspaper and magazine articles are clipped or downloaded, books are ordered and information is gathered from a wide variety of sources, including interest groups, universities and the government. Once the writers are well informed, they develop a detailed outline and begin the interview process. Each report requires a minimum of ten to fifteen interviews with academics, officials, lobbyists and people working in the field. Only after all interviews are completed does the writing begin.

CHAPTER FORMAT

Each issue of *CQ Researcher,* and therefore each selection in this book, is structured in the same way. A selection begins with an introductory overview, which is briefly explored in greater detail in the rest of the report.

The second section chronicles the most important and current debates in the field. It is structured around a number of key issues questions, such as "Should the U.N. help more displaced people?" and "Do small loans for poor entrepreneurs help end poverty?" This section is the core of each selection. The questions raised are often highly controversial and usually the object of much argument among scholars and practitioners. Hence, the answers provided are never conclusive, but rather detail the range of opinion within the field.

Following those issue questions is the "Background" section, which provides a history of the issue being examined. This retrospective includes important legislative and executive actions and court decisions to inform readers on how current policy evolved.

Next, the "Current Situation" section examines important contemporary policy issues, legislation under consideration and action being taken. Each selection ends with an "Outlook" section that gives a sense of what new regulations, court rulings and possible policy initiatives might be put into place in the next five to ten years.

Each report contains features that augment the main text: sidebars that examine issues related to the topic, a pro/con debate by two outside experts, a chronology of key dates and events and an annotated bibliography that details the major sources used by the writer.

CUSTOM OPTIONS

Interested in building your ideal CQ Press Issues book, customized to your personal teaching needs and interests? Browse by course or date, or search for specific topics or issues from our online catalog of *CQ Researcher* issues at http://custom.cqpress.com.

ACKNOWLEDGMENTS

We wish to thank many people for helping to make this collection a reality. Thomas J. Colin, managing editor of *CQ Researcher*, gave us his enthusiastic support and cooperation as we developed this edition. He and his talented staff of editors and writers have amassed a first-class collection of *Researcher* articles, and we are fortunate to have access to this rich cache. We also thankfully acknowledge the advice and feedback from current readers and are gratified by their satisfaction with the book.

Some readers may be learning about *CQ Researcher* for the first time. We expect that many readers will want regular access to this excellent weekly research tool. For subscription information or a no-obligation free trial of *Researcher*, please contact CQ Press at www.cqpress.com or toll-free at 1-866-4CQ-PRESS (1-866-427-7737).

We hope that you will be pleased by the 2010 edition of *Global Issues*. We welcome your feedback and suggestions for future editions. Please direct comments to Elise Frasier, Acquisitions Editor for International Relations and Comparative Politics, College Publishing Group, CQ Press, 2300 N Street, NW, Suite 800, Washington, DC 20037; or send e-mail to efrasier@cqpress.com.

—The Editors of CQ Press

Contributors

Thomas J. Colin, managing editor of *CQ Researcher,* has been a magazine and newspaper journalist for more than 30 years. Before joining Congressional Quarterly in 1991, he was a reporter and editor at the *Miami Herald* and *National Geographic* and editor in chief of *Historic Preservation.* He holds a bachelor's degree in English from the College of William and Mary and in journalism from the University of Missouri.

Irwin Arieff is a veteran journalist now freelancing in New York City. He served for 23 years as a correspondent for the Reuters news agency in Washington, Paris, and New York and at the United Nations. During more than four decades as a writer and editor—including five years writing for the *CQ Weekly*—Arieff covered subjects ranging from international affairs, the White House and U.S. politics to science and medicine, the television industry and financial market regulation. He has a master's degree in journalism from Northwestern University's Medill School.

Peter Behr recently retired from *The Washington Post,* where he was the principal reporter on energy issues and served as business editor from 1987–1992. A former Nieman Fellow at Harvard University, Behr worked at the Woodrow Wilson Center for Scholars and is working on a book about the history of the U.S. electric power grid.

Thomas J. Billitteri is a *CQ Researcher* editor and writer with more than 30 years' experience covering business, nonprofit institutions and public policy for newspapers and magazines, including the *St. Petersburg Times* and the *Chronicle of Philanthropy.* His recent

CQ Researcher reports include "Afghanistan's Future," "Financial Literacy" and "Offshore Drilling." He holds a bachelor's degree in English and a master's in journalism from Indiana University.

John Felton is a freelance journalist who has written about international affairs and U.S. foreign policy for nearly 30 years. He covered foreign affairs for the *Congressional Quarterly Weekly Report* during the 1980s, was deputy foreign editor for *National Public Radio* in the early 1990s and has been a freelance writer specializing in international topics for the past 15 years. His most recent book, published by CQ Press, is *The Contemporary Middle East: A Documentary History.* He lives in Stockbridge, Mass.

Roland Flamini is a Washington-based correspondent who writes on foreign-affairs for *CQ Weekly, The New Republic* and other publications. Fluent in six languages, he served as *Time* bureau chief in Rome, Bonn, Beirut, and Jerusalem and for the European Common Market and later served as international editor at United Press International. His previous reports for *CQ Researcher* were on Afghanistan, NATO, Latin America, nuclear proliferation and U.S.-Russia relations. His most recent reporting trip to China was in November–December 2009.

Karen Foerstel is a freelance writer who has worked for the *Congressional Quarterly Weekly Report* and *Daily Monitor, The New York Post* and *Roll Call,* a Capitol Hill newspaper. She has published two books on women in Congress, *Climbing the Hill: Gender Conflict in Congress* and *The Biographical Dictionary of Women in Congress.* She currently lives and works in London. She has worked in Africa with ChildsLife International, a nonprofit that helps needy children around the world, and with Blue Ventures, a marine conservation organization that protects coral reefs in Madagascar.

Sarah Glazer, a London-based freelancer, is a regular contributor to *CQ Global Researcher.* Her articles on health, education and social-policy issues also have appeared in *The New York Times, The Washington Post* and *The Public Interest.* Her recent *CQ Global Researcher* reports include "Radical Islam in Europe" and "Anti-Semitism in Europe." She graduated from the University of Chicago with a bachelor's degree in American history.

Alan Greenblatt is a freelance writer in the Washington area and former staff writer at *Governing* magazine. He previously covered elections, agriculture and military spending for *CQ Weekly,* where he won the National Press Club's Sandy Hume Award for political journalism. He graduated from San Francisco State University in 1986 and received a master's degree in English literature from the University of Virginia in 1988. His recent *CQ Researcher* reports include "Future of the GOP" and "State Budget Crisis."

Kenneth Jost, associate editor of *CQ Researcher,* graduated from Harvard College and Georgetown University Law Center. He is the author of the *Supreme Court Yearbook* and editor of *The Supreme Court from A to Z* (both from CQ Press). He was a member of the *CQ Researcher* team that won the American Bar Association's 2002 Silver Gavel Award. His previous reports include "Bilingual Education vs. English Immersion" and "Testing in Schools." He is also author of the blog *Jost on Justice* (http://jostonjustice.blogspot.com).

Reed Karaim, a freelance writer living in Tucson, Ariz., has written for *The Washington Post, U.S. News & World Report, Smithsonian, American Scholar, USA Weekend* and other publications. He is the author of the novel, *If Men Were Angels,* which was selected for the Barnes & Noble Discover Great New Writers series. He is also the winner of the Robin Goldstein Award for Outstanding Regional Reporting and other journalism awards. Karaim is a graduate of North Dakota State University in Fargo.

Peter Katel is a *CQ Researcher* staff writer who previously reported on Haiti and Latin America for *Time* and *Newsweek* and covered the Southwest for newspapers in New Mexico. He has received several journalism awards, including the Bartolomé Mitre Award for coverage of drug trafficking from the Inter-American Press Association. He holds an A.B. degree in university studies from the University of New Mexico. His recent reports include "New Strategy in Iraq," "Rise in Counterinsurgency" and "Wounded Veterans."

Barbara Mantel is a freelance writer in New York City whose work has appeared in *The New York Times,* the *Journal of Child and Adolescent Psychopharmacology* and *Mamm Magazine.* She is a former correspondent and senior producer for National Public Radio who has won several journalism awards, including the National Press Club's Best Consumer Journalism Award and the Front Page Award from the Newswomen's Club of New York for her April 18, 2008, *CQ Researcher* report "Public Defenders." She holds a bachelor's degree in history and economics from the University of Virginia and a master's in economics from Northwestern University.

Jason McLure is a correspondent for Bloomberg News and Newsweek based in Addis Ababa, Ethiopia. He previously worked for Legal Times in Washington, D.C., and in *Newsweek's* Boston bureau. His reporting has appeared in *The Economist, Business Week,* the *British Journalism Review* and *National Law Journal.* His work has been honored by the Washington, D.C., chapter of the Society for Professional Journalists, the Maryland–Delaware–District of Columbia Press Association and the Overseas Press Club of America Foundation. He has a master's degree in journalism from the University of Missouri.

Jennifer Weeks is a *CQ Researcher* contributing writer in Watertown, Mass., who specializes in energy and environmental issues. She has written for *The Washington Post, The Boston Globe Magazine* and other publications, and has 15 years' experience as a public-policy analyst, lobbyist and congressional staffer. She has an A.B. degree from Williams College and master's degrees from the University of North Carolina and Harvard University.

1

Afghanistan Dilemma

Thomas J. Billitteri

An Afghan security officer guards two tons of burning heroin, opium and hashish near Kabul, Afghanistan's capital, on March 18, 2009. Nearly eight years after U.S.-led forces first entered Afghanistan, many challenges still confront the U.S., Afghan and coalition forces seeking to stabilize the country: fanatical Taliban and al Qaeda fighters, rampant police corruption, shortages of Afghan troops and a multibillion-dollar opium economy that supports the insurgents.

From *CQ Researcher*,
August 7, 2009.

O n the outskirts of Now Zad, a Taliban stronghold in southern Afghanistan's violent Helmand Province, the past, present and future of the war in Afghanistan came together this summer.

The past: After the U.S.-led invasion of Afghanistan in 2001, Now Zad and its surrounding poppy fields and stout compounds were largely tranquil, thanks in part to the clinics and wells that Western money helped to build in the area. But three years ago, when the war in Iraq intensified and the Bush administration shifted attention from Afghanistan to Iraq, insurgents moved in, driving out most of Now Zad's 35,000 residents and foreign aid workers.

The present: This summer U.S. Marines engaged in withering firefights with Taliban militants dug in on the northern fringes of the town and in nearby fields and orchards.

The future: The situation in Now Zad and the surrounding war-torn region of southern Afghanistan is a microcosm of what confronts the Obama administration as it tries to smash the Taliban, defang al Qaeda and stabilize governance in Afghanistan. "In many ways," wrote an Associated Press reporter following the fighting, Now Zad "symbolizes what went wrong in Afghanistan and the enormous challenges facing the United States."[1]

Nearly eight years after U.S.-led forces first entered Afghanistan to pursue al Qaeda and its Taliban allies in the wake of the Sept. 11, 2001, terrorist attacks, the country remains in chaos, and President Barack Obama faces what many consider his biggest foreign-policy challenge: bringing stability and security to Afghanistan and denying Islamist militants a permanent foothold there and in neighboring nuclear-armed Pakistan.

An Unstable Nation in a Volatile Neighborhood

Almost as large as Texas, Afghanistan faces Texas-size problems, including desperate poverty, an economy dominated by illicit drugs and an unstable central government beset by Taliban militants. Afghanistan's instability is compounded by longstanding tensions between neighboring Pakistan and India, both armed with nuclear weapons. Many Western experts also say Pakistan has failed, despite promises, to rein in Taliban and other Islamist extremists.

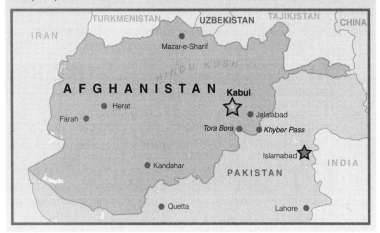

using Pakistan's lawless western border region as a sanctuary.[3]

"The fact that Pakistan has nuclear weapons and the question of the security of those weapons presses very hard on the minds of American defense planners and on the mind of the president," says Bruce Riedel, who led a 60-day strategic policy review of Afghanistan and Pakistan for the Obama administration. "If you didn't have that angle," adds Riedel, who has since returned to his post as a Brookings Institution senior fellow, "I think this would all be notched down one level of concern."

Pakistan is important to the Afghan conflict for reasons that go beyond its nuclear arsenal. Pakistan has been a breeding ground for much of the radical ideology that has taken root in Afghanistan. A failure of governance in Afghanistan would leave a void that Islamist militants on either side of the border could wind up filling, further destabilizing the entire region.

The challenge is heightened by the war's growing casualty figures. July was the deadliest month in Afghanistan for U.S. soldiers since the 2001 invasion began, with 43 killed.[2] Twenty-two British troops also died last month, including eight in a 24-hour period. In nearly eight years of war in Afghanistan, 767 U.S. troops have died there, along with 520 coalition forces, according to the Web site iCasualties.org. Thousands of Afghan civilians also have died.

The Afghanistan-Pakistan conflict —"Af-Pak" in diplomatic parlance — poses a witch's brew of challenges: fanatical Taliban and al Qaeda fighters, rampant corruption within Afghanistan's homegrown police force and other institutions, not enough Afghan National Army forces to help with the fighting and a multibillion-dollar opium economy that supplies revenue to the insurgents.

But those problems pale in comparison with what foreign-policy experts call the ultimate nightmare: Pakistan's nuclear weapons falling into the hands of jihadists and terrorists, a scenario that has become more credible this summer as suicide bombers and Taliban fighters have stepped up attacks in Pakistani cities and rural areas,

In March Obama announced what he called a "comprehensive, new strategy" for Afghanistan and Pakistan that rests on a "clear and focused goal" for the region: "to disrupt, dismantle and defeat al Qaeda in Pakistan and Afghanistan, and to prevent their return to either country in the future."[4]

Key to the strategy is winning over the local Afghan population by protecting it from insurgent violence and improving governance, security and economic development.[5]

The effort includes new troop deployments — a total of 21,000 additional U.S. soldiers to fight the insurgency in Afghanistan and train Afghan security forces, plus other strategic resources. By year's end, U.S. troop levels are expected to reach about 68,000. NATO countries and other allies currently are supplying another 32,000 or so, though many are engaged in development and relief work but not offensive combat operations.[6]

An immediate goal is to heighten security in Afghanistan in the run-up to a high-profile presidential election on Aug. 20. None of Afghan President Hamid Karzai's main challengers are expected to beat him flat out, *The Washington Post* noted, but some observers said other candidates could "do well enough as a group to force a second round of polling, partly because of recent blunders by Karzai and partly because many Afghans are looking for alternative leadership at a time of sustained insurgent violence, economic stagnation and political drift."[7]

Observers say Obama's approach to the Af-Pak conflict represents a middle path between counterterrorism and counterinsurgency — protecting civilians, relying on them for information on the enemy and providing aid to build up a country's social and physical infrastructure and democratic institutions.[8]

Among the most notable features of the new approach is a vow among military officials — beginning with Gen. Stanley A. McChrystal, the newly appointed commander of U.S. and NATO forces in Afghanistan — to avoid civilian casualties. McChrystal pledged to follow a "holistic" approach in which protecting civilians takes precedence over killing militants.[9]

"I expect stiff fighting ahead," McChrystal told the Senate Armed Services Committee at his confirmation hearing. But "the measure of effectiveness will not be the number of enemy killed," he added, "it will be the number of Afghans shielded from violence."[10]

The United Nations said that 1,013 civilians died in the first six months of 2009, up from 818 during the same period last year. The U.N. said 310 deaths were attributed to pro-government forces, with about two-thirds caused by U.S. air strikes.[11]

As part of his strategy, Obama called for a "dramatic" increase in the number of agricultural specialists, educators, engineers and lawyers dispatched to "help the Afghan government serve its people and develop an economy that isn't dominated by illicit drugs." He also supports economic-development aid to Pakistan,

Gates Warns About Civilian Deaths

The number of civilians killed in Afghanistan more than doubled from 2006 to 2008, but based on the toll for the first six months of 2009, the rate may be somewhat lower in 2009 (graph at left). In 2008 nearly half of the civilian deaths were caused by executions or suicide and IED (improvised explosive device) attacks by the Taliban and other anti-government groups (graph at right). Concern over civilian deaths prompted Defense Secretary Robert Gates to call such casualties "one of our greatest strategic vulnerabilities."

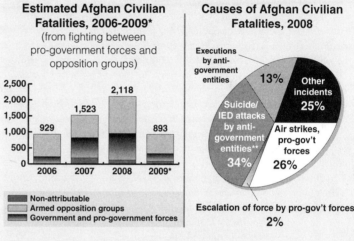

* Through June; the total is 1,013, according to the U.N.

** Includes Taliban and other insurgents

Source: "Afghan Index: Tracking Variables of Reconstruction and Security in Post-9/11 Afghanistan," Brookings Institution, July 15, 2009

including legislation to provide $1.5 billion annually over the next five years. But Obama's approach on Pakistan also reflects long-held Western concerns that the Pakistani government has been at best negligent — and perhaps downright obstructionist — in bringing Taliban and other Islamist extremists to heel. Pakistan, whose situation is complicated by long-standing tensions with nearby India, will get no free pass in exchange for the aid, Obama vowed. "We will not, and cannot, provide a blank check," he said, because Pakistan had shown "years of mixed results" in rooting out terrorism.[12]

As Obama goes after the insurgency, his Af-Pak policy is under the microscope here at home.

Some have demanded that the administration describe its plans for ending military operations in Afghanistan.

Opium Trade Funds Taliban, Official Corruption

"It's clear that drug money is paying for the Taliban's operational costs."

In the crowded Afghan capital of Kabul, opulent marble homes sit behind guard houses and razor wire. "Most are owned by Afghan officials or people connected to them, men who make a few hundred dollars a month as government employees but are driven around in small convoys of armored SUVs that cost tens of thousands of dollars," reporter Tom Lasseter noted recently. "[M]any of the houses were built with profits harvested from opium poppy fields in the southern provinces of Helmand and Kandahar."[1]

The so-called "poppy palaces" are outward signs of a cancer eating Afghanistan to its core: illicit drugs and narcoterrorism, aided by official corruption.

According to the United Nations Office on Drugs and Crime, Afghanistan grows more than 90 percent of the world's opium, which is used to produce heroin and morphine.[2] Total opium production for 2008 was estimated at 7,700 metric tons, more than double the 2002 level.[3]

In her new book, *Seeds of Terror: How Heroin Is Bankrolling the Taliban and Al Qaeda*, journalist Gretchen Peters says militant groups are raising hundreds of millions of dollars a year from the opium trade.

"It's clear that drug money is paying for the Taliban's operational costs within Afghanistan," she told *Time* magazine. "That means that every time a U.S. soldier is killed in an IED attack or a shootout with militants, drug money helped pay for that bomb or paid the militants who placed it. . . . The Taliban have now thrown off their old masters and are a full-fledged criminal force on both sides of the [Afghan-Pakistan] border."[4]

The biggest challenge to curbing the drug trade, Peters said, is corruption. "As much money as the insurgents are earning off the drug trade, corrupt officials in Afghanistan and Pakistan are earning even more," she said. "It's going to be very complex for the U.S. and for the international community, for NATO, to find reliable and trustworthy partners to work with. I don't think that it is widely understood how high up the corruption goes within the Pakistani government, particularly within their military and intelligence forces."

In recent weeks, the Obama administration has shifted U.S. drug policy in Afghanistan from trying to eradicate poppy fields to seizing drugs and related supplies and helping farmers grow alternative crops.[5]

"The Western policies against the opium crop, the poppy crop, have been a failure," Richard C. Holbrooke, the administration's special representative for Afghanistan and Pakistan, said. "They did not result in any damage to the Taliban, but they put farmers out of work and they alienated people and drove people into the arms of the Taliban."[6]

The Bush administration had advocated intense efforts to eradicate poppy fields, but some experts have said the approach is counterproductive.

"The United States should de-emphasize opium eradication efforts," Air Force Lt. Col. John A. Glaze wrote in a 2007 report for the U.S. Army War College. It recommended a multi-pronged strategy including higher troop levels, more economic aid for Afghanistan, pursuit of drug lords and corrupt officials and development of alternative

---

A measure proposed by Rep. Jim McGovern, D-Mass., requiring a report from the Obama administration by the end of the year on its exit strategy, drew significant support from Democrats but was defeated in the House this summer amid heavy Republican opposition.

And some critics question the validity of Obama's rationale for the fighting in Afghanistan, particularly the assumption that if the Taliban were victorious they would invite al Qaeda to return to Afghanistan and use it as a base for its global jihad. John Mueller, a political science professor at Ohio State University and author of *Overblown: How Politicians and the Terrorism Industry Inflate National Security Threats, and Why We Believe*

Them, contends that al Qaeda does not need Afghanistan as a base. The 2001 terrorist attacks were orchestrated mostly from Hamburg, Germany, he points out.

What's more, he argues, "distinct tensions" exist between al Qaeda and the Taliban. Even if the Taliban were to prevail in Afghanistan, he says, "they would not particularly want al Qaeda back." Nor, he says, is it clear that al Qaeda would again view Afghanistan as a safe haven.[13]

But administration officials disagree. The Taliban are "the frontrunners for al Qaeda," said Richard Holbrooke, Obama's special envoy to Pakistan and Afghanistan. "If they succeed in Afghanistan, without any shadow of a

livelihoods for Afghans, plus exploration of the possibility of participating in the market for legal opiates used for morphine and other medicines.

"U.S.-backed eradication efforts have been ineffective and have resulted in turning Afghans against U.S. and NATO forces . . . ," Glaze wrote. "While the process of eradication lends itself well to the use of flashy metrics such as 'acres eradicated,' eradication without provision for long-term alternative livelihoods is devastating Afghan's poor farmers without addressing root causes."[7]

Brookings Institution scholar Vanda Felbab-Brown, an expert on Afghanistan's opium-poppy economy, says rural development, not poppy eradication, is the best way to attack the drug economy. "Any massive eradication right now . . . , we would lose Afghanistan," she says. "In the absence of resources available to farmers, any eradication would just prompt massive destabilization and invite the Taliban in."

Felbab-Brown says the development of new crops is key, but that such crops must be "high-labor-intensive, high-value crops" that offer more than subsistence income.

"People don't have to become rich, but they cannot continue existing in excruciating poverty. Many people will be willing and motivated to switch to a legal crop," she says, but "it needs to offer some chance of advancement."

Vegetable, fruit and horticultural crops are better options, Felbab-Brown says. Wheat, on the other hand, "has no traction" because the prices are low, people in vast parts of the country don't have enough land to make the crop pay, and wheat is much less labor-intensive than poppy growing, affording fewer opportunities for employment, she says.

For rural development to offer an alternative to illicit poppy production, it must include not only access to land,

legal microcredit and other features, but security for Afghan farmers, Felbab-Brown stresses.

"The lack of security in many ways is the key structural driver of illicit crop cultivation, because the risks of cultivating legal crops in insecure settings are just tremendous," she says.

Rural development, for example, "needs to involve roads, and not just their physical presence but also security on the roads," Felbab-Brown says. Roads are now insecure due to both the insurgents and the Afghan National Police.

"In much of the south, travel on the road is three times as expensive as travel in the north because of the number of bribes that one needs to pay at check stops. For many people, simply to take crops from Laskar Gah to Kandahar, by the time they pay the bribes that they need to pay, they will have lost all profit."

----

[1] Tom Lasseter, "Western Military Looked Other Way as the Afghan Drug Trade Boomed," *Charlotte Observer*, May 10, 2009, p. 13A.

[2] "World Drug Report 2009 Highlights Links Between Drugs and Crime," United Nations Office on Drugs and Crime, June 2009, www.unodc.org/unodc/en/press/releases/2009/june/world-drug-report-2009-highlights-links-between-drugs-and-crime.html.

[3] "World Drug Report 2009," United Nations Office on Drugs and Crime, www.unodc.org/documents/wdr/WDR_2009/WDR2009_eng_web.pdf.

[4] Bobby Ghosh, "Q&A: Fighting the New Narcoterrorism Syndicates," *Time*, July 17, 2009, www.time.com/time/nation/article/0,8599,1910935, 00.html.

[5] Rachel Donadio, "New Course for Antidrug Efforts in Afghanistan," *The New York Times*, June 28, 2009, www.nytimes.com/2009/06/28/world/asia/28holbrooke.html?scp=1&sq=holbrooke+drug%20policy+afghanistan+rome&st=cse.

[6] Quoted in *ibid.*

[7] John A. Glaze, "Opium and Afghanistan: Reassessing U.S. Counternarcotics Strategy," U.S. Army War College, www.strategic-studiesinstitute.army.mil/Pubs/Display.Cfm?pubID=804.

doubt al Qaeda would move back into Afghanistan, set up a larger presence, recruit more people and pursue its objectives against the United States even more aggressively."[14]

As the war in Afghanistan continues, here are some of the questions people are asking:

Is the Obama administration pursuing the right course in Afghanistan?

Early in July, thousands of U.S. Marines began a massive assault in Afghanistan's Helmand River valley, the biggest American offensive of the Obama presidency and a key test of his new strategy in the region.

The operation included 4,000 troops from the 2nd Marine Expeditionary Brigade, who poured into the area in helicopters and armored vehicles. The Marines have run into stiff opposition, but the ultimate goal remains intact: protect local Afghans from insurgent violence and strengthen Afghanistan's legal, judicial and security institutions.

"Our focus must be on getting this [Afghan] government back up on its feet," Brig. Gen. Lawrence D. Nicholson, commander of the brigade, told his officers.[15]

But the mission is fraught with huge risks and challenges, and skepticism about it runs deep, even among some of Obama's fellow Democrats.

Social Conditions Worsened in Many Areas

Living conditions deteriorated between 2007 and 2008 in areas such as education, water quality and availability of electricity, according to surveys of Afghan citizens.

Condition of Infrastructure in Localities, 2007 and 2008

	Very/Quite Good (%) 2007	2008	Quite/Very Bad (%) 2007	2008
Availability of clean drinking water	63%	62%	36%	38%
Availability of water for irrigation	59	47	40	49
Availability of jobs	30	21	69	78
Supply of electricity	31	25	68	74
Security situation	66	No data	33	No data
Availability of medical care	56	49	44	50
Availability of education for children	72	70	28	29
Freedom of movement	72	No data	28	No data

Source: "Afghan Index: Tracking Variables of Reconstruction and Security in Post-9/11 Afghanistan," Brookings Institution, July 15, 2009

In May, House Appropriations Chairman David Obey, D-Wis., suggested that if the White House doesn't demonstrate progress by next year, funding for the war could slow. Asked if he could see Congress halting funding completely, Obey said, "If it becomes a fool's errand, I would hope so," according to *The Hill* newspaper. The success or failure of the Afghan policy is not in the hands of the president or Congress, Obey said, but "in the hands of the practicing politicians in Pakistan and Afghanistan. And I'm dubious about those hands."[16]

Much of the American public is similarly dubious. A June *New York Times*-CBS News poll found that 55 percent of respondents believed the war in Afghanistan was going somewhat or very badly for the United States, an increase of two points since April. Only 2 percent said the war was going "very well."[17]

Critics question the prospect of success in a country long divided by ethnic rivalries, a resistance to central governance and rampant graft that ranges from demands for petty bribes to drug corruption in high levels of government.[18]

"To pacify the place in the absence of reconciliation of the main tribes,* you'd need a very large national

army" — one that would have to be financially subsidized by outside powers, says Stephen Walt, a professor of international affairs at Harvard University's Kennedy School of Government. Such an army "would have to be drawn from all these groups and imbued with central loyalty to the state. And there's never been a strong central state. Politics [in Afghanistan is defined by] factional alignments." And, he adds, the challenge is "compounded by levels of corruption and lack of institutions."

"We're sort of trying to impart a Western model of how the Afghan state should be created — with a central government, ministries, defense and so on. That's not the way Afghanistan has been run for centuries. The idea that we know how to do that, especially in the short term," Walt says, is "far-fetched."

Malou Innocent, a foreign-policy analyst at the conservative Cato Institute think tank, says America faces the prospect of an "ambiguous victory" because it is caught amid long-simmering tensions between Pakistan and India, a dynamic, she argues, that the Obama administration has failed to adequately take into account.

Pakistan has long feared an alliance between Afghanistan and India. To hedge its bets, Pakistan aids the insurgency in Afghanistan by providing shelter to the Taliban and other militants, Innocent says. At the same time, she says, Pakistan has accused India of funneling weapons through Afghanistan to separatists in Pakistan's unstable Balochistan province.[19] The ongoing India-Pakistan dispute over Kashmir also remains a cause of friction in the region.

"The regional dynamics are too intractable," Innocent says. "The countries in the region have an incentive to foment and maintain Afghanistan's instability. So we should be looking to get out of Afghanistan within a reasonable time frame — say at least in the next five years."

Innocent sees a U.S. role in training Afghanistan's own security forces and says covert operations against specific insurgent targets could make sense. But the Taliban threat centered along the Afghanistan-Pakistan

---

* The main ethnic groups are the Pashtun (42%), Tajik (27%), Hazara (9%), Uzbek (9%), Aimak (4%), Turkmen (3%) and Baloch (2%).

border cannot be definitively eradicated, she argues. "We can contain the militancy" and weaken it, she says, "but we can't believe we can have a victory with a capital V."

But Peter Bergen, a counterterrorism analyst and senior fellow at the New America Foundation, is more sanguine about the war's prospects in Afghanistan. In a *Washington Monthly* article, he challenged those who say Afghanistan is an unconquerable and ungovernable "graveyard of empires" where foreign armies have come to ignominious ends.

One telling fact, in Bergen's view, is that "the Afghan people themselves, the center of gravity in a counterinsurgency, are rooting for us to win." He cited BBC/ABC polling data indicating that 58 percent of Afghans named the Taliban — viewed favorably by only 7 percent of Afghans — as the biggest threat to their country, while only 8 percent named the United States.

"[T]he growing skepticism about Obama's chances for success in Afghanistan is largely based on deep misreadings of both the country's history and the views of its people, which are often compounded by facile comparisons to the United States' misadventures of past decades in Southeast Asia and the Middle East," wrote Bergen. "Afghanistan will not be Obama's Vietnam, nor will it be his Iraq. Rather, the renewed and better-resourced American effort in Afghanistan will, in time, produce a relatively stable and prosperous Central Asian state."[20]

Stephen Biddle, a senior fellow at the Council on Foreign Relations, a think tank in New York City, said victory in Afghanistan is possible but only if steps are taken to strengthen Afghanistan's governance. "I do think it's possible to succeed," Biddle said in late July after spending a month as part of a group helping McChrystal formulate a strategic assessment report on the war, due this month. But, he added, "there are two very different requirements for success.

"One is providing security, [and] the other is providing enough of an improvement in Afghan governance to

Afghanistan Ranks Low in Developing World

Afghanistan ranked as the second-weakest state in the developing world, after Somalia, in 2008, according to the Brookings Institution* (left). It consistently ranks near the bottom among countries rated for corruption by Transparency International (right).

Afghanistan's Rank					
Index of State Weakness in Developing World, 2008			Corruption Perceptions Index		
Rank	Country	Overall Score	Year	Rank	No. of Countries Surveyed
1	Somalia	0.52	2008	176	180
2	Afghanistan	1.65	2007	172	180
3	Dem. Rep. Congo	1.67	2006	No data	163
4	Iraq	3.11	2005	117	159
5	Burundi	3.21			

* Brookings surveyed 141 nations, allocating a score of 0-10 points for each of four categories: economic, political, security and social welfare. Benin had the median score, 6.36; the Slovak Republic was the least weak, with a score of 9.41.

Source: "Afghan Index: Tracking Variables of Reconstruction and Security in Post-9/11 Afghanistan," Brookings Institution, July 15, 2009

enable the country to function without us. We can keep the patient on life support by providing security assistance indefinitely, but if you don't get an improvement in governance, you'll never be able to take the patient off the ventilator. Of those two challenges, providing security we know how to do. It's expensive, it's hard, it takes a long time, but if we invest the resources there's a substantial probability that we can provide security through our assistance. Governance improvement is a more uncertain undertaking. There are a lot of things we can do that we have not yet done to improve governance, but ultimately the more uncertain of the two requirements is the governance part."[21]

Another member of McChrystal's strategic assessment group, Anthony Cordesman, a scholar with the Center for Strategic and International Studies, also believes the war is winnable, but that the United States and its allies must "act quickly and decisively" in a number of ways, including "giving the Afghan government the necessary legitimacy and capacity" at national, regional and local levels, reducing official corruption and "creating a level of actual governance that can ensure security and stability."[22]

1838-1930s *Afghanistan gains independence, but ethnic and religious conflicts persist.*

1838-42; 1878 Afghan forces defeat Britain in two wars, but Britain retains control of Afghanistan's foreign affairs under 1879 treaty.

1893 British draw Afghan-Pakistan border, split Pashtun ethnic group.

1919 Afghanistan gains independence after Third Anglo-Afghan War.

1934 Diplomatic relations between United States and Afghanistan established.

1950s-1980s *Political chaos wracks Afghanistan during Cold War.*

1950s-1960s Soviets and Americans funnel aid to Afghanistan.

1953 Gen. Mohammed Daoud becomes prime minister, seeks aid from Soviets, institutes reforms.

1964 New constitution establishes constitutional monarchy.

1973 Daoud overthrows king, is killed in Marxist coup in 1978.

1979-1989 Civil war rages between communist-backed government and U.S.-backed Mujahedeen. Soviets withdraw in 1989, 10 years after they invaded.

1990-2001 *Taliban emerges amid postwar chaos; al Qaeda forges ties with Afghan militants.*

1992 Burhanuddin Rabbani, an ethnic Tajik, rises to power, declares Afghanistan an Islamic state.

1994 Taliban emerges; the militant Islamist group is mainly Pashtun.

1996 Taliban gains control of Kabul.

1996 Taliban leader Mullah Omar invites al Qaeda leader Osama bin Laden to live with him in Kandahar.

1997 Osama bin Laden declares war on U.S. in interview with CNN.

2001 U.S. and coalition forces invade Afghanistan on Oct. 7 after Sept. 11 terrorist attacks; Taliban retreats.

2002-Present *U.S.-led invasion of Iraq shifts focus off Afghanistan; Taliban resurges.*

2002 Hamid Karzai elected head of Afghan Transitional Authority; International Security Assistance Force deployed in Kabul; international donors pledge $4.5 billion for reconstruction.

2003 U.S.-led invasion of Iraq begins, leading to charges Bush administration shifted focus and resources away from Afghanistan; commission drafts new Afghan constitution.

2004 Draft constitution approved; Karzai elected president; Pakistani nuclear scientist A. Q. Khan admits international nuclear-weapons trading; President Pervez Musharraf pardons him.

2005 Afghanistan holds its first parliamentary elections in some three decades.

2006 NATO takes over Afghan security; donors pledge $10.5 billion more.

2007 Musharraf and Karzai agree to coordinate efforts to fight Taliban, al Qaeda; allied troops kill Taliban leader Mullah Dadullah.

2008 More than 50 die in suicide bombing of Indian Embassy in Kabul in July. . . . More than 160 die in November terror attacks in Mumbai, India; India accuses Pakistani militants of carrying out the attacks; in July 2009 a young Pakistani admits to taking part in the attacks as a soldier for Lashkar-e-Taiba, a Pakistan-based Islamic group.

2009 Obama announces new strategy "to disrupt, dismantle and defeat al Qaeda in Pakistan and Afghanistan"; Gen. Stanley McChrystal replaces Gen. David McKiernan as top U.S. commander in Afghanistan; Marines attack Taliban in southern Helmand Province; July is bloodiest month for U.S. and foreign troops in Afghanistan, with 43 Americans killed. . . . Concern grows over security surrounding Aug. 20 presidential election.

Are troop levels in Afghanistan adequate?

When the Marine assault in Helmand Province got under way this summer, only about 400 effective Afghan fighters had joined the American force of nearly 4,000, according to *The New York Times*, citing information from Gen. Nicholson.[23]

Commanders expressed concern that not enough homegrown forces were available to fight the insurgency and build ties with the local population. Gen. Nicholson said, "I'm not going to sugarcoat it. The fact of the matter is, we don't have enough Afghan forces. And I'd like more."[24] Capt. Brian Huysman, a Marine company commander, said the lack of Afghan forces "is absolutely our Achilles' heel."[25]

"We've seen a shift over the past few years to put a lot more resources, including money and attention, toward building Afghan national security forces, army and police forces," Seth Jones, a political scientist at the RAND Corporation, told the "NewsHour" on PBS. "I think the problem that we're running into on the ground in Afghanistan, though: There are not enough Afghan national security forces and coalition forces to do what Gen. McChrystal and others want, and that is to protect the local population."[26]

Worries about the size of the Afghan force have been accompanied by concerns over whether U.S. forces are adequate to overcome the Taliban threat and secure local areas long enough to ensure security and build governance capabilities.

According to a report this summer by veteran *Washington Post* reporter Bob Woodward, National Security Adviser James L. Jones told U.S. commanders in Afghanistan the Obama administration wants to keep troop levels steady for now. Gen. Nicholson, though, told Jones that he was "a little light," suggesting he could use more troops, and that "we don't have enough force to go everywhere," Woodward reported.[27]

"The question of the force level for Afghanistan . . . is not settled and will probably be hotly debated over the next year," Woodward wrote. "One senior military officer said privately that the United States would have to deploy a force of more than 100,000 to execute the counterinsurgency strategy of holding areas and towns after clearing out the Taliban insurgents. That is at least 32,000 more than the 68,000 currently authorized."[28]

Adm. Mike Mullen, chairman of the Joint Chiefs of Staff, said on CBS News' "Face the Nation" on July 5

that in southern Afghanistan, where the toughest fighting is expected, "we have enough forces now not just to clear an area but to hold it so we can build after. And that's really the strategy." He noted that Gen. McChrystal was due to produce his 60-day assessment of the war this summer, adding "we're all committed to getting this right and resourcing it properly."[29]

But senior military officials told *The Washington Post* later that week that McChrystal had concluded Afghan security forces must be greatly expanded if the war is to be won. According to officials, the *Post* said, "such an expansion would require spending billions more than the $7.5 billion the administration has budgeted annually to build up the Afghan army and police over the next several years, and the likely deployment of thousands more U.S. troops as trainers and advisers."[30]

As combat has intensified this spring and summer and more troops entered the war zone, commanders focused on one of the most pernicious threats to the U.S.-led counterinsurgency strategy: the potential for civilian casualties, which can undermine efforts to build trust and cooperation with the local population. Concern over civilian deaths rose sharply in May, when a high-profile U.S. air strike in western Farah province killed at least 26 civilians, according to American investigators.[31] This spring commanders instituted strict new combat rules aimed at minimizing civilian deaths, and Defense Secretary Robert M. Gates has called such casualties "one of our greatest strategic vulnerabilities."[32]

While some fear that the deployment of more troops to Afghanistan could heighten civilian casualties, others say the opposite is true.

"In fact, the presence of more boots on the ground is likely to *reduce* civilian casualties, because historically it has been the over-reliance on American air strikes — as a result of too few ground forces — which has been the key cause of civilian deaths," wrote Bergen of the New America Foundation.[33]

Should the United States negotiate with the Taliban?

In early March, shortly before announcing his new strategy for Afghanistan and Pakistan, *The New York Times* reported that Obama, in an interview aboard Air Force One, "opened the door to a reconciliation process in which the American military would reach out to moderate elements of the Taliban."[34]

The Many Faces of the Taliban

Adherents include violent warlords and Islamist extremists.

When President Barack Obama announced his administration's new Afghanistan strategy in March, he declared that if the Afghan government were to fall to the Taliban, the country would "again be a base for terrorists who want to kill as many of our people as they possibly can."[1]

But defining "the Taliban" is tricky. Far from a monolithic organization, the Taliban is a many-headed hydra, and a shadowy one at that. It is a mélange of insurgents and militants, ranging from high-profile Islamist extremists and violent warlords to local villagers fighting for cash or glory. Western military strategists hope to kill or capture the most fanatical elements of the Taliban while persuading others to abandon their arms and work within Afghanistan's political system.

"You have a whole spectrum of bad guys that sort of get lumped into this catch-all term of Taliban . . . because they're launching bullets at us," a senior Defense official told *The Boston Globe*. "There are many of the groups that can probably be peeled off."

The Defense official quoted by *The Globe* was among "hundreds of intelligence operatives and analysts" in the United States and abroad involved in a broad study of tribes tied to the Taliban, the newspaper said. The aim is to figure out whether diplomatic or economic efforts can persuade some to break away, according to the paper. The examination "is expected to culminate later this year in a detailed, highly classified analysis of the different factions of the Taliban and other groups," *The Globe* said.[2]

Many experts break down the Taliban into four main groups:

• **The Early Taliban** — Insurgents emerged under Mullah Omar and other leaders during the civil war that wracked Afghanistan in the mid-1990s, following the end of the Soviet occupation of the country. Early members were a mix of fighters who battled the Soviets in the 1980s and Pashtuns who attended religious schools in Pakistan, where they were aided by the Pakistani Inter-Services Intelligence agency.[3]

• **The Pakistani Taliban** emerged under a separate organizational structure in 2002, when Pakistani forces entered the country's tribal region in the northwest to pursue Islamist militants.[4]

"At the time of the U.S.-led military campaign in Afghanistan in late 2001, allies and sympathizers of the Taliban in Pakistan were not identified as 'Taliban' themselves," wrote Hassan Abbas, a research fellow at Harvard's Belfer Center for Science and International Affairs. "That reality is now a distant memory. Today, Pakistan's indigenous Taliban are an effective fighting force and are engaging the Pakistani military on one side and NATO forces on the other."[5]

• **Hizb-e-Islami** — Formed by the brutal warlord Gulbuddin Hekmatyar, the group is "a prominent ally under the Taliban umbrella," says *Christian Science Monitor* journalist Anand Gopal.[6]

Hizb-e-Islami ("Islamic Party") was allied with the United States and Pakistan during the decade-long Soviet war, Gopal wrote, but after the 2001 U.S. invasion of Afghanistan a segment led by Hekmatyar joined the insurgency. *The New York Times* has described Hekmatyar as having "a record of extreme brutality."[7]

Hizb-e-Islami fighters have for years "had a reputation for being more educated and worldly than their Taliban

In broaching the idea of negotiating with the Taliban, the president cited successes in Iraq in separating moderate insurgents from the more extreme factions of al Qaeda. Still, he was cautious about reconciliation prospects in Afghanistan.

"The situation in Afghanistan is, if anything, more complex" than the one in Iraq, he said. "You have a less governed region, a history of fierce independence among tribes. Those tribes are multiple and sometimes operate at cross-purposes, and so figuring all that out is going to be much more of a challenge."[35]

Nevertheless, the notion of seeking some sort of reconciliation with elements of the Afghan Taliban has received fresh attention recently.

counterparts, who are often illiterate farmers," Gopal wrote last year. In the 1970s, Hekmatyar studied engineering at Kabul University, "where he made a name for himself by hurling acid in the faces of unveiled women."[8]

Today the group has a "strong presence in the provinces near Kabul and in Pashtun pockets in the country's north and northeast," Gopal wrote. In 2008 Hizb-e-Islami participated in an assassination attempt on President Hamid Karzai and was behind a 2008 ambush that killed 10 NATO soldiers, according to Gopal.

"Its guerrillas fight under the Taliban banner, although independently and with a separate command structure," Gopal wrote. "Like the Taliban, its leaders see their task as restoring Afghan sovereignty as well as establishing an Islamic state in Afghanistan."

• **The Haqqani network** — Some of the most notorious terrorist actions in recent months have been linked to the network, including the kidnapping of a *New York Times* reporter and the abduction of a U.S. soldier. Haqqani is "not traditional Taliban, they're more strongly associated with al Qaeda," said Haroun Mir, director of Afghanistan's Center for Research and Policy Studies in Kabul.[9]

Thought to control major parts of eastern Afghanistan, the network in recent years "has emerged . . . as a powerful antagonist to U.S. efforts to stabilize that country and root out insurgent havens in the lawless tribal areas of Pakistan," according to *The Washington Post*.[10]

The network is controlled by Jalaluddin Haqqani and his son, Sirajuddin, the *Post* said. Analysts call the son a "terrorist mastermind," according to *The Christian Science Monitor*.[11]

New York Times reporter David Rohde, who was abducted in Logar Province in Afghanistan and taken across the Pakistani border to North Waziristan, was held by the Haqqani network until he escaped in June after seven months in captivity.[12]

The network also is suspected of the suicide bombing of the Indian Embassy in Kabul in July 2008 that left more than 50 dead, *The Post* said.[13]

According to Gopal, "The Haqqanis command the lion's share of foreign fighters operating in [Afghanistan] and tend to be even more extreme than their Taliban counterparts. Unlike most of the Taliban and Hizb-e-Islami, elements of the Haqqani network cooperate closely with al Qaeda."[14]

---

[1] "Remarks by the President on a New Strategy for Afghanistan and Pakistan," The White House, March 27, 2009, www.whitehouse.gov.

[2] Bryan Bender, "U.S. probes divisions within Taliban," *The Boston Globe*, May 24, 2009, p. 1.

[3] See Eben Kaplan and Greg Bruno, "The Taliban in Afghanistan," Council on Foreign Relations, July 2, 2008, www.cfr.org/publication/10551/taliban_in_afghanistan.html.

[4] *Ibid.*

[5] Hassan Abbas, "A Profile of Tehrik-i-Taliban Pakistan," *CTC Sentinel*, Vol. 1, Issue 2, pp. 1-4, www.ctc.usma.edu/sentinel/CTCSentinel-Vol1Iss2.pdf.

[6] Anand Gopal, "Briefing: Who Are the Taliban?" *The Christian Science Monitor*, April 16, 2009, http://anandgopal.com/briefing-who-are-the-taliban/.

[7] Dexter Filkins, "Taliban said to be in talks with intermediaries about peace; U.S. withdrawal is called a focus," *The New York Times*, May 21, 2009, p. 4.

[8] Anand Gopal, "Who Are the Taliban?" *The Nation*, Dec. 22, 2008, www.thenation.com/doc/20081222/gopal.

[9] Quoted in Issam Ahmed, "Captured U.S. soldier in Taliban video: Held by Haqqani network?" *The Christian Science Monitor*, Global News blog, July 19, 2009, http://features.csmonitor.com/globalnews/2009/07/19/captured-us-soldier-in-taliban-video-held-by-haqqani-network/.

[10] Keith B. Richburg, "Reporters Escape Taliban Captors," *The Washington Post*, June 21, 2009, p. A1.

[11] Ahmed, *op. cit.*

[12] *Ibid.*

[13] Richburg, *op. cit.*

[14] Gopal, *The Nation, op. cit.*

Opponents of the idea argue that it could project an image of weakness and embolden the insurgency and that Taliban leaders cannot be trusted to uphold any deals they may make.

But proponents argue the Taliban is not a unified bloc, but rather an amalgam that includes those who joined the insurgency out of frustration at the lack of security in their villages or because they were forcibly drafted, among other reasons. (*See sidebar, p. 10.*)

"If you look at a security map of Afghanistan between, say, 2003 and today, you have this creep of the insurgency sort of moving up from the south and east into other parts of the country," J. Alexander Thier, senior rule of law adviser with the United States Institute of Peace. That trend, he says, suggests many local communities and commanders that may have once supported the Afghan government have turned neutral or are actively supporting the Taliban. "There's real room in there to deal with their grievances and concerns about security and justice and the rule of law so as to change that tide."

Thier says he's not talking about seeking a "grand bargain" with the Taliban leadership now ensconced in Pakistan. "If what you're envisioning is [Afghan President] Karzai and [Taliban leader] Mullah Omar sitting on the deck of an aircraft carrier signing an armistice, I don't think that's feasible or realistic," he says. What is feasible are "micro level" negotiations.

"There is an enormous opportunity to work on what I would call mid- and low-level insurgents who, for a variety of reasons, were likely not engaged in the insurgency just a few years ago and were either pro-government or at least neutral. And I think they can and should be brought back to that position."

In an article this summer in *Foreign Affairs*, Fotini Christia, an assistant professor of political science at MIT, and Michael Semple, former deputy to the European Union special representative to Afghanistan, wrote that while "sending more troops is necessary to tip the balance of power against the insurgents, the move will have a lasting impact only if it is accompanied by a political 'surge,' a committed effort to persuade large groups of Taliban fighters to put down their arms and give up the fight."[36]

For reconciliation to work, say Fotini and Semple, Afghans first must feel secure. "The situation on the ground will need to be stabilized, and the Taliban must be reminded that they have no prospect of winning their current military campaign," they wrote. "If the Afghan government offers reconciliation as its carrot, it must also present force as its stick — hence the importance of sending more U.S. troops to Afghanistan, but also, in the long term, the importance of building up Afghanistan's own security forces. Reconciliation needs to be viewed as part of a larger military-political strategy to defeat the insurgency."

Some favor waiting to begin negotiation efforts, while others say they should occur simultaneously with the military campaign. Riedel of Brookings says he sees reason to believe that "a fair number" of Taliban foot soldiers and local commanders are not deeply dedicated to the core extremist cause as espoused by leaders such as Omar. Many rank and file Taliban may be "in this for one reason or another" — perhaps because "their tribe is aligned with the Taliban for local reasons, they're getting paid by the Taliban to do this better than they could be paid by anyone else, or simply because if you're a 17-year-old Pashtun male in Kandahar, fighting is kind of how you get your right of passage," Riedel says.

If the momentum changes on the battlefield "and it's a lot more dangerous to support the Taliban," Riedel continues, "my sense . . . is that these people will either defect or simply go home — they just won't fight."

Still, he says, it's not yet time to begin negotiations. First must come intelligence networks and greater political savvy in each district and province to capitalize on any Taliban inclinations to bend, he argues. "That is primarily an Afghan job, because they're the only people who are going to know the ins and outs of this. That's one of the things the new [U.S.] command arrangement needs to focus on the most. I don't think we're there. This requires really intense local information."

Yet, while the hour for negotiating may not be ripe, "the time is now to do the homework to do that," Riedel says, in order to develop "fine-grained knowledge of what's going on."

But Rajan Menon, a professor of international relations at Lehigh University, says "not coupling" the military campaign against the Taliban "with an olive branch is probably not effective."

Because huge challenges face the military operation — from the threat of civilian casualties to the weakness of the country's central government — the prospect of a long and costly war looms, he says. To avoid that, Menon says, the military effort should be occurring simultaneously with one aimed at encouraging "pragmatic" elements of the Taliban to buy into a process in which they "have to sell [their] ideas in the political marketplace."

The Taliban pragmatists, he says, would be offered a choice: either a long, open-ended war with heavy insurgent casualties or the opportunity to enter the political process as a group seeking victory through the ballot box.

"The question is, can you fracture the [insurgency] movement by laying down terms that are pretty stringent and test their will," Menon says. Nobody knows if the arms-and-olive branch approach would work, he says, but "you lose nothing by trying."

BACKGROUND

'Graveyard of Empires'

Afghanistan has long been known as the "crossroads of Central Asia," an apt name given the long list of outsiders who have ventured across its borders. It also is known as the "graveyard of empires," reflecting the difficulty faced by would-be conquerors of its remote terrain and disparate peoples.

The list is long. It includes the Persian king Darius I in the 6th century B.C. and the Macedonian conqueror Alexander the Great in 328 B.C., followed by the Scythians, White Huns, Turks, Arabs (who brought Islam in the 7th century A.D.), and the Mongol warrior Genghis Khan in 1219 A.D.[37]

Afghanistan's more recent history is a story of struggle against foreign domination, internal wrangling between reformists and traditionalists, coups, assassinations and war.

Modern Afghanistan began to take shape in the late 19th century, after a bitter fight for influence in Central Asia between the burgeoning British Empire and czarist Russia in what is known as "the Great Game." The contest led to Anglo-Afghan wars in 1839 and 1878. In the first, Afghan warriors forced the British into a deadly retreat from Kabul. The Afghans also had the upper hand over the British in the second war, which resulted in a treaty guaranteeing internal autonomy to Afghanistan while the British had control of its foreign affairs.

In 1880 Amir Abdur Rahman rose to the throne, reigning until 1901. Known as the "Iron Amir," he sought to institute reforms and weaken Pashtun resistance to centralized power but used methods, later emulated by the Taliban, to bring Uzbeks, Hazaras and Tajiks under Kabul's authority.[38] During his reign, Britain drew the so-called Durand Line separating Afghanistan from what was then India and later became Pakistan.

Rahman's son succeeded him but was assassinated in 1919. Under his successor, Amanullah — Rahman's grandson — Afghanistan gained full independence as a result of the Third Anglo War. Amanullah brought reforms that included ties with other countries and coeducational schools. But the moves alienated traditionalists, and Amanullah was forced to abdicate in 1929. His successor and cousin, Nadir Shah, was assassinated in 1933.

His death led to the 40-year reign of Crown Prince Mohammad Zahir Shah, Nadir Shah's son, who assumed power at 19.

Chaos and War

Under Zahir, Afghanistan sought to liberalize its political system. But the effort collapsed in the 1970s, and the country became a battleground between communist-backed leftists and a U.S.-backed Islamist resistance movement.

Afghanistan had tilted toward the Soviets in the Cold War era of the 1950s, partly because of U.S. ties to Pakistan, a country created by the partition of India in 1947. Afghan leaders wanted independence or at least autonomy for the Pashtun-dominated areas beyond the Durand Line.

Border tensions led Kabul to seek help from the Soviets, who responded with development loans and other aid in 1950. The United States sought to counter the Soviet

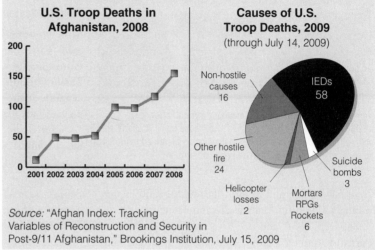

U.S. Troop Deaths Rose Steadily

U.S. troop fatalities have risen steadily since the United States entered Afghanistan in 2001 (graph at left). So far this year, IEDs (improvised explosive devices) caused slightly more than half the deaths (right).

U.S. Troop Deaths in Afghanistan, 2008

200
150
100
50
0
2001 2002 2003 2004 2005 2006 2007 2008

Causes of U.S. Troop Deaths, 2009
(through July 14, 2009)

Non-hostile causes 16
IEDs 58
Other hostile fire 24
Suicide bombs 3
Helicopter losses 2
Mortars RPGs Rockets 6

Source: "Afghan Index: Tracking Variables of Reconstruction and Security in Post-9/11 Afghanistan," Brookings Institution, July 15, 2009

AFP/Getty Images/Massoud Hossaini

Afghan President Hamid Karzai may face a runoff after the presidential election on Aug. 20, partly because many Afghans are looking for alternative leadership in the face of sustained insurgent violence, economic stagnation and political drift.

Union's influence, and in the 1960s both countries were helping to build up Afghanistan's infrastructure.

Between 1956 and 1978, according to Pakistani journalist Ahmed Rashid, Afghanistan received some $533 million in economic aid from the United States and $2.5 billion in both economic and military aid from the Soviets.[39]

In the 1960s Zahir introduced a constitutional monarchy and pressed for political freedoms that included new rights for women in voting, schooling and employment. "These changes, in a deeply traditional Islamic society, were not popular with everyone," the *Times* noted in a 2007 obituary of Zahir. "But his years were characterized by a rare long period of peace. This tranquility is recalled now with immense nostalgia. On the other hand, peace was not accompanied by prosperity, and the king was faulted for not developing the economy."[40]

Zahir's "experiment in democracy" did not lead to many lasting reforms, but "it permitted the growth of unofficial extremist parties on both the left and the right," including the communist People's Democratic Party of Afghanistan that was ideologically aligned with the Soviets, the U.S. State Department noted. The party split into rival groups in 1967 in a rift that "reflected ethnic, class and ideological divisions within Afghan society."[41]

In 1973 Zahir was ousted while in Europe for medical treatment. His cousin, former Prime Minister Sardar Mohammad Daoud Khan, whom Zahir had forced out in the 1960s, seized power in a bloodless coup. Daoud tried to institute reforms, but political unrest persisted.

He aligned closely with the Soviets, but his efforts to build his own political party and forge some links with the United States alienated communist radicals. In 1978, the People's Democratic Party overthrew Daoud, killing him and most of his family.

Soviet Invasion

More upheaval followed. The new leader, Nur Mohammad Taraki, imposed Marxist reforms that angered Islamic traditionalists and ethnic leaders, sparking revolts. Taraki was ousted and killed, and his successor, Hafizullah Amin, who resisted Soviet pressure to moderate his policies, was himself executed in 1979 by the Soviets.

Shortly before Amin's killing, the Soviets mounted a massive invasion of Afghanistan, starting a decade-long war that would permanently alter Afghanistan's profile in world affairs. In Amin's place, the Soviets installed Babrak Karmal. With Soviet military aid, he tried to impose authority throughout Afghanistan but ran into stiff opposition, especially in rural regions. An Islamist resistance movement called the Mujahedeen began receiving weapons and training from the United States and other countries in 1984, and soon the Soviet invasion was on the ropes.

In 1986 Karmal was replaced by Muhammad Najibullah, former head of the Afghan secret police, but the war continued to sour for the Soviets, who also were dealing with powerful political opposition at home. In 1988 Moscow signed agreements, along with the United States, Pakistan and Afghanistan, calling for an end to foreign intervention in Afghanistan. The Soviets withdrew early the following year, and in 1991 the USSR collapsed.

The Soviet invasion affirmed the idea of Afghanistan as a "graveyard" for invaders. Between 1979 and the Soviet withdrawal in 1989, some 14,500 Soviets died.[42] For the Afghan people, however, the war was a bloodbath that all but destroyed the economy and educational system and uprooted much of the population. The U.S. State Department estimates a million died.[43] Some estimates are higher.

Yet the end of the Soviet invasion brought no peace, but rather more chaos. After the Soviets departed, President George H. W. Bush withdrew support from Afghanistan, setting the stage for the conflict engulfing Afghanistan today. "Having won the Cold War," journalist Rashid wrote, "Washington had no further interest in Afghanistan or the region. This left a critical power vacuum for which the United States would pay an enormously high price a decade later."[44]

When the Soviet Union collapsed and the United States disengaged from Afghanistan, they left a country "that had become a cockpit for regional competition, a shattered state with no functioning security forces or civilian political process, a highly mobilized and armed population increasingly dependent on international organizations and cash for livelihood (including through the drug trade), and a multiplicity of armed groups linked transnationally to both state and non-state patrons," wrote Barnett Rubin, director of studies at the Center on International Cooperation at New York University, where he directs a program on Afghan reconstruction.[45]

The Mujahedeen were not a party to the accord leading to Soviet withdrawal, and through the early 1990s they continued fighting the Najibullah regime. In 1992 his government fell, and Burhanuddin Rabbani, an ethnic Tajik, became president. He declared Afghanistan an "Islamic state" but failed to ensure order.

By 1994 Afghanistan "was fast disintegrating," Rashid wrote. "Warlord fiefdoms ruled vast swathes of countryside. President Rabbani . . . governed only Kabul and the northeast of the country, while the west, centered on Herat, was under the control of warlord Ismael Khan. Six provinces in the north were ruled by the Uzbek general Rashid Dostum, and central Afghanistan was in the hands of the Hazaras. In the Pashtun south and east there was even greater fragmentation. . . . Warlords seized people's homes and farms for no reason, raped their daughters, abused and robbed the population and taxed travelers at will. Instead of refugees returning to Afghanistan, more began to leave the south for Pakistan."[46]

In 1994 a militant Islamist group — known as the Taliban and made up mainly of Pashtuns — sprang up in the south to oppose Rabbani. Their rise stemmed directly from the chaos wracking Afghanistan, Rashid wrote. "Frustrated young men who had fought against the Soviets and then returned to madrassas in Pakistan to resume their religious studies or to their villages in Afghanistan gathered around their elders demanding action."[47]

The Taliban took over Kabul in 1996, and by the early 2000s Rabbani's anti-Taliban Northern Alliance was limited to a slice of northern territory. "The Taliban instituted a repressive version of sharia law that outlawed music,

banned women from working or going to school and prohibited freedom of the press," wrote Jones, the RAND political scientist. "While it was a detestable regime that committed gross human rights violations, the Taliban succeeded in establishing law and order throughout most of the country."[48]

At the same time, the Taliban was forging links to al Qaeda. In 1996 Taliban leader Mullah Omar invited Osama bin Laden to stay with him in Kandahar, and even though "the CIA already considered bin Laden a threat . . ., he was left alone to ingratiate himself with Omar by providing money, fighters and ideological advice to the Taliban," Rashid wrote. "Bin Laden gathered the Arabs left behind in Afghanistan and Pakistan from the war against the Soviets, enlisted more militants from Arab countries, and established a new global terrorist infrastructure."[49]

The al Qaeda threat reached full force with the Sept. 11, 2001, attacks on the United States. In October President George W. Bush responded with a military assault called Operation Enduring Freedom. The Taliban promptly collapsed, and its leadership, along with that of al Qaeda, fled, in the view of many analysts, to Pakistan.

Yet still more trouble was to follow.

A Weakening Government

"The collapse of the Taliban government . . . created a condition of emerging anarchy," Jones wrote. In late 2001 a United Nations-sponsored conference in Bonn, Germany, laid down a process to rebuild Afghanistan's political system. With the Bonn agreement, "on paper, Afghanistan looked like it had a central government," Jones wrote. But "in practice . . ., Afghanistan had a fragile government that became weaker over time."[50]

The new government couldn't provide essential services, especially in rural areas, and a 2005 World Bank study found that "the urban elite" were the main beneficiaries of help, Jones wrote.[51] Meanwhile, the Afghan government had various problems, including the inability to provide security outside of Kabul, in large measure due to "the inability of the U.S. government to build competent Afghan security forces, especially the police."[52]

American force levels were low, too, with "the number of U.S. troops per capita in Afghanistan . . . significantly less than in almost every state-building effort since World War II," Jones wrote.[53] Moreover, the United States gave "significant assistance to local warlords, further undermining governance and weakening the ability of the Afghan state to establish law and order."[54]

The Taliban rebounded, aided by what critics have called a lack of focus by the Bush administration after its decision to invade Iraq in 2003. In Afghanistan, reconstruction and security issues were left unattended, critics say, leaving an opening for the Taliban — along with criminals, warlords, drug traffickers and others — to assert brutal control. Afghan opium production soared, al Qaeda sanctuaries in the border region of Pakistan festered and once again the region threatened to unleash a new wave of global terrorism.

The threat came not only from Afghanistan, but Pakistan, too.

In an article last year on the emboldened Taliban and al Qaeda forces in the Pakistani border region, celebrated *New York Times* war correspondent Dexter Filkins noted that Islamist militants continued to be backed by Pakistani military and intelligence services. Then, in 1994, came Pakistan's "most fateful move," he wrote. Concerned about the mayhem that swept through Afghanistan after the Soviet withdrawal, Pakistani Prime Minister Benazir Bhutto and her administration intervened on behalf of the Taliban, Filkins wrote.

"We created the Taliban," Bhutto's interior minister, Nasrullah Babar, told Filkins. "Mrs. Bhutto had a vision: that through a peaceful Afghanistan, Pakistan could extend its influence into the resource-rich territories of Central Asia." Her dream didn't materialize — the Taliban's conquest of Afghanistan fell short, and Bhutto was assassinated in late 2007. But as Filkins noted, the Taliban training camps, sometimes supported by Pakistani intelligence officials, "were beacons to Islamic militants from around the world."[55]

Concerns persist about Pakistan's intentions and security capabilities. In recent weeks, as militants threatened Islamabad and other Pakistani cities, Pakistan has gone after insurgents in the Swat Valley and elsewhere. But Pakistani officials also have criticized U.S. attacks on insurgent strongholds using unmanned drone planes.

The big question, as posed by Filkins and others, is whether Pakistan is willing — or able — to control the radical forces within its border region. "This was not supposed to be a major worry," Filkins wrote, noting that after the Sept. 11 attacks Pakistani President Pervez Musharraf backed the United States, helped find al Qaeda

suspects, attacked militants in Pakistan's remote tribal areas and vowed to fight terrorism — all in return for $10 billion in U.S. aid since 2001.

But Pakistani military and civilian leaders have survived by playing a "double game," Filkins wrote, promising the United States they were cracking down on militants, and sometimes doing so, while also allowing, and even helping, the same militants.

One reason for the "double game" is Pakistan's longstanding tension with India, especially over the disputed border region of Kashmir. "You can't address Pakistan without dealing with India," says Riedel, the Brookings scholar.

Some experts say Pakistan views its support of the Taliban as a hedge against an India-friendly government coming to power in Afghanistan.

"The Pakistanis have convinced themselves that India's objective is a friendly Afghanistan that can pose a second front against Pakistan," says Riedel. "They see the Afghan Taliban, in particular, as a very useful asset. It keeps Afghanistan from becoming an Indian client state, and their conviction is that . . . it's only a matter of time" until the United States leaves Afghanistan. The Pakistanis believe that "if they wait it out, their client will be the dominant power at least in southern and eastern Afghanistan."

The Cato Institute's Innocent says the Obama administration has made a "profound strategic miscalculation" by not recognizing how much Pakistani leaders fear a non-Pashtun, India-leaning government assuming power in Kabul.

India has used its influence in Afghanistan, she says, to funnel weapons to a separatist movement in southwest Pakistan's sprawling Baluchistan region — a movement that some say could pose an existential threat to Pakistan. That, in turn, has given Pakistan an incentive to keep Afghanistan from growing closer to India.

Says Innocent, "This rivalry between [Pakistan and India] is the biggest impediment to stabilizing Afghanistan."

CURRENT SITUATION
Measurable Metrics

In the weeks leading up to this summer's Helmand River operation, Defense Secretary Gates expressed optimism

Should the president announce an Afghanistan exit strategy?

YES   Malou Innocent
Foreign Policy Analyst
Cato Institute

Written for *CQ Researcher*, July 2009

No strategic, political or economic gains could outweigh the costs of America maintaining an indefinite military presence in Afghanistan. Washington can continue to disrupt terrorist havens by monitoring the region with unmanned aerial vehicles, retaining advisers for training Afghan forces and using covert operatives against specific targets.

Many policy makers and prominent opinion leaders are pushing for a large-scale, long-term military presence in Afghanistan. But none of their rationales for such a heavy presence withstands close scrutiny.

Al Qaeda poses a manageable security problem, not an existential threat to America. Washington's response, with an open-ended mission in Afghanistan, is both unnecessary and unsustainable.

Policy makers also tend to conflate al Qaeda with indigenous Pashtun-dominated militias, such as the Taliban. America's security, however, will not necessarily be at risk even if an oppressive regime takes over a contiguous fraction of Afghan territory.

Additionally, the argument that America has a moral obligation to prevent the reemergence of reprehensible groups like the Taliban seems instead a justification for the perpetuation of American empire. After all, America never made a substantive policy shift toward or against the Taliban's misogynistic, oppressive and militant Islamic regime when it controlled Afghanistan in the 1990s. Thus, the present moral outrage against the group can be interpreted as opportunistic.

Some policy makers claim the war is worth waging because terrorists flourish in failed states. But that cannot account for terrorists who thrive in states with the sovereignty to reject external interference. That is one reason why militants find sanctuary in Pakistan. In fact, attempts to stabilize Afghanistan destabilize Pakistan. Amassing troops in Afghanistan feeds the perception of a foreign occupation, spawning more terrorist recruits for Pakistani militias and thus placing undue stress on an already-weakened, nuclear-armed nation.

It's also important to recognize that Afghanistan's land-locked position in Central Asia will forever render it vulnerable to meddling from surrounding states. This factor will make sealing the country's borders from terrorists impossible.

Finally, Americans should not fear appearing "weak" after withdrawal. The United States accounts for almost half of the world's military spending, wields one of the planet's largest nuclear arsenals and can project its power around the globe. Remaining in Afghanistan is more likely to weaken the United States militarily and economically than would withdrawal.

NO   Ilan Berman
Vice President for Policy
American Foreign Policy Council

Written for *CQ Researcher*, July 2009

It has been called the "graveyard of empires," a place that for thousands of years has stymied invading armies. Today, Afghanistan remains one of the West's most vexing international security conundrums — and a pressing foreign policy challenge for the Obama administration.

Indeed, for almost as long as Obama has been in office, critics have counseled the new U.S. president to set a date certain for an American exit from Afghanistan. To his credit, Mr. Obama has done no such thing. To the contrary, through the "Af-Pak" strategy unveiled in March, the White House has effectively doubled down on the American investment in Afghanistan's security. It has done so for two principal reasons.

The first has to do with Afghanistan's importance to the overall struggle against radical Islam. In the years before Sept. 11, Afghanistan became an incubator of international terrorism. And the sinister synergy created there between al Qaeda and the ruling Taliban movement was directly responsible for the most devastating terrorist attack in American history. Preventing a repeat occurrence remains an overriding priority, which is why Washington has committed to propping up the fragile government of Afghan President Hamid Karzai with the troops and training necessary to hold its ground.

The second is an understanding that Afghanistan is essentially a derivative problem. Much of the instability that exists there today is a function of radicalism nurtured next door, in Pakistan. The Taliban, after all, was an invention of Pakistan's Inter-Services Intelligence back in the mid-1990s, and Islamabad's intelligence czars (as well as their military counterparts) remain heavily invested in its future. Today, the Taliban poses perhaps a greater threat to Pakistan's own stability than to that of Afghanistan. But a retraction of U.S. and allied forces from the latter is sure to create a political vacuum that Islamic radicals will be all too eager to exploit.

These realities have defined the Obama administration's approach. Unlike previous foreign powers that have gotten involved in Afghanistan, the United States today is interested simply in what the military calls "area denial." The goal is not to conquer and claim, but to deny the Taliban the necessary breathing room to regroup and re-entrench.

Setting a firm date for an American withdrawal would fundamentally undermine that objective. It would also serve to provide regional radicals with far greater certainty that the U.S. investment in Afghanistan's stability is both limited and reversible.

about the war in Afghanistan, but acknowledged that the American public's patience with its progress could be limited.

"I think what the people in the United States want to see is the momentum shifting to see that the strategies that we're following are working," he said on CBS' "60 Minutes." "And that's why I've said in nine months to a year, we need to evaluate how we're doing."[56]

Part of that evaluation will be done through "metrics," statistical measurements on everything from civilian casualties to the strength of the Afghan National Army. The approach is part of the Obama strategy.

"Going forward, we will not blindly stay the course," Obama said, but rather "we will set clear metrics to measure progress and hold ourselves accountable. We'll consistently assess our efforts to train Afghan security forces and our progress in combating insurgents. We will measure the growth of Afghanistan's economy and its illicit narcotics production. And we will review whether we are using the right tools and tactics to make progress towards accomplishing our goals."[57]

One measure attracting rising attention in recent weeks is that of troop levels. Michael E. O'Hanlon, a senior fellow at Brookings, wrote this summer in the *Washington Examiner* that "for all its virtues," the Obama administration's Afghan strategy "may still lowball requirements for the Afghanistan mission to succeed."

"The administration's decisions in March to increase U.S. troop numbers to 68,000 (making for about 100,000 foreign troops in all), and Afghan army and police to about 215,000 will leave combined coalition forces at only half the levels in Iraq during the surge," O'Hanlon wrote, "and Afghanistan is slightly larger and more populous."

O'Hanlon cautioned against closing the door on adding more troops and pointed to "troubling signs that the Obama administration may be digging in against any future troop requirements." While "we may or may not have enough forces in Afghanistan" to accomplish the mission's full range of goals, he concluded, "let's not close off the conversation until we learn a little bit more."[58]

NATO's Cold Shoulder

Among the thorniest of the troop-level issues is the role of NATO forces in Afghanistan. As of June, countries participating in the NATO-led International Security

Assistance Forces (ISAF), a mission mandated by the U.N. under the 2001 Bonn agreement, have committed about 32,000 troops to Afghanistan, not counting those from the United States, according to the Brookings Institution. The top three were the United Kingdom, which had committed 8,300 troops, Germany (3,380) and Canada (2,830). Several countries, including the U.K. and Germany, were expected to send a small number of additional troops to provide security for the Aug. 20 election.

The Obama administration has been largely unsuccessful in prodding European nations to send more troops to Afghanistan. In April, in what the online edition of the *Times* of London billed as a "charm offensive" by Obama on his "debut international tour," leaders on the European continent "turned their backs" on the president, with British Prime Minister Gordon Brown "the only one to offer substantial help." Brown offered to send several hundred extra troops to provide election security, the *Times* noted, "but even that fell short of the thousands of combat troops that the U.S. was hoping to [gain] from the prime minister."[59]

Nonetheless, Obama has mustered some recent support for his Afghan policy. In late July Spain's prime minister, José Luís Rodriguez Zapatero, said his country was willing to increase its force on long-term deployment to Afghanistan, *The New York Times* reported.[60]

Early this month, NATO approved a reorganized command structure for Afghanistan, agreeing to set up a New Intermediate Joint Headquarters in Kabul under U.S. Lt. General David M. Rodriguez, who will manage the war on a day-to-day basis and report to McChrystal. NATO made the move at the first meeting of its governing body, the North Atlantic Council, under new NATO Secretary General Anders Fogh Rasmussen, former Danish prime minister.[61] Rasmussen, in his first comments as secretary general, called on the United Nations and European Union to help defeat the Taliban. "NATO will do its part, but it cannot do it alone," he said. "This needs to be an international effort, both military and civilian."[62]

The effectiveness of having more NATO troops in Afghanistan has been a matter of debate. At a forum in June, Brookings scholar Jeremy Shapiro, recently back from a visit to southern Afghanistan, suggested U.S. commanders have had little faith in the NATO command structure.

"Each of the main countries there is really running its own provincial war," Shapiro said. "The overall problem is that there really is no unity of command in Afghanistan so we're unable . . . to prioritize and to shift resources to deal with the most important problems. . . . It's related to the fact that for every NATO force in Afghanistan including the Americans, there are two chains of command, one up through the NATO commander who is an American, and one to the national capital, and in case of conflict, the national capital command always takes priority.

"The result is that each of the lead countries in the south, the Canadians in Kandahar, the British in Helmand, the Dutch in Uruzgan, are focused on their own priorities, on improving specific indicators in their piece of the war in their own province or district without a great deal of attention to the impact of that measure on the overall fight."

In impoverished Uruzgan Province, for example, the Dutch are doing "impressive things" with development efforts, but Uruzgan "is to a large degree serving as a sanctuary for insurgents to rest and refit and plan and to engage in the struggle in Kandahar and Helmand" province, Shapiro said.

The Canadians and British "would argue . . . that the priority for Afghanistan is not Uruzgan, it is Kandahar and Helmand and [if] the development of Uruzgan comes at the cost of strengthening the insurgency in other provinces, it's perhaps not the best use of resources."

Shapiro said he believes that as the number of U.S. troops has increased, especially in southern Afghanistan, "the focus for the U.S. military command is on . . . assigning roles to coalition partners that don't require intense coordination. . . . What that presages is an Americanization of the war, including in the south." By next year, Shapiro said, NATO will remain in command, "but I would be very dubious that we'll be truly fighting a NATO war at that point."[63]

Americanizing the War

Such predictions of an Americanized war are at odds with the administration's perception of the Afghan mission. Obama told *Sky News*, a British news outlet, that British contributions to the war effort are "critical" and that "this is not an American mission. The mission in Afghanistan is one that the Europeans have as much if not more of a stake in what we do. . . . The likelihood of a terrorist attack in London is at least as high, if not higher, than it is in the United States."[64]

Any further Americanization of the war will doubtlessly fuel scrutiny of the Afghan strategy in Congress and bolster demands for the Obama administration to set forth an exit strategy.

This summer, the U.S. House of Representatives strongly rejected an amendment calling on the defense secretary to submit a report no later than Dec. 31 outlining an exit strategy for U.S. forces in Afghanistan.

"Every military mission has a beginning, a middle, a time of transition and an end," said Rep. McGovern, the Massachusetts Democrat who sponsored the measure. "But I have yet to see that vision articulated in any document, speech or briefing. We're not asking for an immediate withdrawal. We're sure not talking about cutting or running or retreating, just a plan. If there is no military solution for Afghanistan, then please just tell us how we will know when our military contribution to the political solution has ended."[65]

But "focusing on an exit versus a strategy is irresponsible and fails to recognize that our efforts in Afghanistan are vital to preventing future terrorist attacks on the American people and our allies," argued Rep. Howard McKeon, R-Calif.[66]

The amendment's defeat did nothing to allay scrutiny of the war. Sen. John F. Kerry, D-Mass., chairman of the Senate Foreign Relations Committee, told *GlobalPost*, an online international-news site, that he planned to hold oversight hearings on U.S. involvement in Afghanistan.[67]

"End of summer, early fall," Kerry said, "we are going to take a hard look at Afghanistan."

OUTLOOK
More Violence

Military strategists say the Afghan war is likely to get more violent in coming months as U.S. and NATO forces battle the insurgency.

One immediate concern is whether the Taliban will make good on threats to disrupt this month's presidential election. While additional troops are being deployed to guard against attacks, officials have said ensuring the security of all 28,000 polling places is impossible.[68]

Meanwhile, tensions are likely to remain between those calling for a strict timetable for de-escalating the war and those arguing in favor of staying the course.

"I certainly do not think it would be a wise idea to impose a timeline on ourselves," says Riedel of Brookings, although he points to "political realities" that include the idea "that some measure of improvement in the security situation on the ground needs to be apparent over the course of the next 18 to 24 months."

Riedel expresses confidence that will occur. Once all scheduled troop deployments are in place, he says, "it's reasonable to expect that you can see some impact from [those deployments] in 18 to 24 months. Not victory, not the surrender of [Taliban leader] Mullah Omar, but some measurable decline in the pace of Taliban activity, some increase in the number of districts and provinces which are regarded as safe enough for [non-governmental organizations] to work in."

Beyond demands for on-the-ground progress in Afghanistan, the Obama administration faces other pressures as it struggles to get a grip on the Afghanistan and Pakistan region. One is helping U.S. allies maintain support for the war. In Britain, Prime Minister Brown has faced an uproar over growing British casualties that critics say stem from an underfunded defense budget that led to inadequate troop levels and equipment. [69] At home, as the financial crisis, health-care reform and other issues put pressure on the federal budget, Obama is likely to face opposition in Congress over additional war funding.

And Obama also is under pressure to address incendiary issues left over from the Bush administration. In July, a *New York Times* report detailed how the Bush administration repeatedly sought to discourage an investigation of charges that forces under U.S.-backed warlord Gen. Abdul Rashid Dostum massacred hundreds or even thousands of Taliban prisoners of war during the 2001 invasion of Afghanistan.[70]

In an editorial, the *Times* said Obama has directed aides to study the issue and that the administration is pressing Afghan President Karzai not to return Dostum to power. But, it added, Obama "needs to order a full investigation into the massacre."[71]

In the long run, one of the biggest challenges facing the Obama administration is its effort to instill sound governance in a country saturated with graft.

Afghanistan's corruption "reveals the magnitude of the task," says Walt, the Harvard international affairs professor. "Fixing corrupt public institutions is really hard once a pattern of behavior has been established, where money is flowing in non-regular ways. It's very difficult for outsiders to re-engineer those social and political practices, even if we were committed to staying five or 10 years."

Walt says he hopes he's wrong — "that the injection of the right kind of American power will create space for some kind of political reconciliation." But he's not optimistic. "I believe several years from now, [Afghanistan] will look like a sinkhole."

NOTES

1. Chris Brummitt, "Afghan firefight shows challenge for U.S. troops," The Associated Press, June 21, 2009, http://news.yahoo.com/s/ap/20090621/ap_on_re_as/as_afghan_taking_on_the_taliban.

2. Laura King, "6 U.S. troops killed in Afghanistan," *Los Angeles Times*, Aug. 3, 2009, www.latimes.com/news/nationworld/world/la-fg-afghan-deaths3-2009aug03,0,3594308.story.

3. For background, see Robert Kiener, "Crisis in Pakistan," *CQ Global Researcher*, December 2008, pp. 321-348, and Roland Flamini, "Afghanistan on the Brink," *CQ Global Researcher*, June 2007, pp. 125-150.

4. "Remarks by the President on a New Strategy for Afghanistan and Pakistan," White House, March 27, 2009, www.whitehouse.gov.

5. See www.boston.com/news/nation/washington/articles/2009/07/23/obama_victory_not_right_word_for_afghanistan/.

6. For background, see Roland Flamini, "Future of NATO," *CQ Global Researcher*, January 2009, pp. 1-26.

7. Pamela Constable, "For Karzai, Stumbles On Road To Election," *The Washington Post*, July 13, 2009, www.washingtonpost.com/wp-dyn/content/article/2009/07/12/AR2009071202426.html.

8. See, for example, Fred Kaplan, "Counterinsur genterrorism," *Slate*, March 27, 2009, www.slate.com/id/2214726/.

9. Ann Scott Tyson, "New Approach to Afghanistan Likely," *The Washington Post*, June 3, 2009, www

.washingtonpost.com/wp-dyn/content/article/ 2009/06/02/AR2009060203828.html.

10. *Ibid.*

11. Sharon Otterman, "Civilian death toll rises in Afghanistan," *The New York Times*, Aug. 1, 2009, www.nytimes.com/2009/08/01/world/asia/01afghan .html?scp=1&sq=civilian%20death%20toll%20 rises&st=cse.

12. White House, *op. cit.*

13. See also John Mueller, "How Dangerous Are the Taliban?" *foreignaffairs.com*, April 15, 2009, www .foreignaffairs.com/articles/64932/john-mueller/ how-dangerous-are-the-taliban.

14. Matthew Kaminski, "Holbrooke of South Asia," *The Wall Street Journal*, April 11, 2009.

15. Quoted in Rajiv Chandrasekaran, "Marines Deploy on Major Mission," *The Washington Post*, July 2, 2009, www.washingtonpost.com/wp-dyn/content/ article/2009/07/01/AR2009070103202.html.

16. Jared Allen and Roxana Tiron, "Obey warns Afghanistan funding may slow unless significant progress made," *The Hill*, May 4, 2009, http://thehill .com/leading-the-news/obey-warns-afghanistan-fund ing-may-slow-unless-significant-progress-made- 2009-05-04.html.

17. *The New York Times*/CBS News Poll, June 12-16, 2009, http://graphics8.nytimes.com/packages/ images/nytint/docs/latest-new-york-times-cbs-news- poll/original.pdf.

18. See Dexter Filkins, "Afghan corruption: Everything for Sale," *The New York Times*, Jan. 2, 2009, www .nytimes.com/2009/01/02/world/asia/02iht-corrupt .1.19050534html?scp=2&sq=everything%20for% 20sale&st=cse.

19. See Malou Innocent, "Obama's Mumbai problem," *The Guardian*, Jan. 27, 2009, www.guardian.co.uk/ commentisfree/cifamerica/2009/jan/27/obama-in dia-pakistan-relations.

20. Peter Bergen, "Winning the Good War," *Washington Monthly*, July/August 2009, www.washington- monthly.com/features/2009/0907.bergen.html# Byline.

21. Greg Bruno, "U.S. Needs a Stronger Commitment to Improving Afghan Governance," Council on Foreign Relations, July 30, 2009, www.cfr.org/publi cation/19936/us_needs_a_stronger_commitment_ to_improving_afghan_governance.html?bread crumb=%2Fpublication%2Fpublication_list%3 Ftype%3 Dinterview.

22. Anthony H. Cordesman, "The Afghanistan Campaign: Can We Win?" Center for Strategic and International Studies, July 22, 2009. Cordesman expands on his ideas in a paper available at http:// csis.org/files/publication/090722_CanWeAchieve Mission.pdf.

23. Richard A. Oppel Jr., "Allied Officers Concerned by Lack of Afghan Forces," *The New York Times*, July 8, 2009, www.nytimes.com/2009/07/08/world/ asia/08afghan.html?ref=world.

24. Quoted in Associated Press, "Marines: More Afghan Soldiers Needed in Helmand," CBS News, July 8, 2009, www.cbsnews.com/stories/2009/07/08/ap/ politics/main5145174.shtml.

25. Quoted in Oppel, *op. cit.*

26. Transcript, "Death Toll Mounts as Coalition Forces Confront Taliban," "The NewsHour with Jim Lehrer," PBS, July 15, 2009, www.pbs.org/newshour/bb/ military/july-dec09/afghancas_07-15.html.

27. Bob Woodward, "Key in Afghanistan: Economy, Not Military," *The Washington Post*, July 1, 2009, www.washingtonpost.com/wp-dyn/content/article/ 2009/06/30/AR2009063002811.html.

28. *Ibid.*

29. "Face the Nation," CBS News, July 5, 2009.

30. Greg Jaffe and Karen De Young, "U.S. General Sees Afghan Army, Police Insufficient," *The Washington Post*, July 11, 2009, www.washingtonpost.com/wp- dyn/content/article/2009/07/10/AR2009071002975 .html.

31. Greg Jaffe, "U.S. Troops Erred in Airstrikes on Civilians," *The Washington Post*, June 20, 2009, www.washingtonpost.com/wp-dyn/content/article/ 2009/06/19/AR2009061903359.html.

32. Quoted in Robert Burns, "Analysis: reducing Afghan civilian deaths key goal," The Associated Press, June 13, 2009, www.google.com/hostednews/ap/article/ eqM5hyNJNBigtMGe2M12B2s3w6OCoAbQD98 Q2VP80.

33. Bergen, *op. cit.*

34. Helene Cooper and Sheryl Gay Stolberg, "Obama Ponders Outreach to Elements of Taliban," *The New York Times*, March 8, 2009, www.nytimes.com/2009/03/08/us/politics/08obama.html?scp=1&sq=obama%20ponders%20outreach%20to%20elements%20of%20taliban&st=cse.

35. Quoted in *ibid.*

36. Fotini Christia and Michael Semple, "Flipping the Taliban: How to Win in Afghanistan," *Foreign Affairs*, July/August 2009, p. 34, www.foreignaffairs.com/articles/65151/fotini-christia-and-michael-semple/flipping-the-taliban. Co-author Semple, who has significant background in holding dialogues with the Taliban, was expelled from Afghanistan in 2007 by the Karzai government amid accusations he and another diplomat held unauthorized talks with the Taliban.

37. See, "Background Note: Afghanistan," U.S. Department of State, November 2008, www.state.gov/r/pa/ei/bgn/5380.htm; also, *Grolier Encyclopedia of Knowledge*, Vol. 1, 1991. See also Kenneth Jost, "Rebuilding Afghanistan," *CQ Researcher*, Dec. 21, 2001, pp. 1041-1064.

38. Ahmed Rashid, *Descent into Chaos* (2008), p. 8.

39. *Ibid.*

40. Barry Bearak, "Mohammad Zahir Shah, Last Afghan King, Dies at 92," *The New York Times*, July 24, 2007, www.nytimes.com/2007/07/24/world/asia/24shah.html.

41. U.S. State Department, *op. cit.*

42. *Ibid.*

43. *Ibid.*

44. Rashid, *op. cit.*, p. 11.

45. Barnett R. Rubin, "The Transformation of the Afghan State," in J. Alexander Thier, ed., *The Future of Afghanistan* (2009), p. 15.

46. Rashid, *op. cit.*, pp. 12-13.

47. *Ibid.*, p. 13.

48. Seth G. Jones, "The Rise of Afghanistan's Insurgency," *International Security*, Vol. 32, No. 4, spring 2008, p. 19.

49. Rashid, *op. cit.*, p. 15.

50. Jones, *op. cit.*, p. 20.

51. *Ibid.* The reference to "the urban elite" comes from "Afghanistan: State Building, Sustaining Growth, and Reducing Poverty," World Bank Report No. 29551-AF, 2005, p. xxvi.

52. *Ibid.*, pp. 20, 22.

53. *Ibid.*, p. 24.

54. *Ibid.*, p. 25.

55. Dexter Filkins, "Right at the Edge," *The New York Times*, Sept. 7, 2008, www.nytimes.com/2008/09/07/magazine/07pakistan-t.html.

56. "Bob Gates, America's Secretary of War," "60 Minutes," May 17, 2009, www.cbsnews.com/stories/2009/05/14/60minutes/main5014588.shtml.

57. White House, *op. cit.*

58. Michael O'Hanlon, "We Might still Need More Troops In Afghanistan," *Washington Examiner*, July 7, 2009, www.washingtonexaminer.com/politics/50044002.html.

59. Michael Evans and David Charter, "Barack Obama fails to win NATO troops he wants for Afghanistan," *Timesonline*, April 4, 2009, www.timesonline.co.uk/tol/news/world/us_and_americas/article6032342.ece.

60. Victoria Burnett and Rachel Donadio, "Spain Is Open to Bolstering Forces in Afghanistan," *The New York Times*, July 30, 2009, www.nytimes.com/2009/07/30/world/europe/30zapatero.html?ref=world.

61. Steven Erlanger, "NATO Reorganizes Afghan Command Structure," *The New York Times*, Aug. 4, 2009, www.nytimes.com/2009/08/05/world/05nato.html.

62. Thomas Harding, "New NATO head calls for 'international effort' in Afghanistan," *Telegraph*, Aug. 3, 2009, www.telegraph.co.uk/news/worldnews/asia/afghanistan/5967377/New-Nato-head-calls-for-international-effort-in-Afghanistan.html.

63. "Afghanistan and Pakistan: A Status Report," Brookings Institution, June 8, 2009, www.brookings.edu/~/media/Files/events/2009/0608_afghanistan_pakistan/20090608_afghanistan_pakistan.pdf.

64. "Taliban pushed back, long way to go: Obama," Reuters, July 12, 2009, www.reuters.com/article/topNews/idUSTRE56A2Q420090712?feedType=RSS&feedName=topNews&rpc=22&sp=true.

65. Quoted in Dan Robinson, "U.S. Lawmakers Reject Amendment Calling for an Exit Strategy from Afghanistan," *VOA News*, June 26, 2009, www .voanews.com/english/2009-06-26-voa1.cfm.

66. Quoted in *ibid.*

67. John Aloysius Farrell, "Kerry: 'We are going to take a hard look at Afghanistan,' " *GlobalPost*, updated July 10, 2009, www.globalpost.com.

68. Pamela Constable, "Karzai's Challengers Face Daunting Odds," *The Washington Post*, July 6, 2009, p. 7A.

69. John F. Burns, "Criticism of Afghan War Is on the Rise in Britain," *The New York Times*, July 12, 2009, www .nytimes.com/2009/07/12/world/europe/12britain .html?scp=1&sq=criticism%20of%20afghan%20 war%20is%20on%20the%20rise&st=cse.

70. James Risen, "U.S. Inaction Seen After Taliban P.O.W.'s Died," *The New York Times*, July 11, 2009, www.nytimes.com/2009/07/11/world/asia/11afghan .html?scp=1&sq=U.S.%20Inaction%20Seen%20 After%20Taliban&st=cse.

71. "The Truth About Dasht-i-Leili," *The New York Times*, July 14, 2009, www.nytimes.com/2009/07/14/ opinion/14tue2html?scp=5&sq=U.S.%20 Inaction%20Seen%20After%20Taliban&st=cse.

BIBLIOGRAPHY

Books

Coll, Steve, *Ghost Wars,* **Penguin Press, 2004.**
The former *Washington Post* managing editor, now president of the New America Foundation think tank, traces the CIA's involvement in Afghanistan since the Soviet invasion in the 1970s.

Kilcullen, David, *The Accidental Guerrilla,* **Oxford University Press, 2009.**
A former Australian Army officer and counterterrorism adviser argues that strategists have tended to conflate small insurgencies and broader terror movements.

Peters, Gretchen, *Seeds of Terror,* **Thomas Dunne Books, 2009.**
A journalist examines the role of Afghanistan's illegal narcotics industry in fueling the activities of the Taliban and al Qaeda.

Rashid, Ahmed, *Descent into Chaos,* **Viking, 2008.**
A Pakistani journalist argues that "the U.S.-led war on terrorism has left in its wake a far more unstable world than existed on" Sept. 11, 2001.

Wright, Lawrence, *The Looming Tower,* **Knopf, 2006.**
In a Pulitzer Prize-winning volume that remains a must-read for students of the wars in Afghanistan and Iraq, a *New Yorker* staff writer charts the spread of Islamic fundamentalism and emergence of al Qaeda that gave rise to the Sept. 11 attacks.

Articles

Bergen, Peter, "Winning the Good War," *Washington Monthly,* **July/August 2009, www.washingtonmonthly .com/features/2009/0907.bergen.html.**
A senior fellow at the New America Foundation argues that skepticism about the Obama administration's chances of victory in Afghanistan are based on a misreading of that nation's history and people.

Christia, Fotini, and Michael Semple, "Flipping the Taliban," *Foreign Affairs,* **July/August 2009.**
A political scientist (Christia) and a specialist on Afghanistan and Pakistan who has talked with the Taliban argue that while more troops are necessary, "the move will have a lasting impact only if it is accompanied by a political 'surge' " aimed at persuading large groups of Taliban fighters to lay down arms.

Hogan, Michael, "Milt Bearden: Afghanistan Is 'Obama's War,' " *Vanityfair.com,* **Feb. 5, 2009, www.vanityfair .com/online/politics/2009/02/milt-bearden-afghani stan-is-obamas-war.html.**
Bearden, the former CIA field officer in Afghanistan when U.S. covert action helped expel the Soviet Union, says in this Q&A that "the only thing that is absolutely certain about this war is that it's going to be Obama's war, just as Iraq will be Bush's war."

Jones, Seth G., "The Rise of Afghanistan's Insurgency," *International Security,* **Vol. 32, No. 4, spring 2008, http://belfercenter.ksg.harvard.edu/files/IS3204_ pp007-040_Jones.pdf.**
A RAND Corporation political scientist analyzes the reasons a violent insurgency began to develop in Afghanistan earlier this decade.

Mueller, John, "How Dangerous Are the Taliban?" *Foreignaffairs.com*, April 15, 2009, www.foreignaffairs.com/articles/64932/john-mueller/how-dangerous-are-the-taliban.
An Ohio State University political science professor questions whether the Taliban and al Qaeda are a big enough menace to the United States to make a long war in Afghanistan worth the cost.

Riedel, Bruce, "Comparing the U.S. and Soviet Experiences in Afghanistan," *CTC Sentinel*, Combating Terrorism Center, May 2009, www.brookings.edu/~/media/Files/rc/articles/2009/05_afghanistan_riedel/05_afghanistan_riedel.pdf.
A Brookings Institution scholar and former senior adviser to President Barack Obama examines the "fundamental differences" between the Soviet and U.S. experiences in the region.

Rosenberg, Matthew, and Zahid Hussain, "Pakistan Taps Tribes' Anger with Taliban," *The Wall Street Journal*, June 6-7, 2009, p. A14.
Pakistani anger at the Taliban in tribal regions bordering Afghanistan is growing, and Pakistan's military leaders hope to capitalize on that anger as they mount a grueling campaign against insurgents in North and South Waziristan.

Reports and Studies

Campbell, Jason, Michael O'Hanlon and Jeremy Shapiro, "Assessing Counterinsurgency and Stabilization Missions," Brookings Institution, Policy Paper No. 14, May 2009, www.brookings.edu/~/media/Files/rc/papers/2009/05_counterinsurgency_ohanlon/05_counterinsurgency_ohanlon.pdf.
Brookings scholars examine the status of change in Afghanistan and Iraq and explain why "2009 is expected by many to be a pivotal year in Afghanistan."

Tellis, Ashley J., "Reconciling With the Taliban?" Carnegie Endowment for International Peace, 2009, www.carnegieendowment.org/files/reconciling_with_taliban.pdf.
Efforts at reconciliation today would undermine American credibility and jeopardize the success of the U.S.-led mission in Afghanistan, argues a senior associate at the endowment.

For More Information

American Foreign Policy Council, 509 C St., N.E., Washington, DC 20002; (202) 543-1006; www.afpc.org. Provides analysis on foreign-policy issues.

Brookings Institution, 1775 Massachusetts Ave., N.W., Washington, DC 20036; (202) 797-6000; www.brookings.edu. Liberal-oriented think tank that provides research, data and other resources on security and political conditions in Afghanistan and Pakistan and global counterterrorism.

Cato Institute, 1000 Massachusetts Ave., N.W., Washington, DC 20001; (202) 842-0200; www.cato.org. Libertarian-oriented think tank that provides analysis on U.S. policy toward Afghanistan and Pakistan.

RAND Corp., 1776 Main St., Santa Monica, CA 90401; (310) 393-0411; www.rand.org. Research organization that studies domestic and international policy issues.

United Nations Office on Drugs and Crime, U.N. Headquarters, DC1 Building, Room 613, One United Nations Plaza, New York, NY 10017; (212) 963-5698; www.unodc.org. Helps member states fight illicit drugs, crime and terrorism; compiles data on opium poppy production.

United States Institute of Peace, 1200 17th St., N.W., Washington, DC 20036; (202) 457-1700; www.usip.org. Provides analysis, training and other resources to prevent and end conflicts.

2

U.S. Policy on Iran

Peter Katel

Iranian women demonstrate in support of the country's nuclear development program at the uranium conversion facility in Isfahan, about 250 miles south of Tehran. Contrary to U.S. claims, Iran says the program is for peaceful uses of nuclear energy.

From *CQ Researcher*, November 16, 2007.

While U.S. troops fight in Iraq, the Bush administration is waging a war of words with neighboring Iran. Bad blood has existed between Washington and Tehran for nearly three decades. But the verbal conflict is getting so intense that even Middle East experts — long accustomed to pugnacious rhetoric — say bullets could start flying.

At issue are Iran's nuclear development efforts and its perceived military support of Iraqi insurgents. Washington says Iran is seeking to develop nuclear weapons, but Iranian President Mahmoud Ahmadinejad says the program is for peaceful uses.

In October, President George W. Bush said he had "told people that if you're interested in avoiding World War III, it seems like you ought to be interested in preventing [Iran] from having the knowledge necessary to make a nuclear weapon."[1]

For his part, Ahmadinejad calls the United States an international bully intent on keeping Iraq violent to justify continued occupation.

"No day passes without people [in Iraq] being killed, wounded or displaced," Ahmadinejad said during an address to the U.N. General Assembly in September. "And the occupiers not only refuse to be accountable and ashamed of their adventure, but speak in a report of a new market for their armaments as a result of their military adventure."

"We're in a serious and dangerous situation," says Bruce Riedel, a senior fellow at the Brookings Institution's Saban Center for Middle East Policy, a centrist think tank. "We'd be better served by lowering the rhetoric."

Meanwhile, hundreds of U.S. troops in Iraq have been killed by sophisticated roadside bombs that Bush and his top military commanders say are coming from Iran, which denies supplying them.

A Major Presence in the Middle East

Heartland of the ancient Persian Empire, Iran is the biggest non-Arab country in the Middle East. It has the biggest Shiite population of any nation and the only officially Shiite constitution in the world. It also maintains the region's biggest military force and is among the world's top petroleum producers.

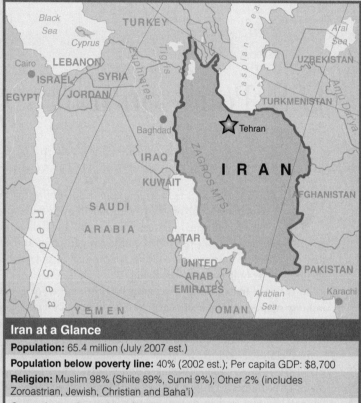

Iran at a Glance

Population: 65.4 million (July 2007 est.)

Population below poverty line: 40% (2002 est.); Per capita GDP: $8,700

Religion: Muslim 98% (Shiite 89%, Sunni 9%); Other 2% (includes Zoroastrian, Jewish, Christian and Baha'i)

Gross domestic product: $222.9 billion (2006)

Military expenditures: 4.5% of GDP (2005)

Percentage of world's total proven oil reserves: 10%

Ranking among OPEC crude oil producers: No. 2 at 3.8 million barrels per day (Saudi Arabia is No. 1, at 9.2 million)

Natural gas reserves: 974 trillion cubic ft., second-highest in world after Russia (1,680 trillion cubic ft.)

Total military manpower: 545,000 (next highest in the region: Saudi Arabia, 199,500)

Sources: CIA *World Factbook*, updated Nov. 1, 2007; Anthony Cordesman and Martin Kleiber, "Iran's Military Forces and Warfighting Capabilities: The Threat in the Northern Gulf," Center for Strategic and International Studies, 2007; Energy Information Administration, Department of Energy; *Political Handbook of the World, 2007*

Amid the fighting and the fighting words, a glimmer of hope appeared in November. Lt. Gen. Raymond T. Odierno, second in command in Iraq behind Gen. David Petraeus, told reporters on Nov. 1 the number of attacks involving deadly EFPs (explosively formed penetrators) had dropped from 177 in July and August to 105 in September and October.

Defense Secretary Robert M. Gates said Iran had promised to clamp down on shipment of EFPs. "I don't know whether to believe them," Gates said. "I'll wait and see."[2]

Some of the skepticism grows out of Iran's reported role in a 33-day war last year between Israel — America's key Middle East ally — and Lebanon's Hezbollah militia, which was created and armed by Iran. Ahmadinejad has expressed the hope that Israel would be wiped off the map, much as the Soviet Union disappeared. "Was it done through war?" he asked at a September news conference at the United Nations. "No. It was through the voice of the people."[3]

Three weeks later, Bush made his "World War III" remark. And four days after that Vice President Dick Cheney called Iran "the world's most active state sponsor of terror," adding: "The Iranian regime needs to know that if it stays on its present course, the international community is prepared to impose serious consequences. The United States joins other nations in sending a clear message: We will not allow Iran to have a nuclear weapon."[4]

The White House followed the tough talk with new economic sanctions designed to halt or slow down business transactions for anyone doing

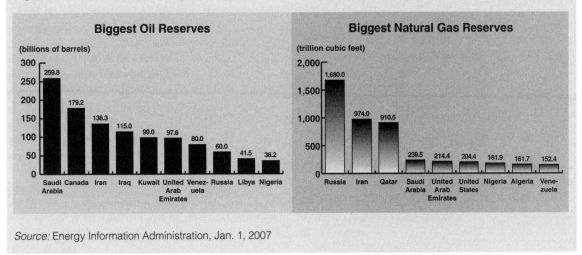

Iran Ranks Among World Leaders in Energy

Iran ranks third in proven oil reserves, with nearly 140 billion barrels; world leader Saudi Arabia has almost twice as much (left). Iran has nearly a quadrillion cubic feet of natural gas reserves, second only to Russia (right).

Biggest Oil Reserves

(billions of barrels)

Saudi Arabia	259.8
Canada	179.2
Iran	136.3
Iraq	115.0
Kuwait	99.0
United Arab Emirates	97.6
Venezuela	80.0
Russia	60.0
Libya	41.5
Nigeria	36.2

Biggest Natural Gas Reserves

(trillion cubic feet)

Russia	1,680.0
Iran	974.0
Qatar	910.5
Saudi Arabia	239.5
United Arab Emirates	214.4
United States	204.4
Nigeria	181.9
Algeria	161.7
Venezuela	152.4

Source: Energy Information Administration, Jan. 1, 2007

business with banks or other companies linked to the Iranian Revolutionary Guard, a military and covert-action agency long accused of supporting and aiding terrorism in the region.

What will the future bring? If past relations between the two countries are a guide, it will be a bumpy ride. In 1953 the United States orchestrated a coup against a nationalist Iranian prime minister, throwing its weight behind the country's pro-Western monarch, Shah Mohammed Reza Pahlavi. The United States, like the then-new state of Israel, saw Iran — successor to the ancient Persian Empire — as a key ally in a dangerous neighborhood. Iran, like other Middle Eastern nations, was Muslim. But Iranians are not Arabs and were seen as distant from the Israeli-Arab confrontation. In 1979 a revolution toppled the shah and installed the anti-American, anti-Israel theocracy that now rules Iran. Since then, U.S.-Iranian relations have been schizophrenic — marked by the 1979-81 hostage crisis involving 52 U.S. Embassy personnel in Tehran but also by quiet cooperation during the U.S.-led invasion of Afghanistan.

Tension has been climbing since Ahmadinejad launched himself globally as a challenger to American power following his election as president in 2005. Yet his real power largely is limited to economic policy. Under Iran's constitution, a clergyman, elected by a clerical Assembly of Experts, has the last word in all major affairs of state. Only the supreme leader, for instance, can declare war.[5]

Despite the confusing division of power, hawks argue that one thing is clear about the Iranian government: It wants to destroy the United States and Israel. "We're under attack; they're at war with us," says Michael A. Ledeen, who holds the title of "freedom scholar" at the conservative American Enterprise Institute and is the author of a new book on Iran.[6] "They're killing Americans [in Iraq] and intend to kill as many as they can. They want to destroy us."[7]

Other foreign-policy watchers deride such arguments as war-mongering fantasy. "Iran has an economy the size of Finland's and an annual defense budget of around $4.8 billion," wrote Fareed Zakaria, editor of *Newsweek International,* in a widely discussed column. "It has not invaded a country since the late 18th century. The United States has a GDP that is 68 times larger and defense expenditures that are 110 times greater."[8]

Hawks and doves alike place great importance on the survival of Iran's pro-democracy/human rights community, or "civil society." Its members have always risked prison and torture, but increased repression this year is

A police patrol boat guards the Neka oil terminal on the Caspian Sea on Iran's northern coast. Despite its huge petroleum reserves, Iran has a faltering economy and an 11 percent unemployment rate.

causing renewed alarm. Among other moves, the government imprisoned several visiting Iranian-American professionals on suspicion of trying to help the Bush administration topple the government. Iran acted after the administration created a $75 million fund to promote civil society in Iran, in part by supporting pro-democracy organizations.

The unintended consequence of that support, some exiled dissidents and their American allies say, is to validate the Iranian government's contention that opposition members are American stooges. "Any Iranian who seeks American dollars will not be recognized as a democrat by his or her fellow citizens," Akbar Ganji, one of Iran's leading democracy activists, wrote in an op-ed in October. "Iran's democratic movement does not need foreign handouts."[9]

U.S. hawks argue that blaming the Bush administration for the latest crackdown ignores history. Iran's government, they point out, was jailing and torturing dissidents long before Bush took office. And, Ledeen says, the dissidents represent Iran's future, so helping them makes more sense than bombing a nuclear site.

In fact, few experts advocate military action. "There's a remarkable consensus across Washington about what the consequences would be," says Michael Rubin, a hawkish American Enterprise Institute scholar who lived in Iran in 1999 and speaks Farsi. "I don't know anyone who thinks a strike is a good idea." Military action, he says, likely would rally Iranians to the government's side. Systematic attacks against U.S. forces in Iraq could also be expected, as could sabotage of oil export facilities in the Persian Gulf, further driving up petroleum prices.[10]

But prominent neoconservative* Norman Podhoretz does advocate air strikes against Iran's nuclear research sites. The United States has "only one terrible choice, which is either to bomb those facilities and retard their program or even cut it off altogether or allow them to go nuclear," said Podhoretz, editor-at-large of *Commentary* magazine."[11]

Podhoretz insisted that Ahmadinejad is today's version of Adolf Hitler. "If we allow Iran to get the bomb," he argued, "people 50 years from now will look back at us the way we look back at the men who made the Munich Pact with Hitler in 1938 and say, 'How could they have let this happen?' "

Most experts scoff at such analogies, despite Iran's hostility to Israel. "The idea that Iran presents to the region and world a threat as big as Hitler's is absurd," says Iranian-born historian Shaul Bakhash of George Mason University, who is Jewish. "Iran is very unlikely to get involved in military adventures abroad."

Israel's reported bombing on Sept. 6 of a possible nuclear site in Syria — an Iranian ally — has fueled fears of U.S. designs on Iran. But even experts concerned about a U.S. attack worry more about the impact of the Iraq War. "I think the president is telling the truth when he says he doesn't intend to bomb," says Riedel, a former Middle East policy director at the National Security Council. "But the war by proxy we're fighting with Iran

---

* "Neoconservative," or neocon, originally referred to a small band of left-wing writers and academics who jumped to the Republican Party in the 1970s and '80s. It now is applied broadly, usually pejoratively, to strongly pro-Israel supporters of the Bush administration.

in Iraq could escalate unpredictably because of events on the ground."

As tension mounts, here are some of the issues being debated:

Would a nuclear-armed Iran endanger the United States?

Concern about Iran's nuclear development program had been simmering for several years. Worries heated up after Ahmadinejad's election in 2005. But the country's nuclear ambitions actually predate the 1979 revolution that led to the Islamic Republic.

Shortly before his overthrow, the shah had been hoping to obtain reactors and other nuclear technology from the United States, his closest ally. Nuclear-generated power would allow Iran to sell more of its oil abroad, bringing in more much-needed revenue. Today, the Islamic Republic — created by the same men who toppled the shah — justifies its nuclear program on the same grounds.[12]

Iranian officials have declared repeatedly their nuclear program excludes plans for any weapons. "We consider the acquiring, development and use of nuclear weapons inhuman, immoral, illegal and against our basic principles," Deputy Foreign Minister G. Ali Khoshroo said in 2003.[13]

To be sure, Khoshroo served in the administration of reformist President Mohammed Khatami. But his successor, Ahmadinejad, sounded the same note. "We are not after an atomic bomb because it is not useful, and our religion does not allow us to have it," he says on his Web site.[14]

In addition, Iran's alternately compliant and defiant dealings with the international nuclear regulatory system — even before Ahmadinejad's rise — have led experts with connections to the Bush administration to be deeply skeptical of Iran's objectives. "Iran has too often dictated the pace of diplomatic progress, giving the impression that it is playing for time," David Albright, president of the Institute for Science and International Security, wrote in 2004. The apparent aim was to stall the regulatory process until its nuclear facilities were up and running, Albright and a colleague wrote.[15]

So widespread are suspicions, in fact, that even critics of the Bush administration's war talk assume Iran's nuclear program is designed to produce weapons. Retired Gen. John Abizaid, former U.S. commander in the Middle East, faced the issue head-on during a talk in Washington last September. "There are ways to live with a nuclear Iran," he said. "Let's face it, we lived with a nuclear Soviet Union; we've lived with a nuclear China; we're living with other nuclear powers as well."[16]

The American Enterprise Institute's Rubin, among the most prominent advocates of a tough policy on Iran, bluntly rejects Abizaid's thesis: "I think he's wrong."

But Rubin isn't worried about nuclear war. Instead, he argued, nuclear weapons will block any attempts to force Iran to play by international rules. He cited a bombing raid by Turkish warplanes on Iranian territory in 1999, apparently aimed at punishing Iran for sheltering a Kurdish guerrilla organization that had been attacking Turkish troops for years. "After that, Iran stopped sheltering them," Rubin says. "But if Iran has a nuclear deterrent, no one is going to risk correcting its behavior."[17]

Brookings' Riedel, the former Middle East policy director at the National Security Council, says the United States has numerous options for pressuring Iran. "I do not see evidence from Iranian behavior over the last 30 years that this is a crazy state," he says. "Iran's behavior shows an understanding of the limits of its capability." He cites fighting between the United States and Iran during the 1980-88 Iran-Iraq War, when U.S. forces were protecting shipping in the Persian Gulf from Iranian attacks. "In the end, they chose to stop the conflict and to de-escalate," he says.

The question of whether Iran is a fundamentally rational power is crucial to the debate over nuclear intentions. True, deterrence worked against America's adversary in the Cold War, says the American Enterprise Institute's Ledeen, a former National Security Council consultant during the Reagan administration. But, he adds, "The Soviet Union was not governed by insane millenarian fanatics. The [Iranian government] wants to rule the world."

"Millenarian" signifies a belief in an approaching end of days, or change on a cataclysmic scale. For many Shiites, including Ahmadinejad, the return of the holy, historic figure known as the Mahdi, or the "Hidden Imam," would herald such a period. "With his 'second coming' there will be a reign of justice until the return of Jesus" — a revered figure to all Muslims — "at which time the world will end," writes Vali Nasr, a political scientist at Tufts University who specializes in the Shiite world.[18]

But Nasr also argues that the key to the future of the Middle East is the evolution of the historic Shiite-Sunni rivalry. And *Newsweek*'s Zakaria, in a television debate with Podhoretz, noted that past communist dictators had their own version of millenarianism that was just as terrifying, on paper — but not in reality — as

Ahmadinejad Takes Aim at the United States

Tough talk is the president's specialty.

Mahmoud Ahmadinejad may be only 5'2" tall, but he looms large as the embodiment of U.S., Israeli and European fears about Iran and its state ideology of religion-laced nationalism.

Seemingly on any given day, if the Iranian president isn't questioning whether the Holocaust occurred, he's accusing the United States of deliberately keeping Iraq unstable to justify the war or defying international nuclear watchdogs.

"Nations and countries don't have to obey the injustice of certain powers," Ahmadinejad told the U.N. General Assembly on Sept. 26, unmistakably referring above all to the United States. "These powers . . . have lost the competence to lead the world because of their hideous acts." And, he went on: "I officially declare that the age of relations arising from the Second World War, as well as materialistic thoughts based on arrogance and domination, is well over now. Humanity has passed a perilous precipice, and the age of monotheism, purity, affinity, respecting others, justice and true peace loving has commenced."[1]

Ahmadinejad's bill of particulars against the United States and its Western allies includes the creation of Israel, their responsibility for poverty and disease in poor countries and the global arms race.

To be sure, any number of developing-nation leaders — including other Iranian presidents — have leveled similar accusations. But Ahmadinejad's talent for provocative oratory, coupled with his position — albeit largely symbolic — as head of a major oil power, has amplified his voice.

Yet, by all accounts, the former mayor of Tehran owes his 2005 election to the presidency less to his international stands than to the political identity he carved out as the voice of the little man hammered by economic problems. Born in 1956, Ahmadinejad is the son of a blacksmith and a veteran of the horrific eight-year war with Iraq. Afterwards, overcoming many hardships, he earned a doctorate in civil engineering.[2]

"Most people voted for Ahmadinejad because he promised they would never have to feel sad again on New Year's Eve in front of their children," Farshid Bakhtieri, a young computer salesman, said in February.[3]

But those promises haven't been fulfilled, Bakhtieri added. Iranians complain they aren't getting the benefits of Iran's status as a major oil power, as the 11.5 percent official jobless rate indicates. And in June, government-imposed gasoline rationing ignited rioting in Tehran and other cities. Although it has the world's third-largest reserves of oil, Iran has built an insufficient number of refineries to produce enough gasoline — which it provides at low, subsidized rates — to meet growing domestic demand. Thus, the country depends heavily on imports, which require cash

Ahmadinejad's. Zakaria quoted the late Chinese ruler, Mao Zedong: "If the worst came to worst and half of mankind died, the other half would remain, while imperialism would be razed from the ground."[19]

Trita Parsi, president of the National Iranian American Council, which advocates a diplomatic resolution of U.S.-Iran tensions, argues that Iran's claim of a peaceful purpose for its nuclear development program is accurate — though weapon construction may be on the agenda as well. If the latter succeeded, he says, the existence of the U.S. and Israeli nuclear deterrent will prevent nuclear war. "Coexistence is possible," he says. The Iranians are deterrable." Parsi is also author of a new book chronicling the post-revolutionary relationship between Iran, the United States and Israel.[20]

Does U.S. support help pro-democracy dissidents influence Iran's policies?

President Ahmadinejad's frequently bellicose speeches may suggest Iran is ruled, and populated, by religious, revolutionary fanatics. But the country's cadre of human-rights campaigners, labor-union organizers, student activists and investigative journalists is bigger than one might think. "Iranian society has refused to be coerced into silence," wrote Shirin Ebadi, a human-rights lawyer who won the Nobel Peace Prize in 2003. "Human-rights discourse is alive and well at the grass-roots level; civil-society activists consider it to be the most potent framework for achieving sustainable democratic reforms and political pluralism."[21]

Ebadi received the Nobel Prize at the moment when expectations of change reached their highest point in recent

outlays. Rationing was designed to reduce Iran's gasoline import payments if international sanctions over the country's disputed nuclear-development activities restrict access to cash.[4]

But average Iranians had little sympathy for the government's rationing strategy. "We live on an ocean of oil," said Kambiz Rahmati, 25, an electronics engineer. "Why should we pay a high price for gasoline or suffer rationing?"[5]

Some Iranian pro-democracy activists tie Ahmadinejad's economic failures to his aggressiveness in the international arena. Indeed, says an exiled dissident, the president might see it in his interest to bait the United States into military action over Iran's insistence on building nuclear facilities. "Limited war would give a good excuse to accuse the foreign states — 'it's their fault that the Iranian economy has problems,' " says Ali Afshari, an exiled student leader who spent nearly three years in prison. "Second, he would use this for a complete militarization of the country, and suppress all dissident activities."

But Iran's supreme leader, Ayatollah Ali Khamenei, doubts even a limited U.S. strike against Iran's nuclear facilities would be strategically advantageous, Afshari theorizes. And Khamenei's opinion counts: Only he can declare war or command the military.[6]

But Khamenei makes few public comments these days. Ahmadinejad has come to be seen as the man in charge because he issues a steady stream of commentary on hot-button issues. About the Holocaust, for instance, he shocked listeners when he said last year: "I will only accept something as truth if I am actually convinced of it." In 2001, Khamenei got only sparse attention when he said Zionists had been "fabricating figures related to the Holocaust."[7]

Such statements don't surprise Shaul Bakhash, an Iranian-born historian at George Mason University in Fairfax, Va. "These statements are not as new as people seem to imagine," he says.

In fact, points out Michael Rubin, a resident scholar at the American Enterprise Institute, Iran's nuclear program has been around much longer than Ahmadinejad. "The presidency in Iran is about style, not substance."

---

[1] Address to 62nd U.N. General Assembly, Sept. 26, 2007, www.president.ir/en/.

[2] See Nazila Fathi, "Blacksmith's Son Emphasized His Modest Roots," *The New York Times*, June 26, 2005, p. A11. See also "Iran-Iraq War (1980-1988)," globalsecurity.org, undated, www.globalsecurity.org/military/world/war/iran-iraq.htm.

[3] Quoted in Kim Murphy, "Iran reformists want U.S. to tone it down," *Los Angeles Times*, Feb. 11, 2007, p. A1.

[4] See Ramin Mostaghim and Borzou Daragahi, "Gas rationing in Iran ignites anger, unrest," *Los Angeles Times*, June 28, 2007, p. A5; Najmeh Bozorgmehr, "Iran pushes on with fuel rationing in face of riots," *Financial Times* (London), June 28, 2007, p. A7. Also see Peter Behr, "Energy Nationalism," *CQ Global Researcher*, July 2007, pp. 151-180.

[5] Quoted in *Los Angeles Times*, ibid.

[6] See Ray Takeyh, *Hidden Iran: Paradox and Power in the Islamic Republic* (2006), pp. 24-25.

[7] Quoted in Christopher De Bellaigue, "Hanging of 'CIA Spy' Dents Iran's Overtures to U.S.," *The Independent* (London), May 24, 2001, p. A19. Ahmadinejad quoted in Michael Slackman, "Deep Roots of Denial for Iran's True Believer," *The New York Times*, Dec. 14, 2006, p. A3.

---

years, during the term of reformist President Khatami. Under Ahmadinejad, those hopes have dimmed.

A crackdown that intensified this year included enforcement of the religious code against revealing clothing, including scanty head scarves on women and tight shirts on men. "Those who damage the system under any guise will be punished," Intelligence Minister Gholamhossein Mohseni Ejei warned in April. He accused the civil-society movement of conspiring to topple the government.[22]

Controversy over direct American aid for Iranian dissidents leapt to the top of the agenda in 2006, when Secretary of State Condoleezza Rice asked Congress for $75 million to fund activities that included expanding Farsi-language news broadcasts into Iran — and support for Iranian civil-society groups. "The United States will actively confront the policies of this Iranian regime, and at the same time we are going to work to support the aspirations of the Iranian people for freedom in their own country," Rice told the Senate Foreign Relations Committee. Congress granted the request. The administration is now asking for the same amount in 2008.[23]

Debate over the usefulness of the money has been raging since the first request, with most supporters of Iranian civil-society groups opposed to the funding. Human Rights Watch is among several groups lobbying against the program as the House and Senate Appropriations committees negotiate the funding. "Iranian activists don't want it and can't get it," Saman Zarifi, Washington advocate for Human Rights Watch,

Haleh Esfandiari, left, appears on Iranian television after her arrest early last year in Tehran. The Middle East Program director of the Woodrow Wilson International Center for Scholars in Washington spent eight months in jail along with several other U.S. pro-democracy activists. She was released in September 2007. Ali Afshari, a former student human-rights activist, spent most of 2000-2003 in prison, where he endured torture and 400 days of solitary confinement.

said in October. "Second, it supports Iranian government efforts to cast activists as foreign agents."[24]

Earlier in the year, Iran added fuel to the conflict by arresting four visiting American human-rights supporters: Haleh Esfandiari, Middle East Program director of the Woodrow Wilson International Center for Scholars in Washington; Kian Tajbakhsh, an urban planner who had been a consultant to the Open Society Institute of the New York-based Soros Foundation; Parnaz Azima, a reporter for Radio Farda, the Persian-language arm of Radio Free Europe/Radio Liberty; and Ali Shakeri, 59, a mortgage broker and a founding board member of the Center for Citizen Peacebuilding at the University of California, Irvine. After solitary confinement and frequent interrogation, the four were freed.[25]

Iranian citizens, however, have spent years in prison. Ali Afshari, a former student human-rights activist, spent most of 2000-2003 in prison, where, he told *CQ Researcher*, he endured 400 days of solitary confinement. He now lives in the United States and is a doctoral student in engineering.

Afshari says U.S. support for the Iranian human-rights movement should be limited to programs that remain within U.S. borders. "In Iranian political culture, it's taboo for any organization to get money from any foreign state," he says. "It harms civil society because the government uses it as an excuse to repress."

Some advocates of tough U.S. action against the Iranian government cite the crackdown as evidence of an urgent necessity for financing as many Iranian pro-democracy organizations as possible. The American Enterprise Institute's Rubin says the arrest of Esfandiari and the other Iranian-Americans shows a government feeling weak. "Governments with self-confidence about their peoples' attitudes don't arrest 67-year-old grandmothers," he says, referring to Esfandiari.

The apparent insecurity begs to be exploited, Rubin argues. As for Afshari's view — which is widely echoed — that U.S. funding would provide a rationale for more repression — Rubin notes that repression is a longstanding tradition in the Islamic Republic. "It's safe to say that crackdowns happened long before democracy funding was an issue," he says.

Bakhash, the Iranian-born historian, disputes the notion that American funding would help those for whom it's intended. "Given the way Iran is now, I don't think it's at all helpful for the American government to be involved directly in such activities," he says. "The sensitivity to foreign funding in the Middle East is huge, enormous. The idea that foreign-funded political groups in-country can cooperate freely with political groups out of the country is a rather difficult concept; it can lead to a charge of treason."

Bakhash has a personal stake in the matter. Esfandiari is his wife, and after her release from eight months of imprisonment she coauthored a piece opposing U.S. government aid to Iranian pro-democracy groups. "Governments should talk to governments," she wrote with Robert Litwak, director of international-security studies at the Wilson Center, "while Iranian and American [non-governmental organizations] should be permitted to interact in a transparent fashion without the intrusion of governments."[26]

But some Iranian exiles argue in favor of American funding. "It's very helpful," says Akbar Atri, a former student activist who was also imprisoned. He dismisses as a well-worn accusation, long predating the Bush administration, that all dissidents are tools of American subversion. "The regime said the American government is helping these Iranians, but before these funds they all the time accused the opposition of being the puppet of U.S. intelligence agencies."

Atri, a longtime student democracy activist who fled Iran in late 2004 while under investigation for his political work, is a member of the Washington-based

Committee on the Present Danger, co-chaired by R. James Woolsey, former CIA director in the Clinton administration, and George P. Shultz, who was secretary of State in the Reagan administration. The organization favors "regime change" in Iran.[27]

Is Iran fomenting instability in Iraq?

The U.S. overthrow of Saddam Hussein did an enormous favor for Iran, which had good reason to consider Iraq's dictator an enormous threat. As the instigator of the 1980-1988 Iran-Iraq War, Saddam was responsible for at least 300,000 Iranians killed and an estimated 700,000 wounded.[28]

U.S. destruction of Iran's enemy would seem to make Iran and the United States de facto allies. But the U.S. military accuses Iran of supplying weapons to anti-American Shiite militias in Iraq. "There is absolutely no question," said Gen. Petraeus, the top U.S. commander in Iraq, "that Iranians are funding, arming, training and even in some cases, directing the activities of extremists and militia elements."[29]

Specifically, Petraeus and Lt. Gen. Odierno say the Iranian Revolutionary Guard Corps is supplying "explosively formed penetrators" (EFPs), roadside bombs that can penetrate vehicle armor.[30]

Iranian officials have consistently denied all such accusations. And U.S. military brass have backed away from disclosing what they call definitive evidence.[31]

But even without conclusive proof, some administration critics call the U.S. allegations plausible. "I think the administration is telling the truth when it says Iran is targeting American soldiers in Iraq and Afghanistan," says Riedel, the ex-CIA and National Security Council official. "What that says to me is that the Iranians are demonstrating that we're vulnerable. I have no doubt the U.S. Air Force and U.S. Navy can inflict enormous pain on Iran, but I also know that Iran can inflict enormous pain on the U.S. in Iraq, the Persian Gulf and diplomatic installations. They're prepared to play hardball with us."

Nonetheless, for some Iran-watchers, the question looming over the war in Iraq is whether Iran could be persuaded to help U.S. forces disengage.

Iran hawks say that hope is futile. Rubin of the American Enterprise Institute argues that Iran has settled on a policy of keeping U.S. forces tied down in Iraq. In testimony last July before the House Foreign Affairs Committee, Rubin cited a July 13 sermon by former Iranian President Hashemi Rafsanjani in which he ridiculed American weakness. "What a superpower is the United States when it can be easily trapped in a small country like Iraq?" he said.[32]

Based on the sermon and other evidence, Rubin testified: "The assumption that Iraq's neighbors seek a peaceful, stable Iraq is false. . . . Iranian strategists believe limited instability [in Iraq] and free rein of pro-Iranian militias to be in their best interest."[33]

Parsi of the National Iranian American Council shares Rubin's analysis, up to a point. "If a larger accommodation doesn't take place, my thinking is that the Iranians will not help stabilize Iraq," he says. "The fear in Iran is that the ultimate goal of the United States is to attack Iran and remove its government." Based on that perception, he says, Iran sees a benefit in American forces facing continued threat in Iraq.

But unlike the Iran hawks, Parsi argues that Iran could become a force for peace in Iraq. "They want something in return — better relations with the United States in which the U.S. recognizes Iranian security interests and doesn't attack Iran."

Hardliners ridicule the notion that any deal can be reached with a government that sees itself as an implacable enemy.

"They're just trying to kill us in Iraq," says Ledeen of the American Enterprise Institute. "We have been looking for a modus vivendi with Iran since 1979." The only conclusion to be drawn, he argues, is that there is no Iranian interest in cooperating with the United States.

Riedel argues that view closes off any possibility of peaceful resolution. "If Iranians believe we are only interested in regime change, we're killing any chance of a serious dialogue," he says. "The Iranians need to know when they enter into any kind of dialogue with us that it is not a subterfuge for overthrowing the Islamic Republic."

In any event, he adds, "If an overthrow is anyone's goal, it's a fantasy." The present Iranian government will not disappear "any time in the near future."

BACKGROUND

Mossadegh Overthrown

Modern U.S.-Iranian relations began with the CIA-engineered overthrow of Prime Minister Mohammed Mossadegh in 1953. Mossadegh, an ardent nationalist,

CHRONOLOGY

1950s-1978 *CIA ousts nationalist prime minister, ushering in an era of close ties to Iran's monarch.*

April 28, 1951 Iran's parliament nationalizes country's oil industry.

Aug. 19, 1953 CIA directs coup that ousts Prime Minister Mohammed Mossadegh, who spearheaded oil nationalization.

1963 Shah Mohammed Reza Pahlavi's U.S.-originated "white revolution" on socioeconomic issues receives 99 percent approval in an obviously rigged referendum that prompts a wave of protests.

1964 More protests greet a new law granting immunity to thousands of Americans working in Iran if they are accused of crimes. . . . Ayatollah Ruhollah Khomeini, a cleric leading the protests, is forced into exile.

1977 President Jimmy Carter toasts the shah in Tehran as a beloved promoter of stability.

Jan. 1978 Officially sponsored publication of an article defaming Khomeini sparks demonstrations.

1979-1989 *Incapable of quelling the protests, the shah flees, and Khomeini returns from exile to become the country's dominant leader under a quasi-parliamentary system dominated by religious leaders.*

Jan. 1979 Shah goes into exile.

Nov. 4, 1979 Shah's arrival in United States for cancer treatment prompts students to storm the U.S. Embassy in Tehran and take 52 hostages.

1980 Iraqi dictator Saddam Hussein, a Sunni, launches a war against Iran's Shiite government — which he perceives as a threat to his regime.

1981 Iran frees the hostages the day Carter leaves office. . . . Crash of a plane carrying Israeli arms for Iran signals Israel's tilt in Iran-Iraq war.

1983 Hezbollah terrorists allied with Iran attack U.S. Embassy and Marine barracks in Beirut, Lebanon, killing 304 Americans.

1986 President Ronald Reagan admits his administration illegally sold weapons to Iran and funneled profits to the "contra" guerrillas fighting Nicaragua's left-wing Sandinista government. . . . U.S. confirms providing intelligence to Iraq to help its bombing campaign against Iran.

1989 Ayatollah Khomeini dies.

1990-2007 *Conservative cleric appointed to Iran's most important post. Relations with the U.S. deteriorate.*

1990 Conservative Ayatollah Ali Khamenei named supreme leader.

1997 Reformist cleric Mohammed Khatami elected president in a landslide.

1998 Khatami seems interested in reopening relations with the U.S.

2000 Dissident journalist Akbar Ganji and other democracy activists imprisoned.

2001 Khatami wins second term. . . . Iranian security forces help U.S. military during invasion of Afghanistan.

2002 Bush calls Iran a member of the "axis of evil," along with North Korea and Iraq.

2005 Populist hard-liner Mahmoud Ahmadinejad elected president following failure of Khatami's reforms.

Dec. 23, 2006 U.S. military says Iran is arming Iraqi militias. . . . U.N. Security Council imposes financial sanctions on Iran for failing to halt uranium enrichment. . . . Iran holds conference on Holocaust, with Holocaust deniers invited.

2007 Security Council orders new sanctions against Iran for its refusal to quit uranium enrichment. . . . Senate resolution demands that the U.S. "combat" Iranian activities in Iraq. . . . President Bush says Iran's nuclear program raises specter of "World War III." . . . Israeli bombing in Syria raises fear of Israeli or U.S. strike on Iran. . . . Ahmadinejad vows no retreat from nuclear program. . . . October talks between Iran and nuclear-watchdog agency produce no agreement.

had been at the center of a crisis that had been building since the late 1940s over the future of Britain's long-standing oil concession, which effectively controlled Iran's major natural resource.[34]

Mossadegh had accepted the post of prime minister from the shah on condition that parliament end the concession, which it did on April 28, 1951. "The anniversary of the passing of the oil nationalization bill," writes historian Ali M. Ansari of the University of St. Andrews in Scotland, "is perhaps the closest thing to an Iranian independence day."[35]

But for the CIA — which worked closely with the British — Mossadegh's nationalization of Britain's Anglo-Iranian Oil. Co. showed him to be a threat to Western interests, and politically unreliable, in a region where the Soviet Union was a looming presence. President Dwight D. Eisenhower approved a coup plan. One attempt failed, leading the shah to take a sudden vacation in Rome. Then, on Aug. 19, 1953, a CIA officer directed a move against Mossadegh, who eventually surrendered. "The shah became the centerpiece of American foreign policy in the Islamic world," writes *New York Times* correspondent Tim Weiner in a recent history of the CIA. But, "A generation of Iranians grew up knowing that the CIA had installed the shah."[36]

Although the United States poured money into Iran after the coup, it didn't buy all Iranians' friendship. Abolhasan Ebtehaj, a government official who lost his post after disputes with American officials, faulted the free-spending U.S. approach. "Not so many years ago in Iran, the United States was loved and respected as no other country, and without having given a penny of aid," he said in a 1961 speech in San Francisco. "Now, after more than $1 billion of loans and grants, America is neither loved nor respected; she is distrusted by most people and hated by many."[37]

The John F. Kennedy administration, which came to power in 1961, pushed the shah even harder to shake up his country's social structure. Arguing that Iran's land-tenure system amounted to "feudalism," creating conditions that made Iran ripe for a communist revolution, the Americans demanded private land ownership for peasants.

But when the shah's so-called "white revolution" occurred, it brought repercussions that the Americans hadn't foreseen. Rural, land-owning aristocrats and members of the clergy, who had been instrumental in pushing out Mossadegh, opposed the change, in some cases more

because it was American-imposed than because of its objectives. The shah, with U.S. encouragement, also proposed the political emancipation of women, which angered conservatives, especially religious leaders.

When a national referendum showed 99 percent approval for the "revolution," riots broke out because the election clearly had been rigged. Ruhollah Khomeini, a previously obscure clergyman, became one of the strongest voices against the shah.

For Iranians, what the shah and his American advisers called reform was something quite different. "The shah's modernization program — which created less an authentic development than a consumer society for privileged elites — quickly enriched the members of the royal family and the court, the entrepreneurs (almost all subcontractors for large Western firms), the powerful merchants, the importers of spare parts and consumer goods, the speculators," wrote French journalist Eric Rouleau in 1980.[38]

Then the United States prompted the shah to introduce legislation granting immunity from the Iranian legal system for any American citizen accused of a crime. On the same day the bill was approved — after the shah fixed the parliamentary vote — Iranian lawmakers also approved a $200 million loan from the United States.

"The dignity of Iran has been destroyed," Khomeini declared. "They wanted a loan, and America demanded this in return." In 1964 Khomeini was sent into exile.[39]

Shah Overthrown

The United States and the shah deepened their relationship in the 1970s. Israel, too, enjoyed close ties to the shah, whose quiet acceptance of the Jewish state enraged Arab governments — and many Iranians. By 1977, there were some 30,000 American government personnel and businesspeople in Iran, President Jimmy Carter noted during a toast to the shah on New Year's Eve in Tehran.[40]

"Iran, because of the great leadership of the shah, is an island of stability in one of the more troubled areas of the world," said Carter, in words that would later embarrass him. "This is a great tribute to you, your majesty, and to your leadership and to the respect and the admiration and love which your people give to you."[41]

Only weeks later, however, the monarchy's collapse began. In January, after the shah-approved publication of a defamatory newspaper article about Khomeini, well-organized street protests broke out in several cities, creating a crisis atmosphere.

Presidential Hopefuls Targeting Iran

Democrats and Republicans disagree on military action.

U.S. military action against Iran may or may not occur, but candidates for the 2008 presidential nomination are fighting about whether it would be a good idea.

For now, the big Iran knockdown is taking place among Democratic candidates. Debate centers on a Sept. 26 Senate resolution urging the United States to "combat, contain and roll back the violent activities and destabilizing influence" of Iran's government inside Iraq and declare the Iranian Revolutionary Guard Corps a terrorist organization. The resolution passed, 76-22.[1]

Former Sen. John Edwards, D-N.C.

Antiwar Democrats called the amendment a barely veiled authorization to scramble warplanes over Iran. "It's an enormous mistake to give George Bush the first step in the authority to move militarily on Iran," said former North Carolina **Sen. John Edwards**. "The resolution on the Iranian Revolutionary Guard did that."[2]

Edwards' comment was aimed not only at the Bush administration but at frontrunner **Sen. Hillary Rodham Clinton**, D-N.Y., who drew fire from antiwar Democrats for supporting the resolution.

Sen. Hillary Rodham Clinton, D-N.Y.

Clinton responded that she hadn't been voting for war. "I oppose any rush to war but also believe doing nothing is not acceptable — diplomacy is the right path," she said in a mailing to prospective primary voters in Iowa.[3]

Perhaps in response to criticism of her vote, Clinton on Oct. 1 signed up as a cosponsor of a bill introduced last March by Sen. Jim Webb, D-Va., that would bar military action against Iran without congressional authorization.[4]

Webb, a Marine combat veteran of Vietnam, was among the critics of the resolution, which had been sponsored by Sen. Joseph Lieberman, I-Conn., whose hawkish views on Iraq cost him the Democratic Senate nomination in his state in 2006, and Sen. Jon Kyl of Arizona, a conservative Republican. "Those who regret their vote five years ago to authorize military action in Iraq should think hard before supporting this approach," he said, "because, in my view, it has the same potential to do harm where many are seeking to do good."[5]

While Clinton's support for Webb's bill might have seemed an opportunistic response to recent attacks, last February she had demanded that Bush make no move against Iran without congressional authorization.[6]

In any case, Clinton's opponents didn't drop the Iran issue. By late October, another front-runner nipping at her heels advocated a sharp break with the Iran policy espoused by the administration — notably going further than Clinton in marking a distance from Bush.

Sen. Barack Obama, D-Ill.

"I would meet directly with Iranian leaders," **Sen. Barack Obama**, D-Ill., told *The New York Times*. "We would engage in a level of aggressive, personal diplomacy. . . . Iran and Syria would start changing their behavior if they started seeing that they had some incentives to do so, but right now the only incentive that exists is our president suggesting that if you do what we tell you, we may not blow you up." Obama didn't vote on the resolution that brought Clinton so much heat.

Among Republican presidential hopefuls, Iran has served mostly as a contest over who can advocate the toughest measures. Arizona **Sen. John McCain** seemed

Sen. John McCain,
R-Ariz.

momentarily to have won that contest. In April, sitting in his tour bus, he sang a few bars of the chorus of "Bomb Iran," by Vince Vance and the Valiants, an AM radio favorite of the 1979-1981 hostage-crisis period (based on the Beach Boys' "Barbara Ann").[7] But after cries of indignation, McCain protested that he'd only been kidding. "People got to lighten up, get a life," McCain said.[8]

Nevertheless, in a more serious setting McCain answered affirmatively when asked at an October debate whether he would take action against Iran — without consulting Congress — to stop it from acquiring nuclear weapons. But he added a proviso — "if the situation . . . requires immediate action to ensure the security of the United States of America."[9]

Former Massachusetts **Gov. Mitt Romney** was widely judged to have stumbled when he answered the same question: "We're going to let the lawyers sort out what he needed to do and what he didn't need to do,"

Former Gov. Mitt
Romney, R-Mass.

Romney said, seemingly referring to whichever president might be facing the issue, "but certainly what you want to do is to have the agreement of all the people in leadership of our government, as well as our friends around the world where those circumstances are available."[10]

Of all the Republican contenders, former New York City Mayor **Rudolph W. Giuliani** has made the most of the Iran issue. His senior foreign policy adviser on Iran is Michael Rubin of the American Enterprise

Former Mayor Rudolph
Giuliani, R-N.Y.

Institute, who advocates stepping up aid to Iranian democracy activists. Also advising is *Commentary* magazine Editor-at-large Norman Podhoretz, a prominent neocon who calls for bombing Iranian nuclear facilities.

During a September visit to London, Giuliani said that if Iran got close to building a nuclear weapon, "We will prevent them or we'll set them back five or 10 years." He added, "That is not said as a threat. That should be said as a promise."[11]

But even if he won the nomination and the election, Giuliani wouldn't be deciding Iran policy until early 2009. For now, the constant stream of events, speculation, declarations and rumors about Iran is fueling the political process to such an extent that liberal *New York Times* columnist Frank Rich theorized that the Bush administration is keeping the tension high mainly to torment Democratic candidates.

"Whatever happens in or to Iran," Rich wrote, "the American public will be carpet-bombed by apocalyptic propaganda for the 12 months to come."

[1] See Senate Amendment 3017 to HR1585: "To express the sense of the Senate regarding Iran," Sept. 20, 2007, www.govtrack.us/congress/amendment.xpd?session=110&amdt=s3017.

[2] Quoted in Dan Balz, "Iran Becomes an Issue in Democratic Contest," *The Washington Post*, Oct. 25, 2007, p. A7.

[3] *Ibid.*

[4] See "Senator Clinton Announces Co-Sponsorship of Webb Legislation Prohibiting the Use of Funds for Military Operations In Iran," press release, Oct. 1, 2007, www.senate.gov/~clinton/news/state ments/details.cfm?id=284618.

[5] Quoted in Shailagh Murray, "Webb Seen as a Potential 2008 Running Mate," *The Washington Post*, Oct. 28, 2007, p. A4.

[6] "Clinton: No Military Action on Iran Without Congressional Authority," press release, Feb. 14, 2007, www.senate.gov/~clinton/news/statements/record.cfm?id=269287.

[7] See "Vince Vance and the Valiants," neworleansbands.net, undated, www.neworleansbands.net/music/bands/161/.

[8] Quoted in Mark Leibovich, "Falling From the Top Lands McCain in a Scaled-Back Comfort Zone," *The Washington Post*, Oct. 7, 2007, p. A1.

[9] Quoted in Adam Nagourney and Marc Santora, "Romney and Giuliani Spar as New Guy Looks On," *The New York Times*, Oct. 10, 2007, p. A1.

[10] *Ibid.*

[11] Quoted in Michael Finnegan, "Giuliani warns Iranians against nuclear ambitions," *Los Angeles Times*, Sept. 20, 2007, p. A15.

To the surprise of observers, the shah and his notorious secret police, SAVAK, proved incapable of coping. In the past SAVAK had arrested, tortured or killed hundreds of thousands of genuine or alleged oppositionists. Israel had a close working relationship with SAVAK, growing out of antagonism between the shah and the Arab states. That relationship fueled popular antagonism toward the Jewish state.

A year later, on Jan. 16, 1979, the shah fled Iran. Two weeks later, Khomeini returned home from exile in Paris, turning the revolutionary process definitively toward his brand of socially conservative, politically aggressive and theocratic Shiite politics. Some secular democrats who were involved in an early provisional government were pushed aside. "At every step of the way, [Khomeini] and his supporters proved more ardent in their faith, more manipulative in their conduct and more merciless in their retaliations," writes Ray Takeyh, a historian and senior fellow at the centrist Council on Foreign Relations.[42]

Khomeini's strategy bore fruit on Dec. 3, 1979, when Iranian voters approved a constitution that created today's Islamic Republic of Iran, directed by a religious leader who would not be accountable to the public or to elected officials. A Guardian Council, mainly clerics, would have the final word on all legislation.

The referendum passed amidst a frenzy of enthusiasm generated by a crisis that still reverberates. A month earlier, on Nov. 4, a band of student militants overran the U.S. Embassy in Tehran, taking 52 hostages, to punish the Carter administration for allowing the shah into the United States for cancer treatment.

Khomeini applauded the takeover, and the United States cut relations with Iran — which haven't been restored to this day. Khomeini's forces, meanwhile, used CIA and other U.S. documents the students found to discredit domestic enemies shown to have connections to the United States. The hostage crisis ended 444 days after it began, with the inauguration of Ronald Reagan on Jan. 20, 1981.

Besides broken diplomatic relations, U.S. sanctions against Iran imposed during the hostage crisis also have survived. The United States first imposed financial penalties on Iran during the crisis, when the Carter administration banned Iranian oil imports and froze Iranian assets in the United States. In 1987, Reagan banned imports of all Iranian goods and services, citing Iranian support for international terrorism. In 1995, Clinton banned U.S. participation in petroleum development in Iran, also citing Iranian support for terrorism as well as efforts to acquire weapons of mass destruction. In 1997 Clinton extended the previous order by explicitly barring Americans from virtually all trade and investments involving Iran — a ban that was eased in 2000 to allow imports of Iranian dried fruits, nuts and caviar.[43]

Israel's Tilt

During the hostage crisis, in September 1980, Saddam Hussein launched a war against Iran over its alleged violation of a bilateral treaty. But, pretext aside, Saddam wanted to crush the new republic. As a Sunni ruling a majority-Shiite populace, Saddam viewed Iran's Shiite government as a powerful threat to his predominantly Sunni regime.

Saddam also posed a serious threat to Israel, given his nuclear ambitions. Iran seemed a lesser danger, despite its anti-Israel rhetoric. But for the United States, still reeling from the hostage crisis, Iran was the main enemy. The Iran-Iraq war would see the United States helping Iraq, while Israel secretly shipped arms to Iran. These alignments later shifted — with the United States toppling Saddam and Israel coming to fear Iran. But even during the 1980s, U.S. officials at one point joined in a scheme with Israel to sell arms to Iran.

During the eight-year war, Israeli leaders occasionally acknowledged their tilt toward Iran. "For 28 of 37 years, Iran was a friend of Israel. If it could work for 28 years . . . why couldn't it [again], once this crazy idea of Shiite fundamentalism is gone?" asked Yitzhak Rabin, Israel's defense minister, in 1987.[44]

But in addition to talking, the Jewish state was supplying arms to Iran. Both countries had reasons to keep the supply line secret, but in July 1981 an Argentine airplane carrying Israeli weapons to Iran crashed, leading to reports of a $200 million arms deal between the two countries.[45]

A few years later, Israeli — and American — arms sales to Iran became front-page news during the so-called "Iran-Contra" scandal. In November 1986, a Beirut newspaper revealed a secret visit to Iran by President Reagan's national security adviser, Robert McFarlane. Weeks later, Reagan admitted his administration had sold weapons to Iran — violating a U.S. arms embargo — and funneled the profits to the "contra" guerrillas fighting Nicaragua's left-wing Sandinista government.

Further complicating an already tangled tale, the Reagan administration also acknowledged it had fed secret intelligence to Iraq from U.S. satellite photos, allowing it to assess damage from bombing strikes on Iranian targets. "Because we could see the fact that Iran at various times clearly had the upper hand, and had the manpower to continue much further than Iraq could," the American assistance was necessary, an unnamed White House official said.[46]

By that time, the United States had another reason to help Iran's enemy. Following the 1982 Israeli invasion of Lebanon, Iran — eager for a base in the Arab countries — helped create the terrorist organization and political movement Hezbollah (Party of God). Its base was Lebanon's marginalized Shiite population, which had turned against Israel.

The following year, Hezbollah was implicated in a deadly bombing that destroyed the U.S. Embassy in Lebanon's capital, Beirut, killing 63 people. Six months later, a Hezbollah truck bomb hit the U.S. Marine barracks in Beirut, killing 241 Marines serving as peacekeepers.

Opinions are divided about whether Iran played a role in a terrorist attack that killed 19 airmen in 1996 at Khobar Towers, an apartment building serving as Air Force quarters near Dhahran, Saudi Arabia. In December 2006, U.S. District Judge Royce C. Lamberth of Washington ruled Iran responsible in connection with a lawsuit by victims' families against the Islamic Republic.[47]

Lamberth's decision echoed Attorney General John Ashcroft's conclusion in June 2001 that "elements of the Iranian government inspired, supported and supervised" the attack. Some experts challenge that conclusion. "There was a paucity of credible evidence," writes historian Ansari.[48]

Rise of Repression

After Khomeini's death in 1989, Iran's clerical overseers chose conservative Ayatollah Ali Khameini as the next supreme leader. "He believes that the mission of the Islamic Republic is to uphold religious norms and resist popular attempts to alter the regime along democratic lines," writes a critic, historian Takeyh.[49]

By the late 1990s, however, the popular call for more democracy was picking up strength. In 1997, by a landslide of nearly 70 percent, voters elected Mohammed Khatami as president. Khatami, a mid-ranking cleric who had emerged as a foe of repression, had studied Western philosophy, from which he quoted freely. And he knew Western social and political norms up close, having lived in Germany. That broader outlook and

experience showed. "State authority cannot be attained through coercion and dictatorship," he had written.[50]

In 1998, Khatami indicated a willingness not only to loosen controls on Iranians but also to enter into negotiations aimed at renewing relations with the United States. Using a 1998 interview with CNN to broadcast his views to the West, Khatami condemned terrorism "in all its forms." And speaking of the hostage crisis — still looming over U.S.-Iranian affairs — Khatami said it grew out of Iranian grievances such as the 1953 coup but also reflected the chaos of a revolutionary period — a condition that no longer applied. "Today, our new society has been institutionalized," he said, "and there is no need for unconventional methods of expression."[51]

In his first year in office, more than 200 new newspapers and magazines and 95 political parties and organizations were permitted. The new freedom sparked public debates on topics that had been out of bounds, including Israel and the Palestinians.

In 2001 Khatami swept into office a second time, with a 77 percent victory. But even supporters admitted that political liberalization had advanced, despite continued repression, while the economy had fallen off a cliff. One-quarter of the workforce was unemployed, and 40 percent of the population lived below the poverty line.[52]

Not surprisingly, the high hopes Khatami had inspired turned into disillusion. Economic disaster aside, Iranians who had hoped for reopening relations with the United States had experienced only disappointment. Iranian-U.S. cooperation early in the invasion of Afghanistan hadn't led to closer ties. "Before and during the war in Afghanistan, the Iranians were quite helpful to the United States," writes Kenneth Pollack, director of Persian Gulf Affairs at the National Security Council in the Clinton administration "They shared our hatred of al Qaeda and the Taliban, and they provided us with extensive assistance on intelligence, logistics, diplomacy and Afghan internal politics."[53]

And yet, the year after the Afghanistan campaign began, Bush in his first State of the Union address called Iran a member of the "axis of evil," along with North Korea and Iraq. "Iran aggressively pursues these weapons [of mass destruction] and exports terror," Bush said, "while an unelected few repress the Iranian people's hope for freedom."[54]

In 2005, Ahmadinejad, then Tehran's mayor, won a presidential-election runoff with 62 percent of the vote. A veteran of the bloody Iran-Iraq War and an engineer of working-class origins, he combined Khomeini-era rhetoric against the United States with denunciations of economic injustice.

Where reformists in Iran had hoped for eventual restoration of relations with the West, the new president and his circle looked to China, India and Russia for capital and trade links. "Our nation is continuing the path of progress and on this path has no significant need for the United States," Ahmadinejad said shortly before his election.[55]

CURRENT SITUATION

New Sanctions

The Bush administration is gearing up to start enforcing a new set of financial sanctions against an Iranian military force that the administration charges with terrorism. The sanctions also are designed to stymie what the administration regards as Iran's nuclear-weapons development program.

On Oct. 25, 2007, the State Department barred U.S. citizens and businesses from dealing with banks, businesses and individuals linked to the Revolutionary Guard, Iran's military logistics agency, or the Aerospsace Industries Organization, both of which the administration says are helping in developing ballistic missiles or nuclear weapons.[56]

The State Department also listed a unit of the Revolutionary Guard — the Qods [Jerusalem] Force — as a terrorist agency. The administration says the force, which has been described as a 5,000-man "unconventional warfare" wing of the Guard, provides "material support" to Lebanon's Hezbollah; three Palestinian organizations, including the militant Palestinian Islamic group Hamas; Afghanistan's Taliban and Shiite militias in Iraq "who target and kill coalition and Iraqi forces and innocent Iraqi civilians."[57]

Administration officials suggested that the sanctions represented a commitment to cracking down on Iran short of war. "We do not believe that conflict is inevitable," said Under Secretary of State for Political Affairs R. Nicholas Burns after the measures were announced. "This decision today supports the diplomacy and in no way, shape or form does it anticipate the use of force."[58]

Whether the sanctions will bite into Iran's nuclear development project is another question. "It is unlikely that these sanctions are going to impede the Iranian pursuit of nuclear capabilities," says Jon Wolfstahl, a senior fellow at the Center for Strategic and International Studies. "It is not going to seriously affect their financial situation because oil prices have risen so high."[59]

But a former National Security Council (NSC) official, Lee Wolosky, sees the sanctions as capable of slowing down Iran's use of the international financial system. European governments may ignore the sanctions, he acknowledges, but European banks could cooperate, if only to avoid complicating their own dealings with the United States. "Already, a great deal of of informal pressure is being applied to European banks to re-analyze relationships with Iran," he says.

"This has had a certain measure of success," he continues. "You're going to see non-U.S. banks cease to do business with [Iranian entities]."[60]

Days after his remarks, according to *The New York Times*, Western diplomats said most major European banks had quit dealing with the Iranian banks named in the sanction orders, or were getting ready to do so.[61]

The new sanctions have reverberated at the World Bank, where officials said in November they were holding up $5.4 million for four projects in Iran — earthquake relief, water and sanitation, environment management and urban housing. The bank acted because the sanctions left it without an Iranian bank through which to funnel funds.[62]

An Iranian official, meanwhile, scoffed at the new measures. "Sanctions have been imposed on us for the past 28 years," said Saeed Jalili, who recently replaced Ali Larijani as Iran's representative before the International Atomic Energy Agency (IAEA). "The new sanctions, like those before, will have no effect on Iran's policies."[63]

Whatever effects the past sanctions may have had, they clearly haven't stopped Iran's nuclear development efforts, according to Paul Pillar, the CIA's former national intelligence officer for the Near East and South Asia. He worries the latest sanctions raise tensions between Iran and the United States. "They strengthen the positions of the relative hard-liners," Pillar says. "I think we played into the Iranian president's hands."[64]

Iran in the U.N.

Amid the new sanctions, and the stepped-up war of words between Washington and Tehran, the U.N. Security Council is jockeying with Iran over its nuclear program.

AT ISSUE

Are President Bush's recent statements on Iran dangerously provocative?

YES
Sen. Robert C. Byrd, D-W. Va.
Chairman, Senate Appropriations Committee

Written for *CQ Researcher*, November 2007

Yes. Every day now, it seems that the confrontational rhetoric between the United States and Iran continues to escalate. The main point of contention is Iran's pursuit of nuclear weapons. While few doubt Iran's desire to attain a nuclear bomb, there is little evidence that they are close to acquiring such a capability.

Yet, the White House has been busy unleashing almost daily claims of an imminent nuclear threat in Iran, as it did with Iraq. Fear, panic and chest-pounding do not work well in the conduct of foreign policy. This is a time to put diplomacy to work. There is ample opportunity to coordinate with our allies to constrain Iran's ambitions. But instead of working with our partners, the Bush administration has unveiled new unilateral sanctions against Iran. Instead of direct diplomatic negotiations with Iran, the administration continues to issue ultimatums and threats.

We have been down that path already. We know where it leads. Vice President Cheney recently threatened "serious consequences" — the exact phrase that he used in the run-up to the invasion of Iraq — if Tehran does not acquiesce to U.S. demands. The parallels are all-too-chilling. President Bush warned that those who wish to "avoid World War III" should seek to keep Iran from attaining nuclear weapons. Secretary of Defense Robert Gates has admitted in the press that the Pentagon has drafted plans for a military option in Iran. The president's $196 billion request for emergency war funding included a request for "bunker-buster" bombs that have no immediate use in Iraq.

Taking all of it together — the bellicose rhetoric, the needlessly confrontational unilateral sanctions, the provocative stationing of U.S. warships in the region, the operational war planning and the request for munitions that seem designed for use in Iran — there are reasons for deep concern that this administration is once again rushing headlong into another disastrous war in the Middle East.

The Bush administration apparently believes that it has the authority to wage preemptive war — and can do so without prior congressional approval. That is why I am cosponsoring a resolution with Sen. Richard Durbin, D-Ill., which affirms that any military action taken against Iran must be explicitly approved by Congress before any such action be initiated. The White House must be reminded of the constitutional powers entrusted to the people's branch. Let us halt this rush to another war. Let us not make the same disastrous mistake as we did with Iraq.

NO
Michael Rubin
Resident Scholar, American Enterprise Institute

Written for *CQ Researcher*, November 2007

On Oct. 17, President Bush raised the specter of war with Iran. "If you're interested in avoiding World War III," he said, it's necessary to deny the Islamic Republic "the knowledge necessary to make a nuclear weapon." Condemnation of his comments was swift. Sen. Robert Byrd, D-W. Va., accused the president of using "rhetorical ghosts and goblins to scare the American people, with claims of an imminent nuclear threat in Iran."

Navel-gazing is a Capitol Hill pastime, but such criticism is misplaced. Since the disclosure of Iran's covert enrichment program, International Atomic Energy Agency (IAEA) inspectors — not the CIA or Iranian exiles — report a litany of lies. IAEA inspectors discovered traces of uranium metal used to build bombs, not fuel reactors. IAEA inspectors also found that Iran had experimented with chemical separation of polonium, a material used to initiate nuclear detonation. Iran still has not revealed what rogue Pakistani scientist A.Q. Khan sold on his trip to Tehran.

Diplomacy should always be the strategy of first resort, but its track record with Tehran does not encourage. While it is fashionable to blame Iran's nuclear desire upon U.S. presence in Iraq and Afghanistan, Tehran's program predates such interventions by 15 years. In the name of engagement, the European Union nearly tripled trade with Iran between 2000 and 2005. But rather than invest that windfall in schools and hospitals, the Iranian government — then under reformist control — poured money into its military and centrifuge programs. Tehran has yet to provide the West a single, confidence-building measure.

Iranian diplomats say their program is peaceful, but officials close to Supreme Leader Ali Khamenei suggest otherwise. On Feb. 14, 2005, Ayatollah Mohammad Baqer Kharrazi, secretary-general of Iranian Hezbollah, said, "We are able to produce atomic bombs, and we will do that." Three months later, Gholam Reza Hasani, Khamenei's representative to West Azerbaijan province said, "An atomic bomb . . . must be produced." And, on Sept. 3, 2007, Khamenei himself said, "Iran will outwit the West on the nuclear issue."

Iran's centrifuge cascade, Syria's surprise nuclear plant and North Korea's role in its construction suggest time is limited. To avert escalation, the White House must demonstrate diplomacy to be Tehran's best option. Bush's rhetoric dampens Iran's overconfidence and underscores U.S. seriousness, both in Tehran and at the United Nations. Bashing Bush may make good politics, but it is irresponsible and may hasten the result which Bush's domestic critics most fear.

Mohammed ElBaradei, director of the IAEA, has been trying to negotiate a program of tough inspections to ensure Iran's uranium-enrichment program stops short of producing weapons-quality fuel. While he has argued against trying to stop enrichment altogether, he has also warned that Iran may have to "come clean" about possible past work on weapons development.[65]

"We cannot give Iran a pass right now, because there's still a lot of question marks," ElBaradei said on CNN in late October. He added that the agency hasn't seen any definitive evidence Iran is pursuing an "active weaponization program."[66]

ElBaradei's remarks came about six weeks before he is scheduled to tell diplomats from the United States, Britain, France, Germany, Russia and China whether doubts over Iran's nuclear intentions have been resolved. If not, at least some of those countries favor new U.N. sanctions designed to force Iran's compliance with IAEA regulations.

In early November, the British Foreign Office announced that all six countries had agreed to approve such sanctions, but China and Russia hadn't confirmed Britain's statement. Days earlier, President Vladimir V. Putin asked, "Why make the situation worse, bring it to a dead end, threaten sanctions or even military action?"[67]

The climate surrounding Putin's statement — already made tense by the Foreign Office's announcement and the earlier statements by Bush and Cheney — was further supercharged by military action by Israel. On Sept. 6, Israeli warplanes bombed a building in Syria that American officials said housed a nuclear project aided by North Korea. Israel has maintained official silence and imposed military censorship on its aggressive press. And Syria has denied doing any nuclear work — with North Korea or without it. "The rumors have been deliberately fabricated by Israel to justify its recent act of aggression against Syria," Syrian Prime Minister Mohammed Naji al-Otri said.[68]

Whatever effect the bombing may have had on Syria, Iran was also indirectly a target, some Washington strategists said. "If you are Israel and you are looking at this, the value of striking Syria is that it sends a signal, including to the Iranians," said Michael Green, a former director of Asian affairs at the National Security Council and now an associate professor at Georgetown University's School of Foreign Service. "This follows the Chinese proverb that sometimes you have to kill the chicken to scare the monkey."[69]

Iranian officials gave no sign of being scared, nor of willingness to bend to international pressure to suspend their efforts to enrich uranium. "Suspension is the crucial issue if the Iranians want to get off the hook of more sanctions," said a participant in talks in Rome in October between Iranian negotiators and Javier Solana, foreign policy director of the European Union. "They seem to think they are doing enough."[70]

Last March, and also in December 2006, the Security Council approved sanctions aimed at forcing Iran to stop its enrichment efforts.[71]

The first of those two sets of sanctions banned the import and export by Iran of materials and technology used in uranium enrichment and ballistic missiles. In addition, the assets of 12 Iranian individuals and 10 companies allegedly involved in nuclear and missile work were frozen.[72]

Then, in March, after Iran still hadn't satisfied objections to its nuclear program, the Security Council approved tougher sanctions, including a ban on all weapons sales to Iran and on any grants or loans to Iran not involving humanitarian and development aid.[73]

In the weeks leading up to the scheduled November meeting, the outlook for Iran to back away from enrichment seemed dim, judging by President Ahmadinejad's blunt remarks just before the Rome talks were to start. "Iran will not retreat one iota," he said. "We are in favor of talks, but we will not negotiate with anyone about our right to nuclear technology."

Ahmadinejad's declaration represents one face that Iranian officials have presented to international bodies who try to control the proliferation of nuclear technology.

The other face showed in statements made after Iranian officials met in Rome with E.U. representatives. "We are after no adventure, and we are after no trouble-making," Larijani told reporters.[74]

But, in a further complication for those trying to decode Iran's strategy, Larijani — seen by some as a voice of moderation — was replaced as Iran's chief negotiator on the nuclear issue. Larijani denied that his removal signaled a hardening of Iran's position. Some Iranian politicians didn't buy the denial. "It is very disappointing that the government does not tolerate even views of a person like Mr. Larijani and would eliminate him in such a manner," said Mohammed Hashemi, a former vice president and the brother of former President Ali Akbar Hashemi Rafsanjani.[75]

Larijani's replacement, in fact, was among the latest in a long sequence of events that have prompted suspicion of

Iran's intentions. In 2005, for example, the IAEA reported that Iran had acquired engineering drawings on how to cast uranium into the exact shape of a nuclear bomb core. Equally important, the source of the drawings was the infamous A.Q. Khan of Pakistan, who had made a mission and a business out of selling nuclear plans to developing countries, especially Muslim-majority nations.[76]

Hovering over the entire issue of Iran and nuclear development is the question of when Iran could be ready to produce a nuclear weapon. Defense Secretary Gates has reported that intelligence agencies estimate 2010 at the earliest, or 2015 at the latest. But Israel's military intelligence research chief, Brig. Gen. Yossi Baidatz, told the Israeli parliament in early November that the date could come as early as 2009. Some Israeli officials have suggested that Israel would never let Iran get that far. Sallai Meridor, ambassador to the United States, said in late October that Israel should always be prepared "to preempt, to deter, to defeat if we can."[77]

But Israel's political-military elite isn't of one mind on the subject. Efraim Halevy, Israel's retired chief spymaster, disputes the notion that Iran poses a threat to Israel's existence. "I believe that Israel is indestructible," Halevy told *The Washington Post*. And if Iran does produce an atomic weapon, he said, Israel has "a whole arsenal of capabilities" to deter nuclear aggression from Iran, whose leaders would consider it a religious violation to put their country's survival at risk.[78]

OUTLOOK

Popular Uprising?

What will Iran be like 10 years from now? George Mason University historian Bakhash refuses to hazard a prediction. "There are too many variables," he says.

Indeed, from the 1953 coup to the flight of the shah to the embassy hostage crisis to the horrific war with Iraq — and more — Iran has experienced enough volatility for 10 countries.

"Iran is a very emotional and changeable society; it's better to forecast the next six months," says human-rights activist Afshari, sounding a similar note of caution. But he does sketch out a possible near-term future.

"In the next 10 years, Iranian society will be in a much better situation in the field of democracy and human rights and justice," he says. "A basic change will

have happened. The government can't continue like this. They have to give in to the Iranian people's demands."

Afshari sees the present government as incapable of maintaining its current nuclear development efforts. "It cannot continue outside the control of the international community," he says.

Moreover, he predicts, citing the collapse of the Soviet Union, sweeping changes will be brought about, but not by popular elections. "There will be big social changes — civil disobedience like in Poland, and also like the Islamic Revolution," he says.

Such a scenario could come about, says Iran hawk Rubin of the American Enterprise Institute. But a far bleaker one is equally possible, he says: "Either you're going to have a Romania-style change, or else the regime will have crushed all dissent."[79]

Rubin agrees with Afshari that working within legal channels won't produce the kind of deep change that democracy activists and their supporters abroad support. "If you believe that your legitimacy comes from God, you don't care what 90 percent of the people think." Hence, any hopes are futile that the government would respond even to a massive negative vote, he says.

Rubin's American Enterprise Institute colleague Ledeen depicts the government's position even more starkly. "The problem is not the fanaticism of the people, it's the fanaticism of the regime — a thin veneer on top of a civilized and cultured country. They're pro-Western and pro-American, they understand a lot about self-government, they're well-educated, and they've had constitutions. Why aren't we working for their freedom?"

Parsi, the Iranian-American advocate of a negotiated reduction in tension in Tehran, argues that lowering the level of hostility between the governments will make democratic change more possible in Iran. "If we manage to avoid conflict, if there is significant reduction of tension between the two countries and if Iran is included in the regional political and security structure — in return for significant changes — then Iran can be a constructive player in the region," he says. Indeed, he adds, "Then pro-democracy forces will have greater maneuverability to move Iran in a more democratic direction."

Riedel of the Brookings Institution's Saban Center says the failure of reformist President Khatami to produce fundamental changes shows the obstacles the democracy movement faces. "It is a pretty dramatic demonstration that it's not going to move as fast as its own supporters — or outsiders — would like.

"I'm not an optimist about civil-society movements in the Middle East — not on a 10-year cycle. Maybe 50 years."

For the moment, though, Riedel and other Iran-watchers are paying much closer attention to the immediate future, and the prospects for peace.

"The possibilities of avoiding war — if we can get through the end of the Bush administration, they're reasonably good," he says.

NOTES

1. Quoted in Sheryl Gay Stolberg, "Nuclear-Armed Iran Risks 'World War III,' Bush Says," *The New York Times*, Oct. 18, 2007, p. A6.

2. Quoted in Thom Shanker, "Gates Says Iran Gave Assurances on Explosives," *The New York Times*, Nov. 2, 2007, p. A10.

3. Quoted in Warren Hoge, "Iran's President Vows to Ignore U.N. Measures," *The New York Times*, Sept. 26, 2007, p. A1, www.nytimes.com/2007/09/26/world/26nations.html.

4. See "Vice President's Remarks to the Washington Institute for Near East Policy," The White House, Sept. 21, 2007, www.whitehouse.gov/news/releases/2007/10/print/20071021.html.

5. See Ray Takeyh, *Hidden Iran: Paradox and Power in the Islamic Republic* (2006), pp. 24-25.

6. Other institute scholars include John R. Bolton, former U.S. ambassador to the United Nations, who now criticizes the administration for being soft on North Korea. See John R. Bolton, "Bush's North Korea Meltdown," *The Wall Street Journal*, Oct. 31, 2007, p. A21.

7. See Michael A. Ledeen, *The Iranian Time Bomb: The Mullah Zealots' Quest for Destruction* (2007).

8. See Fareed Zakaria, "Stalin, Mao and . . . Ahmadinejad?" *Newsweek.com*, Oct. 29, 2007, www.newsweek.com/id/57346.

9. See Akbar Ganji, "Why Iran's Democrats Shun Aid," *The Washington Post*, Oct. 27, 2007, p. A21.

10. For analysis of oil market effects, see Steven Mufson, "Strike on Iran Would Roil Oil Markets, Experts Say," *The Washington Post*, Oct. 26, 2007, p. A1.

11. See "Debate Stirs Over Possible U.S. Military Action Against Iran," transcript, Online News Hour, Oct. 29, 2007, www.pbs.org/newshour/bb/middle_east/july-dec07/iran_10-29.html.

12. See Sharon Squassoni, "Iran's Nuclear Program: Recent Developments," Congressional Research Service, updated Dec. 26, 2006, pp. 1-2, http://fpc.state.gov/documents/organization/78477.pdf; Jonathan C. Randal, "Shah's Economic Projects Hit Snags, Periling His Regime," *The Washington Post*, April 2, 1978, p. A22; Susanna McBee, "Shah Reportedly Pledges Neutrality on Oil Prices," *The Washington Post*, Nov. 16, 1977, p. A1.

13. Quoted in Squassoni, *ibid.*, p. 2.

14. Quoted in Thom Shanker and William J. Broad, "Iran to Limit Cooperation With Nuclear Inspectors," *The New York Times*, March 26, 2007, p. A6.

15. David Albright and Corey Hinderstein, "Countdown to Showdown," *Bulletin of the Atomic Scientists*, November/December 2004, p. 67, http://thebulletin.metapress.com/content/y718r48304663rg9/fulltext.pdf.

16. "Smart Power Speakers Series, Gen. John Abizaid (Ret.)," Sept. 17, 2007 www.csis.org/media/csis/events/070917_smartpower_abizaid.pdf.

17. For brief background on the 1999 bombing raid, see "Iran wants compensation for Turkish air raids," Deutsche Presse-Agentur, Aug. 1, 1999.

18. See Vali Nasr, *The Shia Revival: How Conflicts within Islam Will Shape the Future* (2006), p. 67.

19. See "Debate Stirs. . . .," *op. cit.*; see also Andrew Higgins, "The bomb-makers of Asia," *The Independent* (London), Nov. 21, 1991, p. A29.

20. Trita Parsi, *Treacherous Alliance: The Secret Dealings of Israel, Iran, and the United States* (2007).

21. See Shirin Ebadi and Hadi Ghaemi, "The Human Rights Case Against Attacking Iran," *The New York Times*, Feb. 8, 2005, p. A25. For background on Ebadi see "Shirin Ebadi, The Nobel Peace Prize 2003, Autobiography," http://nobelprize.org/nobel_prizes/peace/laureates/2003/ebadi-autobio.html.

22. Quoted in Bourzou Daragahi, "Iran tightens the screws on internal dissent," *Los Angeles Times*, June 10, 2007, p. A1.

23. Quoted in Glenn Kessler, "Rice Asks for $75 Million to Increase Pressure on Iran," *The Washington Post*, Feb.

16, 2006, p. A1. See also Adam Graham-Silverman, "Family Planning Programs and Policy Fuel Senate Debate on Spending Bill," *CQ Today*, Sept. 26, 2007.

24. Quoted in Robin Wright, "Cut Iran Democracy Funding, Groups Tell U.S.," *The Washington Post*, Oct. 11, 2007, p. A15.

25. See Neil McFarquhar, "Iran Frees One Detainee as Another Family Waits in Hope," *The New York Times*, Sept. 20, 2007, p. A12; Tony Barboza, "Diplomacy in New York: Divestment; OC man freed from Iran prison," *Los Angeles Times*, Sept. 25, p. A10.

26. See Haleh Esfandiari and Robert S. Litwak, "When Promoting Democracy is Counterproductive," *Chronicle of Higher Education*, Oct. 19, 2007, http://chronicle.com/free/v54/i08/08b00701.htm.

27. See Eli Lake, "An Iranian Student Makes His Escape In face of Charges," *The New York Sun*, Jan. 3, 2005, www.nysun.com/article/7065. See also, "Iran — An Update," Committee on the Present Danger, Jan. 23, 2006, www.committeeonthepresentdanger.org/portals/4/iranpaperjan23.pdf.

28. See "Iran-Iraq War (1980-1988)," undated, globalsecurity.org, www.globalsecurity.org/military/world/war/iran-iraq.htm.

29. Quoted in Cesar G. Soriano, "General discusses Iran's, al-Sadr's influence in Iraq," *USA Today*, June 14, 2007, p. A13.

30. See Michael R. Gordon, "U.S. Says Iran-Supplied Bomb Is Killing More Troops in Iraq," *The New York Times*, Aug. 8, 2007, p. A1.

31. Quoted in Sam Enriquez, "Conflict in Iraq: Guarding the Border; Officer Sentenced," *Los Angeles Times*, Oct. 20, 2007, p. A1.

32. For the full report on Rafsanjani's sermon see "Rafsanjani: World should admire Iran's nuclear achievements," IRNA — Islamic Republic News Agency, July 13, 2007, republished at Globalsecurity.org, www.globalsecurity.org/wmd/ library/news/iran/2007/iran-070713-irna02.htm.

33. See "Policy Options in Iraq," House Foreign Affairs Committee, Committee Testimony, July 17, 2007.

34. Except where otherwise indicated, this subsection is drawn from Ali M. Ansari, *Hidden Iran* (2006); and (for details of the CIA's role) Tim Weiner, *Legacy of Ashes: The History of the CIA* (2007), pp. 81-92.

35. See Ansari, *op. cit.*, pp 36-37.

36. See Weiner, *op. cit.*, p. 92.

37. Quoted in *ibid.*, p. 46. See also, Frances Bostock and Geoffrey Jones, *Planning and Power in Iran: Ebtehaj and Economic Development Under the Shah* (1989), pp. 160-161.

38. See Eric Rouleau, "Khomeini's Iran," *Foreign Affairs*, fall 1980.

39. Quoted in Ansari, *op. cit.*, p. 53.

40. Unless otherwise indicated, material in this subsection and the one that follows is drawn from Ansari, *op. cit.*; Takeyh, *op. cit.*; Trita Parsi, *Treacherous Alliances: The Secret Dealings of Israel, Iran, and the U.S.* (2007), p. 62; and Rouleau, *op. cit.*

41. See "Tehran, Iran, Toasts of the President and the Shah at a State Dinner," Dec. 31, 1977, The American Presidency Project, www.presidency.ucsb.edu/ws/index.php?pid=7080&st=&st1=.

42. See Takeyh, *op. cit.*, p. 23. Also see Shaul Bakhash, *The Reign of the Ayatollahs: Iran and the Islamic Revolution* (1990).

43. See Bernard Gwertzman, "Iraq Gets Reports From U.S. for Use in War With Iran," *The New York Times*, Dec. 16, 1986, p. A1. U.S. Department of the Treasury, *op. cit.*

44. Quoted in Glenn Frankel, "Israeli Critical of U.S. Policy in Gulf War," *The Washington Post*, Oct. 29, 1987, p. A33.

45. See Benjamin Weiser, "Behind Israel-Iran Sales, 'Amber' Light from U.S.," *The Washington Post*, Aug. 16, 1987, p. A1.

46. Quoted in Gwertzman, *op. cit.*; See also Bob Woodward, "CIA Aiding Iraq in Gulf War," *The Washington Post*, Dec. 15, 1986, p. A1.

47. See Carol D. Leonnig, "Iran Held Liable in Khobar Attack," *The Washington Post*, Dec. 23, 2006, p. A2.

48. See Ansari, *op. cit.*, p. 180; Ashcroft quoted in Barbara Slavin, "14 indicted in barracks bombing," *USA Today*, June 22, 2001, p. A6.

49. See Takeyh, *op. cit.*, pp. 33-34. For background, see Katel, *op. cit.*

50. Quoted in Takeyh, *op. cit.*, p. 44.

51. See "Iranian President Favors People to People Dialogue," CNN "Worldview," Jan. 7, 1998.

52. See John Ward Anderson, "With Stalemate Ended, Khatami Takes Oath in Iran," *The Washington Post*, Aug. 9, 2001, p. A12.

53. See Kenneth M. Pollack, "Don't Count on Iran to Pick Up the Pieces," *The New York Times*, Dec. 8, 2006, p. A35.

54. See "The President's State of the Union Address," The White House, Jan. 29, 2002, www.whitehouse.gov/news/releases/2002/01/20020129-11 .html.

55. Quoted in Takeyh, *op. cit.*, p. 133.

56. See "Fact Sheet: Designation of Iranian Entities and Individuals for Proliferation Activities and Support for Terrorism," Treasury Department, Oct. 25, 2007, www.treasury.gov/press/releases/hp644.htm.

57. See Anthony H. Cordesman and Martin Kleiber, "Iran's Military Forces and Warfighting Capabilities," Center for Strategic and International Studies, 2007, pp. 78-79.

58. Quoted in Helene Cooper, "In Sanctioning Iran, U.S. Plays Its 'Unilateralism' Card," *The New York Times*, Oct. 26, 2007, p. A12.

59. Wolfstahl spoke during a conference call on Oct. 25, 2007, with journalists arranged by the National Security Network, an organization of former Democratic officials. He served as special policy adviser on non-proliferation at the Department of Energy in the Clinton administration.

60. Wolosky, now a Washington attorney, served as transnational threats director at the National Security Council under Clinton and, briefly, President George W. Bush. He spoke during the National Security Council conference call on Oct. 25, 2007.

61. See Steven R. Weisman, "U.S. Sanctions Force World Bank to Halt Some Iran Aid," *The New York Times*, Nov. 3, 2007, p. A14.

62. *Ibid.*

63. Quoted in Nazila Fathi, "Iranians Dismiss Sanctions From U.S.," *The New York Times*, Oct. 27, 2007, p. A7.

64. Pillar spoke during the National Security Council conference call on Oct. 25, 2007.

65. Quoted in Elaine Sciolino and William J. Broad, "To Iran and its Foes, an Indispensable Irritant," *The New York Times*, Sept. 17, 2007, p. A1. Also see Kenneth Katzman, "Iran: U.S. Concerns and Policy Responses," Congressional Research Service, updated Aug. 6, 2007, p. 20, http://fpc.state.gov/documents/organization/91002.pdf.

66. Quoted in Maggie Farley, "U.N. still probing Iran nuclear case," *Los Angeles Times*, Oct. 30, 2007, p. A4.

67. Quoted in "Britain Reports Plan for New Sanctions on Iran," *The New York Times* [Reuters], Nov. 30, 2007, p. A7.

68. Quoted in Joby Warrick and Robin Wright, "Suspected Location of Syria's Reactor Cleared," *The Washington Post*, Oct. 26, 2007, p. A17. See also, Mark Mazzetti and Helene Cooper, "Israeli Nuclear Suspicions Linked to Raid," *The New York Times*, Sept. 18, 2007, p. A11; Glenn Kessler and Robin Wright, "Israel, U.S. Shared Data on Suspected Nuclear Site," *The Washington Post*, Sept. 21, 2007, p. A1.

69. Quoted in David E. Sanger, "Pre-emptive Caution: The Case of Syria," *The New York Times*, Oct. 14, 2007, p. A8.

70. Quoted in Elaine Sciolino and Peter Kiefer, "Iran Has New Nuclear Negotiator, But Similar Stance," *The New York Times*, Oct. 24, 2007, p. A6.

71. See "Uranium Enrichment," U.S. Nuclear Regulatory Commission, Sept. 20, 2007, www.nrc.gov/materials/fuel-cycle-fac/ur-enrichment.html.

72. See Helene Cooper, "Diplomats to Begin Drafting New U.N. Sanctions on Iran," *The New York Times*, Feb. 27, 2007, p. A9.

73. See "Security Council tightens sanctions against Iran over uranium enrichment," UN News Centre, March 24, 2007, www.un.org/apps/news/story.asp?NewsID=21997&Cr=Iran&Cr1#.

74. *Ibid.*

75. *Ibid.*

76. See David E. Sanger and William J. Broad, "Bush and Putin Want Iran to Treat Uranium in Russia," *The New York Times*, Nov. 18, 2005, p. A1. See also Douglas Frantz, "From Patriot to Proliferator," *Los Angeles Times*, Sept. 23, 2005, p. A1, and Roland Flamini, "Nuclear Proliferation," *CQ Global Researcher*, January 2007, pp. 1-26; and Mary H. Cooper, "Nuclear Proliferation and Terrorism," *CQ Researcher*, April 2, 2004, pp. 297-320.

77. Meridor quoted in Hilary Leila Krieger, *Jerusalem Post*, online edition, Oct. 23, 2007, www.jpost .com/ servlet/Satellite?pagename=JPost%2FJPArticle%2F ShowFull&cid=1192380626865; Baidatz quoted in Mark Weiss and Sheera Claire Frenkel, "Mofaz: 2008 is decisive for stopping Iran's nuclear drive," *Jerusalem Post*, online edition, www.jpost.com/serv let/Satellite?cid=1192380749027&pagename=JPost %2FJPArticle%2FShowFull.

78. Quoted in David Ignatius, "The Spy Who Wants Israel to Talk," *The Washington Post*, Nov. 11, 2007, p. B7.

79. The 1989 Romanian revolution, one of the last nails in the coffin of Eastern and Central European communism, toppled dictator Nicolae Ceausescu, who was shot by firing squad on national television, along with his wife, Elena. See William Horsley, "Romania's bloody revolution," BBC News, Dec. 12, 1999, http:// news.bbc.co.uk/2/hi/europe/574200.stm.

BIBLIOGRAPHY

Books

Ansari, Ali M., *Confronting Iran: The Failure of American Foreign Policy and the Next Great Crisis in the Middle East*, Basic Books, 2006.
A historian at the University of St. Andrews in Scotland chronicles and analyzes the complexities of the U.S.-Iran relationship.

Ledeen, Michael A., *The Iranian Time Bomb: The Mullah Zealots' Quest for Destruction*, St. Martin's Press, 2007.
The Iranian leadership is far more dangerous than most Westerners realize, argues a longtime Iran hawk.

Parsi, Trita, *Treacherous Alliance: The Secret Dealings of Israel, Iran, and the U.S.*, Yale University Press, 2007.
An adjunct professor at Johns Hopkins University's School of Advanced International Studies traces the shifting alliances that have marked the crucial three-way relationship.

Takeyh, Ray, *Hidden Iran: Paradox and Power in the Islamic Republic*, Times Books, 2006.
A Middle East expert at the Council on Foreign Relations explores the twists and turns of Iranian politics.

Articles

Barboza, Tony, "Iranians in U.S. weigh the price of activism," *Los Angeles Times*, Sept. 16, 2007, p. B1.
The imprisonment of liberal Iranian-Americans visiting their homeland sends a chill through the Iranian exile community.

Daragahi, Borzou, "Iran tightens the screws on internal dissent," *Los Angeles Times*, June 10, 2007, p. A1.
The Iranian regime is intensifying its repression of pro-democracy Iranians and those who break dress codes.

Daragahi, Borzou, "U.S.-Iran rivalry has a familiar look," *Los Angeles Times*, July 5, 2007, p. A6.
The complicated, tense standoff between the United States and Iran has parallels to the Cold War.

Hersh, Seymour M., "Shifting targets: The administration's plan for Iran," *The New Yorker*, Oct. 8, 2007, www.newy-orker.com/reporting/2007/10/08/071008fa_fact_hersh.
A leading investigative journalist reports that administration strategy on Iran has met some detours and complications.

Montagne, Renee, (host), "The Evolution of Iran's Revolutionary Guard," National Public Radio, (transcript), www.npr.org/templates/transcript/transcript .php?story Id=9371072.
Iran experts discuss the Iranian force at the center of the U.S.-Iran standoff.

Sciolino, Elaine, "To Iran, Iraq May Be the Greater Satan," *The New York Times*, Nov. 3, 2002, Sect. 4 (*News of the Week in Review*), p. 14.
In the run-up to the Iraq War, a veteran correspondent examines the complicated world of Middle Eastern alliances.

Wright, Robin, "Free Thinker; Iranian Dissident Akbar Ganji at Libert to Speak His Mind, at Least Until he Goes Back Home," *The Washington Post*, Aug. 14, 2007, p. C1.
A celebrated dissident assesses the grim state of civil liberties and democracy in Iran, but plans on returning.

Reports

Clawson, Patrick, and Michael Eisenstadt, "Deterring the Ayatollahs: Complications in Applying Cold War Strategy to Iran," Washington Institute for Near East

Policy, July 2007, www.washingtoninstitute.org/templateC04.php?CID=280.

Washington think tank scholars compiled essays on how Iran might be persuaded not to develop nuclear weapons.

Cordesman, Anthony H., "Iran's Revolutionary Guards, the Al Quds Force, and Other Intelligence and Paramilitary Forces," Center for Strategic and International Studies, Aug. 16, 2007, (draft), www .csis.org/media/csis/pubs/070816_cordesman_report.pdf.

A veteran military analyst describes what is known about the key Iranian military and unconventional-warfare units.

Katzman, Kenneth, "Iran: U.S. Concerns and Policy Responses," Congressional Research Service, Aug. 6, 2007, http://fpc.state.gov/documents/organization/91002.pdf.

A dispassionate run-down of the issues at stake in the faceoff between the United States and Iran.

Sadjadpour, Karim, "Iran: Reality, Options, and Consequences — Iranian People and Attitudes," testimony to House Committee on Oversight and Government Reform, Subcommittee on National Security and Foreign Affairs, Oct., 30, 2007, www.carnegieendowment.org/files/2007-10-30_ks_testimony.pdf.

An associate at the Carnegie Institute for International Peace with extensive experience in Iran reports that public alienation from the government is unlikely to lead to popular revolt in the near future.

Yaphe, Judith S., and Charles D. Lutes, "Reassessing the Implications of a Nuclear-Armed Iran," Institute for National Strategic Studies, National Defense University, 2005, www.ndu.edu/inss/mcnair/mcnair 69/McNair PDF.pdf.

A book-length study examines Iran's nuclear ambitions, including their effects on Israel.

For More Information

American Enterprise Institute, 1150 17th St., N.W., Washington, DC 20036; (202) 862-5800; http://aei.org. Conservative think tank advocates hawkish policies on Iran.

Committee on the Present Danger, P.O. Box 33249, Washington, DC 20033; (202) 207-0190; www.committeeonthepresentdanger.org. Conservative organization favors regime change in Iran.

National Iranian American Council, 1411 K St., N.W., Suite 600, Washington, DC 20005; (202) 386-6325; www.niacouncil.org/index.php. Favors negotiations to establish a new U.S. relationship with Iran.

Saban Center for Middle East Policy, Brookings Institution, 1775 Massachusetts Ave., N.W., Washington, DC 20036; (202) 797-6000; www.brookings.edu/saban.aspx. Studies U.S. policy options in the region.

U.S. Department of State, 2201 C St., N.W., Washington, DC 20520; (202) 647-4000; www.state.gov/p/nea/ci/ir. Web site provides information on events and policy matters regarding Iran.

Washington Institute for Near East Policy, 1828 L St., N.W., Suite 1050, Washington, DC 20036; (202) 452-0650; www.washingtoninstitute.org. Think tank that devotes much attention to Iran.

3

Prosecuting Terrorists

Kenneth Jost

AP Photo

Republican lawmakers say al Qaeda terrorist Khalid Sheikh Mohammed, seen shortly after his capture in Pakistan in 2003, should be treated as an enemy combatant and tried in the military commissions established during the Bush administration. But administration officials and Democratic lawmakers say criminal prosecutions have produced hundreds of convictions since 9/11 compared to only three in the military system.

From *CQ Researcher*,
March 12, 2010.

He has been described as Osama bin Laden's chief executive officer, the man who conceived the plan to crash hijacked airliners into buildings symbolic of America's political, military and financial power.

Some 18 months after the 9/11 attacks, Pakistani intelligence agents, working with the U.S. Central Intelligence Agency, captured Kuwait-born Khalid Sheikh Mohammed at an al Qaeda safe house in Rawalpindi. Rousted out of bed in the middle of the night, he looked like a street person — not the scion of a well-to-do Pakistani family once known for his expensive tastes and elegant dress.[1]

For the next three years, KSM — as U.S. officials and news media dubbed him — was held at a secret CIA site, reportedly in Poland, where interrogators waterboarded him 183 times in the first month of his captivity. In September 2006 he was transferred to the U.S. prison camp at the Guantánamo Bay naval base in Cuba, to be held awaiting trial.

The trial — on 2,973 counts of murder and other charges — began before a military judge on June 5, 2008, but was thrown into disarray six months later, when Mohammed announced that he and his four co-defendants wanted to plead guilty. A month later, the judge, Army Col. Stephen Henley, agreed to put the trial on hold in response to President Obama's decision, on his first full day in office, to suspend the military trials of all suspected "enemy combatants" being held at Guantánamo.

Now, a year after Obama's interim move, the proceedings against KSM remain in limbo thanks to the full-throttle controversy that

Military Commissions Convicted Three

Three of the terrorism suspects who were detained at Guantánamo Bay — Ali Hamza Ahmad Suliman al Bahlul, Salim Ahmed Hamdan and David Hicks — have been convicted after trials before military commissions. Hicks, known as the "Australian Taliban," and Hamdan, identified as the driver for al Qaeda leader Osama bin Laden, have served their sentences already and been released to their home countries. Al Bahlul awaits a decision on his appeal to his life sentence before a U.S. military judge panel. Hamdan's appeal of his conviction is pending before the same panel; Hicks waived his right of appeal after pleading guilty.

Terrorists Convicted in Military Commissions at Guantánamo Bay

AFP/Getty Images

al Bahlul
Nationality:	Yemeni
Conviction date:	Nov. 3, 2008
Charges:	35 counts of solicitation to commit murder, conspiracy and providing material support for terrorism.
Current status:	Sentenced to life in prison; appeal pending before panel of military judges; argued Jan. 26.

AFP/Getty Images

Hamdan
Nationality:	Yemeni
Conviction date:	Aug. 6, 2008
Charges:	Providing material support for terrorism.
Current status:	Returned to Yemen and released; appeal pending before panel of military judges; argued Jan. 26.

Hicks
Nationality:	Australian
Conviction date:	March 30, 2007
Charges:	Providing material support for terrorism.
Current status:	Returned to Australia and released

Getty Images

Source: News reports

erupted after Attorney General Eric Holder announced plans to try the five alleged 9/11 conspirators in a federal court in New York City. In announcing his decision on Nov. 13, Holder said the defendants would "answer for their alleged crimes in a courthouse just blocks away from where the twin towers [of the World Trade Center] once stood."[2]

New York City Mayor Michael Bloomberg and Police Commissioner Raymond Kelly welcomed Holder's decision, but many New Yorkers expressed concerns about the costs and risks of a sensational trial in Lower Manhattan. Some families of 9/11 victims also voiced criticism, saying enemies of the United States deserved military tribunals, not civilian courts.

Holder faced a buzz saw of criticism when he appeared before the Senate Judiciary Committee a week later to defend his decision — which he said he made without consulting the White House. Sen. Jeff Sessions of Alabama, the committee's ranking Republican, called the decision "dangerous," "misguided" and "unnecessary."[3]

Criticism of the decision intensified — and became even more overtly politicized — after the Christmas Day arrest of Umar Farouk Abdulmutallab for the attempted bombing of a Northwest Airlines flight bound from Amsterdam to Detroit. Republican lawmakers and former GOP officials, including former Vice President Dick Cheney and former Attorney General Michael Mukasey, strongly criticized the decision to treat Abdulmutallab as a criminal suspect instead of as an enemy combatant. A major focus of the criticism was the decision to advise Abdulmutallab of his Miranda rights not long after his arrest. (*See sidebar, p. 58.*)

GOP lawmakers raised the stakes on the issue by introducing legislation in Congress to prohibit the use of any funds to try KSM in civilian courts. With administration officials and Democratic lawmakers making little headway in quieting the criticism, the White House let it be known in early February that Obama was personally reviewing the planned location for the trial as part of the broader issue of where and how to try the remaining prisoners at Guantánamo.[4]

The trials have been delayed by controversies that began immediately after President George W. Bush decided to use the base to house alleged enemy combatants captured in the Afghanistan war or rounded up from other locations. Instead of using civilian courts or regular military courts — courts-martial — Bush used his power as commander in chief to create military commissions to try the detainees, with fewer procedural rights than courts-martial.[5]

Critics, including a wide array of civil liberties and human rights organizations, denounced the military commissions as a second-class system of justice. They also lent their support to legal challenges filed by some of the prisoners that eventually resulted in Supreme Court decisions guaranteeing judicial review of their cases and forcing some changes in the rules for the commissions.

Because of the legal uncertainties, the military commissions did not produce their first conviction until March 2007 when David Hicks, the so-called Australian Taliban, pleaded guilty to providing material support for terrorism. Two other Guantánamo prisoners were convicted on material-support counts the next year: Salim Ahmed Hamdan, former driver to bin Laden, and Ali Hamza Ahmad Suliman al Bahlul, an al Qaeda filmmaker and propagandist. (*See box at left.*)

Even as the Guantánamo cases moved at a glacial pace, the Bush administration was using federal courts to prosecute hundreds of individuals arrested in the United States on terrorism-related charges. Among the first was Richard Reid, the so-called shoe bomber, who was charged with attempting to blow up a commercial aircraft en route to the United States on Dec. 22, 2001.

Guidelines Adopted for Detainee Prosecutions

The Justice and Defense departments adopted broadly written guidelines in July 2009 to be used in deciding whether a Guantánamo detainee was to be tried in a civilian court or before a military tribunal. The protocol begins with "a presumption that, where feasible, referred cases will be prosecuted in" federal criminal courts. The two-page agreement lists three categories of factors to be considered in deciding whether "other compelling factors make it more appropriate to prosecute a case in a reformed military commission":

Strength of interest, including where the offense occurred, where the defendant was apprehended and which agency or agencies investigated the case.

Efficiency, including protection of intelligence sources, foreign policy concerns and "legal or evidentiary problems that might attend prosecution in the other jurisdiction."

Other prosecution considerations, including the charges that can be brought and the sentences that can be imposed in one or the other forum.

Source: "Determination of Guantánamo Cases Referred for Prosecution," July 20, 2009, www.justice.gov/opa/documents/taba-prel-rpt-dptf-072009.pdf

Reid, an admitted al Qaeda supporter, is now serving a life sentence.

At various points, Bush himself touted the administration's record of convicting hundreds of individuals in terrorism-related cases in criminal courts. In a budget document in 2008, the Justice Department put the number of convictions or guilty pleas at 319 out of 512 individuals prosecuted.[6]

More recently, a report written for Human Rights First counted 195 convictions or guilty pleas in al Qaeda- or Taliban-related terrorism cases through July 2, 2009, along with 19 acquittals or dismissals. The report, written by two lawyers who had previously served as federal prosecutors in New York, concluded that the criminal justice system "is well-equipped to handle a broad variety of cases arising from terrorism" associated with al Qaeda or similar groups.[7] (*See sidebar, p. 62.*)

Despite that record, GOP lawmakers, ex-Bush administration officials and conservative experts and advocates are arguing strongly for the use of military commissions to try Abdulmutallab and, apparently, most of the prisoners held at Guantánamo. "Wartime alien enemy combatants should be tried by military commissions in the safety of Guantánamo Bay," says Andrew McCarthy, a contributing editor with *National Review Online* and former federal prosecutor.[8]

While in the U.S. attorney's office in Manhattan, McCarthy was lead prosecutor in the 1995 trial of Omar Abdel Rahman, the so-called Blind Sheik, along with nine others for plotting to blow up various civilian targets in the New York City area. Rahman was convicted of seditious conspiracy and is now serving a life sentence.[9]

Human rights advocates, however, say military commissions have failed to produce results while tarnishing the United States' image both at home and abroad. "The only choice should be trial in civilian courts," says Laura Olson, senior counsel for the rule of law program at the Washington-based Constitution Project. "They're both tougher and more reliable than military commissions."

The Obama administration says civilian trials are the presumptive forum for terrorism cases but is continuing the use of what it calls "reformed" military commissions for some cases. A protocol adopted jointly by the Justice and Defense departments in July 2009 says forum selection will depend on a number of factors, including the agency or agencies involved in the investigation and the charges and sentences available in one or the other forum. Holder designated several Guantánamo prisoners for trial by military commissions on the same day he announced the decision to try KSM in New York City. (*See box, p. 64.*)

Meanwhile, administration officials also are saying that 50 or more Guantánamo prisoners may be held indefinitely without trial because they cannot be prosecuted successfully but are too dangerous to release.[10] Conservatives say the prolonged detentions are justifiable as long as the United States is effectively at war with al Qaeda. Civil liberties advocates strongly disagree.

President Obama cheered human rights groups with his initial moves on counterterrorism policies, especially his pledge to close the Guantánamo prison camp within a year. Now that the deadline has been missed and other policies recalibrated, Obama is drawing some complaints from liberal advocacy groups along with sharp criticism from Republicans and conservative groups for the planned use of federal courts to try enemy combatants.

Here are some of the major issues the administration faces:

Should suspected terrorists be tried in civilian courts?

When the FBI got wind of a group of Yemeni Americans who had trained at an al Qaeda camp in 2001 and returned to their homes in the Buffalo, N.Y., suburb of Lackawanna, Bush administration's officials were divided on what to do.

Vice President Dick Cheney and Defense Secretary Donald Rumsfeld wanted to use troops to arrest the men and treat them as enemy combatants to be tried before a military commission. President Bush, however, sided with Attorney General John Ashcroft and FBI Director Robert Mueller, who favored using federal agents to arrest the men and trying them in a federal court.

In the end, the men were arrested without incident on Sept. 14, 2002, and over the next year pleaded guilty and received prison sentences ranging from seven to 10 years for supporting a foreign terrorist organization. They also cooperated with authorities in providing information about al Qaeda, and three of them testified in the 2008 military commission trial of the al Qaeda filmmaker Bahlul.[11]

Supporters of criminal prosecutions — including but not limited to human rights and civil liberties groups — say prosecutions such as the Lackawanna Six case prove civilian courts can mete out effective, tough justice in terrorism-related cases without shortchanging constitutional rights.

"The criminal justice system is reasonably well-equipped to handle most international terrorism cases," New York attorneys Richard B. Zabel and James J. Benjamin Jr. wrote in the Human Rights First report in May 2008. A year later, the two former federal prosecutors reiterated that civilian court prosecutions had generally led to "just, reliable results" without causing security breaches or other harms to national security.[12]

National security-minded critics and some non-ideological experts counter that the rights accorded defendants in the criminal justice system do pose potential obstacles to successful prosecutions in some terrorism cases. "Civilian trials should be a secondary option," says

David Rivkin, a former Justice Department official in the Bush administration now affiliated with the hawkish Foundation for the Defense of Democracies. Among other problems, Rivkin says classified information is harder to protect in a civilian court than in a military commission despite a federal law, the Classified Information Procedure Act (CIPA), which limits disclosure in federal trials.

"The federal courts have some real limitations," agrees Benjamin Wittes, a research fellow at the Brookings Institution and author of several influential reports about war-on-terror policies. He cites as examples the beyond-a-reasonable-doubt standard used in criminal prosecutions and the stricter standard on use of evidence obtained under coercive interrogation. Still, Wittes adds, the problems are "not as big as conservatives claim."

Critics assailed the decision to try the 9/11 conspiracy case in New York City in particular as a security risk. Rivkin complains of "the logistical nightmare" that would be created by a trial in a major metropolitan area such as New York.

When Holder visited New York to discuss plans for the trial in December, however, a Justice Department spokesman declared, "We have a robust plan developed by both federal and local officials to ensure that these trials can be safely held in New York, and everyone is committed to doing that."[13]

Above any practical considerations, however, critics such as Rivkin say simply that criminal prosecutions signal a wrong approach in the nation's fight against al Qaeda. "This is a long and difficult war," he says. "It is essential for any administration to inculcate the notion that this is a real war. And it is utterly jarring in that context to take enemy combatants, particularly high-value ones, and treat them as common criminals."

Benjamin counters that the criminal justice system in fact amounts to one of the United States' most effective weapons in the war on terror. "We are at war," he says. "One of the unique features of this particular war is that many of the people on the other side are violating our criminal law. If we can develop the evidence and successfully put them away, why in the world would we foreclose ourselves from doing that?"

Should suspected terrorists be tried in military tribunals?

Attorney General Holder's decision to try seven Guantánamo detainees in military commissions represents only a modest step toward resolving the cases of the remaining prisoners there. (*See box, p. 64.*) But the trials, if completed, would more than double the number of cases resolved by military tribunals since President Bush authorized them less than two months after the 9/11 attacks.

Supporters say history, law and national security justify the use of military tribunals to try enemy combatants. They blame opponents for the legal controversies that have limited their use so far.

"The record has been underwhelming," concedes ex-Justice Department attorney Rivkin. "Why should we be surprised? There has been a concentrated effort from day one to litigate against them."

Human rights and civil liberties groups counter that the military tribunals were flawed from the outset and, despite some recent reforms, still have significant problems and will face additional legal challenges.

"They remain vulnerable to constitutional challenge," says Olson of the Constitution Project. "We're going to have to go through this litigation for years and years."

In contrast to the three men convicted so far by military commissions, the prisoners that Holder designated in his Nov. 13 announcement for trial by military commissions include figures alleged to have played significant roles in al Qaeda operations. They include Abd al Rahim al Nashiri, a Yemeni accused of plotting the October 2000 attack on the *USS Cole*, and Noor Uthman Mohammed, a Sudanese alleged to have assisted in running an al Qaeda training center in Afghanistan.

The accusations against some of the others, however, depict them as hardly more than al Qaeda foot soldiers. The group includes Omar Khadr, the youngest Guantánamo detainee, who was captured at age 15 after a firefight in Afghanistan. Now 23, the Canadian citizen faces a charge of providing support for terrorism by throwing a grenade that killed a U.S. soldier. The charge goes against the United Nations' position that children should not be prosecuted for war crimes.[14]

AFP/Getty Images/Don Emmert

Omar Abdel Rahman, the so-called Blind Sheik, was convicted in a civilian criminal trial in 1995 along with nine others for plotting to blow up various civilian targets in the New York City area. Rahman is now serving a life sentence. Andrew McCarthy, the then-lead prosecutor for the U.S. attorney's office, is now a contributing editor with National Review Online, a conservative publication. He now says, "Wartime alien enemy combatants should be tried by military commissions in the safety of Guantánamo Bay."

In announcing his decisions on the legal forum to be used, Holder gave no explanation of the reasons for designating some of the prisoners for trial by military commissions. But he did say that recent changes approved by Congress for the commissions "will ensure that commission trials are fair, effective and lawful." Those changes include limits on use of hearsay and coerced testimony and greater access for defendants to witnesses and evidence.

Despite the changes, human rights advocates continue to oppose use of the military commissions. "We don't quarrel with military justice," says Ben Winzer, a staff attorney with the American Civil Liberties Union's (ACLU) national security project. "The problem is that even the modified military commissions are being used to paper over weaknesses in the government's evidence."

"Most of the growing pains have been alleviated," counters Rivkin. "The solution now is to stand them up, make them work, give them the right resources and get out of the way."

For his part, Brookings Institution expert Wittes says the military commissions "have significantly underperformed to date" and continue to face a host of practical and legal difficulties. "We worry that the military commissions will present issues of their own, particularly with respect to challenges to the lawfulness and integrity of the system itself," he says. "And the rules have been used so little that there are a lot of issues about how the system works."

Among the most important pending issues is the question whether material support of terrorism — a mainstay of criminal prosecutions — is an offense that can be tried in a military tribunal. The review panel established to hear appeals from the military commissions currently has that issue under advisement after arguments in two cases in January.

"No one questions that these are crimes, but there are special rules that come into play when we start talking about what crimes military commissions can prosecute," says Stephen Vladeck, a law professor at American University in Washington. "I think there are far fewer cases in which the government realistically has a choice between civilian and military courts than we might think, if for no other reason than the jurisdiction of military commissions is actually tightly circumscribed by the Constitution."

Should some Guantánamo detainees be held indefinitely without trial?

In his first major speech on how to deal with the Guantánamo prisoners, President Obama called in May 2009 for "prolonged detention" for any detainees "who cannot be prosecuted yet who pose a clear danger to the American people." Obama said he would work with Congress to "construct a legitimate legal framework" for such cases, but added: "I am not going to release individuals who endanger the American people."[15]

In the nine months since, neither Congress nor the president has put any appreciable work into possible legislation on the issue. Now, administration officials are estimating 50 or more detainees will have to be held without trial, but they have not listed names or described procedures being used to designate individuals for that category.

The ACLU and other human rights groups immediately denounced Obama's remarks on the issue and continue to oppose detention without trial. The administration's conservative critics approve of holding some prisoners without trial but fault the administration for its efforts to transfer others to their home countries or other host nations because they might return to hostilities against the United States.

"The term is detention for the duration of hostilities," says Rivkin. "Those rules have been in place since time immemorial. They are not meant to punish anybody; they are designed to prevent someone from going back to the battlefield."

Rivkin says the policy of transferring prisoners to other countries — begun by the Bush administration and continued by Obama — amounts to "a revolving door" for terrorists. "We know for sure that they go back to combat," Rivkin says. "This is the first war in human history where we cannot hold in custody a captured enemy. That's a hell of a way to run a war."

ACLU lawyer Winzer calls Obama's detention-without-trial proposal "an extraordinarily controversial statement in a country governed by the rule of law." Anyone "truly dangerous" should be and likely can be prosecuted, Winzer says. "Our material-support laws are so broad that if we don't have legitimate evidence to convict [detainees] under those laws, it's hard to accept that they are too dangerous to release."

Allegations that some of the released Guantánamo prisoners have returned to hostilities against the United States stem from studies released by the Pentagon during the Bush administration and sharply challenged by some human rights advocates. The final of three studies, released in January 2009 only one week before Bush was to leave office, claimed that 61 out of 517 detainees released had "returned to the battlefield."

But an examination of the evidence by Mark Denbeaux, a law professor at Seton Hall University in South Orange, N.J., and counsel to two Guantánamo detainees, depicts the Pentagon's count as largely unsubstantiated. In any event, Denbeaux says the Pentagon's count is exaggerated because it includes former prisoners who have done nothing more after their release than engage in propaganda against the United States.[16]

Supporters of detention without trial cite as authority the first of the Supreme Court's post-9/11 decisions, *Hamdi v. Rumsfeld*.[17] In that 2004 ruling, a majority of the justices agreed that the legislation Congress passed in 2001 to authorize the Afghanistan war included authority for the detention of enemy combatants. In the main opinion, Justice Sandra Day O'Connor said a detainee was entitled to some opportunity to contest allegations against him, but did not specify what kind of procedure.

The court rulings appear to support the government's power "to hold people indefinitely without charge if they are associated with al Qaeda or the Taliban in the same way that a solider is associated with an army," says Benjamin, coauthor of the Human Rights First report. Law professor Vladeck agrees, but says the number of people in that category is likely to be "small."

Brookings Institution expert Wittes defends the practice "philosophically" but acknowledges practical problems, including public reaction both in the United States and abroad. "The first risk is that it's perceived as the least legitimate option, domestically or internationally," he says. "It's not the way you like to do business."

The evidence needed to justify detention has been the major issue in the dozens of habeas corpus petitions filed by Guantánamo prisoners. Federal district judges in Washington who have been hearing the cases have mostly decided against the government, according to a compilation coauthored by Wittes.[18]

Wittes has long urged Congress to enact legislation to define the scope of indefinite detention. In an unusual interview, three of the judges handling the cases agreed. "It should be Congress that decides a policy such as this," Judge Reggie Walton told the online news site *ProPublica*.[19]

But David Cole, a law professor at Georgetown University in Washington and prominent critic of the detention policies, disagrees. The issues, Cole says, "require careful case-by-case application of standards. It's a job for judges, not Congress."[20]

Khalid Sheikh Mohammed and the 9/11 Attacks

Khalid Sheikh Mohammed, self-described mastermind of the Sept. 11 terrorist attacks, faces trial in federal court on 2,973 counts of murder and other charges along with his four co-defendants. Kuwait-born KSM first claimed to have organized the 9/11 attacks during interrogations in which he was waterboarded 183 times. In March 2007, at a hearing at the Guantánamo Bay prison, he said he was responsible for the attacks "from A to Z" — as well as for 30 other terrorist plots. The five co-defendants now face nine charges including conspiracy, terrorism, providing material support for terrorism and murder. Controversy erupted over Attorney General Eric Holder's plan to hold the trial in New York City, and the location of the trial is now being reconsidered. KSM's four co-defendants are:

• **Ramzi Bin al-Shibh (Yemen)** — Alleged "coordinator" of the attacks after he was denied a visa to enter the United States.
• **Walid bin Attash (Saudi Arabia)** — Charged with selecting and training several of the hijackers of the attacks.
• **Ali Abdul Aziz Ali (Pakistan)** — Allegedly helped hijackers obtain plane tickets, traveler's checks and hotel reservations. Also taught them the culture and customs of the West.
• **Mustafa Ahmed al-Hawsawi (Saudi Arabia)** — Allegedly an organizer and financier of the attacks.

BACKGROUND

Power and Precedent

The United States faced the issue of how to deal with captured members or supporters of al Qaeda or the Taliban with no exact historical parallel as guidance. The use of military tribunals for saboteurs, spies or enemy sympathizers dated from the American Revolution but had been controversial in several instances, including during the Civil War and World War II. After World War II, military commissions became — in the words of Brookings expert Wittes — "a dead institution." The rise of international terrorism in the 1980s and '90s was met with military reprisals in some instances and a pair of notable U.S. prosecutions of Islamist extremists in the 1990s.[21]

As commander of the revolutionary army, Gen. George Washington convened military tribunals to try suspected spies — most notably, Major John André, Benedict Arnold's coconspirator, who was convicted, sentenced to death and hanged. During the War of 1812 and the First Seminole War (1817-1818). Gen. Andrew Jackson was criticized for expansive use of his powers as military commander — most notably, for having two British subjects put to death for inciting the Creek Indians against the United States. During the occupation of Mexico in the Mexican-American War, Gen. Winfield Scott established — without clear statutory authority — "military councils" to try Mexicans for a variety of offenses, including guerrilla warfare against U.S. troops.

The use of military tribunals by President Abraham Lincoln's administration during the Civil War provoked sharp criticism at the time and remains controversial today. Lincoln acted unilaterally to suspend the writ of habeas corpus in May 1861, defied Chief Justice Roger Taney's rebuke of the action and only belatedly got Congress to ratify his decision. More than 2,000 cases were tried by military commissions during the war and Reconstruction. Tribunals ignored some judicial orders to release prisoners. Lincoln, however, overturned some decisions that he found too harsh. As the war continued, the Supreme Court turned aside one challenge to the military commissions, but in 1866 — with the war ended — held that military tribunals should not be used if civilian courts are operating.[22]

During World War II, President Franklin D. Roosevelt prevailed in three Supreme Court challenges to expansive use of his powers as commander in chief in domestic settings. Best known are the court's decisions in 1943 and 1944 upholding the wartime curfew on the West Coast and the internment of Japanese-Americans. Earlier, the court in 1942 had given summary approval to the convictions and death sentences of German saboteurs captured in June and tried the next month before hastily convened military commissions. Roosevelt's order

CHRONOLOGY

1970s-2000 *International terrorism era begins, with attacks on civilian aircraft, facilities; prosecutions in foreign, U.S. courts get mixed results.*

1988 Bombing of Pan Am Flight 103 over Scotland kills 270, including 189 Americans; Scottish court later convicts and sentences to life former head of Libyan secret service; ill with cancer, released from Scottish jail in 2009.

1995 Civilian court convicts Omar Abdel Rahman and nine others for conspiring to blow up World Trade Center, other sites, in 1993.

1997 Ramzi Ahmed Yousef draws life sentence after 1997 conviction in civilian court for masterminding 1993 trade center bombing.

2000-Present *Al Qaeda launches 9/11 attacks; Bush, Obama administrations prosecute terrorism cases mainly in civilian courts.*

September-October 2001 Nearly 3,000 killed in al Qaeda's Sept. 11 attacks. . . . Congress on Sept. 14 gives president authority to use force again st those responsible for attacks.

November-December 2001 President George W. Bush on Nov. 13 authorizes military commissions to try enemy combatants captured in Afghanistan, elsewhere. . . . U.S. Naval Base at Guantánamo Bay is chosen as site to hold detainees. . . . Zacarias Moussaoui indicted in federal court in Virginia on Dec. 11 for conspiracy in 9/11 attacks. . . . "Shoe bomber" Richard Reid arrested Dec. 21 for failed attack on American Airlines Flight 63.

2002 First of about 800 prisoners arrive in Guantánamo; first of scores of habeas corpus cases filed by detainees by mid-spring. . . . José Padilla arrested at Chicago airport May 8 in alleged radioactive bomb plot; case transferred to military courts. . . . John Walker Lindh, "American Taliban," sentenced Oct. 4 by a civilian court to 20 years in prison.

2003 Federal judge in Boston sentences Reid to life in prison on Jan. 31.

2004 Supreme Court rules June 28 that U.S. citizens can be held as enemy combatants but must be afforded hearing before "neutral decisionmaker" (*Hamdi v. Rumsfeld*); on

same day, court rules Guantánamo detainees may use habeas corpus to challenge captivity (*Rasul v. Bush*).

2006 Moussaoui is given life sentence May 3. . . . Supreme Court rules June 29 that military commissions improperly depart from requirements of U.S. military law and Geneva Conventions (*Hamdan v. Rumsfeld*). . . . Congress passes Military Commissions Act of 2006 in September to remedy defects.

2007 First conviction in military commission: Australian David Hicks sentenced on March 30 to nine months after guilty plea to material support for terrorism. . . . Padilla convicted in federal court Aug. 16 on material support counts; later sentenced to 17 years.

2008 Supreme Court reaffirms June 12 habeas corpus rights for Guantánamo detainees (*Boumediene v. Bush*). . . . Two more convictions of terrorists in military commissions: Hamdan convicted on material support counts Aug. 6, sentenced to 7-1/2-year term; al Qaeda propagandist Ali Hamza al Bahlul convicted Nov. 3, given life sentence.

January-June 2009 President Obama pledges to close Guantánamo within a year, suspends military commissions pending review (Jan. 21). . . . Obama in major speech says some detainees to be held indefinitely without trial (May 21).

July-December 2009 Defense and Justice departments agree on protocol to choose civilian or military court (July 20). . . . Military Commission Act of 2009 improves defendants' protections (October). Attorney General Eric Holder announces plan to try Khalid Sheikh Mohammed (KSM), four others in federal court in Manhattan for 9/11 conspiracy (Nov. 13); other alleged terrorists designated for military commissions; plan for N.Y. trial widely criticized. . . . Umar Farouk Abdulmutallab arrested Dec. 25 in failed bombing of Northwest Flight 253; decision to prosecute in civilian court criticized, defended.

2010 Administration mulls change of plans for KSM trial. . . . U.S. appeals court backs broad definition of enemy combatant in first substantive appellate-level decision in Guantánamo habeas corpus cases (Jan. 5). . . . Military review panel weighs arguments on use of "material support of terrorism" charge in military commissions (Jan. 26).

The Case Against the 'Christmas Day' Bomber

Critics say prosecutors mishandled Abdulmutallab's arrest.

Caught in the act of trying to bomb a Northwest Airlines aircraft, Umar Farouk Abdulmutallab would appear to offer prosecutors a slam dunk under any of several terrorism-related charges. Indeed, there were dozens of witnesses to his capture.

But the case against the baby-faced Nigerian-born, Yemeni-trained al Qaeda supporter became enmeshed in post-9/11 American politics almost immediately after his Christmas Day flight landed in Detroit.[1]

President Obama invited the subsequent criticism by initially labeling Abdulmutallab as "an isolated extremist" on Dec. 26 before learning of his training in al Qaeda camps in Yemen and history of extreme Islamist views. Homeland Security Secretary Janet Napolitano compounded the administration's political problems by saying on Dec. 27 that Abdulmutallab's capture showed that "the system worked" — a statement she quickly worked hard to explain away, given that a U.S. airliner had nearly been bombed.

The administration also faced criticism for intelligence analysts' failure to block Abdulmutallab from ever boarding a U.S.-bound aircraft after having received a warning from the suspect's father, a prominent Nigerian banker, of his son's radicalization. Obama moved to stanch the criticism by commissioning and quickly releasing a review of the intelligence agencies' "failure to connect the dots" and by ordering other steps, including a tightening of airline security procedures.

The politicization of the case intensified, however, with a broadside from former Vice President Dick Cheney sharply attacking the administration's decision to treat Abdulmutallab as a criminal suspect instead of an enemy combatant to be tried in a military tribunal. Obama "is trying to pretend we are not at war," Cheney told *Politico*, the Washington-based, all-politics newspaper.

"He seems to think if he has a low-key response to an attempt to blow up an airliner and kill hundreds of people, we won't be at war. He seems to think if he gives terrorists the rights of Americans, lets them lawyer up and reads them their Miranda rights, we won't be at war."[2]

White House press secretary Robert Gibbs responded promptly by accusing Cheney of playing "the typical Washington game of pointing fingers and making political hay." But the response did nothing to stop Republican politicians and conservative commentators from keeping up a drumbeat of criticism for several weeks into the new year, focused in particular on the decision to advise Abdulmutallab of his right to remain silent and to confer with a lawyer.

The criticism appears to have been based in part on an erroneous understanding of when FBI agents advised the 21-year-old Abdulmutallab of his Miranda rights. For weeks, critics said he had been "Mirandized" within 55 minutes of his arrest. Only in mid-February did the administration release a detailed, materially different timeline.[3]

The administration's account showed that Abdulmutallab was questioned for 55 minutes and provided some information about his rights before being taken away for surgery. When he returned after the four-hour procedure — a total

convening the seven-member tribunals specified that the death penalty could be imposed by a two-thirds majority instead of the normal unanimous vote. The Supreme Court heard habeas corpus petitions filed by seven of the eight men but rejected their claims in a summary order in the case, *Ex parte Quirin*, on July 31. Six of the men had been executed before the justices issued their formal opinion on Oct. 29.[23]

International law governing wartime captives and domestic law governing military justice were both significantly reformed after World War II in ways that cast doubt on the previous ad hoc nature of military commissions. The Geneva Conventions — signed in 1949 and ratified by the Senate in 1954 — strengthened previous protections for wartime captives by, among other things, prohibiting summary punishment even for combatants in non-traditional conflicts such as civil wars. The Uniform Code of Military Justice, approved by Congress in 1950, brought civilian-like procedures into a system previously built on command and discipline. The United States went beyond the requirements of the Geneva Conventions in the Vietnam War by giving full prisoner-of-war status to

of nine hours after his arrest — Abdulmutallab declined to answer further questions.

Without regard to the precise timing, critics said Abdulmutallab should have been treated outside the criminal justice system to maximize his value as a source of intelligence. Former Attorney General Michael B. Mukasey said the administration had "no compulsion" to treat Abdulmutallab as a criminal defendant "and every reason to treat him as an intelligence asset to be exploited promptly." The administration claimed that Abdulmutallab did begin providing actionable intelligence after family members were brought to the United States from Nigeria, but Mukasey said the five-week time lag meant that "possibly useful information" was lost.[4]

Administration supporters noted, however, that the Bush administration handled all suspected terrorists arrested in the United States as criminal defendants with the concomitant necessity to advise them of their Miranda rights. The administration's defense was substantiated by John Ashcroft, Mukasey's predecessor as attorney general. "When you have a person in the criminal justice system, you Mirandize them," Ashcroft told a reporter for *Huffington Post* when questioned at the conservative Tea Party Conference in Washington in mid-February.[5]

Administration critics appeared to say little about the precise charges brought against Abdulmutallab. He was initially charged in a criminal complaint Dec. 26 with two counts: attempting to blow up and placing an explosive device aboard a U.S. aircraft. Two weeks later, a federal grand jury in Detroit returned a more detailed indictment charging him with attempted use of a weapon of mass destruction and attempted murder of 269 people. If convicted, he faces a life sentence plus 90 years in prison. No trial date is set.

— *Kenneth Jost*

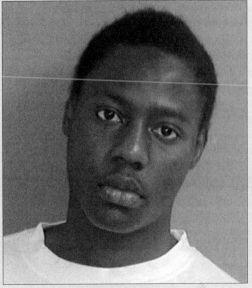

U.S. Marshals Service via Getty Images

Umar Farouk Abdulmutallab, a 23-year-old Nigerian, is charged with attempting to blow up a Northwest Airlines flight as it was landing in Detroit last Christmas Day.

[1] Some background drawn from a well-documented Wikipedia entry: http://en.wikipedia.org/wiki/Umar_Farouk_Abdulmutallab.

[2] Mike Allen, "Dick Cheney: Barack Obama 'trying to pretend,' " *Politico*, Dec. 30, 2009, www.politico.com/news/stories/1209/31054. html, cited in Philip Elliott, "White House Hits Back at Cheney Criticism," The Associated Press, Dec. 30, 2009.

[3] Walter Pincus, "Bomb suspect was read Miranda rights nine hours after arrest," *The Washington Post*, Feb. 15, 2010, p. A6.

[4] Michael B. Mukasey, "Where the U.S. went wrong on Abdulmutallab," *The Washington Post*, Feb. 12, 2010, p. A27.

[5] Ryan Grim, "Ashcroft: 'When You Have a Person in the Criminal Justice System, You Mirandize Them,' " *Huffington Post*, Feb. 19, 2010, www.huffingtonpost.com/2010/02/19/ashcroft-when-you-have-a_n_469384.html.

enemy captives, whether they belonged to the regular North Vietnamese army or the guerrilla Vietcong.

International terrorism grew from a sporadic problem for the United States in the 1970s to a major concern in the 1980s and '90s. The results of foreign prosecutions in two of the major incidents in the '80s left many Americans disappointed. An Italian jury imposed a 30-year sentence in 1987 on Magid al-Molqi after the Palestinian confessed to the murder of U.S. citizen Leon Klinghoffer during the 1985 hijacking of the cruise ship *Achille Lauro*; the prosecution had sought a life term. The bombing of

Pan Am Flight 103 over Scotland in 1988 — and the deaths of 189 Americans among the 270 victims — resulted in the long-delayed trial of Abdel Basset Ali al-Megrahi, former head of the Libyan secret service. Megrahi was indicted in 1991 in the United States and Scotland, extradited only after protracted diplomatic negotiations and convicted and sentenced to life imprisonment in 2001. He was released on humanitarian grounds in 2009, suffering from purportedly terminal pancreatic cancer.

Two prosecutions in the United States stemming from the 1993 bombing of the World Trade Center produced seemingly stronger verdicts. Omar Abdel Rahman, the so-called Blind Sheik, was convicted in federal court in New York City along with nine others in 1995 for conspiracy to carry out a campaign of bombings and assassinations within the United States. Abdel Rahman is now serving a 240-year prison sentence. Two years later, Ramzi Ahmed Yousef was convicted on charges of masterminding the 1993 bombing and given a life sentence. Even after the second verdict, however, questions remained about whether the plot had been sponsored by a foreign state or international organization.[24]

Challenge and Response

The Bush administration responded to the 9/11 attacks by declaring an all-out war on terrorism that combined separate strategies of detaining captured "enemy combatants" at Guantánamo outside normal legal processes and prosecuting hundreds of individuals in federal courts on terrorism-related charges. The improvised system of military tribunals at Guantánamo drew political and legal challenges that stalled their work, resulting in only three convictions late in Bush's time in office. Meanwhile, criminal cases proceeded in federal courts with relatively few setbacks and little hindrance from criticism by some civil libertarians of overly aggressive prosecutions.[25]

Even as the Guantánamo military tribunals were being formed, the administration was initiating criminal prosecutions in other al Qaeda or Taliban-related cases. In the most important, the government indicted Zacarias Moussaoui, sometimes called the 20th hijacker, on Dec. 11, 2001, on conspiracy counts related to the 9/11 attacks. The prosecution dragged on for more than four years, extended by Moussaoui's courtroom dramatics and a fight over access to classified information that ended with a ruling largely favorable to the government. The trial ended on May 3, 2006, after a jury that had deliberated for seven days imposed a life sentence instead of the death penalty — apparently rejecting the government's view of Moussaoui as a central figure in the 9/11 attacks.

Two other early prosecutions ended more quickly. British citizen Richard Reid, the so-called shoe bomber, was charged in a federal criminal complaint on Dec. 24, 2001, two days after his failed explosive attack on American Airlines Flight 63. In January, Attorney General John Ashcroft announced that U.S. citizen John Walker Lindh, the so-called American Taliban captured in Afghanistan,

would be tried in a civilian court in the United States. Both men entered guilty pleas in 2002; Lindh was given a 20-year sentence while Reid was sentenced in January 2003 to life in prison.

The government started two other early cases in the criminal justice system and moved them into the military system only to return later to civilian courts. Ali Saleh Kahlah al-Marri, a Qatari student attending college in Illinois, was detained as a material witness in December 2001 and indicted two months later on credit-card charges. Bush's decision in 2003 to designate him as an enemy combatant led to a protracted appeal that the Obama administration resolved in 2009 by indicting al-Marri on a single count of conspiracy to provide material support for terrorism. In a similar vein, U.S. citizen José Padilla was arrested at the Chicago airport on May 8, 2002, on suspicion of plotting a radioactive attack; designated an enemy combatant a month later and then indicted after drawn-out legal challenges that reached the Supreme Court. Padilla was convicted of terrorism conspiracy charges and given a 17-year prison sentence; al-Marri drew 15 years after pleading guilty.

Meanwhile, the military tribunals had been stymied by a succession of legal challenges before the Supreme Court and responses by the administration and Congress to the justices' rulings. In the pivotal decision in Hamdan's case, the court ruled in June 2006 that the military commissions as then constituted were illegal because the president had not shown a need to depart from established rules of military justice.[26] Reconstituted under the Military Commissions Act of 2006, the tribunals finally produced their first conviction in March 2007 when the Australian Hicks pleaded guilty to a single material-support count. Under a plea agreement and with credit for time served, he was allowed to return to Australia to serve the remaining nine months of a seven-year sentence.

Two more convictions followed in 2008, both after trials. Hamdan was convicted in August of conspiracy and material support but acquitted of more serious charges and given an unexpectedly light sentence of 61 months. With credit for time served, he was transferred to his native Yemen in late November to serve the last month of his term. Earlier, a military tribunal on Nov. 3 had convicted Bahlul of a total of 35 terrorism-related counts after the former al Qaeda propaganda chief essentially boycotted the proceedings. The panel returned the verdict in the morning and then deliberated for an hour before sentencing the Yemeni native to life imprisonment.

As the Bush administration neared an end, the Justice Department issued a fact-sheet on the seventh anniversary of the 9/11 attacks touting its "considerable success in America's federal courtrooms of identifying, prosecuting and incarcerating terrorists and would-be terrorists." The report listed the Padilla and Moussaoui cases among eight "notable" prosecutions in recent years. It also briefly noted the department's cooperation with the Defense Department in developing procedures for the military commissions, defending against challenges to the system and jointly bringing charges against KSM and other high-value detainees.[27]

In an important post-election setback, however, a federal judge in Washington ruled on Nov. 20, 2008, in favor of five of the six Algerians whose habeas corpus petitions had led to the Supreme Court decision guaranteeing judicial review for Guantánamo detainees. Judge Richard Leon said the government had failed to present sufficient evidence to show that the six men, arrested in Bosnia in January 2002, had planned to travel to Afghanistan to fight against the United States. He found sufficient evidence, however, that one of the prisoners had acted as a facilitator for al Qaeda. Three of the five were returned to Bosnia in December; two others were transferred to France in May and November 2009.[28]

Change and Continuity

In his first days in office, President Obama began fulfilling his campaign pledge to change the Bush administration's legal policies in the war on terror. Obama's high-profile decisions to set a deadline for closing Guantánamo, shut down the secret CIA prisons and prohibit enhanced interrogation techniques drew support from Democrats and liberals and sharp criticism from Republicans and conservatives. By year's end, the roles were reversed, with support from the right and criticism from the left of Obama's decision to continue use of military tribunals and claim the power to detain suspected terrorists indefinitely without trial. Meanwhile, the government was continuing to win significant terrorism-related convictions in federal courts but suffering setbacks in many habeas corpus cases brought by Guantánamo prisoners.

Even with the Guantánamo and interrogation policies under attack, the Justice Department was achieving some

significant successes in prosecutions that carried over from the Bush administration. The new administration sidestepped a Supreme Court test of the power to detain U.S. residents by transferring al-Marri to civilian courts in late February and securing his guilty plea in April. Also in April, Wesam al-Delaema, an Iraqi-born Dutch citizen, was given a 25-year prison sentence for planting roadside bombs aimed at U.S. troops in his native country. Al-Delaema had fought extradition from the Netherlands and was to be returned there to serve what was expected to be a reduced sentence. The case marked the first successful prosecution for terrorist offenses against U.S. forces in Iraq.

In May, the government won convictions — after two prior mistrials — in its case against the so-called Liberty City Six (originally, Seven), who were charged with plotting to blow up the Sears Tower in Chicago and selected federal buildings. The jury in Miami convicted five of the men but acquitted a sixth. On the same day, a federal jury in New York City convicted Oussama Kassir, a Lebanese-born Swede, of attempting to establish a terrorist training camp in Oregon. Material-support charges were the major counts in both cases. Kassir was sentenced to life in September; of the six defendants in the Miami case, sentences handed down on Nov. 20 ranged from 84 to 162 months.

By summer, the Justice Department conceded that it would be late with an interim report on closing Guantánamo. In acknowledging the delay in a background briefing on July 20 — the eve of the due date for the report — administration officials claimed some progress in resettling some of the detainees but confirmed expectations to hold some of the prisoners indefinitely. The administration did release the two-page protocol from the Defense and Justice departments on prosecuting Guantánamo cases, with its stated "presumption" in favor of civilian prosecutions "where feasible." The memo outlined a variety of factors to consider in choosing between civilian courts or "reformed" military commissions. With Guantánamo dominating the coverage, the memo drew little attention.[29]

Meanwhile, federal judges in Washington, D.C., were giving mixed verdicts as more of the long-delayed habeas corpus cases by Guantánamo detainees reached decision stage. [30] In the first of the rulings after Obama took office, Judge Leon ruled on Jan. 28 that evidence of serving as a cook for al Qaeda was sufficient to hold a prisoner for

Material-Support Law Called Anti-Terror "Weapon of Choice"

Critics say the broadly written law criminalizes lawful speech.

Oussama Kassir never took up arms against U.S. forces in Afghanistan and never carried out a terrorist attack against Americans in the United States or abroad. But he is serving a life prison sentence today after a federal court jury in New York City found him guilty of attempting to establish a jihadist training camp in Oregon and distributing terrorist training materials over the Internet.

To put Kassir behind bars, federal prosecutors used a broadly written law that makes it a crime to provide "material support" — broadly defined — to any group designated by the government as a "terrorist organization." The law, first passed in 1994 and amended several times since, accounts for roughly half of the al Qaeda-related terrorism convictions since 2001, according to a study by two ex-prosecutors written for the Washington-based group Human Rights First.[1]

The material-support law is "the anti-terror weapon of choice for prosecutors," says Stephen Vladeck, a law professor at American University in Washington, D.C. "It's a lot easier to prove that a defendant provided material support to a designated terrorist organization than to prove that they actually committed a terrorist act."

Kassir, a Lebanese-born Swedish citizen, was convicted on May 12, 2009, after a three-week trial. The evidence showed he came to the United States in 1999 and bought a parcel of land in Oregon with plans to take advantage of lax U.S. gun laws to train Muslim recruits in assembling and disassembling AK-47 rifles. He also established six different Web sites and posted materials about how to make bombs and poisons.

The defense denied that Kassir conspired to train recruits and claimed the Web sites contained only readily available information. The jury deliberated less than a day before returning guilty verdicts on a total of 11 counts. U.S. District Judge John Keenan sentenced him to life imprisonment on Sept. 15.[2]

On the same day as the Kassir verdict, a federal court jury in Miami returned guilty verdicts against five of the so-called "Liberty City Six," who had been charged with plotting to blow up the Sears Tower in Chicago and selected federal buildings. In the Human Rights First report, New York lawyers Richard Zabel and James J. Benjamin Jr. note that the trial shows the importance of the material-support charge because prosecutors won convictions against only two defendants on an explosives charge and against only one defendant for seditious conspiracy.

Zabel and Benjamin, who both served in the U.S. attorney's office in New York City, say the material-support law has similarly been used to convict defendants for such actions as providing broadcasting services to a terrorist organization's television station or traveling to Pakistan for training in a jihadist camp. The law was also invoked against Lynne Stewart, a well-known defense lawyer, for transmitting messages to her terrorism-case client, Omar Abdel Rahman, the "Blind Sheik."

The law defines material support to include not only financial contributions but also any "property" or "service," including "personnel" and "training, expert advice or assistance." Medicine and religious materials are exempted.

Some civil liberties and humanitarian groups contend the law sweeps too broadly. Material support is defined "so expansively and vaguely as to criminalize pure speech furthering lawful, nonviolent ends," the bipartisan Constitution Project says in a recent report. The report

"material support" of terrorism. In 14 cases over the next year, however, the government lost more — eight — than it won (six). In five of the cases granting habeas corpus, judges found the government's evidence either insufficient or unreliable. In one, the judge specifically found the government's evidence had been obtained by torture or under the taint of prior torture. In the two other cases, one of the detainees was found to have been expelled from al Qaeda, while the other was no longer a threat because he was cooperating with U.S. authorities.

recommends amending the law to exempt "pure speech" unless intended to further illegal conduct. It also calls for giving groups the opportunity to contest designation as a terrorist organization.[3]

Appellate courts have generally upheld broad readings of the statute. In a decision in December 2007, however, the San Francisco-based U.S. Court of Appeals for the Ninth Circuit ruled that some of the law's terms —"training," "service," and "expert advice or assistance" — were impermissibly vague or overbroad.

The ruling came in a suit filed originally in 1998 by the Humanitarian Law Project on behalf of individuals or U.S.-based groups that sought to provide assistance to two designated terrorist organizations: the Kurdistan Workers' Party in Turkey or the Liberation Tigers of Tamil Eelam in Sri Lanka. The plaintiffs claimed they wanted to counsel both groups on use of international law and nonviolent conflict resolution.

The Supreme Court agreed to hear the government's appeal of the case as well as the plaintiffs' cross-appeal of the part of the ruling that upheld a broad construction of the term "personnel." The case was argued on Feb. 23; a decision is due by the end of June.[4]

Meanwhile, a military appeals panel is weighing challenges to the use of material-support counts in military commission proceedings. The United States Court of Military Commission Review heard arguments on Jan. 26 in appeals by two of the three men convicted so far in military commissions: Salim Ahmed Hamdan, former driver for al Qaeda leader Osama bin Laden, and al Qaeda filmmaker and propagandist Ali Hamza Ahmad Suliman al Bahlul.

Hamdan, who was freed in late 2008 after about seven-and-a-half years in captivity, and al Bahlul, who was sentenced to life imprisonment, both contend that material support for terrorism is outside the military tribunals' jurisdiction because it is not a traditional war crime. The cases were argued before separate three-judge panels, which gave no indication when rulings would be expected.[5]

— *Kenneth Jost*

[1] Richard B. Zabel and James J. Benjamin Jr., "In Pursuit of Justice: Prosecuting Terrorism Cases in the Federal Courts," Human Rights First,

AFP/Getty Images/Vadim Kramer

Oussama Kassir is serving a life sentence after a federal court jury in New York City found him guilty last year of attempting to establish a jihadist training camp in Oregon and distributing terrorist training materials over the Internet.

May 2008, p. 32, www.humanrightsfirst.info/pdf/080521-USLS-pursuit-justice.pdf. See also by same authors "In Pursuit of Justice: Prosecuting Terrorism Cases in the Federal Courts: 2009 Update and Recent Developments," July 2009, www.humanrightsfirst.org/pdf/090723-LS-in-pursuit-justice-09-update.pdf. Background drawn from both reports.

[2] The press release by the U.S. Attorney for the Southern District of New York can be found at www.humanrightsfirst.org/pdf/090723-LS-in-pursuit-justice-09-update.pdf. See also "Man convicted in NY of trying to start terror camp," The Associated Press, May 12, 2009.

[3] "Reforming the Material Support Laws: Constitutional Concerns Presented by Prohibitions on Material Support to 'Terrorist Organizations,' " Constitution Project, Nov. 17, 2009, www.constitutionproject.org/manage/file/355.pdf.

[4] The case is *Holder v. Humanitarian Law Project*, 08-1498. For materials on the case, including links to news coverage, see SCOTUSWiki, www.scotuswiki.com/index.php?title=Holder_v._Humanitarian_Law_Project.

[5] Material in Bahlul's case can be found at www.defense.gov/news/CMCRHAMZA.html/; materials in Hamdan's case at www.defense.gov/news/commissionsHamdan.html.

In order to prevent leaks, Holder made his decision to try KSM in a federal court with little advance notice to New York City officials. He explained later to the Senate Judiciary Committee that a federal court trial would give the government "the greatest opportunity to present the strongest case in the best forum." The explanation left Republicans, conservatives and many New Yorkers unconvinced of the benefits, dismayed at the potential costs and appalled at the idea of according full legal rights to a self-proclaimed enemy of the United

Cole Bombing Case, Six Others Set for Tribunals

Abd al Rahim al Nashiri, the alleged mastermind of the October 2000 suicide attack on the *USS Cole*, is one of seven Guantánamo detainees designated by Attorney General Eric Holder for trial by military commissions. Seventeen U.S. sailors were killed in the attack on the warship as it lay docked in Aden, Yemen.

The Saudi-born al-Nashiri, now 45, allegedly served as al Qaeda's chief of operations in the Arabian peninsula before his capture in the United Arab Emirates in November 2002. He was held in a secret CIA prison (reportedly in Thailand) until being brought to Guantánamo in 2006.

The CIA has confirmed that al-Nashiri was waterboarded. He claims that he falsely confessed to the *Cole* attack and six other terrorist incidents as a result. It is also reported that he was the target of a mock execution by CIA interrogators.

The six other prisoners designated for trial by military commissions are:

- **Ahmed al Darbi (Saudi Arabia)** — Accused of plotting to bomb oil tankers in the Strait of Hormuz.
- **Mohammed Kamin (Afghanistan)** — Charged with planting mines in Afghanistan.
- **Omar Khadr (Canada)** — Accused of killing a U.S. soldier with a grenade in Afghanistan in 2002; Khadr was 15 at the time.
- **Noor Uthman Mohammed (Sudan)** — Charged with assisting in running al Qaeda training center.
- **Obaidullah (Afghanistan)** — Charged with possessing anti-tank mines.
- **Ibrahim al Qosi (Sudan)** — Accused of acting as Osama bin Laden's bodyguard, paymaster and supply chief.

States. Civil liberties and human rights groups applauded the decision while giving little attention to Holder's simultaneous move to try the alleged *USS Cole* plotter and others in military commissions that the groups had called for abolishing.

The political attacks over the administration's handling of Abdulmutallab's case added to the pressure against trying KSM in New York City. Behind the scenes, Justice Department officials were looking for alternate, more remote sites for a possible civilian trial. And by February Holder was being deliberately ambiguous about whether the case would be tried in a civilian court at all.

"At the end of the day, wherever this case is tried, in whatever forum, what we have to ensure is that it's done as transparently as possible and with adherence to all the rules," Holder said on Feb. 11. [31] "If we do that, I'm not sure the location or even the forum is as important as what the world sees in that proceeding."

CURRENT SITUATION

Watching Appeals

Lawyers for the government and for Guantánamo detainees are watching the federal appeals court in Washington and a specially created military appeals panel for the next major developments on the rules for prosecuting terrorism cases.

The government scored a major victory in early January when the U.S. Circuit Court of Appeals for the District of Columbia decisively backed the government's power to detain a low-level member of a pro-Taliban brigade captured during the Afghanistan war and held at Guantánamo for more than eight years.

Later in the month, the U.S. Court of Military Commission Review heard arguments on Jan. 26 from two of the men convicted so far in the military tribunals challenging the government's power to prosecute material support for terrorism in military instead of civilian courts. Separate three-judge panels convened to hear the appeals by al Qaeda propagandist Bahlul and former bin Laden driver Hamdan gave no indication when they would rule on the cases.

With several other habeas corpus cases pending before the D.C. Circuit, the appeals court is likely to determine both the direction and the pace of the next stage of the litigation from Guantánamo prisoners, according to Brookings Institution scholar Wittes.

If other judges follow the lead of the conservative-dominated panel in the Jan. 5 decision, many of the

Should terrorism suspects ordinarily be tried in civilian courts?

YES

Laura Olson
Senior Counsel, Rule of Law Program
Constitution Project

Written for *CQ Researcher*, March 2010

Civilian courts are the proper forum for trying terrorism cases. Trial in our traditional federal courts is a proven and reliable way to provide justice, while ensuring our national security. This is in stark contrast to the new military commissions that were re-created for the third time in the Military Commissions Act (MCA) of 2009. Like their predecessors, these new commissions remain vulnerable to constitutional challenge.

We should not place some of the most important terrorism trials, and arguably the most important criminal trials, in our nation's history in the untested and uncertain military commissions system.

Since 2001, trials in federal criminal courts have resulted in nearly 200 convictions of terrorism suspects, compared to only three low-level convictions in the military commissions. Two of those three are now free in their home countries. This record demonstrates that prosecutions in our traditional federal courts are tough on terrorists.

To date, the rules to accompany the MCA of 2009 remain to be approved. Therefore, military commission judges are without guidance on how to proceed with these cases. Meanwhile, our traditional federal courts move ahead, applying long-established rules on procedure and evidence. For example, the Classified Information Procedures Act (CIPA) elaborates the procedures by which federal courts admit evidence while protecting national security information from improper disclosure. The MCA of 2009 incorporates CIPA procedures on dealing with classified information into the military commissions system, but military judges have little or no experience with these procedures. Federal judges have worked with CIPA for the last 30 years.

Our Constitution provides a safe and effective way to prosecute terrorism suspects. In fact, Ahmed Kfalfan Ghailani, a former Guantánamo detainee, is now being held in New York City for his trial in federal court there. The judge has issued a protective order on all classified information, and there have been no reports of any increased safety risks or expenses associated with this trial.

I agree with the nearly 140 former diplomats, military officials, federal judges and prosecutors and members of Congress, as well as bar leaders, national-security and foreign-policy experts, and family members of the 9/11 attacks that signed Beyond Guantánamo: A Bipartisan Declaration. This unique and bipartisan group is in favor of trying terrorism suspects in our traditional federal courts. Federal trials are the only way to ensure swift and constitutional trials of terrorism suspects.

NO

Sen. John McCain, R-Ariz.
*From statement in support of the Enemy
Belligerent Interrogation, Detention and Prosecution Act,
March 4, 2010*

This legislation seeks to ensure that the mistakes made during the apprehension of the Christmas Day bomber, such as reading him a Miranda warning, will never happen again and put Americans' security at risk.

Specifically, this bill would require unprivileged enemy belligerents suspected of engaging in hostilities against the U.S. to be held in military custody and interrogated for their intelligence value by a "high-value detainee" interagency team established by the president. This interagency team of experts in national security, terrorism, intelligence, interrogation and law enforcement will have the protection of U.S. civilians and civilian facilities as their paramount responsibility. . . .

A key provision of this bill is that it would prohibit a suspected enemy belligerent from being provided with a Miranda warning and being told he has a right to a lawyer and a right to refuse to cooperate. I believe that an overwhelming majority of Americans agree that when we capture a terrorist who is suspected of carrying out or planning an attack intended to kill hundreds if not thousands of innocent civilians, our focus must be on gaining all the information possible to prevent that attack or any that may follow from occurring. . . . Additionally, the legislation would authorize detention of enemy belligerents without criminal charges for the duration of the hostilities consistent with standards under the law of war which have been recognized by the Supreme Court.

Importantly, if a decision is made to hold a criminal trial after the necessary intelligence information is obtained, the bill mandates trial by military commission, where we are best able to protect U.S. national security interests, including sensitive classified sources and methods, as well as the place and the people involved in the trial itself.

The vast majority of Americans understand that what happened with the Christmas Day bomber was a near catastrophe that was only prevented by sheer luck and the courage of a few of the passengers and crew. A wide majority of Americans also realize that allowing a terrorist to be interrogated for only 50 minutes before he is given a Miranda warning and told he can obtain a lawyer and stop cooperating is not sufficient. . . .

We must ensure that the broad range of expertise that is available within our government is brought to bear on such high-value detainees. This bill mandates such coordination and places the proper focus on getting intelligence to stop an attack, rather than allowing law enforcement and preparing a case for a civilian criminal trial to drive our response.

FEMA News Photo/WireImage/Andrea Booher

Controversy erupted after Attorney General Eric Holder announced plans to try the five alleged 9/11 conspirators in a federal court "just blocks away from where the twin towers [of the World Trade Center] once stood." New York City Mayor Michael Bloomberg and Police Commissioner Raymond Kelly welcomed Holder's decision, but many New Yorkers expressed concern about the costs and risks of a sensational trial in Lower Manhattan.

outstanding issues regarding the government's power to hold enemy combatants could be resolved quickly, Wittes says. But different rulings by panels in other cases could add to what he calls the "cacophony" surrounding the habeas corpus cases and force the Supreme Court to intervene to resolve the conflicts.

The appeals court's decision rejected a habeas corpus petition by Ghaleb Nassar Al-Bihani, a Yemeni native who served as a cook for a Taliban brigade. He argued that he should be released because the war against the Taliban has ended and, in any event, that he was essentially a civilian contractor instead of a combatant.

In a 25-page opinion, Judge Janice Rogers Brown rejected both arguments. Brown, a strongly conservative judge appointed by President George W. Bush, said Bihani's admitted actions of accompanying the brigade to the battlefield, carrying a weapon and retreating and surrendering with the brigade showed that he was "both part of and substantially supported enemy forces."

As for the status of the war, Brown said, it was up to Congress or the president to decide whether the conflict had ended, not the courts. In a significant passage, Brown also said that U.S. instead of international law determined the president's authority to hold enemy combatants. "The international laws of war as a whole have not been implemented domestically by Congress and are therefore not a source of authority for U.S. courts," Brown wrote.

Judge Brett Kavanaugh, another Bush-appointed conservative, joined Brown's opinion. Judge Stephen Williams, who was appointed by President Ronald Reagan, agreed on the result but distanced himself from Brown's comments on the impact of international law. He noted that Brown's "dictum" — the legal term for a passage unnecessary to the decision in the case —"goes well beyond what the government has argued in the case."[32]

Wittes says the ruling is "a huge development if it stands." The appellate panel, he says, was "signaling" to the federal district court judges in Washington handling habeas corpus cases to "lighten up" on the government. District court judges have ruled against the government in somewhat over half of the cases decided so far.

The appeals court for the military commissions was created by the 2006 law overhauling the rules for the tribunals, but it had no cases to review until after Hamdan's and Bahlul's convictions in 2008.

In their appeals, both men claim that their convictions for material support for terrorism were improper because the offense is not a traditional war crime prosecutable in a military court. Bahlul also argues that the First Amendment bars prosecuting him for producing a video documentary for al Qaeda that recounts the bombing of the *USS Cole* and calls for others to join a jihad against the United States.

The government counters by citing cases from the Civil War and World War II to argue that providing support to unlawful enemy combatants has been prosecutable in military courts even if the term "material support for terrorism" was not used. As to Bahlul's free-speech argument, the government contends that the First Amendment does not apply to enemy "propaganda."[33]

Bahlul is also challenging the life sentence imposed in November 2008; Hamdan was freed later that month after being credited with the seven years he had already been held at Guantánamo.

Wittes says the government has "a big uphill climb" on the material-support issue. He notes that in the Supreme Court's 2006 decision in Hamdan's case, four of the justices questioned whether military tribunals could try a conspiracy charge, another of the generally phrased offenses the government has used in terrorism cases. Material support for terrorism would be harder to justify, he says.

Wittes adds that it is important to resolve the issue quickly if the military commissions are to be used in other cases. "What you don't want to happen is to have a whole lot of people sentenced in military commissions and then find out that the charges are invalid," he says.

Making a Deal?

The Obama administration may be on the verge of deciding to try Khalid Sheikh Mohammed and four other alleged 9/11 conspirators in a military tribunal in an effort to gain Republican support for closing the Guantánamo prison camp.

Administration officials are reportedly near to recommending that Obama reverse Attorney General Holder's Nov. 13 decision to hold the 9/11 conspiracy trial in federal court in hopes of securing support for closing Guantánamo from an influential Republican senator, South Carolina's Lindsey Graham.[34]

Graham, a former military lawyer, has strongly advocated use of military tribunals for detainees held at Guantánamo but has not joined other Republicans in attacking Obama's pledge to close the facility. GOP lawmakers have been pushing legislative proposals to block use of funds for closing Guantánamo or for holding the 9/11 conspiracy trial in federal court.

The administration's possible reversal on the KSM trial is drawing a heated response from civil liberties and human rights groups. The decision would "strike a blow to American values and the rule of law and undermine America's credibility," according to the ACLU.

Elisa Massimino, president and CEO of Human Rights First, says failure to support Holder's decision would set "a dangerous precedent for future national security policy."

In the wake of the strong criticism of holding the KSM trial in New York City, Justice Department lawyers and others had been reported to be holding onto the plan for a federal court trial, but in a different location. Among the sites reported to have been under consideration were somewhere else in southern New York, Northern Virginia and western Pennsylvania.[35]

Any of those sites would satisfy the constitutional requirement that trial of a federal criminal case be held in "the district wherein the crime shall have been committed." Besides the World Trade Center in New York City, the 9/11 hijackers also crashed a plane into the Pentagon in Northern Virginia and into a rural location in western Pennsylvania.

Graham, first elected to the Senate in 2002, argued during the Bush administration for a greater role for Congress in defining detention policies. Since Obama's election, he is widely reported to have formed a working relationship on several issues with White House chief of staff Rahm Emanuel, a former colleague in the House of Representatives. Emanuel was described in a flattering profile in *The Washington Post* and elsewhere as having disagreed with Obama's pledge to close Guantánamo and with Holder's decision to try KSM in federal court.[36]

Beyond the KSM trial and Guantánamo issue, Graham is continuing to call for congressional legislation to govern the handling of detention issues. "I want Congress and the administration to come up with a detainee policy that will be accepted by courts and so that the international community will understand that no one is in jail by an arbitrary exercise of executive power," Graham told *The New York Times*.[37]

As outlined, the legislation would authorize holding terrorism suspects inside the United States without charging them with a crime or advising them of Miranda rights; establish standards for choosing between military or civilian court for prosecution; and authorize indefinite detention under standards subject to judicial review. Civil liberties and human rights groups remain opposed to indefinite-detention proposals.

Administration officials were quoted in news accounts as saying Obama hopes to have the KSM trial issue resolved before he begins a trip to Asia on March 18. But officials quoted in *The Washington Post* cautioned against expecting a "grand bargain" with Graham on the full range of detention issues in the near future.

OUTLOOK

Bringing Justice to Bear

When he defended the administration's decision to try Khalid Sheikh Mohammed in a civilian court, deputy national intelligence director John Brennan made clear that he expected the trial would be fair and just, but the result certain and severe.

"I'm confident that he's going to have the full weight of American justice," Brennan said on NBC's "Meet the Press" on Feb. 7. Asked by host David Gregory whether Mohammed would be executed, Brennan initially skirted the question but eventually concluded, "I'm convinced and confident that Mr. Khalid Sheikh Mohammed is going to meet his day in justice and before his maker."[38]

Despite the assurance from Brennan, Attorney General Holder and other administration officials, Americans apparently lack the same confidence in the federal court system. An ABC/*Washington Post* poll conducted in late February showed Americans favoring military over civilian trials for terrorism suspects by a margin of 55 percent to 39 percent. In a similar poll in the fall, Americans showed a statistically insignificant preference for military trials: 48 percent to 47 percent.[39]

A survey by Democratic pollsters similarly finds a majority of respondents opposed to Obama's policy on interrogation and prosecution of terrorism suspects (51 percent to 44 percent). But the survey, conducted in late February for the Democratic groups Democracy Corps and Third Way, also found majority approval of Obama's handling of "national security" (57 percent to 40 percent) and "fighting terrorism" (54 percent to 41 percent).

In a memo, leaders of the two organizations advise Obama to move the issue away from "civilian" versus "military" trials. Instead, they say the administration should "place the debate over terrorism suspects into the broader context of tough actions and significant results."[40]

Even before the memo's release, civil liberties and human rights groups were following the strategy in public lobbying of Obama as the administration was weighing where to hold the KSM trial. In a March 5 conference call for reporters arranged by Human Rights First, three

retired military officers all depicted the military commissions as an unproven forum for prosecuting terrorists. "This is not ready for prime time," said Human Rights First President Massamino.

The ACLU followed with a full-page ad in the Sunday edition of *The New York Times* that compared the 300 terrorism cases "successfully handled" in the criminal justice system to "only three" in military commissions. "Our criminal justice system will resolve these cases more quickly and more credibly than the military commissions," the March 7 ad stated.

Meanwhile, former prosecutor McCarthy conceded in a speech sponsored by a college-affiliated center in Washington, "I don't think the military commission system performed well. By and large, the civilian system has performed well."

Speaking March 5 at the Kirby Center for Constitutional Studies and Citizenship at Hillsdale College in Michigan, McCarthy nevertheless reiterated that discovery procedures available to defendants argued against use of criminal prosecutions. "When you're at war, you can't be telling the enemy your most sensitive national intelligence," the *National Review* columnist said. Massamino noted, however, that a new military commissions law passed in 2009 dictates that defendants are to have access to evidence "comparable" to that provided in civilian courts.

The White House now says a decision on the KSM trial is "weeks" away. On Capitol Hill, Sen. Graham is continuing to push for a deal that would swap Republican support for closing Guantánamo for the administration's agreement to try KSM and other high-level terrorism suspects in military commissions. But Graham has yet to gain any public support for the plan from GOP colleagues.

McCarthy mocks Graham's proposed deal. He says the White House has already "stood down" on the military commissions issues and is only deferring a decision in hopes of getting GOP support for closing Guantánamo. "It makes no sense to horse-trade when Obama was being pushed toward military commissions by reality," McCarthy writes.[41]

Fellow conservative Rivkin also expects military commissions to become the norm for terrorism suspects. "My hope is that we'll come to our senses," he says. The current policies "are not consonant with the traditional law-of-war architecture, and they're not consistent with prevailing in this war."

Liberal groups continue to strongly oppose use of military commissions, but acknowledge congressional politics may determine decision-making. "There's no question that Congress has been trying to hold hostage the president's national security agenda," Massamino says.

For his part, former Assistant U.S. Attorney Benjamin doubts that military commissions will prove as useful as conservatives expect. "It would be great if the military commissions develop into a forum that works," he says. "But I have my doubts about how quickly or how smoothly that will happen."

NOTES

1. Some background information drawn from Farhan Bokhari, *et al.*, "The CEO of al-Qaeda," *Financial Times*, Feb. 15, 2003. See also the Wikipedia entry on Khalid Sheikh Mohammed and sources cited there, http://en.wikipedia.org/wiki/Khalid_Sheikh_Mohammed.

2. Quoted in Devlin Barnett, "NYC trial of 9/11 suspects faces legal risks," The Associated Press, Nov. 14, 2009. For Holder's prepared remarks, see U.S. Department of Justice, "Attorney General Announces Forum Decisions for Guantánamo Detainees," Nov. 13, 2009, www.justice.gov/ag/speeches/2009/ag-speech-091113.html.

3. Quoted in Carrie Johnson, "Holder Answers to 9/11 Relatives About Trials in U0.S.," *The Washington Post*, Nov. 19, 2009, p. A3. See also Charlie Savage, "Holder Defends Decision to Use U.S. Court for 9/11 Trial," *The New York Times*, Nov. 19, 2009, p. A18.

4. See Anne E. Kornblut and Carrie Johnson, "Obama to help pick location of terror trial," *The Washington Post*, Feb. 12, 2010, p. A1.

5. For background, see these *CQ Researcher* reports: Kenneth Jost, "Closing Guantánamo," Feb. 27, 2009, pp. 177-200; Peter Katel and Kenneth Jost, "Treatment of Detainees," Aug. 25, 2006, pp. 673-696; and Kenneth Jost, "Civil Liberties Debates," Oct. 24, 2003, pp. 893-916.

6. "FY 2009 Budget and Performance Summary: Part One: Summary of Request and Performance," U.S. Department of Justice, www.justice.gov/jmd/2009summary/html/004_budget_highlights.htm. See also Mark Hosenball, "Terror Prosecution Statistics Criticized by GOP Were Originally Touted by Bush Administration," *Declassified* blog, Feb. 9, 2010, http://blog.newsweek.com/blogs/declassified/archive/2010/02/09/terror-prosecution-statistics-criticized-by-gop-were-originally-touted-by-bush-administration.aspx.

7. Richard B. Zabel and James J. Benjamin Jr., "In Pursuit of Justice: Prosecuting Terrorism Cases in the Federal Courts: 2009 Update and Recent Developments," Human Rights First, July 2009, www.humanrightsfirst.org/pdf/090723-LS-in-pursuit-justice-09-update.pdf. See also by the same authors, "In Pursuit of Justice: Prosecuting Terrorism Cases in the Federal Courts," Human Rights First, May 2008, www.humanrightsfirst.info/pdf/080521-USLS-pursuit-justice.pdf.

8. Andy McCarthy, "No Civilian Trial — In NYC or Anywhere Else," *Conservative Blog Watch*, Jan. 30, 2010, www.conservativeblogwatch.com/2010/01/30/no-civilian-trial-in-nyc-or-anywhere-by-andy-mccarthy.

9. See Benjamin Weiser, "A Top Terrorism Prosecutor Turns Critic of Civilian Trials," *The New York Times*, Feb. 20, 2010, p. A1.

10. See Del Quentin Wilber, " '08 habeas ruling may snag Obama plans," *The Washington Post*, Feb. 13, 2010, p. A2.

11. The defendants and their respective sentences were Mukhtar Al-Bakri and Yahya Goba (10 years each), Sahim Alwan (9-1/2 years), Shafal Mosed and Yaseinn Taher (eight years each) and Faysal Galab (seven years). For a full account, see Matthew Purdy and Lowell Bergman, "Where the Trail Led: Between Evidence and Suspicion, Unclear Danger: The Lackawanna Terror Case," *The New York Times*, Oct. 12, 2003, sec. 1, p. 1. See also Lou Michel, "Lackawanna officials say troops in city was bad idea," *Buffalo News*, July 26, 2009, p. A1.

12. *In Pursuit of Justice, op. cit.*, p. 2; *In Pursuit of Justice: 2009 Update, op. cit.*, p. 2.

13. Quoted in Bruce Golding, "Holder tours federal courthouse ahead of 9/11 terror trial," *The New York Post*, Dec. 9, 2009.

14. See Peter Finn, "The boy from the battlefield," *The Washington Post*, Feb. 10, 2010, p. A1.

15. "Remarks by the President on National Security," National Archives, May 21, 2009, www.whitehouse .gov/the_press_office/Remarks-by-the-President-On-National-Security-5-21-09/. For coverage, see Sheryl Gay Stolberg, "Obama Would Move Some Terror Detainees to U.S.," *The New York Times*, May 22, 2009, p. A1.

16. Department of Defense comments on the study are at www.defense.gov/Transcripts/Transcript.aspx? TranscriptID=4340. See also Joseph Williams and Bryan Bender, "Obama Changes US Course on Treatment of Detainees," *The Boston Globe*, Jan. 23, 2009, p. A1. See Mark Denbeaux, Joshua Denbeaux and R. David Gratz, "Released Guantánamo Detainees and the Department of Defense: Propaganda by the Numbers?," Jan. 15, 2009, http:// law.shu.edu/publications/GuantánamoReports/pro paganda_numbers_11509.pdf.

17. The case is 542 U.S. 507 (2004). For an account, see Kenneth Jost, *Supreme Court Yearbook 2003-2004*, CQ Press.

18. Benjamin Wittes, Robert Chesney and Rabea Benhalim, "The Emerging Law of Detention: The Guantánamo Habeas Cases as Lawmaking," Brookings Institution, Jan. 22, 2010, www.brook ings.edu/papers/2010/0122_Guantánamo_wittes_ chesney.aspx. See Benjamin Wittes and Robert Chesney, "Piecemeal detainee policy," *The Washington Post*, Jan. 27, 2010, p. A17.

19. Chisun Lee, "Judges Urge Congress to Act on Indefinite Detention," *ProPublica*, Jan. 22, 2010, www.propublica.org/feature/judges-urge-congress-to-act-on-indefinite-terrorism-detentions-122. Walton, an appointee of President George W. Bush, was joined in the interview by Chief Judge Royce Lamberth, an appointee of President Ronald Reagan, and Judge Ricardo Urbina, an appointee of President Bill Clinton.

20. David Cole, "Detainees: still a matter for judges," *The Washington Post*, Feb. 9, 2010, p. A16.

21. Background drawn in part from Jennifer K. Elsea, "Terrorism and the Law of War: Trying Terrorists as War Criminals before Military Commissions," Congressional Research Service, Dec. 11, 2001, www .fas.org/irp/crs/RL31191.pdf. See also Louis Fisher,

Military Tribunals and Presidential Power: American Revolution to the War on Terrorism (2005). Wittes' quote is from his book *Law and the Long War: The Future of Justice in the Age of Terror* (2008), p. 42.

22. The decision is *Ex parte Milligan*, 71 U.S. 2 (1866). *The New York Times'* contemporaneous account is reprinted in Kenneth Jost, *The New York Times on the Supreme Court 1857-2006* (2009), CQ Press, pp. 58-59.

23. The citation is 317 U.S. 1 (1942). The opinion was issued on Oct. 29, almost three months after the July 31 decision. The rulings on the curfew and internments are *Hirabayashi v. United States*, 320 U.S. 81 (1943), and *Korematsu v. United States*, 323 U.S. 214 (1944).

24. Joseph P. Fried, "Sheik Sentenced to Life in Prison in Bombing Plot," *The New York Times*, Jan. 18, 1996, p. A1, and Christopher S. Wren, "Jury Convicts 3 in a Conspiracy to Bomb Airliners," *The New York Times*, Sept. 6, 1996, p. A1. See also Benjamin Weiser, "Judge Upholds Conviction in '93 Bombing," *The New York Times*, April 5, 2003, p. A1.

25. Accounts drawn from *Pursuit of Justice* (2008), *op. cit.*, supplemented by Wikipedia entries or contemporaneous news coverage.

26. The decision is *Hamdan v. Rumsfeld*, 548 U.S. 557 (2006). For an account, see Kenneth Jost, *Supreme Court Yearbook 2005-2006*, CQ Press.

27. U.S. Department of Justice, "Fact Sheet: Justice Department Counter-Terrorism Efforts Since 9/11," Sept. 11, 2008, www.justice.gov/opa/pr/2008/ September/08-nsd-807.html.

28. The Supreme Court decision is *Boumediene v. Bush*, 553 U.S. — — (2008). For an account, see Kenneth Jost, *Supreme Court Yearbook 2007-2008*, CQ Press. For Leon's decision granting habeas corpus to five of the six prisoners, see "Emerging Law of Detention," *op. cit.*, p. 99; William Glaberson, "Judge Declares Five Detainees Held Illegally," *The New York Times*, Nov. 21, 2008, p. A1.

29. See Peter Finn, "Report on U.S. Detention Policy Will Be Delayed," *The Washington Post*, July 21, 2009, p. A2.

30. For summaries of individual cases, see "Emerging Law of Detention," *op. cit.*, appendix II, pp. 88-105.

31. Quoted in Kornblut and Johnson, *op. cit.*

32. The decision is *Al Bihani v. Obama*, D.C. Cir., Jan. 5, 2010, http://pacer.cadc.uscourts.gov/docs/common/opinions/201001/09-5051-1223587.pdf. For coverage, see Del Quentin Wilber, "Court upholds ruling to detain Yemeni suspect," *The Washington Post*, Jan. 6, 2010, p. A3.

33. Material in Bahlul's case can be found at www.defense.gov/news/CMCRHAMZA.html/; materials in Hamdan's case had not been posted by the deadline for this report.

34. See Anne E. Kornblut and Peter Finn, "Obama aides near reversal on 9/11 trial," *The Washington Post*, March 5, 2010, p. A1; Charlie Savage, "Senator Proposes Deal on Handling of Detainees," *The New York Times*, March 4, 2010, p. A12.

35. Richard A. Serrano, "Experts make case for N.Y. terror trial," *Los Angeles Times*, March 3, 2010, p. A12.

36. Jason Horwitz, "Obama's 'enforcer' may also be his voice of reason," *The Washington Post*, March 2, 2010, p. A1.

37. Savage, *op. cit.* (March 4).

38. Transcript: www.msnbc.msn.com/id/35270673/ns/meet_the_press//.

39. http://blogs.abcnews.com/thenumbers/2010/03/911-and-military-tribunals.html

40. "The Politics of National Security: A Wake-Up Call," Democracy Corps/Third Way, March 8, 2010, www.democracycorps.com/strategy/2010/03/the-politics-of-national-security-a-wake-up-call/?section=Analysis. The memo was signed by Stanley B. Greenberg, James Carville and Jeremy Rosner of Democracy Corps, and Jon Cowan, Matt Bennett and Andy Johnson of Third Way.

41. Andrew McCarthy, "Hold the Champagne on Military Commissions — It's a Head Fake," *The Corner*, March 5, 2010, http://corner.nationalreview.com.

BIBLIOGRAPHY

Books

Fisher, Louis, *Military Tribunals and Presidential Power: American Revolution to the War on Terrorism*, University of Kansas Press, 2005.
The veteran separation-of-powers specialist at the Library of Congress examines the development of the president's wartime authority in legal matters. Includes chapter notes, 10-page bibliography and list of cases.

Wittes, Benjamin, *Law and the Long War: The Future of Justice in the Age of Terror*, Penguin Press, 2008.
A leading researcher on national security at the Brookings Institution provides a critical examination of detention and interrogation policies along with his arguments for Congress to pass legislation to authorize administrative detention of suspected enemy combatants and to create a national security court to try terrorism cases. Includes detailed notes. Wittes is also editor of *Legislating the War on Terror: An Agenda for Reform* (Brookings, 2009).

Yoo, John, *War by Other Means: An Insider's Account of the War on Terror*, Kaplan, 2005.
Yoo, a law professor at the University of California-Berkeley who served as deputy assistant attorney general for the Office of Legal Counsel during the George W. Bush administration, provides a combative account of his role in detention and interrogation policies and a strong argument for presidential wartime powers vis-à-vis Congress and the courts. Includes detailed notes. Yoo's other books include *Crisis and Command: The History of Executive Power from Washington to George W. Bush* (Kaplan, 2009); and *The Powers of War and Peace: Foreign Affairs and the Constitution after 9/11* (University of Chicago (2005).

Articles

Mayer, Jane, "The Trial," *The New Yorker*, Feb. 5, 2010, www.newyorker.com/reporting/2010/02/15/100215fa_fact_mayer.
The magazine's prolific staff writer details the legal reasoning behind, and political implications of, Attorney General Eric Holder's decision to prosecute Khalid Sheikh Mohammed and four other alleged 9/11 conspirators in a civilian court instead of a military tribunal.

Reports and Studies

Elsea, Jennifer K., "Comparison of Rights in Military Commission Trials and Trials in Federal Criminal Courts," Congressional Research Service, Nov. 19, 2009, http://assets.opencrs.com/rpts/R40932_20091119.pdf.

The 23-page report provides a side-by-side comparison of the rights accorded to defendants respectively in federal criminal courts under general federal law or in military commissions under the Military Commissions Act of 2009. Elsea, a legislative attorney with CRS, also wrote two previous reports on military commissions: "The Military Commissions Act of 2006 (MCA): Background and Proposed Amendments" (Sept. 8, 2009), http://assets.opencrs.com/rpts/R40752_2009 0908.pdf; and "Terrorism and the Law of War: Trying Terrorists as War Criminals before Military Commissions" (Dec. 11, 2001), www.fas.org/irp/crs/RL31191.pdf.

Laguardia, Francesca, Terrorist Trial Report Card: September 11, 2001-September 11, 2009, Center on Law and Security, New York University School of Law, January 2010, www.lawandsecurity.org/publications/ TTRCFinalJan14.pdf.
The series of reports studies data from federal terrorism prosecutions in the post-9/11 years and analyzes trends in the government's legal strategies.

Wittes, Benjamin, Robert Chesney and Rabea Benhalim, "The Emerging Law of Detention: The Guantánamo

Habeas Cases as Lawmaking," Brookings Institution, Jan. 22, 2010, www.brookings.edu/papers/2010/0122_ guantanamo_wittes_chesney.aspx.
The comprehensive report examines and identifies unsettled issues in decisions by federal courts in Washington, D.C., in several dozen habeas corpus cases filed by Guantánamo detainees. Wittes is a senior scholar and Benhalim a legal fellow at Brookings; Chesney is a law professor at the University of Texas-Austin.

Zabel, Richard B., and James J. Benjamin Jr., "In Pursuit of Justice: Prosecuting Terrorism Cases in the Federal Courts: 2009 Update and Recent Developments," Human Rights First, July 2009, www.humanrightsfirst.org/ pdf/090723-LS-in-pursuit-justice-09-update.pdf.
The 70-page report by two New York City lawyers who formerly served as federal prosecutors finds federal courts to have a "track record of serving as an effective and fair tool for incapacitating terrorists." The report updates the authors' original, 171-page report, "In Pursuit of Justice: Prosecuting Terrorism Cases in the Federal Courts" (May 2008), www.humanrightsfirst.info/pdf/080521-USLS-pursuit-justice.pdf.

For More Information

American Civil Liberties Union, 125 Broad St., 18th Floor, New York, NY 10004; (212) 549-2666; www.aclu.org. Advocates for individual rights and federal civilian trials for suspected terrorists.

Brookings Institution, 1775 Massachusetts Ave., N.W., Washington, DC 20036; (202) 797-6000; www.brookings.edu. Public policy think tank focusing on foreign policy and governance.

Constitution Project, 1200 18th St., N.W., Suite 1000, Washington, DC 20036; (202) 580-6920; www.constitutionproject.org. Promotes bipartisan consensus on significant constitutional and legal issues.

Foundation for Defense of Democracies, P.O. Box 33249, Washington, DC 20033; (202) 207-0190; www .defenddemocracy.org. Nonpartisan policy institute dedicated to promoting pluralism, defending democratic values and opposing ideologies that threaten democracy.

Human Rights First, 333 Seventh Ave., 13th Floor, New York, NY 10001; (212) 845-5200; www.humanrightsfirst. org. Advocates for the U.S. government's full participation in international human rights laws.

National Institute of Military Justice, Washington College of Law, American University, 4801 Massachusetts Ave., N.W., Washington, DC 20016; (202) 274-4000; www.wcl.american .edu/nimj. Promotes the fair administration of justice in the military system.

4

Terrorism and the Internet

Barbara Mantel

Hosam Maher Husein Smadi, a Jordanian teenager in the United States illegally, pleaded not guilty on Oct. 26 of trying to blow up a 60-story Dallas skyscraper. Smadi reportedly parked a vehicle in the building's garage on Sept. 24 hoping to detonate explosives with a cellphone. FBI agents, posing as al-Qaeda operatives, had been keeping tabs on Smadi after discovering him on an extremist Web site earlier this year where he stood out for "his vehement intention to actually conduct terror attacks in the United States."

From *CQ Researcher*, November, 2009.

AP Photo/Ellis County Sheriff's Department

In March 2008 a participant on the pro al-Qaeda online forum ek-Is.org posted six training sessions for aspiring terrorists. The first was entitled: "Do you want to form a terror cell?" Using the name Shamil al-Baghdadi, the instructor described how to choose a leader, recruit members and select initial assassination targets. The second lesson outlined assassination techniques.[1]

"Although the first two training lessons often contain very basic instructions that may be less significant for experienced jihadis, they provide essential training for novices," said Abdul Hameed Bakier, a Jordanian terrorism expert who translated and summarized the training manual.[2]

The sessions then progressed to more sophisticated topics. Lesson three explained in more detail how to carry out assassinations, including: suicide attacks using booby-trapped vehicles or explosive belts; sniper attacks using Russian, Austrian and American rifles and direct attacks through strangling, poison and booby-trapped cellular phones.[3] Lesson four explained how to steal funds, and the final two lessons gave detailed instructions on how to conduct "quality terror attacks," including strikes against U.S. embassies.[4]

While this particular forum can no longer be accessed under its original domain name, Web sites controlled or operated by terrorist groups have multiplied dramatically over the past decade.

"We started 11 years ago and were monitoring 12 terrorist Web sites," says Gabriel Weimann, a professor of communication at Haifa University in Israel and a terrorism researcher. "Today we are monitoring more than 7,000."

73

Internet Offers Vast Potential for Spreading Terror

The Internet has opened global communication channels to anyone with computer access, creating a simple and cheap venue for spreading terrorist ideology. Interestingly, the regions with the largest concentrations of terrorist groups — the Middle East and Asia — have some of the lowest Internet usage rates. The highest rates are in developed countries, such as the United States, Canada, Australia and New Zealand.

World Internet Usage Rates, by Region

Percentage of Population That Uses the Internet

- [ ] Under 20%
- 20%-29%
- 30%-39%
- 40%-49%
- 50%-59%
- 60%-69%
- 70% or more

Major Terrorist Groups with Web Sites, by Region

Middle East: Hamas, Lebanese Hezbollah, al-Aqsa Martyrs Brigades, Fatah Tanzim, Popular Front for the Liberation of Palestine, Palestinian Islamic Jihad, Kahane Lives Movement, People's Mujahidin of Iran, Kurdish Workers' Party, Popular Democratic Liberation Front Party, Great East Islamic Raiders Front

Europe: Basque Euskadi Ta Askatasuna, Armata Corsa, Real Irish Republican Army

Latin America: Tupac-Amaru, Shining Path, Colombian National Liberation Army, Armed Revolutionary Forces of Colombia, Zapatista National Liberation Army

Asia: Al Qaeda, Japanese Supreme Truth, Ansar al Islam, Japanese Red Army, Hizb-ul Mujahidin, Liberation Tigers of Tamil Eelam, Islamic Movement of Uzbekistan, Moro Islamic Liberation Front, Lashkar-e-Taiba, Chechnyan rebel movement

Sources: "World Internet Penetration Rates by Geographic Region," Internet World Stats, June 30, 2009, www.internetworldststs.com/stats.htm; Gabriel Weimann, "Terror on the Internet," 2006

Analysts say nearly every group designated as a foreign terrorist organization by the U.S. State Department now has an online presence, including Spain's Basque ETA movement, Peru's Shining Path, al Qaeda, the Real Irish Republican Army and others.[5] (*See list, p. 74.*)

The Internet appeals to terrorists for the same reasons it attracts everyone else: It's inexpensive, easily accessible, has little or no regulation, is interactive, allows for multimedia content and the potential audience is huge.[6] And it's anonymous.

"You can walk into an Internet café, enter a chat room or Web site, download instructions to make a bomb, and no one can find you," says Weimann. "They can trace you all the way down to the computer terminal, but by then you'll already be gone."

Terrorism on the Internet extends far beyond Web sites directly operated or controlled by terrorist organizations. Their supporters and sympathizers are increasingly taking advantage of all the tools available on the Web. "The proliferation of blogs has been exponential," says Sulastri Bte Osman, an analyst with the Civil and Internal Conflict Programme at Nanyang Technological University in Singapore. Just two years ago, Osman could find no extremist blogs in the two predominant languages of Indonesia and Malaysia; today she is monitoring 150.

The University of Arizona's "Dark Web" project, which tracks terrorist and extremist content in cyberspace, estimates there are roughly 50,000 such Web sites, discussion forums, chat rooms, blogs, Yahoo user groups, video-sharing sites, social networking sites and virtual worlds.[7] They help to distribute content — such as videos of beheadings and suicide attacks, speeches by terrorist leaders and training manuals — that may originate on just a few hundred sites.

Security experts say terrorist groups use the Internet for five general purposes:

- Research and communication: The Sept. 11, 2001, terrorists who attacked the World Trade Center and the Pentagon used the Internet to research flight schools, coordinate their actions through e-mail and gather flight information.[8]
- Training: Global Islamic Media Front, a propaganda arm of al Qaeda, issued a series of 19 training lessons

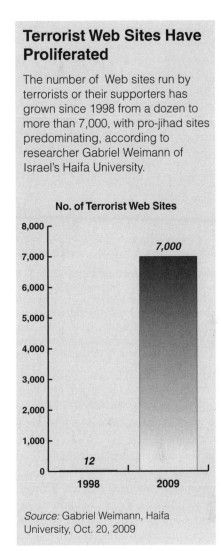

Terrorist Web Sites Have Proliferated

The number of Web sites run by terrorists or their supporters has grown since 1998 from a dozen to more than 7,000, with pro-jihad sites predominating, according to researcher Gabriel Weimann of Israel's Haifa University.

No. of Terrorist Web Sites

Source: Gabriel Weimann, Haifa University, Oct. 20, 2009

in 2003 covering topics like security, physical training, weapons and explosives. The document was later found on a computer belonging to the terrorist cell responsible for the 2004 train bombings in Madrid, Spain, that killed 191 people. But most material is posted by individuals who use the Internet as a training library.[9]

- Fundraising: In 1997 the rebel Tamil Tigers in Sri Lanka stole user IDs and passwords from

AP Photo/Keystone/Karl Mathis

Tunisian Moez Garsallaoui, right, and his wife Malika El Aroud, the widow of an al-Qaeda suicide bomber, were convicted in Switzerland's first Internet terrorism trial of running pro-al-Qaeda Web sites that showed executions. Garsallaoui served three weeks in prison; El Aroud received no jail time. They are continuing their online work from Belgium, where El Aroud is described by Belgian State Security chief Alain Winants as a "leading" Internet jihadist.

faculty at Britain's Sheffield University and used the e-mail accounts to send out messages asking for donations.[10]

- Media operations: Before his death in 2006, Abu Musab al Zarqawi, the mastermind behind hundreds of bombings, kidnappings and killings in Iraq, posted gruesome videos of terrorist operations, tributes immortalizing suicide bombers and an Internet magazine offering religious justifications for his actions.[11]

- Radicalization and recruitment: In 2006, Illinois resident Derrick Shareef pleaded guilty to attempting to acquire explosives to blow up a mall in Rockford, Ill. Although not part of a terrorist organization, he was inspired in part by violent videos downloaded from a Web site linked to al Qaeda.[12]

The use of the Internet for recruitment and radicalization particularly worries some authorities. But experts disagree over the extent to which cyber content can radicalize and convert young men and women into homegrown supporters of — or participants in — terrorism.

The Internet is where "the gas meets the flame," says Evan F. Kohlmann, a senior investigator with the NEFA Foundation, a New York-based terrorism research organization.* "It provides the medium where would-be megalomaniacs can try and recruit deluded and angry young men . . . and magnify that anger to convince them to carry out acts of violence." The Internet replaces and broadens the traditional social networks of mosques and Arabic community centers, which have come under intense government scrutiny since 9/11, says Kohlmann.

A frequent expert witness in terrorism cases, Kohlmann says the Internet comes up in nearly every prosecution. For instance, Hamaad Munshi — a British national convicted in 2008 of possessing materials likely to be used for terrorism — participated in an online British extremist group that shared terrorist videos and used chat rooms to discuss its plans to fight overseas.[13] He was arrested at age 16.

The group's ringleader, then 22-year-old Aabid Khan, another Briton, used the chat rooms to incite Munshi to fight, Kohlmann says; the youth's grandfather also blamed the Internet. "This case demonstrates how a young, impressionable teenager can be groomed so easily through the Internet to associate with those whose views run contrary to true Muslim beliefs and values," Yakub Munshi said after the teen's conviction.[14]

But other researchers say online terrorism sites are largely about preaching to the choir and have limited influence on non-terrorists. "There has been very little evidence that the Internet has been the main or sole driver in radicalization," says Peter Neumann, director of the International Centre for the Study of Radicalisation and Political Violence at King's College in London. "In most cases, radicalization requires would-be terrorists to come in contact with social groups of people in the real world."

For instance, he pointed out, while much of Munshi's extremist activism took place online, "his radicalisation had been initiated in the 'real world.' " Through a friend at a local mosque, Munshi had met Khan, who spotted Munshi's computer expertise and groomed him to become a part of his online network. "It was the early meetings with Khan and some of his friends that helped turn a boy interested in religion into a young man dedicated to killing 'non-believers,' " according to Neumann.[15]

---

* NEFA stands for "Nine Eleven Finding Answers."

"There is anecdotal evidence out there, but no one has done a systematic study to show that radicalization via the Internet is a reality," says Maura Conway, a terrorism expert at Dublin City University in Ireland. Nevertheless, she adds, "governments are certainly acting as if radicalization through the Internet is possible, putting in place legislation that curbs how people can interact online."

As terrorists' presence on the Internet continues to grow, here are some of the questions being asked:

Should governments block terrorist Web sites?

Many of those who think the Internet is a major terrorist recruiting tool say authorities should simply shut down terrorists' sites.

Often the call comes from politicians. "It is shocking the government has failed to shut down a single Web site, even though Parliament gave them that power," Britain's opposition security minister, Baroness Pauline Neville-Jones, said last March. "This smacks of dangerous complacency and incompetence."[16]

In France, a minister for security said she wanted to stop terrorist propaganda on the Internet.[17] And a European Commission official called for a Europe-wide prohibition on Web sites that post bomb-making instructions.[18]

Although governments have shut down terrorist Web sites when they felt the information posted was too great a threat, some critics say such a move is legally complicated, logistically difficult and unwise.

Last year, three of the most important discussion forums used by Islamist terrorist groups disappeared from the Internet, including ek-Is.org, which had posted the six-part training manual. Jordanian terrorism expert Bakier says counterterrorism officials were so worried about the site that he "used to get requests from concerned agencies to translate the exact texts posted on ek-Is.org that were referenced in my articles. It was that serious."

"It is widely assumed that Western intelligence agencies were responsible for removing the three sites," and probably without the cooperation of the Internet service providers (ISPs) that host the sites, says Neumann, of King's College. "It would have required the cooperation of all the ISPs in the world," because those Web sites were not accessible at all, he explains. Instead, he thinks intelligence agencies may have launched so-called

British officials, including Prime Minister Gordon Brown, center right, visit a London cyber security firm on June 25 during the launch of a new government campaign to counter cyber criminals and terrorists.

denial-of-service attacks against the sites, bombarding them with so many requests that they crashed. This September, one of the sites resurfaced; however, many experts believe it is a hoax.[19]

But government takedowns of terrorist sites — by whatever method — are not common, say many researchers. First, there are concerns about free speech.

"Who is going to decide who is a terrorist, who should be silenced and why?" asks Haifa University's Weimann. "Who is going to decide what kind of Web site should be removed? It can lead to political censorship."

Concern about free speech may be more acute in the United States than elsewhere. Current U.S. statutes make it a crime to provide "material support" — including expert advice or assistance — to organizations designated as terrorist groups by the State Department.[20] However, the First Amendment guarantee of free speech may trump the material support provisions.

"Exceptions to the First Amendment are fairly narrow" says Ian Ballon, an expert on Internet law practicing in California. "Child pornography is one, libelous or defamatory content another. There is no terrorism exception per se." Words that would incite violence are clearly an exception to the First Amendment, he says, "but there is a concept of immediacy, and most terrorism sites would not necessarily meet that requirement." A 1969 Supreme Court case, *Brandenburg v. Ohio*, held that the

Southeast Asian Sites Now Espouse Violence

Extremist Web sites using the two main languages in Indonesia and Malaysia have evolved since 2006 from mostly propagandizing to providing firearm and bomb-making manuals and encouraging armed violence.

How the Sites Evolved

2006-July 2007	Posted al-Qaeda and Jemaah Islamiyah propaganda (videos, photographs, statements, etc.); articles about how Muslims are victimized and the necessity to fight back; celebrations of mujahidin victories; conspiracy theories; anger directed at the West; local grievances linked to global jihad; endorsements of highly selective Islamic doctrines
August 2007	First posting of manual on how to hack Web sites
February 2008	First posting of bomb-making manual and bomb-making video compilation in Arabic; emergence of a password-protected forum
April 2008	First posting of a firearm manual
Present	All of the above posted/available

Source: "Contents of Bahasa and Malay Language Radical and Extremist Web Sites, 2006 to 2009," in "Countering Internet Radicalisation in Southeast Asia," S. Rajaratnam School of International Studies, Singapore, and Australian Strategic Policy Institute, 2009

government cannot punish inflammatory speech unless it is inciting or likely to incite imminent lawless action.[21]

In Europe, where free-speech rights are more circumscribed than in the United States, the legal landscape varies. Spain, for instance, outlaws as incitement "the act of performing public ennoblement, praise and/or justification of a terrorist group, operative or act," explains Raphael Perl, head of the Action Against Terrorism Unit at the Organization for Security and Co-operation in Europe, a regional security organization with 56 member nations, based in Vienna, Austria. And the U.K. passed the Terrorism Acts of 2000 and 2006, which make it an offense to collect, make or possess material that could be used in a terrorist act, such as bomb-making manuals and information about potential targets. The 2006 act also outlaws the encouragement or glorification of terrorism.[22] Human Rights Watch says the measure is unnecessary, overly broad and potentially chilling of free speech.[23]

Yet, it does not appear that governments are using their legal powers to shut down Web sites. "I haven't heard from any ISP in Europe so far that they have been asked by the police to take down terrorist pages," says Michael Rotert, vice president of the European Internet Service Providers Association (EuroISPA).

For one thing, says Rotert, there is no common, legal, Europe-wide definition of terrorism. "We are requesting a common definition," he says, "and then I think notice and takedown procedures could be discussed. But right now, such procedures only exist for child pornography."

But even if a European consensus existed on what constitutes terrorism, the Internet has no borders. If an ISP shuts down a site, it can migrate to another hosting service and even register under a new domain name.

Instead of shutting down sites, some governments are considering filtering them. Germany recently passed a filtering law aimed at blocking child pornography, which it says could be expanded to block sites that promote terrorist acts. And Australia is testing a filtering system for both child pornography and material that advocates terrorism.

The outcry in both countries, however, has been tremendous, both on technical grounds — filtering can slow down Internet speed — and civil liberties grounds. "Other countries using similar systems to monitor Internet traffic have blacklisted political critics," wrote an Australian newspaper columnist. "Is this really the direction we want our country to be heading? Communist China anyone? Burma? How about North Korea?"[24]

Ultimately, filtering just may not be that effective. Determined Internet users can easily circumvent a national filter and access banned material that is legal elsewhere. And filtering cannot capture the dynamic parts of the Internet: the chat rooms, video sharing sites and blogs, for instance.

Even some governments with established filtering laws seem reluctant to remove terrorist sites. The government owns Singapore's Internet providers and screens all Web sites for content viewed as " 'objectionable' or a potential threat to national security."[25] Yet Osman, of the Nanyang Technological University, says the government is not blocking Web sites that support terrorism. "I can still get access to many of them," she says, "so a lot of other people can, too."

In fact, counterterrorism officials around the world often prefer to monitor and infiltrate blogs, chat rooms, discussion forums and other Web sites where terrorists and sympathizers converse. If the sites remain active, they can be mined for intelligence.

"One reason [for not shutting down sites] is to take the temperature, to see whether the level of conversation is going up or down in terms of triggering an alert among security agencies," says Anthony Bergin, director of research at the Australian Strategic Policy Institute.

Another purpose is to disrupt terrorist attacks, says Bergin. Just recently, the violent postings of Texas resident Hosan Maher Husein Smadi to an extremist chat room attracted the attention of the FBI, which was monitoring the site. Agents set up a sting operation and arrested the 19-year-old Jordanian in late September after he allegedly tried to detonate what he thought was a bomb, provided by an undercover agent, in the parking garage beneath a Dallas skyscraper.[26]

Should Internet companies do more to stop terrorists' use of the Web?

Between 100 and 200 Web sites are the core "fountains of venom," says Yigal Carmon, president of the Middle East Media Research Institute, headquartered in Washington, D.C., with branch offices in Europe, Asia and the Middle East. "All the rest, are replication and duplication. You need to fight a few hundred sites, not thousands."

And many of these sites, he says, are hosted in the West. American hosting services, for instance, are often cheaper, have sufficient bandwidth to accommodate large video files and enjoy free-speech protection. But the companies often don't know they are hosting a site that, if not illegal, is perhaps violating their terms-of-service agreements.

Most Internet Service Providers, Web hosting companies, file-sharing sites and social networking sites have terms-of-service agreements that prohibit certain content. For instance, the Yahoo! Small Business Web hosting service states that users will not knowingly upload, post, e-mail, transmit or otherwise distribute any content that is "unlawful, harmful, threatening, abusive, harassing, tortious, defamatory, vulgar, obscene, libelous, invasive of another's privacy, hateful or racially, ethnically or otherwise objectionable."

It also specifically forbids users from utilizing the service to "provide material support or resources . . . to any organization(s) designated by the United States government as a foreign terrorist organization."

But Yahoo! also makes clear that it does not pre-screen content and that "You, and not Yahoo!, are entirely responsible for all Content that you upload, post, transmit, or otherwise make available."[27]

Some policy makers want Internet companies to begin screening the sites they host. Last year in the U.K., for instance, the House of Commons' Culture, Media and Sport Select Committee recommended that the "proactive review of content should be standard practice for sites hosting user-generated content."[28]

Internet companies, as well as civil libertarians and privacy advocates, disagree. "We do not think that ISPs should monitor anything since they are just in the business of transferring bits and bytes," says Rotert of EuroISPA. "We still believe in privacy laws."

David McClure, president and CEO of the U.S. Internet Industry Association, concurs. "If I'm a Web hoster, it is not my job to go snooping through the files and pages that people put on those Web sites," says McClure. "It's my job to keep the servers and the hosting service running." And, according to McClure, no U.S. law compels them to do more. Under the Telecommunications Act of 1996, McClure says, companies that host Web sites are not legally responsible for their content.

Still, ISPs and Web hosting companies do remove sites that violate their terms-of-service agreements, once

AP Photo/Sankei Shimbum/Kiyohiro Oku

Members of the Peruvian revolutionary movement Tupac Amaru flash victory signs after seizing the Japanese ambassador's residence in Lima in December 1996, along with hundreds of hostages. The morning after the seizure, the rebels launched a new era in terrorist media operations by posting a 100-page Web site, based in Germany. As the four-month siege dragged on, the group updated the site periodically, using a laptop and a satellite telephone. The hostages were eventually rescued in a raid by the Peruvian military.

they are aware of them. Since 9/11 a variety of private watchdog groups — like the SITE Intelligence Group and Internet Haganah — have made it their business to track jihadi Web sites.

Some anti-jihadist activists, like Aaron Weisburd — who created and runs Internet Haganah — have even contacted ISPs in an effort to shame them into taking down sites. Perhaps hundreds of sites have been removed with his help. "It is rare to find an Internet company that does not care or that actively supports the terrorist cause," he says.

Weisburd says some sites should be left online because they are good sources of intelligence, "while many other sites can — and arguably should — be taken down." He says the main reason to remove them is not to get them off the Internet permanently — which is extremely difficult to do — but to track individuals as they open new accounts in order to gather evidence and prosecute them.

But ISPs don't always follow through. "Even when you get a complaint about a Web site that may be violating the terms of service, many Web hosting services may

be unlikely to pursue it," says McClure. Investigating complaints is time-consuming and expensive, he says, and "once you start pursuing each complaint, you are actively involved in monitoring, and the complaints will skyrocket."

To monitor how the big Internet platforms respond to user complaints, Neumann, of King's College, suggests forming an Internet Users Panel, which could name and shame companies that don't take users' complaints seriously. "We don't want the panel to be a government body," says Neumann. "We are proposing a body that consists of Internet users, Internet companies and experts." It could publicize best practices, he says, and act as an ombudsman of last resort. ISPs would fund the panel.

But Neumann's proposal does not sit well with the ISPs. "A lot of people propose that ISPs do a lot of things," says McClure, "and what they want is for ISPs to do a lot of work for nothing."

Carmon also objects to relying on ISPs and Web hosting companies to respond to user complaints. "It's a totally untrustworthy system because you don't know who is making the complaint and why," Carmon says. "I issue a complaint against your Web site, but I may be settling an account against you, I may be your competitor in business." So ISPs must be very careful in evaluating complaints, which takes time, he says; ISPs don't want to be sued.

Instead, Carmon proposes creating what he calls a Civic Action Committee, based at an accredited research organization, which would monitor the Web and recommend sites that ISPs should consider closing. The committee would be made up of "intellectuals, writers, authors, people known for their moral standing, activists and legislators from different political parties," says Carmon.

Rotert is doubtful. "The ISPs in Europe would follow only government requests for notice and takedown procedures," he says, "because the ISPs know they cannot be held liable for destroying a business by taking down a site if the order came from the police."

Conway, of Dublin City University, has another objection to private policing of the Internet. "The capacity of private, political and economic actors to bypass the democratic process and to have materials they find politically objectionable erased from the Internet is a matter of concern," she said. Governments might want to consider legislation not just to regulate the Internet — "perhaps, for example, outlawing the posting and dissemination of beheading videos — but also writing into law more robust protections for radical political speech."[29]

Does cyberterrorism pose a serious threat?

Last year Pakistani President Asif Ali Zardari issued the following decree: "Whoever commits the offence of cyberterrorism and causes death of any person shall be punishable with death or imprisonment for life."[30]

In March India's cabinet secretary warned an international conference that cyber attacks and cyberterrorism are looming threats. "There could be attacks on critical infrastructure such as telecommunications, power distribution, transportation, financial services, essential public utility services and others," said K. M. Chandrasekhar. "The damage can range from a simple shutdown of a computer system to a complete paralysis of a significant portion of critical infrastructure in a specific region or even the control nerve centre of the entire infrastructure."[31]

Politicians, counterterrorism officials and security experts have made similarly gloomy predictions about cyberterrorism since 9/11 — and even before. But to date there have been no such attacks, although an ex-employee of a wastewater treatment plant in Australia used a computer and a radio transmitter to release sewage into parks and resort grounds in 2000.

Cyberterrorism is generally defined as highly damaging computer attacks by private individuals designed to generate terror and fear to achieve political or social goals. Thus, criminal hacking — no matter how damaging — conducted to extort money or for bragging rights is not considered cyberterrorism. (Criminal hacking is common. A year ago, for instance, criminals stole personal credit-card information from the computers of RBS WorldPay and then used the data to steal $9 million from 130 ATMs in 49 cities around the world.[32]) Likewise, the relatively minor denial-of-service attacks and Web defacements typically conducted by hackers aligned with terrorist groups also is not considered cyberterrorism.[33]

Skeptics say cyberterrorism poses only a slim threat, in part because it would lack the drama of a suicide attack or an airplane crash. "Let's say terrorists cause the lights to go out in New York City or Los Angeles, something that has already happened from weather conditions or human error," says Conway, of Dublin City University. "That is not going to create terror," she says, because those systems have been shown they can rapidly recover. Besides, she adds, terrorist groups tend to stick with what they know, which are physical attacks. "There is evolution but not sea changes in their tactics."

Even if terrorists wanted to launch a truly destructive and frightening cyber attack, their capabilities are very limited, says Irving Lachow, a senior research professor at the National Defense University in Washington, D.C. "They would need a multidisciplinary team of people to pull off a cyberterrorism attack," he says.

"A lot of these critical facilities are very complicated, and they have hundreds of systems," he continues. To blow up a power plant, for instance, a terrorist group would need an insider who knows which key computer systems are vulnerable, a team of experienced hackers to break into these systems, engineers who understand how the plant works so real damage can be done, a computer simulation lab to practice and lots of time, money and secrecy.

"At the end of the day, it's a lot easier just to blow something up," Lachow says.

But others fear that as governments continue to foil physical attacks, terrorists will expand their tactics to include cyberterrorism. Some analysts warn that terrorists could purchase the necessary expertise from cyber criminals. That, said Steven Bucci, IBM's lead researcher for cyber security, would be "a marriage made in Hell."[34]

According to Bucci, cybercrime is "a huge (and still expanding) industry that steals, cheats and extorts the equivalent of many billions of dollars every year." The most insidious threat, he said, comes from criminal syndicates that control huge botnets: worldwide networks of unwitting personal computers used for denial-of-service attacks, e-mail scams and distributing malicious software.[35]

The syndicates often rent their botnets to other criminals. Some analysts fear it's only a matter of time before a cash-rich terrorist group hires a botnet for its own use. "The cyber capabilities that the criminals could provide would in short order make any terrorist organization infinitely more dangerous and effective," said Bucci, and the permutations are "as endless as one's imagination."

Governments Now Prosecute Suspected Online Terrorists

New laws apply to online activities.

Governments around the world have prosecuted suspected terrorists before they carry out acts of violence, but not many have been prosecuted solely for their alleged online activities in support of terrorism.

Those cases have been hampered by concerns about restricting free speech, the desire to monitor terrorist-linked sites for intelligence and the difficulty of identifying individuals online. Here are some examples of such cases:

Sami Al-Hussayen — A 34-year-old graduate student in computer science at the University of Idaho, Al-Hussayen was arrested in February 2003 and accused of designing, creating and maintaining Web sites that provided material support for terrorism. It was the U.S. government's first attempt at using statutes prohibiting material support for terrorism to prosecute activity that occurred exclusively online. The definition of "material support" used by the prosecutors had been expanded under the Patriot Act of 2001 to include "expert advice or assistance."

Al-Hussayen had volunteered to run Web sites for two Muslim charities and two Muslim clerics. But prosecutors alleged that messages and religious fatwas on the sites encouraged jihad, recruited terrorists and raised money for foreign terrorist groups. It didn't matter that Al-Hussayen had never committed a terrorist act or that he hadn't written the material. Prosecutors said it was enough to prove that he ran the Web sites and knew the messages existed.

Jurors were not convinced, however. They acquitted Al-Hussayen in June 2004. "There was no direct connection in the evidence they gave us — and we had boxes and boxes to go through — between Sami and terrorism," said one juror.[1]

The case attracted national attention, and according to University of Idaho law professor Alan Williams, "triggered a heated debate focused mainly on a key question: Were Al-Hussayen's Internet activities constitutionally protected free speech or did they cross the line into criminal and material support to terrorism?"[2]

The U.S. Supreme Court is scheduled to hear challenges to the material support statute — which critics complain is too vague — in two related cases this session.[3]

Younis Tsouli — In late 2005, British police arrested 22-year-old Tsouli, a Moroccan immigrant and student who prosecutors alleged was known online as "Irhaby 007" — or Terrorist 007. The government linked Tsouli and his accomplices Waseem Mughal and Tariq al-Daour to "the purchase, construction and maintenance of a large number of Web sites and Internet chat forums on which material was published which incited acts of terrorist murder, primarily in Iraq."[4]

Tsouli had been in active contact with al Qaeda in Iraq and was part of an online network that extended to Canada, the United States and Eastern Europe. In July 2007, Tsouli, Mughal and Al-Daour "became the first men to plead guilty to inciting murder for terrorist purposes" under the U.K.'s Terrorism Act of 2000.[5]

Samina Malik — In November 2007 the 23-year-old shop assistant became the first woman convicted of terrorism in the United Kingdom when she was found guilty of "possessing information of a kind likely to be useful to a person committing or preparing an act of terrorism."[6]

Malik had downloaded and saved on her hard drive *The Terrorist's Handbook*, *The Mujahideen Poisons Handbook* and

---

For example, terrorists could "open the valves at a chemical plant near a population center," replicating the deadly 1984 chemical accident in Bhopal, India.[36]

And a full-fledged cyberterrorism attack is not the only disturbing possibility, say Bucci and others. Perl at the Organization for Security and Co-operation believes terrorists are much more likely to use a cyber attack to amplify the destructive power of a physical attack. "One of the goals of terrorism is to create fear and panic," says Perl, "and not having full access to the Internet could greatly hamper governments' response to a series of massive, coordinated terrorist incidents." For example,

other documents that appeared to support violent jihad. She had also written violent poems about killing nonbelievers. Her defense portrayed her as a confused young woman assuming a persona she thought was "cool."

Her conviction sparked public outrage. Muhammed Abdul Bari, secretary general of the Muslim Council of Britain, said, "Many young people download objectionable material from the Internet, but it seems if you are Muslim then this could lead to criminal charges, even if you have absolutely no intention to do harm to anyone else." An appeals court later overturned her conviction and clarified a new requirement that suspects must have a clear intent to engage in terrorism.[7]

Ibrahim Rashid — In 2007 German prosecutors charged the Iraqi Kurdish immigrant with waging a "virtual jihad" on the Internet. They argued that by posting al-Qaeda propaganda on chat rooms, Rashid was trying to recruit individuals to join al Qaeda and participate in jihad. It was Germany's first prosecution of an Islamic militant for circulating propaganda online.[8]

"This case underscores how thin the line is that Germany is walking in its efforts to aggressively target Islamic radicals," wrote Shawn Marie Boyne, a professor at Indiana University's law school. "While active membership in a terrorist organization is a crime . . . it is no longer a crime to merely sympathize with terrorist groups or to distribute propaganda."[9] Thus, the prosecution had to prove that Rashid's postings went beyond expressing sympathy and extended to recruiting. The court found him guilty in June 2008.

Saïd Namouh — On Oct. 1, the 36-year-old Moroccan resident of Quebec was convicted under Canada's Anti-Terrorism Act of four charges largely related to his online activities. In March 2007 he had helped publicize a video warning Germany and Austria that they would suffer a bomb attack if they didn't withdraw their troops from Afghanistan. He also distributed violent videos on behalf of Global Islamic Media Front, a propaganda arm of al Qaeda. Intercepted Internet chats revealed Namouh's plans to explode a truck bomb and die a martyr. "Terrorism is in our

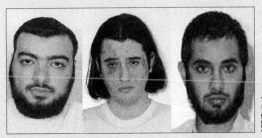

Tariq al-Daour, Younis Tsouli and Waseem Mughal (left to right), in 2007 became the first to plead guilty to inciting murder for terrorist purposes online under the U.K.'s Terrorism Act of 2000.

blood, and with it we will drown the unjust," Namouh said online.[10]

— *Barbara Mantel*

[1] Maureen O'Hagan, "A terrorism case that went awry," seattletimes. com, Nov. 22, 2004, http://seattletimes.nwsource.com/html/localnews/2002097570_sami22m.html.

[2] Alan Williams, "Prosecuting Website Development Under the Material Support in Terrorism Statutes: Time to Fix What's Broken," *NYU Journal of Legislation & Public Policy*, 2008, p. 366.

[3] The cases are *Holder v. Humanitarian Law Project; Humanitarian Law Project v. Holder*, 08-1498; 09-89. See http://onthedocket.org/cases/2009.

[4] Elizabeth Renieris, "Combating Incitement to Terrorism on the Internet: Comparative Approaches in the United States and United Kingdom and the Need for an International Solution," *Vanderbilt Journal of Entertainment and Technology Law*, vol. 11:3:673, p. 698, 2009.

[5] *Ibid.*

[6] *Ibid.*

[7] *Ibid.*, pp. 699-700.

[8] Shawn Marie Boyne, "The Criminalization of Speech in an Age of Terror," working paper, June 12, 2009, p. 7, http://ssrn.com/abstract=1418496.

[9] *Ibid.*

[10] Graeme Hamilton, "Quebec terror plotter undone by online activities," *National Post*, Oct. 1, 2009, www.nationalpost.com/news/story.html?id=2054720.

terrorists might try to disable the emergency 911 system while blowing up embassies.

Some experts are particularly concerned that al Qaeda could launch a coordinated attack on key ports while simultaneously disabling their emergency-response systems, in order to immobilize the trade-dependant global economy. Al-Qaeda leaders have made it clear that destroying the industrialized world's economy is one of the group's goals.

But Dorothy Denning, a professor of conflict and cyberspace at the Naval Postgraduate School in Monterey, Calif., said, "Terrorists do not normally integrate multiple modes of attack." If coordinating cyber and physical attacks did become their goal, Denning would expect to see evidence of failed attempts, training, discussions and planning. "Given terrorists' capabilities today in the cyber domain, this seems no more imminent than other acts of cyberterror," she said. "At least in the near future, bombs remain a much larger threat than bytes."[37]

But that doesn't mean critical infrastructure is secure from cyber criminal syndicates or nation-states, which do have the technical know-how, funds and personnel to launch a damaging attack, Denning said. "Even if our critical infrastructures are not under imminent threat by terrorists seeking political and social objectives," she said, "they must be protected from harmful attacks conducted for other reasons, such as money, revenge, youthful curiosity and war."[38]

BACKGROUND

Growth and Evolution

After seizing the Japanese embassy in Lima, Peru, on Dec. 17, 1996, the Tupac Amaru communist rebels "launched a new era in terrorist media operations," wrote Denning. The next morning the group had a Web site with more than 100 pages up and running out of Germany, which it updated using a laptop and a satellite telephone.[39]

"For the first time, terrorists could bring their message to a world audience without mediation by the established press or interference by the government," Denning said. They could offer the first news accounts to the media, and they could use the Web site to communicate directly with their members and supporters. "The advantage the Web offered was immeasurable and recognized by terrorist groups worldwide."[40]

By the end of 1999, nearly all of the 30 organizations designated by the U.S. State Department as foreign terrorist organizations had a presence on the Internet. By 2005, there were more than 40 designated terrorist groups and more than 4,300 Web sites serving them and their supporters. Today, the number of such Web sites exceeds 7,000, according to Weimann, of Haifa University.[41]

Of these groups, Islamic terrorists have perhaps made the most use of the Internet. When al Qaeda suffered defeat in Afghanistan directly after 9/11, its recruiters in Europe "who had previously encouraged others to travel to mujahidin training camps in Afghanistan, Bosnia-Herzegovina and Chechnya began radically changing their message," wrote Kohlmann, of the NEFA Foundation. "Their new philosophy emphasized the individual nature and responsibility of jihad."[42] Recruits did not necessarily have to travel abroad; they could learn what they needed online.

Thus the Internet became a vital means for communication amid a global law enforcement clampdown on suspected terrorists.

Al Qaeda's first official Web site was the brainchild of a senior Saudi operative — and one-time Osama bin Laden bodyguard — Shaykh Youssef al-Ayyiri. The site contained audio and video clips of the al-Qaeda leader, justification for the 9/11 attacks and poetry glorifying the attackers and — on its English version — a message to the American people.[43]

After al-Ayyiri's 2003 death during a clash with Saudi security forces, his top lieutenant, Abdelaziz al-Muqrin, took control. He was a "firm believer in using the Web to disseminate everything from firsthand accounts of terrorist operations to detailed instructions on how to capture or kill Western tourists and diplomats," according to Kohlmann. Before he was killed by Saudi forces in 2004, al-Muqrin created several digital magazines, including *Sawt al-Jihad*, or *The Voice of Jihad*. The author of an article in its inaugural issue told readers, "The blood [of the infidels] is like the blood of a dog and nothing more."[44]

While al Qaeda's Saudi Arabian network pioneered the use of online publications, Kohlmann said, "The modern revolution in the terrorist video market has occurred in the context of the war in Iraq and under the watchful eye of Jordanian national Abu Musab al-Zarqawi." Until his death in 2006, Zarqawi led al Qaeda in Iraq and was known for "his penchant for and glorification of extreme violence — particularly hostage beheadings and suicide bombings," many of them captured on video, including the murder of American civilian contractor Nicholas Berg.[45]

"Images of orange-clad hostages became a headline-news staple around the world — and the full, raw videos of their murders spread rapidly around the Web."[46]

Content on militant Islamist Web sites in Southeast Asia tends to "mimic the contents and features of their Arabic and Middle Eastern online counterparts," according

CHRONOLOGY

1990s *Terrorist groups discover the Internet's usefulness for fundraising and publicity.*

1996 After seizing the Japanese embassy in Lima, Peruvian revolutionary movement Tupac Amaru creates a Web site to publicize its actions.

1997 Sri Lanka's Tamil Tigers use stolen Sheffield University faculty members' computer IDs and passwords to solicit donations.

1998 Researchers looking for online terrorism sites discover al Qaeda's Web site, www.alneda.com.

1999 Nearly all 30 U.S.-designated foreign terrorist organizations have an Internet presence.

2000-2005 *Extremist Web sites and discussion forums multiply; first prosecution of man accused of providing material online in support of terrorists fails.*

July 20, 2000 Terrorism Act of 2000 makes it illegal in the U.K. to collect, make or possess information likely to be used in terrorism.

2001 The 9/11 attackers use the Internet to research flight schools and flights and to coordinate their actions. On Oct. 26, 2001, President George W. Bush signs the USA Patriot Act, which prohibits "material support" for terrorists.

2003 Abdelaziz al-Muqrin, leader of al Qaeda in Saudi Arabia, pioneers several digital magazines, including *Sawt al-Jihad* (*The Voice of Jihad.*)

2004 Video of the decapitation of kidnapped U.S. businessman Nicholas Berg is released on a Malaysian Web site.... University of Idaho graduate student Sami Omar al-Hussayen is acquitted of fostering terrorism online after his lawyers raise freedom of expression issues. Autobiography of Imam Samudra, mastermind of the 2002 Bali nightclub bombings that killed 202, promotes online credit-card fraud to raise funds.... Saudi Arabia launches the Sakinah Campaign, in which Islamic scholars steer religious questioners away from online extremists.

2005 YouTube, launched in February, quickly becomes repository for jihadist video content and commentary.

More than 4,000 Web sites connected to terrorist groups are on the Internet.

2006-Present *Governments reauthorize and expand antiterrorism laws; U.K. begins prosecuting those who use the Internet to "incite" others to commit terrorist acts.*

2006 President Bush reauthorizes Patriot Act.... U.K. passes Terrorism Act of 2006, outlawing encouragement or glorification of terrorism; civil libertarians raise concerns about free speech.... U.S. State Department creates Digital Outreach Team with two Arabic-speaking employees who converse online with critics of U.S. policies.

2007 EU police agency Europol begins "Check the Web" program, in which member states share in monitoring and evaluating terrorists' Web sites.... In July, U.K. resident Younis Tsouli pleads guilty to inciting terrorism after he and two associates used stolen credit cards to register Web site domains that promote terrorisim.... Samina Malik becomes the first woman convicted of terrorism in the U.K. for having documents that support violent jihad on her computer. A court of appeals later overturns her conviction, questioning her intent to engage in terrorism.

2008 Three important Islamist terrorist discussion forums disappear from the Internet; analysts assume counterterrorism agencies bombarded the sites with denial-of-service attacks.... On Nov. 6, Pakistan's president makes cyberterrorism punishable with death or life imprisonment.... In its first prosecution for promoting terrorism online, a German court finds Iraqi Kurdish immigrant Ibrahim Rashid guilty of waging a "virtual jihad" for attempting to recruit individuals online to join al Qaeda and participate in jihad.

2009 Canadian resident Saïd Namouh is convicted on Oct. 1 of planning terrorist acts and distributing jihadist propaganda via the Internet.... On Oct. 26 Jordanian teenager Hosam Maher Husein Smadi pleads not guilty of plotting to blow up a Dallas skyscraper on Sept. 24. FBI agents had been keeping tabs on Smadi after discovering him on an extremist Web site earlier this year.... Researchers are tracking more than 7,000 Web sites connected to terrorist groups and their supporters.

'Terrorists Are Trying to Attract Young Recruits'

An interview with the director of the Dark Web project.

The University of Arizona's Dark Web project, funded by the National Science Foundation, studies international terrorism using automated computer programs. The project has amassed one of the world's largest databases on extremist/terrorist-generated Internet content. Author Barbara Mantel recently interviewed Hsinchun Chen, the project's director.

CQ: What is the purpose of Dark Web?

HC: We examine who terrorists talk to, what kind of information they disseminate, what kind of new violent ideas they have, what kind of illegal activities they plan to conduct. We're looking at Web sites, forums, chat rooms, blogs, social networking sites, videos and virtual worlds.

CQ: How difficult is it to find terrorist content on the Web?

HC: From Google you can find some, but you won't be able to get into the sites that are more relevant, more intense and more violent.

CQ: So how do sympathizers find these sites?

HC: Typically people are introduced by word of mouth, offline. And there are different degrees of openness on these sites.

CQ: For example?

HC: There are many sites that require an introduction; they may require a password; moderators may also ask a series of questions to see if you are from the region, if you are real and if you are in their targeted audience.

CQ: How does the Dark Web project find these sites?

HC: We have been collaborating for six or seven years with many terrorism study centers all around the world, and they have been monitoring these sites for some time. So they know how to access these Web sites and whether they are legitimate forums. But most of them do not have the ability to collect all the content; they can do manual review and analysis.

So these researchers will give us the URLs of these sites, and they'll give us the user names and passwords they've been using to gain access. Once we get this information, we load it into our computer program, and the computers will spit out every single page of that site and download that into our database.

CQ: How much material are we talking about?

HC: The researchers we work with can analyze maybe hundreds or thousands of pages or messages, but we collect and analyze maybe half a million to 10 million pages easily.

CQ: How do you know that a site is actually linked to a terrorist group or supporter?

HC: Remember we start off with the URLs that terrorism researchers think are important. We also do "crawling" to find new sites. Any Web site will have links to other sites, and by triangulating those links from legitimate sites, we can locate other legitimate sites.

CQ: After finding the content, do you analyze it?

HC: Our claim to fame is analysis. We have techniques that look at social network linkages, that categorize the content into propaganda, training, recruiting, etc., and techniques that determine the sophistication of Web sites. We have a technique that looks at the extent of the violent sentiment in these sites and techniques that can determine authorship.

---

to a study from the Australian Strategic Policy Institute. "Although they aren't yet on par in operational coordination and tradecraft, they are catching up."[47]

Between 2006 and July 2007, extremist content on radical Bahasa Indonesia (the official language of Indonesia) and Malay language Web sites consisted of propaganda from al Qaeda and the Indonesian jihadist group Jemaah Islamiyah. The sites celebrated mujahidin victories, aired local grievances linked to the global jihad and posted highly selective Koranic verses used to justify acts of terror. In

August 2007, one of the first postings of instructions on computer hacking appeared, and in the first four months of 2008 the first bomb-making manual, bomb-making video and a password-protected forum emerged.[48] (*See box, p. 78.*)

Not all terrorist organizations use the Internet to showcase violence. Many, such as FARC (Revolutionary Armed Forces of Colombia), focus on human rights and peace. "In contrast to al Qaeda's shadowy, dynamic, versatile and often vicious Web sites," wrote Weimann, "the

CQ: *None of this is done manually?*

HC: Everything I talk about — almost 90 percent — is entirely automated.

CQ: *What trends you are noticing?*

HC: I'm not a terrorism researcher, but there are trends that we observe on the technology end. Terrorists are trying to attract young recruits, so they like to use discussion forums and YouTube, where the content is more multimedia and more of a two-way conversation. We also see many home-grown groups cropping up all over the world.

CQ: *Do you share this information with government agencies?*

HC: Many agencies — I cannot name them — and researchers from many countries are using the Dark Web forum portal.

CQ: *How does the portal work?*

HC: There is a consensus among terrorism researchers that discussion forums are the richest source of content, especially the forums that attract sometimes 50,000 members to 100,000 members. So we have created this portal that contains the contents from close to 20 different, important forums. And these are in English, Arabic and French. The French ones are found in North Africa.

We also embedded a lot of search, translation and analysis mechanisms in the portal. So now any analyst can use the content to see trends. For example, they can see what are the discussions about improvised explosive devices in Afghanistan, or they can look at who are the members that are interested in weapons of mass destruction.

CQ: *Are these forums mostly extremist jihadi forums?*

HC: Yes, they are. That's what analysts are primarily interested in. We are also creating another portal for multimedia content that will be available in another month or two. That would contain material from YouTube, for instance.

CQ: *Do you collect information from U.S. extremist sites?*

HC: We collect from animal-liberation groups, Aryan Nation and militia groups, but that is just for our research

AP Photo/John Miller

Hsinchun Chen oversees the University of Arizona's Dark Web project, which analyzes terrorists' online activities.

purposes. We don't make it available to outsiders. Government lawyers advise us against giving that kind of information out to them or to the outside world. It's a civil liberty issue.

CQ: *Even if that material is open source material, available to anyone who finds their Web site?*

HC: Even if it is open source.

FARC sites are more 'transparent,' stable and mainly focused on information and publicity."

Established in 1964 as the military wing of the Colombian Communist Party, FARC has been responsible for kidnappings, bombings and hijackings and funds its operations through narcotics trafficking.[49] Yet there are no violent videos of these attacks. Instead, FARC Web sites offer information on the organization's history and laws, its reasons for resistance, offenses perpetrated by the Colombian and U.S. governments, life as a FARC member

and women and culture. Weimann called the sophisticated FARC Web sites "an impressive example of media-savvy Internet use by a terrorist group."[50]

From Web 1.0 to 2.0

Terrorist content can now be found on all parts of the Internet, not just on official sites of groups like FARC and al Qaeda and their proxies. Chat rooms, blogs, social networking sites and user groups allow conversation and debate among a wide variety of participants.

Political Change Is Main Attack Motivation

Four out of six types of cyber attacks or threats are politically motivated. Attackers typically use "malware," or malicious software that spreads viruses, or denial-of-service attacks to disrupt Web sites of individuals, companies, governments and other targets.

Cyber Threat	Motivation	Target	Method
Cyberterror	Political or social change	Innocent victims	Computer-based violence or destruction
Hacktivism*	Political or social change	Decision-makers or innocent victims	Web page defacements or denial of service
Black Hat Hacking**	Ego, personal enmity	Individuals, companies, governments	Malware, viruses, worms or hacking
Cybercrime	Economic gain	Individuals, companies	Malware for fraud or identity theft; denial of service for blackmail
Cyber Espionage	Economic or political gain	Individuals, companies, governments	Range of techniques
Information War	Political or military gain	Infrastructures, information-technology systems and data (private or public)	Range of techniques

* Hacking to promote an activist's political ideology.

** Hacking just for the challenge, bragging rights or due to a personal vendetta.

Source: Franklin D. Kramer, Stuart H. Starr and Larry Wentz, eds., "Cyber *Threats:* Defining Terms," Cyberpower and National Security (2009)

"Yahoo! has become one of al Qaeda's most significant ideological bases of operations," wrote researchers Rita Katz and Josh Devon in 2003. "Creating a Yahoo! Group is free, quick and extremely easy.... Very often, the groups contain the latest links to jihadist Web sites, serving as a jihadist directory."[51] A Yahoo! user group is a hybrid between an electronic mailing list and a discussion forum. Members can receive posted messages and photos through e-mail or view the posts at the group's Web site.

While much of the original content on the terrorist-linked sites was text-based, videos began to play a much larger role after 2003, especially for militant Islamist organizations and their supporters. "Nevertheless, much of this video content remained quite difficult to access for Westerners and others, as it was located on Arabic-only Web sites" that were often frequently changing domain names and were therefore used "only by those who were strongly committed to gaining access," according to a study co-authored by Conway, of Dublin City University.[52]

But the advent of YouTube in 2005 changed the situation dramatically, Conway wrote, playing an increasing role in distributing terrorist content. Not only did YouTube become an immediate repository for large amounts of jihadist video content, but the social-networking aspects of the site allowed a dialogue between posters and viewers of videos.[53]

Terrorists-linked groups also have used mass e-mailings to reach broad audiences, according to Denning. "The Jihadist Cyber-Attack Brigade, for example, announced in May 2008 they had successfully sent 26,000 e-mails to 'citizens of the Gulf and Arab countries explaining the words of our leader Usama Bin Ladin.' "[54]

Terrorists and Cybercrime

Terrorists increasingly have turned to the Internet to raise funds, often through cybercrime. "We should be extremely concerned about the scope of the credit-card fraud problem involving terrorists," according to Dennis Lormel, a retired special agent in the FBI. Although there is "limited or no empirical data to gauge the extent of the problem . . . there are compelling signs that an epidemic permeates," he wrote.[55]

In his jailhouse autobiography, Imam Samudra — convicted of masterminding the 2002 nightclub bombings in Bali, Indonesia, that killed 202 people — includes a rudimentary outline of how to commit online credit-card fraud, or "carding."

"If you succeed at hacking and get into carding, be ready to make more money within three to six hours than the income of a policeman in six months," Samudra writes. "But don't do it just for the sake of money." Their main duty, he tells readers, is to raise arms against infidels, "especially now the United States and its allies."[56] Although Samudra's laptop revealed an attempt at carding, it's not clear he ever succeeded.

But others have. Younis Tsouli, a young Moroccan immigrant in London who made contact with al Qaeda online, and two associates used computer viruses and stolen credit-card accounts to set up a network of communication forums and Web sites that hosted "everything from tutorials on computer hacking and bomb making to videos of beheadings and suicide bombing attacks in Iraq," said Lormel.[57]

The three hackers ran up $3.5 million in charges to register more than 180 Web site domains at 95 different Web hosting companies and purchased hundreds of prepaid cellphones and more than 250 airline tickets. They also laundered money through online gaming sites.[58]

Even though both Samudra and Tsouli are in jail, "they left their successful tradecraft on Web pages and in chat rooms for aspiring terrorists to learn and grow from," noted Lormel.[59]

CURRENT SITUATION

Alternative Voices

Western governments and terrorism experts are concerned that the United

The Top 10 Jihadi Web Forums

The most influential jihadi online forums serve as virtual community centers for al Qaeda and other Islamic extremists, according to Internet Haganah — an online network dedicated to combating global jihad. Jihadi Web addresses, which are often blocked, change frequently.

1 al-Faloja
Highly respected among terrorists; focuses on the Iraq War and the Salafi-jihadi struggle.

2 al-Medad
Was associated with Abu Jihad al-Masri, the al-Qaeda propaganda chief killed in a U.S. missile strike in Pakistan on Oct. 30, 2008; disseminates Salafi-jihadi ideology.

3 al-Shouaraa
Originally named el-Shouraa, it was blocked, but later reemerged with a new name; has North African influences; no longer active.

4 Ana al-Muslm
Very active; was used by al Qaeda to communicate with Abu Musab al-Zarqawi (Osama bin Laden's deputy in Iraq) until he was killed by U.S. forces in 2006.

5 al-Ma'ark
Has been slowly and steadily building an online following in recent years.

6 al-Shamukh
Successor to al-Mohajrun, a militant Islamic organization that was banned in the U.K. in 2005; provides radio broadcasts.

7 as-Ansar
Features English and German invitation-only spin-off sites; a favorite among Western jihadists.

8 al-Mujahideen
Attracts a strong contingent of Hamas supporters, with an overall global jihad perspective; especially focused on electronic jihad.

9 al-Hanein
Has a significant amount of jihadi content tinged by Iraqi, Egyptian and Moroccan nationalism.

10 at-Tahaddi
Sunni jihadist; recruits from Somali, Taliban and other terrorist groups.

Source: "Top Ten List of Jihadi Forums," Internet Haganah, a project of The Society for Internet Research, Aug. 3, 2009, www.http://internet-haganah.com/harchives/006545.html; Jamestown Foundation

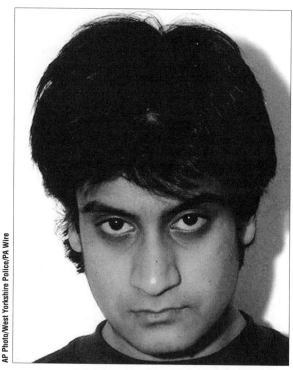

Hamaad Munshi — a British national convicted in 2008 of possessing materials likely to be used for terrorism — was 16 when he was arrested after participating in an online British extremist group. The trial revealed that Munshi had downloaded details on how to make napalm and grenades and wished to become a martyr by fighting abroad.

States and other nations are not providing a counter message to online militant Islamists.

"The militant Islamist message on the Internet cannot be censored, but it can be challenged," says Johnny Ryan, a senior researcher at the Institute of International and European Affairs in Dublin, Ireland. But governments and societies, he says, for the most part, have ceded the dialogue in cyberspace to extremists, who are highly skilled at crafting their message.

That message "is mostly emotional," according to Frank Cilluffo, director of the Homeland Security Policy Institute at The George Washington University in Washington, D.C. It "uses images, visuals and music to tell a powerful story with clear-cut heroes and villains."

Societies interested in countering that message should not shy away from emotion either, he argues. "Who are the victims of al Qaeda?" Cilluffo asks, "and why don't we know their stories?" Western and Arab-Muslim media

rarely reveal victims' names unless they are famous or foreign, he points out. Personal stories about victims "from the World Trade Center to the weddings, funerals, schools, mosques and hotels where suicide bombers have brought untold grief to thousands of families, tribes and communities throughout the Muslim world" could be told in online social networks, he suggested, "creating a Facebook of the bereaved that crosses borders and cultures."[60]

Raising doubts is "another powerful rhetorical weapon," says Ryan, who suggests exploiting the chat rooms and discussion forums frequented by prospective militants and sympathizers. Moderate Islamic voices should question the legitimacy of al Qaeda's offensive jihad, disseminate the arguments of Muslim scholars who renounce violence and challenge militant Islamists' version of historical relations between the West and Islam, according to Ryan.[61]

The U.S. Department of State has begun its own modest online effort. In November 2006 it created a Digital Outreach Team with two Arabic-speaking employees. The team now has 10 members who actively engage in conversations on Arabic-, Persian- and Urdu-language Internet sites, including blogs, news sites and discussion forums. Team members identify themselves as State Department employees, but instead of posting dry, policy pronouncements they create "engaging, informal personas for [their] online discussions." The team's mission is "to explain U.S. foreign policy and to counter misinformation," according to the State Department.[62]

No one knows the full impact of the team's efforts, but the project has come in for criticism. "They should be larger," says Matt Armstrong, an analyst and government advisor who writes a blog on public diplomacy at mountainrunner.us, "and they should be coordinated to a much greater degree with the production side of the State Department." The team's Internet conversations should directly shape a post on the State Department Web site or on its radio program, he says.

But Duncan MacInnes, principal deputy coordinator at the State Department's Bureau of International Information Programs, says the scale of the Digital Outreach Team is about right, although it could use one or two more Persian speakers and possibly expand into more languages. "Having too many people blogging in a fairly small blogosphere would raise our profile, and we felt [it] would create a reaction against us. You don't want to overdo it." Also, he says, the team does not work in isolation. It writes

Is cyberterrorism a significant global threat?

YES
Mohd Noor Amin
Chairman, International Multilateral Partnership Against Cyber Threats Selangor, Malaysia

Written for *CQ Researcher* November 2009

Alarm bells on cyberterrorism have been sounding for more than a decade, and yet, hacktivism aside, the world still has not witnessed a devastating cyber attack on critical infrastructure. Nothing has occurred that caused massive damage, injuries and fatalities resulting in widespread chaos, fear and panic. Does that mean the warnings were exaggerated?

On the contrary, the convergence of impassioned politics, hacktivism trends and extremists' growing technological sophistication suggests that the threat of cyberterrorism remains significant — if not more urgent — today. Although hacktivists and terrorists have not yet successfully collaborated to bring a country to its knees, there is already significant overlap between them. Computer-savvy extremists have been sharpening their skills by defacing and hacking into Web sites and training others to do so online. Given the public ambitions of groups like al Qaeda to launch cyber attacks, it would be folly to ignore the threat of a major cyber assault if highly skilled hackers and terrorists did conspire to brew a perfect storm.

Experts are particularly concerned that terrorists could learn how to deliver a simultaneous one-two blow: executing a mass, physical attack while incapacitating the emergency services or electricity grids to neutralize rescue efforts. The scenario may not be so far-fetched, judging from past cyber attacks or attempts, although a certain level of technical skill and access would be needed to paralyze part of a nation's critical infrastructure. However, as shown by an oft-cited 2000 incident in Australia, a single, disgruntled former employee hacked into a wastewater management facility's computer system and released hundreds of thousands of gallons of raw sewage onto Sunshine Coast resort grounds and a canal.

Vital industrial facilities are not impenetrable to cyber attacks and, if left inadequately secured, terrorists and hackers could wreak havoc. Similarly, the 2008 cyber attacks that caused multicity power outages around the world underscore the vulnerabilities of public utilities, particularly as these systems become connected to open networks to boost economies of scale.

If this past decade of terrorist attacks has demonstrated the high literacy level, technological capability and zeal of terrorists, the next generation of terrorists growing up in an increasingly digitized and connected world may hold even greater potential for cyberterrorism. After all, if it is possible to effect visibly spectacular, catastrophic destruction from afar and still remain anonymous, why not carry it out?

NO
Tim Stevens
Associate, Centre for Science and Security Studies, King's College London

Written for *CQ Researcher* November 2009

Cyberterrorism is the threat and reality of unlawful attacks against computer networks and data by an individual or a non-governmental group to further a political agenda. Such attacks can cause casualties and deaths through spectacular incidents, such as plane crashes or industrial explosions, or secondary consequences, such as crippled economies or disrupted emergency services.

We have seen many attempts to disrupt the online assets of governments, industry and individuals, but these have mercifully not yet caused the mass casualties predicted by the term "cyberterrorism." The assumption that terrorists might use cyberspace in such attacks is not in question, but the potential threat that cyberterrorism poses is accorded disproportionate weight in some circles.

Cyberterrorism resulting in civilian deaths is certainly one possible outcome of the convergence of technology and political aggression. That it has not happened yet is a function of two factors. First, the ongoing vigilance and operational sophistication of national security agencies have ensured that critical infrastructure systems have remained largely unbreached and secure. And second, like all self-styled revolutionaries, terrorists talk a good talk.

Although a terrorist group might possess both the intent and the skill-sets — either in-house, or "rented" — there is little evidence yet that any group has harnessed both to serious effect. Most attacks characterized as "cyberterrorism" so far have amounted to mere annoyances, such as Web site defacements, service disruptions and low-level cyber "skirmishing" — non-violent responses to political situations, rather than actions aimed at reaping notoriety in flesh and blood.

It would be foolish, however, to dismiss the threat of cyberterrorism. It would also be disingenuous to overstate it. Western governments are making strides towards comprehensive cyber security strategies that encompass a wide range of possible scenarios, while trying to overcome agency jurisdictional issues, private-sector wariness and the fact that civilian computer systems are now seen as "strategic national assets."

As it becomes harder to understand the complexities of network traffic, identify attack vectors, attribute responsibility and react accordingly, we must pursue integrated national and international strategies that criminalize the sorts of offensive attacks that might constitute cyberterrorism. But designating the attacks as terrorism is a taxonomic firewall we should avoid.

a biweekly report about the issues, concerns and misunderstandings members encounter online, which goes to hundreds of people inside the State Department.

Others question whether the government should be the one to hold this dialogue. "The state is not in a position to be the primary actor here because it lacks credibility in online forums," says Ryan.

"The best approach is to provide young people with the information and the intellectual tools to challenge this material themselves on various Web forums," says Bergin, of the Australian Strategic Policy Institute. "It's got to be provided by stakeholders in the Muslim community themselves, from community workers, religious figures and parents."

The Sakinah Campaign

Many terrorism analysts cite Saudi Arabia's Sakinah Campaign as a model program. Internet use in the kingdom has grown rapidly since access first became available there 10 years ago. Since 2000, the kingdom's total number of Internet users has risen from roughly 200,000 to more than 7 million today, out of an overall population of nearly 29 million.[63]

Meanwhile, extremist Web sites in the kingdom have multiplied from 15 sites in 1998 to several thousand today, even though the Saudi government controls Internet access and blocks sites featuring gambling, pornography and drug and alcohol use, according to Christopher Boucek, a researcher at the Carnegie Endowment for International Peace. Extremist sites "often appear faster than they can be identified and blocked," said Boucek.[64]

Responding to that trend, the Sakinah Campaign since 2004 has used volunteer Islamic scholars "to interact online with individuals looking for religious knowledge, with the aim of steering them away from extremist sources." These scholars have "highly developed understandings of extremist ideologies, including the religious interpretations used to justify violence and terrorism," according to Boucek.[65] The campaign is officially an independent, nongovernmental project, even though several government ministries encourage and support it.

According to Abdullah Ansary, a lawyer and former lecturer at King Abdul-Aziz University in Saudi Arabia, al Qaeda has issued several statements over the Internet cautioning their followers not to engage in dialogues with members of the Sakinah Campaign, a sign that the campaign is having an impact on al Qaeda's membership.[66] The campaign itself periodically releases the number of people it says it has turned away from extremism. In January 2008, it announced it had "convinced some 877 individuals (722 male and 155 female) to reject their radical ideology across more than 1,500 extremists Web sites."[67]

But in 2007, after the government arrested members of seven terrorist cells operating in the kingdom, several columnists complained that the Sakinah Campaign and other government supported programs trying to reform extremists were ineffective and not getting to the root of the problem. According to translations from the Middle East Media Research Institute, columnist Abdallah bin Bajad Al-'Utaibi wrote in the Saudi daily *Al-Riyadh*: "There are schoolteachers, imams in the mosques, preachers and jurisprudents who do nothing but spread hatred and *takfir** in our society. They should be prosecuted for their actions, which lay down the foundations for terrorism."[68]

Ansary said the government must make wider reforms if it wants to prevent young people from turning to extremism. The government must "speed up the process of political reform in the country, widening popular participation in the political process, improving communication channels of both the government and the public, creating effective communication among branches of government, continuing the efforts in overhauling the Saudi educational system and boosting the role of women in the society."[69]

In late 2006, the Sakinah Campaign expanded its role and created its own Web site designed to "serve as a central location for people to turn to online with questions about Islam."[70]

Government-funded Sites

Similar Web sites have been set up in other countries to offer alternative messages to terrorist propaganda.

The Islamic Religious Council of Singapore — the country's supreme Islamic authority, whose members are appointed by the country's president — has several interactive Web sites to counter extremist strands of Islam. The sites feature articles, blogs and documentary videos targeted at young people and host an online forum where religious scholars answer questions about Islam. One site specifically challenges the ideology of Jemaah Islamiyah, the jihadist group responsible for the deadly 2002 nightclub

---

* *Takfir* is the act of identifying someone as an unbeliever.

bombing in Bali and the July 2009 bombings of the Marriott and Ritz Carlton hotels in Jakarta. The organization wants to establish a pan-Islamic theocratic state across much of Southeast Asia.[71]

But the effectiveness of such sites is difficult to gauge. "To a certain extent it is helping to drown out extremist voices online," says Osman, of Nanyang Technological University in Singapore, "but for those who are actively seeking extremist ideology, these kinds of Web sites don't appeal to them."

A similar project in the United Kingdom also meets with skepticism. On its Web site, the Radical Middle Way calls itself "a revolutionary grassroots initiative aimed at articulating a relevant mainstream understanding of Islam that is dynamic, proactive and relevant to young British Muslims."[72] It rejects all forms of terrorism, and its site has blogs, discussions, videos, news and a schedule of its events in the U.K. Its two dozen supporters and partners are mostly Muslim organizations as well as the British Home Office, which oversees immigration, passports, drug policy and counterterrorism, among other things.

"We are arguing that this is not money well spent," says Neumann of King's College. "The kind of money the government is putting into the Web site is enormous, and the site doesn't attract that much traffic."

The government money has also caused at least some young people to question the group's credibility. One blogger called the group "the radical wrong way" and wrote that "because the funding source is so well known, large segments of alienated British Muslims will not have anything to do with this group. . . . If anything, such tactics will lead to even further alienation of young British Muslims — who will rightly point out that this kind of U.S./U.K.-funded version of Islam is just another strategy in the ongoing war on Islam."[73]

Neumann and Bergin recommend instead that governments give out many small grants to different Muslim organizations with ideas for Web sites and see if any can grow to significance without dependence on government funds.

In the end, individual governments' direct role in providing an online alternative narrative to terrorist ideology may, out of necessity, be quite small because of the credibility issue, say analysts. Instead, they say, governments could fund Internet literacy programs that discuss hate propaganda, adjust school curriculums to include

Above, an Internet café in Sydney. Many Australians oppose government plans to build what critics call the Great Aussie Firewall — a mandatory Internet filter that would block at least 1,300 Web sites prohibited by the government.

greater discussion of Islam and the West and encourage moderate Muslim voices to take to the Web. Cilluffo, of the Homeland Security Policy Institute, said the United Nations could lead the way, sponsoring a network of Web sites, publications and television programming.

"The United Nations can and should play a significant role," Cilluffo said, "bringing together victims to help meet their material needs and raising awareness by providing platforms through which to share their stories."[74]

OUTLOOK

Pooling Resources

Web sites that promote terrorism are here to stay, although governments and Internet companies will occasionally shut one down if it violates the law or a terms-of-service agreement. Such decisions can only be reached after prolonged monitoring and "must weigh the intelligence value against the security risk posed by the Web site," says Jordanian terrorism expert Bakier.

But monitoring the thousands of Web sites, discussion forums, chat rooms, blogs and other open sources of the Web requires trained personnel with expertise in the languages, cultures, belief systems, political grievances and organizational structures of the terrorist groups online. Because such personnel are scarce, most experts agree that nations should pool their resources. "It is hardly possible for one individual member state to cover all suspicious terrorism-related activities on the Internet," according to a European Union (EU) report.[75]

Good intentions aren't enough. "There are lots of conferences, lots of declarations, lots of papers, but in reality, you have different counterterrorism agencies not sharing information, competing, afraid of each other, sometimes in the same state and also across borders," says Haifa University's Weimann.

Europol, the EU police agency, began a program in 2007 called Check the Web, which encourages member nations to share in monitoring and evaluating open sources on the Web that promote or support terrorism. The online portal allows member nations to post contact information for monitoring experts; links to Web sites they are monitoring; announcements by the terrorist organizations they are tracking; evaluations of the sites being monitored and additional information like the possibility of legal action against a Web site.

Weimann, who calls the program a "very good idea and very important," says he cannot directly evaluate its progress, since access is restricted to a handful of counterterrorism officials in each member nation. But he does speak to counterterrorism experts at workshops and conferences, where he hears that "international cooperation — especially in Europe — is more theoretical than practical."

When asked if barriers exist to such cooperation, Dublin City University's Conway says, "Emphatically, yes! These range from protection-of-institutional-turf issues — on both a national and EU-wide basis — to potential legal constraints." For instance, she says, some member states' police are unsure whether or not they need a court order to monitor and participate in a Web forum without identifying themselves. Others disagree about the definition of a terrorist and what kinds of sites should be watched.

These barriers may not be the program's only problem. "It might be a disadvantage that so far just EU countries participate," according to Katharina von Knop, a professor of international politics at the University of the Armed Forces, in Munich, Germany, thus limiting the expertise available.[76]

NOTES

1. Abdul Hameed Bakier, "An Online Terrorist Training Manual — Part One: Creating a Terrorist Cell," *Terrorism Focus*, vol. 5, no. 13, The Jamestown Foundation, April 1, 2008. The ek-Is.org Web site has also gone under various other names, including ekhlass.org.

2. *Ibid.*

3. Bakier, *op. cit.*, "Part Two: Assassinations and Robberies," vol. 5, no. 14, April 9, 2008.

4. Bakier, *op. cit.*, "Part Three: Striking U.S. Embassies," vol. 5, no. 15, April 16, 2008.

5. Gabriel Weimann, *Terror on the Internet*, United States Institute of Peace Press (2006), p. 51.

6. *Ibid.*, p. 30.

7. University of Arizona, "Artificial Intelligence Lab Dark Web Project," www.icadl.org/research/terror/.

8. "The 9/11 Commission Report," www.9-11com mission.gov/report/index.htm.

9. Anne Stenersen, "The Internet: A virtual training camp?" Norwegian Defense Research Establishment, Oct. 26, 2007, p. 3, www.mil.no/multimedia/ archive/00101/Anne_Stenersen_Manu_101280a.pdf.

10. Dorothy Denning, "Terror's Web: How the Internet Is Transforming Terrorism," Handbook on Internet Crime, 2009, p. 19, http://faculty.nps.edu/deden nin/publications/Denning-TerrorsWeb.pdf.

11. *Ibid.*, p. 4.

12. "Violent Islamic Extremism, the Internet, and the Homegrown Terrorist Threat," U.S. Senate Committee on Homeland Security and Governmental Affairs, May 8, 2008, pp. 2, 13, http://hsgac.senate.gov/pub lic/_files/IslamistReport.pdf.

13. "Safeguarding Online: Explaining the Risk Posed by Violent Extremism," Office of Security and Counter Terrorism, Home Office, Aug. 10, 2009, p. 2, http:// security.homeoffice.gov.uk/news-publications/pub lication-search/general/Officers-esafety-leaflet-v5. pdf?view=Binary.

14. *Ibid.*

15. Peter Neumann and Tim Stevens, "Countering Online Radicalisation: A Strategy for Action," The International Centre for the Study of Radicalisation and Political Violence, Kings College London, 2009, p. 14, www.icsr.info/news/attachments/123676844 5ICSROnlineRadicalisationReport.pdf.

16. Clodagh Hartley, "Govt Can't Stop 'Web of Terror,' " *The Sun* (England), March 20, 2009, p. 2.

17. "Interview given by Mme. Michèle Alliot-Marie, French Minister of the Interior, to Le Figaro," French Embassy, Feb 1, 2008, www.ambafrance-uk.org/ Michele-Alliot-Marie-on-combating.html.

18. Greg Goth, "Terror on the Internet: A Complex Issue, and Getting Harder," IEEE Computer Society, March 2008, www2.computer.org/portal/web/csdl/ doi/10.1109/MDSO.2008.11.

19. Howard Altman, "Al Qaeda's Web Revival," *The Daily Beast*, Oct. 2, 2009, www.thedailybeast .com/blogs-and-stories/2009-10-02/is-this-al-qae das-website.

20. Gregory McNeal, "Cyber Embargo: Countering the Internet Jihad," *Case Western Reserve Journal of International Law*, vol. 39, no. 3, 2007-08, p. 792.

21. *Brandenburg v. Ohio*, www.oyez.org/cases/1960-1969/1968/1968_492/.

22. "Safeguarding Online: Explaining the Risk Posed by Violent Extremism," *op. cit.*, p. 3.

23. Elizabeth Renieris, "Combating Incitement to Terrorism on the Internet: Comparative Approaches in the United States and the United Kingdom and the Need for an International Solution," *Vanderbilt Journal of Entertainment and Technology Law*, vol. 11:3:673, 2009, pp. 687-688.

24. Fergus Watts, "Caught out by net plan," *Herald Sun* (Australia), Dec. 29, 2008, p. 20, www.heraldsun .com.au/opinion/caught-out-by-net-plan/story-e6frfifo-1111118423939.

25. Weimann, *op. cit.*, p. 180.

26. "Jordanian accused in Dallas bomb plot goes to court," CNN, Sept. 25, 2009, www.cnn.com/2009/ CRIME/09/25/texas.terror.arrest/index.html.

27. http://smallbusiness.yahoo.com/tos/tos.php.

28. Neumann and Stevens, *op. cit.*, p. 32.

29. Maura Conway, "Terrorism & Internet Governance: Core Issues," U.N. Institute for Disarmament Research, 2007, p.11. www.unidir.org/pdf/articles/ pdf-art2644.pdf.

30. Isambard Wilkinson, "Pakistan sets death penalty for 'cyber terrorism,' " *Telegraph.co.uk*, Nov 7, 2008, www.telegraph.co.uk/news/worldnews/asia/ pakistan/3392216/Pakistan-sets-death-penalty-for-cyber-terrorism.html.

31. "Cyber attacks and cyber terrorism are the new threats," *India eNews*, March 26, 2009, www.indiae-news.com/print/?id=187451.

32. Linda McGlasson, "ATM Fraud Linked in RBS WorldPay Card Breach," Bank info Security, Feb. 5, 2009, www.bankinfosecurity.com/articles.php?art_ id=1197.

33. Dorothy Denning, "A View of Cyberterrorism Five Years Later," 2007, pp. 2, 3, http://faculty.nps.edu/ dedennin/publications/Denning-TerrorsWeb.pdf.

34. Steven Bucci, "The Confluence of Cyber-Crime and Terrorism," Heritage Foundation, June 15, 2009, p. 6, www.heritage.org/Research/NationalSecurity/ upload/hl_1123.pdf.

35. *Ibid.*, p. 5.

36. *Ibid.*, p. 6.

37. Dorothy Denning, *op. cit.*, p. 15.

38. *Ibid.*

39. Denning, "Terror's Web: How the Internet is Transforming Terrorism," *op. cit.*, p. 2.

40. *Ibid.*

41. Weimann, *op. cit.*, p. 15.

42. Evan Kohlmann, " 'Homegrown' Terrorists: Theory and Cases in the War on Terror's Newest Front," *The Annals of the American Academy of Political and Social Science*, July 2008; 618; 95. p. 95.

43. Denning, "Terror's Web: How the Internet is Transforming Terrorism," *op. cit.*, p. 3.

44. Kohlmann, *op. cit.*, p. 101.

45. *Ibid.*

46. David Talbot, "Terror's Server," *Technology Review. com*, Jan. 27, 2005, www.militantislammonitor.org/ article/id/404.

47. Anthony Bergin, *et al.*, "Countering Internet Radicalisation in Southeast Asia," The Australian Strategic Policy Institute Special Report, March 2009, p. 5.

48. *Ibid.*, p. 6.

49. Weimann, *op. cit.*, pp. 75-76.

50. Weimann, *op. cit.*, p. 75.

51. Rita Katz and Josh Devon, "WWW.Jihad.com," *National Review Online*, July 14, 2003, http://nationalreview.com/comment/comment-katz-devon071403.asp.

52. Maura Conway and Lisa McInerney, "Jihadi Video & Auto-Radicalisation: Evidence from an Exploratory YouTube Study," 2008, p. 1, http://doras.dcu.ie/2253/2/youtube_2008.pdf.

53. *Ibid.*, p. 2.

54. Denning, "Terror's Web: How the Internet is Transforming Terrorism," *op. cit.*, p. 5.

55. Dennis Lormel, "Terrorists and Credit Card Fraud . . . A Quiet Epidemic," Counterterrorism Blog, Feb. 28, 2008, http://counterterrorismblog.org/2008/02/terrorists_and_credit_card_fra.php.

56. Alan Sipress, "An Indonesian's Prison Memoir Takes Holy War Into Cyberspace," *The Washington Post*, Dec. 14, 2004, p. A19, www.washingtonpost.com/wp-dyn/articles/A62095-2004Dec13.html.

57. Lormel, *op. cit.*

58. Dennis Lormel, "Credit Cards and Terrorists," Counterterrorism Blog, Jan. 16, 2008, http://counterterrorismblog.org/2008/01/credit_cards_and_terrorists.php.

59. Dennis Lormel, "Terrorists and Credit Card Fraud . . .," *op. cit.*

60. Frank Cilluffo and Daniel Kimmage, "How to Beat al Qaeda at Its Own Game," *Foreign Policy*, April 2009, www.foreignpolicy.com/story/cms.php?story_id=4820.

61. Johnny Ryan, "EU must take its anti-terrorism fight to the Internet," *Europe's World*, Summer 2007, www.europesworld.org/EWSettings/Article/tabid/191/ArticleType/ArticleView/ArticleID/21068/Default.aspx.

62. Digital Outreach Team, U.S. Department of State, www.state.gov/documents/organization/116709.pdf.

63. "Middle East Internet Usage and Population Statistics," *Internet World Stats*, www.internetworldstats.com/stats5.htm.

64. Christopher Boucek, "The Sakinah Campaign and Internet Counter-Radicalization in Saudi Arabia," *CTC Sentinel*, August 2008, p. 2, www.carnegieendowment.org/files/CTCSentinel_Vol1Iss9.pdf.

65. *Ibid.*, p. 1.

66. Abdullah Ansary, "Combating Extremism: A brief overview of Saudi Arabia's approach," *Middle East Policy*, Summer 2008, vol. 15, no. 2, p. 111.

67. *Ibid.*

68. Y. Admon and M. Feki, "Saudi Press Reactions to the Arrest of Seven Terrorist Cells in Saudi Arabia," Inquiry and Analysis, no. 354, MEMRI, May 18, 2007.

69. Ansary, *op. cit.*, p. 111.

70. Boucek, *op. cit.*, p. 3.

71. Bergin, *op. cit.*, p. 19.

72. www.radicalmiddleway.co.uk.

73. "A radical wrong way," Progressive Muslims: Friends of Imperialism And Neocolonialism, Oct. 31, 2006, http://pmunadebate.blogspot.com/2006/10/radical-wrong-way.html.

74. Cilluffo and Kimmage, *op. cit.*

75. "Council Conclusions on Cooperation to Combat Terrorist Use of the Internet ("Check the Web")," Council of the European Union, May 16, 2007, p. 3, http://register.consilium.europa.eu/pdf/en/07/st08/st08457-re03.en07.pdf.

76. Katharina von Knop, "Institutionalization of a Web-Focused, Multinational Counter-Terrorism Campaign," *Responses to Cyber Terrorism* (2008), p. 14.

BIBLIOGRAPHY

Books

Jewkes, Yvonne, and Majid Yar, eds., *The Handbook on Internet Crime*, Willan Publishing, 2009.
British criminology professors have compiled essays by leading scholars on issues and debates surrounding Internet-related crime, deviance, policing, law and regulation in the 21st century.

Kramer, Franklin D., Stuart H. Starr and Larry K. Wentz, eds., *Cyberpower and National Security*, Potomac Books, 2009.

Experts write about cyber power and its strategic implications for national security, including an assessment of the likelihood of cyberterrorism.

Sageman, Marc, *Leaderless Jihad: Terror Networks in the Twenty-First Century*, University of Pennsylvania Press, 2008.

A senior fellow at the Center on Terrorism, Counter-Terrorism, and Homeland Security in Philadelphia examines the impact of the Internet on global terrorism, including its role in radicalization, and strategies to combat terrorism in the Internet age.

Weimann, Gabriel, *Terror on the Internet*, United States Institute of Peace Press, 2006.

A professor of communication at Haifa University in Israel explores how terrorist organizations exploit the Internet to raise funds, recruit members, plan attacks and spread their message.

Articles

Boucek, Christopher, "The Sakinah Campaign and Internet Counter-Radicalization in Saudi Arabia," *CTC Sentinel*, August 2008.

Saudi Arabia enlists religious scholars to engage in dialogue on the Internet with individuals seeking out religious knowledge in order to steer them away from extremist beliefs.

Cilluffo, Frank, and Daniel Kimmage, "How to Beat al Qaeda at Its Own Game," *Foreign Policy*, April 2009, www.foreignpolicy.com.

Two American terrorism experts recommend using Web sites, chat rooms, social networking sites, broadcasting and print to tell the stories of Muslim victims of militant Islamist terror attacks.

Goth, Greg, "Terror on the Internet: A Complex Issue, and Getting Harder," *IEEE Distributed Systems Online*, vol. 9, no. 3, 2008.

Counterterrorism agencies cringe when posturing by politicians leads to the dismantling of terrorist Web sites they've been monitoring.

Labi, Nadya, "Jihad 2.0," *The Atlantic Monthly*, July/August, 2006.

With the loss of training camps in Afghanistan, terrorists turned to the Internet to find and train recruits.

Talbot, David, "Terror's Server — How radical Islamists use Internet fraud to finance terrorism and exploit the Internet for Jihad propaganda and recruitment," *Technology Review.com*, Jan. 27, 2008.

Terrorists use the Internet for fundraising, propaganda and recruitment, but government and the Internet industry responses are limited by law and technology.

Reports and Studies

Bergin, Anthony, *et al.*, "Countering Internet Radicalisation in Southeast Asia," Australian Strategic Policy Institute, March 2009.

The director of research at the institute traces the evolution of extremist and terrorist-linked content from static Web sites to the more dynamic and interactive parts of the Internet.

Boyne, Shawn Marie, "The Criminalization of Speech in an Age of Terror," Indiana University School of Law-Indianapolis, working paper, June 12, 2009.

A law professor compares prosecution of incitement to terror in Germany, the U.K. and the United States.

Conway, Maura, "Terrorism & Internet Governance: Core Issues," *Disarmament Forum*, 2007.

A terrorism expert at Dublin City University in Ireland explores the difficulties of Internet governance in light of terrorists' growing use of the medium.

Denning, Dorothy, "Terror's Web: How the Internet is Transforming Terrorism," Naval Postgraduate School, 2009.

A professor of conflict and cyberspace discusses the implications of shutting sites down versus continuing to monitor sites or encouraging moderate voices to engage in dialogue online with terrorist sympathizers.

Neumann, Peter R., and Tim Stevens, "Countering Online Radicalisation: A Strategy for Action," The International Centre for the Study of Radicalisation and Political Violence, 2009.

Shutting down terrorist sites on the Internet is expensive and counterproductive, according to the authors.

Renieris, Elizabeth, "Combating Incitement to Terrorism on the Internet," *Vanderbilt Journal of Entertainment and Technology Law*, vol. 11:3:673, 2009.

The author compares U.S. and U.K. laws used to prosecute incitement to terrorism on the Internet.

For More Information

Australian Strategic Policy Institute, 40 Macquarie St., Barton ACT 2600, Australia; (61) 2 6270 5100; www.aspi.org.au. Nonpartisan policy institute set up by the Australian government to study the country's defense and strategic policy choices.

EuroISPA, 39, Rue Montoyer, B-1000 Brussels, Belgium; (32) 2 503 2265; www.euroispa.org. World's largest association of Internet service providers.

Homeland Security Policy Institute, George Washington University, 2300 I St., N.W., Suite 721, Washington, DC 20037; (202) 994-2437; www.gwumc.edu/hspi. A think tank that analyzes homeland security issues.

Institute of International and European Affairs, 8 North Great Georges St., Dublin 1, Ireland; (353) 1 8746756; www.iiea.com. A think tank that analyzes how global and European Union policies affect Ireland.

International Centre for Political Violence and Terrorism Research, Nanyang Technological University, South Spine S4, Level B4, Nanyang Ave., Singapore 639798; (65) 6790 6982; www.pvtr.org. Studies threats and develops countermeasures for politically motivated violence and terrorism.

International Centre for the Study of Radicalisation, King's College London, 138-142 Strand, London, WC2R 1HH, United Kingdom; (44) 0 207 848 2098; http://icsr.info/index.php. A think tank set up by King's College London, the University of Pennsylvania, the Interdisciplinary Center Herzliya (Israel) and the Jordan Institute of Diplomacy.

Internet Haganah, http://internet-haganah.com/haganah/index.html. Tracks, translates and analyzes extremist Islamic sites on the Web.

The Jamestown Foundation, 1111 16th St., N.W., Suite #320, Washington, DC 20036; (202) 483-8888; www.jamestown.org. Informs policy makers about trends in societies where access to information is restricted.

Middle East Media Research Institute, P.O. Box 27837, Washington, DC 20038-7837; (202) 955-9070; www.memri.org. Provides translations of Arabic, Persian, Turkish and Urdu-Pashtu media and analyses political, ideological, intellectual, social, cultural and religious trends in the Middle East.

NEFA Foundation, (212) 986-4949; www1.nefafoundation.org. Exposes those responsible for planning, funding and executing terrorist activities, with a particular emphasis on Islamic militant organizations.

Norwegian Defence Research Establishment, FFI, P.O. Box 25, NO-2027 Kjeller, Norway; (47) 63 80 70 00; www.mil.no/felles/ffi/english. The primary institution responsible for defense-related research in Norway.

Organization for Security and Co-operation in Europe, Action Against Terrorism Unit, Wallnerstrasse 6, 1010 Vienna, Austria; (43) 1 514 36 6000; www.osce.org/atu. Coordinates anti-terrorism initiatives among European nations.

5

President Barack Obama called for new efforts to stop the spread of nuclear weapons during an address before the U.N. General Assembly on Sept. 23. The next day the Security Council called for nuclear reductions and disarmament and tighter controls on nuclear technology. Many experts warn that abolishing nuclear weapons would make the world less safe, in part by enabling terrorists and rogue states to threaten other nations.

From *CQ Researcher*,
October 2, 2009.

Nuclear Disarmament

Jennifer Weeks

Speaking to the United Nations General Assembly on Sept. 23, President Barack Obama pledged his administration would work with other nations to strengthen world peace and prosperity.

"First, we must stop the spread of nuclear weapons, and seek the goal of a world without them," Obama said. "If we fail to act, we will invite nuclear arms races in every region, and the prospect of wars and acts of terror on a scale that we can hardly imagine."[1]

It is an ambitious goal, especially for the United States. Nuclear weapons have been integral to U.S. defense policy since the end of World War II. Even today, nearly 20 years after the Cold War ended, the United States still spends more than $50 billion every year on nuclear armaments and related programs, including weapons systems, missile defenses and environmental and health costs from past nuclear weapons production.[2]

Many civilian and military experts say abolishing nuclear weapons is impossible. Moreover, they argue, doing so would make the world less safe, because rogue states and terrorists would feel freer to threaten other countries.

But in 2007, four men who had shaped U.S. national security policy for decades — both Democrats and Republicans — warned that relying on nuclear weapons to keep the peace was "becoming increasingly hazardous and decreasingly effective." The problem, said former secretaries of state Henry Kissinger and George Shultz, former Defense Secretary William Perry and former Senate Armed Services Committee Chairman Sam Nunn, was that countries like India, Pakistan, North Korea and Iran were seeking the bomb, and

Nuclear Weapons Network Spans Seven States

Eight nuclear facilities in seven states make up the U.S. nuclear weapons complex. Responsibilities at each site range from the design and production of the nation's nuclear arsenal to testing and improving bomb yield.

The U.S. Nuclear Weapons Network

1. **Pantex:** Tests, retrofits and repairs weapons in the stockpile and dismantles surplus nuclear weapons.

2. **Kansas City Plant:** Produces non-nuclear components for nuclear weapons.

3. **Y-12:** Produces and reworks nuclear weapon components and stores enriched uranium and plutonium.

4. **Savannah River:** Produces radioactive tritium to boost the yield of nuclear weapons.

5. **Los Alamos National Laboratory:** Designs and certifies the safety and reliability of the explosive cores of nuclear weapons; oversees refurbishment of all weapons in the stockpile.

6. **Lawrence Livermore National Laboratory:** Designs and certifies safety and reliability of nuclear weapons; conducts research on weapons physics.

7. **Sandia National Laboratory:** Designs the non-nuclear components of nuclear weapons.

8. **Nevada Test Site:** Performed nuclear tests until 1992; conducts underground sub-critical tests and maintains the capability to resume testing if so directed.

Source: "Nuclear Matters: A Practical Guide," Office of the Under Secretary of Defense for Acquisition, Technology and Logistics, 2008

President Obama agrees. His proposed fiscal 2010 budget eliminates funds for designing new nuclear warheads, which his predecessor, George W. Bush, had argued were needed to replace older weapons in the U.S. arsenal. On April 5, in Prague, Czechoslovakia, Obama laid out a broad agenda for moving toward nuclear abolitio n. First, he said, the U.S. would reduce the role of nuclear weapons in its own security strategy by:

- Negotiating new strategic (long-range) arms reductions with Russia;
- Ratifying a treaty ending nuclear weapons testing; and
- Seeking a new international treaty to end production of fissile materials for nuclear weapons.[4]

Obama also proposed strengthening the Nuclear Non-Proliferation Treaty (NPT), under which 188 nations have pledged not to seek nuclear weapons, by:

- Giving international inspectors more authority;
- Agreeing on consequences when nations break the rules; and
- Creating an international nuclear-fuel bank so countries with nuclear power reactors would not need nuclear technology to produce their own fuel.

Finally, Obama announced new actions to keep nuclear weapons away from terrorists, including measures to secure vulnerable nuclear materials worldwide and stronger programs to detect nuclear smuggling.

a global black market in nuclear materials was expanding. Instead, they argued, the best way to reduce nuclear dangers was to work toward completely eliminating nuclear weapons.[3]

"I'm not naïve. This goal will not be reached quickly — perhaps not in my lifetime," Obama said. "But now we, too, must ignore the voices who tell us that the world cannot change."[5]

Obama took another important step in mid-September, canceling Bush administration plans to deploy antimissile defense systems in Poland and the Czech Republic. The installations were intended to defend Europe against missile strikes from Iran. But Russian leaders saw them as a provocative intrusion into Eastern Europe and argued that the system might be expanded and reconfigured to threaten Russia. Instead, the Obama administration said it would field shorter-range interceptors, initially based on ships, which could be targeted more easily against Iranian threats.[6]

Russian Prime Minister Vladimir Putin called Obama's move a "correct and brave decision."[7] But conservatives said Obama was undermining U.S. security commitments to European allies. "Given the serious and growing threats posed by Iran's nuclear and missile programs, now is the time when we should look to strengthen our defenses, and those of our allies," said Republican senator and former presidential candidate John McCain of Arizona. "I believe the decision to abandon [the land-based system] unilaterally is seriously misguided."[8]

On Sept. 24 the Security Council unanimously passed a resolution urging all countries to work toward nuclear reductions and disarmament and to put tighter controls on nuclear technologies and materials.[9] U.N. Secretary-General Ban Ki-Moon welcomed the council's new resolve and urged states to follow through on the resolution. "Together we have dreamed about a nuclear-weapon-free world. Now we must act to achieve it," he said.

Other heads of state who had long supported faster nuclear reductions echoed the secretary-general. "While we sleep, death is awake. Death keeps watch from the warehouses that store more than 23,000 nuclear warheads, like 23,000 eyes open and waiting for a moment

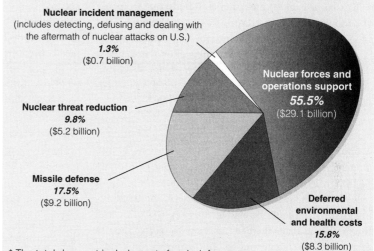

Budget on Nuclear Weapons Exceeds $52 Billion

At least $52 billion was appropriated for nuclear weapons and related expenses in fiscal 2008.* Most of the money was allocated for nuclear forces and operations support.

U.S. Nuclear Weapons-Related Appropriations, FY 2008 (includes nuclear delivery systems, warheads and bombs)

Nuclear incident management
(includes detecting, defusing and dealing with the aftermath of nuclear attacks on U.S.)
1.3%
($0.7 billion)

Nuclear threat reduction
9.8%
($5.2 billion)

Missile defense
17.5%
($9.2 billion)

Nuclear forces and operations support
55.5%
($29.1 billion)

Deferred environmental and health costs
15.8%
($8.3 billion)

* The total does not include costs for air defense, antisubmarine warfare, classified programs and most nuclear weapons-related intelligence programs.

Note: Percentages do not total 100 due to rounding.

Source: Stephen I. Schwartz and Deepti Choubey, "Nuclear Security Spending: Assessing Costs, Examining Priorities," Carnegie Endowment for International Peace, 2009

of carelessness," said Oscar Arias Sanchez, president of Costa Rica.[10]

The world has lived with nuclear threats for more than 60 years, but today's challenges differ dramatically from those during the Cold War, when the greatest global security risk was war between the United States and the Soviet Union. Under the doctrine of "mutual assured destruction," each country fielded tens of thousands of nuclear weapons to ensure that it could survive a first strike and still inflict catastrophic damage on its enemy. The policy kept the peace, advocates argued, by making each side afraid to start a war.

But accidents and misread signals nearly caused nuclear explosions more than once, when nations came close to nuclear exchanges or troops mishandled their own nuclear weapons. (*See sidebar, p. 100.*) Many experts still worry that too many nuclear weapons are on high alert, and that U.S. or Russian leaders might misinterpret an accidental launch as a planned strike and respond by launching more missiles and killing millions of people.

Now the threat of terrorism has compounded the danger. "The greatest threat to our security is that al Qaeda will acquire a nuclear weapon from Pakistan's or Russia's arsenal, or the material to build one from any of a dozen countries that don't guard their material adequately," says Joseph Cirincione, president of the Ploughshares Fund, which supports efforts to prevent the spread of nuclear weapons. "Another risk is that nuclear weapons could be used in a regional war — for example, between India and Pakistan."

The United States and Soviet Union (succeeded by Russia) have always possessed nearly all the nuclear weapons in the world. Together they have about 24,500 nuclear weapons today, down from a peak of roughly 64,000 in 1986.[11] (*See graph, p. 101.*) More than half of these weapons are held as spares, in reserve, or are awaiting dismantlement. But advocates say the U.S. and Russia should make further cuts, both to reduce the risk of a nuclear exchange and to build support for strong, global nonproliferation policies.

"The NPT requires the nuclear powers to move toward disarmament," says Daryl Kimball, executive director of the nonprofit Arms Control Association. "If we don't, other countries will be less willing to support tough controls on nuclear bomb material and sanctions on countries that try to develop nuclear weapons. Treading water is not a feasible option. And nuclear weapons aren't practical tools to deal with terrorist threats or conventional conflicts. Their only defensible purpose is to deter use of nuclear weapons by another country, and only Russia has an arsenal as big as ours."

Most advocates agree the U.S. should maintain a strong deterrent force as long as other countries have nuclear weapons. Earlier this year, a congressionally appointed bipartisan commission concluded the United States could make more nuclear reductions jointly with Russia, but it recommended retaining bombers, land-based missiles and submarines to deliver them. The report also left open an option for developing new warheads, and commission members disagreed over ending U.S. nuclear testing.[12]

Defense hawks argue that treaties constrain the U.S. but do nothing to reduce threats from countries determined to acquire nuclear weapons. One of their prime examples, Iran, made headlines less than 24 hours after the Security Council's disarmament resolution, when it was revealed that Iran was building a secret underground plant to enrich uranium.[13]

Obama and his British and French counterparts accused Iran — a member of the NPT — of flouting its non-nuclear pledges. Obama warned that if Iran did not disclose all of its nuclear activities immediately, it would face "sanctions that bite." But critics said negotiations would not curb Iran's alleged bomb program.

"In the bitter decades of the Cold War, we learned the hard way that the only countries that abide by disarmament treaties are those that want to be disarmed," *The Wall Street Journal* argued in an editorial.[14]

In the debate over U.S. nuclear policies, here are some issues under consideration:

Can all nuclear weapons be eliminated?

The United States has officially supported abolishing nuclear weapons ever since President Lyndon B. Johnson signed the Non-Proliferation Treaty in 1968. Article VI requires the five countries that then possessed nuclear weapons (United States, Soviet Union, Britain, France and China) to "negotiate in good faith on effective measures relating to the cessation of the nuclear arms race at an early date and to nuclear disarmament."[15] But advocates disagreed then and now about how quickly that should happen.

Today, arms reduction advocates say key steps to nuclear abolition include:

- Ending nuclear testing so that nations cannot develop new weapons;
- Ceasing production of fissile material for military use;
- Setting up a global civilian nuclear fuel bank so nations won't need to build plants that can produce bomb-usable material; and
- Drastically reducing U.S. and Russian nuclear arsenals.

Disarmament advocates argue that once the superpowers have made major cuts, perhaps below 1,000 warheads each, other nations with nuclear weapons would join the disarmament process. As arsenals shrink toward zero, they say, all countries then would have to accept intrusive inspections and monitoring to show that they were keeping their pledges.

Some supporters envision such a scenario within several decades. For example, Global Zero, an international coalition led by more than 100 former political and military leaders from the United States, Russia, China, Britain, and other countries, issued a plan last June to eliminate nuclear weapons by 2030.[16] "It's in the national interest of every country to live in a world free of nuclear weapons," says former U.S. Air Force nuclear weapons launch officer Bruce Blair, president of the World Security Institute in Washington and a Global Zero coordinator.

As evidence of worldwide support for abolition, Blair notes that 188 countries have signed the NPT, and only nine nations worldwide — the five recognized in the treaty plus India, Pakistan, Israel and North Korea — possess nuclear weapons.[17] What's more, a number of countries have abandoned once-secret nuclear weapons programs since the 1970s, including South Korea, Brazil, Argentina, Taiwan, South Africa and, most recently, Libya.[18]

In Blair's view, serious efforts to eliminate nuclear weapons will make it increasingly hard for the four holdout nations to keep going against the tide. "All other countries are currently members of the NPT, which obligates them to remain nuclear weapons-free. So they would have no reason not to sign a Global Zero accord, and strong reason to support the trend toward zero," Blair says.

Others believe disarmament will take more than political pressure. "You would have to believe that there will be a time when Russia doesn't feel beleaguered and dependent on nuclear weapons, that Israel feels at peace with its neighbors and that India isn't at war with Pakistan," says Linton Brooks, who headed the National Nuclear Security Administration during George W. Bush's administration. "Then you have to ask how we'll know that people have given up nuclear weapons. Then you have to figure out what to do if you discover somebody is cheating."

In Brooks' view, the solution will take many decades and should not divert attention from current nuclear challenges. "Abolition has focused a lot of intellectual energy in the think-tank community on something that will happen in 40 and 50 years, instead of current problems like what we'll do if we can't keep Iran from producing nuclear weapons," he warns. "I think we're not spending enough intellectual time on near-term problems."

Another argument often raised against going to zero points out that the basics of how nuclear weapons work are widely known. "Proliferating states, even if they abandoned these devices under resolute international pressure, would still be able to clandestinely retain a few of their existing weapons — or maintain a standby, break-out capability to acquire a few weapons quickly, if needed," wrote former Defense Secretary Harold Brown and former Energy Secretary and CIA Director John Deutch in 2007.[19]

But others say a breakout nation could not achieve very much with a handful of nuclear bombs. "Nuclear weapons make it harder for other people to threaten you and conquer you, but they're not good for blackmailing or getting your way in many international political situations," says Stephen Walt, a professor of international affairs at Harvard University.

Going nuclear actually may be counterproductive for would-be regional powers like Iran, Walt contends, because their neighbors will arm in response. "Iran will have more influence in the Persian Gulf if no one has nuclear weapons, so I think it's in their interest not to develop nuclear weapons," he says. "The way we make that point is to stop holding a gun to their heads and try to persuade them that they're better off not weaponizing their technology. They should know that if they produce weapons they'll go to the top of our potential terrorist source list. Our goal should be persuading them to be more like Japan and less like Pakistan."

Making disarmament viable for countries like Pakistan with enemies next door will require creative strategies for taming regional conflicts. "Pakistani leaders are worried about an attack from India, so giving them enough political will to abandon nuclear deterrence may mean creating a demilitarized zone between Pakistan and India," says Sharon Squassoni, a senior associate at the Carnegie Endowment for International Peace. "The weakest nation with nuclear weapons will have to feel comfortable letting go of that safety net and believe that it will be better off without it."

Should the United States end nuclear testing?

From 1945 through 1992 the United States detonated more than 1,000 nuclear weapons. Most other nuclear nations, including Russia, Britain, France, China, India, Pakistan and North Korea, are known to have also carried out nuclear tests.

Arms control advocates have long sought a global ban on nuclear testing to keep nations from developing and validating new warhead designs. Since 1996 148 countries have signed and ratified the Comprehensive Test-Ban Treaty (CTBT), which bars members from carrying out or helping with nuclear explosions and sets up an international monitoring system to detect clandestine tests. If a member country is suspected of conducting a test, other countries can request on-site inspections of its facilities.[20] But for the CTBT to enter into force, it must be ratified by nine more states: the U.S., China, North Korea, Egypt, India, Indonesia, Iran, Israel and Pakistan.[21]

President Bill Clinton signed the CTBT in 1996, but the Republican-controlled Senate delayed action on ratifying the treaty. Although the United States had adopted a moratorium on nuclear tests five years earlier (initiated by a Democratic Congress), many conservative critics argued the treaty was not verifiable because cheaters could easily hide low-level nuclear tests. They also contended tests were essential to assure that U.S. nuclear weapons remained safe and reliable over time, and that ending U.S. tests would have little impact on proliferator countries.[22]

In 1999 Senate Republicans forced a quick debate and rejected the CTBT on a 51-48 vote. Support fell far short of the 67 votes required under the Constitution to ratify a treaty, even though the Energy and Defense departments and Joint Chiefs of Staff urged approval. In his Prague speech earlier this year, President Obama promised to try again.

"After more than five decades of talks, it is time for the testing of nuclear weapons to finally be banned," Obama said.

But critics argued that without testing the nation's nuclear deterrent would be weakened. Sen. Jon Kyl, R-Ariz., and former Assistant Secretary of Defense Richard Perle asserted that ending nuclear testing, together with Obama's decision not to fund new nuclear warhead designs, amounted to "unilateral disarmament by unilateral obsolescence."[23]

CTBT supporters predict that all Senate Democrats will support ratification and that some Republicans who voted no in 1999 will reconsider their positions, including Sens. Richard Lugar of Indiana and Arizona's McCain. (As a presidential candidate in 2008, McCain promised to keep an open mind on the issue.) But others still believe the treaty undercuts U.S. security interests.

"I know of no information that suggests that the matters that led the Senate to reject the treaty have changed for the better," said Sen. Kyl earlier this year. "CTBT, a bad idea shrouded in good intentions, would not even be capable of detecting political tantrums like the North Korean test [in May], even when the international monitoring system is told where and when to look."[24]

In fact, the CTBT's international monitoring system — with 130 seismic monitoring stations worldwide — detected North Korea's first test in 2006 as well as last May's test, which registered as far away as Texas. On the day of the test, CTBT officials said the system could pinpoint the location of the explosion to an area the size of Berlin, and would be able to make its estimate much more precise with further analysis.[25]

Such findings indicate the CTBT can detect cheaters, advocates say. "The design objective for the monitoring system was to be able to detect explosions measuring one kiloton or less in any medium anywhere in the world, and it looks as though we're doing better than that," says Princeton University physicist Frank von Hippel, a former arms control adviser during the Clinton administration. "North Korea's test was a fraction of a kiloton. Seismologists have become very sophisticated at discriminating between explosions and other signals like earthquakes. A nuclear test is a sudden expansion of a gas in all directions, and that creates a very different signal from two sides of a fault shifting against each other." (See "At Issue," p. 115.)

Advocates of continued testing question whether the Department of Energy can maintain a robust nuclear weapons stockpile without conducting tests, in part because some of the precisely engineered materials in nuclear weapons change over time, including plutonium cores and the chemical explosives that compress bomb cores to critical mass. A 2002 National Academy of Sciences study acknowledged that aging would make stewardship of the U.S. stockpile increasingly challenging, but said, "[W]e see no reason that the capabilities of those mechanisms . . . cannot grow at least as fast as the challenge they must meet."[26]

The directors of the three DOE laboratories that design and build nuclear weapons (Los Alamos and Sandia in New Mexico and Lawrence Livermore in California) must certify annually to Congress that U.S. nuclear weapons are safe and reliable. (*See map, p. 100.*) So far they have made that certification each year, but questions persist. "[A]s the weapons age, a thing that is referred to as margins begins to decrease," said Gen. Kevin Chilton, head of the U.S. Strategic Command, early last year. "A simple way to think of [margin] is the likelihood it's going to work the way you want it to work the day you need it. . . . And margin, because of shelf life and chemistry, is decreasing."[27]

Siegfried Hecker, a professor of management science and engineering at Stanford University and former director of Los Alamos National Laboratory, argues that stockpile stewardship creates some uncertainty and is a slower and more expensive way to resolve certain questions than testing. But Hecker nonetheless supports ratifying the CTBT because, in his view, other nations need nuclear tests more than the U.S. does.

"The single most important reason to ratify the CTBT is to stop other countries from improving their arsenals — China, India, Pakistan, North Korea, and Iran if it ever progresses that far," says Hecker. "We gain substantially more from limiting other countries than we lose by giving up testing — even with a gradual loss of confidence, which stockpile stewardship has held to an acceptable level. The U.S. has carried out more than 1,000 nuclear tests, and the Chinese have done about 45. You can see the difference in the sophistication of our arsenals."

Does the United States need new nuclear weapons?

The United States built its last nuclear weapon in 1992 — nearly 20 years ago — and today experts sharply

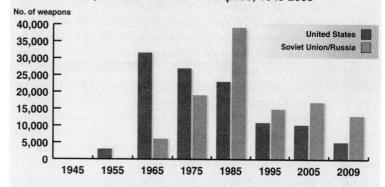

Global Stockpiles on the Decline

The United States has a little more than 5,200 nuclear weapons stockpiled this year, about one-sixth of the amount it had in the mid-1960s when stockpiles were at their highest. Similarly, stockpiles have steadily declined for Russia since the collapse of the Soviet Union.

U.S., Russian Nuclear Stockpiles, 1945-2009

Note: France, China and the United Kingdom have a few hundred nuclear weapons each.

Source: Natural Resources Defense Council

disagree over whether new weapons are needed. New-construction advocates say the thousands of weapons in the current stockpile were not designed for shelf lives longer than about 20-30 years, and that simply refurbishing them would leave uncertainty about how they will perform. Opponents say the stockpile is reliable and can be kept that way through regular maintenance, and that producing new models would signal an expanding role for nuclear weapons in U.S. security policy.

After the Persian Gulf War in 1991, when air strikes failed to destroy many of Iraq's underground military facilities, some defense planners proposed developing low-yield nuclear weapons that could destroy buried targets. Congress rejected the idea in 1993, barring work on "mini-nukes" with explosive yields of five kilotons or less. But conservative legislators and weapon designers continued to press the issue of usable nuclear weapons to destroy "very hard targets."[28]

Spurred by its search for al Qaeda leader Osama bin Laden in the caves of Afghanistan, the Bush administration sought funding from Congress starting in 2003 for a Robust Nuclear Earth Penetrator (RNEP). But critics, led by Rep. David Hobson, R-Ohio, argued the so-called "bunker buster" would cause too much damage in the area surrounding a target, and that building it would undermine U.S. nonproliferation policy. "It gave people a lot of reason to build their own weapons," Hobson later said.[29]

After Congress zeroed out bunker buster funding in 2004 and 2005, Hobson urged the Bush administration instead to develop what became known as the Reliable Replacement Warhead (RRW) program to design safer, more durable replacements for the most problematic weapons in the stockpile. But when DOE responded by proposing an entire new generation of nuclear warheads, Hobson and other critics zeroed funding for RRW, arguing that first the U.S. needed to develop post-Cold War deterrence strategies and decide how many weapons it needed to carry them out.[30]

Although Obama did not include RRW in his fiscal 2010 budget request, some senior administration officials are on record supporting new nuclear weapons. In October 2008, Defense Secretary Robert Gates described the long-term outlook for the U.S. nuclear stockpile as "bleak," thanks to aging weapons and an aging nuclear work force. RRW, said Gates, "is not about new capabilities — suitcase bombs or bunker busters or tactical nukes. It is about safety, security and reliability. It is about the future credibility of our strategic deterrent, and it deserves urgent attention."[31]

At a congressional hearing last March, the Strategic Command's Gen. Chilton said, "We do not need a new weapon with new capabilities. But I do believe we have a great opportunity here to develop modern nuclear weapons . . . that have 21st-century requirements put into their designs," such as higher reliability and better security features in case a weapon is stolen by terrorists.

Then-Rep. Ellen Tauscher, D-Calif., who is now Under Secretary of State for Arms Control and International Security, agreed, "as long as the [constraints] include no testing; no new capabilities for the weapons in the sense that we're not increasing yield . . . and that it is all done in a context of ratifying [the CTBT] and taking down weapons and dismantling them."[32]

Opponents counter that warheads in the stockpile are safe and reliable. The 2002 National Academy of Sciences study on technical issues associated with the CTBT concluded that thanks to investments in nuclear weapons science that do not involve testing, "confidence in the reliability of the stockpile is better justified technically today than it was [in 1992 when the U.S. stopped testing]."[33]

More recently, studies released in 2006 by the JASON group, a panel of high-level experts that provides independent scientific advice to the U.S government, and by the Livermore and Los Alamos national laboratories, concluded that plutonium "pits," or cores, for most U.S. nuclear weapons would be reliable for at least 85 years — about twice as long as scientists had previously estimated. The JASON report concluded that the weapons laboratories "have also made significant progress in prioritizing the unresolved questions regarding the aging of stockpile weapons" and have "identified key metrics to assess the effects of aging."[34]

In addition to studying scientific problems like plutonium aging, the DOE is carrying out "life extension" programs on each of the major weapon types in the U.S. stockpile. Designed to extend the lives of warheads by 20 to 30 years, the programs involve refurbishing some components and replacing others that have degraded or pose technical problems. As of mid-2009, DOE had completed a life extension on the B61, an air-delivered bomb, and was working on the W76 warhead, which is carried on submarine-launched ballistic missiles.[35]

Debate over building new nuclear weapons is part of a larger discussion about the future of the aging DOE nuclear complex and the increasing challenge of recruiting talented scientists to maintain the U.S. nuclear stockpile and develop new weapons if they ever are needed (a stated U.S. policy goal).[36] "The U.S. is experiencing a serious brain drain in the loss of veteran nuclear weapons designers and technicians," Gates said last October. "Half of our nuclear lab scientists are over 50 years old, and many of those under 50 have had limited or no involvement in the design and development of a nuclear weapon."[37]

But it is less obvious that U.S. military leaders want new nuclear weapons. In a 2008 poll of more than 3,400 senior active-duty and retired military officers, only about 2 percent of respondents thought the U.S. needed to develop a new generation of nuclear weapons.[38] "Nuclear weapons don't factor into the kinds of missions that most military officers perform day to day, and it's civilian leaders who make the decision about pressing the button," says Carnegie Endowment analyst Squassoni. "Military leaders are much more focused on issues like getting their forces to the theater and communicating with them."

Many observers predict that to win votes for CTBT ratification, Obama may strike a deal that increases funding and activities related to nuclear weapon design (but not production). "There are a lot of things you can do to ensure the safety and reliability of the arsenal in between nothing and developing new warheads, and that's where the discussion is happening now," says the Ploughshares Fund's Cirincione. "You can already see the outlines of a compromise around robust research and development at the labs. We need to find a balance between making sure that our nuclear weapons work as intended and avoiding activities that make other countries think we're improving our capabilities while we tell them to reduce theirs."

BACKGROUND

Dawn of Arms Race

The United States made the world's first nuclear weapons, drawing on work by researchers in England, Italy, France and Germany. Through the 1930s and early '40s these scientists solved pieces of the central challenge — splitting the atom and releasing huge quantities of energy. But only the United States, its research ranks swelled by top European physicists fleeing the Nazi government, undertook a full-scale effort to build the bomb.

In October 1941, with the nation on the brink of war, President Franklin D. Roosevelt ordered advisers to find out whether an atomic bomb could be built and what it would cost. Three months later, after Japan's surprise attack on Pearl Harbor, Roosevelt approved the Manhattan Project — a crash program to develop nuclear weapons. Working in secret, the Army Corps of Engineers built a nuclear production complex by 1945 that was as large as the U.S. auto industry. At its peak the Manhattan Project employed some 130,000 people from Washington state to South Carolina.[39]

On July 16, 1945, the world's first nuclear test lit up the desert at Alamogordo, New Mexico. Describing it, J. Robert Oppenheimer, the Manhattan Project's scientific director, recalled a statement in Hindu scripture by the god Vishnu: "Now I am become Death, the destroyer of worlds." A month later U.S. bombers dropped two atomic bombs in three days on the Japanese cities of Hiroshima and Nagasaki, killing more than 100,000 people immediately, and perhaps twice that number within weeks from radiation poisoning.[40]

Although scientists urged Roosevelt and his successor, President Harry S Truman, to tell the Soviet Union about the bomb program, Truman only told Premier Josef Stalin that the U.S. was working on "a new weapon of great force" 12 days before the Hiroshima bombing.[41] In 1946 U.S. negotiator Barnard Baruch presented a plan to the United Nations to destroy all existing atomic bombs and put atomic energy technology under international control. But the Soviet Union, which by then had launched its own atomic bomb program, rejected the plan.

In 1949 the Soviets tested their first atomic bomb. Truman then approved development of even more powerful thermonuclear, or hydrogen, bombs. By 1953 both superpowers had tested H-bombs and were expanding their nuclear stockpiles rapidly, each seeking the ability to respond instantly and massively to a sudden nuclear attack.

President Dwight D. Eisenhower renewed the idea of international control in his 1953 "Atoms for Peace" speech, which urged the United Nations to promote peaceful uses of atomic energy. The proposal led to establishment of the International Atomic Energy Agency in 1957 but did not slow the growth of nuclear arsenals. Emulating the United States and Soviet Union, Britain had tested a nuclear weapon in 1952. France and China would follow in the 1960s.

The arms race intensified in 1957, when the Soviet Union launched its *Sputnik* satellite into orbit, demonstrating that it could build a long-range ballistic missile.[42] *Sputnik* raised U.S. fears of falling behind and becoming vulnerable to nuclear blackmail. Concerns about a "missile gap" persisted until 1961, when satellite photographs showed that the U.S.S.R. had deployed only four long-range ballistic missiles.[43] The United States had more than 24,000 nuclear weapons — roughly 10 times as many as the Soviets.[44]

Early Agreements

Democratic President John F. Kennedy (1961-63) came to office supporting limits on nuclear testing, but friction with the Soviet Union obstructed progress. In 1962 the

CHRONOLOGY

1940s–1960s *Atomic Age begins.*

August 1945 U.S. drops atomic bombs on Hiroshima and Nagasaki, Japan, killing 250,000 people.

1949 Soviet Union tests atomic bomb.

1952 Britain tests first nuclear bomb; U.S. tests hydrogen bomb.

1957 International Atomic Energy Agency (IAEA) is created to promote peaceful uses of nuclear energy.

1960 France tests nuclear bomb.

1962 Cuban Missile Crisis brings U.S., Soviet Union to brink of nuclear war.

1963 Limited Test Ban Treaty bars tests in atmosphere, space, underwater.

1964 China tests its first nuclear bomb.

1968 Nearly 100 countries sign Nuclear Non-Proliferation Treaty (NPT).

1970s–1980s *Developing countries start acquiring nuclear arms.*

1972 U.S. and U.S.S.R. conclude Strategic Arms Limitation Talks (SALT I).

1974 India carries out "peaceful" underground nuclear explosion.

1979 U.S. and U.S.S.R. sign SALT II, cutting long-range missiles.

1983 U.S. deploys nuclear missiles in Western Europe, triggering widespread protests.

1986 President Ronald Reagan and Soviet Premier Mikhail Gorbachev discuss eliminating nuclear weapons at summit in Reykjavik, Iceland. Talks collapse but lay base for 1987 Intermediate-Range Nuclear Forces Treaty.

1989 Pakistan is revealed to be developing "nuclear capability."

1990s–2000s *U.S., Russia reduce Cold War arsenals; other proliferation threats increase.*

July 31, 1991 President George H. W. Bush and Gorbachev sign Strategic Arms Reduction Treaty (START I). . . . Inspectors begin destroying Iraq's nuclear weapons research sites. . . . Soviet Union collapses; U.S. provides aid to safeguard nuclear weapons.

1993 U.S., Russia sign START II treaty, reducing number of deployed strategic warheads by end of 2007. Russia conditions ratification on preservation of ABM Treaty's limits on development of missile defense systems.

1994 North Korea agrees to stop producing plutonium in return for food and energy aid. . . . START I enters into force for 15 years.

1996 Comprehensive Test Ban Treaty (CTBT) signed by 71 nations.

1998 India, Pakistan test nuclear weapons.

1999 U.S. Senate votes 51-48 against CTBT.

2002 U.S. withdraws from ABM Treaty, which President George W. Bush says prevents protection of Americans from rogue or terrorist attacks. Russia repudiates START II. The two countries conclude Strategic Offensive Reduction Treaty (SORT).

2003 U.S. invades Iraq, claiming it is developing weapons of mass destruction; no nuclear weapons program is found. . . . North Korea withdraws from NPT. . . . Libya agrees to dismantle clandestine nuclear weapons program.

2006 North Korea conducts nuclear test. . . . U.N. Security Council learns Iran has uranium enrichment program.

2008 Poland, Czech Republic agree to host U.S. missile defense systems; Russia says it will deploy missiles near Poland.

2009 President Barack Obama pledges steps toward nuclear-free world, including new nuclear reduction agreements with Russia and CTBT ratification and cancels missile defense deployment in Eastern Europe. . . . North Korea conducts second nuclear test. . . . Obama and Russian President Dmitry Medvedev sign joint understanding on treaty to reduce nuclear forces.

superpowers came to the brink of nuclear war when U.S. satellite photographs revealed that Russians were installing nuclear missiles in Cuba that could reach U.S. territory.[45]

Some advisers recommended conventional air strikes on the Cuban missile sites, but instead Kennedy imposed a naval quarantine on Cuba and insisted that the weapons be removed. After a 13-day standoff, Soviet Premier Nikita Khrushchev agreed to remove the missiles. In return the U.S. promised not to invade Cuba (a fear that had spurred the Soviets to install the missiles), and also agreed confidentially to remove its own nuclear missiles from Turkey.

After the Cuban Missile Crisis, Kennedy renewed efforts to limit nuclear testing, hoping to make it harder for other countries to develop nuclear weapons. In March 1963 Kennedy said, "I see the possibility in the 1970s of the president of the United States having to face a world in which 15 or 20 or 25 nations may have these weapons. I regard that as the greatest possible danger and hazard." And he argued that even if a test ban constrained the U.S., it would still make the nation safer.[46]

The Limited Test Ban Treaty, signed later that year, banned nuclear tests in the atmosphere, outer space and under water, but allowed underground tests to continue.[47]

Under Kennedy's successor, Lyndon B. Johnson, the U.S. and Russia joined with other countries to negotiate the Nuclear Non-Proliferation Treaty, which barred members other than the current nuclear powers (the U.S., Soviet Union, Britain, France, and China) from acquiring nuclear weapons. In return signatories were guaranteed access to peaceful nuclear energy technologies, and the five nuclear states agreed to negotiate toward disarmament, although without any time frame.[48] Ninety-eight countries signed the NPT when it was completed in 1968, and many more joined later.

By this time the United States had more than 28,000 nuclear weapons, down from a peak of 31,700 in 1966, and the Soviet Union had nearly 10,000.[49] Both sides were developing weapons that could deliver multiple warheads to different targets, known as MIRVs (multiple independently targetable reentry vehicles), and anti-ballistic missile defense systems that could shoot down attacking missiles.

Unable to agree on a broad nuclear disarmament plan, the superpowers shifted to a more modest goal in the late 1960s: setting some upper limits on their arms race. In 1972 U.S. and Soviet leaders signed an interim agreement (referred to as SALT I because it was negotiated during the Strategic Arms Limitation Talks) freezing the number of each side's long-range ballistic missiles, bombers and submarines, and also the Anti-Ballistic Missile (ABM) Treaty, which limited each country to a single defensive system around its capital and another at a missile launch area.[50] By preventing either country from developing a nationwide missile defense system, the ABM Treaty sought to maintain the so-called "balance of terror" that kept the superpowers from attacking each other.

Negotiations during the Ford and Carter administrations produced the SALT II treaty in 1979, which set permanent limits on many types of nuclear weapons but did not require any existing weapons to be destroyed. After the Soviet Union invaded Afghanistan in 1980, President Jimmy Carter asked the Senate to put SALT II ratification on hold and signed a directive that stated, "To continue to deter in an era of strategic nuclear equivalence . . . we must be capable of fighting [a nuclear war] successfully," so that the enemy would recognize that it could not possibly benefit from attacking.[51]

New Directions

President Ronald Reagan (1981-1989) ran on a platform that called for rebuilding U.S. military power, and some of his senior advisers alarmed the public with statements about planning for nuclear war. For example, in 1981 Deputy Under Secretary of Defense T. K. Jones argued that with a robust civil defense program, most Americans could survive a nuclear attack. "Dig a hole, cover it with a couple of doors and then throw three feet of dirt on top," Jones said.[52]

Many Americans rejected such views and supported proposals to freeze and reduce nuclear arsenals. One of the biggest anti-nuclear rallies, in New York's Central Park in 1982, drew 700,000 people.[53] When the U.S. started deploying medium-range nuclear missiles in Western Europe in 1983 (a step approved during the Carter administration to balance new Soviet missiles), protests spread to European capitals. The U.S. Conference of Catholic Bishops weighed in with a pastoral letter that argued, "The arms race is one of the great curses on the human race; it is to be condemned as a danger, an act of aggression against the poor, and a folly which does not provide the security it promises."[54]

What If an Armed Nuclear Bomber Crashed?

Potentially catastrophic accidents have occurred.

The terms are vaguely military, but innocent-sounding: "bent spears" and "broken arrows." But they refer to a dreadful reality: potentially catastrophic incidents involving nuclear weapons.

"Broken arrows" are the most serious, such as the accidental or unauthorized launch of a nuclear weapon that could lead to nuclear war, an explosion of nuclear or non-nuclear weapon components, radioactive contamination or loss or seizure of a nuclear weapon. To date, the U.S. military has logged 32 such incidents — all before 1983 and none resulting in a nuclear detonation.[1]

But some came close. In 1966 an American B-52 bomber carrying four hydrogen bombs collided with a tanker plane during mid-air refueling off the coast of Spain. The bomber broke apart, and three of the bombs fell on land near a small fishing village; the bombs didn't detonate, but non-nuclear explosives in two of the bombs did go off, contaminating a square mile with radioactive material. The fourth bomb landed in the Mediterranean Sea and was recovered intact two months later.[2]

"Bent spears" involve the mishandling of nuclear weapons or incidents that pose a risk of explosion, radioactive contamination or damage to the weapon.[3] The most recent bent spear occurred in 2007, when crewmen loaded what they thought were 12 unarmed cruise missiles onto a bomber at Minot Air Force Base in North Dakota. The airmen and the officer in charge didn't realize that six of the missiles carried nuclear warheads. The loaded plane stood unguarded on the runway for 15 hours before flying to a base in Louisiana, where the nuclear missiles were discovered nine hours later.[4]

Afterwards, seven officers at Minot were reassigned, and 90 service members temporarily lost authority to handle nuclear weapons.[5] In 2008, after it was disclosed that another Air Force unit had mislabeled fuses for nuclear missiles and accidentally shipped them to Taiwan, Defense Secretary Robert Gates ordered an investigation of the Air Force's problems handling nuclear weapons. In June, the Air Force's military chief of staff and civilian secretary were forced to resign.[6]

Many security experts say the risk of accidental nuclear war has grown since the end of the Cold War, largely because the United States and Russia still maintain hundreds of nuclear weapons at a high stage of alert. In addition, Russia's computer systems degraded after the Soviet Union disintegrated, raising concerns that leaders might misinterpret a malfunction or false signal as an attack and launch weapons in response. Indeed, false alarms indicating a Soviet attack occurred in the United States in 1979 and 1980, and in 1995 Russian leaders almost launched a nuclear attack on the U.S. in response to what turned out to be a Norwegian research rocket.[7]

"About 800 to 900 U.S. warheads, and a comparable number of Russian warheads, are launch ready — fuelled, armed, targeted and will instantly fire if they receive a very short stream of computer launch signals," says Bruce Blair, president of the World Security Institute and a former Air Force nuclear missile launch officer. "Nothing has been done to change these legacy postures, except for a cosmetic detargeting agreement between [President Bill] Clinton and [Soviet President Boris] Yeltsin in 1994." The U.S. and Russia agreed not to target each other, but nuclear weapons can be retargeted in seconds.

Military leaders maintain that launch-ready warheads are under rigorous controls, including design features, safety rules and procedures, accident prevention or mitigation measures, physical security and coded control systems.[8] U.S. Strategic Command head Gen. Kevin Chilton said in 2008 that nuclear weapons are "in the holster" with two combination locks, which must be opened by two people who can only act under authenticated orders from the president.[9]

Reagan opposed a nuclear freeze and argued that increasing U.S. military power was the best way to preserve peace. But he also believed that once Soviet leaders saw that they could never win an arms race, nuclear weapons could be eliminated. In 1983 Reagan further complicated arms control discussions when he called for "rendering nuclear weapons impotent and obsolete" by developing a national missile defense system.

Reagan envisioned sharing missile defense technology with the Soviet Union, but Soviet leaders and U.S. critics

Nonetheless, former Senate Armed Services Committee Chairman Sam Nunn, D-Ga., has urged the United States and Russia to remove all nuclear weapons from high-alert status. "We are running the irrational risk of an Armageddon of our own making," Nunn said in 2004.[10]

During the 2008 presidential campaign, President Barack Obama pledged to "work with Russia to take U.S. and Russian ballistic missiles off hair-trigger alert." That issue will be addressed during the congressionally mandated Nuclear Posture Review, a study of U.S. nuclear forces and policies scheduled for completion by the end of this year.

Cyber-intrusion by computer hackers could also pose a risk.[11] "If outside actors, perhaps with insider collusion that provides passwords and other access information, manage to break into 'closed' nuclear communications and computer networks, then this risk could become high as long as nuclear missiles remain on launch-ready alert," Blair warns.

In fact, since 2006 hackers have breached the networks at the Defense, Commerce and State departments, the Federal Aviation Administration and the military's U.S. Central Command, according to the Center for Strategic and International Studies, a Washington think tank.[12] The Defense Department is creating a new military command to manage offensive and defensive computer warfare, in coordination with a new civilian cyber-security initiative announced by President Obama last May.[13]

No other countries keep their forces on launch-ready alert, according to Blair, and other nations usually keep warheads separated from delivery vehicles. However, he worries that India, Pakistan and China may start mating warheads with missiles and adopting quick-launch postures.

"If there's a crisis, they will be more likely to assemble weapons and bombs, mate them to delivery vehicles and prime them for use," Blair says. "That's the context in which mistaken or unauthorized launch becomes a concern."

To avoid that scenario, Blair recommends that all countries with nuclear weapons agree to prohibit launch-ready postures except in extreme circumstances and require pre-notification and information exchange about steps governments take to alert their forces.

"A joint warning center with multinational crews from all of the nuclear weapons countries (except North Korea) and links to all their national early-warning centers would also help to minimize misinterpretation of missile launches," he says.

— *Jennifer Weeks*

[1] Office of the Deputy Assistant to the Secretary of Defense (Nuclear Matters), *Nuclear Matters: A Practice Guide* (2008), p. 183, www.acq.osd .mil/ncbdp/nm/nmbook/index.htm.

[2] For details see Barbara Moran, *The Day We Lost the H-Bomb: Cold War, Hot Nukes, and the Worst Nuclear Weapons Disaster in History* (2009).

[3] Office of the Assistant to the Secretary of Defense for Nuclear and Chemical and Biological Defense Programs, Nuclear Weapons Accident Response Procedures, Feb. 22, 2005, pp. 28-29, www.dtic.mil/whs/direc tives/corres/pdf/315008m.pdf.

[4] Joby Warrick and Walter Pincus, "Missteps in the Bunker," *The Washington Post*, Sept. 23, 2007.

[5] Marc V. Schanz and Suzann Chapman, "No More Bent Spears," *Air Force Magazine.com*, Feb. 15, 2008.

[6] Kristin Roberts, "U.S. Mistakenly Sent Nuclear Missile Fuses to Taiwan," Reuters, March 25, 2008; "Moseley and Wynne Forced Out," *Air Force Times*, June 9, 2008.

[7] Lachlan Forrow, *et al.*, "Accidental Nuclear War — A Post-Cold War Assessment," *New England Journal of Medicine*, vol. 338, no. 18 (April 30, 1998), pp. 1326-32; Geoffrey Forden, "False Alarms on the Nuclear Front," NOVA, updated December 2001, www.pbs.org/wgbh/nova/mis sileers/falsealarms.html.

[8] E-mail from U.S. Strategic Command to Arms Control Association, Nov. 28, 2007, www.armscontrol.org/interviews/20071204_STRATCOM.

[9] Elaine M. Grossman, "Top U.S. General Spurns Obama Pledge to Reduce Nuclear Alert Posture," Global Security Newswire, Feb. 27, 2009.

[10] "Nunn Urges U.S. and Russia to Remove All Nuclear Weapons from Hair-Trigger," Nuclear Threat Initiative, June 21, 2004.

[11] See Peter Katel, "Homeland Security," *CQ Researcher*, Feb. 13, 2009, pp. 129-152.

[12] James Andrew Lewis, "Cyber Events Since 2006," Center for Strategic and International Studies, June 11, 2009, http://csis.org/publication/ cyber-events-2006.

[13] David E. Sanger and Thom Shanker, "Pentagon Plans New Arm to Wage Cyberspace Wars," *The New York Times*, May 29, 2009.

argued that the Strategic Defense Initiative (SDI), popularly known as "Star Wars," would escalate the nuclear arms race and make cuts in offensive weapons impossible. Many scientists also argued that it was technically impossible to build effective defenses against a large-scale nuclear attack.[55] In a 1986 summit meeting at Reykjavik, Iceland, Reagan and Soviet General Secretary Mikhail Gorbachev nearly agreed on a proposal to eliminate nuclear weapons but deadlocked over missile defense. Gorbachev insisted that the U.S. should adhere to the

U.S. Seeks New Roles for Bomb Builders

Nation's science leadership faces "precipitous decline."

As the United States downsizes its nuclear arsenal and makes cutbacks at its nuclear weapons laboratories, managers are finding it harder and harder to recruit and retain top-level nuclear scientists and engineers.

"We've slowly but steadily lost the capabilities that have made these places incredibly good scientific institutions," says former Los Alamos Director Siegfried Hecker.

More broadly, "Our nation is witnessing a precipitous decline in global science and technology leadership," warned a task force last spring convened by the Henry L. Stimson Center think tank in Washington, D.C. To start reversing that decline, members called for diversifying the labs' core mission so they can "address an array of 21st-century national security challenges."[1]

The nation's three nuclear weapons laboratories — Los Alamos and Sandia in New Mexico and Livermore in California — face both budget challenges and bureaucratic red tape, says Hecker. While other agencies use the labs' world-class facilities and technology in joint non-nuclear projects — such as developing advanced conventional munitions — those initiatives have not provided steady funding for the labs. "Other agencies have typically come into the labs as users of the technologies, not builders of it," he says, "so they've never supported the underlying science and technology base." Furthermore, he adds, "It's hard to do anything experimentally because the labs have been driven toward a zero-risk environment."

Still, the labs have made important contributions to non-weapons initiatives. In the 1980s, for instance, Los Alamos created the human DNA libraries that laid the groundwork for the Human Genome Project, which identified all of the genes in human DNA. And both Los Alamos and Livermore have developed strong climate-modeling programs.

To expand the labs' core mission, the task force recommended moving them from the Energy Department's National Nuclear Security Administration (NNSA) to a new, independent Agency for National Security Applications. The agency's mission would still be nuclear-related but also would include verifying compliance with arms control treaties; nuclear forensics (analyzing recovered nuclear materials to identify their sources); counter-terrorism research; and analysis of intelligence information on foreign nuclear weapons programs.

"Almost everyone understands the labs' role poorly," says Stimson Center senior fellow and study director Elizabeth Turpen. "They have been servicing broader national security needs beyond the nuclear stockpile since before the end of the Cold War, and they're huge in the nuclear nonproliferation arena. But they should be bigger."

The challenge is most urgent for Los Alamos and Livermore, which were created to design nuclear weapons and today are primarily focused on ensuring the safety and reliability of those weapons. Sandia, which designs and produces non-nuclear components of nuclear weapons, "has already turned the corner," says Turpen. "Only about 42 percent of their current budget comes from defense

ABM Treaty, but Reagan refused, saying that would constrain SDI.[56]

A year later, however, Reagan and Gorbachev signed the Intermediate Nuclear Forces (INF) Treaty, the first agreement to eliminate an entire class of nuclear weapons (ground-launched missiles with ranges of 500 to 5,500 kilometers).[57] Negotiations continued, and in 1991 Gorbachev and President George H. W. Bush signed the Strategic Arms Reduction Treaty (START I) — the first agreement to require each side to make major cuts in long-range nuclear weapons. START I limited each side

to 6,000 "accountable" (deployed) warheads and set up an intrusive verification system.

Opportunities and Threats

In December 1991, a few months after START I was signed, the Soviet Union dissolved. Now Russia posed a new kind of nuclear threat: with its economy in crisis and its borders no longer secured, many leaders worried that nuclear weapons and materials from former Soviet republics might be stolen or sold on the black market.

programs, so they already think of themselves as a national security laboratory."

In 2000 the NNSA was split off as an autonomous agency within the Department of Energy (DOE) after security lapses and alleged Chinese spying at the labs raised congressional concerns that DOE was not overseeing the weapons complex effectively.[2] But that made it harder to broaden their portfolios, partner with other agencies and attract talented young scientists, the Stimson task force concluded.

"NNSA has never achieved the autonomy that Congress intended, just an overlay of bureaucracy," says Turpen. "And DOE's bureaucratic culture is very risk-averse in all of its decisions about the labs. There are lots of stovepipes, and anyone can stop a decision."

Early this year the Office of Management and Budget (OMB) asked for a cost-benefit analysis of putting the labs under the control of the Pentagon or another agency. Housing them within DOE "hasn't been a good marriage," said former Sandia Director C. Paul Robinson.[3] But others point out that the United States has had a longstanding policy of civilian control.

"For the past 63 years non-military control over the development of nuclear weapons technology has ensured independence of technical judgment over issues associated with our nuclear arsenal, has attracted the best scientific and technical talent to these important programs and has served to underline the crucial differences between nuclear weapons and conventional military munitions," a bipartisan group of U.S. senators wrote to OMB in March.[4]

The future of the labs is part of a larger debate over what kind of nuclear weapons complex the U.S. needs to support a post-Cold War arsenal. Some former production sites have been closed for cleanup, but the DOE still conducts weapons-related activities at eight sites. (*See map, p. 100.*) A Bush administration plan — originally called Complex 2030 and later renamed Complex Transformation — would have modernized many facilities and equipped them to produce a new stockpile of Reliable Replacement Warheads and maintain sizeable nuclear reserves.[5]

Now, however, the replacement warhead is off the table, and President Obama has called for further nuclear reductions. Many observers say the United States should complete its ongoing Nuclear Posture Review before deciding what goals nuclear weapons will serve. Then the size and scope of the nation's nuclear weapons infrastructure can be shaped accordingly.

— *Jennifer Weeks*

[1] "Leveraging Science for Security: A Strategy for the Nuclear Weapons Laboratories in the 21st Century," Henry L. Stimson Center, March 2009, p. 9, www.stimson.org/cnp/pdf/Leveraging_Science_for_Security_FINAL.pdf.

[2] "Congress Approves DOE Reorganization; Clinton Leaves Control with Energy Secretary," *Arms Control Today*, September/October 1999.

[3] Sue Vorenberg, "Feds Ponder Switching Labs to Military Agency," *Santa Fe New Mexican*, Feb. 4, 2009.

[4] "Senators Ask Obama Administration to End Study of Proposal to Move DOE Weapons Labs to Defense Department," Senate Energy and Natural Resources Committee, March 18, 2009. The senators were Sens. Jeff Bingaman (D-NM), Lisa Murkowski (R-AK), Byron Dorgan (D-ND), Robert Bennett (R-UT), and Bill Nelson (D-FL).

[5] For details see National Nuclear Security Administration, "Complex Transformation SPEIS," www.complextransformationspeis.com/index.html, and Philip Coyle III, "The Future of the DOE Complex Transformation Program," testimony before the House Committee on Appropriations, Subcommittee on Energy and Water, March 17, 2009, www.cdi.org/pdfs/CoyleHouseDOE3.09.pdf.

In response the U.S. started providing aid for so-called Cooperative Threat Reduction (CTR) — joint work by the superpowers to secure weapon-usable nuclear materials and destroy the Soviet Union's surplus nuclear weapons. Starting at $400 million in 1991, the initiative (popularly known as Nunn-Lugar after its lead Senate sponsors, Sens. Sam Nunn, D-Ga., and Indiana Republican Richard Lugar), grew into a multi-agency, multi-year program. Through fiscal 2008 the U.S. had provided about $15 billion to help other countries destroy or improve controls over nuclear, chemical, biological and missile technologies, weapons and materials.[58]

The end of the Cold War and Russia's economic collapse undercut many of the assumptions underlying U.S. nuclear policies. Just before leaving office, President Bush and Russian President Boris Yeltsin took another big step by signing the START II treaty, which called for each side to reduce its deployed strategic warheads to between 3,000 and 3,500 by 2007. START II also set other limits, such as barring multiple warheads on land-based missiles.

To assess what these changes meant for U.S. security policy, Congress ordered the Clinton administration to carry out an assessment of U.S. nuclear forces and policies in a post-Cold War world. The first Nuclear Posture Review, completed in 1994, stuck to the status quo in many ways. It endorsed continued reliance on a triad of nuclear delivery systems (bombers, land-based missiles and submarine-launched missiles). And it recommended that the U.S. should "lead but hedge" on arms control by supporting nuclear reductions but keeping warheads removed from service in storage, where they could be reloaded quickly onto missiles and bombers if U.S.-Russian relations deteriorated.[59]

Clinton was the first world leader to sign the Comprehensive Test Ban Treaty (CTBT) when it was completed in 1996. But a Republican-led Senate rejected the treaty in 1999, with opponents arguing it would not keep other countries from going nuclear (India and Pakistan had each tested nuclear weapons a year earlier), and that ending U.S. nuclear testing would make it harder to ensure that U.S. nuclear weapons were safe and reliable.

President George W. Bush's administration (2001-2009) was cooler toward nuclear arms control and argued that the U.S. needed many options to deter rogue countries or terrorist groups with nuclear weapons. In 2002 a second Nuclear Posture Review by Bush's Defense Department argued that the ABM Treaty and the CTBT were not applicable to current security conditions.[60]

A leaked version of the study named countries against which the U.S. should be ready to use nuclear weapons — including Russia, China, Iran, Iraq, Libya, North Korea, and Serbia — and proposed developing new warheads, spurring charges that Bush was expanding U.S. reliance on nuclear weapons.[61] But the administration rejected that view. "We were trying to make nuclear weapons less usable, not more usable," says Brooks, the former National Nuclear Security Administration director under Bush.

In 2002 Bush traveled to Moscow and with Russian President Vladimir Putin signed the Strategic Offensive Reduction Treaty (SORT), a pact to reduce U.S. and Russian deployed strategic warheads to between 1,700 and 2,200 each by 2012. The agreement superseded START II, which had never been enacted because Russia's legislature conditioned its approval of that agreement on the U.S. adhering to the ABM Treaty. Unlike START II, the Moscow treaty did not specify how each side's pledges would be verified or dictate what would be done with warheads removed from service.[62] A few weeks later the U.S. withdrew from the ABM Treaty and pledged to deploy missile defenses against growing threats from countries like North Korea and Iran.

Russia's response was subdued at first, but the issue heated up in 2007 when the Bush administration started negotiating to put missile interceptors and radar in Poland and the Czech Republic. U.S. officials said they were needed to counter Iranian attacks on European and American targets, but Russian leaders argued the new sites could become part of a defensive network against Russian missiles. Putin said the U.S. defense system would lead to "an inevitable arms race" and suggested Russia might target its own weapons on Poland and the Czech Republic.[63]

CURRENT SITUATION

Reshaping U.S. Forces

The Obama administration is currently carrying out the third U.S. Nuclear Posture Review (NPR) since the end of the Cold War. This study, due in December, will establish policies for the next five to 10 years governing U.S. nuclear deterrence doctrine, strategies, and the makeup of U.S. nuclear forces. Congress, executive branch officials, and many advocacy groups expect the NPR to define how nuclear weapons fit into President Obama's foreign and military agendas.

"The most important measure of whether President Obama is serious about pursuing a nuclear-free world will be how the NPR defines the future role of U.S. nuclear weapons," says Kimball of the Arms Control Association. "The president ought to articulate that nuclear weapons no longer play a useful role in deterring or fighting wars that start as conventional conflicts. They're not useful to deter or counter chemical and biological warfare threats. Mission statements dictate targets and requirements, so if the Obama administration crafts that kind of nuclear vision, the U.S. and Russia will be able to reduce their stockpiles to 1,000 warheads or fewer apiece. That will let us engage other countries in a discussion about multilateral nuclear disarmament."

To conservatives, however, nuclear weapons serve many important security functions, including reassuring U.S.

Can we detect Nuclear Test Ban cheaters?

YES Richard L. Garwin
Fellow Emeritus, Thomas J. Watson Research Center, IBM

Written for *CQ Researcher*, September 2009

I have been involved in detecting clandestine nuclear explosions since before December 1958, when I had a role in the U.N. Conference of Experts in Geneva devoted to seismic detection. The weapons that destroyed Hiroshima and Nagasaki were in the 10-kiloton range, but stockpile nuclear weapons today range to considerably more than a megaton yield (1 million tons of TNT equivalent).

Now 247 of the 337 facilities planned for the International Monitoring System (IMS) have been certified. These include primary and auxiliary seismic stations, infrasound sensors, hydroacoustic detectors and radionuclide laboratories.

The seismic sensors in particular are augmented by thousands of university seismometers in cooperative networks, with advancing capabilities to detect earthquakes. These networks can be focused even after the fact on nuclear test sites or suspect locations. The technology of detection has continuously improved, as well as the ability to distinguish underground explosions from background earthquakes. There has been no such evolution in means of hiding nuclear explosions.

According to a 2002 National Academy of Sciences study that analyzed the planned capability for Comprehensive Test Ban Treaty (CTBT) verification and possible military advances by any foreign testing that might evade detection, "[T]he only evasion scenarios that need to be taken seriously at this time are cavity decoupling and mine masking." The IMS network readily meets its goal of confident detection of a one-kiloton explosion non-evasively tested anywhere in the world, and has sensitivity a thousand times greater to explosions in the oceans.

In general, advanced nuclear weapon states that could hide a one-kiloton explosion would have little to gain from successfully doing so, and much to lose if concealment failed. Emerging nuclear powers are unlikely to be successful in such concealment and would also have little benefit, because the test explosive would have to be so modified to limit its yield as to bear little resemblance to an actual weapon.

The CTBT provides for on-site inspections (OSI) following a questionable seismic detection, allowing the search of 1,000 square kilometers of terrain. An OSI exercise of similar size was practiced in Kazakhstan in August 2008, with good results.

Former U.S. arms control negotiator Paul Nitze wrote in 1999 that the CTBT can be verified "with great confidence," more than meeting his prior general requirement that an arms control agreement be "adequately verifiable." I am now involved in a reassessment of this question.

NO Thomas Scheber
Vice President, National Institute for Public Policy

Written for *CQ Researcher*, September 2009

To be effective, a CTBT detection and verification regime would need to be highly intrusive and guarantee timely on-site inspections to resolve indications of cheating. The planned treaty regime is incapable of doing that.

First, there cannot be confidence in verification if major parties to the treaty don't agree on what is banned and permitted. The treaty is not clear. The CTBT prohibits all nuclear explosions. The U.S. interprets this prohibition strictly as zero-yield. Apparently Russia and possibly China do not accept the U.S. criterion and conduct low-yield nuclear tests.

Second, a zero-yield treaty poses an unattainable verification challenge. Evasion techniques can reduce the signature of a nuclear explosion by factors of 50 to 100; evidence can be obscured by natural geologic activity or man-made explosions. A National Academy of Sciences report on the CTBT addressed testing techniques to evade detection or attribution and concluded that, with evasive techniques, verification of testing below a kiloton could be problematic. These techniques include cavity decoupling, masking, or testing in an environment that makes attribution difficult. A CIA assessment concluded: "an evader could successfully contain a decoupled test in hard rock, using a cautious experimental approach, and thereby avoid detection by sensors external to its country."

Third, nuclear tests below a kiloton can provide valuable data — perhaps more valuable for the Russians than for the U.S. Russia has extensive experience with low-yield nuclear testing and a system to fully contain very low-yield tests. When U.S. personnel helped clean up a former Soviet test site in Kazakhstan, they discovered that 20 percent of the tests conducted there had escaped detection. These tests were low-yield and designed for special weapon effects. Recently, Russia has gone to great expense to restore its nuclear testing infrastructure.

Fourth, even the planned, inadequate verification provisions won't be fully implemented because CTBT cannot enter into force until it is ratified by North Korea, Iran, China, India, Pakistan, Israel, and Egypt.

Finally, verifying compliance would require timely on-site challenge inspections to investigate evidence of cheating. The CTBT requires that 30 of 51 members of an Executive Council consider the evidence and vote for inspection. Only 10 of the 51 member-states would be from North America or Western Europe; the U.S. is not even guaranteed a vote. This is a prescription for inaction.

Bottom line: A "zero-yield" nuclear test ban treaty is not verifiable.

allies that they are protected under a strong nuclear umbrella. "The key elements of a robust deterrent are under extreme stress today and will be imperiled further by a presidential determination to pursue a 'world without nuclear weapons' and the attendant policy of not investing in modernization of the stockpile," a group of former U.S. security officials warned in July.[64] The authors, with years of service in mainly Republican administrations, argued that modernizing U.S. nuclear weapons and delivery systems and developing national missile defenses should take priority over negotiating any new nuclear reduction agreements with Russia.

In that same month, however, Obama and Russian President Dmitry Medvedev agreed on new warhead reduction targets for a follow-on treaty to START I, which expires in December. Under the new targets the United States and Russia pledge to reduce their deployed strategic nuclear warheads from the current limit of 2,200 each by 2012 to between 1,500 and 1,675 each by 2016. Both sides would also make some cuts in nuclear bombers and missiles.[65]

Alarmed over these new proposed reductions, Senate conservatives attached several non-binding resolutions to a defense spending bill stating that the new treaty should not limit missile defenses, space capabilities or advanced conventional weapons, and endorsing the Bush administration's proposed missile defense system based in Poland and the Czech Republic. "I have yet to hear a convincing strategic rationale that would justify going this low [on warheads and delivery vehicles]," said Sen. Jeff Sessions, R-Ala., who warned that he would condition his support for any START follow-on agreement on "a serious commitment by the administration to modernize our nuclear deterrent."[66]

Some observers predict that with hawks pushing back, President Obama may have trouble making radical policy changes in the Nuclear Posture Review. "There are a lot of Bush administration holdovers in the nuclear bureaucracy, so the NPR may not end up being all that path-breaking," says Carnegie Endowment analyst Squassoni. "The real question is whether the president will step in and make a difference."

North Korea and Iran

As the U.S. reexamines its own nuclear weapons policies, it is also working to limit options for proliferators, especially North Korea and Iran. North Korea expelled international inspectors and withdrew from six-nation denuclearization talks in April, then conducted its second nuclear test in May. Although security experts estimate North Korea has produced enough plutonium for perhaps four to eight bombs, they mainly fear Pyongyang will sell nuclear materials and technology to other countries or groups.[67]

Because North Korea is diplomatically isolated, the U.S. has little direct leverage over its behavior. In the short term, U.S. leaders want to keep the North from spreading nuclear technology abroad. "You can't do anything about North Korea until it wants to have a different kind of relationship with the world, so the problem is to contain its impact," says Harvard's Walt.

Other nations also support containment of North Korea. In June the U.N. Security Council unanimously condemned its May nuclear test, tightening trade sanctions and calling on member countries to inspect and destroy all banned cargo coming to or from North Korea. China and Russia, both former allies of North Korea, both condemned the test.[68]

"We still want North Korea to come back to the negotiating table, to be part of an international effort that will lead to denuclearization," said Secretary of State Hillary Rodham Clinton in July. "But we're not going to reward them for doing what they said they would do in 2005 and 2006."[69]

Defense Secretary Gates said after the May test that the U.S. "will not accept North Korea as a nuclear state."[70] However, many observers believe North Korea hopes the U.S. will ultimately do just that — much as it opposed but ultimately recognized India's and Pakistan's nuclear programs.[71]

The challenge is different with Iran, which still belongs to the Nuclear Non-Proliferation Treaty and maintains that its nuclear research activities are strictly for peaceful purposes. But that position rings hollower than ever after last month's disclosure that Iran had built a second secret uranium enrichment plant.[72] President Obama's emphasis on diplomatic engagement and enforcing international treaties will be tested as the United States works to rally a strong international response.

The United States wants Iran to suspend enrichment activities, declare all of its nuclear activities, and open its nuclear facilities to international inspections.

"[I]f the U.S. extends a defense umbrella over the region, if we do even more to support the military capacity of those in the [Persian] Gulf, it's unlikely that Iran will be any stronger or safer, because they won't be able to intimidate and dominate, as they apparently believe they can, once they have a nuclear weapon," Secretary Clinton said in July. Officials in Washington said this was the first time the U.S. had publicly discussed offering defensive support to other Middle Eastern countries like Saudi Arabia and Egypt if Iran continued to pursue a nuclear capability.[73]

One of Obama's major diplomatic goals will be persuading Russia and China to support strong international sanctions on Iran if its leaders refuse to disclose their nuclear activities. Both countries have trade relationships with Iran and have resisted sanctions in the past. However, they also supported the Security Council resolution, which reaffirms the need to strengthen the NPT.

"It's all very well and good for the U.N. to condemn proliferator countries, but state actions supporting those measures determine whether they'll work or not," says Squassoni. "We can't be the global nuclear weapons policemen on our own. We need collaboration from our allies and Russia and China and a lot of other states."

New START with Russia

President Obama's administration came into office determined to "press the reset button with Russia," in Vice President Joseph Biden's words, and restore cooperation with Moscow on many issues — particularly arms control — where cooperation had deteriorated under President Bush.[74]

"We can and should cooperate to secure loose nuclear weapons and materials to prevent their spread, to renew the verification procedures in the START Treaty, and then go beyond existing treaties to negotiate deeper cuts in both our arsenals," Biden said in February. "The United States and Russia have a special obligation to lead the international effort to reduce the number of nuclear weapons in the world."[75]

Obama and Russian President Medvedev issued a joint statement in April affirming that they had committed both nations to "achieving a nuclear free world" through steps including a follow-on agreement to the START Treaty and efforts to strengthen international nuclear

non-proliferation policies, bring the Comprehensive Test Ban Treaty into force and negotiate a fissile production cutoff treaty. They also noted the possibility of U.S.-Russian cooperation on missile defense issues — no longer a far-fetched prospect in the wake of Obama's decision not to base mid-range defenses in Eastern Europe.[76]

But putting these agreements into action will require much more work. For example, the July agreement on post-START reductions identified ranges, not final numbers. Nuclear warheads would be limited to between 1,500 and 1,650 on each side, while delivery vehicles (bombers and missiles) would be reduced to between 500 and 1,100 each. Russia reportedly favors the lower numbers, while U.S. negotiators pushed for the higher figures. Nonetheless, observers saw the targets as a good first step.

"Russia is eager to do a START follow-on because its nuclear forces are coming down anyway," says former NNSA administrator Brooks. "And the transparency measures in the new treaty will be important, because we're still deeply suspicious of Russia's technology efforts, and they're suspicious of ours."

Since 1992 the United States and Russia have worked together under the Cooperative Threat Reduction (CTR) partnership, popularly known as the Nunn-Lugar initiative, to deactivate more than 7,000 warheads and destroy hundreds of bombers and long-range ballistic missiles.[77] CTR has also greatly improved security at many sites that store warheads and nuclear materials, although much remains to be done to consolidate the former Soviet Union's sprawling nuclear complex.[78]

"This work is essential in preventing nuclear terrorism and deserves greater support and government resources," said Nunn last May after the United States, Russia and the International Atomic Energy Agency helped remove 162 pounds of weapon-grade uranium (enough for about three bombs) from Kazakhstan.[79]

But even the popular Nunn-Lugar program faces constant budget pressures. Indeed, while Obama announced a new international effort in his Prague speech to "secure all vulnerable nuclear material around the world within four years," his 2010 budget request for nuclear threat reduction and related programs totals about $2.8 billion, about $150 million below the current level.[80]

OUTLOOK

Tipping Point?

In April 2010, members of the Nuclear Non-Proliferation Treaty (NPT) will hold their next five-year review conference to assess how well the pact is working. Most observers see the meeting as a critical decision point. If governments agree that progress is being made toward international arms control goals, they will be likely to make new commitments to support it. Conversely, if nations cannot agree on how to achieve key non-proliferation goals — as happened at the 2005 review conference — some experts worry that more proliferation, not less, could be the result.

"The 2005 review conference was a total disaster," says the Arms Control Association's Kimball. "The nonproliferation regime was in crisis: North Korea was withdrawing from the NPT and producing plutonium, Iran had been discovered to be developing a nuclear capability and the Bush administration had rejected the Comprehensive Test Ban Treaty as counter to U.S. interests. It was an important time for the world to come together and strengthen the treaty, and it didn't, partly because the United States didn't lead."

The tone has been more optimistic in preparatory meetings for the 2010 conference, and progress toward new U.S. and Russian reductions will help to demonstrate that the nuclear superpowers are serious about their disarmament commitments. "Obama's new approach is already producing some results," says Kimball, "but the U.S. and other countries will have to work hard to build consensus for an action plan that sets new limits on nuclear weapon development."

Many steps could be taken to strengthen the NPT regime. For example, says the Carnegie Endowment's Squassoni, states could endorse limits on reprocessing plutonium and enriching uranium. In addition, supporting the creation of an international nuclear fuel bank to replace national facilities would take the moral high ground away from countries like Iran that use civilian nuclear programs as cover for military activities.

"In 2005 countries like Iran talked about their rights to enrichment, reprocessing and peaceful use of nuclear energy under the NPT, and a lot of nonaligned states bought it," she says. "The debates were very polemical, not constructive."

Other helpful steps could include agreement on how NPT members should react if another state emulates North Korea and withdraws from the treaty, or more states adopt so-called additional protocols (intrusive inspections and monitoring) to their basic nuclear safeguard agreements with the International Atomic Energy Agency. As of mid-2009, 42 countries had not brought additional protocols into force, including Iran.[81]

Either as part of the review conference or separately, many experts would like to see cooperative threat reduction (CTR) programs expanded globally, as President Obama pledged in Prague. "I'd like to see it extended to all countries that have fissile materials," says Stanford University's Hecker, who has discussed protection, control and accounting for nuclear materials with officials in countries including Russia, India and North Korea. "There's very little uniformity across the world in how countries handle these materials or what they think needs to be done to provide a comprehensive safeguards system."

Some observers say that CTR programs could be much more effective. Rens Lee, an independent security consultant and author of a book on nuclear smuggling, argues that Obama needs a more proactive strategy that includes sharing intelligence with Russia about nuclear trafficking. "[A]ctual sharing remains woefully inadequate, both bilaterally and with international organizations such as the International Atomic Energy Agency," Lee wrote in July.[82]

But the basic concept of CTR has broad support. A congressionally mandated National Academy of Sciences study, released earlier this year, called for dramatically scaling up CTR programs to reduce threats from weapons of mass destruction in regions including the Middle East and Asia.

"The world is smaller than it was in 1992," the study said. "Ignoring globalization is not an option, whether in economics, public health, combating terrorism, or reducing the threat of WMD [weapons of mass destruction]. While our technological and military capabilities will continue to play an essential role, engagement is also one of the most important tools in the national security arsenal."[83]

NOTES

1. "Text of Obama's speech to the United Nations General Assembly," *The New York Times*, Sept. 23, 2009.

2. Stephen I. Schwartz with Deepti Choubey, *Nuclear Security Spending: Assessing Costs, Examining Priorities* (2009), p. 7, www.carnegieendowment.org/files/nuclear_security_spending_low.pdf.

3. George P. Shultz, *et al.*, "A World Free of Nuclear Weapons," *The Wall Street Journal*, Jan. 4, 2007.

4. Nuclear weapons get their explosive power from materials that are fissile, meaning that their atoms can be split by certain types of sub-atomic particles (neutrons). The main fissile materials are uranium-233, uranium-235, and plutonium-239.

5. Remarks by President Barack Obama, Prague, Czech Republic, April 5, 2009, www.whitehouse.gov/the_press_office/Remarks-By-President-Barack-Obama-In-Prague-As-Delivered/.

6. "U.S. Scraps Missile Defense Shield Plans," CNN.com, Sept. 17, 2009.

7. Clifford J. Levy and Peter Baker, "Putin Applauds Brave U.S. Decision on Missile Defense," *The New York Times*, Sept. 19, 2009.

8. "Statement of Senator John McCain," Sept. 17, 2009, http://mccain.senate.gov/public/.

9. "Historic Summit of Security Council Pledges Support for Progress on Stalled Efforts to End Nuclear Weapons Proliferation," United Nations, Sept. 24, 2009.

10. *Ibid.*

11. Natural Resources Defense Council, "Archive of Nuclear Data: Table of Global Nuclear Weapons Stockpiles, 1945-2002," www.nrdc.org/nuclear/nudb/datab19.asp.

12. America's Strategic Posture: Final Report of the Congressional Commission on the Strategic Posture of the United States (2009), chapters 2, 5 and 9, www.usip.org/files/file/strat_posture_report_adv_copy.pdf.

13. David E. Sanger and Helene Cooper, "Iran is Warned Over Nuclear Deception," *The New York Times*, Sept. 26, 2009.

14. "The Disarmament Illusion," editorial, *The Wall Street Journal*, Sept. 26, 2009.

15. For the treaty's history and full text, see www.state.gov/www/global/arms/treaties/npt.html.

16. www.globalzero.org/files/pdf/gzap_3.0.pdf.

17. For background see Mary H. Cooper, "Nuclear Proliferation and Terrorism," *CQ Researcher*, April 2, 2004, pp. 297-320.

18. Joseph Cirincione, *Bomb Scare: The History & Future of Nuclear Weapons* (2007), pp. 126-127.

19. Harold Brown and John Deutch, "The Nuclear Disarmament Fantasy," *The Wall Street Journal*, Nov. 19, 2007.

20. Treaty text is at www.state.gov/www/global/arms/treaties/ctb.html.

21. Annex 2 of the treaty lists 44 countries that must sign and ratify the treaty for it to enter into force. As of mid-2009, 35 of these countries had done so.

22. Damien J. LaVera, "Looking Back: The U.S. Senate Vote on the Comprehensive Test Ban Treaty," Arms Control Today, October 2004.

23. Jon Kyl and Richard Perle, "Our Decaying Nuclear Deterrent," *The Wall Street Journal*, June 30, 2009.

24. Congressional Record, June 8, 2009, p. S6238.

25. Comprehensive Nuclear Test Ban Treaty Organization, "CTBTO's Initial Findings on the DPRK's 2009 Announced Nuclear Test," May 25, 2009, www.ctbto.org/press-centre/press-releases/2009/ctbtos-initial-findings-on-the-dprks-2009-announced-nuclear-test/.

26. National Academy of Sciences, Technical Issues Related to the Comprehensive Nuclear Test Ban Treaty (National Academy Press, 2009), p. 5.

27. Speech at Strategic Weapons in the 21st Century Conference, Washington, D.C., Jan. 31, 2008, pp. 2-3, www.lanl.gov/conferences/sw/docs/chilton-speech-SW21-31Jan08.pdf.

28. Charles D. Ferguson, "Mini-Nuclear Weapons and the U.S. Nuclear Posture Review," Monterey Institute of International Studies, April 8, 2002, http://cns.miis.edu/stories/020408.htm.

29. James Sterngold, "Failure to Launch," *Mother Jones*, January 2008.

30. Jonathan Medalia, "The Reliable Replacement Warhead Program: Background and Current Developments," Congressional Research Service, Sept. 12, 2008, pp. 45-46, www.fas.org/sgp/crs/nuke/RL32929.pdf.

31. Robert Gates, "Nuclear Weapons and Deterrence in the 21st Century," speech at Carnegie Endowment for International Peace, Oct. 28, 2008, p. 5, www.carnegieendowment.org/files/1028_transcrip_gates_checked.pdf.

32. Hearing before House Armed Services Committee, March 17, 2009, www.stratcom.mil/speeches/21/.

33. *Technical Issues Related to the Comprehensive Nuclear Test Ban Treaty*, National Academy of Sciences (2002), p. 5.

34. "Pit Lifetime," MITRE Corporation, Nov. 20, 2006, p. 16, www.nukewatch.org/facts/nwd/JASON_ReportPuAging.pdf; National Nuclear Security Administration, "Studies Show Plutonium Degradation in U.S. Nuclear Weapons Will Not Affect Reliability Soon," Nov. 29, 2006.

35. National Nuclear Security Administration, "Life Extension Programs," http://nnsa.energy.gov/defense_programs/life_extension_programs.htm.

36. For details see U.S. Government Accountability Office, "Nuclear Weapons: Annual Assessment of the Safety, Performance, and Reliability of the Nation's Stockpile," Feb. 2, 2007, p. 14.

37. Gates, *op. cit.*, p. 5.

38. "The U.S. Military Index," *Foreign Policy*, March/April 2008, p. 77.

39. U.S. Department of Energy, Office of History and Heritage Resources, "The Manhattan Project: An Interactive History," www.cfo.doe.gov/me70/manhattan/retrospect.htm.

40. *Ibid.*

41. McGeorge Bundy, *Danger and Survival: Choices About the Bomb in the First Fifty Years* (1988), p. 113.

42. A ballistic missile is powered during the launch phase of its flight and then falls freely toward its target.

43. Bundy, *op. cit.*, p. 350.

44. Natural Resources Defense Council, "Table of Global Nuclear Weapons Stockpiles, 1945-2002," www.nrdc.org/nuclear/nudb/datab19.asp.

45. For an account and analysis of the crisis, see Bundy, *op cit.*, pp. 391-452. Bundy was President Kennedy's national security adviser during the missile crisis.

46. News conference 52, March 21, 1963, www.jfklibrary.org/Historical+Resources/Archives/Reference+Desk/Press+Conferences/.

47. Text and background at www.state.gov/www/global/arms/treaties/ltbt1.html.

48. *Ibid.*

49. Natural Resources Defense Council, *op. cit.*

50. Text and background at www.state.gov/www/global/arms/treaties/salt1.html and www.state.gov/www/global/arms/treaties/abm/abm2.html.

51. Presidential Directive 59, July 25, 1980, www.fas.org/irp/offdocs/pd/pd59.pdf.

52. Robert Scheer, *With Enough Shovels: Reagan, Bush and Nuclear War* (1983), p. 20.

53. Michael Goodwin, "Antinuclear Protest Cost the City $1.8 Million," *The New York Times*, July 25, 1982.

54. U.S. Catholic Bishops' Pastoral Letter on War and Peace, May 3, 1983, www.nuclearfiles.org/menu/key-issues/ethics/issues/religious/us-catholic-bishops-pastoral-letter.htm.

55. For background see Mary H. Cooper, "Missile Defense," *CQ Researcher*, Sept. 8, 2000.

56. Nikolai Sokov, "Reykjavik Summit: the Legacy and a Lesson for the Future," Nuclear Threat Initiative, December 2007.

57. Text and background at www.state.gov/www/global/arms/treaties/inf1.html.

58. Compiled from Nuclear Threat Initiative, "Threat Reduction Budgets," www.nti.org/e_research/cnwm/overview/cnwm_home.asp.

59. Nuclear Threat Initiative, "U.S. Nuclear Posture Reviews," www.nti.org/f_wmd411/f2c.html.

60. *Ibid.*

61. Philipp C. Bleek, "Nuclear Posture Review Leaks: Outlines Targets, Contingencies," *Arms Control Today*, April 2002.

62. Arms Control Association, "START II and Its Extension Protocol at a Glance," January 2003, www.armscontrl.org/print/2562; Nuclear Threat Initiative, "The SORT Treaty," updated July 2009, www.nti.org/f_wmd411/f2b2_1.html.

63. Steven A. Hildreth and Carl Ek, "Long-Range Ballistic Missile Defense in Europe," Congressional Research Service, June 22, 2009, p. 17, www.fas.org/sgp/crs/weapons/RL34051.pdf.

64. New Deterrent Working Group, "U.S. Nuclear Deterrence in the 21st Century: Getting It Right," Center for Security Policy, July 2009, p. 12, http://204.96.138.161/upload/wysiwyg/center%20publication%20pdfs/NDWG-%20Getting%20It%20Right.pdf.

65. Clifford J. Levy and Peter Baker, "U.S.-Russia Nuclear Agreement is first Step in Broad Effort," *The New York Times*, July 7, 2009.

66. Congressional Record, July 22, 2009, p. S7850.

67. Siegfried S. Hecker, "The Risks of North Korea's Restart," Bulletin of the Atomic Scientists, May 12, 2009; David E. Sanger, "Tested Early by North Korea, Obama Has Few Options," *The New York Times*, May 26, 2009. For background see Mary H. Cooper, "North Korean Crisis," *CQ Researcher*, April 11, 2003, pp. 321-344.

68. United Nations Department of Public Information, "Security Council, Acting Unanimously, condemns in Strongest Terms Democratic People's Republic of Korea Nuclear Test, Toughens Sanctions," June 12, 2009.

69. Interviewed on Meet the Press, July 26, 2009, www.msnbc.msn.com/id/32142102/ns/meet_the_press/.

70. Neil Chatterjee, "U.S. Says Will Not Accept N. Korea as Nuclear State," Reuters, May 30, 2009.

71. See Martin Fackler, "Test Delivers a Message for Domestic Audience," *The New York Times*, May 26, 2009,

72. David E. Sanger and Helene Cooper, "Iran Is Warned Over Nuclear Deception," *The New York Times*, Sept. 26, 2009.

73. Mark Landler and David E. Sanger, "Clinton Speaks of Shielding Mideast from Iran," *The New York Times*, July 23, 2009.

74. For background see Roland Flamini, "Dealing with the 'New' Russia," *CQ Researcher*, June 6, 2008, pp. 481-504.

75. "Biden's full remarks at the Munich conference," *Politico.com*, Feb. 7, 2009, www.politico.com/news/stories/0209/18535.html.

76. "Joint Statement by President Obama and President Medvedev," The White House, April 1, 2009.

77. Office of Sen. Richard G. Lugar, "The Nunn-Lugar Scorecard," http://lugar.senate.gov/nunnlugar/scorecard.html.

78. Matthew Bunn, "Securing the Bomb 2008," Harvard University, November 2008, pp. vi-xi, www.nti.org/e_research/STB08_Executive_Summary.pdf.

79. "NTI Co-chairman Sam Nunn Commends Successful Removal of Dangerous Nuclear Material from Kazakhstan," Nuclear Threat Initiative, May 19, 2009.

80. Kingston Reif and Cuyler O'Brien, "Obama Nuclear Nonproliferation Budget Disappointing," Center for Arms Control and Non-Proliferation, June 2, 2009.

81. International Atomic Energy Agency, "Strengthened Safeguards System: Status of Additional Protocols," July 9, 2009, www.iaea.org/OurWord/SV/Safeguards/sg_protocol.html.

82. Rens Lee, "Toward an Intelligence-Based Nuclear Cooperations Regime," Foreign Policy Research Institute, July 2009.

83. Committee on International Security and Arms Control, National Academy of Sciences, *Global Security Engagement: A New Model for Cooperative Threat Reduction* (2009), p. 9.

BIBLIOGRAPHY

Books

Allison, Graham, *Nuclear Terrorism: The Ultimate Preventable Catastrophe*, Times Books, 2004.
A Harvard professor and former Defense Department official explores the risk of terrorist nuclear attacks on the U.S.

Bundy, McGeorge, *Danger and Survival: Choices About the Bomb in the First 50 Years*, Vintage, 1990.
A national security adviser to presidents Kennedy and Johnson examines factors that led nations to pursue or forswear nuclear weapons during World War II and the Cold War.

Moran, Barbara, *The Day We Lost the H-Bomb: Cold War, Hot Nukes, and the Worst Nuclear Weapons Disaster in History*, Presidio Press, 2009.
Journalist Moran revisits the 1966 collision of a U.S. B-52 bomber carrying four hydrogen bombs with a refueling plane over Spain.

Shultz, George P., *et al.*, eds., *Reykjavik Revisited: Steps Toward a World Free of Nuclear Weapons*, Hoover Institution Press, 2008.
National security experts examine the steps required to reduce threats from nuclear weapons and move toward their elimination.

Articles

Bender, Bryan, "Obama Seeks Global Uranium Fuel Bank," *The Boston Globe*, June 8, 2009.
Bender outlines an idea advocated by many arms control specialists: creating an international nuclear fuel supply so that countries would not need to build fuel production systems that could produce weapon-grade nuclear material.

Broad, William J., and David E. Sanger, "Obama's Youth Shaped His Nuclear-Free Vision," *The New York Times*, July 5, 2009.
President Obama's support for nuclear abolition dates back to his college years.

DeSutter, Paula A., "The Test Ban Treaty Would Help North Korea," *The Wall Street Journal*, June 1, 2009.
A former Bush administration official argues that ending nuclear testing would erode U.S. nuclear credibility.

Kimball, Daryl, "Change Nuclear Weapons Policy? Yes, We Can," *Foreign Policy in Focus*, Nov. 25, 2008.
The director of the Arms Control Association contends that without action by the Obama administration to shrink nuclear arsenals and transform U.S. nuclear policy, global risks of nuclear proliferation and terrorism will increase.

Suri, Jeremi, "The Nukes of October: Richard Nixon's Secret Plan to Bring Peace to Vietnam," *Wired*, Feb. 25, 2008.
A professor details how in 1969 President Richard M. Nixon sent nuclear-armed bombers to the edge of Soviet airspace to convince Soviet leaders and their North Vietnamese allies that unless they joined talks to end the Vietnam War, the United States might end it with nuclear weapons.

Reports and Studies

"Leveraging Science for Security: A Strategy for the Nuclear Weapons Laboratories in the 21st Century," Henry L. Stimson Center, March 2009, www.stimson.org/cnp/pdf/Leveraging_Science_for_Security_FINAL.pdf.
A task force co-chaired by former senior officials from the Clinton and Bush administrations recommends moving nuclear weapons laboratories in the United States into a new agency that would maintain the nuclear arsenal and analyze national security problems.

"U.S. Nuclear Weapons Policy," Council on Foreign Relations, Independent Task Force Report No. 62, 2009, www.cfr.org/content/publications/attachments/Nuclear_Weapons_TFR62.pdf.
Nuclear security experts recommend how to reshape U.S. nuclear forces and policies to address nuclear proliferation and other post-Cold War security threats.

"White Paper on the Necessity of the U.S. Nuclear Deterrent," National Institute for Public Policy, Aug. 15, 2007, www.nipp.org/Publication/Downloads/Publication%20Archive%20PDF/Deterrence%20Paper%20-%20version%202.pdf.
Conservative security scholars and former government officials contend the United States still needs nuclear weapons for deterring attacks, destroying strategic military targets and stemming nuclear proliferation.

Perkovich, George, *et al.*, "Abolishing Nuclear Weapons: A Debate," Carnegie Endowment for International Peace, February 2009, www.carnegieendowment.org/files/abolishing_nuclear_weapons_debate.pdf.
Security experts in 13 countries examine what would be required to achieve nuclear disarmament.

Schwartz, Stephen I., with Deepti Choubey, *Nuclear Security Spending: Assessing Costs, Examining*

Priorities (2009), p. 7, www.carnegieendowment.org/files/nuclear_security_spending_low.pdf.
A review of U.S. funding for programs related to nuclear weapons finds that the nation is still spending more than $50 billion annually in this area nearly two decades after the Cold War.

For More Information

Alliance for Nuclear Accountability, 903 West Alameda St., #505, Santa Fe, NM 87501; (505) 473-1670; www.ananuclear.org. A network of local, regional and national organizations working to control pollution from nuclear weapons production.

Arms Control Association, 1313 L St., N.W., Suite 130, Washington, DC 2005; (202) 463-8270; www.armscontrol.org. A nonprofit, nonpartisan organization that promotes public understanding of and support for effective arms control policies.

Atomic Heritage Foundation, 910 17th St., N.W., Suite 408, Washington, DC 20006; (202) 293-0045; www.atomicheritage.org. A nonprofit organization working to preserve and interpret the Manhattan Project and its legacy.

Center for International Security and Cooperation, 616 Serra St., E200, Stanford University, Stanford, CA 94305-6055; (650) 723-9265; http://cisac.stanford.edu. Studies nuclear weapons strategy and proliferation.

National Institute for Public Policy, 9302 Lee Hwy., Suite 750, Fairfax, VA 22301-1214; (703) 293-9181; www.nipp.org. A nonprofit education organization focusing on foreign and defense policy from a conservative perspective.

National Nuclear Security Administration, U.S. Department of Energy, 1000 Independence Ave., S.W., Washington, DC 20585; (800) 342-5363; http://nnsa.energy.gov. Manages the nation's nuclear stockpile and related laboratories and production plants.

Nuclear Threat Initiative, 1747 Pennsylvania Ave., N.W., 7th Floor, Washington, DC 20006; (202) 296-4810; www.nti.org. Works to strengthen global security by preventing the spread of weapons of mass destruction.

Ploughshares Fund, Fort Mason Center B-330, San Francisco, CA 94123; (415) 775-2244; www.ploughshares.org. Opposes the spread of nuclear weapons.

6

Attacking Piracy

Kenneth Jost

A Chinese destroyer escorts two Chinese freighters in the pirate-infested waters off the coast of Somalia. Warships from dozens of nations, including the United States, the European Union, China, India and Russia now patrol the region against a sudden upsurge in piracy, which costs the global shipping industry up to $50 billion a year. Despite the show of force, many experts argue that given Somalia's grinding poverty, eradicating piracy requires more than a naval solution.

From *CQ Researcher*,
August 11, 2009.

Hassan Abdalla was on his way to deliver rice to starving Somalis when his freighter, the *Semlow*, was surrounded by small boats manned by pirates with AK-47 assault rifles and rocket-propelled grenades (RPGs).

Claiming to belong to the so-called Somali Marines — the largest of the many pirate gangs operating off the Somali coast — the hijackerstook over the *Semlow* and began using it as a "mother" ship — for launching smaller, faster boats to attack other ships. Four months later Abdalla and his fellow mariners were released, after more than $500,000 in ransom was paid to the pirates.

"I knew they would hijack again, because ransom money is sweet," Abdalla told Daniel Sekulich, a reporter with *The Globe and Mail* in Toronto and author of a new book about piracy, *Terror on the Seas*. "Once you've tasted it, you want more."[1]

Indeed, the lure of easy money has turned the seas around the Horn of Africa into danger zones for commercial ships. Some 30,000 vessels per year use the region's shipping lanes to deliver oil and other goods between Europe, the Middle East and Asia.[2] In the first half of this year, armed Somali pirates attacked at least 150 oceangoing vessels in the area, a sixfold jump in attacks in that region over the same period in 2008.[3]

More than 250 years since the end of the so-called Golden Age of Piracy — the days of Blackbeard, Captain Kidd and other legendary figures — pirates have returned to the high seas, threatening maritime security, commerce and, some terrorism experts say, global security. "Piracy, the scourge of the 17th and 18th centuries, has emerged from the history books and has returned with deadly, terrifying results,"

Piracy Spans the Globe

Piracy occurs in most of the world's tropical oceans — including the Pacific waters off Peru, the east and west coasts of Africa and the seas of Southeast Asia. More than 60 percent of the 240 attacks in the first half of 2009 were attributed to heavily armed Somalis attacking ships in the Gulf of Aden and off the coast of Somalia. The second-largest number of pirate attacks this year occurred in the Southeast Asia/Far East region.

Successful and Attempted Pirate Attacks
(January–June, 2009)

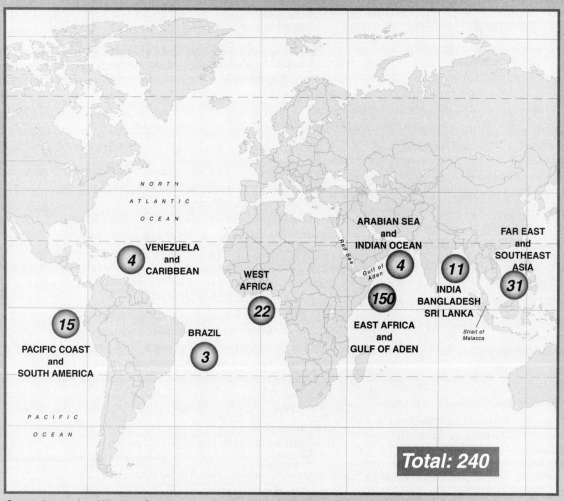

Source: International Maritime Bureau

writes John Burnett, a London-based maritime security consultant and former reporter, in his 2002 book *Dangerous Waters.*[4]

A record 889 crew members were taken hostage in 2008 — a 207 percent increase over 2007, according to Peter Chalk, a maritime security analyst with the RAND Corporation think tank. Although ransom negotiations are kept confidential, pirates collected an estimated $30 million to $150 million in booty last year. Many worry that such big — and rapidly growing — sums will only encourage, and fund, further attacks. Currently, Somali pirates are holding 10 foreign vessels hostage, awaiting ransom payments.[5]

Piracy costs the shipping industry overall — in ransoms, lost cargoes, higher insurance premiums and interrupted shipping schedules — from $10 billion to $50 billion a year, according to Sekulich. "Even the low-ball estimates," he notes, are "well above the gross domestic product of numerous nations [and] virtually unprecedented in our global economic history."[6]

And, while no direct link has been established between the Somali pirates and terrorists, some worry the weaknesses in maritime security exploited by pirates will prove useful to those seeking to spread terror. (*See sidebar, p. 132.*) Martin N. Murphy, a senior research fellow at the Center for Strategic and Budgetary Assessments in Washington and author of a 2009 book on piracy and marine terrorism, says Web traffic and intelligence intercepts clearly indicate that Islamic extremist groups "are watching what's happening off Somalia. It reveals a clear weakness, and terrorists can exploit this."

While most pirate attacks today occur near Somalia, pirates also operate off the coasts of other countries, including Peru, Brazil and Nigeria. Private yachts in the Caribbean and Gulf of Mexico also have been attacked. For decades, pirates plagued Southeast Asia, especially the

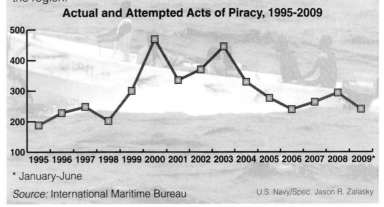

Piracy Could Set New Record This Year

In the first half of 2009 there were 240 attempted and successful pirate attacks worldwide — twice the number in the same period last year. The increase is due largely to attacks by Somali pirates in the Gulf of Aden and off the coast of Somalia. At the current rate, global piracy this year will surpass its modern peak of 469 attacks in 2000. Most of those attacks occurred in Southeast Asia and the Malacca Strait between Malaysia, Indonesia and Singapore. After those governments jointly cracked down, piracy declined dramatically in the region.

Actual and Attempted Acts of Piracy, 1995-2009

* January-June

Source: International Maritime Bureau

U.S. Navy/Spec. Jason R. Zalasky

Malacca Strait — the strategic waterway that runs between Singapore, Indonesia and Malaysia and links northeast Asia with the Indian Ocean. But a tough, new, regional anti-piracy campaign has helped to control the attacks in recent years.

Recent pirate attacks have been concentrated off Somalia and in the Gulf of Aden/Red Sea area: Attacks by Somalis in the first six months of this year accounted for more than 60 percent of the world's 240 pirate incidents. At that rate, total attacks in 2009 could surpass the modern-day record of 469 incidents in 2000, when most piracy was occurring in Southeast Asia. But experts say shipowners only report about a third of actual attacks, because they don't want their voyages delayed further by criminal or insurance investigations.

One of the most dramatic attacks occurred in April, when Somali pirates boarded the *Maersk Alabama* — the first such incident against a U.S. vessel manned by an American crew. The captain, Richard Phillips, gave himself up as a hostage in exchange for the release of his crew and ship. Several days later he was dramatically rescued

Piracy Shifts From Asia to East Africa

The world's piracy hot spot has shifted dramatically from Southeast Asia to East Africa over the last decade. In 2000, nearly half of the 469 pirate attacks occurred in Southeast Asia, and only 5 percent in East Africa. But since Singapore, Malaysia and Indonesia jointly adopted a strong anti-piracy program in 2004, pirate attacks in the region have plummeted. In the first half of 2009, Southeast Asia experienced only 10 percent of the world's pirate attacks, and 60 percent occurred in Somalia, the Gulf of Aden and the Red Sea.

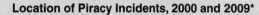

Location of Piracy Incidents, 2000 and 2009*

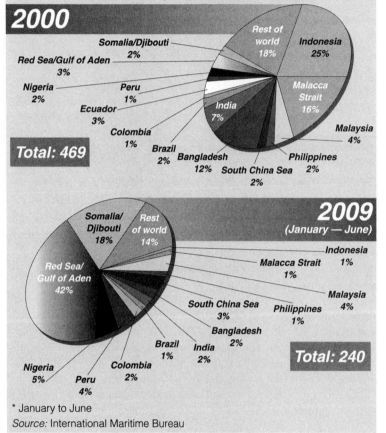

2000

- Rest of world 18%
- Indonesia 25%
- Somalia/Djibouti 2%
- Red Sea/Gulf of Aden 3%
- Nigeria 2%
- Peru 1%
- Ecuador 3%
- India 7%
- Malacca Strait 16%
- Colombia 1%
- Brazil 2%
- Bangladesh 12%
- South China Sea 2%
- Philippines 2%
- Malaysia 4%

Total: 469

2009 (January — June)

- Somalia/Djibouti 18%
- Rest of world 14%
- Red Sea/Gulf of Aden 42%
- Indonesia 1%
- Malacca Strait 1%
- Malaysia 4%
- South China Sea 3%
- Philippines 1%
- Bangladesh 2%
- Brazil 1%
- India 2%
- Colombia 2%
- Nigeria 5%
- Peru 4%

Total: 240

* January to June

Source: International Maritime Bureau

when three Navy SEAL snipers shot and killed his three captors.

Some in the shipping industry complained afterwards that killing pirates might endanger future hostages, who until now have mainly been unharmed. Some Somali pirates at the time boasted they would now target and kill American sailors, but that hasn't happened.[7]

The debate about the use of force reflected a larger point: Navies are uncertain how to handle the problem. They don't engage with pirates until after an attack has occurred, and, even when they do capture pirates, it's not always clear what they should do with them or who has jurisdiction over crimes committed in international waters. Because many Western nations lack clear anti-piracy statutes, dozens of captured pirates have been disarmed and released. Some have been taken to neighboring countries, especially Kenya, for prosecution. (*See sidebar, p. 138.*)

In the past year the ranks of Somali pirates have burgeoned, as more and more citizens of the failed state — lucky to earn $2 a day and attracted by the lucrative spoils — have joined their ranks. Today there are at least 3,000 Somali pirates, up significantly from the roughly 200 that were operating in early 2008, according to Burnett. Russian Vice Admiral Oleg Burtsev puts the number at 5,000 or more.[8]

"If you're young and able-bodied, what else can you do but join the pirates?" asks Peter Lehr, a terrorism-studies lecturer at the University of St. Andrews in Scotland. "It's like the California Gold Rush."

Regardless of the exact number, Somali pirates have grown bolder in recent months, targeting large container ships and even supertankers like the *Sirius Star*, which was carrying $100 million worth of oil and eventually was ransomed for an estimated $3 million.

Up to 90 percent of the world's goods travel by boat, making ships at sea the weak link in the global trading system. Given the threat, warships from nearly two-dozen countries, part of a "combined task force" set up by the United States in January, are now patrolling the area. The European Union is running a separate escort and patrol operation to protect food aid shipments like the one carried by the *Semlow*. It is the EU's first naval mission and the first time Britain's Royal Navy has been on an anti-piracy mission in nearly 200 years.[9] In addition, France, China, India, South Korea and Russia have sent their own vessels.

Despite the show of force, naval officials concede it's not enough. Patrolling more than half a million square miles of water would take hundreds of warships, not a couple dozen. "The weird thing is, piracy has increased while we have the heaviest presence of naval warships in that region that's ever been seen," says author Sekulich.

Many argue that ending piracy requires more than a naval solution. Piracy, particularly the Somali brand, reflects that country's poverty, limited opportunities and lack of a functioning central government. Since the fall of a dictatorial regime in 1991, Somalia has had a new government about once every 14 months, on average.[10] It's also awash in arms, after decades of civil war and Cold War efforts to play the Soviets off against the Americans.

But while Somalia has devolved into a failed state, its pirate gangs have become increasingly sophisticated, Sekulich points out. "Somalia has transformed itself, or rather the pirates have transformed themselves, into the most advanced and effective type of pirates we've seen in centuries."

The pirates often turn a portion of the ransom money over to their backers — sophisticated organized crime figures — who reinvest much of it in high-powered weaponry, faster boats, global positioning systems (GPS) and satellite phones. And the pirates now are apparently sharing intelligence about the movement of merchant ships.

"The most recent evidence shows that the mother vessels are telling each other about potential targets," British Rear Adm. Philip Jones, commander of the EU naval task force, said in May. "They are exchanging positional information, . . . information about ships they have seen or may have tried to attack. Obviously, that is a significant development."[11]

Given the enormous profits Somalis are pulling in, some analysts worry that the piracy problem will spread.

As the global community struggles to combat piracy, here are some of the questions people are debating:

Can navies defeat piracy?

Piracy has been a menace since ancient times. Cicilian pirates from what is now Turkey disrupted commerce between cities and kidnapped important officials until 67 B.C., when a Roman commander, Gnaeus Pompeius Magnus ("Pompey the Great"), shut down the pirate operation in less than two months with a massive naval and land campaign.

Pompey divided his massive fleet into 13 naval squadrons responsible for various sections of the Mediterranean. He kept 60 ships under his direct command, using them to harass pirates into the areas patrolled by his commanders. Within 40 days, he cleared the western Mediterranean of pirates and chased them inland using tens of thousands of soldiers, attacking pirate strongholds in Turkey.

Similarly, the rise of modern-day piracy off Somalia has attracted the attention of the world's great navies, and their warships are having an effect. The United Nations had stopped sending food aid to Somalia for nearly three years due to pirate raids on the shipments. But since the EU launched its "Operation Atalanta" mission in December, not a single escorted U.N. shipment has been stopped, and 1.6 million Somalis are being fed by the U.N.'s World Food Programme (WFP) every day. In addition to protecting food shipments, Atalanta's ships and helicopters escort commercial vessels and provide aerial surveillance and other measures to deter piracy in the region.

"We hope very much that with this anti-piracy operation in the Horn of Africa — one of the busiest transit routes in the world — we can bring these piracy activities down," says Cristina Gallach, spokeswoman for the European Union's high Representative for the Common Foreign and Security Policy.

Although the EU recently extended the Atalanta mission for another year, Gallach says it's not a panacea. Pirates who can't hit ships along their accustomed corridors now attack ships as far south as the Seychelles. "It's just like any other criminal activity," says RAND's Chalk. "They'll exploit some other area where there isn't so much law enforcement."

Shippers want navies to disrupt piracy before attacks occur, says Pottengal Mukundan, director of the International Chamber of Commerce's International Maritime Bureau. Capturing or sinking the mother ships would be particularly helpful, he says.

Reuters/Crack Palinggi

Indonesian naval personnel guard pirates suspected of hijacking the palm oil tanker MT Kraton in the Strait of Singapore. Although the pirates changed the ship's name, a joint anti-piracy campaign by Indonesia, Malaysia and Singapore used a new international database to uncover the name change and apprehend the pirates in September 2007.

The Indian navy sank a mother ship last November, 325 miles southwest of Oman's port of Salalah. And in April, a French frigate sailing under the EU banner intercepted a mother ship in the Gulf of Aden, detaining 11 pirates.

"Navies have to increase their deterrent efforts — before pirates get on board," says Lee Willett, head of the maritime studies program at the Royal United Services Institute for Defence and Security Studies in London. "Stop them on shore, create exclusion zones bigger than the current corridors, stop any vessel out there with small engines, which are obviously out there for no good reason."

But aside from the "balloon effect" of pushing pirates out to new, unguarded areas, the battle against piracy ultimately must be won on land, says Gallach. "The problem of piracy is on land, not on the high seas."

Many observers agree the problem is "land-based," the result of Somalia's 18 years without a functioning government. Without law enforcement or any sense of order, Somali gangs and warlords have become increasingly sophisticated in their sponsorship of crimes extending out to the high seas. "Piracy is the maritime ripple effect of anarchy on land," wrote foreign policy journalist Robert D. Kaplan.[12]

Piracy has prospered because pirates have safe havens back home, and the ruined economy is not producing legitimate jobs for young Somalis. Since Somalia's 2,000-mile-long coastline sits near a key transit corridor — the Gulf of Aden — the country's problems have filtered far out to sea.

"You've got the most powerful naval armada assembled in recent history to fight the scourge of pirates who are really lightly armed in some puny boats, and they still can't stop them," says Burnett.

Historical battles against piracy have generally required action on land, from Pompey's use of 120,000 infantry to clemency deals cut with Chinese and Caribbean pirates. More recently, piracy in the Strait of Malacca and the surrounding region dropped from 187 attacks in 2003 to 65 in 2008 after Singapore, Indonesia, Malaysia and Thailand — with Japanese prodding and funding — launched a coordinated anti-piracy campaign.[13]

But without a functioning government in Somalia, "there's no way of controlling pirates internally," Burnett says. "There are efforts to build a coast guard there, but that's so far down the road."*

Chris Trelawny — head of maritime security for the U.N.'s London-based International Maritime Organization (IMO) — is more hopeful. He points out that 17 countries in the region drafted a code of conduct in January vowing to seize pirate ships and cooperate in the arrest and prosecutions of pirates.

---

* The Transitional Federal Government, formed in 2004, is the latest in a string of efforts to establish a central government in Somalia in the last 18 years. President Sheikh Sharif Sheikh Ahmed, elected in January, has not yet been able to provide essential services or maintain security. The externally funded, ultra-conservative jihadist al-Shabaab group controls much of the southern part of the country and some parts of the capital.

Until a land-based solution can be instituted in Somalia, Trelawny says, "We welcome the work of the navies in carrying out what are essentially constabulary efforts."

The International Maritime Bureau's Mukundan disagrees. "It is a naval problem," he says. "In today's world, navies have the responsibility to protect maritime trade routes. They have stepped up to the mark splendidly." But he concedes that naval efforts are only a "temporary measure."

Willett concurs, saying naval action is needed to buy time for Somalia and other regional countries to get a handle on the problem. "While navies are a short-term element in the process," he says, "navies need to be there to keep a lid on it."

Despite the recent EU extension of its convoy program, some wonder whether the great powers will sustain their presence in the region for the years it undoubtedly will take for the Somali government to get its house in order enough to start prosecuting piracy.

The relatively low incidence of pirate attacks — only 240 so far this year on the tens of thousands of ships plying the world's oceans — has implications for how military resources are allocated, Michèle Flournoy, undersecretary of Defense for policy, told the Senate Armed Services Committee in May. She noted that merchant ship crews had thwarted 78 percent of the unsuccessful attacks, while military or law enforcement interventions had blocked only 22 percent.[14]

The millions being spent on naval patrols might even be counterproductive, suggests RAND's Chalk. "We're investing too much in naval solutions, to the detriment of long-term solutions."

"Navies cannot defeat piracy," insists EU spokeswoman Gallach. "Navies can . . . give protection to those who are in transit — the merchants, the ships that are transporting humanitarian aid."

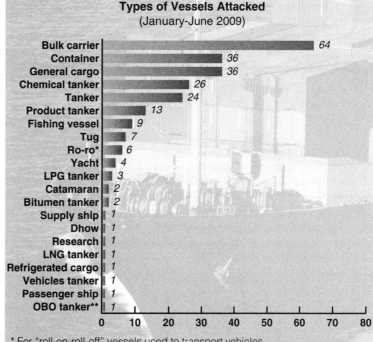

Bulk Carriers Are Main Pirate Target

More than a quarter of the 240 pirate attacks in the first half of 2009 were on bulk carriers that transport commodities like grain. Container ships and general cargo vessels were attacked 36 times each.

Types of Vessels Attacked
(January-June 2009)

Bulk carrier	64
Container	36
General cargo	36
Chemical tanker	26
Tanker	24
Product tanker	13
Fishing vessel	9
Tug	7
Ro-ro*	6
Yacht	4
LPG tanker	3
Catamaran	2
Bitumen tanker	2
Supply ship	1
Dhow	1
Research	1
LNG tanker	1
Refrigerated cargo	1
Vehicles tanker	1
Passenger ship	1
OBO tanker**	1

* For "roll-on-roll-off" vessels used to transport vehicles

** For oil, bulk commodities or ore

Source: "Piracy and Armed Robbery Against Ships," International Maritime Bureau, January-June 2009

Besides, as Flournoy and others suggest, chasing down pirates would divert their resources and attention from their fundamental strategic defense missions. "Prosecuting detained pirates . . . is simply not our business," said Cmdr. Achim Winkler, who heads an EU flotilla in the Gulf of Aden.[15]

Should shipping crews be armed?

A growing chorus of voices — including *Maersk Alabama* Capt. Phillips — are now convinced that maritime crews should be armed and trained to defend their ships.

"Arming the crew as part of an overall strategy could provide an effective deterrent under certain circumstances," Phillips told the Senate Foreign Relations Committee on

No Link Seen Between Pirates and Terrorists

But some fear terrorists could adopt pirates' tactics.

Given the logistical difficulties involved, it's not surprising that terrorists have struck on land much more often than they've tried to strike at sea. Since the 1960s, there have been fewer than 200 maritime terror attacks worldwide, compared with over 10,000 terrorist incidents overall.[1]

But there is now some concern among defense analysts that the rapid growth of piracy might lead to more terror at sea. "Similar forces allow piracy and maritime terrorism to flourish," says Peter Chalk, a policy analyst with the RAND Corporation think tank. "The model of piracy could be mimicked by terrorists, including ransom demands."

Chalk notes that piracy can weaken political systems by encouraging corruption among public officials. And it's clear that piracy has been used as a fundraising tool by some terrorists, including the Free Aceh Movement in Indonesia and the Tamil Tigers in Sri Lanka. The two-decade-long Tiger insurgency was defeated by the Sri Lankan government in May.

"In the last year, we have seen structures related to al Qaeda that are taking advantage of the lawlessness that exists in Somalia," says Christina Gallach, a spokeswoman for the European Union.[2]

As Gallach and others point out, however, there appears to be no credible evidence of a direct link between pirates off the Somali coast and terrorists. "We are working very firmly in the belief that there is no proven link between piracy and al Qaeda-type terrorism," says Chris Trelawny, security chief of the International Maritime Organization. "What makes Somali piracy unique is that they are purely taking ships for kidnap and ransom."

In fact, pirates and terrorists work at cross-purposes, suggests Daniel Sekulich, author of the 2009 book, *Terror on the Seas: True Tales of Modern-Day Pirates*. Pirates' tools are subterfuge and anonymity, while terrorists want, more than anything else, to attract attention for their deeds.

"Pirates and terrorists have diametrically opposed goals," Sekulich says. "Pirates are seeking economic gain that comes from a steady supply of the world's shipping. They love all those container ships. Terrorists want to slow [or disrupt] shipping . . . for their own nefarious means."

Still, both piracy and terror are dangers because of the vulnerable nature of ocean-going trade. Piracy is a reflection of the fact that the weakest link in world trade is the lone vessel at sea, which could also be hit by politically motivated attackers.

April 30, just weeks after his spectacular rescue by Navy sharpshooters. But he doesn't think it would be "the best or ultimate solution to the problem."[16]

Vice Admiral James Winnefeld, director of strategic plans and policy for the Joint Chiefs of Staff, agrees. "It's a capacity issue," he told the Senate Armed Services Committee. "We believe this is something private industry needs to do for themselves."

The idea that shipowners should arm and train crew members — or hire private security forces to accompany ships or their escorts — appears to be gaining currency with U.S. defense officials. "It may be useful for Congress to consider developing incentives to encourage merchant ships to invest in security measures," Defense undersecretary Flournoy told the Armed Service Committee. "These could range from tax credits to reduced insurance rates for ships with enhanced security."

In other countries, however, proposals to arm crewmen or hire mercenaries remain highly controversial. Shipowners, insurers and seafarers all cite increased risks and legal and logistical complications posed by having firearms aboard merchant ships.

"Arming seafarers — that is totally out of the question," says Arild Wegener, chief of security for the Norwegian Shipowners Association.

Arming crews would trigger an arms race between the pirates and the crews and could increase the risk of serious harm and death onboard, even without a pirate attack, he says. So far, Somali pirates have shown little interest in harming their hostages, because they want to be able to collect ransom payments for them. But arming ship crews could change the equation.

"Arming merchant sailors may result in the acquisition of even more lethal weapons and tactics by the

"We believe the division between piracy and terrorism is much more blurred than some people seek to argue," says Andrew Linington, spokesman for the Nautilus International seafarers' union. "Certainly, our big worry is that a dozen guys in a fiberglass boat can take command of a ship like the *Sirius Star*, a massive vessel with millions of dollars of oil on board.

"We think that's an intolerable situation and should be sending huge warning signals out to governments about the fragility of safety at sea," he continues.

The deadliest terror attack at sea occurred in 2004, when 116 people were killed in the bombing of the Philippine *SuperFerry 14*. The ferry was blown up by 16 sticks of dynamite hidden in a hollowed out television set by members of the Abu Sayyaf Islamist separatist group. Such attacks worry security officials because they areso cheap and easy to carry out. Planning for the bombing took only a couple of months and cost no more than $400t.[3]

Marine terrorism is not new in the region of the world where piracy now dogs the shipping industry. In 2002, two suicide bombers attacked the oil tanker *Limburg* off Yemen, killing themselves and one crew member. The attack triggered a rise in the price of oil and area shipping insurance rates, causing a 93 percent drop in the container business at the Port of Aden.[4]

The disproportionate impact of such terrorist attacks is why some worry about the potential for piracy to lead to increases in maritime terrorism. Some experts worry, for example, that a liquefied natural gas tanker could be hijacked and turned into a massive bomb.

"No matter how well-protected, every ship afloat — and this includes those that carry enough reactor fuel to build a few nuclear devices — is physically highly vulnerable," writes maritime security consultant John Burnett.[5]

A more likely scenario, though, is that terrorists could take over or blow up a ship along one of the major shipping chokepoints, such as the Strait of Hormuz or the Suez Canal, disrupting the flow of oil or other crucial cargo. "With deliberate preparation and the occasional well-placed attack, a few men with small boats can keep the navies churning for years," writes journalist William Langewiesche in his 2004 book *The Outlaw Sea*.[6]

"If terrorists like al Qaeda want to keep Western powers tied up, would it not be logical for them to open another front to get attention off Afghanistan and Pakistan?" asks Lee Willett, a British naval security expert.

---

[1] Martin N. Murphy, *Small Boats, Weak States, Dirty Money* (2009), p. 185.

[2] For background, see Jason McLure, "The Troubled Horn of Africa," *CQ Global Researcher*, June 2009, pp. 149-176.

[3] Peter Chalk, "The Maritime Dimension of International Security: Terrorism, Piracy and Challenges for the United States," RAND Corporation, 2008, p. 26.

[4] *Ibid.*, p. 24.

[5] John S. Burnett, *Dangerous Waters* (2002), p. 288.

[6] William Langewiesche, *The Outlaw Sea* (2004), p. 39.

pirates, a race that merchant sailors cannot win," John Clancey — chairman of the energy and shipping company Maersk Inc., which owns the *Maersk Alabama* — said during congressional testimony on April 30.[17]

"It has been our very strong policy that seafarers should not be armed," echoes Andrew Linington, a spokesman for Nautilus International, a British and Dutch seafarers' union. "It would be counterproductive and actually make things worse, partially because of the fear that in the wrong hands guns could actually inflame the situation."

For example, in a commonly cited case, New Zealander Sir Peter Blake, who had twice won the America's Cup, was anchored in the Amazon in 2001, when his ship was attacked by several armed men. Although Blake had a rifle and fired it in defense, he was shot and killed.[18]

Besides crew members being shot, Linington adds, gunfire could ignite a shipboard fire or cause other serious damage. Moreover, further problems would crop up when ships want to dock. Merchant ships are allowed to sail freely through territorial waters and come into port if they are not a threat to the security of the coastal state. That right of "innocent passage" could be forfeited if they were armed. The U.S. Coast Guard, for instance, considers armed vessels within U.S. territorial waters a threat.

"In many jurisdictions, a crew member could be arrested for possessing weapons," says John Bainbridge, who represents the International Transport Workers' Federation before the IMO on piracy issues. Most sailors also oppose having to undergo training and be responsible for protecting their workplaces along with their many other duties. "When asked, the

United States Navy/SFC Eric L. Beauregard

Sailors from the guided-missile cruiser USS Gettysburg stop suspected pirates in the Gulf of Aden as part of the multinational task force conducting anti-piracy operations throughout the region. Since patrols began earlier this year, more than three times as many pirates have been interdicted as in all of 2008.

overwhelming majority of seafarers have rejected this option," Bainbridge says.

"The shipping industry is entirely against arming crews," says Neil Roberts, senior technical executive with Lloyd's Market Association, a London-based insurer.

But private security companies are anxious to offer their services. Blackwater Worldwide, a U.S. security firm, has offered dozens of shipping and insurance companies various options, such as a 181-foot long escort ship and certified mariners with small-arms training.

"The pirates are going after soft targets," said Jeff Gibson, vice president for international training and operations at Blackwater. "If a ship is being escorted by another boat, or some small boats or even a helicopter overhead, [the pirates] are going to decide, let's not make the effort."[19]

But hiring private security companies would be expensive — viable only for ships carrying the most valuable cargoes. And using private security companies "is fraught with difficulties," Roberts says, "not least because owners are unable to gauge the quality of various companies," since they are unregulated. If security guards kill someone, the shipping company could also be held liable.

And, many worry that hiring private security forces would ratchet up the potential for violence. Hiring armed security guards just escalates the situation "on both sides,"

says David M. Crane, a Syracuse University law professor. "Then you have a type of combat situation."

Despite such concerns, however, the rapid growth of piracy has led at least some analysts to rethink the longstanding prohibition against arming merchant ships. "Today's personnel, in signing up for a maritime career, do not wish to take upon themselves the responsibility and risk of providing for their own security in this way," says Graham Gerard Ong-Webb, a research fellow at the Centre for Defence and International Security Studies in London. "But I think these added responsibilities are inescapable today."

"We simply have to pay them more to do so," he continues. "I believe all maritime seafarers either have to undergo the requisite training to perform the basic defensive measures in deterring or staving off a pirate attack, or their employers should contract private security companies to do the job for them."

Those who argue that arming merchant ships will deter attackers rather than escalate the violence point out that Israeli and Russian merchant ships — which are assumed to be armed — are generally not attacked. For instance, in 2001, Burnett notes, no Russian or Israeli ships were attacked by pirates, compared to 27 attacks on U.S. and British ships.[20]

"It's very difficult to create a defense against armed pirates with unarmed ships," author Burnett says.

Nevertheless, he prefers that unarmed crew members use defenses such as water cannon, barbed wire around the decks or long-range acoustic devices that can destroy the eardrums of attackers — along with evasive maneuvers and general vigilance. "Guns aboard ships, unless they're military, just don't belong," he says.

Recalling the time when his own ship was boarded by pirates, Burnett says, "If I had been armed, if I had had my 12-gauge on board when I was attacked, I'd be dead today."

"If weapons are on board, they will get used," says Willett, of the Royal United Services Institute for Defence and Security Studies.

Should shipowners pay ransom?

Early pirate history is full of tales of extreme violence and even torture being used against captives. And earlier in this decade, when the greatest area of concern was in the Strait of Malacca, pirates generally stole the ships and cargo and killed crew members or set them adrift.

But Somali pirates are not out to kill: They need the crew alive for ransom from shipowners and insurance companies. The IMO's Trelawny points out that only two hostages have died in recent years while in pirate hands — one killed by a ricocheting bullet, another of a heart attack.[21]

"They were never nice to us and treated us the whole time as a potential threat," said Leszek Adler, an officer on the *Sirius Star*, the Saudi oil tanker taken by Somali pirates last November. But, "other than a few minor episodes, they weren't hostile toward us all, although there were a few of them that had a hotter temper."[22]

"Crew members are lots of money on two legs," says Lehr, the lecturer in terrorism studies at the University of St. Andrews.

A Congressional Research Service report points out that "while individual ransom payments can be significant," the payment of ransoms has kept Somali piracy violence "relatively low."[23] And because only a small percentage of ships in the area are successfully attacked and captured, some commercial entities view the overall risk of paying ransoms as low.

"What's the practical alternative?" asks Linington of Nautilus, the seafarers' union. "What are you going to do if you're not going to pay? Nobody seems to have a proper answer to that."

Indeed, once pirates control a ship, few alternatives remain. Navies can attempt rescues, but the casualty risk is high. French special forces storming a yacht taken by pirates in April may have killed its skipper during the firefight to rescue him and other hostages.[24]

But even the successful rescue of Capt. Phillips sparked criticism that it could lead pirates to greater violence. "Paying ransom certainly does encourage piracy, but they really don't have much alternative," says RAND's Chalk. "The amount of money paid for ransom is insignificant compared to the value of the ship.

"Shipowners remain concerned that should pressure be brought against them to not pay ransom, it will increase the danger that pirates might kill off a couple of crew members to establish the seriousness of their demands," he continues.

"The last people who want to pay a ransom are the industry," says the International Maritime Bureau's Mukundan. "They don't want to have to pay millions of dollars to get their ships and crews back. But . . . they don't have a choice. Inside Somali waters, no one else can help them. They have to do whatever they can. Today it means paying a ransom."

Governments don't pay ransoms. "We as a government do not condone the paying of ransom," said U.S. Defense undersecretary Flournoy. "We seek to end the paying of ransom."

But private shipping companies view paying ransom — or having their insurance companies pay — as the cheapest alternative and the most compassionate for the crew. "There is a concern that it sets a precedent, but ransoms do get paid," says Willett, of the Royal United Services Institute for Defence and Security Studies. "The amount tends to be only a small percentage of the value of the ship."

But even if paying ransoms is the more prudent course, is it the wisest? Trelawny feels it only exacerbates the situation. "Five years ago, the ransoms were in the tens of thousands, now they're in the millions," he says.

Though final payments are generally kept confidential, estimates of the total amount of ransoms paid to Somali pirates in 2008 range from $30 million up to $150 million.[25]

"At the moment, we seem to be approaching the worst of all possible worlds," wrote Bloomberg columnist Matthew Lynn. "Shipping companies either avoid the African coastline or . . . agree to pay what amounts to protection money for safe passage. Neither is satisfactory in the long term. Over time, the pirates will just grow stronger, the attacks will cover a wider area, and the ransom demands will get bigger."[26]

Little of the money stays with the pirates who carried out the crime. Usually, most of it goes to their backers — organized-crime syndicates or warlords. "In a typical ransom payment, 70 percent of that money is not returned to the pirates that undertake the operation. That goes to businessmen on land," Chalk writes.[27]

"To make matters worse, we know pirates use much of the ransom money paid to them to buy heavier and larger caliber weapons and bigger engines for their skiffs to make it even easier to overtake larger vessels," Senate Foreign Relations Committee Chairman John F. Kerry, D-Mass., said at the April 30 hearing. "They also use ransom money to arm and equip private militias. This is a dangerous and a vicious cycle, and it needs to be addressed."

Inevitably, the pirates' price comes down as negotiations drag on, sometimes for months. The pirates who took the *Sirius Star*, for instance, initially demanded $25 million but settled for an estimated $3 million after nearly two months of talks.

"What we want for this ship is only $25 million, because we always charge according to the quality of the ship and the value of the product," one of the hijackers told a reporter during the standoff.[28]

Delivering the ransoms has become another big business. Lawyers in London often handle the negotiations on behalf of shipowners, and private companies charge up to $1 million to deliver the ransoms, which are always paid in cash to avoid computer tracking. Bundled bills might be parachuted directly on board captured ships or delivered in suitcases to middlemen in cities such as Nairobi and Djibouti or to villages along the coast.

Recently, pirates have become more sophisticated, demanding only $50 and $100 bills and refusing easily traceable years of issue. The *Sirius Star*'s hijackers even brought a counting machine and a counterfeit-money detector on board with them.

However, the $3 million ransom they collected apparently was too much to carry away. The small getaway boat some of them took capsized. Five of the pirates drowned along with their shares, with one reportedly washing ashore with $153,000 in his pockets.[29] "The small boat was overloaded and going too fast," pirate leader Mohammed Said told the Agence France-Presse news agency. "The survivors told us they were afraid some foreign navies would attempt to catch them."[30]

Ong-Webb, of the Centre for Defence and International Security Studies, says it's perfectly understandable that shipping companies pay ransoms for their crews, but "it is not sustainable in the long term." Too much depends on global shipping to make payments to criminals a normal cost of doing business, he says.

Some countries, such as the United Kingdom, want to discourage private industry from paying ransom. But it will be difficult to come up with an alternative, since the decision about paying ransoms is made among shipping companies, insurers, national governments and captured crew members' families.

"Payment does encourage further attacks, and each one raises the bar, but unless shipowners pay ransoms they will be faced with a total loss of their ships," says Roberts, of Lloyd's Market Association.

But, he says, "While ships trade through such waters, there is no practical alternative to ransoms."

BACKGROUND

Piracy's 'Golden Age'

The poet Homer recorded an act of piracy in *The Odyssey*, written around 800 B.C., and in 75 B.C. the imperial barge carrying Roman Emperor Julius Caesar was apparently hijacked during a Mediterranean crossing.[31]

But piracy was tolerated — and even encouraged — by some rulers, who gave "letters of marque," or licenses, to privateers, legalizing their plundering so long as the ruler received a cut. "Piracy has always benefited from the support of unscrupulous great men only too happy to receive bribes and cheap pirated goods at no risk to themselves," writes British historian Peter Earle.[32]

Perhaps the most famous privateer was Francis Drake, who plundered gold and jewels from Spanish ships in the 1570s in support of Britain's Elizabeth I. Investors in Drake's voyage, including Elizabeth, received 47 British pounds for every pound they'd invested.[33]

"Elizabeth was not a weak monarch," writes Murphy of the Center for Strategic and Budgetary Assessments, "but she depended for the defense of her realm upon the sea power she could not afford."[34]

The most infamous pirates of all — Blackbeard, Captain Kidd and Henry Morgan — sacked towns in the Caribbean and North America and attacked ships during the so-called Golden Age of Piracy from the 1650s until the 1720s. Many were based in the lawless British colony of the Bahamas.

The pirates successfully eluded the British navy for years. Even when they were caught, the legal procedure for dealing with them, which dated from 1536, required them to be tried by an admiralty court in London. In 1700, Parliament passed the Act for the More Effectual Suppression of Piracy, which allowed trials outside England and authorized the death penalty outside of Great Britain.[35]

The new law allowed the British Navy to more aggressively dispatch armadas to drive pirates from their lairs and bring them to justice. Between 1716 and 1726 more than 400 men were hanged for piracy, effectively eliminating most of the leaders and decimating the general ranks.[36] "The Golden Age of Piracy . . . was conducted by a clique of 20 to 30 pirate commodores and a few thousand crewmen," writes journalist and author Colin Woodard.[37] Their trials and executions were highly public, with Captain

CHRONOLOGY

1700s-1800s *Rampant piracy in the Caribbean, Mediterranean and South China Sea is crushed.*

1700 Britain updates its piracy laws, enabling prosecution of pirates and use of the death penalty overseas. More than 400 men are hanged for piracy in the Atlantic and Caribbean.

Late 1700s U.S. builds a navy to fight state-sponsored piracy in North Africa. Two Barbary Wars ensue (1801-1805 and 1815-1816).

1810 China asks Western powers to help combat piracy in the South China Sea. Female pirate leader Cheng I Sao accepts amnesty deal, leading to surrender of hundreds of ships and more than 17,000 pirates.

1980s *Maritime piracy reemerges, especially in Southeast Asia.*

1985 Palestinian terrorists attack the Italian cruise ship *Achille Lauro*, prompting an international convention on maritime terrorism.

1988 Rome Convention makes seizing or endangering ships illegal.

1990s-2000s *Piracy and maritime terrorism grow in Asia and Africa.*

1990 In early example of "phantom ship" piracy, the *Marta* is hijacked en route to Korea, with pirates knowing all the details in advance about its whereabouts and cargo.

1991 *MV Naviluck* is attacked, ransacked and burned and the crew killed or thrown overboard on Jan. 12 — the first recorded modern piracy incident off Somalia. . . . Gen. Mohamed Siad Barre's dictatorship later collapses, triggering Somalia's "failed state" status and widespread piracy in the region.

1992 Oil tanker *Valiant Carrier* is attacked, sparking creation of the International Maritime Bureau's Piracy Reporting Centre. . . . Indonesia, Malaysia and Singapore begin anti-pirate patrols in Strait of Malacca; program is dropped due to cost.

1999 India captures and prosecutes hijackers of Japanese freighter *Alondra Rainbow*.

2000 Suicide bombers attack the *USS Cole* in Yemen, killing 17 sailors.

2002 In a post-9/11 security measure, President George W. Bush allows Navy to intercept merchant ships on high seas. . . . Al Qaeda suicide bombers damage the oil tanker *Limburg*, temporarily interrupting Gulf of Aden shipping.

2004 Terrorists bomb Philippine ferry, killing 116. . . . Singapore, Malaysia and Indonesia adopt coordinated anti-piracy policy.

2005 International Maritime Organization calls for action against piracy.

2006 Congress allows Pentagon to help other countries improve maritime security.

2008 Somali pirates seize French yacht *Le Ponant* and release the hostages; French commandos capture six of the pirates in the Djibouti desert (April 4). . . . Separatist attack forces Royal Dutch Shell to close its largest Nigerian offshore oil well (June 19). . . . Supertanker *Sirius Star* is hijacked near Kenya (Nov. 15). . . . Indian frigate destroys Somali pirate "mother ship" (Nov. 18). . . . U.N. authorizes all necessary measures to suppress Somali piracy (Dec. 16).

2009 International task force begins patrolling Gulf of Aden (Jan. 8), and capture more than 100 pirates in the first few months. . . . 17 nations adopt anti-piracy Code of Conduct (Jan. 29). . . . Capt. Richard Phillips of American freighter *Maersk Alabama* is taken hostage, freed by Navy sharpshooters off the Somali coast, (April 8). . . . Pirate survivor of *Maersk Alabama* incident is indicted in New York (May 19). . . . International Maritime Bureau says pirates struck 240 times during first half of 2009 — more than double the rate in the same period of 2008 — with Somali pirates responsible for more than 60 percent of the attacks and 86 percent of the 561 hostages taken in 2009 (July 15). . . . Trials scheduled to resume in Yemen for more than 20 Somali pirates captured by Indian and Russian forces (October).

Countries Outsource Piracy Prosecutions

Western nations try pirates in Kenyan courts.

Francis Kadima has suddenly gotten very busy. The Kenyan defense attorney is taking on new clients by the dozen, brought to him by a variety of countries asking that Kenya become the venue of choice for Western countries wanting to bring captured pirates to trial.

Yemen has 30 alleged pirates awaiting trial in its courts, and Seychelles has 20, according to the International Maritime Organization. But Kenya has some 250 suspected pirates awaiting trial, sent there by the United Kingdom, United States and European Union. Those nations all signed memorandums of understanding offering Kenya — as one of Somalia's closest neighbors with a functioning judicial system — funding, computers and legal assistance if it would prosecute pirates.

Justice is being outsourced to Kenya largely because of the murkiness of the laws regarding piracy. According to maritime -law experts, under international law — including the U.N. Convention on the Law of the Sea — piracy is a universal crime and can be prosecuted by any country. However, because piracy had abated for centuries, few Western countries still have specific anti-piracy statutes on their books.

"In the majority of European Union states, piracy is not a crime," says Christina Gallach, an EU spokeswoman. "It's not in the criminal code anymore. It's something that happened many years ago."

Another obstacle: Pirates are jurisdictional orphans. Because of the multinational nature of global shipping, it is unclear who has jurisdiction to prosecute a pirate. For instance, if Somali pirates are captured in international waters by an Indian warship after they attacked a Panamanian-registered ship owned by a Japanese company and crewed by Filipinos, which country prosecutes the pirates?

Under current practice, the capturing country does the prosecuting. That's what India did in the scenario described above, when it caught pirates who had stolen goods from the *Alondra Rainbow* in 1999. But it's still a logistical and linguistic nightmare to bring foreign witnesses in to testify against foreign offenders. That's why several nations prefer to try the alleged pirates as close to the point of capture as possible, especially if the captor's home country has no anti-piracy statute.

Because of the legal limbo and logistical issues, many captured pirates are merely disarmed and released. Canadian and Dutch warships have caught pirates this year only to let them go, in what critics have mocked as "catch and release." "They can't stop us," Jama Ali, a pirate aboard a hijacked Ukrainian freighter, told *The New York Times* last December. "We know international law."[1]

"While nobody would advocate the ancient naval tradition of just making them walk the gangplank, equipment like GPS [receivers], weapons (and) ladders are often just tossed overboard and the pirates let go," said a Kenya-based diplomat.[2]

In fact, naval powers making up the combined international task force on piracy in the Gulf of Aden and Somalia have disarmed and released 121 pirates since it was established in January and turned 117 others over to Kenya for prosecution, U.S. Navy officials told Congress in March.

At one point the U.S. Navy held a piracy suspect for seven months because of confusion over where he would be prosecuted.[3]

And in the only modern piracy case being tried in the United States, an 18-year-old Somalians captured during the April attack on the *Maersk Alabama* was indicted in New York in May for piracy and conspiracy to seize a ship and take hostages. U.S. piracy laws are still on the books

Kidd's tarred body left to hang in a gibbet — an iron cage — over the Thames for years as a warning.

Barbary Piracy

About the same time, North Africa's Barbary corsairs — Muslim pirates and privateers who had long plagued the southern Mediterranean Sea — earned a special place in early U.S. naval history. In the late 1700s the pirates

thought they had found easy pickings in merchant ships from the newly independent United States, which had lost the protection of the British Royal Navy. For years the Barbary pirates captured American ships and held the crews for ransoms and annual "tribute" payments from the U.S. government — just as they had traditionally extracted money from European governments. Signing treaties to buy off the pirates' state

but haven't been used in 100 years. Once punishable by death, piracy has carried a mandatory life sentence in the United States since 1819.[4]

"It is a workable model," Pottengal Mukundan, director of the International Maritime Bureau, a London-based office of the International Chamber of Commerce, says of the Kenya prosecution contracts. He hopes to see more international arrangements to bring pirates to trial within the region, noting that countries such as China are not party to the agreements with Kenya.

utsourcing piracy justice to Kenya, however, presents a major obstacle: Kenya's judicial system already has a backlog of 800,000 cases of all kinds in its courts. Suspects often spend a year or more in jail just waiting for a hearing.[5]

"What we would like to see is some measures coming from the International Maritime Organization or from the U.N., which allows for . . . all the countries with naval vessels in the region to hand over pirates for prosecutions to countries in the area," Munkundan says. "If the [navies] can't prosecute, then they might let them go or not pursue them with full vigor."

But Daniel Sekulich, a Canadian journalist and author of *Terror on the Seas*, says it's a mistake to outsource pirate justice. He prefers that nations update their laws and set up an international court.

"It is not going to result in the conviction of every captured suspect, but it is a reflection of the resolve of nations to not only dispatch warships but also prosecute suspects to the full extent of the law," he says.

The idea of an international court for piracy has received a fair amount of attention, but it remains controversial and would take years to implement. (*See "At Issue," p. 142.*)

In the interim, there are concerns that Kenya won't be able to handle the load. Aside from the heavy case backlog, there have been allegations that Kenya's courts are prone to corruption and questions about whether the country can provide western standards of due process.

"The problem is that Kenya itself cannot handle hundreds of pirate cases," Mukundan says, arguing for more

Suspected Somali pirates appear in court in Mombasa, Kenya, on April 23, 2009, after being apprehended by the French navy, which is part of Operation Atalanta, the EU anti-piracy effort.

AFP/Getty Images/Tony Karumba

international support. "It may grind down their own legal system." The critical question, then, is how much money and support rich nations will pour in to build judicial capacity there.

The fact that Kenya's parliament itself hasn't fully signed off on the international agreements is an issue Kadima has raised on behalf of his clients. "You can't just go around making up laws, you know," he said. "There is a process."[6]

[1] Jeffrey Gettleman, "Pirates in Skiffs Still Outmaneuvering Warships Off Somalia," *The New York Times*, Dec. 16, 2008, p. A6, www.nytimes.com/2008/12/16/world/africa/16pirate.html.

[2] Katharine Houreld and Mike Corder, "Navies ask: What do you do with a captured pirate?" The Associated Press, ABC News, April 17, 2009, http://abcnews.go.com/US/wireStory?id=7365467.

[3] Mike Corder, "Nations Look to Kenya as Venue for Piracy Trials," The Associated Press, April 17, 2009.

[4] Houreld and Corder, *op. cit.*

[5] *Ibid.*

[6] Jeffrey Gettleman, "Rounding Up Suspects, the West Turns to Kenya as Piracy Criminal Court," *The New York Times*, April 24, 2009, p. A8, www.nytimes.com/2009/04/24/world/africa/24kenya.html.

sponsors — Tripoli, Tunis, Morocco and Algiers — was considered cheaper for the new country, still in debt from its Revolutionary War, than building its own navy.[38]

The ransoms and tributes prompted a debate that echoed today's controversy over whether paying ransom only encourages more piracy. Then-Ambassador to France Thomas Jefferson felt that paying ransom only invited more

demands, so he tried to organize an international naval coalition to battle the pirates and their state sponsors.

"The states must see the rod," Jefferson wrote in an Aug. 18, 1786, letter to future president James Monroe, then a member of Congress. And in a letter to Yale College president Ezra Stiles, Jefferson wrote, "It will be more easy to raise ships and men to fight these pirates into reason, than money to bribe them."[39]

AP Photo/French Defense Ministry

Crew members of the French tourist yacht Le Ponant prepare to board a French frigate after Somali pirates released them on April 11, 2008. The ship had been hijacked a week earlier in the Gulf of Aden. French commandos captured six of the pirates after the hostages were released.

Although Jefferson was unable to establish a coalition, the payoffs were a blow to national pride. And in 1794, in response to Algerian seizures of American ships and crews, Congress appropriated $688,888 to build six frigates "adequate for the protection of the commerce of the United States against Algerian corsairs."[40]

After becoming president in 1801, Jefferson refused Tripoli's demands for $225,000, followed by annual payments of $25,000. Tripoli declared war, and the two Barbary Wars (1801-1805 and 1815-1816) ensued.

The first war involved a series of daring raids and bombardment of Tripoli. The turning point came in 1805, when a handful of U.S. Marines led 500 Greek, Arab and Berber mercenaries on a dramatic overland march across the desert from Alexandria, Egypt, to capture the Tripolitan city of Derna. When they raised the American flag in Derna, it was the first time the flag was raised in victory on foreign soil — an act memorialized in the "shores of Tripoli" line in the Marines' Hymn.

The Barbary nations were emboldened by the War of 1812, when the British chased U.S. ships from the Mediterranean. But eventually the Americans captured some Algerian ships, leading Algeria to foreswear further demands for tribute. In 1816, a massive bombardment of Algiers by an Anglo-Dutch fleet helped to end piracy in the Mediterranean.

Following their heyday, pirates were seen by some people as folk heroes. "Reason tells us that pirates were no more than common criminals, but we still see them as figures of romance," writes David Cordingly in *Under the Black Flag*.[41]

Part of that heroic image — at least to some — may have stemmed from the democratic way they ran their ships, unlike the navies of the time. Pirates elected their own captains and shared their booty according to set terms. "A hundred years before the French Revolution, the pirate companies were run on the lines in which liberty, equality and brotherhood were the rule rather than the exception," Cordingly writes.[42]

As piracy declined, the image of pirates as romantic buccaneers began to grow. In 1814, Lord Byron's poem "The Corsair" sold out seven editions in its first month of publication.[43] Pirates were further romanticized by novelists such as Walter Scott and Robert Louis Stevenson, whose *Treasure Island* in 1883 created the template for much pirate lore. (*See story, p. 141.*) In the 20th century, Hollywood also portrayed pirates as heroes — played by such romantic leading men as Errol Flynn, Douglas Fairbanks and Johnny Depp — whose playful portrayal of pirate Jack Sparrow in the "Pirates of the Caribbean" film series has grossed $2.7 billion worldwide for the Disney company.

Cold War's End

But portraying violent thieves as romantic or comedic characters was fundamentally misleading, argues author Murphy. It was "as if the period that began at the end of the 19th century, when piracy became a nursery story and later was thrown up on the silver screen, formed an impervious barrier through which the reality of maritime depredation could not seep into the modern era," he writes.[44]

In addition, he notes, the rise of sea power and the vast reach of Britain's Royal Navy led Westerners to believe by the early 20th century that piracy was obsolete.[45] "Piracy was seen as a problem out of history," with little relevance to the modern world, wrote Murphy.[46]

However, when the fall of the Soviet Union ended the Cold War, the super powers were no longer routinely patrolling the world's oceans. And merchant ships became more vulnerable as automation allowed shipowners to hire skeleton crews and rising fuel costs led to slower cruising speeds.

Meanwhile, modern pirates were gaining high-tech advantages, including satellite phones, GPS devices and faster fiberglass boats.

Romantic Pirate Lore Is Mostly Fiction

Aarrgh, but they did have parrots and peg legs.

By the early 19th century, piracy had been largely eliminated from the Atlantic and Mediterranean seas, but pirates lived on in the Western imagination as glamorous outlaws.

Like cowboys, pirates starred as highly romanticized heroes in movies and novels, such as Robert Louis Stevenson's 1883 classic, and heavily embroidered, *Treasure Island*. And as a result, much of what most people believe today about pirates isn't actually true.

"The effect of *Treasure Island* on our perception of pirates cannot be overestimated," writes David Cordingly, a former curator at England's National Maritime Museum. "Stevenson linked pirates forever with maps, black schooners, tropical islands and peg-legged seamen with parrots on their shoulders."[1]

Here's a brief guide to sorting out pirate fact and fiction:

• **Walking the plank — Myth.** Captain Hook may have planned to make the "Lost Boys" of J. M. Barrie's *Peter Pan* walk the plank, but real pirates rarely made time for such dastardly deeds. There is no mention of pirates making anyone walk the plank during the so-called Golden Age of Piracy, although an account from a later era survives. "However," writes Canadian journalist and author of a book about pirates Daniel Sekulich, "throwing individuals overboard is another thing altogether and a common enough occurrence in the annals of piracy."[2]

• **Treasure chests and maps — Myth.** Although 18th-century pirates certainly stole doubloons and pieces of eight when they could get them, their typical booty consisted of bales of silk and cotton, barrels of tobacco, spare sails, carpenters' tools and the occasional slave. And maps with an X marking the location of buried treasure were the invention of the illustrator of *Treasure Island*. Pirates usually spent their money in port on gambling, prostitutes and alcohol before they could bury it. The legend grew largely out of reports that Captain Kidd had buried gold and silver from a plundered ship near his home before he was arrested.

• **Peg legs, earrings and parrots — Fact.** "Pirates really did tie scarves or large handkerchiefs around their heads, and they did walk around armed to the teeth with pistols and cutlasses," Cordingly writes.[3] They also wore frock coats, which were typical of the Stuart period, when the Caribbean buccaneers were most active. Tricorn hats were also typical of the period, but skull-and-crossbones emblems were an embellishment added by Barrie in *Peter Pan*.

The common depiction of pirates wearing earrings is accurate. Many people at the time believed that wearing gold or silver in the earlobe improved eyesight or offered protection from drowning.[4] Expressions such as "Aarrgh," "avast" and "shiver me timbers" were part of the seafarers' vocabulary of the day.

As for the wooden legs and parrots, pirates were vulnerable to serious injury, and historical accounts describe several pirates who had lost limbs having replacements fitted by ship's carpenters. And seamen traveling in the tropics often picked up birds and animals as souvenirs. Parrots were popular because they commanded a good price in the London bird markets and were easier to keep on board than monkeys and other wild animals.

---

[1] David Cordingly, *Under the Black Flag* (1995), p. 7.

[2] Daniel Sekulich, *Terror on the Seas* (2009), p. 285.

[3] Cordingly, *op. cit.*, p. xiv.

[4] David Pickering, *Pirates* (2006), p. 160.

And, while piracy largely disappeared from the Atlantic and Mediterranean, it continued almost without interruption in Asia.

Asian Straits

Shih Fa-Hsien, a Buddhist monk from Sri Lanka, recorded cases of piracy in the Malacca Strait and South China Sea in 414 A.D. And 14th-century Moroccan traveler Ibn Battuta described being victimized by pirates off western India and commercial ships crossing the Indian Ocean in armed convoys for protection.[47]

"Slightly earlier," writes journalist Kaplan, "Marco Polo described many dozens of pirate vessels off Gujarat, India, where the pirates would spend the whole summer at sea with their women and children, even as they plundered merchant vessels."[48]

Should an international piracy court be established?

YES Peter Lehr
Lecturer, Terrorism Studies
University of St. Andrews, Scotland

NO John Knott
Consultant
Holman Fenwick Willan LLP*
London, England

Written for *CQ Researcher*, August 2009

Written for *CQ Researcher*, July 9, 2009

Let's face it: Responding to piracy off the coast of Somalia took us quite a while. Now, relatively effective anti-piracy patrols have been established, acts of piracy foiled and scores of pirates arrested. But what should be done with them?

Most nations cannot legally try foreign nationals attacking crews and ships of another foreign country at a foreign location. In the absence of such laws, many pirates simply were disarmed and sent back to their own shores, in their own skiffs.

Since such a response to a serious crime is quite underwhelming, an agreement with Kenya was hastily cobbled together envisioning that pirates would have to stand trial in Mombasa and serve a prison sentence in a Kenyan prison — at least until the Somalian government could establish its own court. So, mission accomplished?

Legal experts in Germany and the Netherlands beg to differ. Since the 2007 post-election riots in Kenya, they point out, the Kenyan judiciary system has been overstretched, and, in any case, it does not meet Western standards. Thus, dumping Somali pirates on the already creaking Kenyan judicial system is hardly a long-term solution. And the Somalis do not have a monopoly on piracy — so an agreement with Kenya addresses only one part of global piracy.

Creating an international piracy tribunal would speed up proceedings and guarantee a fair and efficient trial matching Western standards. It would also solve jurisdictional problems that have marred too many piracy cases in the past.

The Netherlands and Russia are exploring the details of such a tribunal, and some German politicians suggest extending the brief of the Hamburg-based International Tribunal for the Law of the Sea (ITLOS). Hamburg has the facilities and experts for such trials and would thus be a good place.

Sentenced pirates could then serve their terms in states that have adopted the U.N. Convention on the Law of the Sea (which don't include the United States, by the way).

Setting up an international piracy tribunal will cost money, of course, but it's a better solution to a problem that won't go away any time soon. It is politically viable at the moment, and it most definitely is a much fairer solution in the long run than yet another quick fix in the shape of a kangaroo court.

Amid continuing pirate attacks off the coasts of Somalia and legal difficulties in prosecuting captured pirates, it is not surprising that an international piracy tribunal — similar to the International Criminal Court (ICC) at The Hague — has been proposed. While there are some superficial attractions in such a plan, an examination reveals it to be impractical.

Such tribunals take a long time to set up, are very expensive to run and their trials often last for years. The ICC was created by the Rome Statute of 1998 and took four years to become effective, when 60 states ratified it in 2002. That followed the many years it took to draft and negotiate the statute. Even so, the ICC does not include China, India, Russia or the United States. A solution is needed for dealing with Somali pirates that can be implemented much sooner.

A rather vague, hybrid proposal to establish a "regional tribunal" and "an international tribunal" in an unnamed country in the region was considered at a July 7 meeting at The Hague. But more focused, practical and simpler solutions are available.

For instance, the catchment area could be expanded for trials among the African and Arab nations that in January signed a regional Code of Conduct for repressing piracy. Early signatories were Djibouti, Ethiopia (the only non-coastal state), Kenya, Madagascar, the Maldives, the Seychelles, Somalia, Tanzania and Yemen. The code called for participating nations to review their legislation to ensure that adequate laws were in place to criminalize piracy and related crimes and that captured pirates would be treated with a degree of uniformity in the region.

To simplify prosecutions, law enforcement detachments from these countries could be stationed aboard warships operating in the region (under the auspices of NATO, the Combined Task Force 151 and Operation Atalanta) to serve as arresting officers and to ensure that a single legal system is applied throughout a pirate's captivity.

Another possibility: A Somali-constituted court could sit in another country (as did a Scottish court when dealing with the Lockerbie air disaster), and convicted pirates could be housed in special U.N.-funded piracy jails in Puntland and Somaliland. There would be clear advantages in encouraging Somalia to help solve its own problems in this way, while avoiding the need for an international court in any guise.

* The firm represented shipowners and underwriters in over 30 Somali hijacking cases last year.

In the early 19th century, about 40,000 pirates on hundreds of junks dominated the South China Sea coastal waters. From 1807, they were led by Cheng I Sao — known as "Mrs. Cheng" — a former prostitute from Canton, who took command after her husband died. She enforced a stricter code than the West Indies pirates, with punishments including beheading for disobeying orders or stealing from the common treasury.

By 1809, she had amassed a fleet larger than most navies. The following year, the Chinese enlisted the help of Portuguese and British warships in their battle against the pirates. As it became clear that an all-out attack on piracy was imminent, Mrs. Cheng reportedly showed up unannounced at the governor-general's mansion in Canton — surrounded by women and children — to negotiate a peace settlement. The government allowed her to keep her plunder but executed some of her pirates while allowing others to join the Chinese army. Two days later, 17,382 pirates formally surrendered, and 226 junks were handed over to authorities.[49]

Although the large-scale threat was eliminated, local attacks remained a constant. In recent years, Chinese provincial officials were accused of being complicit in smuggling and theft, until the country's growing role in world trade led to an official crackdown in the 1990s.

But piracy remained acute in the strategic Strait of Malacca, where some 70,000 vessels each year transport half the world's oil and more than a third of its commerce, including supply ships heading to and from China and Japan.[50] Batam, an Indonesian island just across the Singapore Strait from Singapore, became a haven for criminals, including pirates.

In 1992, Indonesia, Malaysia and Singapore began aggressively patrolling the region, virtually eliminating piracy for a while. But due to the high cost, including air support and surveillance, they dropped the strategy after six months.[51]

By the early 2000s, the Malacca Strait was the world's piracy hot spot, giving rise to the brutal phenomenon of "phantom ship" piracy. Pirates would board vessels and kill or cast off the crews, stealing not just the cargo but the ships themselves. They would then repaint the ships and change their names and registries — creating "phantoms" that they used as mother ships.

By 2006, piracy in the region was so bad that many fishermen simply stayed home. Roughly half the 300

United States Navy/SFC Eric L. Beauregard

A Singaporean Navy ship patrols Singapore harbor, which faces the busy Strait of Malacca. Half the world's oil supplies pass through the narrow strait, which until recently was a popular target of pirates. Officials fear the strategic waterway could become a target of terrorists seeking to cripple world shipping.

locals who fished off the coast of the Malaysian city of Melaka, for instance, refused to go out.[52]

To address the problem, the International Maritime Organization (IMO) instituted a unique ship-numbering system. Pirates also lost their markets for phantom ship cargo when the Chinese government and customs agents began cracking down on the illicit trade. Equally important, smaller neighboring countries renewed their efforts at aggressive patrols after receiving prodding and funding from outside powers such as Japan and the United States.

Besides conducting joint patrols, the littoral states share data. Pirates who hijacked the tanker *MT Kraton* in September 2007 thought they could hide their deed by changing the ship's name to *Ratu*. But a new international database allowed Malaysian authorities to inform other countries about the name change. Using additional information from Singapore, the Indonesian navy intercepted the tanker off southern Johor and nabbed all 13 hijackers.[53]

According to the latest IMB annual report, there were only two pirate incidents in the Malacca Strait in 2008, down from 34 in 2004. And only 65 attacks occurred within all of Southeast Asia, compared with 187 in 2003. "If pirates here were to try a copycat attack like in Somalia, it won't be easy for them because the governments in this region won't hesitate to take action," said Noel Choong, head of the bureau's Malaysia-based Piracy Reporting Centre.[54]

AFP/Getty Images/Bay Ismoyo

A U.S. Navy SEAL trains Indonesian marines during joint anti-piracy exercises in 2006. Since Southeast Asian governments began coordinating their efforts in 2004, piracy has declined dramatically in the region.

Growth in Somalia

Most piracy experts agree that getting regional powers together to combat piracy around the Horn of Africa like they have in Southeast Asia won't happen anytime soon. The IMO has been leading talks in the area for years, resulting in January in the adoption of a "code of conduct" by 17 nations regarding interdiction, investigation and prosecution of pirates, as well as the establishment of information and training centers.

But the lack of a functioning Somali government makes the country a "black hole," author Murphy says. Coastal waters were already lawless before dictator Mohamed Siad Barre's regime collapsed in 1991. Reportedly the Somali National Movement — which eventually overthrew Barre — seized three ships as early as 1989.[55]

The first officially recorded modern Somali piracy incident, however, took place on Jan. 12, 1991, when three boatloads of pirates attacked the Russian ship *MV Nauviluck*, killing three crew members and forcing the rest overboard. They were later rescued by a trawler.[56]

Somali piracy initially appealed to fishermen "fed up with the depletion of their fisheries" by big, foreign factory ships, says maritime security consultant Burnett, who served as a United Nations official in Somalia, in the 1990s. "The foreign fishing fleets were basically raping the Somali fishing grounds." Fishing within another country's territorial waters is illegal under international law but is a common problem off Africa's coasts.

"The foreign vessels gave no consideration to the welfare and future growth of the marine life," says Abdulkareem Jama, chief of staff for the newly elected Somali president, Sheikh Sharif Sheikh Ahmed.

The Somalis say Europeans were not only destroying their fishing grounds but were dumping a variety of toxic materials, including radioactive uranium, lead, cadmium and mercury and industrial, hospital and chemical wastes.

Somali regional administrators eventually authorized small groups of fishermen to capture and fine vessels caught illegally fishing or dumping wastes in Somali waters. "What started as law enforcement effort became a lucrative business for individuals and groups," says Jama. Soon, every ship that came near Somali waters was a target for ransom.

Some Somali pirates still fancy themselves as eco-warriors, guarding the coast for local fishermen and protecting it against international toxic-waste dumping. But it's clear the area is now plagued by maritime criminals who are not above attacking ships bringing humanitarian food shipments to Somalia's starving millions.

The attacks — on everything from cruise ships and oil tankers to fishing vessels and container ships — began drawing serious attention from the world's great powers last year. Media attention and shipowners' pleas eventually triggered formation of an impressive armada — warships from NATO, the European Union, France, the United States, China, Russia, India and two-dozen other countries.

"All these powers are showing up for these guys with AK-47s and flip-flops," says Abukar Arman, a Somali journalist and activist based in Ohio.

CURRENT SITUATION

Organized Gangs

In the first six months of 2009, Somali pirates have been responsible for more than 60 percent of the world's attacks, 86 percent of the world's maritime hostage-takings and virtually all of the growth in piracy.[57]

The pirate gangs come alongside trawlers and merchant ships in fast-moving skiffs and scamper on board using ladders or grappling hooks. They are typically armed with rocket-propelled grenades and AK-47s. "All you need is three guys and a little boat, and the next day you're millionaires," said Adullahi Omar Qawden, a former captain in Somalia's long-defunct navy.[58]

Several pirate gangs operate in Somalia, undoubtedly with connections to politicians and organized criminal gangs. "Believe me, a lot of our money has gone straight into the government's pockets," Farah Ismail Eid, a captured pirate, told *The New York Times*.

He said his team typically gave 20 percent to their bosses and 30 percent to government officials, allocating 20 percent for future missions and keeping 30 percent for themselves.[59] Abdi Waheed Johar, director general of Puntland's fisheries and ports ministry, acknowledges that some government officials are working with the pirates.

When Somali pirates attacked the *MV Faina*, a Ukrainian ship carrying tanks and ammunition to Mombasa last September, "they knew the number of crew on board and even some names," says Somali journalist Arman. "These are illiterate people — they're being given information."

"Without any form of domestic law and order within Somalia, organized militia groups and pirate gangs have managed to fill this vacuum," says Sekulich, the Canadian journalist and author. "They have it all — command-and-control structures, logistics people, armories, financiers."

In a country with an average annual income of $600, pirates now drive the biggest cars, run many businesses and throw the best parties, sometimes with foreign bands brought in for the occasion. "Entire clans and coastal villages now survive off piracy," *The New York Times* reported in December, "with women baking bread for pirates, men and boys guarding hostages and others serving as scouts, gunmen, mechanics, accountants and skiff builders."[60]

Pirates are also the best customers for retailers. "They pay $20 for a $5 bottle of perfume," Leyla Ahmen, a

Two dozen crew members were taken hostage when this Norwegian chemical tanker was hijacked off the Somali coast on March 26, 2009. Both the ship and crew were released on April 10 after a $2.6 million ransom was paid. Somali pirates are still holding 10 cargo ships.

shopkeeper in Xarardheere, a coastal Somali pirate hangout, told the *Times*.

The huge amounts of cash flooding northeastern Somalia have created serious inflation in the region and corrupts the morals of youths and women in the conservative Muslim society, says Somali presidential chief of staff Jama. "Young men started paying $100 for a cup of tea and telling the waiter to 'Keep the change,' " he explained. And some women have left their husbands for rich, young pirates. "These ill-gotten fast riches . . . are as damaging to the very fabric of the society onshore as it is damaging to international trade offshore."

While the pirates may move freely on land, their movements at sea are now being curtailed. The massive new international armada has captured dozens of pirates and deterred attacks on vessels carrying food aid. Stephen Mull, U.S. acting assistant secretary of State for political and military affairs, says nearly three times as many pirates were interdicted in the first four months of the year as in all of 2008. Under the new international agreements, many of the prisoners are now being sent to Kenya and other area countries for trial. (*See sidebar, p. 138.*)

But Burnett, author of *Dangerous Waters*, attributes the southwest monsoon season — which makes the water too rough for small boats — to a temporary reduction in piracy attacks this summer. The pirates will be back in force by October, he predicts.

A Somali fisherman hauls his catch to market in Mogadishu. Environmentalists and Somali officials say that after the government collapsed in 1991, foreign vessels illegally entered the country's territorial waters to exploit the rich fishing grounds or dump toxic wastes. Initially, the government encouraged Somali fishermen to collect fines from the foreign vessels, but those efforts soon morphed into full-blown piracy, the government says.

Meanwhile, the United States recently sent 40 tons of weapons and ammunition to shore up Somalia's Transitional Federal Government (TFG) against the Islamist al-Shabaab rebels who control much of southern Somalia. And the European Union is considering helping to train Somali police and create courts and other legal infrastructures.[61]

"We are not being utilized as much as we could be," Somali Prime Minister Omar Abdirashid Ali Sharmarke told the *Los Angeles Times* in April. "We need to fight pirates on land. We have information about how they function and who they are. The long-term objective should be to build institutions that will deal with pirates from inside the country."[62]

"The solution is easy if the will-power is there," says Jama. "If a team of 500 Somali soldiers are given special advanced training in, say, Djibouti or Uganda for three months and are given swift boats equipped with good firepower, GPS tracking and 10 helicopters, piracy can be eliminated or severely curtailed in 6 months.

"Only Somalis can deny pirates the land to use their ill-gotten loot," he continues. "The international community would be wise to try this solution with little to lose and much to gain. Insurance companies in the UK have offered to help fund a local solution. Other governments would be wise to join."

However, at the moment Sheikh Ahmed's fledgling government is fighting for its survival against foreign-funded extremists, Jama acknowledged.

The administration of President Sheikh Ahmed is the 16th government that has tried to control the country since the fall of Barre in 1991. And while the moderate cleric is regarded by many as one of the few men whose clan base and political skills might bring peace to the war-ravaged country, many foreign observers are skeptical about the TFG's chances of restoring law and order. Currently, the TFG only controls part of Mogadishu, the capital, and fighting breaks out there frequently.

Moreover, suggests terrorism lecturer Lehr of the University of St. Andrews, the summer lull in piracy due to the monsoon season has stalled momentum toward devising a regional anti-piracy strategy, which had garnered particular interest in nearby countries such as Oman and Saudi Arabia.

A better idea, Lehr says, would be to aid stable provincial governments in Puntland, a semi-autonomous region in northeastern Somalia — home to much of the piracy problem — and neighboring Somaliland, a stable, democratically run state in northwestern Somalia that declared its independence in 1991. Although neither "republic" has received international recognition, they may be more capable of imposing law and order than the fragile central government in Mogadishu.

Puntland President Abdirahman Mohamed Farole may have been complicit in piracy at one time, says piracy author Murphy, of the Center for Strategic and Budgetary Assessments, but he now wants it stopped because the lawlessness and corruption could undermine his regime and make it more vulnerable to insurgencies such as al-Shabaab.

"The piracy is happening in Puntland, not Mogadishu," Murphy says. "We can't address it in Mogadishu." Puntland has already begun imposing 15- to 30-year prison sentences for piracy.

Supporting provincial efforts, Lehr says, "would be a much better option in the long run" and "would take the thunder out" of the Islamist movements, which denounce the presence of foreign navies offshore as Western militarism, he says.

"It would be cheaper and would regionalize the issue," he continues. "They should have a bigger interest in securing their own waters than we have."

Defensive Maneuvers

Although Somali pirates have garnered the most attention, piracy is a problem across the globe, from the Philippines to Peru. In West Africa, Nigerian rebel activity has spilled out of the Niger Delta into the Gulf of Guinea, where violent attacks on mariners occur almost weekly. Seaborne assaults on offshore oil facilities have cut Nigeria's oil exports by more than a quarter since 2006.[63]

In the Indian Ocean, pirates prey on Bangladeshi fishermen in the Ganges Delta and international ships anchored in Chittagong port in Bangladesh. And Somali pirates have extended their reach south along the East African coast to Kenya, Tanzania and the Seychelles.

Although worldwide piracy declined between 2003 and 2006, after Southeast Asian countries cracked down on regional piracy, it's been on the upswing since then, as pirates began ramping up activity in the Horn of Africa.[64] Maritime crimes largely stem from the inability of poor coastal nations to police their territorial waters.

As Murphy writes, "common piracy can be suppressed, or at least contained, by onshore police work supported by vigorous maritime patrolling."[65] But, he notes, the 1982 U.N. Law of the Sea Treaty gave countries greater jurisdiction over their territorial waters — extending jurisdiction 200 nautical miles out to sea, without regard to their ability to exercise authority over that expanded area. Shortly after the law was adopted, a Nigerian official said it "imposes on coastal states, regardless of their resources, an undue burden for providing security in long stretches of sea."[66]

While weak coastal states have allowed piracy to fester, the extent of the Somali piracy problem has forced larger nations to flex their naval muscles. Great Power politics are at work in the anti-piracy armada — a sort of dress rehearsal for further influence or combat in the Indian Ocean.

Japan, for instance, wants to escape the post-World War II constitutional constraints that limit its military posture to self-defense. On June 19, Japan's House of Representatives approved a bill authorizing the Self-Defense Forces to protect any commercial ships, regardless of nationality. Other countries, including China, are trying to determine which waters they may need to patrol to ensure oil shipments.

"They're learning the long-distance deployment ropes," says Murphy.

And the shipping industry is learning how better to defend itself. The International Maritime Organization now recommends ships stay at least 600 nautical miles off the coast of Somalia.

The U.S. Coast Guard issued new rules in May requiring U.S. ships plying pirate-infested waters to post lookouts and be ready to fend off pirates with water hoses and high-speed maneuvers.[67] "Anything over 14 or 15 knots tends to be fast, as far as the pirates are concerned," said Marcus Baker, managing director of the global marine practice at Marsh Ltd., an insurance broker in London.[68]

Many companies are fitting their ships with barbed wire and high-decibel long range acoustic devices — which are louder than standing behind a 747 jet during take-off and can be pointed at pirates up to 1,000 feet away. Some are stationing security guards on board for the most dangerous stretches of water.

"There's a bit of everything" being tried, says Wegener, the Norwegian Shipowners Association's security chief. "It does cost more, and so much more management time must be put into finding preventive measures."

Most of the world's shippers — predominantly those with larger ships — are following "best practice" security guidelines, but smaller ships that account for two-thirds of the Somali attacks remain more vulnerable. "Shipping companies are also hit very hard by the economic downturn," says Lehr. "You can't make much money right now with cargo ships, so they're not very keen at throwing more money at security."

OUTLOOK

No Quick Fix

Although the recent surge in piracy has momentarily captured the world's attention, most maritime experts say sustained, concerted effort is needed over the long term.

"Piracy off the Horn of Africa is not a problem we will cure overnight, nor is there a single solution," Vice Admiral Winnefeld told the Senate Armed Services Committee in May.

Criminal activity that has long occurred on land in Somalia — kidnapping, roadblocks and violence — has migrated out to sea, so "something has to be done on land in Somalia," says Wegener. "They operate safe havens, and it's totally risk-free on the part of the pirates."

Although the Europeans and Americans recently have stepped up aid to Somalia, it remains to be seen whether external assistance will have much impact, given the long history of unsuccessful attempts to establish a functioning government.

Most observers expect it to take years for stability to come to Somalia. "That's a long-term endeavor, and a costly one," says RAND's Chalk.

"In Somalia, let us hope that in 10 years there is the beginning of some kind of solution ashore," says the International Maritime Bureau's Mukundan.

Somalia's internal problems create a particularly fertile breeding ground for maritime piracy, says Mukundan. So he doubts similar problems will arise elsewhere. But others aren't so sure.

"There is a risk of this being contagious, when criminals in other parts of the world see how profitable this can be," Wegener says.

For their part, the Somalis say if the international community were serious about halting piracy, foreign in the region would try to halt the illegal fishing or toxic dumping that triggered the upsurge in piracy in the first place. But that's not happening.

"It would be much cheaper to prevent these illegal activities and provide some basic support for the fishing villages and central government so they could deny the pirates land to operate from," says Somali presidential aide Jama.

It's also unclear how long the world's major powers will maintain their naval presence in the region. Historically, says Murphy — the author and Center for Strategic and Budgetary Assessments research fellow — it has taken decades to defeat piracy, using both political and economic measures.

Western nations must decide what level of piracy is tolerable. "None of the people I spoke to — shipping insiders, government officials, naval people — ever said that piracy could be completely eradicated," says author Sekulich. "The best you can do is to suppress and contain it. What's different now is a greater awareness of the economic impact that maritime piracy can have on the global community."

But if piracy is seen as mostly a nuisance, rich nations may decide it's not worth the expense to aggressively patrol for pirates. "Like most other crimes, piracy will not go away," says Ong-Webb, of the Centre for Defence and International Security Studies. "The question we need

to answer is what levels of piracy we are prepared to live with."

It's important that the great powers continue to combat the problem, suggests Bainbridge of the International Transport Workers' Federation. "Piracy always has and always will be around," he says. "The trick is not to let the message out that it is easy and safe to do and highly profitable."

NOTES

1. Daniel Sekulich, *Terror on the Seas* (2009), p. 6.

2. www.eaglespeak.us/2009/04/somali-pirates-convoys-could-work.html.

3. "ICC-IMB Piracy and Armed Robbery Against Ships Report — Second Quarter 2009," ICC International Maritime Bureau, July 2009, pp. 5-6.

4. John S. Burnett, *Dangerous Waters* (2002), p. 9.

5. Sahal Abdulle and Rob Crilly, "Rich pickings for pirates hook fishermen," *The Times* (London), April 7, 2009, p. 33, www.timesonline.co.uk/tol/news/world/africa/article6045092.ece.

6. Sekulich, *op. cit.*, p. 80.

7. Elizabeth A. Kennedy, "Pirates Target, Vow to Kill U.S. Crews," The Associated Press, April 16, 2009, www.boston.com/news/world/africa/articles/2009/04/16/pirates_target_vow_to_kill_us_crews/.

8. "Over 5,000 pirates operate off Somali coast: Russian Navy," *Hindustan Times*, July 19, 2009, www.hindustantimes.com/StoryPage/StoryPage.aspx?sectionName=HomePage&id=adf76ecd-a7be-41ca-a08f-072def60b7e0&Headline='Over+5K+pirates+operate+off+Somali+coast.

9. Andy Crick, "Pirates," *The Sun* (England), June 8, 2009, p. 1, www.thesun.co.uk/sol/homepage/showbiz/tv/2468907/Ross-Kemps-yo-ho-no-go.html.

10. For background, see Jason McLure, "The Troubled Horn of Africa," *CQ Global Researcher*, June 2009, pp. 149-176.

11. "ICC-IMB Piracy and Armed Robbery Against Ships Report — Second Quarter 2009," *op. cit.*, p. 34.

12. Robert D. Kaplan, "Anarchy on Lands Means Piracy at Sea," *The New York Times*, April 12, 2009, p. WK9,

www.nytimes.com/2009/04/12/opinion/12kaplan. html.

13. Ian Storey, "What's Behind Dramatic Drop in S-E Asian Piracy?" *The Straits Times* (Singapore), Jan. 19, 2009, http://app.mfa.gov.sg/pr/read_con tent.asp?View,11946,.

14. "Statement for the Record, Ms. Michèle Flournoy. Undersecretary of Defense (Policy) and Vice Admiral James A. Winnefeld, Director for Strategic Plans and Policy, Joint Chiefs of Staff," Senate Armed Services Committee, May 5, 2009, www.marad.dot.gov/doc uments/Flournoy-Winnefeld_05-05-09.pdf.

15. Katharine Houreld, "Navies ask: What do you do with a captured pirate?" The Associated Press, April 18, 2009, http://abcnews.go.com/US/wireStory?id=7365467.

16. His testimony is at http://foreign.senate.gov/ testimony/2009/PhillipsTestimony090430p.pdf.

17. His testimony is at http://foreign.senate.gov/ testimony/2009/ClanceyTestimony090430p.pdf.

18. Burnett, *op. cit.*, p. 85.

19. Peter Spiegel and Henry Chu, "Grappling With a Forgotten Scourge," *Los Angeles Times*, Nov. 20, 2008, p. A1, http://8.12.42.31/2008/nov/20/world/ fg-highseas20.

20. Burnett, *op. cit.*, p. 88.

21. Lauren Ploch, *et al.*, "Piracy off the Horn of Africa," Congressional Research Service, April 21, 2009, p. 8, www.fas.org/sgp/crs/row/R40528.pdf.

22. Paul Alexander, "Boredom, Hunger and Fear for Pirates' Hostages," The Associated Press, April 19, 2009, http://abcnews.go.com/International/ wireStory?id=7373830.

23. Ploch, *et al.*, *op. cit.*

24. Henry Samuel, "Pirates' Hostage 'Shot by French Rescuers,'" *The Daily Telegraph*, May 5, 2009, p. 15, www.telegraph.co.uk/news/worldnews/europe/ france/5272730/French-skipper-held-hostage-by- pirates-shot-dead-by-special-forces.html.

25. "Trial of Somali pirates opens in Yemen," *RIA Novosti*, July 2, 2009, www.globalsecurity. org/military/library/news/2009/07/mil-090702-ri anovosti05.htm.

26. Matthew Lynn, "Ignoring Piracy Poses Risk for World Economy," *Sydney Morning Herald*, Dec. 8, 2008, p. 45, www.bloomberg.com/apps/news?pid=n ewsarchive&sid=aRgDvDy5TQpU.

27. David Osler, "Preventing Piracy," *Lloyd's List*, May 28, 2009, p. 7.

28. Sharon Otterman, "Pirates Said to Ask for $25 Million Ransom," *The New York Times*, Nov. 20, 2008, www.nytimes.com/2008/11/21/world/ africa/21pirates.html.

29. Mohamed Olad Hassan, "Five Pirates Drown With Share of $3 Million Ransom a Day After Freeing Saudi Tanker," The Associated Press, Jan. 10, 2009, www.cbsnews.com/stories/2009/01/10/world/ main4711893.shtml.

30. Jean-Marc Mojon, "Ransom Payments: The Hole in Somali Pirates' Net," Agence France-Presse, Jan. 12, 2009, www.google.com/hostednews/afp/article/ ALeqM5gGilBVHvFJS-ae2dlsyDb84aDiKg.

31. Burnett, *op. cit.*, p. 75.

32. Peter Earle, *The Pirate Wars* (2004), p. 20.

33. Sekulich, *op. cit.*, p. 33.

34. Martin P. Murphy, *Small Boats, Weak States, Dirty Money* (2009), p. 11.

35. David Cordingly, *Under the Black Flag* (1995), p. 203.

36. *Ibid.*, p. 277.

37. Colin Woodard, *The Republic of Pirates* (2007), p. 1.

38. Bill Weinberg, "Book Review: Jefferson's War: America's First War on Terror, 1801-1805," *Journal, Middle East Policy Council*, fall 2006, www.mepc .org/journal_vol13/0609_Weinberg2.asp.

39. Gerard W. Gawalt, "America and the Barbary Pirates: An International Battle Against an Unconventional Foe," The Thomas Jefferson Papers, Library of Congress, http://memory.loc.gov/ammem/collec tions/jefferson_papers/mtjprece.html.

40. Michael B. Oren, *Power, Faith and Fantasy* (2007), p. 35. Also see "Barbary Wars," U.S. Department of State, www.state.gov/r/pa/ho/time/jd/92068.htm.

41. Cordingly, *op. cit.*, p. xiii.

42. *Ibid.*, p. 96.

43. *Ibid.*, p. xx.

44. Murphy, p. 1.

45. *Ibid.*, p. 9.

46. *Ibid.*, p. 13.

47. *Ibid.*, p. 10.

48. Kaplan, *op. cit.*

49. Cordingly, *op. cit.*, p. 77.

50. Sean Yoong, "Pirate Abduction in Malacca Strait After Long Quiet," The Associated Press, Feb. 21, 2009, www.thejakartapost.com/news/2009/02/21/pirate-abduction-malacca-strait-after-long-quiet.html.

51. Murphy, *op. cit.*, p. 32.

52. Sekulich, *op. cit.*, p. 46.

53. K. C. Vijayan, "Data-Sharing System Boost for Malacca Strait Security," *The Straits Times* (Singapore), March 29, 2008, http://app.mfa.gov.sg/pr/read_content.asp?View,9678,.

54. Storey, *op. cit.*

55. See McLure, *op. cit.*

56. Murphy, *op. cit.*, p. 31.

57. "ICC-IMB Piracy and Armed Robbery Against Ships Report — Second Quarter 2009," *op. cit.*, p. 11.

58. Jeffrey Gettleman, "Somali's Pirates Flourish in a Lawless Nation," *The New York Times*, Oct. 31, 2008, p. A1, www.nytimes.com/2008/10/31/world/africa/31pirates.html.

59. *Ibid.*

60. Jeffrey Gettleman, "Pirates in Skiffs Still Outmaneuvering Warships Off Somalia," *The New York Times*, Dec. 16, 2008, p. A6, www.nytimes.com/2008/12/16/world/africa/16pirate.html.

61. Mary Beth Sheridan, "U.S. Has Sent 40 Tons of Munitions to Aid Somali Government," *The Washington Post*, June 27, 2009, p. A5, www.washingtonpost.com/wp-dyn/content/article/2009/06/26/AR2009062604261.html.

62. Edmund Sanders, "Let Us Handle Pirates, Somalis Say," *Los Angeles Times*, April 15, 2009, p. A22, http://articles.latimes.com/2009/apr/15/world/fg-somalia-pirates15.

63. "A Clear and Present Danger," *The Economist*, April 18, 2009, www.economist.com/displaystory.cfm?story_id=13496711.

64. Peter Chalk, "The Maritime Dimension of International Security: Terrorism, Piracy and Challenges for the United States," RAND Corporation, 2008.

65. Murphy, *op. cit.*, p. 161.

66. *Ibid.*, p. 32.

67. "US Beefs Up Anti-Piracy Action for Ships," Agence France-Presse, May 13, 2009, www.blnz.com/news/2009/05/13/beefs_anti-piracy_action_ships_9407.html.

68. "Nigerian Pirates Blamed for Hike in Marine Premium," *Africa News*, June 30, 2009, http://allafrica.com/stories/200907010274.html.

BIBLIOGRAPHY

Books

Burnett, John S., *Dangerous Waters: Modern Piracy and Terror on the High Seas*, Dutton, 2002.
After being robbed at sea, a former UPI reporter — now a marine security consultant — investigates the rise of modern piracy, talking with leading authorities and riding on board an oil tanker crossing the Indian Ocean.

Cordingly, David, *Under the Black Flag: The Romance and the Reality of Life Among the Pirates*, Random House, 1995.
The former head of exhibitions at England's National Maritime Museum recounts the history of 17th- and 18th-century pirates and the legends they inspired.

Langewiesche, William, *The Outlaw Sea: A World of Freedom, Chaos, and Crime*, North Point Press, 2004.
A writer for *The Atlantic* and *Vanity Fair* looks at the oceans post-9/11, finding that piracy and terror are

symptomatic of the stateless, "inherently disorderly" nature of the seas, which are largely beyond the reach of nations and their laws.

Murphy, Martin N., *Small Boats, Weak States, Dirty Money: Piracy and Maritime Terrorism in the Modern World*, **Columbia University Press, 2009.**
A research fellow at King's College, London, thoroughly assesses piracy and terrorism, drawing careful distinctions between them but explaining how the two problems may overlap.

Sekulich, Daniel, *Terror on the Seas: True Tales of Modern-Day Pirates*, **Thomas Dunne Books, 2009.**
A Canadian journalist travels around the Indian Ocean, tracing the origins of contemporary piracy through interviews with experts and personal experiences.

Woodard, Colin, *The Republic of Pirates: Being the True and Surprising Story of the Caribbean Pirates and the Man Who Brought Them Down*, **Houghton Mifflin Harcourt, 2007.**
A journalist and author tells the story of the Caribbean pirates of the 18th century and the colonial governors and the former privateer who brought them to justice.

Articles

Alexander, Paul, "Boredom, Hunger and Fear for Pirates' Hostages," The Associated Press, April 19, 2009.
Hostages released by Somali pirates share accounts of fear and deprivation.

Bradsher, Keith, "Captain's Rescue Revives Debate Over Arming Crews," *The New York Times*, **April 12, 2009, p. A8.**
Amid growing calls for arming merchant ship crews against pirates, questions persist about whether it would escalate the level of violence.

Carney, Scott, "Cutthroat Capitalism," *Wired*, **July 2009, www.wired.com/images/multimedia/magazine/ 1707/Wired1707_Cutthroat_Capitalism.pdf.**
A graphics-heavy "economic analysis of the Somali pirate business model" examines the ratio of risk vs. rewards of attacking multiple ships when only a few pay off big. The package includes interviews with a pirate, a security contractor and a former hostage.

Gettleman, Jeffrey, "Rounding Up Suspects, the West Turns to Kenya as Piracy Criminal Court," *The New York Times*, **April 24, 2009, p. A8.**
Kenya will prosecute Somali pirates captured by the European Union, the United Kingdom and the United States.

Kaplan, Robert D., "Anarchy on Land Means Piracy at Sea," *The New York Times*, **April 12, 2009, p. WK9.**
Maritime piracy is a ripple effect of anarchy on land and could potentially serve as a platform for terrorism.

Storey, Ian, "What's Behind Dramatic Drop in S-E Asian Piracy," *The* **[Singapore]** *Straits Times*, **Jan. 19, 2009.**
Although worldwide piracy reached record levels in 2008, the number of regional incidents in Southeast Asia has dropped by two-thirds since 2003, thanks to improved security cooperation among Singapore, Indonesia and Malaysia.

Sudderuddin, Shuli, and Debbie Yong, "It's a Terrible Time to be a Seaman," *The* **[Singapore]** *Straits Times*, **Nov. 23, 2008.**
Seafarers describe being hijacked and held hostage by pirates.

Reports and Studies

Chalk, Peter, "The Maritime Dimension of International Security: Terrorism, Piracy and Challenges for the United States," RAND Corporation, 2008; available at www.rand.org/pubs/monographs/2008/RAND_ MG697.pdf.
A policy analyst with the California think tank finds no nexus between maritime piracy and terrorism in the early years of this decade. Chalk does suggest, however, that the vulnerabilities that have encouraged piracy also apply to terrorism.

Ploch, Lauren, et al., "Piracy off the Horn of Africa," Congressional Research Service, April 24, 2009, www .fas.org/sgp/crs/row/R40528.pdf.
The United Nations allows international ships to combat piracy in Somali waters, but anarchy in Somalia feeds the problem. U.S. officials pledge a more robust response.

For More Information

Congressional Research Service, 101 Independence Ave., S.E., Washington, DC 20540; (202) 707-7640; www.loc.gov. The research arm of the U.S. Congress that has produced detailed reports about maritime piracy and its effects on insurance.

International Maritime Bureau, 26 Wapping High Street, London E1W 1NG, United Kingdom; (44) 0 20 7423 6960; www.icc-ccs.org. A division of the International Chamber of Commerce that aims to identify and investigate fraud and other threats; manages the Piracy Reporting Centre in Kuala Lumpur, which issues warnings to shippers and reports pirate attacks to local law enforcement.

International Maritime Organization, 4, Albert Embankment, London SE1 7SR, United Kingdom; (44) 20 7735 7611; www.imo.org. A U.N. agency responsible for helping to improve the safety and security of international shipping.

International Shipping Federation, 12 Carthusian Street, London EC1M 6EZ, United Kingdom; (44) 20 7417 8844; www.marisec.org. The principal international shipowners organization.

International Transport Workers' Federation, 49-60 Borough Road, London, SE1 1DR, United Kingdom; (44) 20 7403 2733; www.itf.org.uk. A federation of 654 transport workers' unions, representing 4.5 million workers in 148 countries.

International Union of Marine Insurance, c/o Swiss Insurance Association, C.F. Meyer-Strasse 14, Postfach 4288, CH-8022 Zurich, Switzerland; (41) (44) 208-2870; www.iumi.com. A professional association that provides a forum for exchanging information on issues of importance to the marine shipping and insurance sectors.

Nautilus International, 750-760 High Road, Leytonstone, London E11 3BB, United Kingdom; (44) 20 8989 6677; www.nautilusint.org. A union representing 25,000 seafarers and other workers employed by British and Dutch shipping companies.

RAND Corporation, 1776 Main Street, Santa Monica, CA 90401 USA; (310) 393-0411; www.rand.org. A think tank that has produced reports about piracy and maintains a comprehensive database of terrorism incidents worldwide.

7

The Troubled Horn of Africa

Jason McLure

A Somali woman wounded in fighting between government soldiers and Islamist insurgents last June is among thousands of civilians killed or wounded in Somalia's 18-year civil war. The conflict has destabilized the entire region, forcing nearly 1.3 million people from their homes and creating a lawless safe haven for pirates and terrorists.

AFP/Getty Images/Mustafa Abdi

From *CQ Researcher*, June 2009.

Halima Warsame's husband and son were killed two years ago after a mortar shell landed on their shop in Mogadishu, the war-torn capital of Somalia. But the impoverished nation's long civil war wasn't finished with her yet.

After living in a camp for people who had fled the fighting, she returned home in April. But in mid-May renewed fighting forced her to return to the camp.

"I thought with the Ethiopian troops gone and the new government [in place] everything would be alright, only it got worse," she says. "I don't see any hope that our situation will ever improve."[1]

Indeed, there is little reason for optimism. During just two weeks in May, at least 67,000 people were driven from their homes in the beleaguered seaside capital by clashes between the country's U.N.-backed transitional government and Islamist extremists. But they are just the latest victims. Somalia's 18-year civil war has killed tens of thousands, forced nearly 1.3 million people from their homes and created a lawless safe haven for pirates and suspected terrorists.[2]

Once a gem of Italian colonial architecture overlooking the Indian Ocean, parts of Mogadishu have been reduced to a moonscape of gutted buildings where warring militias wielding shoulder-fired grenade launchers and AK-47s periodically wreak havoc, sending civilians fleeing to dozens of primitive camps surrounding the city.

The fighting has continued despite more than a dozen attempts to establish a central government — including the latest, in January, when moderate Islamist Sheikh Sharif Sheikh Ahmed became

Grinding Poverty Afflicts Most of Africa's Horn

The four nations in the Horn of Africa cover an arid swathe about three times the size of Texas. More than 100 million people live in the war-torn region — 85.2 million of them in landlocked Ethiopia, Africa's second-most populous country. Tiny Djibouti is the smallest with half a million people. Ethiopia and Eritrea are near the bottom on the U.N.'s 179-nation Human Development Index, which ranks countries by life expectancy and other factors. Somalia doesn't even make the list, since it has no way to collect statistics. Some analysts say the area's poverty and weak or corrupt governments make it a safe haven for Islamic terrorists and pirates.

Source: The World Factbook, Central Intelligence Agency; U.N. Development Programme

president. In fact, Ahmed's government is said to have, at best, a tenuous hold on just a few blocks of the capital itself. The ongoing security vacuum has encouraged the clan violence and anarchy that make Somalia a global poster child for a "failed state."

But the fighting in Somalia is only part of an inter-related web of conflicts plaguing the Horn of Africa — one of the most benighted corners of the world's poorest continent. Archrivals Ethiopia and tiny Eritrea have backed factions in Somalia's civil war and continue to arm rebel groups destabilizing the region. And both nations have kept tens of thousands of troops dug in along their mutual border since the end of a 1998-2000 border war that killed 70,000.

In January, Ethiopia ended a two-year occupation of Mogadishu, where it initially succeeded in ousting an Islamist alliance that U.S. officials feared was courting links with the al Qaeda terrorist group. Western nations have showered Ethiopia with billions of dollars in aid and avoided criticizing the regime's recent clampdown on opposition parties, journalists and human rights activists.

Eritrea, once admired for its self-sufficiency and discipline, has become an isolated dictatorship facing possible international sanctions for having backed the Islamist insurgents in Somalia. Meanwhile Eritrea's effort to build a military counterweight to much-larger Ethiopia has kept more than a third of its productive population serving in the military.[3]

"Eritrea and Ethiopia are battling to determine which will be the dominant power in the region," says Dan Connell, a former adviser to the Eritrean government and author of the book *Against All Odds: A Chronicle of the Eritrean Revolution.* "The border issue is more excuse than cause."

Thus beleaguered by poor governance, conflict and poverty, Ethiopia and Eritrea rank near the bottom on the United Nations' 179-country Human Development Index, which ranks countries by life expectancy, literacy and other factors. Somalia, with no functioning central government to collect statistics, doesn't even make the list.[4] But with 40 percent of the population needing emergency aid, U.N. officials describe Somalia as the world's worst humanitarian and security crisis.[5]

Horn of Africa at a Glance

Somalia

Area: 246,201 sq. miles (slightly smaller than Texas)
Population: 9.8 million (July 2009 est.)
GDP per capita: $600 (2008 est.)
Unemployment rate: n/a
UN Human Development Index rank: not included
Religion: Sunni Muslim
Government: Sheikh Sharif Sheikh Ahmed was elected president in January 2009; Somaliland in the north remains autonomous, having declared its own local government in 1991 but has not been recognized internationally. Puntland, in the northeast, declared itself the Puntland State of Somalia in 1998 but has refrained from making a formal bid for independence.

Ethiopia

Area: 435,186 sq. miles (about twice the size of Texas)
Population: 85.2 million (July 2009 est.)
GDP per capita: $800 (2008 est.)
Unemployment rate: n/a
UN Human Development Index rank: 169 (out of 179)
Religion: Christian, 61%; Muslim, 33%; other 6%
Government: Federal republic, bicameral Parliament; Prime Minister Meles Zenawi was elected in 2000.

Eritrea

Area: 46,842 sq. miles (slightly larger than Pennsylvania)
Population: 5.6 million (July 2009 est.)
GDP per capita: $700 (2008 est.)
Unemployment rate: n/a
UN Human Development Index rank: 164 (out of 179)
Religion: Muslim, Coptic Christian, Roman Catholic, Protestant
Government: Provisional government since independence from Ethiopia in 1991, constitutional options presented but none yet implemented; single-party state run by the leftist People's Front for Democracy and Justice; President Isaias Afwerki elected by National Assembly in 1993 in country's only election so far.

Djibouti

Area: 8,880 sq. miles (about the size of New Jersey)
Population: 516,055 (July 2009 est.)
GDP per capita: $3,700 (2008 est.)
Unemployment rate: 59% in urban areas, 83% in rural areas (2007 est.)
UN Human Development Index rank: 151 (out of 179)
Religion: Muslim 94%, Christian 6%
Government: Republic; President Ismail Omar Guelleh has held office since 1999.

Source: The World Factbook, Central Intelligence Agency; U.N. Development Programme

"The region seems to be going backwards fast," says Ioan Lewis, a retired professor at the London School of Economics who has written several books on Somalia. "Whether it can change gear and change course, I really don't know."

The region's human rights record worries the international community as much as its dire economic

AFP/Getty Images/Mustafa Abdi

AFP/Getty Images/Adrian Dennis

Death and Demonstrations

The remains of Somalis killed during Ethiopia's two-year occupation are recovered near a former Ethiopian military camp in Somalia (top). More than 10,000 people reportedly were killed during the occupation, which ended in January. Ethiopia also has come under international criticism for a recent crackdown on opposition leaders, the press and human rights organizations. Protesters demonstrate against Prime Minister Meles Zenawi during the April meeting of world leaders in London (bottom).

conditions. The European Parliament on Jan. 15 expressed its "great concern" for the state of "human rights, the rule of law, democracy and governance in all countries of the Horn of Africa," where there were "credible reports of arbitrary arrests, forced labour, torture and maltreatment of prisoners, as well as persecution of journalists and political repression."[6]

The chaos has provided refuge to suspected al Qaeda terrorists and allowed pirates to wreak havoc on

international shipping. The conflict and poverty have sent millions of refugees fleeing to neighboring countries or to camps in Somalia for internally displaced persons (IDPs) where they depend on international aid agencies for food and shelter — aid that is often blocked by violence, theft or piracy. (*See graph, p. 159.*)[7]

Somalia's civil war has been fuelled in large part by distrust and competition between the country's Byzantine network of clans and subclans and by warlords with a vested interest in instability. A brief flicker of hope accompanied the withdrawal of Ethiopian troops in January and the accession of Sheikh Ahmed to the presidency of the country's Transitional Federal Government. But that hope was dimmed by fierce fighting in April and May and the capture of key towns by Islamist insurgents. Even veteran observers of Somalia marvel at the seeming senselessness of the fighting.

"All I can say now is that I have felt it a privilege to observe a people who shot themselves in the foot with such accuracy and tumbled into the abyss in such style," Aidan Hartley, a Kenyan-born Reuters correspondent who covered Somalia in the early 1990s, wrote in a 2003 book.[8]

Such sentiments are still echoed today. "We are all . . . shocked that Somalis keep finding reasons to kill Somalis," said Ahmedou Ould-Abdallah, a Mauritanian diplomat who is the U.N. special envoy to Somalia, during a Feb. 2 press conference.

The four nations of Africa's Horn — Somalia, Ethiopia, Eritrea and the micro-state Djibouti — cover an arid swathe about three times the size of Texas. About 100 million people live in the region — 85.2 million of them in Ethiopia, Africa's second-most populous country after Nigeria. To the north, tiny Eritrea — which split away from Ethiopia in 1993 — maintains Africa's largest army in an effort to deter its southern neighbor from invading.

Conflict is not new to the Horn of Africa, where the predominately Christian highlanders of the Ethiopian plateau have been fighting with the Muslim lowlanders of eastern Ethiopia (known as the Ogaden) and Somalia for centuries. But the region is also periodically plagued by famine, due to a rapidly growing population and increasingly unpredictable rainfall. This year the warfare and drought will force about 15.5 million people in Somalia and Ethiopia to seek humanitarian aid.[9]

And the long-term trends are equally worrying. About 80 percent of Ethiopians and Eritreans are subsistence farmers or herders. Agricultural production per capita has declined in Ethiopia since the 1960s, while the population has more than tripled.[10] Eritrea's government-controlled economy has eliminated nearly all private enterprise, and its farmers don't produce enough food to feed the country, a situation exacerbated by the government's decision not to demobilize tens of thousands of farmers from the military.[11] Somalia, which imports about 60 percent of the grain needed to feed its estimated 8 to 10 million people, has little prospect of feeding itself anytime soon.

"Ethiopia adds to its population between 1.5 to 2 million people a year," says David Shinn, U.S. ambassador to the country from 1996 to 1999. "That is not sustainable for a country that has been unable to feed itself for more than three decades."

While Somalia's humanitarian disaster is the region's most pressing issue, a longer-term question is whether the war-wracked country as presently configured can survive. Its northwestern region, known as Somaliland, has declared independence after building a functional administration and maintaining a comparatively peaceful, democratic existence for the last decade.

"The hard questions have not been asked as to what sort of a nation-state Somalia should look like," says Rashid Abdi, a Nairobi-based analyst for the International Crisis Group, a conflict-resolution think tank. "The focus has been on creating a national government. Unfortunately, in spite of a lot of investment in the last 15 years, we are nowhere near a functioning, credible nation-state."

Western policy in the region has been influenced largely by the perception that Somalia's lawlessness provides a safe haven for al Qaeda. Somalia's radical Islamist al-Shabaab militia, the most powerful group battling the transitional government, has links to al Qaeda and reportedly has been recruiting jihadists in the United States.[12] And while recent reports indicate that hundreds of foreign fighters from the Middle East and Muslim communities in North America and Europe have arrived in Somalia, analysts disagree over whether Somalia's Islamic radicals pose any real threat outside of the Horn.[13] Some blame the George W. Bush administration in particular for fomenting chaos in Somalia by arming warlords whose sole virtues were their willingness to fight Islamic groups.

"Violent extremism and anti-Americanism are now rife in Somalia due in large part to the blowback from policies that focused too narrowly on counterterrorism objectives," writes Kenneth Menkhaus, an American Horn of Africa specialist from Davidson College who worked as a U.N. official in Somalia in the 1990s.[14]

If there is reason for optimism, it is that the new Obama administration in Washington has signaled its willingness to focus more on human rights and stability and less on waging war against radical Islamists and their allies. Such a move would involve both pressing Ethiopia to resolve its border dispute with Eritrea and showing a greater willingness to work with moderate Islamists in Somalia, who many believe are the only force capable of bridging the divide between the country's constantly warring clans.

As analysts and diplomats discuss the Horn of Africa's future, here are some of the questions being debated:

Is there a real threat of international terrorism from Somalia?

When 17-year-old Burhan Hassan didn't come home from school in Minneapolis last Nov. 4, his mother thought he was at a local mosque. Unfortunately he wasn't. Although his family had fled Somalia when he was a toddler, Burhan — it turned out — had embarked that day for the southern Somali port town of Kismayo, a stronghold of al-Shabaab, the military wing of the Islamic Courts Union (ICU) that briefly controlled southern Somalia in 2006 before being ousted by Ethiopian troops.

U.S. law enforcement and counterterrorism officials fear Burhan is one of about 20 young Somali-Americans who may have left the United States since mid-2007 to join the group, which the State Department considers a terrorist organization.[15] The fear is that they may return to the United States or Europe as part of a sleeper cell, sent by a group that is increasingly vociferous about its links to international terrorism. Since 2007 some American generals have considered Somalia a "third front in the war on terror,"[16] and U.S. military planes are a common sight over the nation.[17]*

A spokesman for al-Shabaab said it began seeking links with al Qaeda after it was listed as a terrorist group

---

* In 2003, the U.S. opened a military base in Djibouti, less than 30 miles from the border of Somalia. Camp Lemonier houses about 2,000 U.S. personnel who monitor suspected terrorists in the Horn of Africa and train the militaries of Ethiopia and other U.S. allies.

AFP/Getty Images/Simon Maina

Newly elected Somalia President Sheikh Sharif Sheikh Ahmed is regarded by many as one of the few men whose clan base and political skills might bring peace to the war-ravaged country. Somalia has had no effective central authority since former president Mohamed Siad Barre was ousted in 1991, touching off an endless cycle of war between rival factions.

by the Bush administration in 2008. Before that, Shabaab "had no official links with al Qaeda," Sheikh Mukhtar Robow, a spokesman for the group, said in 2008. Now, however, "we're looking to have an association with them. Al Qaeda became more powerful after it was added to the list; we hope that it will be the same with us."[18]

Experts differ on whether the links are substantive. Those who worry that Somalia has become a safe haven for terrorists point out that several Somali Islamist leaders were trained in al Qaeda camps in the Afghanistan-Pakistan border regions in the 1990s before returning to Somalia to help form al-Ittihad al-Islamiya, a forerunner of al-Shabaab.

"We face a very serious counterterrorism challenge in Somalia, with extremists affiliated with al Qaeda training and operating in substantial portions of southern Somalia," said Susan Rice, the Obama administration's U.N. ambassador, during confirmation hearings in January. "And that has the potential to pose a serious and direct threat to our own national security."

Those concerned about the terrorism threat from Somalia often cite Gouled Hassan Dourad, a Somali national who was trained in Afghanistan, captured in Somalia in 2004 and held in the CIA's secret prison system before being transferred to Guantánamo Bay in 2006. The United States claims he supported al Qaeda's

East Africa cell and was privy to plots to attack an Ethiopian airliner and the U.S. military base in Djibouti in 2003.[19] Likewise, Fazul Abdullah Mohammed — a Comoran national accused of involvement in the 1998 bombings of U.S. embassies in Kenya and Tanzania and suspected in the 2002 truck bombing of the Paradise Hotel in Mombasa that killed 15 — is also thought to have taken refuge in Somalia.[20] A third figure, Hassan al-Turki, is said to run a training camp for Islamist militants in southern Somalia, and, like Mohammed, has been the target of an unsuccessful U.S. air strike in Somalia.[21]

"Definitely you have the al Qaeda East Africa cell that has only been able to function in Somalia with the protection of Somali Islamist movements," says Andre LeSage, an American Horn of Africa specialist at the Pentagon's National Defense University. "Previously, it had been with the protection of al-Ittihad, now it's with the protection of al-Shabaab."

But others say the international terrorism threat from Somalia has been exaggerated, both by al Qaeda and by the United States and its allies. "There is very strong documentation, using declassified al Qaeda documents, indicating that it was in and out of Somalia starting in 1992-1993," says Shinn, the former ambassador to Ethiopia. "They had relatively little success, however. They thought it was going to be relatively easy pickings until they learned Somalis could be just as obstreperous with them as with everyone else. It was very tough sledding."

"Over time they've had increasing success. But I think there is a certain amount of hype here," he says, especially when the West compares al-Shabaab to the ultra-conservative Taliban in Afghanistan. "The idea that the Taliban is moving into Somalia is just utter nonsense."

Indeed, some argue that U.S. support for Ethiopia's 2006 invasion of Somalia and subsequent U.S. air strikes in Somalia that have often mistakenly killed civilians have been counterproductive and have helped to radicalize the population — increasing the terrorism threat. But so far, these analysts point out, no Somali-born citizens have been involved in successful acts of international terrorism.

"The Ethiopian invasion was totally negative," says Lewis, the Somali historian. "The terrorist threat is much more real now than before the interventions."

Coordinated suicide attacks last October on five separate targets in the autonomous Somali regions of Somaliland and Puntland — apparently carried out by

Aid to Ethiopia Spiked Dramatically

The Horn of Africa in 2007 received more than $3 billion in aid from the 30 developed countries that make up the Organization for Economic Cooperation and Development (OECD). Drought-plagued Ethiopia received the most — $2.3 billion — in part because of its consistent support for the West's war on terrorism.

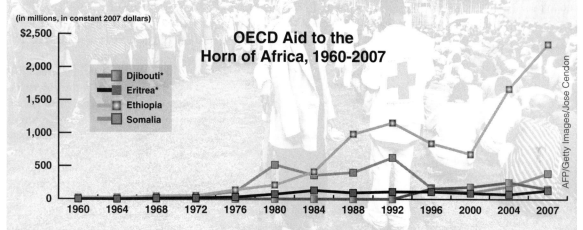

(in millions, in constant 2007 dollars)

OECD Aid to the Horn of Africa, 1960-2007

Legend:
- Djibouti*
- Eritrea*
- Ethiopia
- Somalia

AFP/Getty Images/Jose Cendon

* Djibouti was a French colony until 1977. Eritrea declared its independence from Ethiopia in 1993.

Source: Organization for Economic Cooperation and Development

al-Shabaab — have raised fears the group's capacity for such tactics is growing.[22]

"The suicide bombings in Puntland and Somaliland were clear evidence that these guys have the capacity to work outside their comfort zone," says Menkhaus. "They've also demonstrated their capacity to induce some young men to commit suicide, which is fairly new to Somalia."

"Where will the next threat present itself? Kenya, Ethiopia, Djibouti? Shabaab has every reason to keep this conflict internationalized," he adds.

Is Somalia a viable state?

In the 18 years since the fall of dictator Mohamed Siad Barre, Somalia's foundations have steadily crumbled, with two large northern swathes of the country declaring themselves autonomous or independent entities.

In some ways, the Somalia that existed in the three decades before 1991 — a unified Somalia with a capital in Mogadishu — was an historical anomaly. It never existed previously and has not existed since. Though some analysts express optimism about the newest U.N.-backed Transitional Federal Government (TFG) formed

in February, the fact remains that its 14 predecessors since 1991 have all failed.[23]

The TFG struggles to control the port of Mogadishu, which is its main source of revenue, and has authority over just a tiny fraction of Somali territory. Though the current government has 36 cabinet ministers, most of the ministries have no employees and no budget.[24] The situation is so chaotic that businessmen print their own currency, and educated Somalis seek passports from neighboring countries to facilitate international travel.

Despite a string of U.N.-funded peace-and-reconciliation conferences in neighboring countries, a constantly shifting array of militia groups has defied outside attempts at reconciliation. In 2008, World Food Programme convoys bringing aid from Mogadishu to refugee camps 18 miles away needed to pass through more than a dozen checkpoints controlled by different militia groups, according to Peter Smerdon, a spokesman for the program.

"There are too many separate interests on the ground in Somalia," says LeSage, of the National Defense University. "You have so many different power centers there, and each one is being held by a different faction

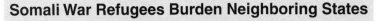

Somali War Refugees Burden Neighboring States

Nearly a half-million Somalis have fled into neighboring countries to escape the country's 18-year civil war. Most have gone to Kenya and Yemen. Only 10 percent have remained in other Horn of Africa countries.

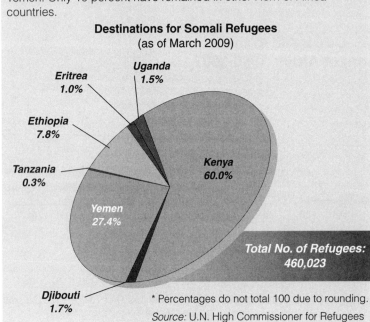

Destinations for Somali Refugees
(as of March 2009)

Uganda 1.5%
Eritrea 1.0%
Ethiopia 7.8%
Tanzania 0.3%
Yemen 27.4%
Kenya 60.0%
Djibouti 1.7%

Total No. of Refugees: 460,023

* Percentages do not total 100 due to rounding.
Source: U.N. High Commissioner for Refugees

"We don't know who to talk to now in Somalia," he continues. "There is no central government. They are so fragmented. They have been killing and killing and killing and oppressing. The people of Somaliland have enjoyed peace, security and democracy, and they're confident they can continue."

Because of the lack of international recognition, however, the region has not garnered needed development aid or political support. Many countries are reluctant to recognize break-away states unless it is politically expedient to do so, and there is no coherent international policy for recognizing separatist states.[25]

"There is no way Somaliland will rejoin Somalia, not in my lifetime," says Abdi, the International Crisis Group analyst. "They are dead-set on independence. If we don't reward Somaliland with some form of recognition, they risk sliding back. I think they are the most democratic administration in the Horn of Africa."

leader. They don't all share the same agenda for the way forward for the government. . . . You've already got 30-odd political groups just in Mogadishu."

The notable exception is Somaliland, formerly controlled by Britain. It declared independence from Somalia in 1991, ratified a national constitution in 2001 and has remained relatively peaceful since then. Its autonomous government, based in Hargeysa, prints money, operates a police force and issues passports. The region's combination of electoral democracy and clan-based power-sharing has drawn widespread praise, though so far no other government has recognized its independence.

"Somalia hasn't been functioning as a unified state at all, and Somaliland is virtually a separate state that really requires international recognition," says historian Lewis. "I don't think Somalia needs to exist in its present fashion."

Mohamed Hassan, Somaliland's ambassador to Ethiopia, says his homeland's independence was inevitable: "It was a bad marriage, and when a marriage is bad you have to separate.

Neighboring Puntland also has functioned largely autonomously from both the Islamist militias and the Western-backed transitional government in the south. Dominated by the Majerteyn subclan of Somalia's Darod clan, the region declared itself the Puntland State of Somalia in 1998 but has refrained from making a formal independence bid.[26] That's in part because Abdullahi Yusuf, a native of Puntland, served as president of the TFG in Mogadishu for four years until being pressured to resign in December.

Puntland also has made democratic strides. The regional president was ousted in a parliamentary election in January by Abdirahman Mohamed Farole, a former finance minister.[27] But the area's reputation has been harmed by its status as a launching point for dozens of pirate attacks in 2008 and 2009. In December a U.N. report expressed concern "about the apparent complicity in pirate networks of Puntland administration officials at all levels" — a charge Puntland officials have disputed.[28] (*See sidebar, p. 166.*)

"They are somewhere between secession and union with the rest of Somalia," says Abdi. "Depending on how things evolve in the next few months, Puntland is just hedging its bets. If they think union with Somalia is a dead-end, they will go their own way."

Recognition for either autonomous region would likely have to come first from Ethiopia, the regional power and a close ally of both administrations, or from the African Union (AU). So far both have refrained from doing so. "Those areas are pretty well-secured," Jean Ping, the Gabonese chairman of the African Union Commission, told a Jan. 27 press conference. "But the AU is characterized by respect for the territorial integrity of Somalia."

The United States has said it prefers a unified Somalia. "We will stay in line with the AU; that was the Bush administration's policy," says Jendayi Frazer, the U.S. assistant secretary of state for African affairs from 2005 to 2008. And it's a policy the Obama administration is likely to continue.

Most analysts say a unified Somalia would need a decentralized administrative system in order to be effective. "Our insistence that Somalis remake themselves in our image with ministries of this and this and this isn't realistic," says Menkhaus, the former U.N. official in Somalia. "A state that could emerge in a more organic way is possible. That might include a full array of local Islamic courts, municipalities and hybrid arrangements involving professional groups and clerics."

Should the United States reconsider its policies toward Ethiopia?

Ethiopia's human rights record is among the worst on the continent. But because the predominantly Christian nation — Africa's second-most populous country — cooperates in counterterrorism efforts, the United States and its European allies rarely criticize Prime Minister Meles Zenawi's government.

"There has been full support largely because they view the region through the counterterrorism lens, and Ethiopia has been considered the primary partner in the region," says Leslie Lefkow, a researcher at Human Rights Watch. "This has been problematic because it's ignored the very serious downward trajectory of Ethiopia's human rights record."

Indeed, the Zenawi government has become increasingly repressive in recent years:

- During an ongoing offensive against insurgents in eastern Ethiopia's Somali-speaking Ogaden region, Ethiopian troops have been accused of burning villages, raping women and summarily executing civilians suspected of supporting the separatist Ogaden National Liberation Front.[29]
- Opposition leader Birtukan Mideksa has been held in solitary confinement since December, when she was jailed for life for disputing terms of a pardon agreement that freed her and other opposition leaders from prison in 2007.[30]
- In April 2008, the ruling party and its allies swept to victory in local elections after major opposition parties withdrew, citing government intimidation.
- In January Ethiopia's parliament effectively banned foreign aid agencies from funding groups that promote democracy and human or women's rights.[31]

Lefkow also points out that U.S. support for Ethiopia's invasion of Somalia has not been rewarded by the death or capture of major terrorist suspects. "The small number of people that the U.S. was interested in have not been detained," she says. "The scores of people who were detained in 2007 were either not implicated at all in anything or were very minor people."

Western support for Ethiopia's 2006 invasion of Somalia — as well as Ethiopia's continued occupation of territory awarded to Eritrea in 2002 by the Eritrea-Ethiopia Boundary Commission — have led to growing resentment toward the West among Ethiopia's rivals.

"Sovereign Eritrean territories are still under Ethiopian occupation," Eritrean President Isaias Afwerki said in April 2008.[32] "This is basically the problem of the United States. Ethiopia doesn't have the power to occupy Eritrean territory without the support and encouragement of the U.S. administration. And this is the core of the problem."

"U.S. support for the Ethiopian invasion and pursuit of terrorist targets in Somalia in the name of the war on terrorism have further weakened Washington's credibility in the Horn of Africa and galvanised anti-American feeling among insurgents and the general populace," says a December 2008 report from the International Crisis Group.[33]

Connell, the former adviser to Eritrea, says Ethiopia has manipulated U.S. support to its own ends. "Ethiopia

Ethiopia Takes On Malaria

New effort attacks a deadly foe.

When malaria swept through the green hills of his village in southwest Ethiopia three years ago, Biya Abbafogi was lucky. The 35-year-old coffee farmer and three of his children were stricken with the deadly, mosquito-borne disease, but they all survived. Thirteen neighbors and friends in Merewa didn't.

"We would take one child to the hospital and come back and another one would be sick," he says.

The treatment Abbafogi and his family received was cheap by Western standards — just $40. But that was about a third of his annual coffee earnings, and the bills from the medical clinic — located two hours away by foot — forced Abbafogi to sell one of the oxen he used to plow his small corn field.

But today things are much better for Merewa's 4,335 residents, thanks to two young women trained to treat and prevent malaria and other common ailments. They're not doctors or nurses, and they haven't been to college. But with just one year of training they've cut malaria rates during the infectious season from 15 to 20 new cases per day to one to three.

Merewa's success has been replicated all across Ethiopia, where the government has dispatched an army of up to 30,000 "health extension workers" in the past four years. With money from donors like the Geneva-based Global Fund and the Carter Center in Atlanta, the women have distributed 20 million mosquito-repelling nets and offered basic malaria testing and treatment in isolated villages dozens of miles from the nearest paved road.

Every year 4 million Ethiopians contract malaria, which is particularly deadly for children. As many as one in five youngsters under age 5 who get the disease die from it. In response, Ethiopia is at the forefront of two major public-health initiatives in poor countries. The first, known as task-shifting, trains lower-skilled health professionals — who are cheaper to pay and easier to retain — to provide basic treatments and teach prevention. The second aims to distribute anti-malarial bed nets to 600 million Africans living in mosquito-infested regions by 2011.

Ethiopia's poverty helped drive the new approach. As one of the world's poorest countries, Ethiopia has trouble keeping doctors from moving to better-paying jobs overseas, says Tedros Adhanom, Ethiopia's health minister. "Right now, 50 percent of the doctors Ethiopia trains will emigrate," he says. To compensate, he says, Ethiopia is training more doctors — medical schools admitted 1,000 students in 2008, four times more than in 2007 — and shifting as much work as possible to nurses and health extension workers.

Lower-skilled extension workers don't emigrate, and they're also willing to work for less and to serve in rural areas, Adhanom says. "To tackle our health problems, the solutions are simple," he says. "You don't need highly skilled people to tell you how to prevent malaria."

Health workers learn 16 different health-education and treatment interventions, including midwifery, malaria treatment and hygiene education. They also make sure villagers are vaccinated and organize insecticide spraying to kill malaria-transmitting mosquitoes.

The mosquito net distribution program faces many obstacles in a country where many of the 85 million citizens live miles from paved roads. But improved technology offers hope the new anti-malaria effort will succeed where earlier attempts failed.

Bed nets not only provide a physical barrier against malaria-bearing mosquitoes but also kill the pests with insecticide sprayed on the nets. In the past, bed nets had to be dipped in chemicals annually to retain their potency. But newer nets are treated with long-lasting chemicals that require re-dipping only once every three to four years.

Dipping the older nets every year posed "a huge logistical problem" in rural places, Adhanom says. "Fewer than 40 percent of villagers would show up to have their old nets dipped. That really compromised the whole program."

So far, the combined initiatives seem to be working. Malaria prevalence dropped by 67 percent in Ethiopia between 2001 and 2007, according to a World Health Organization study, while the number of deaths of children under 5 has dropped 56 percent.[1]

---

[1] "Impact of the Scale-Up of Anti-Malarial Interventions Measured Using Health Facility-Based Data in Ethiopia," World Health Organization, Feb. 1, 2008.

is embroiled in a self-interested effort to promote its interests at the expense of its neighbors," he says. "We cannot build relations with so-called anchor states under such circumstances. Tamp down the regional confrontations, however, and the relationship again makes sense from our perspective. Let it fester and we will again and again be drawn into fights that are not of our own making and not in our interests."

Others say the United States won't offend Ethiopia because it has contributed peacekeepers to help monitor the conflicts in Sudan's Darfur region and Burundi and supports the Comprehensive Peace Agreement between north and south Sudan. And despite human rights abuses, Ethiopia's governance looks good in comparison with neighboring Eritrea, Sudan and Somalia.

"What you have is a very difficult balancing act where you try to push Ethiopia to open up on human rights . . . without jeopardizing Ethiopia's help on regional issues," says Shinn, the former ambassador to Ethiopia. "I don't take the opinion that you should just hammer them on human rights and let the other side drop off. On the other hand, I don't think their help in counterterrorism and peacekeeping is so important you ignore human rights."

While some critics of the regime say the United States and other Western countries should cut economic aid to Ethiopia over concerns about rising oppression, others say that would be naïve. (See "At Issue," p. 173.)

The Bush administration's top diplomat for Africa agrees. "Obviously, we have a lot of interests in Ethiopia," says Frazer. "Ethiopia has one of the largest, best-trained militaries in Africa. There are many Ethiopians in the United States, and Ethiopia is a major player within the African Union."

The Obama administration is still formulating its policy toward the region but has suggested that democratic reforms will have a higher priority than counterterrorism cooperation.

"It is extremely important that Ethiopia . . . not close down its democratic space, that it allow its political opposition — its civil society — to participate broadly in the political life of that country," Johnnie Carson, Obama's assistant secretary of state for African affairs, told a Senate subcommittee on April 29. "We have our strongest relationships among our democratic partners where we share ideals and values together, rather than

where we share common enemies together. A balanced relationship is absolutely essential."

BACKGROUND
Christian Kingdoms

Christianity arrived in Ethiopia in the early 4th century A.D., about 300 years before it arrived in England. According to tradition, two shipwrecked Syrian sailors brought the religion to what the Romans called Abyssinia.[34] A series of Christian kingdoms would rise and fall in the Ethiopian highlands until the 14th century, when feudalism descended over the country.

The dark ages lasted until the 1850s, when central authority was resurrected by the emperors Tewodros II, Yohannes IV and Menelik II. By the 1890s, Italy — a latecomer to the race for colonies in Africa — had conquered much of present-day Eritrea, which had only sporadically been under Ethiopian rule. But Italy's colonial ambitions were checked when Menelik's troops resoundingly beat back an Italian invasion from its Eritrean colony in 1896, ensuring that Ethiopia would remain the lone African nation never colonized by Europeans.

After becoming emperor in 1930, Haile Selassie, a former noble from the eastern city of Harar, barely had time to consolidate his rule before facing another challenge from Italy. In 1935 up to 100,000 Italian troops invaded northern Ethiopia. Selassie appealed to the League of Nations for help, but was rebuffed by France and the United Kingdom. Backed by bombers and tanks, the Italians had conquered most of Ethiopia's main cities by 1936, forcing Selassie into exile in Britain.[35]

But the Fascist Italians never controlled the countryside, and by 1941 a British-backed Ethiopian insurgency had ousted them.[36] Selassie reasserted the country's sovereignty in 1942 and turned to a new patron, the United States, to escape falling into Britain's colonial sphere.[37]

Compared with Ethiopia's rich history of ancient lords and kings ruling over peasant farmers in the cool highlands, Somalia's history is one of desert nomads who appeared in the Horn of Africa relatively late. Newly Islamized Somalis first began expanding south from the coastal area near the modern port of Berbera in northwestern Somalia in the 10th century. Fiercely independent camel and goat herders, Somalis have only rarely been brought under

CHRONOLOGY

1850s-1940s *Britain, France, Italy and Ethiopia divvy up the Horn of Africa, setting the stage for later ethnic disputes.*

1950s-1970s *Emperor Haile Selassie's grip on Ethiopia and Eritrea weakens as Somalia gains independence.*

1952 U.N. panel rules Eritrea should become part of a federation with Ethiopia rather than gain independence.

1960 Somalia gains independence, uniting British Somaliland with Italian Somalia, but not Somali-speaking regions of Kenya, Ethiopia and Djibouti. . . . Eritrean exiles in Egypt found Eritrean Liberation Front to fight for independence, beginning a three-decade-long struggle.

1969 Somalia's democratically elected president is assassinated. Military seizes power under Gen. Siad Barre, who proclaims Somalia a socialist state.

1974 Coup deposes Ethiopia's Selassie. Military group called the Derg takes control under Col. Mengistu Haile Mariam, establishing communist government.

1977-1978 Somalia conquers much of southeastern Ethiopia before Soviet Union enters war on Ethiopia's side. Barre turns away from communist bloc.

1980s-1990s *Civil wars overthrow authoritarian rulers across the Horn, but Somalia fails to recover.*

1983-1985 Drought triggers massive famine in Ethiopia, exacerbated by Mengistu's efforts to block food supplies to northern areas held by Eritrean and Tigray rebels. . . . Up to a million people die.

1991 As Soviet Union collapses, Ethiopia's Derg is overthrown by Eritrean and Tigrayan rebels from the North. Clan militias oust Barre regime in Somalia and then turn on one another. Somalia's civil war begins.

1992-1995 U.N. and U.S. try to help Somalia after up to 300,000 die from famine due to civil war and drought. U.S. withdraws in 1994 after U.S. troops die in "Black Hawk Down" incident.

1993 Eritreans vote for independence.

1998-2000 Ethiopia and Eritrea go to war over economic and border disputes. Ethiopia advances into Eritrea by 2000, capturing disputed town of Badme. U.N. peacekeepers begin patrolling border zone.

2000s *U.S. focus on anti-terrorism in the Horn leads to realigned loyalties.*

2001 Somaliland, which declared independence in 1991, ratifies constitution that endorses independence from southern Somalia, still mired in civil war. . . . Sept. 11 terrorist attacks on U.S. put focus on fighting al Qaeda threats in Somalia. Eritrean President Isaias Afwerki arrests Eritrean dissidents and closes private press.

2002 Eritrea-Ethiopian Boundary Commission awards Badme to Eritrea, but Ethiopia continues occupation.

2005 Ethiopia's first multiparty elections end badly as opposition leaders protest government claims of victory. At least 193 protesters are killed by Ethiopian security forces in Addis Ababa and thousands more injured. Government jails more than 120 opposition leaders, journalists and human rights activists.

2006 Islamic Courts Union (ICU) defeats U.S.-backed warlords in Mogadishu to take control of southern Somalia. Eritrean-armed ICU threatens jihad against Ethiopia.

December 2006 U.S.-backed Ethiopian troops invade Somalia, eventually ousting ICU. Efforts to install U.N.-backed Transitional Federal Government (TFG) amid Islamist insurgency fail due to resentment of Ethiopian occupation and intransigence of TFG President Abdullahi Yusuf.

December 2008-Present Ethiopian troops withdraw from Somalia; Islamist militias still control much of the south. Yusuf resigns. Sheikh Sharif Sheikh Ahmed, former ICU chairman, becomes president of U.N.-backed Somali government. . . . Shabaab and hardline militias declare war on Sheikh Ahmed's new government. Islamists capture additional towns in southern Somalia.

the control of a central state. A notable exception occurred during the holy wars against Ethiopia in the 13th-16th centuries, which culminated in the mid-16th century, when a predominantly Muslim army under Ahmed Gragn — "Ahmed the Left-Handed" — conquered much of the Ethiopian highlands.

The clan is the foundation and defining feature of Somali society. It is also at the root of the nation's problems, fostering factionalism and competition for resources rather than a sense of nationhood. The four major clan groups — Darod, Hawiye, Isaq and Dir — are each divided into sub-clans and sub-sub-clans, defined by shared ancestors going back hundreds of years.[38]

By the 19th century, France, Britain and Italy were competing with the rulers of Zanzibar, Egypt, Oman and Ethiopia for control of Somali lands. By the 1890s, the French had taken control of what is now Djibouti; Britain had established a protectorate in Somaliland; the Italians controlled central and southern Somalia and the Ethiopians ruled the Ogaden — now eastern Ethiopia.[39]

After World War II Italy was given "trusteeship" of its Somali territory, where it had developed banana and mango plantations using forced labor during the colonial era. But as independence movements swept the continent in the 1950s, the U.N. decided to unify British and Italian Somalia into a single independent state.[40] The move dashed nationalists' hopes for a Greater Somalia encompassing Somali-speaking populations in Djibouti, northern Kenya and the Ogaden.

Rise of Dictatorships

In the 1960s Somalia's young, democratically elected government unsuccessfully tried to expand its territory through a brief war with Ethiopia and by sponsoring Somali rebels in Kenya's Somali-speaking Northern Frontier District.[41] The assassination of President Abdirashid Ali Sharmarke in 1969 by one of his bodyguards heralded the end of those aspirations and of the country's nine-year-old democracy.

The army seized power under Gen. Barre, who quickly moved the government toward communism. On the first anniversary of the coup in 1970, Barre announced that his nation of nomadic herders henceforth would pursue "Scientific Socialism," Barre's own strain of Marxism.

"The Big Mouth," as he was known colloquially, soon established internal-security services and security courts to prosecute political crimes and "Victory Pioneers," modeled on China's Red Guards, to defend the revolution.[42] Exerting unprecedented political authority over the people, he tried to quell tribalism by prohibiting citizens from referring to their clan affiliations and by building rural schools and clinics.[43]

Meanwhile, Ethiopia's Selassie won a major diplomatic victory after World War II, when he persuaded the U.N. to unite Eritrea and Ethiopia, dashing the hopes of Eritrea's fledgling independence movement. But by the 1960s, the emperor's reign — backed by the landowners who ruled millions of peasants like medieval serfs — was chafing at the currents of the 20th century. His Amhara-dominated government faced rebellion from Tigrays in Eritrea and Oromos in southern Ethiopia. He also faced war with Somalia, which still sought control of the Ogaden.[44]

By 1973 the imperial regime's denial and botched response to a famine in northern Ethiopia, combined with soaring inflation and pressure from the Somali and Eritrean rebellions, led to a military revolt. The next year, "His Imperial Majesty Haile Selassie I, King of Kings, Lord of Lords, Conquering Lion of the Tribe of Judah, and Elect of God" was ousted.[45]

The new military government — headed by Lt. Col. Mengistu Haile Mariam and calling itself the Derg, the Amharic word for committee — aligned itself with the communist bloc and nationalized all private land, giving each peasant family 10 hectares (25 acres). The aging Selassie mysteriously died the same year. Many Ethiopians believe he was smothered with a pillow by Mengistu himself.

In 1977, the Derg was still struggling to consolidate its rule. To eliminate civilian Marxist rivals, it launched the so-called Red Terror, during which tens of thousands of students, businessmen and intellectuals suspected of disloyalty to the military government were murdered.[46] Meanwhile, with rebellions widening in the southeast and north, Somalia seized the opportunity to invade the Ogaden in hopes of fulfilling the grand dream of a Greater Somalia.

Although the Ogaden War pitted two of the Soviet Union's client states against each other, the U.S.S.R. eventually supported Ethiopia. Reinforced with Cuban troops and Soviet airpower, the Derg's army drove the Somalis out of the Ogaden in early 1978.[47]

Somali Pirate Attacks on the Increase

Sophisticated gangs rake in millions in ransoms, thwart navy patrols.

"I will never go back to sea," 25-year-old seaman Jiang Lichun told the *China Daily* after being held hostage for seven months by Somali pirates in the Gulf of Aden.[1]

During his harrowing 2007 ordeal, a shipmate was murdered after ship owners initially refused to pay a $300,000 ransom. "We heard six gunshots, but no one could believe Chen was dead," he said. Later, when the hostages were allowed up on deck, it was covered with blood.[2]

More recently, American sea captain Richard Phillips did not have to wait seven months to escape the clutches of Somali pirates. After his U.S.-flag ship carrying humanitarian aid for Africa was attacked in April, he gave himself up as a hostage so his shipmates could go free. He spent several days in a lifeboat with the pirates before U.S. Navy snipers killed his captors and freed Phillips.[3] Since then the pirates have seized several more ships with dozens of hostages.

The uptick in piracy in the Gulf of Aden has become the face of the lawlessness that engulfs Somalia. Until recently, the chaos had been largely contained within Somalia's borders. But in recent years what began as the occasional attack by local fishermen, angry at foreign vessels vacuuming their coastal waters, has morphed into one of Somalia's biggest sources of revenue, with sophisticated criminal gangs ramping up the hunt for ransoms.

Attacks on commercial ships off Somalia's coast increased from 20 to 111 between 2006 and 2008. Last fall, a vessel was attacked on average once every other day. Though killings have been rare, about 300 seamen and 18 vessels were being held by Somali pirates in late April. Ransoms paid in 2008 alone amounted to between $50 million and $80 million.[4]

The growth of Somali piracy was an unforeseen consequence of the 2006 U.S.-backed Ethiopian invasion of Somalia. The invasion ousted Somalia's governing Islamic Courts Union (ICU), which had effectively stamped out

French soldiers take suspected Somali pirates into custody on the French warship *Le Nivose* on May 3, 2009. Attacks on commercial ships increased from 20 in 2006 to 111 in 2008. Last fall, a vessel was attacked on average once every other day.

AFP/Getty Images/Pierre Verdy

piracy during its brief reign in 2006. "The Islamic Courts, for some reason known only to themselves, decided to take action against maritime piracy," says Pottengal Mukundan, director of the International Maritime Bureau. "They made a public announcement saying those guilty of piracy would be punished in 2006. During the summer of 2006, there were no attacks at all."

Since the ICU was ousted, piracy has exploded. Armed with rocket launchers and machine guns, Somalia's buccaneers prowl the seas in small vessels that can range as far as 200 miles off shore. Often they'll approach a boat disguised as fishermen or traders, then fire weapons at the bridge and attempt to climb aboard using ropes and grappling hooks. Once aboard there is little foreign militaries can do. The pirates quickly take the crew hostage and steam the hijacked ship back to Eyl and other pirate bases along Somalia's Indian Ocean coast to await ransom payments.

The pirate gangs have become highly organized and intertwined with Somalia's various militias. "They have

Civil Wars

The 1983-1984 famine that would make Ethiopia synonymous with images of emaciated children resulted not just from drought but also from government policies intended to starve rebel-held areas.[48] With the Derg preoccupied with preparations for a lavish 10th anniversary celebration of the communist revolution, up to a million Ethiopians died in the famine as the government

spies," says Gérard Valin, a vice admiral in the French navy, who led a successful raid on pirates in April 2008 after the payment of a ransom to free a French yacht. "They have people in Djibouti, Nairobi and the Gulf giving them intelligence about the good ships to take. It's a business. They have people for taking ships, and they have people for negotiations."

The millions of dollars flowing into Somali fishing villages from piracy have overwhelmed the local economy. Pirates have built luxurious new homes and support hundreds of others who supply food, weapons and khat leaf, a stimulant popular with the pirate gangs. Ilka Ase Mohamed lost his girlfriend to a pirate who wore a black cowboy hat, drove a Land Cruiser and paid a $50,000 dowry to his girlfriend's mother.

"This man was like a small king," the 23-year-old Mohamed told *The Washington Post*. "He was dressed like a president. So many people attended him. I got so angry, I said, 'Why do they accept this situation? You know this is pirate money!' "[5]

The wave of attacks in late 2008 climaxed with the hijacking of the *Sirius Star*, a Saudi supertanker carrying $100 million worth of crude oil. Since then, foreign navies, which had largely ignored the problem, have rallied to the cause. As of late March as many as 30 warships from 23 countries were patrolling the area in a loose anti-pirate alliance that includes the United States, Iran, India and Pakistan.[6] Still, the problem won't be solved at sea, says Valin. Even with two dozen warships on patrol, he says, it's often difficult to distinguish between a fishing boat and a pirate skiff until the pirates are nearly aboard a commercial vessel, and many countries struggle with how to prosecute pirates picked up in international waters.

What's needed, experts say, is a functioning government on land that will shut down pirate safe havens. That's no easy task for either the newly elected Somali government of Sheikh Sharif Sheikh Ahmed — which controls just a few small areas in southern and central Somalia — or the Puntland regional government, which is the nominal authority over the

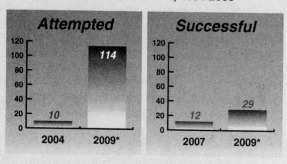

Somali Piracy Up Sharply

The 114 pirate attacks in the Gulf of Aden and Indian Ocean so far this year represent an 11-fold jump over 2004. This year 29 of the attacks were successful, more than twice the 2007 number.

Somali Pirate Attacks, 2004-2009

Attempted — 2004: 10; 2009*: 114

Successful — 2007: 12; 2009*: 29

* Through May 12, 2009

Source: International Maritime Bureau

areas where most of the pirates operate. Pirate ransom revenues last year were greater than either government's budget, and a U.N. report in December accused the Puntland administrators of complicity with pirate gangs.[7]

---

[1] "Chinese Sailor Recalls Terror of Somali Kidnapping," Agence France-Presse, Jan. 4, 2009.

[2] *Ibid.*

[3] Josh Meyer, "Snipers kill pirates in dramatic rescue," *Chicago Tribune*, April 13, 2009, p. 1.

[4] "Somalia: Anti-pirate Alliance," *Africa Confidential*, March 20, 2009, p. 8.

[5] Stephanie McCrummen, "Somalia's Godfathers: Ransom-Rich Pirates; Coastal Villagers Find Blessings and Ruin at Hands of Sea Robbers," *The Washington Post*, April 20, 2009, p. A1, www.washingtonpost.com/wp-dyn/content/article/2009/04/19/AR2009041902236.html.

[6] "Somalia: Anti-pirate Alliance," *op. cit.*

[7] "Report of the Monitoring Group on Somalia," United Nations, Dec. 10, 2008, www.un.org/sc/committees/751/mongroup.shtml.

---

systematically tried to hide images of starving peasants from the outside world while using aid to buttress government control rather than to alleviate suffering.[49] In an effort to undermine support for the rebels, entire regions

of Tigray peasants in the north were forcibly moved to government camps — a policy known as villagization.[50]

Meanwhile, the humiliation of the Ogaden War led to an unsuccessful coup attempt in Somalia against Barre,

U.N. Somalia Funding Falls $12 Million Short

The Office of the U.N. High Commissioner for Refugees (UNHCR) says it needs more than $32 million to aid refugees in Somalia but has received only about $20 million from member states.

Funding for UNHCR Operations in Somalia

(in $ millions as of April 2009)

Source: U.N. High Commissioner for Refugees

led by officers from the Darod's Majerteyn sub-clan. From then on Barre maintained power by playing off the clans against each other. After the war, 700,000 Ethiopian Somalis poured across the border into Somalia, swelling the population by up to 20 percent. The collapse of the banana and mango plantations under socialism made Somalia's economy increasingly dependent on foreign aid.

The result was a widening civil war. By 1990, with government control of the countryside collapsing, Barre's enemies referred to him as the "Mayor of Mogadishu." In January 1991 he was chased from Mogadishu by a Habar Gida (a subgroup of the Hawiye clan) militia headed by a former heroin smuggler and police chief, Gen. Muhammad Farah "Aideed," whose nickname means "one who does not take insults lying down."[51] After a long sickness, the Somali state was now dead.

In Ethiopia, Mengistu's demise came the same year. By 1988 the Ethiopian Army was demoralized by the failure to win a military victory or reach political compromise with Isaias Afwerki's Eritrean People's Liberation Front. With Eritrean rebels controlling access to the Red Sea and Zenawi's Tigrayan rebels pushing south into central Ethiopia, Mengistu fled to Zimbabwe, and rebels occupied Asmara and Addis Ababa.[52]

Somalia's Descent

Back in Mogadishu, Barre's 1991 ouster led to an orgy of bloodshed. A period of "ethnic cleansing" ensued, mostly along clan lines. The Darod were especially targeted for their links with the hated Barre. Individual militia groups took control of the port, the airfield and major intersections.

At checkpoints, travelers were asked to recite the names of their ancestors — a Somali ritual that identifies people by clan and sub-clan. Those with the wrong lineage were often shot on the spot.[53] Darod militias retreated south, laying waste to the villages of smaller clans and killing and terrorizing civilians and stealing their grain. The ensuing famine claimed some 300,000; a million more were forced from their homes in search of food.

In reaction, the United States sent 28,000 troops to join 5,000 international peacekeepers under the optimistic banner Operation Restore Hope.[54] Though the mission initially succeeded in delivering aid to tens of thousands, it quickly became bogged down in street battles with militias and efforts to capture Aideed. In October 1993 several U.S. helicopters sent on a mission to arrest two of Aideed's top lieutenants were shot down over Mogadishu. In the ensuing effort to rescue trapped U.S. pilots and commandos, 18 American soldiers were killed and 84 injured in fighting that left hundreds of Somalis dead. Afterwards, the naked bodies of American soldiers were dragged through the streets as residents celebrated.

Immortalized by Mark Bowden's book *Black Hawk Down*, the battle led U.S. forces to withdraw by March 1994 and the remaining U.N. peacekeepers to leave a year later.[55] The stinging humiliation suffered by the U.S. military in Somalia is widely credited with leading to America's hesitancy in 1994 to intervene in a month-long genocidal rampage in Rwanda that left nearly a million people dead.[56]

After the U.S. withdrawal Aideed's militias expanded their control of southern Somalia, allying themselves with Islamists aligned with hard-line Saudi and Egyptian clerics. Aideed declared himself "interim president" but was killed in 1996 in fighting with rival Hawiye militias from the Abgal subclan.[57] Thereafter, the international community largely ignored Somalia until the terrorist attacks on New York and the Pentagon on Sept. 11, 2001, led to a renewed focus on Somalia as a haven for Islamic terrorists.[58]

One-Party Rule

Ethiopia embarked on a new path after 1991. The Derg had been defeated primarily by the separatist Eritrean People's Liberation Front. Zenawi's Tigray People's Liberation Front (TPLF) claimed power in Addis Ababa and agreed that Eritreans should be allowed a national referendum on independence. By 1993, Eritrea was independent, and Afwerki was in power in Asmara.

To expand his base, Zenawi reconstituted the TPLF as the Ethiopian People's Revolutionary Democratic Front (EPRDF) during the last years of the civil war. The party, still dominated by Tigrayans from the north, became the foundation of a one-party state. Opposition parties faced harassment, intimidation and imprisonment while politically favored businessmen were given control of economic assets. Tension over economic disputes soon emerged between former allies Zenawi and Afwerki: Eritrea raised port fees on its landlocked southern neighbor and destabilized the Ethiopian birr, still used by both countries, by establishing its own currency market.[59]

The friction erupted into warfare in 1998 in the town of Badme. An estimated 70,000 were killed and 750,000 displaced by the fighting before the Organization of African Unity helped arrange a cease-fire in 2000. By then Ethiopian troops had conquered Badme, and a 25-kilometer demilitarized buffer zone had been established inside Eritrean territory, patrolled by U.N. peacekeepers.

After the war, Afwerki quashed dissent in Asmara, arresting those who questioned his war strategy and abolishing the private press. Rule by the increasingly isolated Afwerki has evolved into a personality cult, and the economy has stagnated as military conscription decimated the labor force. Although an independent boundary commission awarded Badme to Eritrea in 2002, Ethiopia has never fully accepted the decision, and Eritrea — lacking both diplomatic support and military equipment — lacked the power to enforce it.

Ethiopia then briefly moved toward democracy. During political campaigning in 2005, the opposition Coalition

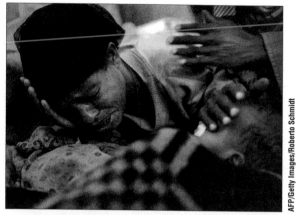

A mother in the Ethiopian town of Kuyera grieves over her sick child at a medical center run by Doctors Without Borders on Sept. 3, 2008. Earlier that day two children in nearby beds had died of malnutrition. Food shortages caused by a 2008 drought left at least 75,000 Ethiopian children under age 5 at risk, according to the U.N.'s Office for the Coordination of Humanitarian Affairs.

AFP/Getty Images/Roberto Schmidt

for Unity and Democracy (CUD) debated ruling party officials on state television and was allowed to stage large rallies in several cities.

After the election, the ruling party claimed an outright victory in parliament, but the CUD disputed the claim. In ensuing demonstrations, 193 people were killed by government security forces, and 127 top opposition leaders, journalists and human rights activists were jailed. Since then democratic freedoms in Ethiopia have been steadily scaled back. In 2008 local and parliamentary elections, opposition parties managed to win just three of 3.6 million races.[60]

In Somalia, the roots of the country's latest attempt at governance trace to 2004, when the Transitional Federal Government was formed with Ethiopian support under the leadership of President Abdullahi Yusuf, a Darod warlord from the Puntland semi-autonomous region. Yusuf's government was viewed skeptically from the beginning by many Somalis, who saw it as a puppet of Ethiopia.[61]

The fledgling TFG largely stayed in exile in its initial years, and by 2006 all-out war had erupted in Mogadishu between a group of CIA-backed anti-Islamist warlords calling themselves the Alliance for the Restoration of Peace and Counterterrorism and supporters of the Islamic Courts Union (ICU), a group of Islamists that sought to bring order to the lawless country by settling disputes and

AFP/Getty Images/Khaled Fazaa

The increasingly harsh government of Ethiopian Prime Minister Meles Zenawi has triggered calls for Western governments to withhold aid from the regime. But in part because Ethiopia has staunchly supported the West's anti-terror campaign, international aid to Ethiopia has grown dramatically in recent years.

bringing criminals to trial under Islamic law. By mid-2006 the alliance, widely despised by ordinary Somalis for its corruption and criminality, was defeated and replaced by the ICU — which ended fighting in much of southern Somalia while instituting a strict form of sharia law.[62]

But the ICU, openly supported by Ethiopia's nemesis Eritrea, laid claim to Ethiopia's Ogaden region. By December 2006 it had succeeded in provoking an Ethiopian invasion. The United States, hoping to capture al Qaeda suspects linked to ICU radicals, gave the Ethiopians intelligence and logistical support, and U.S. Special Forces accompanied Ethiopian troops in the invasion.[63]

Ethiopia's technologically superior army quickly smashed the ICU's militia. But it soon found controlling Mogadishu more difficult than invading it. Within weeks remnants of the ICU's military wing — al-Shabaab — had

allied with disaffected local clans to begin a bloody guerrilla campaign against the Ethiopian occupation. Ethiopia sought African Union peacekeeping troops to replace its forces in Mogadishu, but less than a quarter of the 8,000 authorized AU troops arrived in the first year after the Ethiopian invasion.[64]

Meanwhile the TFG under Yusuf's leadership proved both corrupt and inept. Reliant on Ethiopian soldiers for security in Mogadishu, it failed to bring functioning schools or clinics to the areas of southern Somalia nominally under its control. As the insurgency grew in Mogadishu, hundreds of thousands of people fled the fighting for makeshift refugee camps west of the city. Members of the government were accused of looting food aid from World Food Programme trucks. Radio stations that broadcast critical news were shuttered, and journalists were arrested.

Two years after Yusuf returned to Mogadishu, a U.N. report found that his government's central bank and finance ministry appeared to exist "in name only" and that Yusuf kept a printing press inside his presidential compound to print Somali shillings.

Ethiopian efforts to train a Somali security force to bolster the TFG failed dramatically. By October 2008, an estimated 14,000 of the 17,000 troops trained by the Ethiopians had deserted.[65] The Islamists recruited hundreds of the armed deserters by paying them $200 a month and playing on resentment of the Ethiopian occupation.[66]

By late 2008 Islamists and other opposition militias controlled most of southern Somalia, including the key ports of Kismayo and Merka. Disillusioned with Yusuf's failure to make peace with moderate Islamists, Ethiopia gave notice that it would withdraw troops even if that meant the Islamists would reclaim control.

Yusuf resigned in December 2008 after neighboring states threatened to freeze his assets. Ethiopian troops headed for the exit within weeks, opening the door for a new attempt at peace in the Horn of Africa.

CURRENT SITUATION

Fledgling Government

On May 24, a suicide bomber driving a Toyota Land Cruiser exploded a bomb at the gates of a TFG military compound in Mogadishu, killing six soldiers and a civilian.[67] The bombing was just the latest incident in a new spasm of violence between the TFG and Shabaab insurgents that has seen the Islamist militants tighten their grip over southern and central Somalia.

It wasn't supposed to be this way. After Ethiopian troops, widely despised by ordinary Somalis, pulled out of Mogadishu in January, Yusuf was replaced as president of the TFG by Sheikh Ahmed, the moderate Islamist who had chaired the Islamic Courts Union before the Ethiopian invasion and, from exile in Djibouti, had opposed both the occupation and Yusuf's corrupt government. Though 14 previous U.N.-backed Somali governments had failed to bring peace and stability to the country, it was hoped that Ahmed, as a Hawiye clan leader with previous links to some of the insurgent groups' leaders, could make peace with the Hawiye and Islamist militias opposed to the TFG.

Instead, bolstered by as many as 300 foreign fighters and arms from Eritrea, al-Shabaab has rejected Ahmed's overtures and moved from strength to strength, capturing Ahmed's hometown of Jowhar and neighboring Mahaday, cutting government links with central Somalia.[68] Ahmed has been forced to take refuge in a compound in Mogadishu, protected by foreign troops from the African Union. The growing chaos has led the TFG's new prime minister, Omar Abdirashid Ali Sharmarke, to all but rule out peace talks with insurgents.

"I don't think there is a chance to just sit with them and discuss issues with these people," Sharmarke told Reuters in late May. "The only way to deal with them that they can understand is to fight, and we are prepared to eradicate them."[69]

As fighting intensified in May, Ethiopia launched an apparent strike into Somalia, raising the specter of a possible re-invasion should the TFG collapse and al-Shabaab take control.[70] "Ahmed and the new TFG face an increasing challenge from al-Shabaab and an allied organization known as Hizbul Islam," says Shinn, the former ambassador to Ethiopia. "Al-Shabaab, although not centrally controlled, is well financed from outside and relying on a growing number of foreign fighters."

"The euphoria with which Sheikh Sharif's government was greeted has evaporated," says Abdi, of the International Crisis Group. "Things are very difficult. Unless something happens to unlock this logjam, this is just one of those cycles of transitions that will end up in a failure."

The TFG's reliance on 4,000 Ugandan and Burundian troops in Mogadishu — operating under the African Union — also hurts the fledgling government's legitimacy. "As foreigners [the AU troops] are also resented," says Shinn. "They are keeping the port and the airport out of the hands of al-Shabaab and protecting the presidency. The TFG probably could not accomplish this on its own."

Additional outside help seems remote. The U.N. has repeatedly declined requests from African nations to send a force to stabilize the country, while the AU has struggled to find more countries willing to contribute to the force. An uptick in attacks on AU peacekeepers last year has raised fears that the mission could end in a debacle as the U.S.-U.N. mission did 15-years ago.

"The AU peacekeepers haven't kept any peace because there is no peace to keep," says historian Lewis. "They're just useless."

Still, al-Shabaab also faces risks, especially since its brand of Islam is more radical than Somalia's traditional Sufi Islam. Among the moves that have provoked public revulsion: the amputation of the hands of accused thieves, public flogging of criminals and desecration of the graves of Sufi saints. Most dramatically, in October Islamist clerics in Kismayo ordered the public stoning of a young woman who may have been as young as 13 for committing adultery. Human rights groups said the woman, who was killed in a stadium in front of as many as 1,000 onlookers, had been raped.[71] More recently, al-Shabaab's decision to continue its war after Ethiopia withdrew has also tarnished its identity as a liberation movement fighting Ethiopian occupiers.

"In Mogadishu, public disappointment towards al-Shabaab militants is growing," says Faizal Mohammed, a Somali columnist for the Addis Ababa-based *Sub-Saharan Informer.* "Hawiye elders and some religious leaders have criticized al-Shabaab's move to continue the war after the Ethiopian withdrawal and to target AU peacekeepers."

The TFG also received a recent boost when Islamist warlord Yusuf Indahaadde, the former ICU defense minister, decided to support Ahmed and the TFG after Ahmed announced his government would implement Islamic law.[72]

"It will be messy and slow and it will be subject to reversals, but there is no reason why the right coalition of political and religious and business interests could not

AFP/Getty Images/Abdirashid Abdulle

Somalis displaced from their homes in war-torn Mogadishu prepare a meal at the Dayniile camp — one of dozens that surround the Somali capital. The ongoing civil war and poverty have sent more than a million refugees fleeing to neighboring countries or to camps inside Somalia, where they depend on international assistance for food and shelter — aid that is often blocked by violence, theft or piracy.

pull something together," says Menkhaus, the former U.N. official. "This new coalition government, it's the type of government that could work."

Meanwhile, the country continues to be a source of terrorism. On March 15 a suicide bomber allegedly trained in Somalia killed four South Korean tourists in Yemen. Three days later a second bomber attempted to kill a group of Koreans investigating the attack.[73]

Some analysts say the U.S. and Ethiopian intervention in Somalia has worsened the threat of terrorism by radicalizing the Islamists. "The problem has grown into a much bigger, hydra-headed problem because of that policy," says Lefkow, of Human Rights Watch. "That was a very ill-judged strategy on the part of both the Ethiopians and the U.S."

Ethiopia has a different view. "Ethiopia successfully neutralized" the Islamic Courts, says Ethiopian Foreign Minister Seyoum Mesfin. "Today there is only al-Shabaab and a few terrorist groups working as small units without any formidable organization. Their military backbone [and] organizational structure have been completely shattered."

Frazer, the former Bush administration diplomat, says the Ethiopian intervention had little effect on the threat. "When Ethiopia wasn't there, they were opening the

country to jihadists," she says. "When Ethiopia was there, they were continuing to do it. After Ethiopia left, the country is still open to jihadists."

Standoff Continues

In February Ethiopian state-run television was filled with images of troops parading through Ethiopian cities, celebrating their withdrawal from Somalia. Though the two-year occupation of Somalia began with the ouster of one anti-Ethiopian Islamist group and ended with a more radical anti-Ethiopian group taking control of much of the country's south, Ethiopia's foreign ministry declared "Mission Accomplished."[74]

"We believe a great victory has been secured," Prime Minister Zenawi said on March 19. But the withdrawing troops have not had much time to rest. Despite official denials from Zenawi's government, Somali residents along the border between the two countries have reported repeated Ethiopian incursions since January.[75] In March the Ogaden National Liberation Front — an Eritrean-backed ethnic Somali separatist group in eastern Ethiopia — claimed it killed 24 Ethiopian troops near the town of Degehebur, not far from the Somalia border.[76]

Meanwhile, the standoff between Ethiopia and Eritrea continues to feed regional instability. Throughout 2008 Eritrea delivered up to $500,000 a month to a faction that was battling both Ethiopian troops and TFG security forces inside Somalia. And Eritrea regularly delivers arms and ammunition by small boat to Somali insurgents. It has also supplied arms and funding to the militia of Mohamed Sai'd "Atom," whose Shabaab-affiliated fighters have battled Puntland security forces. Atom's militia was also implicated in the kidnapping of a German aid worker in 2008 and a bombing that killed 20 Ethiopian migrants waiting for transport to Yemen in the Puntland port of Bossasso.[77]

"The Eritreans, under Isaias, are pursuing the same sort of strategy they followed in winning their independence: setting out to weaken Ethiopia from as many directions as possible," says Connell, the former adviser to the Eritrean government. "This results in steady support for all of Ethiopia's enemies, within Ethiopia's borders and without. Hence the support for Islamists in Somalia, whom you might least expect Eritrea to favor."

Eritrea's support of such groups has hindered its diplomatic efforts to get international enforcement for the

Should the West cut aid to Ethiopia over human rights concerns?

YES

Berhanu Nega
Exiled former mayor, Addis Ababa
Leader of opposition group Ginbot 7
Professor of Economics, Bucknell University

Written for *CQ Researcher*, May 2009

The West's policy toward Ethiopia has been a disaster, and President Barack Obama and European leaders must reconsider their support to its government. Ethiopia received more than $1 billion in U.S. aid last year plus generous support from the United Kingdom and European Union. However, the country's human rights record is among the worst on the continent and getting worse by the day.

The possibility of a peaceful transition to democracy vanished in 2005 after Prime Minister Meles Zenawi's security forces killed 193 innocent civilians for peacefully protesting a stolen election and jailed tens of thousands of democracy activists, including 127 opposition leaders, journalists and civil society activists — including me.

Ethiopia is now a totalitarian police state with a human rights record comparable to that of Robert Mugabe's Zimbabwe. Meles and his inner circle have cowed the parliament, the courts and the press. Human rights groups claim the government has killed civilians in several regions. The government held local elections last year with more than 95 percent of the candidates from the ruling party; passed a restrictive new press law; jailed opposition leader Birtukan Mideksa and banned most human rights, democracy and gender-equality organizations.

Why shore up such a brutal dictatorship? Ethiopia is one of the poorest nations in the world, and Western policy makers say aid helps the poor more than the government. But after 18 years in power, Meles' regime still cannot feed its people: Some 14 million Ethiopians required foreign food aid last year. Donors have little control over how aid is delivered, and the government deliberately withholds foreign food aid to punish villages sympathetic to ethnic-Somali rebels.

The West's aid props up an anti-democratic regime and is ineffective in helping the poor. But proponents say Ethiopia — bordered by war-torn Sudan, a belligerent Eritrea and lawless Somalia — needs aid to remain stable in one of the world's toughest neighborhoods. But that's hard to swallow, given that Ethiopia's disastrous, two-year occupation of southern Somalia ended up ejecting a moderate Islamist government while empowering radicals; its nine-year border dispute with Eritrea remains unresolved; and numerous, armed indigenous groups wage domestic attacks with increasing ferocity.

U.S. and European economic pressure could make Meles' government negotiate a peaceful settlement to the country's explosive political problems.

NO

Patrick Gilkes
Adviser to Ethiopia's Ministry of Foreign Affairs; Author, The Dying Lion, Conflict in Somalia and Ethiopia; *and, with Martin Plaut,* Conflict in the Horn: Why Eritrea and Ethiopia are at War

Written for *CQ Researcher*, May 2009

Activists who call for cuts in foreign aid to Ethiopia are seriously misguided. Ethiopia's government is far from perfect, but those who pressure the U.S. Congress and other Western governments to slash assistance to Ethiopia should remember it has averaged economic growth of 11 percent from 2003 to 2008, nearly double Africa as a whole and comparable to that of the Asian "tiger" economies in the 1990s.

The country launched a five-year Sustainable Development and Poverty Reduction Program in 2006 and is devoting about 60 percent of its federal budget to "pro-poor spending," as defined by the World Bank. This is one of the best rates in Africa.

The government has held defense spending to less than 1.5 percent of gross domestic product, even as it has fought a two-year anti-terrorism engagement in Somalia and strives to deter Eritrean aggression. Ethiopia remains a desperately poor nation, but there have been massive investment and major advances in infrastructure, education and health.

Despite the opposition's failure to take up seats in the first multiparty federal elections in 2005 and ensuing violence, local elections took place last year without incident. Ethiopia's federal structure has produced widespread acceptance of self-rule and meaningful fiscal and political devolution. Ethiopia provides a very clear demonstration of the effective use to which aid can and should be put. These must be developments well worth nurturing.

Much has been done in human rights — despite exaggerated opposition claims and poor research by Human Rights Watch and other groups. This includes major training programs for the judiciary, armed forces and police as well as the recent establishment of a government ombudsman and a Human Rights Commission. The recently enacted law regulating nongovernmental organizations (NGOs) has been controversial, but its critics wildly overstate its ramifications. The goal is protection and transparency for NGO humanitarian and development activity.

Ethiopia's long and close relations with the United States and Europe have been enormously important to development. Amidst international financial crisis and climate change, Ethiopia needs support to ensure development efforts don't falter, as it successfully implements its long-term strategy of democratization and poverty reduction. There's still much to do. This is certainly not the time to interrupt the process or threaten regional stability.

A Somali insurgent holds a rocket-propelled grenade launcher in Mogadishu in January 2009, shortly after Ethiopian troops ended a two-year occupation of parts of Somalia. Some analysts say U.S. support for Ethiopia's 2006 invasion of Somalia radicalized many Somalis and increased the threat of anti-U.S. terrorism from Somalia.

Ethiopia-Eritrea Boundary Commission's 2002 decision awarding Badme to Eritrea.[78] With a strong push from Ethiopia, the African Union's Peace and Security Council in May called for international sanctions against Eritrea for its role in arming Somali militants.

Ethiopia also backs proxies. In May 2008 it hosted a conference of Eritrean rebel groups and opposition parties in Addis Ababa.[79] Last August, Ethiopia delivered 3,000 to 5,000 AK-47 assault rifles to the Puntland semi-autonomous government and has provided weapons and training to at least one other anti-Islamist militia in Somalia.[80]

Tens of thousands of troops from the two armies remain dug in across their shared border, sometimes only meters apart. And without U.N. peacekeepers, who were forced to withdraw in February 2008, the border skirmish could again flare up into all out war.

But many analysts believe such an outcome is unlikely. "Eritrea doesn't have diplomatic might or military strength to challenge the status quo," says Shinn, the former U.S. ambassador to Ethiopia. "It's not in either of their interests to resume that war, and they both know it."

However, both regimes have used the continuing presence of an external threat to sharply reduce democratic freedoms. "The stalemate on the border feeds and in turn is fed by growing authoritarianism in both states," said a

June 2008 International Crisis Group report. "The ruling regimes rely on military power and restrictions on civil liberties to retain their dominant positions."[81]

However, it continued, "Both regimes have an interest in keeping the conflict at a low simmer rather than resolving it."

OUTLOOK
Unresolved Conflicts

Few analysts are optimistic that the Horn of Africa's political and economic status will be vastly improved over the next decade.

For the moment, Ethiopia's future looks the brightest. The government says economic growth averaged 11 percent between 2003 and 2008, bolstered by large inflows of aid and debt forgiveness. Some independent economists say the figure is overstated, and that real growth has been around 7 or 8 percent — still a remarkable figure for a land-locked country with no significant oil or mineral reserves.

But, problems abound. The global financial crisis will undoubtedly slow growth. Exports of coffee, Ethiopia's largest foreign-exchange earner, appear likely to decline for the second consecutive year while hospitals and factories face shortages of key supplies. And with dim prospects for a breakthrough with Eritrea, Ethiopia will probably face continuing conflict on at least three fronts: in Somalia, in the Ogaden and along its northern border with Eritrea.

"The future is impossible to predict so long as this simmering confrontation remains unresolved," says former Eritrean adviser Connell. Ethiopia and Eritrea "have enormous potential for growth, but the conflict between them and attendant repression of rights within each country hold both back."

Ethiopia's government, dominated by ethnic Tigrayan Christians from the northern highlands, remains unpopular with the ethnic Amharas and Oromos from central, southern and western Ethiopia, who together make up nearly two-thirds of the population. And the recent crackdown on opposition leaders, the press and human rights groups casts a pall over upcoming 2010 elections.

"I'm not optimistic that 2010 is going to be a breakthrough," says former U.S. Ambassador Shinn. "The tip-off was the local elections in 2008. I think that's a pity."

The government's failure to improve food self-sufficiency also leaves the ongoing threat of drought and famine, which helped trigger the demise of both the communist Derg regime and the Selassie government. "Ethiopia has a relatively high population growth rate," says Shinn. "If you can't feed your people and you're constantly at the mercy of foreign handouts, you've got to do something about it."

In Eritrea the outlook is decidedly dim. The economically and politically isolated government offers few prospects for improving its citizens' lives. "Eritrea is a one-man dictatorship masquerading as a one-party state," says Connell, who formerly worked for the Afwerki government. "The ruling party is little more than a cabal of Isaias Afwerki loyalists, whom he plays off against one another to maintain his iron-fisted rule. The closest analog I can imagine is North Korea." Afwerki's repressive rule, he adds, "is far more effective and all-encompassing than that of, say, [President Robert] Mugabe in Zimbabwe."

In April Human Rights Watch accused Eritrea of becoming a "giant prison" and issued a 95-page report detailing government atrocities against dissidents and evangelical Christians. Thousands of Eritreans risk the government's shoot-to-kill policy to flee to neighboring Sudan and Ethiopia each year, the report said.[82]

"The country is hemorrhaging," said an independent analyst, who asked that his name not be used so that he can continue traveling to Eritrea. "It's largely a police state. I don't see how the regime can survive in the long term. The government has control at the moment, but at some point something will give way."

In Somalia, analysts say probably only an Islamist government can reach across clan divisions to bring a semblance of order to the country's south. "It wouldn't surprise me if an Islamist movement took hold," says the historian Lewis. "How severe it will be and how rigorous is up for grabs."

Unfortunately, he continues, "the radical Islamist movement that they have now developed is particularly poorly educated and poorly informed about the world. It's taking the Somalis really back almost to colonial times."

Rebuilding the country after 18 years of civil war will be a long and difficult task.

"The best-case scenario is that [TFG President] Sharif may succeed in bringing in the hardline groups and — after a bumpy five to six years of transition — we may see a moderate Islamist government take control and become a regional player," says Abdi, of the International Crisis Group. "The worst-case scenario is Sharif's government will collapse, and insurgents will step up their attacks and Ethiopia will invade Somalia again. Somalia is by no means out of the woods."

If the radicals succeed, the threat from terrorism is likely to grow. The recent recruitment of Somali-American jihadis to fight in Somalia raises the question of whether radical Islamists in Somalia might be able to export suicide bombers to Western countries with Somali immigrant communities.

"Would they be able to use U.S. passport holders from places like Minneapolis as sleepers?" asks Menkhaus, the former U.N. official in Somalia. "It's something we need to pay attention to."

The Obama administration should take a more low-key, comprehensive strategy in helping Somalia than the short-term counterterrorism goals followed by the Bush administration, according to Menkhaus. "In fighting terrorism on land and piracy at sea, U.S. national security interests will be better secured if we aligned ourselves more with the interest of most Somalis in better security and effective governance," he writes. "Helping to build the house and using the back door will be much more effective than barging into the front door of a house that has yet to be built."[83]

NOTES

1. "Somalia: Exodus Continues Despite Lull in Mogadishu Fighting," IRIN News, May 21, 2009, www.irinnews.org/report.aspx?Reportid=84483.

2. "Escalating Violence Displaces Somalis," U.N. High Commissioner for Refugees, summary of briefing by spokesman Ron Redmond, May 26, 2009, www.unhcr.org/news/NEWS/4a1bbefb2.html. See also "Some 45,000 Somali Civilians Flee Mogadishu in Past Two Weeks," U.N. High Commissioner for Refugees, May 20, 2009, www.unhcr.org/cgi-bin/texis/vtx/news/open doc.htm?tbl=NEWS&id=4a140e5b2, May 26, 2009.

3. "Beyond the Fragile Peace Between Ethiopia and Eritrea: Averting New War," International Crisis Group, June 17, 2008, p. 10, www.crisisgroup.org/home/index.cfm?id=5490&l=4.

4. "United Nations Human Development Indices: A Statistical Update 2008," U.N. Development Programme, http://hdr.undp.org/en/statistics.

5. "Consolidated Appeal for Somalia 2009," U.N. Office for the Coordination of Humanitarian Assistance, Nov. 19, 2008, www.relief web.int/rw/dbc.nsf/doc104?OpenForm&rc=1&cc=som. See also "Somalia is Worst Humanitarian Crisis: U.N. Official," Global Policy Forum, Jan. 30, 2008, www.globalpolicy.org/component/content/article/205/39493.html.

6. See "European Parliament resolution of 15 January 2009 on the situation in the Horn of Africa," European Parliament, www.europarl.europa.eu/document/activities/cont/200901/20090122ATT46879/20090122ATT46879EN.pdf.

7. For background, see John Felton, "Aiding Refugees," *CQ Global Researcher*, March 1, 2009, pp. 59-90.

8. Aidan Hartley, *Zanzibar Chest* (2003), p. 187.

9. "Horn of Africa Media Briefing Note," U.N. Development Programme, Feb. 11, 2009, www.reliefweb.int/rw/rwb.nsf/db900sid/EDIS-7P6MR3?OpenDocument. Note: The U.N. does not have statistics for those in need of emergency aid in Eritrea, which evicted most foreign aid organizations following the 1998-2000 Ethiopia-Eritrea war.

10. Derek Byerlee and David Spielman, "Policies to Promote Cereal Intensification in Ethiopia: A Review of Evidence and Experience," International Food Policy Research Institute, June 2007.

11. "Eritrea," *CIA World Fact Book*, Central Intelligence Agency, www.cia.gov/library/publications/the-world-factbook/geos/er.html.

12. Dina Temple-Raston, "Al Qaeda Media Blitz Has Some on Alert," National Public Radio, April 8, 2009, www.npr.org/templates/story/story.php?storyId=102735818.

13. Lolita C. Baldor, "Terrorists Moving from Afghan Border to Africa," The Associated Press, April 28, 2009, http://abcnews.go.com/Politics/wireStory?id=7445461.

14. Ken Menkhaus, "Somalia After the Ethiopian Occupation: First Steps to End the Conflict and Combat Extremism," Enough Project, www.enoughproject.org/publications/somalia-after-ethiopian-occupation-first-steps-end-conflict-and-combat-extremism.

15. Dan Ephron and Mark Hosenball, "Recruited For Jihad?" *Newsweek*, Feb. 2, 2009, www.newsweek.com/id/181408.

16. Alex Perry, "Somalia's War Flares Up Again," *Time*, Nov. 12, 2007, www.time.com/time/world/article/0,8599,1682877,00.html.

17. Scott Johnson, "An Unclenched Fist: Barack Obama Has a Unique Opportunity to Bring Something Resembling Stability to Africa's Horn," *Newsweek*, Feb. 2, 2009, www.newsweek.com/id/181313.

18. Scott Johnson, "Dilemmas of the Horn," *Newsweek*, April 21, 2008, www.newsweek.com/id/131836.

19. "Biographies of High Value Terrorist Detainees Transferred to the U.S. Naval Base at Guantánamo Bay," Office of the Director of National Intelligence, Sept. 6, 2006, www.dni.gov/announcements/content/DetaineeBiographies.pdf.

20. Lloyd de Vries, "Elusive Al Qaeda Suspect Was Real Deal," CBS News, Jan. 10, 2007, www.cbsnews.com/stories/2007/01/10/world/main2347258.shtml.

21. Alisha Ryu, "US Airstrike in Somalia Targets al-Qaida Suspect," Voice of America, March 3, 2008, www.voanews.com/english/archive/2008-03/2008-03-03-voa15.cfm?CFID=141624149&CFTOKEN=26521211&jsessionid=de308dbc94966565a9d81e432739512c471d.

22. Hamsa Omar and Jason McLure, "Somali Breakaway Regions Targeted by Suicide Bombers (Update1)," Bloomberg News, Oct. 29, 2008.

23. Jeffrey Gettleman, "The Most Dangerous Place in the World," *Foreign Policy*, March/April 2009, www.foreignpolicy.com/story/cms.php?story_id=4682.

24. Akwei Thompson, "Somali's New 36-Member Cabinet Larger Than Speculated," Voice of America, Feb. 22, 2009, www.voanews.com/english/Africa/2009-02-22-voa20.cfm, March 14, 2009.

25. For background, see Brian Beary, "Separatist Movements," *CQ Global Researcher*, April 2008, pp. 85-114.

26. I. M. Lewis, *A Modern History of the Somali Nation and State in the Horn of Africa* (2002), p. 289.

27. Alisha Ryu, "New Puntland President Faces Stiff Challenges," Voice of America, Jan. 15, 2009, www.voanews.com/english/archive/2009-01/2009-01-15-voa51.cfm.

28. "Report of the Monitoring Group on Somalia," United Nations, Dec. 10, 2008, www.un.org/sc/committees/751/mongroup.shtml.

29. Jason McLure, "Caught in Ethiopia's War," *Newsweek.com*, Jan. 22, 2008, www.newsweek.com/id/98033. See also Jeffrey Gettleman, "In Ethiopia, Fear and Cries of Army Brutality," *The New York Times*, June 18, 2007, and "Collective Punishment: War Crimes and Crimes Against Humanity in the Ogaden Area of Ethiopia's Somali Retion," Human Rights Watch, June 11, 2008, www.hrw.org/en/node/62175/section/1.

30. Jason McLure, "Ethiopian Police Re-arrest Opposition Leader Mideksa," Bloomberg News, Dec. 29, 2008.

31. "Clean Sweep for Ethiopian Party," BBC News, May 19, 2008, http://news.bbc.co.uk/2/hi/africa/7408185.stm. Also see Jason McLure, "Ethiopian Law Curbs Promotion of Rights, Critics Say," Bloomberg News, Jan. 6, 2009, www.bloomberg.com/apps/news?pid=20601116&sid=ahIahjCUZMz0&refer=africa.

32. "President Isaias Afwerki's Interview with Al-Jazeera Television," Eritrean Ministry of Information, April 24, 2008, www.shabait.com/cgi-bin/staging/exec/view.cgi?archive=17&num=8190.

33. "Somalia: To Move Beyond the Failed State," International Crisis Group, Dec. 23, 2008, p. 26, www.crisisgroup.org/home/index.cfm?id=5836&l=1.

34. Graham Hancock, *The Sign and the Seal* (1992), pp. 12-13.

35. Harold G. Marcus, *A History of Ethiopia* (2002), pp. 99-104, 138-142.

36. Sebastian O'Kelly, *Amedeo: The True Story of an Italian's War in Abyssinia* (2003).

37. Marcus, *op. cit.*, pp. 150-152.

38. Lewis, *op. cit.*, pp. 22-23.

39. *Ibid.*, p. 48.

40. *Ibid.*, p. 181.

41. *Ibid.*, pp. 201-202.

42. Ayaan Hirsi Ali, *Infidel* (2007), p. 55.

43. Lewis, *op. cit.*, pp. 210-212, 224.

44. For a first-person account of the student ferment that led to Haile Selassie's ouster, disillusionment under the succeeding Derg regime and the 1977 Ogaden War, see Nega Mezlekia, *Notes From The Hyena's Belly* (2000).

45. Marcus, *op. cit.*, pp. 173-178, 180.

46. Mezlekia, *op. cit.*, p. 295.

47. John Lewis Gaddis, *The Cold War* (2005), pp. 207-208.

48. See Robert Kaplan, *Surrender or Starve: Travels in Ethiopia, Sudan, Somalia and Eritrea* (2003).

49. See Myles F. Harris, *Breakfast in Hell: A Doctor's Eyewitness Account of the Politics of Hunger in Ethiopia* (1987).

50. Marcus, *op. cit.*, pp. 208-209.

51. Lewis, *op. cit.*, pp. 245-246, 259-263.

52. Michela Wrong, *I Didn't Do It For You: How the World Used and Abused a Small African Nation* (2005), pp. 349-352.

53. Hartley, *op. cit.*, p. 184.

54. Lewis, *op. cit.*, pp. 264-265, 268-269.

55. See Mark Bowden, *Black Hawk Down: A Story of Modern War* (1999).

56. For background, see Sarah Glazer, "Stopping Genocide," *CQ Researcher*, Aug. 27, 2004, pp. 685-708.

57. Lewis, *op. cit.*, p. 280.

58. *Ibid.*, pp. 305-306.

59. Marcus, *op. cit.*, pp. 237, 242, 249-250.

60. "2008 Human Rights Report: Ethiopia," U.S. Department of State, April 24, 2009, www.state.gov/g/drl/rls/hrrpt/2008/af/119001.htm.

61. Ken Menkhaus, "Somalia: A Country in Peril, A Policy Nightmare," Enough Project, Sept. 3, 2008, www.enoughproject.org/files/reports/somalia_rep090308.pdf.

62. *Ibid.*

63. Gettleman, *op. cit.*

64. Jason McLure, "Nigeria Needs Helicopters, Tanks to Send Troops to Somalia," Bloomberg News, June 28, 2008.

65. "Report of the Monitoring Group on Somalia," *op. cit.*

66. "Somalia: To Move Beyond the Failed State," *op. cit.*

67. Mustapha Haji Abdinur, "Suicide Attack on Somali Military Camp Kills Seven," Agence France-Presse, May 25, 2009.

68. Derek Kilner, "Somali Insurgents Take Another Town North of Capital," Voice of America, May 18, 2009, www.voanews.com/english/2009-05-18-voa18.cfm.

69. Abdiaziz Hassan, "Somali PM: Little Hope of Talks with Insurgents," Reuters, May 21, 2009.

70. "Ethiopian Forces Return to Somalia: Witnesses," Agence France-Presse, May 19, 2009.

71. "Stoning Victim 'Begged for Mercy,'" BBC News, Nov. 4, 2008, http://news.bbc.co.uk/2/hi/africa/7708169.stm. See also "Somali Justice — Islamist Style," BBC News, May 20, 2009, http://news.bbc.co.uk/2/hi/africa/8057179.stm.

72. "Residents: Islamic Insurgents Seize Somalia Town," The Associated Press, May 20, 2009.

73. "Man Blows Himself Up in Failed Yemen Attack," Reuters, March 18, 2009, www.reuters.com/article/latestCrisis/idUSLI290474.

74. Jason McLure, "Ethiopia Quits Somalia, Declares 2-Year 'Mission Accomplished,'" Bloomberg News, Jan. 5, 2009, www.bloomberg.com/apps/news?pid=20601116&sid=aJqblcQ0bUCo.

75. Abdi Sheikh and Abdi Guled, "Ethiopia Denies Its Troops Enter Somalia," Reuters, Feb. 3, 2009. See also "Ethiopian Forces Return to Somalia: Witnesses," Agence France-Presse, May 19, 2009.

76. Ogaden National Liberation Front Military Communique, March 7, 2009.

77. "Report of the Monitoring Group on Somalia," *op. cit.*, p. 33.

78. "Beyond the Fragile Peace Between Ethiopia and Eritrea: Averting New War," *op. cit.*

79. Jason McLure, "Eritrean Group Calls for 'Popular Uprising' Against Government, Bloomberg News, May 8, 2008.

80. "Report of the Monitoring Group on Somalia," *op. cit.*

81. "Beyond the Fragile Peace Between Ethiopia and Eritrea: Averting New War," *op. cit.*

82. "Service for Life: State Repression and Indefinite Conscription in Eritrea," Human Rights Watch, April 16, 2009. See also Jason McLure, "Eritrea a 'Giant Prison,' Human Rights Watch Says (Update 1)," Bloomberg News, April 16, 2009.

83. Ken Menkhaus, "Beyond Piracy: Next Steps to Stabilize Somalia," Enough Project, www.enough-project.org/publications/beyond-piracy-next-steps-stabilize-somalia.

BIBLIOGRAPHY

Books

Ali, Ayaan Hirsi, *Infidel*, Free Press, 2007.
This coming-of-age tale of a Somali girl living in Somalia, Saudi Arabia, Ethiopia, Kenya, the Netherlands and, finally, the United States explores how Somali culture and Islamic codes subordinate women.

Hartley, Aidan, *The Zanzibar Chest*, Harper Perennial, 2003.
A Reuters correspondent's memoir of covering wars in Somalia, Ethiopia and Rwanda in the early 1990s is interlaced with his family's British colonial history in East Africa and Yemen. Highlights include his eyewitness account of entering Addis Ababa in 1991 with Tigrayan rebels for the fall of the communist Derg regime and witnessing the U.S. military's "Black Hawk" assault on Mogadishu.

Lewis, I. M., *A Modern History of the Somali*, James Currey Ltd., 2002.
One of the few Western academics to have spent his career studying Somalia, anthropologist Lewis focuses on how clan identities have shaped Somalis' history.

Marcus, Harold G., *A History of Ethiopia*, University of California Press, 2002.
This brief history begins with the famed fossil of Lucy, a human ancestor who roamed eastern Ethiopia 4 million years ago, and ends shortly after the 1998-2000 Ethiopia-Eritrea war.

Mezlekia, Nega, *Notes from the Hyena's Belly: An Ethiopian Boyhood*, Picador USA, 2000.
An Ethiopian writer's memoir of growing up during the 1970s provides a first-person account of the country's communist revolution and the ethnic tensions between Somalis and Ethiopian highlanders that still shape regional politics.

Wrong, Michela, *I Didn't Do It For You: How the World Used and Abused A Small African Nation*, Harper Perennial, 2005.
Mixing history and travelogue, a British journalist traces Eritrea's four-decade battle for independence after World War II. Wrong shows how the stubborn and resourceful Eritrean resistance becomes a pawn of Cold War powers and documents post-independence disillusionment under the dictatorial regime of former rebel leader Isaias Afwerki.

Articles

Ephron, Dan, and Mark Hosenball, "Recruited for Jihad?" *Newsweek*, Feb. 2, 2009, www.newsweek.com/id/181408.
Two Washington journalists uncover efforts by Somali Islamists to recruit fighters from U.S. refugee communities.

Gettleman, Jeffrey, "In Ethiopia Fear and Cries of Army Brutality," *The New York Times*, June 18, 2007, www.nytimes.com/2007/06/18/world/africa/18ethiopia.html.
The only Western journalist to enter Ethiopia's Somali region without being accompanied by Ethiopian security forces in recent years gives an account of atrocities by Ethiopian soldiers. Gettleman was arrested by the Ethiopian government during the trip.

Gettleman, Jeffrey, "The Most Dangerous Place in the World," *Foreign Policy*, March/April 2009, www.foreignpolicy.com/story/cms.php?story_id=4682.
The New York Times East Africa correspondent gives a short history of how Ethiopia and the United States exacerbated Somalia's civil war between 2005 and 2008.

Perry, Alex, "Somalia's War Flares Up Again," *Time*, Nov. 12, 2007, www.time.com/time/world/article/0,8599,1682877,00.html.
Perry outlines the motivations of the various actors in Somalia's civil war, including the transitional government, Islamist militias, Ethiopia and the United States.

Reports and Studies

"Beyond the Fragile Peace Between Ethiopia and Eritrea: Averting New War," International Crisis Group, June 17, 2008, www.crisisgroup.org/home/index.cfm?id=1229.
The continuing cold war between Ethiopia and Eritrea after their 1998-2000 war is fueling a host of regional conflicts.

"2008 Human Rights Report: Ethiopia," U.S. Department of State, Feb. 25, 2009, www.state.gov/g/drl/rls/hrrpt/2008/af/119001.htm.
Despite its close ties with Ethiopia's government, the U.S. State Department provides one of the most rigorous and detailed reports on human rights violations under Prime Minister Meles Zenawi.

"Report of the Monitoring Group on Somalia," United Nations, Dec. 10, 2008, www.un.org/sc/committees/751/mongroup.shtml.
The U.N. team that monitors Somalia's arms embargo describes the various militias and their links to foreign governments, piracy and other illicit activities.

Menkhaus, Kenneth, "Somalia: A Country in Peril: A Policy Nightmare," Enough Project, Sept. 3, 2008, www.enoughproject.org/files/reports/somalia_rep090308.pdf.
A former U.N. official in Somalia dissects the missteps by Somali regional and international powers that led Somalia to the brink and suggests how to bring peace to the troubled country.

For More Information

African Union, P.O. Box 3243, Addis Ababa, Ethiopia W21K19; (251) 11 551 77 00; www.africa-union.org. Seeks political and economic cooperation among the 53 member nations.

Amnesty International, 1 Easton St., London, WCIX 0DW, United Kingdom; (44) 20 74135500; www.amnesty .org. Advocates for human rights around the globe and publishes periodic reports on abuses.

Council on Foreign Relations, 1777 F St., N.W., Washington, DC 20006; (202) 509-8400; www.cfr.org. Nonpartisan think tank that offers extensive resources, data and experts on foreign policy issues.

Enough Project, 1225 I St., N.W., Suite 307, Washington, DC 20005; (202) 682-1611; www.enoughproject.org.

Lobbies for ending genocide and crimes against humanity.

Human Rights Watch, 350 Fifth Ave., 34th Floor, New York, NY 10118-3299; (212) 290-4700; www.hrw.org. Investigates human rights abuses worldwide with a team of lawyers and researchers.

Institute for Security Studies, P.O. Box 1787, Brooklyn Square, Tshwane (Pretoria) 0075, South Africa; (27) 012 346 9500; www.iss.co.za. African foreign policy think tank that provides a range of views on African issues.

International Crisis Group, 149 Avenue Louise, Level 24, B-1050 Brussels, Belgium; (32) 2 502-9038; www.crisisgroup .org. Provides independent research on international relations and the developing world.

8

Middle East Peace Prospects

Irwin Arieff and Peter Katel

Palestinian militants stand guard during an Islamic Jihad rally in Bureij, Gaza, on Dec. 26, 2008 — the day before Israel launched its deadly, three-week assault on the Hamas-governed Palestinian territory. Israel says the invasion was necessary to stop persistent Palestinian shelling of Israeli territory from the Gaza Strip. Despite a six-month cease-fire that began last June, at least 1,750 rockets and 1,520 mortar shells landed in Israeli territory in 2008 — more than double the number in 2007.

From *CQ Researcher*,
May 2009. (Updated June 10, 2010)

Ezzeldeen Abu al-Aish is a Palestinian physician and media personality well known in Israel. He speaks Hebrew, champions Israeli-Palestinian reconciliation and during Israel's controversial assault on Gaza earlier this year regularly briefed Israeli broadcast audiences on the fighting.

He was at home in Gaza giving a phone interview to Israeli television in mid-January when two Israeli tank shells suddenly struck his house — killing three of his eight children and a niece.

"My daughters, they killed them," sobbed Abu al-Aish on the broadcast. "Oh God. They killed them, Allah. . . . They died on the spot."[1]

The wrenching interview dramatically drove home for Israelis the impact their government's brutal 22-day assault against Gaza was having on innocent Palestinian civilians.

"I cried when I saw this," then-Israeli Prime Minister Ehud Olmert said later. "How could you not? I wept."[2]

The Israeli military later defended the tank-fire as "reasonable" because it was the result of mistaken intelligence that militants were using the doctor's home to fire on Israeli troops.[3]

Israel has justified its deadly Dec. 27 invasion into Hamas-governed Gaza on the grounds that it needed to stop Palestinian militants in the Gaza Strip from firing rockets into Israeli territory. Some 1,750 rockets and 1,520 mortar shells landed in Israel in 2008, killing eight people, according to Israel's nonprofit Intelligence and Terrorism Information Center. That was more than double the number in 2007, the center says, despite a six-month cease-fire that began in mid-June of 2008.[4]

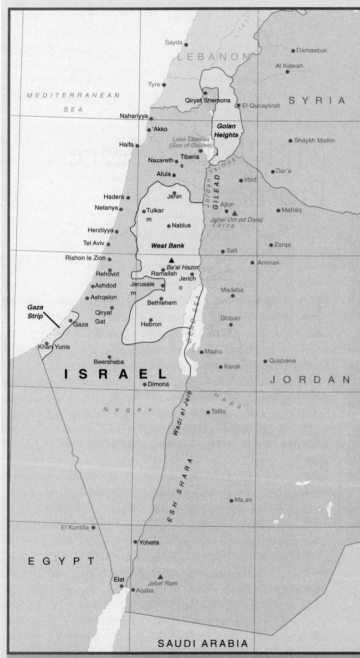

Neighbors, But Worlds Apart

Israel's economy is flourishing compared to the territories it occupied after the 1967 Six-Day War. Israel's gross domestic product (GDP) of $28,000 per capita makes it among the world's wealthiest nations, while the West Bank and Gaza Strip are two of the world's poorest areas. Similarly, the unemployment rate in Israel is a relatively low 6 percent compared with 16 in the West Bank — and a staggering 41 percent in Gaza.

Israel

Area: 8,019 square miles (slightly smaller than New Jersey)

Population: 7,233,701 (July 2009 est., including Israeli settlers in the West Bank, Golan Heights and in East Jerusalem

Religion: Jewish 76%, Muslim 16%, Christians 2%, Druze 2%, unspecified 4%

GDP per capita: $28,200 (2008 est.)

Unemployment rate: 6.1% (2008 est.)

West Bank

Area: 2,263 square miles (slightly smaller than Delaware)

Population: 2,461,267 (July 2009 est.)

Religion: Muslim 75%, Jewish 17%, Christian and other 8%

GDP per capita: $2,900 (2008 est.)

Unemployment rate: 16.3% (June 2008)

Gaza Strip

Area: 139 square miles (about twice the size of Washington, D.C.)

Population: 1,551,859 (July 2009 est.)

Religion: Muslim 99%, Christian 1%

GDP per capita: $2,900 (2008 est.)

Unemployment rate: 41.3% (June 2008)

Note: Statistics for Israel include the Golan Heights — a hilly, 444-square-mile strip of land in northeastern Israel occupied during the Six-Day War and unilaterally annexed by Israel in 1981.

Source: The World Factbook, Central Intelligence Agency

"We wanted to stop the rockets on our cities," says Asaf Shariv, Israel's consul general in New York City. "The goal was to change the security reality on the ground — meaning that they won't shoot without paying a price for that."

During a visit to southern Israel five months before the Gaza war started, then-presidential candidate Barack Obama appeared to support Israel's reasoning. "If somebody was sending rockets into my house where my two daughters sleep at night, I'm going to do everything in my power to stop that. And I would expect Israelis to do the same thing," Obama had said in July 2008.[5]

Palestinian militants say their rockets were fired in retaliation for Israel's continuing stranglehold on Gaza, including regular military raids and tight control over the movement of goods and people in and out of the territory.

But as the deaths of Abu al-Aish's children tragically demonstrated, Middle East violence produces other innocent victims than just Israelis killed by Palestinian rocket fire. According to the Palestinian Centre for Human Rights in Gaza City, of the 1,417 Palestinians killed during Israel's 22-day assault on the densely populated territory, 926 were civilians, including 313 children.[6]

The Israel Defense Forces (IDF) dispute those figures, putting the total at 1,166 Palestinians killed, 709 of them Hamas militants and fewer than 300 of them innocent civilians — including 89 children.[7] The military said it had tried hard to avoid civilian casualties but that the militants often chose to fight in heavily populated areas, effectively using civilians as human shields.

Hamas, one of the two main Palestinian political groups along with Fatah, is a hard-line Islamic organization backed by Iran and Syria that refuses to recognize Israel's right to exist. It also embraces violence — including rocket launches and suicide attacks against Israel — in its fight for what it sees as Palestinian land.

"When we are fired upon, we need to react harshly," then-Foreign Minister Tzipi Livni said on March 9 in Jerusalem after discussing the Gaza war with visiting U.S. Secretary of State Hillary Rodham Clinton.[8]

Ultimately, however, only 13 Israelis died in the conflict — 10 soldiers in combat and three civilians to rocket fire. The disparity in casualties triggered widespread international criticism of Israel's use of fighter jets, tanks and other heavy weapons to target poorly armed urban

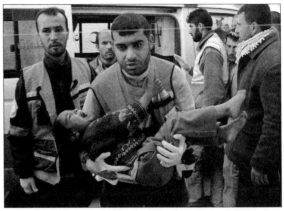

AP Photo/Fadi Adwan

A Palestinian medic rushes an injured child to the hospital during the Israeli invasion of Gaza on Jan. 4, 2009. According to the Palestinian Centre for Human Rights, 926 of the 1,417 Palestinians killed during the three-week assault on the densely populated territory were civilians, including 313 children. Israel Defense Forces estimated that 1,166 Palestinians were killed, fewer than 300 of them civilians, including 89 children.

guerrillas in a densly populated enclosed territory — and accusations of war crimes.[9]

Israel's initial air campaign unleashed 88 attack aircraft on 100 targets in three minutes and 40 seconds. "It was intense, probably more so than any conflict since the January 1991 start of the Iraq War," said Paul Rogers, an international security expert for the London-based Oxford Research Group. The degree of destruction "far exceeded what Hamas planners had anticipated."[10]

"There is a feeling in the Arab world that this kind of disproportionality has been used in the electoral process — that the [then-governing] Kadima and Labor parties were using [harsh military tactics] to increase their chances in the Israeli election," says Maged Abdelaziz, Egypt's ambassador to the United Nations.

Indeed, Israel's invasion occurred just before a major election on Feb. 10 for Israel's single-chamber parliament, the Knesset. Israeli frustration over the rocket launches and the lack of progress from years of peace efforts resulted in a sharp shift to the right, and the installation of conservative Benjamin Netanyahu as prime minister. (*See sidebar, p. 196.*)

During the several weeks it took for Netanyahu to assemble his governing coalition, former Prime Minister Olmert's caretaker government continued its tight rein on the flow of humanitarian and commercial goods into

Getty Images/Abid Katib

AP Photo/Tsafrir Abayov

Suffering on Both Sides

Israeli air strikes on Jan. 9, 2009, turned entire blocks of the Jabalia refugee camp in the Gaza Strip (top) into piles of rubble. Throughout Gaza, the U.N. estimates that 4,000 Palestinian homes were destroyed and 20,000 severely damaged during the three-week war — about 20 percent of the territory's housing stock. In the Israeli city of Ashdod, a man surveys a house (bottom) damaged by a Palestinian rocket on Jan. 18, 2009.

war-torn Gaza, fueling tensions in the territory just as the international community was trying to calm things down.[11] Although both sides unilaterally agreed to stop fighting in January — and Egypt is mediating long-term cease-fire talks — Palestinian militants quickly resumed their rocket fire, and Israel continued to block full access to Gaza — stirring fresh anguish in southern Israel and Palestinian pleas for international help to rebuild a shattered Gaza. The rocket fire also triggered retaliatory Israeli strikes, leading to more Palestinian casualties.

The developments were only the latest in a seemingly endless cycle of Israeli-Palestinian violence since the

Jewish state's creation in May 1948. But a glimmer of hope that change might be in the wind appeared on Jan. 20, when Barack Obama moved into the White House pledging to court global Muslim public opinion and personally strive for a comprehensive Middle East peace. Within days of his inauguration, he named former Sen. George Mitchell, D-Maine, a veteran international mediator, as his special Middle East peace envoy.

"We're not going to wait until the end of my administration to deal with Palestinian and Israeli peace, we're going to start now," Obama said.[12]

His pledge underlined the reality that, despite years of talks and numerous military clashes, Israelis are fed up with years of fruitless peace negotiations while they remain under attack from Palestinian militants, and the Palestinian population bridles at continued Israeli restrictions and sees little hope for a homeland of their own.

Further complicating peace efforts, right-wing fundamentalists are pressuring each side not to accept a two-state solution: Militant Jewish settlers insist that all of the occupied territories rightfully belong to the Jews, while radical Muslims believe Israel itself occupies land wrongfully taken from them.

Moreover, the entire region's geopolitical landscape has been reshaped in recent years by the growing strategic importance of its vast oil reserves, the 2003 U.S. invasion of Iraq, the Muslim world's widening Shiite-Sunni schism and simmering tensions between Syria and Lebanon. In addition, the U.S. toppling of strongman Saddam Hussein's Sunni regime in Iraq unintentionally strengthened predominantly Shiite Iran next door, which worries other Sunni neighbors, such as Saudi Arabia, Jordan and Egypt.

Tehran is also accused by the West of seeking nuclear weapons — a charge it denies — and is openly hostile toward Israel, which is widely presumed to have its own nuclear arsenal. Israel now sees Tehran, not the Palestinians, as its greatest threat, particularly after Iranian President Mahmoud Ahmadinejad repeatedly called for Israel to be "wiped off the map."[13] Iran also supports Hamas as well as Hezbollah, an anti-Israeli militant group that is now a part of the government of Lebanon, Israel's northern neighbor.

In a bold challenge to President Obama's often-stated hopes for swift progress toward Palestinian statehood, a top Israeli official announced in April that Israel's new government would condition entering peace talks with the Palestinians on Washington first making progress in derailing Iran's suspected pursuit of nuclear weapons and curtailing Tehran's regional ambitions.[14]

"It's a crucial condition if we want to move forward," Israeli Deputy Foreign Minister Daniel Ayalon said. "If we want to have a real political process with the Palestinians, then you can't have the Iranians undermining and sabotaging."

Obama has repeatedly warned against delay in addressing the Israeli-Palestinian conflict, and since taking office on Jan. 20 his administration has been simultaneously working to resolve both that crisis and that of Iran — although the global recession has gotten top priority.

Because the United States is Israel's closest ally and arms supplier, the ongoing Israeli-Palestinian conflict continues to fuel anti-American sentiment in the Arab world, perhaps energizing Washington to try harder to resolve the conflict. As part of his post-9/11 war on terror, U.S. President George W. Bush strongly supported Israel's aggressive campaign against Palestinian militants, even though in June 2002 he became the first U.S. leader to publicly embrace the goal of Palestinian statehood.[15]

Nevertheless, the combination of America's pro-Israel stance and its invasion of Iraq have been interpreted by many Muslims as a thinly veiled war on Islam rather than a war on "terrorists." As a result, Islamic militants in Iraq and elsewhere declared holy war against the United States.

After a fruitless year of Middle East diplomacy launched in 2007 in Annapolis, Md., the Bush administration in its final days put the blame squarely on Hamas for the harsh Israeli attack on Gaza, even as many U.S. allies — including moderate Muslim states with normally friendly ties to Israel like Egypt and Turkey — called for Israeli moderation.[16]

In a dramatic moment at this year's World Economic Forum in Davos, Switzerland, Turkish Prime Minister Recep Tayyip Erdogan lashed out at Israeli President Shimon Peres: "When it comes to killing, you know well how to kill."[17]

Some analysts accused Washington of undermining its own interests by blindly supporting Israel.[18] Former President Jimmy Carter drew fire from both U.S. and Israeli officials by meeting with representatives of Hamas, which the United States and Israel shun because it refuses to renounce violence, acknowledge Israel's right to exist and uphold previous Palestinian agreements.[19]

The war, its ratcheting up of regional and international tensions plus the possibility of change have reopened the debate on virtually all aspects of the peace process. Among them: whether Palestinian statehood remains a desirable goal, whether the internationally crafted "roadmap" to peace needs revising and whether the so-called Quartet of international mediators can help the parties along the path to peace.

The Quartet — representing the United States, the United Nations, the European Union and Russia — was pulled together in 2002 by former U.N. Secretary-General Kofi Annan and Spanish Foreign Minister Miguel Angel Moratinos, former European Union (EU) special envoy for the Middle East. The next year the Quartet published its "roadmap" to peace, aimed at Palestinian statehood by the end of 2005.[20]

The roadmap was meant to build on the landmark 1993 Oslo Accords. In those agreements and in accompanying letters, Palestinian leaders recognized Israel's right to exist, Israel recognized the Palestinians' right to eventual self-government and they both agreed to negotiate a final, comprehensive peace agreement gradually over a five-year period.[21]

As it turned out, neither plan did the trick. Six years after the roadmap and 16 years after Oslo, Arab-Israeli peace and Palestinian statehood appear as elusive as ever.

As the search for a peaceful solution in the Middle East continues, here are some questions being debated:

Is a two-state solution still a viable possibility?

Palestinian statehood was not widely accepted as a central focus of the Middle East peace process until recently. The 1993 Oslo Accords did not even mention statehood. (*See box, p. 190.*) And although the idea was central to the failed 2000 Camp David Two peace talks, President Bill Clinton — the host of the summit — didn't publically acknowledge that fact until January 2001, his final month in office.

Palestinian statehood was formally affirmed as a U.S. goal in June 2002, when President Bush declared in a White House speech, "My vision is two states, living side by side, in peace and security."[22] Since then, both sides

Expanding Israeli Settlements Undermine Peace Efforts

The continuing growth of Israeli settlements in Palestinian territories occupied by Israel during the 1967 Six-Day War poses a major barrier to Middle East peace. Although Israel has evacuated its Gaza Strip settlements and repeatedly promised to cap growth in West Bank and East Jerusalem settlements, they have grown steadily. Israel has also been walling off many settlements to bar suicide bombers but also blocking Palestinian access to the land. The Israelis also have built more than two dozen settlements in the Golan Heights, which was abandoned by the Syrian population when the Israelis invaded in 1967.

Source: Foundation for Middle East Peace

have endorsed the idea, and the U.N. Security Council has incorporated it in several resolutions. But the lack of progress over the last seven years has prompted questions about the viability and desirability of statehood.

In fact, in a reflection of growing Arab impatience with the peace process, Libyan leader Muammar Qaddafi recently has called for a single state, on the grounds that a two-state solution would neither satisfy Israeli security concerns nor give Palestinians the borders they desire. "In absolute terms, the two movements must remain in perpetual war or a compromise must be reached. The compromise is one state for all, an 'Isratine' that would allow the people in each party to feel that they live in all of the disputed land, and they are not deprived of any one part of it," he argued.[23]

In time, he predicted, "these two peoples will come to realize, I hope sooner rather than later, that living under one roof is the only option for a lasting peace." Years before Qaddafi's article, the idea had caught on with some Palestinians and liberal Israelis, who argue that Israel will never actually allow a separate Palestinian state — despite past commitments.

But Israeli leaders say the one-state idea is a nonstarter due to changing demographics. Within about a decade Jews will comprise a minority in "Greater Israel" — the original state plus the lands it acquired in the 1967 Six-Day War — because its Arab population is growing faster than the Jewish population. Thus, a single state would be run, eventually, by Arabs rather than by Jews.

The demographic trend leaves Israel precious little time to negotiate Palestinian statehood, Prime Minister Olmert warned a Knesset committee in September. "Ever-growing segments of the international community are adopting the idea of a binational state," he said. "[But] I see a Jewish state as a condition for our existence."[24]

Israeli concerns about a single state strengthened during the Gaza invasion, after many Israeli Arabs participated in anti-Israel demonstrations.

And while some Palestinians may dream of controlling a greater Israel, the idea that "Israel would give equal rights to Palestinians in such a model is a bit of an illusion," says Dutch diplomat Robert H. Serry, the U.N. special coordinator for the Middle East peace process.

For the Palestinian Authority, the internationally acknowledged administrator of the Palestinian territories, the two-state plan remains the best option, but the two sides cannot close a deal on their own, says Riyad Mansour, Palestine's non-voting observer at the United Nations. "They need a third party that they know and trust, and if that third party could act decisively, then the deal could be closed," he says. "And we hope that President Obama is the third party that will help us to reach that conclusion."

Since taking office, the Obama administration has repeatedly reaffirmed the two-state model. "The inevitability of working toward a two-state solution seems inescapable," Secretary of State Clinton said during a visit to Israel in March. "We happen to believe that moving toward the two-state solution, step by step, is in Israel's best interest."[25]

But following the Israeli elections, many diplomats and analysts began wondering whether the parties might instead end up with what some call the "non-state" solution — a continuation of the status quo in which the peace process is indefinitely frozen. Netanyahu, Israel's new prime minister, has consistently refused to express support for Palestinian statehood, preferring instead to focus on Palestinian economic development and security issues and giving a higher priority to the potential nuclear threat from Iran.

Moreover, despite Palestinian efforts to form a national unity government that could include Hamas, Netanyahu insists he would not negotiate with a Palestinian government that includes Hamas — a movement he sees as an enemy of the Jewish state that must be defeated. "We won't negotiate with Hamas, because we won't negotiate with people who only want to negotiate our funeral arrangements," says Israeli Consul General Shariv.

But, he adds, if Hamas agrees to the three key principles set out by the Quartet as a prerequisite for Hamas to be accepted by the international community, "we negotiate with Hamas. It's as simple as that."

A Quartet statement issued after Hamas won the 2006 Palestinian election advised all world governments against dealing with any new Palestinian administration that did not reject violence, recognize Israel and accept all prior Palestinian commitments and obligations — including the roadmap.[26]

Hamas has so far refused to honor those principles, leaving it and Gaza increasingly isolated. After the 2006 elections, the isolation fueled a fierce rivalry between Hamas and Fatah, the other main Palestinian political

Israeli Settlements Continue to Grow

Despite repeated calls for Israel to withdraw its settlers from the West Bank and East Jerusalem and freeze further settlement expansion, the population in West Bank settlements rose 61 percent from 1999 to 2008. The Israeli population in East Jerusalem in 2006, the latest year for which data are available, was 8 percent more than in 2000. Israel withdrew all settlers from Gaza in 2005.

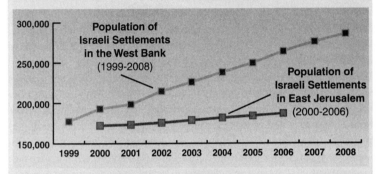

Source: Foundation for Middle East Peace, based on data from Israel's Central Bureau of Statistics and The Jerusalem Institute for Israel Studies.

organization, leading to a civil war that left Hamas in control of the Gaza Strip and Fatah running the West Bank.

Hamas believes Israel was established on land belonging to the Palestinians, regardless of what this or any other Israel government believes about an eventual Palestinian state. But Palestinian President Mahmoud Abbas, whose Fatah party is more moderate than Hamas, said the shared goal of Palestinian statehood — as embraced by past Israeli governments — should not be affected by elections. "We respect the choice of the Israeli people, and we respect the elections that took place in Israel," he said when Secretary Clinton visited the West Bank on March 4. "But we demand that the Israeli government also commits itself to the roadmap plan and the two-state vision."[27]

But Shariv says it is not Netanyahu who is blocking Palestinian statehood but the deep divisions between Hamas and Fatah. "The Palestinians understand that they cannot go to a Palestinian state without Gaza," he says. "They don't want to have a three-state solution."

Has the "roadmap for peace" become a fig leaf for inaction?

The idea of an international overseer — the Quartet — that would push Israelis and Palestinians toward peace

grew out of the lack of progress that followed the Oslo Accords. The Quartet was set up in 2002 when its members concluded the Israelis and Palestinians could not work together on their own to reach a final peace agreement. The Quartet then gave them a "roadmap" to follow.

"They saw that the parties were not capable of producing any peace agreement. You needed the U.S. and the Quartet to hold the hand of both parties," says Norwegian diplomat Terje Roed-Larsen, a former U.N. special coordinator for the Middle East peace process and an architect of the Quartet. "So the roadmap was negotiated between the European Union, the United Nations, the United States and Russia, and then presented to the parties."

The roadmap set out parallel paths for each side to pursue simultaneously, in three phases, culminating in a permanent and comprehensive peace agreement in 2005. "Both parties accept this vision. But we can reach it only if we move rapidly and in parallel on all fronts. The so-called 'sequential' approach has failed," U.N. chief Annan explained at the time.[28] (*See box, p. 190.*)

But in practice the roadmap didn't work. While the Quartet monitored the process and met on an irregular basis to comment on developments and appeal to the parties, there was no mechanism to enforce or even document the parties' performance. And Israel quickly announced that it viewed its obligations under the plan as conditioned on an immediate end to Palestinian violence.

"Full performance will be a condition for progress between phases and for progress within phases," the Israeli cabinet said in attaching 14 reservations to its acceptance of the plan.[29]

The roadmap made its debut during one of the lowest points of the peace process. The 2000 Camp David Two summit — attended by Palestinian leader Yasser Arafat and Israeli leader Barak — had failed to produce a peace agreement, instead triggering a Second Intifada, or Palestinian uprising against Israeli occupation. The violence lasted more than four years and caused the deaths of more than 4,000 people, three-quarters of them Palestinians.[30]

With the Intifada raging, President Clinton asked former Sen. Mitchell to look for ways to bring the violence to an end. Mitchell's first foray into high-stakes Middle East diplomacy called for a freeze on Israeli settlements in occupied territories and a Palestinian crackdown on terrorism. The roadmap later built on Mitchell's 2001 recommendations.[31]

But progress stalled when each side argued that its actions should be contingent on the other side's performance, rather than occur simultaneously. Israel insisted that Palestinian attacks end before Israel would take such required political steps as dismantling settlements erected since March 2001 and easing restrictions on the movements of people and goods; the Palestinians have said the attacks would not end until Israel honors its commitments.

While the Quartet called on both sides to take specific steps, some analysts and diplomats say the Quartet has been softer on Israel overall, due to the United States' close ties to the Jewish state.

"Even though there has developed a generally agreed approach on some aspects of what should be demanded of the Palestinian side, this is not the case as regards Israel," wrote Peruvian diplomat Alvaro de Soto, who served as the chief U.N. Middle East peace envoy from 2005 to 2007, in his confidential end-of-mission report. The report, which cited Washington's "very serious qualms about exerting pressure on Israel," was quickly leaked and ended up on the Internet.[32]

Harvard University professor Stephen Walt, a critic of Israel's outsized political influence in the United States, has argued that, because the roadmap is unevenly enforced, "defending the two-state solution has become a recipe for inaction, a fig leaf that leaders can utter at press conferences while ignoring the expanding settlements and road networks on the West Bank that are rendering it impossible."[33]

Egypt's U.N. ambassador Abdelaziz agrees. "There was a period of calm for about two years immediately after the roadmap was introduced, but during this entire time settlement activities continued, roadblocks continued, confiscation of land continued."

According to the most recent statistics, the number of Israeli settlers living in the Palestinian West Bank grew from 223,954 in 2003 — the year the roadmap was issued — to 276,462 in 2007.[34]

"The Israelis argue that calm is required before steps along the roadmap can be taken," Abdelaziz says. "We need to prove the contrary: If there is to be calm, we want the political process to move forward."

U.N special Middle East coordinator Serry hopes Sen. Mitchell's appointment will be just one part of Obama's strategy. "I very much hope also that the Americans will be using the Quartet a bit more, and a bit more effectively, in a determined international role here," he says.

"Quartet meetings have so far been very much ad hoc. They need to be more structured. And top envoys need to be present more on the ground [in the region] rather than just meeting in capitals," adds Serry, who is based in Jerusalem. Other Quartet members agree the group should be more effective and not be abandoned.

The Obama administration believes "the Quartet remains the most effective instrument for advancing the international community's engagement in the effort to bring lasting peace to the Middle East," Susan Rice, Washington's new U.N. ambassador, told the Security Council in February.[35]

"This is one of the best things we have," says Russia's U.N. ambassador, Vitaly Churkin.

"It is easy to blame the Quartet for not having made peace in the Middle East in so many years. But nobody else has, or has even tried," adds the EU ambassador to the Middle East, Marc Otte, a Belgian. "The Quartet has been useful in harmonizing and coordinating action and has been a plus for EU-U.S. cooperation."

Can the Palestinians form a national unity government?

Hamas' 2006 election victory, its takeover of Gaza in 2007 and the recent Israeli assault on Gaza have left Palestinians deeply divided at a time when they face enormous domestic and international challenges.

To restore its economy, for instance, postwar Gaza must obtain basic food, medicine and commercial goods and rebuild its institutions and shattered housing. The U.N. estimates that 4,000 Palestinian homes were destroyed and 20,000 severely damaged during the three-week war — about 20 percent of the housing stock.[36] In March, at a conference in the Egyptian resort town of

Major Milestones in Israeli-Palestinian Peace Process

The Israeli-Palestinian conflict began immediately after Israel declared itself a state in May 1948, but progress toward peace has been painfully slow and elusive. The U.S.-mediated Camp David Accords led to the first peace treaty between Israel and an Arab state. The Oslo Accords, negotiated secretly between Israeli and Palestinian officials in Norway, set out a plan for a Palestinian Authority to gradually take over administration of lands seized by Israel in the 1967 Six-Day War. The 2003 Roadmap for Peace was drafted by the United States, the United Nations, the European Union and Russia — a self-proclaimed Quartet of international mediators — to guide Israelis and Palestinians to establishment of a Palestinian state as part of a comprehensive peace agreement. While Israel and Egypt remain at peace today, the Oslo Accords and the Roadmap were never carried out.

Here are three major milestones reached along the way:

Camp David Accords (1978)

- Negotiated in secret at the Camp David, Md., U.S. presidential retreat under the guidance of then-President Jimmy Carter.
- Signed at the White House by Egyptian President Anwar El Sadat and Israeli Prime Minister Menachem Begin.

- Led to the Israel-Egypt Peace Treaty of 1979, in which both countries agreed to mutual recognition.
- Established a framework for Egyptian-Israeli relations and for an autonomous, self-governing authority in the West Bank and Gaza Strip.
- Deliberately excluded the fate of Jerusalem.
- Established U.S. economic and military aid packages for each country that over the past 30 years have totaled $142 billion.
- Led to Sadat and Begin winning 1978 Nobel Peace Prize.

Oslo Accords (1993)

- Signed by Israeli Prime Minister Yitzhak Rabin and PLO Chairman Yasser Arafat on Sept. 13, 1993, in the White House Rose Garden with President Bill Clinton. Highlight of the ceremony was the first public handshake between Israeli and Palestinian leaders.
- Called for withdrawal of Israeli forces from certain parts of West Bank and Gaza Strip; creation of a transitional Palestinian Authority to administer the territories under its control, and democratic election of a transitional representative council.
- Called for the two sides to negotiate a comprehensive and permanent peace agreement within five years,

Sharm el-Sheikh, international donors pledged nearly $4.5 billion in aid for the Palestinians.

But Israel and Egypt tightly control all access to Gaza, including financial flows. And under the Quartet principles, none of the aid can pass through Hamas. Since the Palestinian Authority is not present on the ground in Gaza, that effectively leaves only international agencies in charge of reconstruction.

To address the problem, Egypt has pressed Fatah and Hamas to try to form a government of national unity. If the talks succeed, some U.N. and European diplomats have said such a government might also be accepted by Israel and the international community as a negotiating partner in peace talks.

"If we succeed in having a national unity government the U.S. and the Quartet should accept that," says Palestinian U.N. envoy Mansour.

To U.N. Secretary-General Ban Ki-moon, unity is crucial. "For any sustainable political progress to occur, and for Gaza to properly recover and rebuild, Palestinians must engage in reconciliation," Ban told a Feb. 10 news conference.[37] He appealed to Palestinians to "overcome divisions and to work toward one Palestinian government within the framework of the legitimate Palestinian Authority."

But how can a unity government include Hamas, which has refused to accept the Quartet principles that all Palestinian factions must renounce violence, recognize Israel and accept past Palestinian peace deals?

Looking back, it was a mistake for the international community to isolate Hamas after its 2006 election victory, argued de Soto, who was the U.N. Middle East envoy at that time. Hamas "has become a formidable political player. They cannot be ignored in the search

based on principles previously established by the U.N. Security Council.

- Divided the West Bank and Gaza into three zones, pending a final agreement: Areas under complete control of the Palestinian Authority; areas under Palestinian civil control and Israeli security control and areas under complete Israeli control.

- Established a framework for future relations between the two parties, with particular emphasis on regional development and economic cooperation. In side letters (agreements) to the accords, Arafat said the Palestine Liberation Organization (PLO) recognized Israel's right to exist in peace and security and renounced the use of terrorism and other acts of violence, and Rabin said Israel recognized the PLO as the representative of the Palestinian people and would begin negotiations with the PLO within the Middle East peace process.

Roadmap for Peace (2003)

Set out a performance-based and goal-driven roadmap to a comprehensive and final settlement of the Israeli-Palestinian conflict by 2005, in three phases:

- **Phase I** (to be completed by May 2003): end Palestinian violence; implement Palestinian political reform; Israeli withdrawal and freeze on expansion of settlements in the West Bank and Gaza Strip; Palestinian elections.

- **Phase II** (to be completed by December 2003): hold international conference on Palestinian economic

President Bill Clinton gleams with pride as Palestinian Liberation Organization leader Yasser Arafat (right) and Israeli Prime Minister Yitzhak Rabin (left) shake hands in the White House Rose Garden on Sept. 13, 1993. It was the first direct, face-to-face meeting between Israeli and Palestinian political representatives.

recovery; establish a process leading to an independent Palestinian state.

- **Phase III** (to be completed by the end of 2005): Israel and Palestinians conclude a permanent agreement that ends their conflict, ends the Israeli occupation that began in 1967, defines Palestinian refugees' right to return to their former homes, establishes Jerusalem's borders and status and fulfills the vision of two states — Israel and Palestine — living side by side in peace and security. Arab states agree to establish full diplomatic relations and make peace with Israel.

---

for peace with Israel," he wrote recently. "And yet ignore them, and beyond, undermine them and sidestep them, is precisely what the international community has done since their election to a majority in the Palestinian legislature. . . . It should not surprise us that many in Hamas have interpreted this as meaning that there is no interest in a move by them toward democracy and peace, leaving no other recourse but continued armed struggle."[38]

For the time being, however, Israel and most of the key international players, including most Arab donors, appear to be sticking with the three principles and ensuring their aid bypasses Hamas. The three principles are "not the United States talking. That is the Quartet and the Arab League," Secretary of State Clinton said in March during a tour of the region. "Everyone knows what Hamas must do, and it is up to Hamas."[39]

While Egypt has said the unity talks show that Hamas and Fatah want a unity deal, Israeli Consul General Shariv says: "They have been saying that for approximately two years now." The talks will drag on, he says, because "the hate between Fatah and Hamas is bigger than the hate between the Palestinians and Israelis."

Egypt has an uneasy relationship with Hamas, due in part to its repression of the Muslim Brotherhood in Egypt, with which Hamas is allied. But Egypt argues that isolating Hamas unfairly harms all Gazans, most of whom are not Hamas supporters. "We deal with Hamas as part of the Palestinian population. Whether we believe that this national unity government is going to be successful or not, we must first achieve some kind of reconciliation among the Palestinian people themselves," says Egypt's U.N. envoy Abdelaziz.

Obama's Middle East Troubleshooter Gets Mixed Reception

Arab-American George Mitchell is expected to take an even-handed approach.

President Barack Obama's appointment of George Mitchell as his special envoy to the Middle East was widely greeted as a potential game-changer in one of the world's most enduring trouble spots. But he is certainly not the first special envoy to be dispatched to the region.

Former British Prime Minister Tony Blair currently fills that bill for the Quartet — the "pressure group" of diplomats from the United States, Russia, the European Union and the United Nations — with a mandate to focus on beefing up the Palestinian economy. Veteran U.S. diplomat Dennis Ross spent years shuttling between Washington and the region and remains a special envoy to the Obama administration, although this time for Iran.

Mitchell, a 14-year veteran of the U.S. Senate representing Maine, has gained a global reputation as a skilled international troubleshooter for helping tame violence in Northern Ireland and expose steroid use among U.S. Major League Baseball players. His mother migrated to the United States from Lebanon at 18 and he identifies himself as an Arab-American.

After a previous stint in the Middle East at the request of President Clinton, Mitchell in 2001 called on Palestinians to reform their security forces and end violence and for Israel to halt the expansion of settlements on land seized in the 1967 Six-Day War. Clinton had asked Mitchell to investigate the causes of the Second Intifada, or Palestinian uprising, which began in mid-2000 after a Clinton-hosted peace initiative failed.

Mitchell's recommendations had little impact, however, and the Intifada raged on for years, resulting in thousands of Palestinian and Israeli deaths. Palestinian rockets and mortars remain a top international concern, as do Israel's ever-expanding West Bank settlements. Israel withdrew its settlers from Gaza when it pulled out of the territory in 2005.

Obama's appointment of Mitchell was greeted warmly in the Arab world while Israel has reacted more coolly. "George Mitchell has rich experience in solving conflicts — in Northern Ireland, for example — and he has a lot of respect among parties in the region," says Palestinian U.N. Ambassador Riyad Mansour.

But Asaf Shariv, Israel's consul general in New York, stopped short of praising the former senator. Asked if Mitchell made Israel nervous, he responded: "If Sen. Mitchell can help us reach a peace agreement, we would be the most happy people in the world. That is what we want. We know who our friends are, and the United States is the best friend we have, and we want to have peace."

The Mitchell appointment is significant for three reasons, said Paul Rogers, a global security expert with the Oxford Research Group in London. "Mitchell has family knowledge of the Middle East combined with a reputation for evenness in his work in Northern Ireland," Rogers said. "He is not regarded as close to the Israel lobby in Washington, and . . . President Obama made it clear that this was his [personal] initiative" rather than the action of an underling.[1]

However, many Israelis warn that even if the Palestinian Authority led the unity government initially, Hamas could soon end up in control, because President Abbas' four-year term expired in January. He is calling for new presidential and legislative elections by Jan. 24, 2010.[40]

A recent poll showed Hamas gaining popularity after the Gaza war, the opposite of what Israel had hoped. The survey of 1,270 people in the West Bank and Gaza, conducted March 5-7 by the Palestinian Center for Policy and Survey Research, showed Hamas leader Ismail Haniyeh defeating Abbas in a hypothetical election for Palestinian president, which could give Hamas a political foothold in the West Bank and East Jerusalem as well as Gaza.[41] The Fatah leadership has been plagued for years by criticism that the party is corrupt and resists needed financial and security reforms, and this is undoubtedly hurting Fatah among Palestinian voters.

"According to Palestinian public-opinion experts, Hamas emerged from the recent Gaza war stronger than

"For the Arabs, the Americans are the only ones who can actually deliver the Israelis," says a U.N. Middle East analyst, who spoke on condition of anonymity because he is not authorized to speak for the world body. During the George W. Bush administration, "the U.S. appeared to them to be more and more wedded to the Israeli side. So the Arab world is so enthralled with Obama because they see him as a change."

But Egyptian U.N. Ambassador Maged Abdelaziz warns that, while he is "cautiously optimistic" about the role Sen. Mitchell can play, it will take him a while to learn the terrain and identify openings to a solution. "The Americans are still learning to drive, and for them, it is a new car," he says.

He adds, however, "We don't want to repeat the experience of those other envoys, who come every month and have the same round of discussions with everybody, and then go back to Washington, and then come back the next month, and nothing moves forward. We need a time-bound plan, that we are going to do this now, and then that the next month."

EU Middle East envoy Mark Otte also advises caution. "Mitchell is held in very high regard in the region, and also in Europe, due to his involvement in resolving the Northern Ireland conflict. And true statesmanship actually occasionally happens, even in the Middle East," he says. "But I think there is a delusion that just because we — the U.S., the Europeans — want a problem to be solved, that people are ready to solve it."

"There is a new opportunity in that the U.S. government is willing to deal up-front with the problem," he continues. "But there is also a negative side, in that time is running out for a number of strategic problems of the region, including the confrontation with Iran on the nuclear issue and its regional ambitions that are scaring off the Arab governments. There is a potential for a deal between Arabs and Israelis. But the opportunity should not

President Barack Obama's envoy to the Middle East, former Democratic Sen. George Mitchell (left), has a global reputation as a skilled international troubleshooter. A Lebanese-American, Mitchell is expected to take an even-handed approach to discussions with both sides, including hard-line Israeli Foreign Minister Avigdor Lieberman (right).

be lost before something else maybe more radical or catastrophic happens."

[1] Paul Rogers, "Gaza — The Aftermath," Oxford Research Group, January 2009, www.oxfordresearchgroup.org.uk/publications/monthly_briefings/index.html.

ever, especially in the West Bank, where the Fatah party has been neither reformed nor rebuilt," said Yossi Alpher, an Israeli blogger and former director of the Jaffee Center for Strategic Studies at Tel Aviv University. "This means a unity government could quickly confront Israel with the challenge of Hamas rule rather than 'unity' rule in the West Bank as well as Gaza."[42]

"Then Hamas takes over, and then we will see rockets landing on Tel Aviv, certainly on Ben Gurion Airport, and of course where I live in the center of Jerusalem,"

adds Amnon Lord, an Israeli writer and former editor of the *Makor Rishon* newspaper.

International diplomats say that unity could be achieved without Hamas by establishing a government of technocrats — skilled administrators without political affiliations — such as the current Palestinian Authority cabinet.

That may be the only way to keep Israel on board, predicts a veteran European diplomat with long experience in the Middle East. To include Hamas in a unity government "would be the perfect cover for those in Israel who do not want a two-state solution, who want a non-state solution," he says, speaking on condition of anonymity due to his continued involvement in the matter.

"They will never agree to a Hamas role," he continues. "Given that thousands of rockets have flown into Israel, given that those rockets continue to fly, public opinion in Israel is so strong on these issues that there is no government in Israel that could engage with a Palestinian government like that and survive."

BACKGROUND

Decades of Deadlock

While the Israeli-Palestinian conflict has continued for years, the broad outlines of a plan for ending the conflict have long been known to the parties. At one time or another, both sides have endorsed most of the major elements of an agreement.[43]

"All the issues have been negotiated so many times before that we know what the solutions will be," says Palestinian U.N. Ambassador Mansour.

Yet a final resolution remains elusive, say Middle East peacemakers, in part because the two sides view virtually every issue and every development in a fundamentally different way, and thus discussions tend to proceed in endless circles of blame and retribution.

Outside mediators say they try to steer the parties to focus on the future and avoid eternal debate over events long past. But the two sides seem to prefer to dwell on past wrongs: on how to interpret them and how to correct them.

The result has been decades of deadlock.

"It is a conflict over a very small piece of land, and it is a conflict between two rival nationalist movements, with all the rancor and violence that can come with nationalism," says U.N. Middle East specialist Markus Bouillon, a German. "The divergent points of view are fueled by historical experience: For the Jewish people, there is the Holocaust, having no home, the diaspora. And that completely clashes with the Palestinian perspective — that 'this is our land, we have always been here, everybody else has their state, why did you come and steal our land?' These arguments are driven by morality and emotion, making for a powerful argument on both sides."

So the parties in effect end up pitting the Arab grandmother living in a Palestinian refugee camp and still clutching the keys to the family home abandoned in 1948 against the Jewish grandmother with the concentration camp number tattooed on her arm, Bouillon says.

In search of the roots of the conflict, a convenient starting point is the surge in Jewish immigration to the Middle East shortly after the start of the 20th century. Starting in 1904, Jews escaping Russia's anti-Semitic massacres — called pogroms — began creating a state-within-a-state in a region of the Ottoman Empire known as Palestine, where an Arab population was already long established.

Earlier, in the 19th century, Austro-Hungarian journalist Theodor Herzl, considered the father of Zionism, and other Jews began calling for Jews to settle in "Zion," their historic homeland. They argued that Europe had never accepted their presence and never would. The Zionists based their claim to Palestine on the Jews' ancient presence there, which had ended when the Romans destroyed Jerusalem and dispersed most of the Jews in 70 A.D.

The nascent state grew even stronger after a fresh wave of immigration following World War I, when Great Britain took over Palestine under a mandate from the League of Nations, the predecessor of the United Nations. The new arrivals further stoked tensions with the longtime Arab population. Under the so-called Balfour Declaration of 1917, Britain committed itself to allowing the establishment of a Jewish "national home" in Palestine, with the proviso that "nothing shall be done which may prejudice the civil and religious rights of existing non-Jewish communities in Palestine." The measure was endorsed by France, Italy, Japan and, in principle, by the U.S. Congress in 1922.[44]

After the genocide of 6 million Jews by the Nazis in World War II, thousands of Holocaust survivors flooded into Palestine, many joining the ranks of a determined and effective underground army called the Haganah and other similar militias. Their guerrilla-style attacks on British and Arab targets and Palestinian Arab violent resistance to growing Zionist strength prompted the United Nations General Assembly to vote in November 1947 to partition the Palestinian territory into separate countries for Arabs and Jews — Israel and Palestine.

CHRONOLOGY

1948-1977 *Israel becomes a nation, opening new era regularly punctuated by war with its Arab neighbors.*

1948 Israel declares statehood on May 14; Arab armies attack a day later. Israel emerges as victor within months, but 750,000 Palestinians are uprooted.

1965 Exiled Fatah leader Yasser Arafat, now heading new Palestine Liberation Organization (PLO), declares armed struggle against Israel to reclaim former Arab lands.

1967 In Six-Day War, Israeli troops repulse Arab attack, enter Jerusalem and occupy west bank of Jordan River, Gaza Strip along Mediterranean.

1973 Egypt and Syria launch initially successful surprise attack on Israel on Oct. 6, the Jewish holiday of Yom Kippur. Israel makes major territorial gains in the Golan Heights and in the Sinai desert before a U.N.-sponsored cease-fire takes effect, just weeks after the conflict started.

1978-2000 *Peace attempts alternate with periods of heightened violence.*

1978 After secret talks hosted by President Jimmy Carter at Camp David, Egyptian President Anwar Al-Sadat and Israeli Prime Minister Menachem Begin sign agreement leading to 1979 peace treaty, the first between Israel and an Arab neighbor.

1987 Palestinians rise up against Israeli occupation in first Intifada ("uprising"); violence continues for six years.

1993 In secretly negotiated Oslo Accords, Israel agrees to gradually transfer administration of West Bank and Gaza to Palestinians; PLO, in accompanying letter, recognizes Israel's right to exist.

2000 President Bill Clinton fails in push for final Palestinian-Israeli peace deal at second Camp David summit. Second Intifada erupts. Clinton appoints former Sen. George Mitchell, D-Maine, to lead an international inquiry into how to end it.

2001-2007 *Bush administration initially steers clear of involvement in Middle East peace efforts.*

2001 Mitchell tells President George W. Bush Israel should freeze its settlements and the Palestinians end terrorism. Arab terrorists attack United States on Sept. 11, prompting Bush's global war on terror and increasing Muslim-Western tensions.

2002 U.S., European Union, Russia and U.N. form Quartet of global mediators to help resolve Arab-Israeli differences. Bush endorses Palestinian statehood.

2003 United States and allies topple Saddam Hussein in a move widely seen as a grab for Iraqi oil. Quartet's two-year plan (roadmap) calls for Palestinian state.

2005 Israel abandons its Gaza settlements and withdraws from the area.

2006 Hamas wins Palestinian elections. Arab guerrillas capture Israeli soldier Gilad Shalit and demand release of imprisoned Palestinians. Israel invades southern Lebanon on July 12 after Hezbollah guerrillas capture two Israeli soldiers.

2007 Hamas defeats Fatah in Palestinian civil war and takes full control of Gaza on June 15. Bush convenes conference in Annapolis, Md., to seek Israeli-Palestinian peace deal.

2008-Present *Israelis elect new conservative government after controversial invasion of Gaza.*

2008 Palestinian militants in Gaza fire thousands of rockets and mortars into southern Israel. Mid-year truce ends on Nov. 4 after Israeli and Hamas forces clash along Gaza border. On Dec. 27 Israel launches 22-day invasion of Gaza. Annapolis conference ends without a deal.

2009 Barack Obama becomes U.S. president, says time is ripe for new Middle East negotiations and names Mitchell his special Middle East envoy. In Feb. 10 elections, Israel elects Likud Party leader Benjamin Netanyahu to head new right-leaning government. Obama plans to meet with Netanyahu on May 18 and later with Palestinian and Egyptian leaders.

2009

June 4 President Barack Obama, in a heavily publicized speech in Cairo, says Americans "will not turn our backs on the legitimate Palestinian aspiration for dignity, opportunity and a state of their own."

June 12 Iranian President Mahmoud Ahmadinejad wins landslide election victory, triggering street protests by opposition supporters claiming the voting was rigged.

Sept. 15 U.N. fact-finding mission led by South African jurist Richard Goldstone accuses both Israelis and Palestinians of war crimes during Israel's 22-day incursion into Gaza, launched in December 2008.

Sept. 23 President Obama tells U.N. General Assembly the time has come to resume Israeli-Palestinian negotiations aimed at ending their decades-old conflict.

Oct. 31 Palestinian officials rebuff U.S. Secretary of State Hillary Rodham Clinton's call for resumption of peace talks based on what she terms an "unprecedented" offer by Israeli Prime Minister Benjamin Netanyahu to slow but not stop the expansion of Jewish settlements in the West Bank while imposing no restraints on East Jerusalem settlements.

2010

March 9 U.S. Vice President Joseph Biden, thinking he is close to making a deal for the resumption of peace talks during a visit to Israel, is blindsided by Israel's announcement of plans for 1,600 new housing units in a Jewish settlement in East Jerusalem.

March 16 U.S. Gen. David Petraeus says the Israel-Palestinian conflict threatens U.S. security because it "foments anti-American sentiment, due to a perception of U.S. favoritism for Israel."

May 9 U.S. State Department announces the completion of an initial round of indirect peace talks between Israeli and Palestinian officials, with U.S. special envoy George Mitchell acting as a go-between.

May 31 Israel sets off an international furor by deploying commandos to board a Turkish ship carrying pro-Palestinian activists intent on breaking an Israeli naval blockade by delivering humanitarian aid to Gaza. The commandos kill nine activists after they are attacked.

June 9 U.N. Security Council votes 12 to 2 to impose a fourth round of sanctions on Iran. Brazil and Turkey oppose the measure; Lebanon abstains. The measure reinforces economic, high-tech and military sanctions against Iran and imposes travel bans and an asset freeze targeting more than 40 wealthy Iranians and companies linked to the nation's nuclear program.

Israel's New Government Could Block Quick Peace

Netanyahu: No peace talks until progress is made on Iran.

While the Palestinian Authority, President Barack Obama and most world governments are calling for a quick, new push for Palestinian statehood, Israel has signaled through its votes in Feb. 10 parliamentary elections that it is not in any hurry.

What's more, even as critics express concern over Israel's aggressive tactics in Gaza, some Israeli officials are warning of fresh military action over the rocket fire still raining down on southern Israel from Gaza. Sporadic rocket attacks resumed within days of the end of the Gaza operation in January, undermining initial Israeli boasts about the success of its initial assault, launched mainly to stop the attacks.

Continuing rocket fire "will be answered with a painful, harsh, strong and uncompromising response from the security forces," caretaker Prime Minister Ehud Olmert warned on March 1, a month before turning power over to his successor, conservative Likud Party leader Benjamin Netanyahu.[1]

But Hamas — the militant political party that governs Gaza and refuses to recognize Israel's right to exist — was not firing the rockets launched in the months after the Gaza operation, Israeli government and private experts say. "It is only independents — very small and extreme groups — that are shooting. It is not Hamas. We can tell by the rocket and who manufactured it who is shooting," Asaf Shariv, the Israeli consul general in New York and one-time media spokesman for former Prime Minister Ariel Sharon, said in late March. Should Hamas later resume fire, Israel could "go back in" to Gaza, he added.

But the lull continued in April, says Reuven Erlich, head of the Intelligence and Terrorism Information Center, a private organization in Ramat Hasharon, Israel. "It is in Hamas' interest to keep a low profile and calm down the situation at this time. But this won't necessarily continue for the long run," he continues, speculating that Hamas may be using the lull to rebuild its military or enable the reconstruction of Gaza to get under way.

The threat of renewed military action in Gaza is just one sign of Israelis' unhappiness with the peace process. Judging by the election results, "Israel realizes that the so-called peace process has led it to the brink of great peril for its own existence," says Amnon Lord, an Israeli writer and former newspaper editor.

Netanyahu argues that now is not the time for a Palestinian state. He wants to focus instead on Palestinian economic development and security issues. He also champions Israeli settlements in the West Bank and East Jerusalem, despite multiple U.N. Security Council demands to freeze all settlement activity.

Netanyahu also wants to focus above all on the threat from Iran. Israel's deputy foreign minister, Daniel Ayalon, said in April that his country's new government would not begin peace talks with the Palestinians until Washington first made progress in ensuring that Tehran does not develop nuclear weapons.[2]

But the Obama administration has been pushing for a comprehensive approach that aims for progress on the

But borders were never established for the two separate states, and Palestine's Arabs and Jews engaged in a spiral of deadly clashes in the months following the U.N. vote. When Britain's mandate to administer Palestine ran out, Israel simply declared itself an independent nation on May 14, 1948. Immediately, the Arab League went to war to reclaim the land. But Israel defeated the league — made up of Egypt, Syria, Lebanon, Transjordan (now Jordan), Iraq, Saudi Arabia and Yemen — in what Israelis call the "War of Independence." Palestinians call it "the catastrophe" ("al-Naqba") because it led to the departure or expulsion of hundreds of thousands of Arabs from the new country of Israel — creating the

root of today's conflict. Debate over whether the Palestinians were forced out or fled on their own has since become part of the two sides' divergent historical narratives.[45]

Israel's founding triggered a succession of Middle Eastern wars that essentially continues to this day. The 1948 War of Independence was followed by the Six-Day War of 1967 against the region's major Arab countries — led by Syria and Egypt — and the Yom Kippur War of 1973. After the Six-Day War Israel occupied lands now known as the Palestinian territories — the West Bank (of the Jordan River) and the Gaza Strip, which runs along the Mediterranean.

Palestinian and Syrian peace tracks as well as Iran. "The United States is committed to a comprehensive peace between Israel and its Arab neighbors, and we will pursue it on many fronts," Secretary of State Hillary Rodham Clinton said during a March Middle East visit that included trips to Jerusalem, the West Bank city of Ramallah and the Egyptian resort town of Sharm el-Sheikh.[3]

During her tour of the region, Clinton made it clear that, unlike the previous U.S. administration, Washington would press Israel on its commitments to freeze settlement activities and speak out when it disagreed with Israeli leaders.[4]

In elections for the 120 seats in Israel's single-chamber parliament, the Knesset, Likud won 15 additional seats — for a total of 27 — but still finished in second place behind the centrist Kadima Party's 28 seats, despite months of polls suggesting Likud would end up leading the pack. The biggest surprise was the right-wing Yisrael Beitenu Party of Avigdor Lieberman, which captured four new seats — for a total of 15 — putting it in third place.

While Kadima normally would have been tasked with assembling a coalition government supported by more than half of Knesset members, the job in this case went to Netanyahu because right-wing and religious parties enjoyed an overall strong majority.

As coalition talks dragged on, Netanyahu managed to cut deals with the center-left Labor Party as well as with Yisrael Beitenu that assigned the post of foreign minister to Lieberman, whose campaign was widely seen by Israelis as extremist, racist or advocating ethnic cleansing of the Palestinians.[5]

Netanyahu's new government took power on March 31.

Analysts saw the agreement with Labor as helping to shield Netanyahu from U.S. criticism that the government was too right-wing and too opposed to the peace process.

But Lieberman has called for all Israeli citizens — including Israeli Arabs, who make up a fifth of the population — to swear an oath of loyalty to the state in order to retain their rights. Critics said the proposal was aimed at driving Israeli Arabs out of the country. Others, however, have painted Lieberman as more difficult to categorize.

"Lieberman is an enigma for me," says one international diplomat, speaking on condition he not be identified because he will have to work with the Israeli politician. "If you look at what he is saying, it is very, very dangerous to talk of an ethnic Jewish state with no place at all for Israeli Arabs. But on the other hand, Lieberman is for a two-state solution, he wants a Palestinian state. He even wants to think about parts of Jerusalem being part of it."

Adds Israel's Shariv: "It is true that he had a very interesting campaign that made everyone in the world raise some questions about him, but he is a very practical person."

[1] Matti Friedman, "Israeli leader vows 'painful' response to rockets," The Associated Press, March 1, 2009, http://news.yahoo.com/s/ap/20090301/ap_on_re_mi_ea/ml_israel_palestinians;_ylt=Aizxs6J4fCD8EJDs_WfT2RRI2ocA.

[2] Howard Schneider and Glenn Kessler, "Israel Puts Iran Issue Ahead of Palestinians," *The Washington Post*, April 22, 2009, www.washingtonpost.com/wp-dyn/content/article/2009/04/21/AR2009042103998.html?hpid=topnews.

[3] Hillary Rodham Clinton, "Intervention at the International Conference in Support of the Palestinian Economy for the Reconstruction of Gaza," Sharm el-Sheikh, Egypt, March 2, 2009, www.state.gov/secretary/rm/2009a/03/119900.htm.

[4] "Secretary Clinton, Palestinian President Abbas in Ramallah," March 4, 2009, www.america.gov/st/texttransEnglish/2009/March/20090304125709eaifas0.3768885.html?CP.rss=true.

[5] See for example, Lily Galili, "Avigdor Lieberman said to be ex-member of banned radical Kach movement," *Haaretz.com*, Feb. 3, 2009, www.haaretz.com/hasen/spages/1061172.html.

During the second half of the 20th century, nationalism grew among Palestinian Arabs, who demanded the return of their homeland. By 1964, a group of exiles that included Fatah leader Arafat founded the Palestine Liberation Organization (PLO), which brought together religiously oriented political activists and left-wing Arab nationalists. The following year, they declared an armed struggle against Israel to reclaim the formerly Arab lands.

Peace Accords

Just as there was a series of Arab-Israeli wars, there has been a series of peace summits to settle the intractable conflict.

The first Camp David summit, hosted by President Carter in 1978, led to a formal peace treaty between Israel and Egypt in 1979. As part of the deal, the United States agreed to provide $7.5 billion in economic and military aid to the two countries that year, with the lion's share going to Israel. Over the following three decades, seeking to encourage continued friendly ties, Washington has funneled an average of $4.3 billion a year in aid (three-quarters of it to Israel) to the two Middle East neighbors — a costly arrangement that could well be repeated in future Middle East agreements mediated by the United States.[46]

Support for the Palestinian cause eroded, however, with the collapse of the Eastern European bloc — a strong financial and political backer of the Arab world — as the Cold War began to wind down in the late 1980s. Palestinians, frustrated by the continued Israeli occupation of their lands, rose up in 1987 in what is now called the First Intifada, an uprising that lasted until 1993.

In response to the violence, a secret peace initiative was launched in Oslo with the help of Norwegian diplomat Roed-Larsen, leading to the first face-to-face negotiations between Israel and the PLO and ultimately to the so-called 1993 Oslo Accords.[47] The agreements were signed on Sept. 13, 1993, in an historic White House Rose Garden ceremony in which Arafat and Israeli Prime Minister Yitzhak Rabin shook hands as a beaming President Clinton looked on.

Under the accords, the parties committed themselves to negotiate the final details of a comprehensive peace agreement by 1999. The final details — concerning such crucial issues as borders, the disposition of Jerusalem and Palestinian refugees' "right of return" to their former home — became known as the "final status" or "permanent status" issues and remain unresolved today.

The accords also provided for Israel to gradually transfer power and responsibility for the West Bank and Gaza to the Palestinians, and to recognize Arafat's Palestine Liberation Organization as the representative of the Palestinian people and as a negotiating partner.

For its part, the PLO in a letter accompanying the accords formally recognized Israel's right to exist and renounced the use of "terrorism and other acts of violence." The agreement also divided up security responsibilities among the two parties.

But extremists on both sides were unhappy with the accords and in 1995 essentially sabotaged the negotiations toward a comprehensive peace: Palestinian militants stepped up their attacks against Israel, and a Jewish extremist assassinated Rabin.

Five years after that, in May 2000, Israel withdrew its forces from southern Lebanon, which it had first invaded in 1978 in hopes of ending cross-border guerrilla attacks on civilians in northern Israel. Years of occupation and low-intensity warfare between the Israeli occupiers and Hezbollah militia had taken a political toll on Israel, and most Israelis saw the conflict with Palestinians in the West Bank and Gaza as a more pressing concern.[48]

Two months later, the Clinton administration came the closest ever to a broad agreement ending the Israeli-Palestinian conflict by luring Arafat and then-Israeli Prime Minister Barak to the Camp David presidential retreat near Washington.

Their talks, known as Camp David Two, convened on July 11, 2000, and at first made significant progress. But they ran out of steam and ended after two weeks without a deal.[49]

Blame for the failure of Camp David Two has since been hotly debated, with each side blaming the other for failure to go the final mile.[50] Following the talks' collapse, Palestinian frustration boiled over, leading to the popular uprising in September 2000 that became known as the Second Intifada. Dismayed by the deadly violence, Clinton asked former Sen. Mitchell to chair a commission to identify its causes and recommend how to end the uprising.

Clinton left office in January 2001, and Mitchell turned over his findings to President George W. Bush, whose administration avoided direct involvement in the conflict even as it offered strong support for Israeli policies. Mitchell's May 4, 2001, report split the blame, calling for an end to Palestinian violence and a freeze on Israeli settlements. Mitchell saw the settlements as undermining Israel's earlier commitments to the general principle of "land for peace," under which Israel would cede land gained in the Six-Day War in exchange for peace with the Palestinians.[51]

But both sides largely ignored Mitchell's recommendations.

War on Terror

Less than four months after Mitchell's report was published, Islamic extremists hijacked airliners and crashed them into the World Trade Center and the Pentagon, radically altering Washington's relationship with the Middle East and greatly complicating peace efforts while drawing the United States more deeply into the region's political woes.

Bush declared a global war on terror in which the United States vowed to use all its power against radical Islamists. The campaign started with a coalition-led invasion of Afghanistan to oust the ultraconservative Taliban regime, which was harboring al Qaeda leader Osama bin Laden, the architect of the 9/11 attacks. At the same time, Israel adapted Washington's war on terror to its own ends, citing it to defend a crackdown on Palestinian militants.

Following a deadly suicide bombing in the northern town of Netanya during the Jewish Passover holiday in 2002, Prime Minister Ariel Sharon sent the military into the West Bank to reoccupy towns evacuated as part of the Oslo Accords. Israeli forces surrounded Arafat, confining him to his Ramallah offices.[52]

As Middle East violence picked up, U.N. Secretary-General Annan convened a meeting of top diplomats from the United States, the European Union and Russia, urging them to join the United Nations in a pressure group of four, which they dubbed the Quartet. The group began drafting a roadmap to peace to present to the Israelis and Palestinians.

To counter accusations that he was biased against the Arab world, Bush in a June 24, 2002, White House address became the first U.S. president to publicly embrace the so-called two-state solution — separate Palestinian and Israeli states, existing side by side within secure borders.[53] Palestinian statehood was included as a provision of the roadmap, which became international law upon adoption by the U.N. Security Council on Nov. 19, 2003.[54]

But Bush inflamed the Arab world anew with his March 2003 invasion of Iraq to rid it of alleged chemical, biological and nuclear weapons. The weapons were never found, and Washington ended up occupying the oil-rich country. The invasion, building on Bush's war on terror and his unwavering support for Israel, prompted fresh Arab accusations that Washington was waging a war on Islam.[55]

With violence persisting in Gaza, Sharon pushed through a domestically unpopular plan to shut down Israeli settlements there and withdrew from the territory in September 2005. The pull-out initially was widely hailed as a fulfillment of Israeli commitments to end its occupation of Palestinian areas.

But Israel, worried that weapons and fighters would enter Gaza through Egypt, continued to clamp down on border crossings into Gaza from Israel and Egypt. That severely limited the commerce on which Gaza's economic future depended.[56]

Within months, Israel was attacking militants inside Gaza with artillery and air strikes. Militants in Gaza in turn continued their attacks on the Jewish state, arguing they remained under occupation despite the withdrawal.[57]

Getty Images/Yoray Liberman

A Jewish settler cries out in despair when Israeli policemen tell her she must abandon her home in the Atzmona settlement in Gaza Strip on Aug. 21, 2005. All Israeli settlers were forced to leave Gaza under an unpopular plan engineered by Prime Minister Ariel Sharon. Although the pull-out was widely hailed as a fulfillment of Israeli commitments to end its occupation of Palestinian areas, Israel has continued to expand its settlements in other occupied areas.

In the January 2006 elections, the militant Gaza-based Hamas movement defeated long-dominant Fatah to win a majority of the seats in the Palestinian Legislative Council. Bush had been promoting Middle East democracy, but when Hamas won power, Israel and the Quartet refused to deal with it or recognize its authority. To gain recognition, the Quartet declared, Hamas would have to recognize Israel's right to exist, foreswear violence and honor all agreements reached by previous Palestinian administrations.[58] The Quartet principles, presented as recommended policy to all world governments, ended up isolating the Gazan population as well as Hamas from the international community.

Growing tension between Hamas and Fatah soon led to intermittent civil war that ended in the seizure of Gaza by Hamas fighters in mid-2007. That left the Palestinian Authority effectively in charge only of the West Bank, although in international eyes it remains the leader of both territories.[59]

To the north, meanwhile, Lebanon's Hezbollah paramilitary forces resumed targeting Israel from a second front, launching rockets at northern Israeli towns and then kidnapping two Israeli soldiers in a daring cross-border raid. In July 2006 Israel responded by sending troops back into southern Lebanon with orders to wipe out Hezbollah forces. Like Sharon's 2002 reoccupation of the West Bank and the December 2008 incursion into Gaza, the 34-day operation started out with great fanfare but soon began rolling up heavy civilian casualties even as it fell short of its goals, triggering international criticism of the Israeli military's tactics.[60]

Although Hezbollah ended up suffering militarily, it was politically strengthened by the Israeli assault in Lebanon. Within a year, a new Lebanese government had been formed in which the group and its allies held effective veto power over government actions.[61]

With time running out on his presidency, Bush in November 2007 gave a final try to advancing the Israeli-Palestinian peace process from Washington, convening an international peace conference in Annapolis, Md. But even as the conference began, participants played down expectations of a dramatic result, and Bush — shying from specifics — called on the parties only to try to finish whatever they chose to accomplish by the end of 2008.[62]

In line with expectations, the Annapolis initiative produced no agreement before time ran out 13 months later. The U.N. Security Council on Dec. 16, 2008, adopted a resolution supporting the failed initiative's attempt at peace and welcoming the idea of another international conference, as yet unscheduled, in Moscow in 2009.[63] On Dec. 27, four days before the deadline for an Annapolis deal, Israel sent its troops into Gaza.

CURRENT SITUATION

U.S. Role

With new U.S. and Israeli governments settling in, and Palestinian leaders crippled by internal divisions, the Middle East peace process seems on hold for now. In the region and around the world, interested governments are standing on the sidelines, putting off any initiatives until they hear what the Obama administration has in mind.

Meanwhile, Israel, the Palestinians and outsiders involved with the region all agree on at least one thing: The United States must continue to play a central role in Middle East diplomacy.

Washington's key role, of course, can cut both ways. Washington's disinterest has nipped some initiatives in

the bud, while U.S. support has breathed life into other proposals. Washington is Israel's closest and most trusted ally and the world's lone superpower. International diplomats say Washington alone has the power to influence — although not necessarily alter — Israeli policy, and Washington's deep pockets will make it a necessary partner in any agreement.

"U.S. commitment to the resolution of this conflict is indispensable," says Otte, the EU's Middle East ambassador.

For his part, President Obama appears eager to get involved but cautious about the outcome. "I am a strong supporter of a two-state solution, and I think that there are a lot of Israelis who also believe in a two-state solution," he told reporters on April 21 during a visit to Washington by King Abdullah of Jordan. "Unfortunately, right now what we've seen not just in Israel but within the Palestinian territories, among the Arab states, worldwide, is a profound cynicism about the possibility of any progress being made whatsoever.

"What we want to do is to step back from the abyss," he continued, "to say, as hard as it is, as difficult as it may be, the prospect of peace still exists, but it's going to require some hard choices, it's going to require resolution on the part of all the actors involved, and it's going to require that we create some concrete steps that all parties can take that are evidence of that resolution. And the United States is going to deeply engage in this process to see if we can make progress."[64]

Obama's caution is understandable. Months of Palestinian negotiations on a national unity government have gone nowhere. Because of Hamas' pariah status with the Quartet, most international donors refuse to provide it with direct funding, and it can only participate indirectly in the multibillion-dollar international program to rebuild Gaza.

Meanwhile, Egyptian-led talks between Israel and the Palestinians seeking a long-term Gaza cease-fire are at an impasse. Hamas' refusal to release kidnapped Israeli soldier Gilad Shalit, held by Gaza militants since June 2006, has been a major stumbling block. And Israel, furious over continued rocket fire from Gaza, has maintained a tight rein on the movement of people and goods in and out of the area. Despite Israel's insistence that it is not slowing the shipment of food and medicine into Gaza, U.N. officials say otherwise.[65]

Since the 2007 Hamas takeover of Gaza, both before and after its invasion of the territory, Israel has pursued a policy "of near-total closure of the Gaza Strip," Lynn Pascoe, the U.N. undersecretary-general for political affairs, told the Security Council on April 20.[66] Israeli officials say vital supplies are not being blocked. But Pascoe pointed out that while basic emergency needs such as food and blankets have been met, broader humanitarian and reconstruction aid has been "impossible" due to restrictions on the flow of fuel, cash and construction materials.

"The lack of access to Gaza is deeply frustrating," he continued. "Without the materials for recovery and reconstruction, the process cannot begin, and that requires a substantial easing by Israel of its policy of closure of the Gaza Strip."

Besides promoting negotiations between Israel and the Palestinians, the Obama administration also hopes to revive the so-called Syrian track of the Middle East peace process, which centers on the Golan Heights. Israel captured the tract of Syrian land in the 1967 Six-Day War, and Syria wants it back.

Despite being neighbors, Syria and Israel have no diplomatic relations. They held secret, indirect peace talks under Turkish mediation in 2008, but Damascus put the talks on hold after Israel invaded Gaza in December. But in February President Bashar al-Assad told a visiting U.S. official that an agreement with Israel was still possible and that Syria was prepared to resume the talks if Washington joined them.[67]

Syria — a close ally of Iran and a backer of Hamas and Hezbollah — has been listed as a state sponsor of terrorism by the United States since 1979.[68] But Secretary of State Clinton in March dispatched two U.S. envoys to Damascus to explore bilateral and regional issues. "We have no way to predict what the future with our relations concerning Syria might be," she said. "But I think it is a worthwhile effort to go and begin these preliminary conversations."[69]

Israel's Role

The new coalition government formed by Israeli Prime Minister Netanyahu teams right-wing parties cool to Palestinian statehood and the peace process with the Labor Party, which supports negotiations for a Palestinian state. Netanyahu assembled a cabinet after his Likud Party finished first in the Feb. 10 parliamentary elections.

Global Reaction

Israel's harsh three-week campaign against Hamas militants in the Gaza Strip sparked demonstrations around the world, both in support of the assault and in condemnation. Demonstrators outside the Israeli embassy in Madrid (top) show their support for Israel on Jan. 18, 2009, while protesters in Ankara, Turkey, on Jan. 3, 2009, show their outrage (bottom).

Netanyahu said during the campaign that he would continue negotiating with the Palestinians, but not about statehood. Instead, he would grant the Palestinians some degree of sovereignty over any territory they govern while maintaining Israeli control over their borders and airspace.

"Netanyahu has already announced that he will continue the negotiations, especially in the West Bank, about these issues, and to strengthen what he calls the economic peace — to make the Palestinian economy much stronger, to build infrastructure, to encourage companies to work there, to make life better," says Shariv, the Israeli consul general.

Under its coalition agreement with the Labor Party, Likud agreed to respect all of Israel's international agreements — which presumably would include the roadmap to Palestinian statehood.

But Netanyahu thus far has avoided the word "statehood," seemingly seeking to divert international attention from peace talks with the Palestinians and keep it focused instead on containing Iran. While some observers worry that Tehran may be just months away from being able to make nuclear weapons, the timetable on Palestinian statehood "is open-ended," Israeli Deputy Foreign Minister Daniel Ayalon said in April, defying President Obama's insistence that ending the Israeli-Palestinian conflict is an urgent global priority.[70]

"The Palestinians should understand that they have in our government a partner for peace, for security and for rapid economic development of the Palestinian economy," Netanyahu said in late March. "If we have a strong Palestinian economy, that's a strong foundation for peace."[71]

Israelis are also heatedly debating whether a second military thrust into Gaza might be needed to halt the renewed rocket fire into southern Israel. While the continued attacks on Israeli civilians show the 22-day military campaign fell short of its goals, the invasion also prompted a flood of international criticism of aggressive Israeli tactics in Gaza's densely populated urban area as well as of Hamas' rocket fire at Israeli civilians.

Within days after the war ended, New York-based Human Rights Watch called for an international investigation into allegations of war crimes by both Hamas and Israel.[72] A U.N. human rights investigator issued a similar appeal several weeks later. Gaza's civilian population was subjected to "an inhumane form of warfare that kills, maims and inflicts mental harm," said Richard Falk, the U.N. special rapporteur on human rights in the Palestinian territories. "As all borders were sealed, civilians could not escape from the orbit of harm." Israel has prevented Falk — who is a professor emeritus on international law at Princeton — from visiting Gaza, so he based his findings on "preliminary evidence" that was available.[73]

The Geneva-based U.N. Human Rights Council announced in April that famed South African judge Richard Goldstone, who has been involved in human-rights investigations and prosecutions in South Africa, Yugoslavia and Rwanda, would lead an investigation into the allegations on both sides.[74]

International efforts to promote peace in the region will also focus in the coming months on the steady growth of Israeli settlements, diplomats said. All settlements in Gaza were dismantled in 2005, when Israel withdrew from the area. But despite repeated Israeli commitments to freeze them, settlements in the West Bank and East Jerusalem have grown steadily, reaching a combined population of at least 472,657 by the end of 2008, according to the latest available Israeli figures.[75]

"Illegal settlement activity continues, prejudicing final status negotiations and undermining Palestinians who seek a negotiated peace," U.N. envoy Serry told the Security Council in February. "The approach taken since Annapolis to secure implementation of roadmap commitments to freeze settlement activity, including natural growth, and remove outposts, has not worked. This is a clear challenge that must be addressed," Serry said, adding that in 2008, there were 69 percent more new structures built in settlements than in 2007.[76]

"When the Quartet repeatedly states that Israel must freeze all settlement activity and dismantle all outposts, and the Quartet does not do anything, then the Quartet is marginalizing itself," says Mansour, the Palestinian U.N. observer.

But Israel's Shariv dismisses the settlement concerns as overwrought. "When the Palestinians completely stop the terror, we are going to take a few bulldozers or tractors and soldiers, and we are going to evacuate according to the agreement," he says. Israel "should do a better job" of meeting its commitments on settlements, "but you cannot compare terror to settlements."

Discussion of the future of the settlements almost certainly will be on the agenda in May, when Obama meets for the first time with Netanyahu, Abbas and Egyptian President Hosni Mubarak to discuss new U.S. priorities for the region. Obama and Netanyahu are scheduled to meet May 18.[77]

Palestinians' Role

While Israel's political divisions represent an enormous challenge to international peacemakers, Palestinian disunity — specifically the intense hatred between Fatah and Hamas — seems far more untenable.

International donors have offered to pour billions of dollars into Gaza's reconstruction, but tight Israeli border controls and Quartet restrictions on Hamas prevent the people of Gaza from reaping the benefits. Palestinian leaders demand evidence of good faith from the Israelis on fulfilling their commitments, including freezing settlement activities, easing access to Gaza and pursuit of a Palestinian state. But the Israelis say the Palestinians must prevent militants from firing rockets into Israel.

Talks among Palestinians on a national unity government drag on in a fitful way without result. Palestinian Authority bureaucrats scramble to clean up the West Bank's finances and reform their security forces, only to come under fire from hardliners who either question their competence or say they don't deserve to govern because they are cozying up to Israel. Talks aimed at ensuring a lasting cease-fire between Gaza and Israel have stalled over a Hamas plea for the release of some of the 11,000 Palestinian prisoners — a mix of criminals, alleged terrorists and political prisoners — held in Israeli jails in exchange for the freeing of kidnapped Israeli soldier Shalit.

In early April, nearly two weeks passed without violence in Gaza and southern Israel. But during the previous four-week period, 30 rockets and mortar rounds were launched into southern Israel by Palestinian militants, according to Pascoe, the U.N. undersecretary-general for political affairs. The Israeli military retaliated by carrying out two air strikes on the Gaza Strip.[78]

In addition, the Israeli army reported that a Palestinian ship loaded with explosives had blown up in the vicinity of an Israeli naval vessel in mid-April, though without causing injury to the Israeli ship. Egyptian police seeking to prevent the smuggling of arms into Gaza — whether by underground tunnel, the sea or donkey cart — found nearly 2,000 pounds of explosives along Egypt's border with Gaza, Pascoe reported.

While Palestinian Authority security forces stepped up their activity in the West Bank in April — bearing down on criminal gangs and shutting down a suspected explosives manufacturing lab in the West Bank city of Qalqilia — a Palestinian wielding an axe killed a 13-year-old boy and injured a 7-year-old in the Israeli settlement of Bat Ayin, triggering clashes between Israeli settlers and Palestinians that ultimately was halted only after Israeli military intervention, Pascoe told the U.N. council.

The sprawling Ramot housing development in East Jerusalem is built on land Israel captured from Jordan during the 1967 Six-Day War. Despite repeated Israeli commitments to freeze expansion of such settlements in the West Bank and East Jerusalem, they have continued to grow in recent years — undermining peace talks.

Getty Images/David Silverman

Such violence makes a durable end to the war in Gaza just one of peacemakers' many priorities, Secretary of State Clinton said during her early March visit to the region.

"That can only be achieved if Hamas ceases the rocket attacks. No nation should be expected to sit idly by and allow rockets to assault its people and its territories," she said. "These attacks must stop and so must the smuggling of weapons into Gaza."

There have been recent indications that Hamas leaders may be softening their refusal to participate in the peace process, although probably not enough to fully satisfy the Quartet principles. Hamas leader Khaled Meshal said in early May that the group had made a conscious decision to curtail militants' rocket fire into southern Israel.

"Not firing the rockets currently is part of an evaluation from the movement which serves the Palestinians' interest," he said. "After all, the firing is a method, not a goal."[79]

OUTLOOK
'Mammoth Job'

With so little progress in the Middle East peace process, how can the search for peace emerge headed in the right direction? Much will depend on Sen. Mitchell's recommendations and President Obama's resolve to carry them out, say international diplomats.

Did Israel's military action in Gaza make Israel more secure?

YES

Yoaz Hendel
Security and Military Affairs Analyst and Research Fellow, Begin-Sadat Center for Strategic Studies Bar-Ilan University, Israel

Written for *CQ Researcher*, April 2009

The Israeli operation in Gaza started too late and ended too early. For the past eight years, southern Israeli citizens have been under a continuous rain of rockets from Gaza. Repeated threats of military action have done nothing to deter Gaza terror organizations from strikes on Israeli civilians.

The fighting between the Israel Defense Forces (IDF) and Gaza terrorist groups is different from other conflicts pitting conventional armies against guerrilla groups. Intelligence reports show deep Iranian involvement in Gaza. Right under Israel's nose, Iran has established a foothold with the potential to threaten most IDF southern bases, including major air force facilities.

When the IDF withdrew from Gaza in summer 2005, then-Prime Minister Ariel Sharon warned of a strong reaction to any violation of Israeli sovereignty. But Palestinian groups including Hamas only intensified their attacks.

Last summer, the Israeli government — then led by Ehud Olmert — approved a six-month cease-fire with Gaza despite continued attacks on Israeli civilians. During the cease-fire, intelligence reports warned that the terrorists intended to use new weapons from Iran to alter the power balance in the area. The rockets kept falling, even as Hamas prepared for renewed war with Israel.

Part of any state's responsibility is to protect its citizens. But the IDF, established to provide this protection, was not deployed for this purpose until last December.

The basic assumption for Israel in fighting terror across borders is that its forces will pay a heavy price for attacking. The IDF had assumed since its 2005 withdrawal from Gaza that it risked significant casualties by sending its forces back across the border to fight terror. This assumption had been upheld in the 2006 war between Israel and Hezbollah, when 119 Israeli soldiers and 44 Israeli civilians were killed.

But the decisive military tactics in Gaza forced the terrorists to retreat and go into hiding, with just one Israeli soldier killed by a direct Hamas attack. The IDF was just a step short of absolute victory when the fighting was halted. The Israeli military was on the verge of a historic opportunity to alter the basic conditions that had allowed Hamas to steadily increase its military might.

The Israeli government decision to end the operation was a mistake that will lead us in the near future to another war in Gaza — but this time with a higher price in lives for both Israelis and Palestinians.

NO

Paul Rogers
Global Security Consultant, Oxford Research Group, and Professor of Peace Studies, University of Bradford, United Kingdom

Written for *CQ Researcher*, April 2009

Israel's military assault on Gaza had the stated aim of so weakening Hamas' paramilitary capabilities that it could no longer fire unguided rockets into Israeli territory.

As the war began, senior Israeli sources made it clear that the aim extended beyond this, toward destroying Hamas' political and administrative infrastructure in order to weaken and possibly destroy the movement as a functioning entity. The actual conduct of the war suggests that this more extensive operation was indeed being implemented.

Indeed, the war started with a remarkably intensive and sudden air assault in which 88 aircraft attacked 100 targets in under four minutes. The initial assault included an attack on a police graduation ceremony in which 60 people reportedly were killed.

Four hundred more targets were hit during the first week, including numerous police stations and agricultural facilities, government offices and the main campus of the Islamic University.

At the end of the three-week war, the United Nations estimated that 1,300 Gazans had been killed, including 412 children. More than 5,000 people were injured, 4,000 homes were destroyed and 20,000 severely damaged — about 20 percent of the entire housing stock.

Although Hamas' paramilitary was undoubtedly caught by surprise in the initial assault, it reacted very quickly, and most of the personnel went to ground. There was some limited engagement with Israeli ground troops, but for the most part Hamas' military wing recognized the futility of engaging the vastly superior Israeli firepower and escaped with little damage. Rockets continued to be fired into Israel throughout the war. Afterward, Hamas quickly resumed control, returning police and security personnel to the streets and repairing smuggling tunnels to Egypt.

Claims of Israeli attacks on civilians were persistently rebutted by the Israeli Defense Force, but sources within the Israeli Army have recently provided evidence to support the claims. Israel might have expected a strong Arab public reaction to the war, but what was much less expected was considerable antagonism across much of Europe. With Hamas still in control of Gaza and substantially more popular among Palestinians, with rockets still being fired and with Israel losing public support in the wider world, the end result has been counterproductive to Israel's long-term security interests. It may, however, have some impact in persuading Israelis that a state of permanent war is not the best way to ensure the country's long-term survival.

"In spite of all the wars and the difficulties and the rise of extremists on both sides, I still believe that, if there is a decisive political will in Washington, D.C. — and potentially there is one — then . . . a peace deal could be reached between the two sides in a relatively short period of time," says Palestinian U.N. envoy Mansour.

"Honestly I really don't know if it is five minutes before 12, or five past," adds U.N. envoy Serry. "An early engagement of the Americans will be very much needed."

But even then, a deal is likely to remain out of reach for now, diplomats caution. "We face serious difficulties," says EU envoy Otte. "Nobody has really concentrated on the ability of the parties to implement such an agreement."

For example, any deal likely would require the Palestinians to give up the right of refugees to return home to what is now Israel. Its two feuding factions would have to agree to work closely together in governing their new state. At the same time, given the current realities, such a state's economy and security likely would remain heavily dependent on Israel.

Meanwhile, Israel would have to evacuate as many as hundreds of thousands of settlers from the West Bank and East Jerusalem and find a place for them to live and work. It also would have to accept the reality of the Palestinians, former foes, as permanent neighbors and friends.

"It's not something that is done easily," Otte says. "It's not impossible, but it would take years to implement."

Each side also must have the confidence that what it offers will be politically acceptable to its people. Is a new Israeli government capable of delivering on the two-state solution? Is the institutional chaos on the Palestinian side capable of accepting it?

"Both are highly unlikely," laments a veteran Middle East mediator, speaking on condition of anonymity on grounds that his grim view could damage future negotiations. "That is why any kind of significant diplomatic breakthrough at this time — I wish it had happened yesterday — is totally unrealistic." Doing the necessary groundwork, he continues, "is a mammoth job, and it will take time."

With those difficulties in mind, the Israeli approach during the year-long Annapolis discussions was to consider peace talks as only theoretical. The process was aimed at reaching what was referred to as a "shelf agreement" because it would, if reached, be put aside until conditions were right for it to take effect.

Since nothing was changing on the ground, "Prime Minister Olmert said, 'Let's change the sequence. Let's start with negotiation on a final status agreement,'" explains Israel's Shariv. "If we reach an agreement, we'll put it on a shelf. . . . This will show the Palestinians something they can wish for."

But Rashid Khalidi, a prominent U.S. scholar of Arab descent at Columbia University's Middle East Institute, sounds a more urgent note. "Current discussions of whether [to seek] a one-state or a two-state solution . . . have an unrealistic quality at the present moment," says Khalidi. "What has to be devised is how to reverse — very rapidly — the current dynamic, which is a highly inequitable, de facto, one-state solution that looks more and more entrenched — and will become more and more untenable as time goes on."

UPDATE

Israel shocked the world in late May 2010 by dropping marines from helicopters in total darkness onto a cruise ship from Turkey, its closest ally in the Arab world, in a botched and deadly effort to prevent the vessel from breaking the Jewish state's controversial blockade of Gaza.

In the chaos that ensued, the marines opened fire on pro-Palestinian activists on board the vessel, the *Mavi Marmara,* killing nine people, including four Turks.[80] The attack and the deaths infuriated Israel's friends and foes alike and threatened to scuttle indirect peace talks between Israelis and Palestinians that had started less than a month earlier.

The Turkish ship was part of a six-vessel flotilla carrying nearly 700 activists from more than 35 countries challenging the naval blockade imposed after Israel's 22-day assault on Gaza, launched in December 2008. Israel insisted the blockade was required to prevent dangerous weapons from entering Gaza and argued the nighttime deaths had occurred because its commandos had been attacked and had to fire their weapons in self-defense.

But activists argued that the blockade was illegal, the flotilla justified to remedy a humanitarian crisis in Gaza and the shootings unjustified. "Israel's behavior should definitely, definitely be punished," said Turkish Prime Minister Tayyip Erdogan. The United Nations Security Council later called for an impartial investigation of the incident, but the council's statement did not specify whether the inquiry should be carried out by an international body or by Israel itself, leading to prolonged discussions of possible next steps.

In its defense of the assault on the Turkish ship, "the Israeli propaganda machine has managed to convince only brainwashed Israelis," wrote Gideon Levy, an editor and columnist for the Israeli daily newspaper *Haaretz*. "And once more no one asked the question: What was it for? Why were our soldiers thrown into this trap of pipes and ball bearings? What did we get out of it?"[81]

Earlier in May, Israelis and Palestinians had taken a baby step toward resolving six decades of Middle East conflict, resuming negotiations after an 18-month hiatus. But the prospects for peace remained muddy despite a 16-month drive by U.S. President Barack Obama to bring the two sides together.[82]

Obama, who began the effort shortly after taking office in January 2009, encountered numerous obstacles. At times, both Palestinians and Israelis dug in their heels. But the two parties finally consented to indirect talks, using U.S. special envoy George Mitchell as an intermediary.[83]

The so-called proximity talks fell short of Obama's stated goal of direct and substantive negotiations between the parties, without preconditions.[84] He wanted the parties to resolve the conflict's core issues—including ensuring security, setting final borders between Israel and a neighboring Palestinian state, deciding on the rights of Palestinian refugees to return to former homes in Israel and determining the status of East Jerusalem, claimed by Israel and also by the Palestinians as their future capital.

The start of even indirect talks crowned months of U.S. diplomacy. Direct talks had ended 18 months earlier, and the peace process had collapsed altogether by December 2008 when Israel launched its assault on Gaza, the Palestinian territory run by the hard-line Islamic organization Hamas.[85]

The talks did not include Hamas, which seized control of Gaza in June 2007 in a civil war with the more moderate Fatah faction. That left the Palestine Liberation Organization (PLO), an umbrella group chaired by Palestinian Authority President Mahmoud Abbas, to represent the Palestinian side. A Palestinian unification drive, launched by Egypt in early 2009, never bore fruit. And Gaza-based militants continued to sporadically fire rockets at nearby Israeli towns after the Israeli incursion ended. Hamas also continued to

hold captured Israeli soldier Gilad Shalit, despite 120 rounds of talks, mediated by Egypt and Germany and aimed at freeing the young man who has been held since June 2006.[86]

U.S. Secretary of State Hillary Rodham Clinton has stressed that Hamas could join in the quest for peace only if it met longstanding international demands to renounce violence, recognize Israel and honor Middle East agreements signed earlier by the Palestinians.[87] "To those disillusioned by a peace process that has delivered too little, Hamas peddles the false hope that a Palestinian state can somehow be achieved through violence and uncompromising resistance," Clinton said in a mid-April speech. At the same time, she said, "the PLO has emerged as a credible partner for peace. It has rejected violence, improved security, made progress on combating incitement and accepted Israel's right to exist."[88]

The talks were repeatedly delayed by a Palestinian demand, backed by Washington, that talks should only resume once Israel froze expansion of settlements in the West Bank and East Jerusalem. "We have agreed that the final status negotiations will last 24 months, and we hope that in the four months of proximity talks we can achieve results that enable us to go for direct talks," Palestinian negotiator Saeb Erekat said. "Israel needs to choose between peace and settlements."[89]

However, hopes that new talks could resume in March 2010 were dashed when Israeli officials announced plans, during a visit by U.S. Vice President Joseph Biden, to build 1,600 new homes for Jewish settlers in East Jerusalem, where the Palestinians want their future capital.[90] The Israeli announcement infuriated Biden, who reportedly told his Israeli hosts they had damaged not only the peace process but U.S. security.

"This is starting to get dangerous for us," Biden was quoted as telling Israeli Prime Minister Benjamin Netanyahu.[91] "What you're doing here undermines the security of our troops who are fighting in Iraq, Afghanistan and Pakistan. That endangers us, and it endangers regional peace."

The dispute soured ties between the Jewish state and the United States, its closest ally. Many Israelis and American Jews questioned Obama's motives in pushing for a settlement freeze. Netanyahu's brother-in-law, Hagai Ben Artzi, described the U.S. leader as an anti-Semite, a comment rejected by Netanyahu.[92] Dozens of members of Congress urged Obama to drop demands for a freeze.[93]

"Jerusalem is not a settlement; it's our capital," Netanyahu told a pro-Israel lobbying group in Washington shortly after Biden's visit to Israel.[94]

Meanwhile, Gen. David Petraeus, leader of the U.S. Central Command, appeared to reinforce Obama's hand, echoing Biden by telling the U.S. Senate the Israeli-Palestinian conflict was "a major concern" for the U.S. military."[95] "The conflict foments anti-American sentiment, due to a perception of U.S. favoritism for Israel," Petraeus continued. "Arab anger over the Palestinian question limits the strength and depth of U.S. partnerships with governments and peoples in the AOR [Area of Responsibility] and weakens the legitimacy of moderate regimes in the Arab world. Meanwhile, al Qaeda and other militant groups exploit that anger to mobilize support. The conflict also gives Iran influence in the Arab world through its clients, Lebanese Hezbollah and Hamas."[96]

In addition, the international "Quartet" of Middle East mediators—the European Union, United States, Russia and the United Nations—appealed anew to Israel "to freeze all settlement activity" and "refrain from provocative actions."[97] Israel's annexation of East Jerusalem after the 1967 war was "not recognized by the international community," and its ultimate status must be determined through negotiations between the parties, the Quartet's statement added.

In the end, Netanyahu agreed the 1,600 new homes would not be built in East Jerusalem for two years, the U.S. State Department announced.[98] At the same time, Palestinian Authority President Mahmoud Abbas promised to "work against incitement of any sort," according to a State Department statement. "As both parties know, if either takes significant actions during the proximity talks that we judge would seriously undermine trust," the statement said, "we will . . . hold them accountable and ensure that negotiations continue."

An even earlier U.S. drive for a resumption of talks was thrown off by a statement by Secretary of State Clinton. Rejecting a settlement freeze, Netanyahu in the fall of 2009 had offered instead to show restraint, and only in the West Bank—by limiting building there to some 3,000 settler homes that Israel had already approved. During a one-day visit to Israel on Oct. 31, 2009, Clinton praised Netanyahu's offer as "unprecedented" and said talks should resume so his offer could be examined.[99]

The Palestinians reacted angrily to the apparent policy shift. Before talks could be revived, all settlement activity must halt, Palestinian negotiator Erekat said. "Pressuring Palestinians to make further concessions to accommodate Israeli intransigence is not the answer."[100]

While the Obama administration pushed for new peace talks, the Israeli government was grappling with a broad international effort to denounce the Jewish state over its December 2008 invasion of Gaza. A September 2009 report—based on a U.N. fact-finding investigation led by South African jurist Richard Goldstone—accused both the Israeli army and Palestinian militants of war crimes and possibly crimes against humanity.[101]

The 575-page report, commissioned by the Geneva-based U.N. Human Rights Council, faulted the Israeli military for its war tactics and faulted Palestinian militants for triggering the incursion by firing rockets at civilian Israeli areas with no military targets. It recommended that both conduct full and independent investigations of the allegations. Israel did not cooperate with the U.N. inquiry and rejected the report as one-sided. Israel said it had launched the war in self-defense after being repeatedly attacked, complaining that the report did not sufficiently fault Hamas' use of civilians as human shields. Israel also said it was investigating various individual incidents by its own soldiers that had been brought to its attention. Hamas said it would look into the allegations but insisted that Palestinian militants, like the Israeli forces, had acted in self-defense.[102] Washington, after three days of silence on the report, concluded it was unfair to Israel.[103]

In October 2009, the U.N. Human Rights Council censured Israel without referring to any Hamas wrongdoing. The vote was 25 to six, with 11 abstentions. China and Russia backed the measure, while the United States voted against it. Four nations did not vote, including France and Britain.[104] In November, the U.N. General Assembly voted 114–18 with 44 abstentions to ask both sides for an independent investigation.[105] The United States voted against the measure.

Neither side has complied, but Goldstone said on May 3 that if the two sides do not make good-faith investigations into the report's findings, the U.N. could refer its findings to the International Criminal Court (ICC) in The Hague. "That is still a course open to it and if adopted and implemented in good faith, would effectively put an end to calls for international criminal investigations." [106]

Earlier that year during a June speech in Cairo, Egypt, President Obama had called for peaceful co-existence between Muslims and the West and declared to the Arab world his ambition for a two-state solution to the

Arab-Israeli stalemate. "The only resolution is for the aspirations of both sides to be met through two states, where Israelis and Palestinians each live in peace and security," Obama said. "That is in Israel's interest, Palestine's interest, America's interest and the world's interest. And that is why I intend to personally pursue this outcome with all the patience and dedication that the task requires."[107]

While most praised the speech, political science Professor Eytan Gilboa at Bar-Ilan University in Tel Aviv said that while he agrees with Obama's call for a two-state solution, "Israelis will need to be convinced that they'll be living next to a Palestinian state that isn't Hamastan."[108]

He also chided Obama for his lack of attention to the Iranian nuclear issues, calling his inattentiveness a problem for both sides. "It seemed like Iran's nuclear issue was low on his priorities, and that's a main problem not just for Israelis but Arabs, too."[109]

Shortly after Obama entered the White House in January 2009, Israel began pressing him to make Iran's suspected pursuit of nuclear arms his top Middle East priority, arguing that Tehran was a greater threat to global security than the Israeli-Palestinian conflict. Fearing an Israeli military strike against Iranian nuclear facilities, which might further destabilize the oil-rich region, Washington pressed Israel for time to seek a diplomatic solution to the Iran problem. Obama focused his efforts on further tightening international sanctions already imposed on Tehran by the U.N. Security Council in three stages over the years, and the Security Council obliged on June 9, 2010, with a fourth round of sanctions.[110]

But Iran appeared no closer to agreeing to a diplomatic solution to the impasse.[111] Tehran was resisting, despite widespread anti-government protests after the June 12, 2009, re-election of President Mahmoud Ahmadinejad.[112] Ahmadinejad won by a landslide, but opposition candidates said the election was rigged.

In April 2010, President Obama hosted leaders from 47 nations—as well as the United Nations and European Union—for a two-day Nuclear Security Summit aimed at addressing the safeguarding of weapons-grade uranium and plutonium and the prevention of nuclear terrorism by states such as Iran.[113] Israeli Prime Minister Benjamin Netanyahu canceled his plans to attend the Summit—sending Deputy Prime Minister Dan Meridor in his stead—amid anticipated pressure for Israel to sign the Nuclear Non-Proliferation Treaty (NPT), which would oblige it to get rid of its unacknowledged nuclear arsenal.

Asked after the summit about Israel's reported nuclear stockpile, Obama urged Israel to sign the NPT but stopped short of criticizing its ambitions. "And as far as Israel goes, I'm not going to comment on their program," he said. "What I'm going to point to is the fact that consistently we have urged all countries to become members of the NPT."[114]

A U.N. meeting of 189 nations on the NPT, held in New York the next month, adopted with U.S. support a declaration calling for an international conference in 2012 to begin work on the creation of "a Middle East zone free of nuclear weapons and all other weapons of mass destruction."[115]

NOTES

1. "Israeli TV airs Gaza doctor's pleas after children killed," Israel's Channel 10 via YouTube, www.youtube.com/watch?v=OLUJ4fF2HN4.

2. " 'I wept,' Olmert says of death of Gaza children," Reuters, Jan. 23, 2009, www.reuters.com/article/latestCrisis/idUSLN571480.

3. "Agency Says Hamas Took Aid Intended for Needy," *The New York Times*, Feb. 5, 2009, www.nytimes.com/2009/02/05/world/middleeast/05mideast.html?ref=world.

4. "Summary of Rocket Fire and Mortar Shelling in 2008," Intelligence and Terrorism Information Center, Jan. 1, 2009, www.terrorism-info.org.il/malam_multimedia/English/eng_n/pdf/ipc_e007.pdf.

5. "Obama's Speech in Sderot, Israel," *The New York Times*, July 23, 2008, www.nytimes.com/2008/07/23/us/politics/23text-obama.html?ref=politics.

6. "PCHR Contests Distortion of Gaza Strip Death Toll," Palestinian Centre for Human Rights, press release 44/2009, March 26, 2009, www.pchrgaza.org/files/PressR/English/2008/44-2009.html.

7. "Israel challenges Palestinian claims on Gaza death toll," Ynetnews, March 26, 2009, www.ynetnews.com/articles/0,7340,L-3692950,00.html.

8. "Remarks With Israeli Foreign Minister Tzipi Livni: Hillary Rodham Clinton, Secretary of State,"

Jerusalem, March 3, 2009, U.S. Department of State transcript, www.state.gov/secretary/rm/2009a/03/119956.htm.

9. Dan Williams, "Israel fends off censure over Gaza civilian deaths," Reuters, Jan. 19, 2009, http://uk.reuters.com/article/usTopNews/idUKTRE50I2LU20090119.

10. Paul Rogers, "Gaza — The Aftermath," Oxford Research Group, January 2009, www.oxfordresearchgroup.org.uk/publications/monthly_briefings/2009/02/gaza-aftermath.html.

11. "Gaza: situation at border crossings 'intolerable,' Ban says," U.N. Department of Public Information, March 10, 2009, www.un.org/apps/news/story.asp?NewsID=30138&Cr=gaza&Cr1=.

12. "Transcript: Obama's interview with Al Arabiya," Al Arabiya News Channel, Jan. 27, 2009, www.alarabiya.net/articles/2009/01/27/65096.html.

13. "Iranian President Stands by Call to Wipe Israel Off Map," *The New York Times*, Oct. 29, 2005, www.nytimes.com/2005/10/29/international/middleeast/29iran.html.

14. Howard Schneider and Glenn Kessler, "Israel Puts Iran Issue Ahead of Palestinians," *The Washington Post*, April 22, 2009, www.washingtonpost.com/wp-dyn/content/article/2009/04/21/AR2009042103998.html?hpid=topnews.

15. "Text of U.S. President George W. Bush's Middle East speech," June 24, 2002, www.bitterlemons.org/docs/bush.html.

16. Robert Pear, "White House Puts Onus on Hamas to End Violence," *The New York Times*, Dec. 28, 2008, www.nytimes.com/2008/12/28/world/middleeast/28diplo.html.

17. Katrin Bennhold, "Leaders of Turkey and Israel Clash at Davos Panel," *The New York Times*, Jan. 29, 2009, www.nytimes.com/2009/01/30/world/europe/30clash.html.

18. See, for example, John J. Mearsheimer and Stephen M. Walt, *The Israel Lobby and U.S. Foreign Policy* (2007).

19. "Israel's U.N. envoy calls Jimmy Carter 'bigot,'" Reuters, April 24, 2008, www.reuters.com/article/politicsNews/idUSN2448131520080425.

20. "A Performance-Based Road Map to a Permanent Two-State Solution to the Israeli-Palestinian Conflict," the Quartet (of the United States, the European Union, the United Nations and Russia), April 30, 2003, www.bitterlemons.org/docs/roadmap3.html.

21. "Declaration of Principles on Interim Self-Government Arrangements," Government of the State of Israel and the P.L.O. Team, Sept. 13, 1993, www.bitterlemons.org/docs/dop.html. Also see "Israel-PLO Recognition: Exchange of Letters between PM Rabin and Chairman Arafat — Sept. 9, 1993," Israel Ministry of Foreign Affairs, www.mfa.gov.il/MFA/Peace+Process/Guide+to+the+Peace+Process/Israel-PLO+Recognition+-+Exchange+of+Letters+bet we.htm.

22. "Text of U.S. President George W. Bush's Middle East speech," *op. cit.*

23. Muammar Qaddafi, "The One-State Solution," *The New York Times*, Jan. 22, 2009, www.nytimes.com/2009/01/22/opinion/22qaddafi.html.

24. Shahar Ilan and Barak Ravid, "Olmert warns of binational state if no peace deal reached," *Haaretz.com*, Sept. 16, 2008, *Haaretz.com*, www.haaretz.com/hasen/spages/1021689.html.

25. "Remarks With Israeli Foreign Minister Tzipi Livni: Hillary Rodham Clinton, Secretary of State," *op. cit.*

26. "Quartet Statement," *London*, Jan. 30, 2006, www.un.org/news/dh/infocus/middle_east/quartet-30jan2006.htm.

27. "Secretary Clinton, Palestinian President Abbas in Ramallah," transcript of joint press conference, March 4, 2009, www.america.gov/st/texttrans-english/2009/March/20090304125709eaifas0.3768885.html?CP.rss=true.

28. "Kofi Annan's speech to the General Assembly," *The Guardian*, Sept. 13, 2002, www.guardian.co.uk/world/2002/sep/13/iraq.united nations1.

29. "Israel's road map reservations," *Haaretz.com*, May 27, 2003, www.haaretz.com/hasen/pages/ShArt.jhtml?itemNo=297230.

30. "Intifada toll 2000-2005," BBC News, Feb. 8, 2005, http://news.bbc.co.uk/2/hi/middle_east/3694350.stm.

31. "The Sharm el-Sheikh Fact-Finding Committee," April 30, 2001, www.al-bab.com/arab/docs/pal/mitchell1.htm.

32. "Secret UN report condemns US for Middle East failures," *The Guardian*, June 13, 2007, www.guardian.co.uk/world/2007/jun/13/usa.israel.

33. Stephen Walt, "What do we do if the 'two-state' solution collapses?" *ForeignPolicy.com*, Feb. 10, 2009, http://walt.foreignpolicy.com/posts/2009/02/10/what_do_we_do_if_the_two_state_solution_collapses.

34. "Settlement population," based on figures obtained from Israel's Central Bureau of Statistics and the Jerusalem Statistical Yearbook, *B'tselem*, www.btselem.org/English/Settlements/Settlement_population.xls.

35. "Statement by Ambassador Susan E. Rice, U.S. Permanent Representative, Middle East Consultations in the Security Council," Feb. 18, 2009, www.usun newyork.usmission.gov/press_releases/20090218_031.html.

36. See Rogers, *op. cit.*

37. Transcript of press conference by Secretary General Ban Ki-moon, U.N. headquarters, Feb. 10, 2009, www.un.org/News/Press/docs/2009/sgsm12092.doc.htm.

38. Alvaro de Soto, "Few will thank UN when this war ends," *The Independent*, Jan. 16, 2009, www.independent.co.uk/opinion/commentators/alvaro de-soto-few-will-thank-un-when-this-war-ends-1380408.html.

39. Hillary Rodham Clinton, "Press Availability at the End of the Gaza Reconstruction Conference," Sharm el-Sheik, Egypt, March 2, 2009, www.state.gov/secretary/rm/2009a/03/119929.htm.

40. "Secretary Clinton, Palestinian President Abbas in Ramallah," *op. cit.*

41. "Hamas's popularity rises after Israel's Gaza war," Reuters, March 9, 2009, www.reuters.com/article/worldNews/idUSTRE52841Q20090309.

42. Yossi Alpher, "Not now," bitterlemons.org, March 2, 2009, www.bitterlemons.org/previous/bl020309ed9.html#isr1.

43. For background, see the following *CQ Researchers*: Peter Katel, "Middle East Tensions," Oct. 27, 2006, pp. 889-912; Nicole Gaouette, "Middle East Peace," Jan. 21, 2005, pp. 53-76; and David Masci, "Prospects for Mideast Peace," Aug. 30, 2002, pp. 673-696.

44. This section is drawn from Reinhard Schulze, *A Modern History of the Islamic World* (2002); Thomas L. Friedman, *From Beirut to Jerusalem* (1989); Ali M. Ansari, *Confronting Iran: The Failure of American Foreign Policy and the Next Great Conflict in the Middle East* (2006); and Walter Laqueur, *A History of Zionism* (2003).

45. See, for example, Daniel Williams, "New Conflicts of Historic Interest Rack the Heart of the Holy Land," *Los Angeles Times*, May 14, 1989, Part 5, p. 2; Joel Greenberg, "Israel's History, Viewed Candidly, Starts a Storm," *The New York Times*, April 10, 1998, p. A8.

46. Figures from Jeremy M. Sharp, author of two Congressional Research Service reports: "Egypt: Background and U.S. Relations," March 26, 2009, and "U.S. Foreign Aid to Israel," Feb. 3, 2009.

47. "Declaration of Principles on Interim Self-Government Arrangements," *op cit.*

48. "Q & A: Leaving Lebanon," BBC, May 23, 2000, http://news.bbc.co.uk/1/hi/world/middle_east/636594.stm.

49. Jane Perlez and Elaine Sciolino, "High Drama and Hard Talks at Camp David, Against Backdrop of History," *The New York Times*, July 29, 2000, www.nytimes.com/2000/07/29/world/high-drama-and-hard-talks-at-camp-david-against-backdrop-of-history.html.

50. See, for example, Hussein Agha and Robert Malley, "Camp David: The Tragedy of Errors," *The New York Review of Books*, Aug. 9, 2001, www.nybooks.com/articles/14380.

51. "The Mitchell Report," May 4, 2001, www.jewish-virtuallibrary.org/jsource/Peace/Mitchellrep.html.

52. Yoav Peled, "Dual War: The Legacy of Ariel Sharon," *Middle East Report Online*, March 22, 2006, www.merip.org/mero/mero032206.html.

53. Text of U.S. President George W. Bush's Middle East speech, *op. cit.*

54. "Security Council Adopts Resolution Endorsing Road Map Leading Towards Two-State Resolution of Israeli-Palestinian Conflict," U.N. Security Council press release SC/7924, Nov. 19, 2003, www.un.org/News/Press/docs/2003/sc7924.doc.htm.

55. See, for example, "Bush Says US Not At War With Islam," *Sky News*, Sept. 20, 2006, http://news.sky.com/skynews/Home/Sky-News-Archive/Article/20080641234424.

56. See, for example, Greg Myre, "Envoy in Mideast Peace Effort Says Israel Is Keeping Too Tight a Lid on Palestinians in Gaza," *The New York Times*, Oct. 25, 2005, www.nytimes.com/2005/10/25/international/middleeast/25mideast.html.

57. Greg Myre, "Because of Attacks, Israel Declares Part of Gaza Off Limits," *The New York Times*, Dec. 29, 2005, www.nytimes.com/2005/12/29/international/middleeast/29mideast.html.

58. "Quartet Statement," *op. cit.*

59. "Hamas takes full control of Gaza," BBC, June 15, 2007, http://news.bbc.co.uk/2/hi/middle_east/6755299.stm.

60. "Why They Died: Civilian Casualties in Lebanon during the 2006 War," Human Rights Watch, Sept. 5, 2007, www.hrw.org/en/reports/2007/09/05/why-they-died-0.

61. Laila Bassam, "Lebanon forms unity government with Hezbollah," Reuters, July 11, 2008, www.reuters.com/article/homepageCrisis/idUSL1159875._CH_.2400.

62. Sheryl Gay Stolberg, "Peace? Sure, I'll See What I Can Do," *The New York Times*, Dec. 2, 2007, http://query.nytimes.com/gst/fullpage.html?res=9802E5D61638F931A35751C1A9619C8B63.

63. "Adopting Text on Middle East Conflict, Security Council Reaffirms Support for Annapolis Outcomes, Declares Negotiations 'Irreversible,' " press release SC/9539, U.N. Department of Public Information, Dec. 16, 2008, www.un.org/News/Press/docs/2008/sc9539.doc.htm.

64. "President Obama Discusses Mideast During Visit of Jordan's King Abdullah," CQ Transcriptswire, April 21, 2009, www.cqpolitics.com/wmspage.cfm?parm1=5&docID=news-000003099340.

65. "Efforts to end current Gaza 'impasse' imperative — UN political chief," U.N. News Centre, March 25, 2009, www.un.org/apps/news/story.asp?NewsID=30290&Cr=gaza&Cr1=.

66. U.N. Undersecretary-General for Political Affairs Lynn Pascoe, "Briefing to the Security Council on the Situation in the Middle East," April 20, 2009, http://domino.un.org/UNISPAL.NSF/e872be-638a09135185256ed100546ae4/b24712e38d4c2a0a8525759f004bc662!OpenDocument.

67. "Peace with Israel possible, says Syria's Assad," Reuters, March 9, 2009, www.reuters.com/article/worldNews/idUSTRE5281NL20090309.

68. "Background Note: Syria," U.S. Department of State Web site, www.state.gov/r/pa/ei/bgn/3580.htm. Also see "State Sponsors of Terrorism Overview," U.S. Department of State, April 30, 2008, www.state.gov/s/ct/rls/crt/2007/103711.htm.

69. "Remarks With Israeli Foreign Minister Tzipi Livni: Hillary Rodham Clinton, Secretary of State," *op. cit.*

70. Schneider and Kessler, *op. cit.*

71. Jeffrey Heller, "Netanyahu says will negotiate peace with the Palestinians," Reuters, March 25, 2009, www.reuters.com/article/middleeastCrisis/idUSLP254174.

72. "Israel/Gaza: International Investigation Essential," Human Rights Watch, Jan. 27, 2009, www.hrw.org/en/news/2009/01/27/israelgaza-international-investigation-essential.

73. Stephanie Nebehay, "U.N. rights envoy sees Israeli war crimes in Gaza," Reuters, March 20, 2009, www.reuters.com/article/middleeastCrisis/idUSLJ155314.

74. "Richard J. Goldstone Appointed to Lead Human Rights Council Fact-Finding Mission on Gaza Conflict," U.N. Human Rights Council, press release, April 3, 2009, www.unhchr.ch/huricane/huricane.nsf/view01/2796E2CA43CA4D94C125758D002F8D25?opendocument.

75. "Settlement Population," *op. cit.*

76. "The situation in the Middle East, including the Palestinian question," U.N. Security Council, Feb. 18, 2009, http://domino.un.org/UNISPAL.NSF/e872be638a09135185256ed100546ae4/44906205538f760085257562004be029!OpenDocument.

77. See Barak Ravid, "Netanyahu aides fear 'surprise' demands from Obama," *Haaretz.com*, May 2, 2009, www.haaretz.com/hasen/spages/1082144.html.

78. "Briefing to the Security Council on the situation in the Middle East," April 20, 2009, http://domino.un.org/UNISPAL.NSF/e872be638a09135185256ed100546ae4/b24712e38d4c2a0a8525759f004bc662!OpenDocument.

79. Quoted in Taghreed El-Khodary and Ethan Bronner, "Addressing U.S., Hamas says it Grounded Rockets," *The New York Times*, May 5, 2009, p. A5, www.nytimes.com/2009/05/05/world/middleeast/05meshal.html?_r=1&ref=world.

80. "Israel deports flotilla activists after world outcry," Reuters, June 1, 2010, www.reuters.com/article/idUSTRE65005R20100601.

81. "Operation Mini Cast Lead," *Haaretz.com*, June 1, 2010, www.haaretz.com/print-edition/news/operation-mini-cast-lead-1.293417.

82. "Transcript: Obama's interview with Al Arabiya," *Al Arabiya News Channel*, Jan. 27, 2009, www.alarabiya.net/articles/2009/01/27/6507.html.

83. "No R. Shlomo building for 2 years," *The Jerusalem Post*, May 10, 2010, www.jpost.com/MiddleEast/Article.aspx?id=175134.

84. "Remarks by the President to the United Nations General Assembly," Office of the Press Secretary, White House, Sept. 23, 2009, www.whitehouse.gov/the-press-office/remarks-president-united-nations-general-assembly.

85. Allyn Fisher-Ilan, "U.S. envoy, Netanyahu hold inconclusive talks," Reuters, May 5, 2010, http://uk.reuters.com/article/idUKTRE6444V420100505.

86. "Al-Zahar says Israel, Hamas held 120 rounds of talks," *Ynetnews.com*, April 28, 2010, www.ynetnews.com/articles/0,7340,L-3882178,00.html.

87. Secretary of State Hillary Rodham Clinton, "Remarks at the Dedication of the S. Daniel Abraham Center for Middle East Peace," U.S. Department of State, April 15, 2010, www.state.gov/secretary/rm/2010/04/140297.htm.

88. *Ibid.*

89. Aron Heller, "Israel's PM welcomes progress toward peace talks," *Guardian.co.uk*, May 2, 2010, www.guardian.co.uk/world/feedarticle/9057632.

90. Mark Landler, "Clinton Rebukes Israel on Housing Announcement," *The New York Times*, March 12, 2010, www.nytimes.com2010/03/13/world/middleeast/13diplo.html.

91. As quoted by Laura Rozen, "Joe Biden delivers 'hardest truth' in Israel," *Politico.com*, March 12, 2010, www.politico.com/news/stories/0310/34300_Page2.html#ixzz0mcownExA.

92. David Sanger and Isabel Kershner, "U.S. Mulls Own Plan for Mideast Talks," *The New York Times*, March 17, 2010, www.nytimes.com/2010/03/18/world/middleeast/18diplo.html.

93. Mark Landler, "Opportunity in a Fight with Israel," *The New York Times*, March 16, 2010, www.nytimes.com/2010/03/17/world/middleeast/17diplo.html.

94. Mark Landler, "Netanyahu Takes Hard Line on Jerusalem Housing," *The New York Times*, March 22, 2010, www.nytimes.com/2010/03/23/world/middleeast/23diplo.html.

95. Tony Karon, "Pressure Grows on U.S. to Tamp Down Its Spat with Israel," *Time.com*, March 17, 2010, www.time.com/time/world/article/0,8599,1972840,00.html.

96. *Ibid.*

97. "Joint Statement by the Quartet," full text, U.S. Department of State, March 19, 2010, www.state.gov/r/pa/prs/ps/2010/03/138583.htm.

98. "No R. Shlomo building for 2 years," *op. cit.*

99. Andrew Quinn and Alastair Macdonald, "Clinton urges Abbas to talk without settlement halt," Reuters, Oct. 31, 2009, www.reuters.com/article/idUSLV11497220091031.

100. Jeffrey Heller, "Palestinians accuse U.S. of killing peace prospects," Reuters, Nov. 1, 2009, www.reuters.com/article/idUSLV11497220091102.

101. Louis Charbonneau, "Evidence of Israel, Hamas war crimes in Gaza-UN," Reuters, Sept. 15, 2009, www .reuters.com/article/idUSN15401801. The Goldstone report is at www2.0hchr.org/english/bodies/hrcouncil/ specialsession/9/docs/UNFFMGC_Report.pdf.

102. Isabel Kershner, "Israel Rejects Call for Gaza Inquiry," *The New York Times,* Sept. 16, 2009, www.nytimes . com/2009/09/17/world/middleeast/17gaza.html.

103. "U.N. Study Is Called Unfair to Israel," *The New York Times,* Sept. 19, 2009, www.nytimes. com/2009/09/19/world/middleeast/19policy.html.

104. Laura MacInnis, "U.N. rights council criticizes Israel over Gaza," *Reuters.com,* Oct. 16, 2009, www .reuters.com/article/idUSLG308346.

105. Patrick Worsnip, "U.N. assembly votes for probes of Gaza war charges," *Reuters.com,* Nov. 5, 2009, www .reuters.com/article/idUSN05146640._CH_.2400.

106. "Israel Can Still Probe Gaza: Goldstone," *Times Live* (South Africa), May 4, 2010, www.timeslive .co.za/local/article433225.ece/Israel-can-still-probe-Gaza—Goldstone.

107. "Remarks by the President on a New Beginning," Office of the President, White House, June 4, 2009, www.whitehouse.gov/the_press_office/Remarks-by-the-President-at-Cairo-University-6-04-09/.

108. Jamil Hamad and Aaron J. Klein, "Speech Stirs Mixed Feelings in Holy Land," *Time,* June 4, 2009, www .time.com/time/world/article/0,8599,1902758,00 .html#ixzz0mtSfzRek.

109. *Ibid.*

110. "UN approves new sanctions on Iran," *BBC News,* March 4, 2008, http://news.bbc.co.uk/2/ hi/7274902.stm. Also see Colum Lynch, "U.N. Security Council approves Iran sanctions on 12 to 2 vote," *The Washington Post,* June 9, 2010, www .washingtonpost.com/wp-dyn/content/article/ 2010/06/09/AR2010060902876.html.

111. Matt Spetalnick and Ross Colvin, "U.S. sees sanctions by May; Iran lobbies against West," Reuters, April 22, 2010, www.reuters.com/article/idUS-TRE63L50020100422.

112. "Opposition leader says Iran in crisis—website," Reuters, April 25, 2010, www.reuters.com/article/ idUSHAF548447.

113. "Nuclear Security Summit," www.state.gov/nucle-arsummit/.

114. "Obama: All countries should join NPT," *Jerusalem Post,* April 14, 2010, www.jpost.com/International/ Article.aspx?id=173096.

115. Edith M. Lederer, "Israel key to conference on banning nuclear arms," The Associated Press, May 29, 2010, www.google.com/hostednews/ap/article/ ALeqM5iP_c47WRWDs-U5bRaYXA9xgrrmh-wD9G0MK900.

BIBLIOGRAPHY

Books

Hirst, David, *The Gun and the Olive Branch: The Roots of Violence in the Middle East,* **Nation Books, 2003.**
The Middle East correspondent for the *Manchester Guardian* traces the history of the Israeli-Palestinian conflict from the 1880s through the Sept. 11, 2001, terrorist attacks in the United States.

Indyk, Martin, *Innocent Abroad: An Intimate Account of American Peace Diplomacy in the Middle East,* **Simon & Schuster, 2009.**
A former U.S. ambassador to Israel dissects the successes and failures of President Bill Clinton's intensive and highly personal pursuit of a peace deal.

Khalidi, Rashid, *Sowing Crisis: The Cold War and American Dominance in the Middle East,* **Beacon Press, 2009.**
The director of Columbia University's Middle East Institute explores how George W. Bush's global war on terror spilled over into the Middle East.

Kurtzer, Daniel, and Scott Lasensky, *Negotiating Arab-Israeli Peace,* **United States Institute of Peace Press, 2008.**
A veteran U.S. diplomat and lecturer in Middle Eastern policy at Princeton University's Woodrow Wilson School of Public and International Affairs (Kurtzer) and a researcher at the U.S. Institute of Peace analyze two decades of U.S. peace efforts in the Middle East.

Miller, Aaron David, *The Much Too Promised Land: America's Elusive Search for Arab-Israeli Peace*, Bantam, 2008.

A former adviser on Middle East negotiations to six U.S. secretaries of state (1978-2003) provides a frank, insightful walk through decades of diplomacy in the region.

Oz, Amos, *A Tale of Love and Darkness*, Harcourt, 2004.

An Israeli writer traces his family history from 19th-century Ukraine to the Palestine of the 1930s to Jerusalem in the 1940s and '50s, illuminating some of the human drama leading to Israel's birth.

Tolan, Sandy, *The Lemon Tree: An Arab, A Jew, and the Heart of the Middle East*, Bloomsbury, 2007.

A journalist and producer of radio documentaries views the Middle East crisis through the eyes of two families — one Arab and one Jewish — that lived at different times in a house near Tel Aviv with a lemon tree in its garden.

Articles

"Timeline: Israel, the Gaza Strip and Hamas," *The New York Times*, Jan. 4, 2009, www.nytimes.com/interactive/2009/01/04/world/20090104_ISRAEL-HAMAS_TIME LINE.html.

This interactive Web-based timeline traces the history of Israel and the Gaza Strip from Israel's statehood to the withdrawal of Israeli troops from Gaza on Jan. 21, 2009.

Qaddafi, Muammar, "The One-State Solution," *The New York Times*, Jan. 22, 2009, www.nytimes.com/2009/01/22/opinion/22qaddafi.html.

The Libyan leader argues that Israelis and Palestinians will never find peace until they band together in a single state he calls "Isratine."

Walt, Stephen, "What do we do if the 'two-state' solution collapses?" ForeignPolicy.com, Feb. 10, 2009.

A professor of international relations at Harvard University argues that U.S. support for Palestinian statehood makes it sound reasonable and moderate without actually having to do anything to bring about that goal.

Reports and Studies

"Israeli settlements in the Occupied Palestinian Territory, including Jerusalem, and the occupied Syrian Golan: Report of the Secretary-General," U.N. General Assembly, Nov. 5, 2008.

This annual report documents Israeli settlement activity through mid-2008 and recommends steps for both Israel and the Palestinians to comply with international law.

"The Middle East Quartet: A Progress Report," CARE, Christian Aid, Oxfam, Save the Children Alliance, World Vision, et al., Sept. 25, 2008, www.reliefweb.int/rw/rwb.nsf/db900sid/VDUX-7JSSZD.

This report by a consortium of nongovernmental relief organizations finds that the Quartet of international Middle East mediators falls short in addressing an ongoing humanitarian crisis in Palestinian areas.

"The Six Months of the Lull Arrangement," Intelligence and Terrorism Information Center, December 2008, www.terrorism-info.org.il/malam_multimedia/English/eng_n/pdf/hamas_e017.pdf.

This report by an Israeli nongovernmental organization documents Palestinian rocket and mortar fire into southern Israel from Gaza during 2008. Includes many color photos and charts.

Migdalovitz, Carol, "Israeli-Arab Negotiations: Background, Conflicts, and U.S. Policy," Congressional Research Service, updated March 9, 2009.

A Middle East expert documents decades of efforts to find a peaceful solution to the region's longest-running conflict.

For More Information

American Israel Public Affairs Committee, 440 First St., N.W., Suite 600, Washington, DC 20001; (202) 639-5200; www.aipac.org. Widely known as AIPAC, the leading lobbying group for Israel in the United States.

Bitterlemons.org; www.bitterlemons.org. Presents weekly commentary from both the Palestinian and Israeli point of view on key developments in the Middle East conflict; features a helpful archive of key historic documents dating back to 1947.

B'Tselem, 8 HaTa'asiya St. (4th Floor), P.O. Box 53132, Jerusalem 91531, Israel; (972-2) 673-5599; www.btselem .org/English. Leading Israeli human-rights organization that seeks to document human-rights violations in the occupied territories and to promote the protection of Palestinians' human rights.

Intelligence and Terrorism Information Center, Maj. General Aharon Yariv Blvd., P.O. Box 3555, Ramat Hasharon 47134, Israel; (972-3) 760-3579; www.terror-ism-info.org.il/. A private organization focuses on issues linked to terrorism and intelligence; reports available on its Web site on a broad range of related topics including Palestinian policies concerning terrorism, Palestinian groups it considers terrorist groups, terrorism-related activities in other countries including Syria and Iran and global terrorism financing mechanisms.

J Street, Washington, D.C.; (202) 248-5870; http://jstreet .org/. Launched in April 2008; a nongovernmental organization that represents Americans who support both a secure Jewish homeland and a sovereign Palestinian state; advocates strong U.S. leadership to end the Arab-Israeli and Israeli-Palestinian conflicts through diplomatic rather than military means.

Jerusalem Center for Public Affairs, Beit Milken, 13 Tel Hai St., Jerusalem 92107, Israel; (972-2) 561-9281; http:// jcpa.org. A private, nonprofit Israeli think tank that focuses on analysis of various global challenges facing Israel, including Islamic extremism and global anti-Semitism. The group's president, Dore Gold, is a close associate of Israel's new prime minister, Benjamin Netanyahu.

Oxford Research Group, Development House, 56-64 Leonard St., London EC2A 4LT; (44-20) 7549-0298; www.oxfordresearchgroup.org.uk. Independent British think tank that promotes nonviolent resolution of international conflicts, with a special focus on the Middle East.

Palestinian Centre for Human Rights, 29 Omar EL Mukhtar St., Near Amal Hotel, P.O. Box 1328 Gaza City; (972-8) 282-4776 or (972-8) 282-5893; www.pchrgaza. org. Private nonprofit organization dedicated to protecting human rights and promoting the rule of law and democratic principles in the occupied Palestinian territories. It has branch offices in the West Bank town of Ramallah and three in the Gaza Strip.

United Nations, First Avenue at 46th St., New York, NY 10017; (212) 963-1234; www.un.org/english. Supports Middle East programs ranging from economic development and humanitarian aid to human rights, peacekeeping and diplomacy. Its Web site has two main sections devoted to the region, on U.N.-related Middle East news (www.un.org/ apps/news/infocusRel.asp?infocusID=22&Body=middle& Body1=east) and on Palestinian programs (http://un.org/ Depts/dpa/qpal/).

9

Evaluating Microfinance

Sarah Glazer

Nolberta Melara of San Marcos, El Salvador, sells her homemade embroidered aprons in shops across the country. She got her start with a $30 loan from a nonprofit microlender. Since the first microfinance bank was established in 1983, thousands of banks and credit cooperatives around the world have been created to help small entrepreneurs. Supporters say microloans lift millions out of poverty, but critics say lenders' exorbitant rates lure many borrowers deeper into debt and may even be creating a microcredit bubble.

From *CQ Researcher*,
April, 2010.

AFP/Getty Images/Yuri Cortez

Two years ago, Siyawati, a mother of three, lived on a meager income brought in by her husband's work as a construction day laborer in Uttar Pradesh, India's most populous state. Then she got a $212 microfinance loan from SKS India, the country's largest microfinance institution, and invested it in a candle-making machine. That enabled her to increase the number of candles she was making for sale.

Since then, with the help of additional microloans, her small business has become a small factory employing eight people. Her monthly income has risen from $42 to $425, permitting her to send her children to a good school. "She is proud that her expertise could bring her family out of poverty" reports SKS' Web site.[1]

This is the promise of microfinance: helping to end poverty and spur economic development one entrepreneur at a time by offering microloans — typically averaging a few hundred dollars — to help the impoverished, especially women, who lack collateral for a conventional loan. Popular among philanthropists for nearly 30 years, the movement has become increasingly attractive in recent years to equity funds, foreign investors and profit-making banks, drawn by the industry's extraordinary returns on investment, largely due to its high interest and repayment rates of up to 98 percent.[2]

Microlenders' high annual interest rates — averaging around 30 percent but sometimes reaching more than 100 percent — result from the added cost of sending an agent to collect weekly payments on very small loans, often to remote villages. However, microloans are generally lower-cost and more reliable than those offered by the

217

Few People in Poor Nations Have Bank Loans

In the world's poorest nations, largely in sub-Saharan Africa, fewer than 5 percent of adults hold bank loans. Credit is more available in China, India and other African countries, where about one in three adults receives a loan. By contrast eight out of 10 adults in the U.S., Japan, Australia and Western Europe have bank loans.

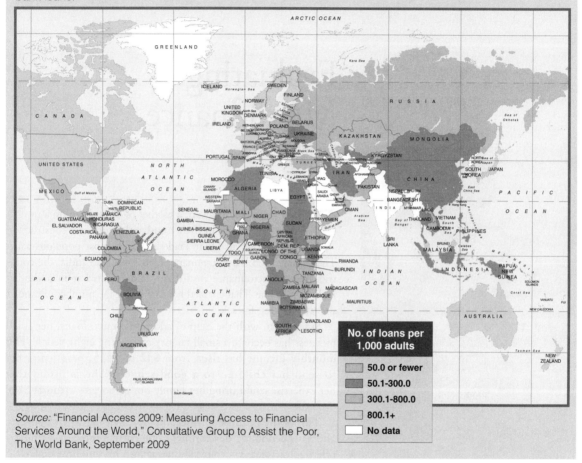

No. of loans per 1,000 adults

- 50.0 or fewer
- 50.1-300.0
- 300.1-800.0
- 800.1+
- No data

Source: "Financial Access 2009: Measuring Access to Financial Services Around the World," Consultative Group to Assist the Poor, The World Bank, September 2009

moneylenders that many poor villagers and slum-dwellers have depended on for decades.

Countless stories like Siyawati's have attracted billions of dollars in loans — more than $44 billion worldwide in 2008, according to one estimate — creating an average growth rate of 34 percent since 2003.[3]

The idea of microcredit finds its roots in Nobel Prize-winning economist Muhammad Yunus' discovery that even very poor people with no collateral, who would never qualify for a bank loan, could be amazingly

diligent in repaying loans. The key, according to Yunus, was for borrowers to band together in small groups of neighbors and guarantee one another's loans. So effective was microcredit as an economic engine in improving the livelihoods of the poor, Yunus famously predicted that it would help create a world where "poverty museums" would be the only place to see poverty.[4]

But increasingly, these cheery anecdotes have been mixed with more disturbing tales of exorbitant interest rates and strong-armed debt recovery practices. Some borrowers who can't make their microloan payments resort to extortionist moneylenders who charge even higher interest rates, sending the borrower ever deeper into debt. Even Yunus' renowned peer-pressure approach has its down side: Members of some neighborhood lending clubs have been known to haul off delinquent debtors' property, attack their houses and ostracize them from their communities.

Malcolm Harper, chairman of M-CRIL, an India-based financial rating company for microfinance lenders, tells of an Indian woman he met in a small village east of Hyderabad. Like many microborrowers, she had taken out a small loan, not for business purposes but to pay for her sister's medical care. Then her husband became ill. When she fell behind on her repayments, the other group members locked her and her young daughters out of their hut. After living on the road for days, she despaired and tried to throw herself and her children into the village well. She was stopped just in time when someone pointed out that she had enough savings with the group to pay off her loan. Her debt was cleared but she was expelled from the group.[5]

The rapid growth of the microfinance sector in recent years and its growing attraction to Western investors have awakened fears that microfinance could create a credit "bubble" akin to the recent U.S. subprime loan craze. Some experts fear that as microfinance institutions seek to reach even more borrowers, especially in areas like southern India where numerous microlenders operate, poor people will be encouraged to take out yet more loans, miring them in a cycle of debt they can never repay.

Microfinance "has put hundreds of millions of people into deeper debt than they were," says Harper. "Now that microfinance is becoming fashionable and profitable, a lot more companies are entering the field, and that leads to overborrowing just like it did with house owners in

Microlending Totaled at Least $44 Billion

At least $44.2 billion was loaned in 2008 to 86 million impoverished borrowers, mainly in Latin America, Eastern Europe and Central Asia. The loans were made by the 1,400 microfinance institutions (MFIs) — nonprofit organizations, regulated financial institutions and commercial banks — that are tracked by the Microfinance Information Exchange (MIX).

Total MFI Outstanding Loans
(in $ billions)

Sub-Saharan Africa	$3.3
East Asia and Pacific	$8.2
Eastern Europe and Central Asia	$10.0
Latin America	$16.7
Middle East and North Africa	$1.2
South Asia	$4.7
All Regions	$44.2

Source: "Microfinance at a Glance — 2008," Microfinance Information Exchange, Dec. 31, 2009

Indianapolis" during the giddy days of subprime mortgages, he maintains. "People are borrowing more than they can afford; it is over-indebting people, and they pay Peter from what they borrow from Paul" — often the high-priced local moneylender.

Because borrowers rarely report their outstanding moneylender debts to microfinance lenders, they may look like better credit risks than they are. Some analysts believe the still-thriving moneylender loans are keeping microcredit loans afloat.[6]

"We fear a bubble," Jacques Grivel of Luxembourg-based Finethic, an investment fund that raises money from institutional investors to channel to microfinance lenders in Latin America, Eastern Europe and Asia, recently told *The Wall Street Journal.* "Too much money is chasing too few good candidates."[7]

But many experts in the field point out that if there really were a credit bubble, it would have had plenty of time over the past 25 years to burst. Instead, microborrowers have consistently maintained high repayment rates. As abusive as it may get, the borrowing group's collective guarantee — known as "solidarity lending" — usually gets people to repay their loans on time. The borrowers want to maintain access to a highly valued service — reliable loans at lower interest rates than are offered by their local moneylenders.

Yet some fear that for-profit companies will themselves become "microloan sharks," and will charge exorbitant interest, focusing more on profits than on helping the poor, in the words of Jonathan C. Lewis, chair and founder of the nonprofit MicroCredit Enterprises, which makes loans to microlenders.

The commercial industry responds that as more capital and competition enter this market, interest rates will likely come down and more impoverished borrowers can be reached. "There will never be enough donor money to solve the world's ills. We need to find market-driven solutions," says Joan Trant, executive director of the New York-based International Association of Microfinance Investors.

Some question the very premise of microcredit — that it offers an escape from poverty — arguing that China-style economic growth and factory jobs offer the better solution. Defenders respond that while microcredit may not lift everybody completely out of poverty, it has been crucial in tiding families over during economic emergencies like health crises.

For the poorest families, "It's a buffer to prevent them from totally collapsing — going into destitution," says Geeta Rao Gupta, president of the International Center for Research on Women, in Washington, D.C. On that score, critics and supporters alike are starting to emphasize ways to help the poor build savings accounts — which may be more appropriate than expensive loans for tiding families over in emergencies.

In 2005, the international charity Catholic Relief Services announced it would divest its holdings in microcredit and focus on savings. Microcredit was making poor borrowers "poor twice" through high interest rates, in the words of Kim Wilson, former director of the organization's microfinance unit.[8]

Wilson, now a lecturer at Tufts University's Fletcher School, says she was disturbed by the "vigilante" enforcement of loan repayments by fellow borrowers. And she was uncomfortable with microcredit's traditional formula of giving borrowers a new loan as soon as they repaid the old one — leading to a "treadmill" of debt, in her view.

Concerns about extortionist interest rates, deceptive information about the interest charged and abusive collection practices have spurred calls for the kind of consumer protection regulation common in the United States but rare in developing countries. The microfinance industry has taken several steps towards self-regulation — including voluntary codes of conduct and more transparent information about interest rates — in an effort to forestall government regulation.

Most economists believe microloans don't necessarily lift people out of poverty but that the loans help them "manage their poverty better," in the words of David Roodman, a research fellow at the Center for Global Development, in Washington, D.C., who is writing a book on microfinance and maintains a popular blog on the subject (http://blogs.cgdev.org/open_book/).

Microfinance gives the poor "a choice to do something to feed their kids and a chance to have a slightly better life," Lewis says. "We should stop romanticizing it." For the billion people who live on $1 a day, he says, "their economic development question is 'How do I feed my kids today? And do I?' And a lot of days they don't."

Increasingly experts agree that the more than 2 billion people living on less than $2 a day, most without access to banks, deserve access to financial services — not just loans but also savings accounts and insurance, which may help them even more in escaping poverty.[9]

As the industry, academia and the philanthropic world ponder the future of microfinance, here are some of the questions being debated:

Does microcredit help the poor, especially women, out of poverty?

When economist Yunus, the father of microfinance, started giving poor Bangladeshi villagers loans as an experiment in the 1970s, he made some startling discoveries that turned standard economic assumptions on their head. Noticing that even the poorest villages were beehives of small-scale trading, he questioned the conventional wisdom that creating jobs, rather than encouraging entrepreneurial activity, is the best way to help the poor.[10]

"An ever-expanding cycle of economic growth," he predicted, could be created by giving repeat loans to poor borrowers for productive enterprises.[11]

Making loans to women brought more benefits to the family than lending money to men, he discovered. "When men make money they tend to spend it on themselves" for items like drink and cigarettes, he said, "but when women make money they bring benefits to the whole family" by spending it on their children for schooling and better food.[12]

Yunus, who founded the Grameen Bank in 1983 specifically to make microloans, says "64 percent of our borrowers" who have been with the bank for five years or more have left poverty. By his own simple checklist, a family has risen out of poverty when it has a house with a tin roof, clean drinking water, warm clothes for winter and can afford to send all the children to school.[13]

Yet, according to some researchers, the claim that business microloans lift most families out of poverty is, on average, unfounded.

"Few live up to the mythology that their business grows and they climb out of poverty," says researcher Roodman. "The majority don't climb out of poverty but get some assistance in managing their poverty" by taking out loans that permit them to pay for school fees or medical and other household crises.

Two recent studies of microcredit borrowers, conducted by researchers at the Massachusetts Institute of Technology (MIT) and Yale University, found no improvement in household income or consumption — two standard measures of poverty.[14] Moreover, the researchers found, microcredit often helps men's businesses more than women's and is most helpful to those who already have businesses or are better-off to start with. (*See sidebar, p. 230.*)

Indeed, studies question almost every element of the famous Yunus narrative — from the dominant role of women to the focus on entrepreneurship. One study found that about half of loans made by Grameen Bank are not for business purposes at all, even though they were labeled as such, but go instead to household consumption, such as school fees or medical expenses.[15]

That raises the question: What types of desperate measures will impoverished borrowers take to pay the high interest rates, which can range from 20 percent to over 100 percent, if they're earning no profits? Some go to moneylenders, who charge even higher rates but can quickly produce the cash needed for a loan installment, according to *The Wall Street Journal*. The number of moneylenders in India rose 56 percent from 1995-2006, when microfinance was growing rapidly. "Group pressure makes us go to moneylenders," one woman told *The*

Bangladeshi economist Muhammad Yunus was awarded the 2006 Nobel Peace Prize for creating Grameen ("village") Bank, the world's first microcredit bank. The idea grew out of a famine in Bangladesh in the mid-1970s, when Yunus lent $27 of his own money to 42 poor villagers for small enterprises and, to his surprise, all the loans were promptly repaid.

Getty Images/Junko Kimura

Journal. "If you lag behind, the rest of the group members can't get new loans."[16]

As for empowering women, loans made to the women who show up at the weekly debt collection meetings often get passed on to the male breadwinners in their families, especially in India and Pakistan, according to Sarita Gupta, vice president for global resources and communications at New York-based Women's World Banking, which works with 40 microfinance providers and banks in 28 countries. That's partly because women may perceive their husbands' businesses as the ones most likely to succeed, she suggests, although women may invest in their own enterprises with later loans.

Yet, even if the loans are used for business, most poor women earn too little from their tiny enterprises to make a significant improvement in their lives, argues Aneel Karnani, associate professor of strategy at the University of Michigan's Ross School of Business. In a typical isolated village in India, he points out, "you see a lot of women sitting next to each other selling the same product — bananas" — to equally impoverished villagers.

"They don't earn enough to get lifted out of poverty. [T]he alternative to microfinance is finding jobs for the poor," he asserts. Rather than making tiny loans to five women, it would be more effective to loan one entrepreneur a large enough sum to start a clothing factory that could provide jobs to those five, he argues. Poor entrepreneurs prefer the same thing most people in rich countries want: the security of a salaried job, he says. "They're not entrepreneurs by choice but by necessity," he claims.

Some economists also question whether microfinance can be the engine of economic growth it's touted to be. "We know that broad-based economic growth is the most powerful way to reduce poverty," says Jonathan Morduch, professor of public policy and economics at New York University's (NYU) Wagner School, noting that standard-of-living improvements in China, which has little microfinance, and India, which has a lot, have been driven by growth in gross domestic product. "Frankly, we don't have a sense (even if all the loans went to business) of the degree to which microfinance has contributed to economic growth."

As for Yunus' claim that more than half of Grameen borrowers have left poverty, Morduch says, "The question an economist like myself asks is, 'What would have happened without Grameen?' This happened at a time when poverty was falling in Bangladesh generally. What's the net impact?"

Microfinance advocates say just because they don't have research evidence that meets the highest standards used by economists doesn't mean microcredit doesn't work. They point to some 25 years of direct experience and growing demand for the loans. "I just think researchers haven't proved it yet," says Alex Counts, president and CEO of the Washington-based Grameen Foundation, which spreads the Grameen philosophy worldwide.

A recent summary of the research from the World Bank-affiliated Consultative Group to Assist the Poor (CGAP), a consortium of government and private development organizations that studies microfinance, concludes the jury is still out as to whether microfinance lifts millions out of poverty. Financial services are, however, "vital tools in helping them to cope with poverty," concluded author Richard Rosenberg, an advisor at CGAP.[17]

Microloans have been used more often to "smooth consumption" over the course of a month of uneven earnings rather than to grow enterprises, studies suggest. But if we find that finding disappointing, it may be because well-to-do Westerners don't have the impoverished person's experience of earning $4 one day and zero the next, Rosenberg suggests.[18]

The microloan can make it possible to eat on that no-earning day. "This is basic survival stuff," says MicroCredit Enterprises founder Lewis.

Will for-profit investors continue to benefit the very poor and women?

Microfinance suddenly became a hot market for Western investors after Banco Compartamos, the largest microfinance lender in Mexico, went public in 2007. Stock in the former nonprofit was soon valued at more than $1.5 billion, offering a mouth-watering rate of return to investors of more than 50 percent a year.[19]

Even more attention-grabbing was the news that Compartamos routinely charged its impoverished borrowers an astoundingly high annual interest rate of more than 100 percent, in sharp contrast to the 31 percent average annual rate charged by microlending institutions worldwide at the time.[20]

Microfinance godfather Yunus, along with others in the industry, was outraged. "Microcredit was created to fight the moneylender, not to become the moneylender," he said.[21]

In an article entitled "Microloan Sharks," MicroCredit Enterprises founder Lewis concurred, "[T]he mission of microfinance is to make a difference in the lives of poor families and to end the scourge of poverty, not build a new asset class based on profiteering."[22]

Yet commercialization boosters say it's just these kinds of highly attractive returns that will draw more capital and more lenders to the sector, permitting it to reach more borrowers. The resulting competition, they say, will ultimately lead to lower interest rates.

Does Falling Repayment Rate Signal a Loan Bubble?

Bangladesh-based Grameen Bank, which pioneered providing tiny loans to the poor, is seeing a drop in repayment rates. Founded by Nobel Peace Prize-winner Muhammad Yunus, the bank has nearly doubled its membership rolls since 2004, reaching almost 8 million members in 2009 (bottom). But after the 2008 global recession, the bank reported its collection rate dropped below 97 percent for the first time in recent years, to 96.55 in 2009 (top). Some observers caution this could be a red flag warning that more borrowers will have trouble repaying their loans in the future. But there's been no epidemic of defaults yet in Bangladesh. Even at this new low, repayment rates for microcredit are significantly higher than for American credit card debt, which fell as low as 85.5 percent for Bank of America last year.

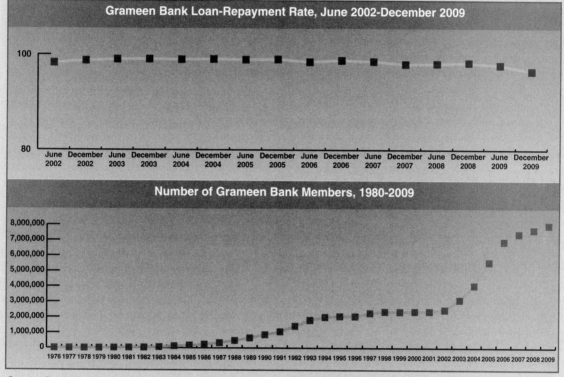

Source: David Roodman, "Grameen Bank, Which Pioneered Loans for the Poor, Has Hit a Repayment Snag," Center for Global Development, February 2010

Even though Compartamos took a lot of heat for its high returns, "you also saw a rush into the Mexican microfinance sector," says Mary Ellen Iskenderian, president and CEO of Women's World Banking, which supports microfinance institutions converting into for-profit banks. "People thought there was money to be made there, and you've seen some real competition," reports Iskenderian, whose organization is starting an equity fund for investors in microfinance institutions.

Bolivia, a microlending market with vigorous competition, has seen some of the world's steepest declines in interest rates, she points out. (Bolivia's rates have dropped from 50 percent in the mid-1990s to just over 20 percent as their market grew from about 200,000 borrowers to more than 600,000.)[23]

"You have 1.5 billion potential customers who need access to microfinance," estimates Trant, of the International Association of Microfinance Investors. If you multiply them by a typical microloan size (about $200), you'll need about $300 billion to meet the demand, she says. But with only about $44 billion now in microfinance funding portfolios around the world, that leaves a funding gap of more than $250 billion to reach all the unbanked poor.[24]

"Charity's not going to cover that gap. We have to find business solutions," maintains Trant. "People's enlightened self-interest — if they know they can make a buck while doing some good in the world — that's what's driving investment in microfinance."

Yet scaling up microfinance could just as well create monopolies, warns Lewis, especially in small, impoverished regions that may never support more than one microfinance bank. In those cases, he writes, "A poor woman driven by economic adversity has very little power to negotiate interest rates with a microlender."[25]

Some companies say they plow their increased profits into reducing their interest rates. For example, Compartamos has reduced its interest rates by about 30 percent since 2000, when it was charging 115 percent, according to a spokesman. "As we grow and are more efficient, we move that efficiency to our clients" in the form of lower interest rates, said spokesman Jorge Daniel Manrique Barrigan.[26] Critics point out, however, that the bank's average loan size also has increased over the same time, reducing its servicing cost per loan. Considering the 50 percent return Compartamos has consistently given investors over the years, "they are clearly only passing on a small amount to the poor and keeping much more for themselves," says Chuck Waterfield, CEO and founder of MFTransparency, an industry-supported group that reports interest rates.

Lewis says the microfinance sector has split between those who want to commercialize it and his own anti-poverty faction. "We didn't get into this to start banks; we're interested in poverty reduction," he says. "And so we really need to look at the problems the poor have and combine the microfinance services with health, education, financial literacy, malaria bed nets. We need to keep interest rates low; it's not about returns for Western investors."

A recent Women's World Banking study of 25 microfinance institutions seems to confirm his fears. The researchers found that the percentage of women borrowers falls off sharply when nonprofit lenders convert themselves into profit-seeking banks.[27]

That's partly because commercial banks shift to larger loans to improve their profit margins, since they're less costly to administer than very small loans, the report found. And women's loans are typically smaller than men's. Women reinvest less in their businesses than men, because their businesses are smaller, often home-based, with household duties competing for their time. Women also tend to have smaller profit margins than men because they're in highly competitive sectors like food preparation, sewing and beauty salons.[28]

However, the same study also found that more women ended up getting loans from lenders that went commercial, despite being a smaller proportion of the total borrowers — largely because the banks scaled up to serve more people overall, both women and men.

"That's the goal — to reach more people," says Trant. "We want to get economic access to people who haven't had it in the past, whether they're male or female."

The free-enterprise nature of microfinance has attracted millions from investors who see a way to make money while doing good. In 2005, Pierre Omidyar, the billionaire founder of eBay, gave a $100 million donation to Tufts University, specifying it should be invested in microfinance institutions. Omidyar was attracted to microfinance because it demonstrated free-market principles, much like eBay. Omidyar hoped donor funding would become unnecessary once microfinance could raise money in the capital markets, he told *The New Yorker* in 2006.[29]

Yet nonprofits continue to serve poorer borrowers than those sought out by commercial banks, research suggests. Surprisingly, a study of 346 leading microfinance institutions co-authored by NYU economist Morduch found that nonprofit, nongovernmental organizations (NGOs) actually tend to charge higher interest rates — a 25 percent median — compared to banks' 13 percent. That occurs because NGOs' poorer clients take out smaller loans, which are more expensive to administer. "Profit-maximizing investors would have limited interest in most of the institutions that are focusing on the poorest customers and women," the researchers conclude.[30]

"[E]veryone thinks you can do it in a win-win way," helping the poor and maximizing profits at the same time, says Morduch. "But in reality, some nonprofits will continue to need donors' help to reach the very poorest.

"There's a lot of stuff going on commercially but it can't reach everybody," he says.

Should microfinance lenders be more tightly regulated?

The astoundingly high interest rates charged by some microlenders have prompted calls for mandated caps on interest rates.

For instance, a populist debtors' rebellion in Nicaragua — the "No Pago" (I Won't Pay) movement — has spurred mass demonstrations protesting high rates and demanding a legal rate ceiling.[31] Part of the outrage stems from the fact that for nearly three decades many microlenders have presented interest rates to illiterate borrowers in a way that makes them look deceptively low.

Until recently, Compartamos charged an annual interest rate of 129 percent, including all up-front fees and taxes, according to a 2008 calculation by MFTransparency's Waterfield.[32] But "Compartamos didn't actually say, 'We charge 129 percent a year.' . . . They said to the borrowers, 'We charge 4 percent a month,' " according to Waterfield.[33]

That 4 percent is deceptively low because it is based on a so-called "flat" rate. Many microfinance lenders charge such flat rates on the entire amount borrowed, but flat fees turn out to be nearly double the annual percentage rate (APR) — the standard used on loans in the United States, which calculates the interest on a declining balance over the life of the loan. For instance, a loan advertised at 36 percent "flat" actually works out to 65.7 percent APR, according to Waterfield.[34] That rate is even higher when up-front fees like security deposits and insurance fees are factored in.[35]

"As soon as some [microlenders] start lying, you've created an environment where everyone else has to lie" within the same regional market, Waterfield says, in order to look as (deceptively) cheap as their competitors. He hopes to break that syndrome by persuading all lenders in a country to submit their interest rates to him in a sealed envelope; then his Web site will disclose all annual rates on the same day.

Compartamos now charges 78.7 percent annually for its core microcredit loan, according to a company spokesman. But Waterfield says even that number is deceptive. Adding taxes and a mandatory 10 percent security deposit brings the rate up to 110 percent annually, he

calculates, lower than the 129 percent of two years ago but still breathtakingly high.[36]

"Compartamos has made serious efforts in order to reduce our rates," spokesman Barrigan said in an e-mail. In fact, he notes, the company has lowered its rates "more than 30 percent" since 2000, when it was charging 115 percent annually according to its own calculation, not including tax or up-front fees.

Citing misleading — and sometimes deceptive — practices, Karnani of Michigan's Ross School of Business wants governments to cap the rates microlenders can charge, prohibit abusive debt collection practices and require interest rate disclosure according to a standardized method.[37] (*See "At Issue," p. 235.*)

Such legal protections are virtually nonexistent for microborrowers overseas, according to Wilson at Tufts' Fletcher School. By contrast, in the United States, usury laws at the state level limit interest rates, and federal truth-in-lending rules stipulate a consistent method of disclosing rates. The Fair Debt Collection Practices Act attempts to limit harassment of debtors.[38]

But mandated interest rate caps are almost universally opposed by the microfinance industry. If politicians were to set caps too low to cover lenders' costs, microfinance organizations would be forced out of business, Grameen Foundation's Counts contends, and borrowers would be driven into the jaws of unregulated loan sharks.

Nonprofits that offer assistance in health, education and training along with loans would be hit hardest, because those extra program costs would no longer be covered, Counts predicts, "The most vulnerable isolated communities would be driven off the map," he says.

Karnani says these kinds of objections assume that free-market competition is keeping interest rates reasonable. That may be true in a rich country like the United States, where numerous banks compete to drive rates down. But in poor villages "there may be [only] one or two [lenders], so there is no competition," he asserts. "So the tendency is to charge above what would be a competitive rate."

Calls to require transparent disclosure of interest rates find some support among industry practitioners like Waterfield. But he believes his voluntary experiment, launched in 2008, will get the job done faster.

"It will take us a decade to get transparency regulation" in all 100 countries that have microfinance, he

The Poor Are Active Money Managers

Financial diaries clarify how the poor manage their money.

People living on $2 a day or less — like Bangladeshi rickshaw driver Hamid and his wife Khadeja — have something in common with the rich: They are also active money managers.

The couple live with their child in one room in the slums of Dhaka, sharing a toilet with seven other families. They survive on an average of 78 cents a day per person. But some days Hamid gets no work and no earnings. To ensure cash flow, they've built up reserves in six different instruments — from money saved at home to a life-insurance policy.[1]

They also have six debts outstanding to lenders ranging from a microlender to the grocer. Between the money they've pushed into savings ($451) and pulled out by taking loans or withdrawing savings ($514), their total turnover ($965) is $125 more than their total income for the year. As a result they have managed to extend each dollar of income earned to $1.15 through a combination of savings, loans and guarding money for others for a fee.

Hamid's story is just one of the 250 portraits gleaned from financial diaries kept by borrowers in Bangladesh, India and South Africa and described by a team of economists in a ground-breaking book last year — changing the way experts think about the "unbanked" poor.

The book, *Portfolios of the Poor*, revealed that while microfinance is often touted as replacing expensive moneylenders for the poor, 88 percent of the loans made actually were taken out through an informal network of friends, relatives and moneylenders — even in Bangladesh where most of the families had access to microfinance banks.

Informal loans, the authors found, sometimes are interest-free, in the cases of relatives, or more flexible, in the case of moneylenders. And loans from microfinance lenders, ostensibly for business enterprises, were frequently used for household needs. Khadeja used part of her microloan to buy gold — a form of secure savings.

Another Bangladeshi rickshaw driver decided that spending his loan to buy his own rickshaw was too risky, because the vehicle could be stolen. Instead, he used the loan to stock up on rice and to buy a cupboard; then he loaned $20 of it to a fellow rickshaw driver for 17.5 percent interest per month, permitting him to make some money.

Moneylenders are often thought to be the main predators on the poor, charging exorbitant interest rates. But the authors were surprised to discover that some of the highest rates in South Africa, for example, were charged by savings clubs. These groups of conservative ladies pool their savings together and then lend a portion of it out at 30 percent per month — over 2,000 percent on an annual basis. That should have yielded hedge-fund sized profits, but because so many loans were not repaid or partly forgiven, the yield came to only about 1 percent a month.

Still, how are poor people able to pay such enormous interest rates? Whether to moneylenders or microfinance banks, interest rates can range from 20 percent to more than 100 percent a year. The authors suggest a 25-cent fee charged for a moneylender loan of $10 for a week may seem reasonable to Hamid, who earns just $2.33 a day as a rickshaw driver, even though on an annual basis, such a loan costs 261 percent per year. That $10 may be the difference between buying new clothes for the Muslim holiday of Eid and going to the mosque in rags.

"It can be a few pennies a week; they're repaying in small bits," explains Jonathan Morduch, a coauthor of *Portfolios* and a professor of public policy and economics at New York University's Wagner School of Business. "Very expensive loans are out for a few weeks, and it's a fee for service — not big." Most microfinance loans made by Bangladesh-based Grameen Bank, a pioneer in microlending, "are 20-40 percent for a year; it's a big chunk of cash you pay back in dribs and drabs."

Many of the diarists also were found to be paying a fee to accumulate their savings in a safe place but earned no interest on their deposits — something a Westerner would find difficult to understand. The fees might be paid to a woman who comes to the village once a week to collect or to a neighbor to act as "money guard," keeping the money out of temptation from a spouse. These savers may not see loans as very different from savings — in each case they are paying a fee each week to procure a large lump sum, the authors note.

But even these nest eggs can disappear. Similarly, informal lenders may not come up with the cash when it's promised. And there can be cheating even among friends.

Having reliable financial tools — whether savings or loans — would make a big difference to those with such low incomes, according to the authors, who find it surprising that cash-flow management has received little attention from the microfinance sector. Although microfinance loans historically have been oriented towards business, the diaries show that households need to borrow for a wide range of needs and "are prepared to find ways of repaying loans from ordinary household cash flow."

— *Sarah Glazer*

---

[1] Information from this story comes from Daryl Collins, *et al.*, *Portfolios of the Poor: How the World's Poor Live on $2 a Day* (2009).

says. "But in a couple of weeks I can go to India, we can go to the microfinance institutions and say, 'Why wait for government to tell us to do the right thing? Why don't we ourselves do the right thing?'"

In Cambodia and Bosnia and Herzegovina, the first two countries his organization approached, all lenders agreed to disclose their APR's on his Web site, www.mftransparency.org. However, he concedes, this doesn't necessarily mean their loan officers tell new borrowers the true rate — though he hopes they eventually will.

However, even that information may be insufficient in places like India, where 39 percent of adults are illiterate.[39]

"I want to tell people, 'Here's exactly what you'll pay' in dollars and cents [and] let them figure out that's three meals of food on the table," says Wilson, who points out interest rates may be a hard concept for an illiterate person to grasp.

Media coverage of Indian and Mexican lenders who hired thugs to collect debts has recently drawn attention to abusive debt collection, the other area Karnani wants regulated.[40]

More than 900 microfinance lenders and other organizations have signed an industry code of conduct, dubbed the Smart Campaign, promising neither to engage in "abusive or coercive" debt collection, nor to market loans to people who can't afford them. They also pledge to present their interest rates in a form understandable to clients.[41]

"The main reason for starting the campaign was watching the U.S. subprime meltdown and recognizing that it arose from a failure of consumer protection — and seeing that regulation hadn't stopped it," says Elisabeth Rhyne, managing director of the Center for Financial Inclusion, the Washington-based industry group that initiated the campaign.

Borrowing from the organic and fair trade labeling movements, Grameen Foundation's Counts has proposed a "certification" for those lenders who agree to abide by an ethical code — including disclosing their interest rates and eschewing unethical debt collection.[42]

Karnani is skeptical, especially in the absence of a government enforcer to assure compliance. "Vague and platitudinous appeals for self-restraint by companies and self-regulation by the industry are not effective at protecting microclients," he has charged.[43]

A microcredit borrowers' group in Kolkata, India, meets to make payments on loans. Peer pressure ensures that the poor pay loans promptly. Weekly payments typically are made in public in the village "center," and everyone in the group can be denied subsequent loans if one member defaults.

BACKGROUND

Early Beginnings

Efforts to organize financial services for the poor stretch back to rural credit cooperatives organized in Europe in the 19th century. By 1910, there were more than 15,000 such institutions operating in small communities in Germany alone.[44]

Members contributed savings to the cooperatives, which then allocated loans to members who needed money for investments or living expenses. Participants, whether borrowers or savers, were all shareholders in the cooperative and made key decisions democratically about interest rates and loan sizes.

The modern microfinance movement's roots date back to 1974 when Yunus, then an economics professor in Bangladesh, became dissatisfied with the free-market theories he was teaching in the classroom as a solution to ending poverty. Since the 1950s, foreign aid had been based on the theory that the route to economic development in poor countries like Bangladesh was technical assistance in modernizing their agriculture and industry.

But Yunus noticed that the poorest of the poor in Jobra, where he was helping farmers improve their crop yields, received no benefit from his assistance. They owned no land and eked out a daily living as day laborers, craft

Tattoo artist Filipe Gil started his parlor in Lisbon, Portugal, after receiving a small loan from a private microcredit bank. Unsecured microcredit loans appeal to the poor, who lack the collateral required by commercial banks. High interest rates charged by microlenders are attracting many private investors to the field, and critics say some microcredit lenders use strong-armed collection tactics.

workers or beggars. A village woman, Sufiya Begum, told Yunus that she relied on a local moneylender for the cash to make the bamboo stools she sold. But the moneylender would only give her the cash if she agreed to sell him what she produced at a price he set. Together with the high interest on her loan, this left her only two pennies a day as income.[45]

In an experiment starting in 1976, Yunus decided to lend $27 of his own money to 42 villagers who were beholden to moneylenders. When he asked a local bank to make more such loans, they objected that the borrowers had no property to offer as collateral and no credit histories.

Yunus persuaded the bank to make the loans by offering to act as guarantor. He was "stunned" when the poor paid back their loans "on time, every time." Unable to persuade local banks to expand this program further, he created the now world-renowned Grameen ("village") Bank in 1983, to lend money to the poor without requiring collateral. [46]

Power of Peer Pressure

The bank grew explosively, largely credited to its innovative group lending, in which poor borrowers acted as guarantors for one another. Each group consisted of five friends, all of whom had to approve of a new loan; if a member defaulted and fellow group members did not pay off the debt, everyone in the group could be denied subsequent loans.[47]

This so-called "joint liability" became the most celebrated feature of the Grameen contract, according to economist Morduch. For many years, microfinance was linked inextricably to the idea of group lending. It gave customers incentives to pay promptly, to monitor their neighbors and to select responsible acquaintances when forming the groups. The requirement that weekly payments be made in public in the village "center" in the presence of 10 or 12 such groups, placed even more peer pressure on timely repayment. To many economists, it was the linchpin that explained why loans to poor people without collateral worked.[48]

Today Grameen has branches covering virtually all villages in Bangladesh, according to Grameen's Web site. The Grameen bank gives loans to more than 8 million poor people, 97 percent of whom are women. Grameen has long boasted an impressive 98 percent repayment rate, but it recently reported a surprising drop to just 96.55 percent of loans paid on time at the end of last year. (*See graph, p. 223.*)[49]

The 'Debt Treadmill'

Grameen's group lending model has been widely imitated by microfinance institutions around the world. By June 2009, microlending had spread to 100 countries, where more than 1,400 microfinance institutions were making loans to more than 86 million borrowers, according to the Microfinance Information Exchange (MIX).

But the model has been criticized in recent years for putting some borrowers into more debt than they could repay and abusively pressuring those who can't repay in time. Loan officers, paid according to how many loans they collect, have sometimes insisted that everyone be held at the village meeting until defaulters paid up. In some cases that meant a rushed visit to an expensive moneylender to come up with the money. In other cases, loan officers harassed borrowers, sometimes refusing to leave someone's house until they came up with the money, according to Anton Simanowitz, a socioeconomist at the University of Sussex Institute of Development Studies in England.

C H R O N O L O G Y

1860s-1940s *Credit cooperatives offering savings and low-cost loans to the poor spread from Europe to India, Senegal and the U.S.*

1864 German village mayor Freidrich Raiffeissen pioneers lending to poor farmers through cooperatives.

1904 In British-ruled India, Cooperative Credit Societies Act creates co-ops that lend to poor farmers.

1946 Indian co-ops have 9 million members.

1950s-1970s *Foreign aid focuses on economic development in the Third World.*

1970s Bangladeshi professor Muhammad Yunus begins experimenting with loans to poor villagers.

1974-75 Bangladesh famine leaves many families destitute.

1976 Yunus lends $27 to 42 villagers, launching his lending experiments with the poor; all loans are repaid.

1980s *Bangladeshi banks begin lending to the poor to start tiny businesses; the idea spreads to Latin America, Asia and Africa.*

1983 Yunus creates Grameen Bank in Bangladesh, first bank devoted to making microfinance loans to poor people with no collateral.

1990s *Microfinance lending grows rapidly; Grameen eases lending rules, microfinance becomes more professional.*

1991 Grameen hits millionth member, growing 40 percent per year.

1995 Consultative Group to Assist the Poor, a group of major donors and agencies, created at World Bank.

1997 Microcredit Summit Campaign — a coalition of lenders, donors and advocates — sets goal of reaching 100 million families with microloans.

1998 Worst flood in Bangladesh's history leaves over 30 million homeless, killing over 1,000.

1999 Grameen suffers large-scale defaults.

2000s *Grameen Bank makes microlending more flexible; profit-seeking investors take stakes in microfinance; worldwide credit crisis begins to affect microfinance. Reports of over-indebted microborrowers raise specter of loan "bubble"; microfinance industry initiates consumer-protection efforts to avoid regulation.*

2001 "Grameen II" is introduced, making loan terms more flexible.

2004 Grameen's savings deposits exceed its loans for the first time.

2005 U.N. declares it the Year of Microcredit.

2006 Yunus receives Nobel Peace Prize for bringing microcredit to the poor.

2007 California venture capital firm Sequoia Capital's $11.5 million equity investment in giant microlender SKS India signals attraction to purely profit-seeking investors.

2008 Worldwide credit crisis erupts (March 17). . . . By year-end, growth of new borrowings slows and delinquency rates rise.

2009 First randomized study finds microlending has no impact on poverty (July). . . . *Wall Street Journal* reports poor residents of southern India get "carpet-bombed" with offers of multiple microloans, raising fear of a credit bubble (August). . . . Microlenders criticized for concealing high interest rates with deceptive marketing; industry responds by disclosing true price of microlenders' loans in three countries, at www.mftransparency.org (Oct. 19).

2010 Bill & Melinda Gates Foundation announces $38 million grant to microfinance lenders in 12 countries in Asia, Africa and Latin America to create savings accounts for the very poor — signaling new focus on savings.

Do Microcredit Loans Alleviate Poverty?

New studies question old assumptions.

Many impoverished borrowers rise above the poverty level after receiving a microfinance loan. But was the loan the crucial factor, as advocates have claimed?

Not necessarily, economists have argued. Since people who take small loans tend to be entrepreneurs with drive and ambition, they could have found some other way besides microfinance to better their situation — through social networks, other loans or business aptitude. Dean Karlan, a professor of economics at Yale University, argues that the better question is: "How would their lives have been different had they not received the loan?"[1]

Karlan and economist Jonathan Zinman of Dartmouth College are two of the first researchers to employ the randomized control trial — the gold standard of scientific research — to determine the effectiveness of microfinance. In this approach, one group of people is randomly assigned to receive a loan, and another group gets no loan. Last year, in one of two studies that appear to overturn widely held beliefs about microcredit's power to alleviate poverty, they compared two such groups in the Philippines.[2]

The results were surprising. They found no evidence that household income improved among those who got a loan. Although women are the traditional recipients of microcredit, male borrowers were more likely to increase their small-business profit as a result of their loan. Men also tended to spend their profits on their children's education — in contrast to the conventional wisdom that it's mainly women who can be counted on to do so.

A second study using randomized groups in the slums of urban Hyderabad, India, did see some benefit: Borrowers who already had a business saw some increase in profit. Conducted by economists Abhijat Banerjee and Esther Duflo at the Massachusetts Institute of Technology (MIT), the study found that overall household spending — a crucial sign of financial health — stayed about the same. The authors found "no impact on health, education or women's decision-making" power in the family — three benefits often claimed for microfinance. For example, households that took a loan were no more likely to have children in school than those that did not.[3]

In at least half the Hyderabad cases, borrowers said they planned to use their loan for a nonbusiness purpose, such as repaying another loan, buying a TV or meeting household expenses. The authors conclude that those borrowers who didn't start a business but increased their consumption when they got a loan "may eventually become poorer" because they are "borrowing against the future."

However, critics said both studies measured a period of time — up to 18 months — that was too short to determine whether poverty would be overcome. "You need about two-and-a-half years worth of loans to see a real impact," says Mary Ellen Iskendarian, CEO of Women's World Banking, which works with 40 microfinance lenders in 28 countries. In Pakistan, she says, that's when "you start to see a substantial improvement in the house: The tin roof goes on or the mud floor becomes wood, or another child is registered for school."

Leading microfinance advocates say the studies can't disprove improvements in people's lives that they've seen with their own eyes. "We don't have the evidence in the sense academics want to have it," partly because randomized trials are expensive, says Susan Davis, president and CEO of BRAC USA, a New York-based nonprofit that supports the leading microlender BRAC. In addition, Bangladesh now has so many microlenders that it's hard to find people

Most microfinance institutions pay cash incentives to loan officers based on how many new clients they bring in and how much money they lend, according to Simanowitz. "It doesn't matter if you're not careful about assessing [the borrower's] ability to repay and their business capacity" when recruiting new clients, he says.

As a result of how they're paid, some loan officers put excessive pressure on borrowers to pay their loans — even in desperate situations. For example, says Simanowitz, a group of women in Kenya had fallen behind in their payments because of a drought. Despite being on the verge of starvation, they sold one of their last chickens to pay their loans.[50]

"That's irresponsible lending . . . accepting money from people selling food when they're starving," says Simanowitz. Theoretically, the business supported by a microloan is expected to generate enough income to repay the loan.

who have never received a loan to use as a control group, she points out.

"If I hadn't talked to hundreds and hundreds of microfinance borrowers directly, maybe I wouldn't be such a supporter," says Davis, who lived in Bangladesh for four years. "I'm not worried about what the research says. I could see the difference between a mom who got access to finance in the size of their children," who weren't stunted with malnourishment, she recalls. "We have way too many people who have seen the stories. And the fact that millions want access to the service is an indication of the demand."

Jonathan Morduch, a professor of public policy and economics at New York University's Wagner Graduate School of Public Service, is a longtime skeptic about the traditional claims for microfinance. "The boldest claim for microfinance — that it can single-handedly eliminate a large share of world poverty — outpaces by a long distance the evidence accumulated to date," he said in 2006.[4]

That conclusion is "even more true now," with the release of last year's randomized studies from Yale and MIT, he says. But surprisingly, he also insists that "microfinance could be good in its own right without poverty reduction" by giving poor people the kinds of banking services that permit them to send a child to school or deal with a health problem. Something as simple as having money on hand to go to the hospital for childbirth could have a big impact on infant mortality, he says.

However, the underlying question remains: Would governments and aid agencies make a bigger dent in poverty by spending their money on something else? A year of primary schooling probably helps poor people more than a year of microfinance lending, some experts say. But microfinance costs much less in subsidies.[5]

"What interventions do we have that have even repaid 1 percent of the investment?" asks Jonathan C. Lewis, founder and CEO of the nonprofit MicroCredit Enterprises, which makes loans to microlenders. "Do we have vaccination programs or schools that provide self-financing?"

Carpenter Anil Sutradhr works in the backyard shop he opened in Manikganj, Bangladesh, with a microloan from Grameen Bank. Recent studies have shown that microloans are less effective at decreasing poverty than was widely thought.

As for the recent studies, he concludes, "Every single value that you hold dear you don't measure with a spread sheet. We don't say, 'Before you start school, we need to know what benefit society will get.' We have a general sense this is the way it's going to work."

— Sarah Glazer

[1] Dean Karlan, "Measuring Microfinance," *Stanford Social Innovation Review*, Summer 2008, p. 53.

[2] Dean Karlan and Jonathan Zinman, "Expanding Microenterprise Credit Access: Using Randomized Supply Decisions to Estimate the Impacts in Manila," July 2009, http://financialaccess.org/sites/default/files/Expanding%20Credit%20Access%20Manila.pdf.

[3] Abhijit Banerjee, *et al.*, "The Miracle of Microfinance? Evidence from a Randomized Evaluation," October 2009.

[4] Connie Bruck, "A Reporter at Large: Millions for Millions," *The New Yorker*, Oct. 30, 2006.

[5] Richard Rosenberg, "Does Microcredit Really Help Poor People?" January 2010, Focus Note No. 59, Consultative Group to Assist the Poor, www.cgap.org.

But the longer a borrower is with the lender, he says, the more likely are microfinance lenders to "give bigger and bigger loans, so the gap between business and loan size gets bigger until people are extremely vulnerable."

The common practice of pressuring members to take a new loan as soon as they've repaid their last loan also disturbed Wilson, the former director of microfinance for Catholic Relief Services. In 2005, the organization announced that it was withdrawing from the business as a direct investor and lender, citing a fundamental conflict between seeking financial profits and its mission of serving the poor.[51] (The organization still lends technical assistance to microlenders but has shifted emphasis to encouraging savings.) Wilson believes savings, rather than loans, meet the kinds of emergency health and household needs poor families have most often.

AP Photo/Esteban Felix

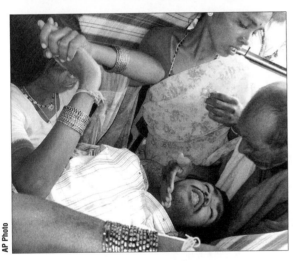

AP Photo

Desperate Microfinance Borrowers

Riot police arrest a farmer in San Benito, Nicaragua, during a January 2009 demonstration in which hundreds of farmers blocked the Pan-American Highway to protest high interest rates charged by microfinance firms (top). Demonstrators associated with Nicaragua's populist "No Pago" (I Won't Pay) rebellion have held mass protests across the country demanding a legal cap on interest rates. In an Indian village in Andhra Pradesh state, family members grieve the suicide death of a 26-year-old farmer, who had been despondent about his debts. In 2006 more than 200 people in the state reportedly committed suicide because of intimidation by microfinance institutions. The government closed down 50 branches of two major microlenders and charged them with extortionate interest rates and intimidating borrowers with strong-armed debt recovery.

"The problem I've seen with most microcredit is they have a formula: once you get a customer hooked, you don't want them to graduate [out of indebtedness] because it's expensive to get that first customer — you've got to do organizing and outreach. Now you've got a live one and don't want to let them go, so you keep selling them more loans. That's a treadmill" of debt, Wilson says.

After the Flood

In 1998 Grameen itself recognized problems with its group lending approach after being hit with large-scale loan defaults following Bangladesh's worst flood in history. When the bank studied which borrowers were defaulting in 1999, it discovered many of them had been struggling to repay for years before the flood. [52]

Recognizing underlying flaws in its approach, Grameen made some radical changes. It began offering more flexible loans — not just for business but also for family needs like student fees — allowing borrowers to change the rigid weekly payment schedule and putting less emphasis on the group to enforce loans. [53]

In 2001 Yunus introduced "Grameen II," which shifted away from the previous inflexible lending system in which every loan term was one year and repayments had to be in weekly installments even if that didn't match the cash flows of many poor households. The new approach removed the requirement that a member borrow continuously. Grameen II also stepped back from the group approach, outlawing an arrangement that makes borrowers responsible for repaying each other's loans. [54]

In addition, the bank intensified its collection of villagers' savings. By the end of 2004, savings deposits amounted to more than its loans for the first time and have continued growing faster than loans.

In 2006, Yunus received the Nobel Peace Prize for his work in microfinance.

CURRENT SITUATION

Rising Delinquencies

Having grown from a small philanthropic movement in the 1970s, microfinance institutions (MFIs) today provide financial services to 86.2 million borrowers and nearly 100 million savers in the developing world.[55] And while dozens of banks in the developed world met their demise during the world financial crisis in mid-2008, the MFIs appeared to be surprisingly nimble.

"No microfinance bank has gone under yet," according to Trant, of the International Association of Microfinance Investors. "We've seen some show stress in repaying loans; but we haven't had a bankruptcy or liquidation."

Iskenderian of Women's World Banking attributes the industry's adaptability to the fact that the microborrowers tend to have small, short-term loans that they can get out of quickly and maintain small inventories so they can shift easily to a new business.

While the industry may have been resilient at first, the most recent reports suggest it is not impervious. By the end of 2008, the rapid 25 percent annual growth rate in borrowers worldwide had slowed to 15 percent, according to the MIX. A major reason: Rising delinquency rates in some areas forced loan officers to focus on getting current clients to pay their debts rather than attracting new borrowers.[56]

Delinquency rates rose particularly in high-growth markets; Morocco and Bosnia and Herzegovina saw their unpaid loan rate double, though defaults still represented less than 5 percent of their loans.[57]

Contrary to early hopes that they would be insulated from broader economic shocks, microlenders now see themselves as "vulnerable to them through financial markets, credit conditions and the fortunes of their customers," the London-based Centre for the Study of Financial Innovation recently reported. Indeed, a survey of 430 lenders and investors showed that they were most worried about borrowers being unable to repay their loans — a radical change from its last survey in early 2008, when many lenders were growing at double-digit rates.[58]

Fear of growing overindebtedness — borrowers who've taken on more debt than they can repay — dominated the list of concerns. In disturbing echoes of the subprime mortgage market collapse, many lenders worried that in high-competition regions like Latin America and Asia, where growing numbers of lenders are jockeying for market share, standards for determining the

A Jordanian woman who obtained a microloan from the private Microfund for Women displays her embroidered wares at a microfinance conference in Amman. Studies show that when nonprofit lenders convert themselves into profit-seeking banks, the percentage of female borrowers declines sharply. Commercial banks seek higher profit margins, but women generally operate in highly competitive sectors like food preparation, sewing and beauty salons, which have smaller profit margins.

credit-worthiness of borrowers are declining, and more borrowers are defaulting.[59]

In Bosnia and Herzegovina, loan officers are being forced to fill "crazy" monthly quotas of new borrowers, one survey respondent said, based on this come-on: "Just take a loan, you'll pay it back some way."[60]

Looming Crisis?

Even before the international credit crisis hit, there had been growing concern in the industry about regions where borrowers seemed to be over their head in microfinance debt, with rising delinquency rates. A potential repayment crisis is brewing in several "hotspots" — South India, Morocco, Nicaragua and Bosnia and Herzegovina, according to industry experts. [61]

Experts say borrowers owing multiple debts to several microlenders are driving the problem. Typically, microfinance borrowers don't develop individual credit histories.

Members of the Fikina Kibiashara ("think business") borrowers' group in Nairobi, Kenya, gather to make payments on their microloans. The group's tailors, vegetable and grain vendors and used clothing and wastepaper dealers are just the kind of small entrepreneurs the microfinance movement targets.

"Group lending . . . the very thing that makes it possible to reach poorer people, means the institution knows less about each individual client," says Rhyne, of the Center for Financial Inclusion.

Could this overlending lead to a bubble like the U.S. subprime crisis? "We should be worried," says the Center for Global Development's Roodman. Since credit bureaus are rare in these countries, "No one except the borrower has the whole picture," Roodman observes.

In Karnataka, one of the Indian states worst-hit by defaults, the four largest microfinance lenders recently pooled their data to determine how many of their borrowers had multiple loans. They found less of a problem than many imagined. Only 11 percent of borrowers said they were getting loans from two or more institutions, according to the Grameen Foundation's Counts.

Yet, more and more the industry and trade press are asking if a subprime-size bubble could develop. Some argue that a bubble already exists in three states of southern India that account for nearly half of all Indian microclients — Andhra Pradesh, Karnataka and Tamil Nadu — yet are also experiencing some of the fastest growth.[62]

In August *The Wall Street Journal* reported that poor neighborhoods in southern India were being "carpet-bombed" with offers of loans. The reporter found two aspects reminiscent of the subprime bubble: loan officers paid on commission and undocumented loans.[63]

Industry defenders are quick to point out the sector's admirable history of on-time repayment by 98 percent of borrowers. But people living on $2 a day typically have many unreported loans in the informal sector — from moneylenders, storekeepers, friends and family — in addition to one or more microfinance loans.[64]

This is only one of the reasons why Trant, of the International Association of Microfinance Investors, says, "The general consensus is the 98 percent repayment rate is probably not 100 percent realistic." A study by her organization discovered that microfinance organizations often restructured loans — giving borrowers who can't pay extra time — but counted that as part of their renowned 98 percent repayment rate.

Nevertheless, industry experts say, even the highest default rates among microlenders — about 5 to 10 percent of their portfolios — are less than American credit card defaults in the past year, which rose as high as 14.5 percent for Bank of America customers.[65]

Government Crackdowns

As the specter of overindebtedness looms, several governments have introduced consumer protection measures. Some countries in West Africa are encouraging the creation of credit bureaus. Nigeria has imposed interest rate caps on microlenders. And India has clamped down on what it considers exorbitant rates and abusive debt-collection policies by microlenders.[66]

Such "political interference" worries Latin American microfinance industry leaders, according to a recent survey, some of whom complain that interest rate caps in Colombia and Venezuela are stunting the growth of the market.[67]

In Nicaragua, the "No Pago" movement, supported by thousands of angry borrowers, scored a major victory last October when legislators recommended a bill capping interest rates at 12 percent and giving debtors up to five years to repay loans.[68] The movement in Nicaragua, first sparked by inflammatory remarks against microfinance lenders by President Daniel Ortega, has the industry worried about measures that populist governments might take.

Indeed, according to MFTransparency's Waterfield, fear of government caps is one reason why the industry "lied for three decades" about the interest rates they charge. "If the Ortegas of the world knew what we were really charging, they would freak out and put a limit on interest rates," he says.

Should governments cap microloan interest rateds?

YES
Aneel Karnani
Associate Professor of Strategy, Stephen M. Ross School of Business, University of Michigan

Written for *CQ Researcher*, April 2010

The microcredit industry resists regulation on the grounds that microcredit is an open and competitive market. I disagree. The industry is characterized by a lack of competition, imperfect information and vulnerable consumers. In an ironic twist on the original microcredit mission, microfinance institutions (MFIs) are making a fortune in microcredit — by exploiting the poor! The government should impose an interest rate ceiling to protect the poor.

Microcredit interest rates are very high. Grameen Bank founder Muhammad Yunus argues that if the interest rate is more than 15 percent above the cost of funds, then it is "too high…. You are moving into the loan shark zone." A study by the Consultative Group to Assist the Poor (CGAP), (a consortium dedicated to promoting microcredit) showed MFIs charge a median interest rate of 28 percent per year, and 5 percent of MFIs charge rates above 50 percent. Generously allowing 10 percent for cost of funds implies that more than half of MFIs charge interest rates that Yunus would consider too high.

High interest rates have made many MFIs very profitable. In the CGAP study, MFIs earned an average 2.1 percent return on assets annually, well above the 1.4 percent earned by banks in the same countries. In 2006 10 percent of MFIs earned a return on equity above 35 percent. These are high profits by any business criteria. Even the CGAP study concludes that MFI profits are high because "the microcredit market is still immature . . . and [has] little competition so far."

The industry responds that the high interest rates are due to high costs. But empirical analysis shows that costs (and prices) vary widely across MFIs in a country. Since this analysis holds the loan size and the environment constant, the cost differential is likely due to some MFIs having unreasonably high controllable costs. In a competitive industry, such wide differentials in costs would not persist, and firms with inefficient operations and high prices would be penalized.

Financial literacy is a major problem for microcredit clients, who are poor, ill-informed and often illiterate and innumerate. The volatile combination of profit-seeking companies, minimal competition and vulnerable borrowers has opened up a dangerous potential for exploiting the poor. MFIs have much market power and can earn monopoly rents. Expecting microcredit organizations to exercise self-restraint and self-regulation is naively optimistic. Regulating interest rates is the only feasible solution. This does not mean that all, or even most, MFIs abuse monopoly power; but enough of them do exploit the poor to warrant regulation.

NO
Alex Counts
President, Grameen Foundation

Written for *CQ Researcher*, April 2010

When we hear about poor microfinance clients paying interest rates well above the rates paid by businesses and middle-class consumers, in the same country, it is tempting to argue for government-imposed interest rate caps on microfinance institutions. But I am convinced it would be counterproductive in practice.

Caps might spur some needed innovation and cost-cutting in a few markets if the imposed rate was within striking distance of the rates currently being charged. But in most cases, it would drive microfinance lenders out of business and force their former clients to increase their dependence on moneylenders who can charge rates well above 100 percent annually (as we saw happen in India in 2006).

And the MFIs that survive would likely suspend outreach to the poorest and most isolated clients (where initial transaction costs are highest); cut back on social-empowerment services (mostly related to health and education) that often magnify the poverty-reduction impact of microfinance; and attempt to circumvent the interest rate caps by charging additional fees (effectively negating the cost savings to clients).

Rather than take this crude though possibly popular approach, a more subtle strategy would be preferable. First of all, let competition on a level playing field — rather than government mandates — drive reductions in pricing (as has occurred in Bangladesh and Bolivia, two mature and highly efficient markets where there have been no government-imposed rates). Second, have donors and others invest in industry-wide initiatives that could bring widespread efficiency gains, such as documenting and driving adoption of best practices in (a) low-cost capital mobilization (especially from deposits), (b) optimization of human resources and (c) cutting-edge technology applications.

Grameen Foundation has made significant commitments to all these areas. Governments can play a role by helping to ensure a level playing field by, among other actions, defining price transparency in a way that helps clients find the lowest cost for particular products and requiring microfinance providers to implement consumer protection measures.

Rather than impose interest rates set by bureaucrats and politicians, it would be safer and more in the interests of the poor for governments to work with microfinance stakeholders to accelerate a market-based process that has been under way for years — which is bringing down rates 2-3 percent on an annual basis thanks to competition, media scrutiny, efficiency-enhancing innovation and price transparency.

AFP/Getty Images/Roberto Schmidt

Women seeking loans in Sauir, Kenya, rest in the shade of an Albizia tree as they wait to speak with a representative from a microcredit lender.

India also has cracked down on microfinance organizations over exorbitant rates and abusive debt collection. In Andhra Pradesh more than 200 people committed suicide in 2006 allegedly because of intimidation by microfinance institutions. Government authorities closed down 50 branches of two major microlenders and charged them with extortionist interest rates and intimidating borrowers with strong-armed debt recovery.[69]

Last month, Bangladesh Finance Minister AMA Muhith charged that high interest rates and charges were forcing borrowers to sign up with several microlenders simultaneously to pay back their loans, placing them in a "debt trap."[70] Yunus called on the Bangladesh Microcredit Regulatory Authority to come up with standardized interest rates to establish transparency and remove suspicion among borrowers about interest rates.[71] The authority has announced that it plans to publish microlenders' interest

rates regularly and to frame a policy to make rates more transparent.[72]

Other than these scattered official efforts, Counts says, no big government backlash has occurred. "There are more threats than outright laws," he says.

Have the recent government actions been effective? "The problem is there's very little ability to enforce regulation in most of the countries in which microfinance operates," says Rhyne. "Most of the time you have a few scattered laws here and there and a very weak regulatory apparatus; it's not clear who is responsible for consumer protection in the financial industry."

OUTLOOK
Soaring Needs

To many in the banking world, microcredit offers enormous opportunity as 2010 marks the beginning of a demographic window in which the developing world's working-age population will surge to its highest point relative to the nonworking old and young. Millions of the "unbanked" will join the formal banking system, and "the need for microfinance will also soar," predicted HSBC Chairman Stephen Green. If all the working-age adults earning $2 a day or less are counted, some estimate the demand for microfinance is already 10 times the current supply.[73]

But many uncertainties hang in the balance, including worries about exploiting the poor to pay Western investors and questions about whether governments will clamp down on the industry.

Revealing microlenders' true interest rates is particularly important now that more profit-oriented investors are getting into the act. "We all agreed to lie [about interest rates] to help the poor, and now we've created the perfect environment for new people to come in and say, 'We can make a lot of money,' " Waterfield, of MFTransparency, says bluntly about his industry. "We're working to rapidly correct that before the damage gets out of control."

Meanwhile, the industry has "a long way to go" before attracting for-profit investors in a big way, according to Tryfan Evans, director of the Omidyar-Tufts Microfinance Fund. Illiterate borrowers placing their thumbprint on a hand-written receipt are a long way from providing Western-style credit ratings. The industry must become far more sophisticated to attract private investors on a large scale.

Despite all the excitement about high profits, average investor returns for microfinance banks overall fall well below the returns for either a commercial bank like Citibank or high-flying Compartamos, according to a recent study. Thus, for the immediate future, the industry probably will continue to depend on "social investors" — those willing to settle for a lower return in exchange for the knowledge they are helping the poor.[74]

And subsidies will continue to be important — perhaps even more so as microlenders struggle with the effects of the worldwide recession. About half of the foreign investment in microfinance in 2008 still came from donors and aid agencies, according to CGAP.[75]

The growing trend of MFIs providing savings accounts to the poor could address concerns that microloans are often used for emergency household needs, rather than entrepreneurial investment. Financial diaries reveal that those living on $2 a day are willing to pay neighbors to guard their savings for emergencies. Citing that finding, the Bill & Melinda Gates Foundation recently provided a $38 million grant to microcredit institutions in 12 countries to encourage them to offer savings accounts for the very poor.[76]

New technology — such as banking via cell phones, which is already widely used in Kenya and the Philippines — could help spread financial services to the poor, potentially offering more flexibility to borrowers than microcredit, with its group attendance requirements and lack of privacy.

Whatever the contributions and faults of the microcredit system, almost everyone agrees that the poor should have access to the same kinds of financial services — whether for credit or savings — that those in the West take for granted.

NOTES

1. See www.sksindia.com.

2. See "Microfinance at a Glance-2008," updated Dec. 31, 2009, Microfinance Information Exchange. www.themix.org/publications/microfinance=glance. The average loan balance per borrower reported by almost 1,400 microlenders is $1,588 — heavily influenced by higher average loans in Eastern Europe and Central Asia. Average loan balances reported by region were Africa: $626; East Asia and Pacific: $684; Eastern Europe and Central Asia: $4,008; Latin America: $1,341; Middle East and North Africa: $746; south Asia: $912.

3. This is the compound average annual growth rate according to "Microfinance at a Glance-2008," Updated Dec. 31, 2009. The $44 billion gross loan portfolio is based on reporting from 1,395 microfinance lenders to the Microfinance Information Exchange, *op. cit.*

4. Muhammad Yunus, "Poverty Is a Threat to Peace," Nobel Peace Prize lecture delivered Oslo, Norway, Dec. 10, 2006, http://nobelprize.org/nobel_prizes/peace/laureates/2006/yunus-lecture-en.html.

5. Malcolm Harper, "Some Final Thoughts," in Thomas Dichter and Malcolm Harper, eds., *What's Wrong with Microfinance?* (2008), p. 257.

6. Ketaki Gokhale, "As Microfinance Grows in India, So do its Rivals," *The Wall Street Journal*, Dec. 15, 2009, http://online.wsj.com/article/SB12605511 7322287513.html.

7. Ketaki Gokhale, "A Global Surge in Tiny Loans Spurs Credit Bubble in a Slum," *The Wall Street Journal*, Aug. 13, 2009, http://online.wsj.com/article/SB125012112518027581.html.

8. Kim Wilson, "The Moneylender's Dilemma," in Dichter and Harper, *op. cit.*, p. 97.

9. The World Bank counted 2.5 billion people living on less than $2 a day in 2005 — two fifths of the world population. See Daryl Collins, *et al.*, *Portfolios of the Poor* (2009), p. 1.

10. Muhammad Yunus, *Creating a World Without Poverty* (2007), p. 54.

11. *Ibid.*, p. 56.

12. *Ibid.*, p. 55.

13. *Ibid.*, pp. 52, 111.

14. For a summary of the studies, See Richard Rosenberg, "Does Microcredit Really Help the Poor?" Focus Note 59, Consultative Group to Assist the Poor, January 2010, www.cgap.org/p/site/c/template .rc/1.9.41443/.

15. Cited in Robert Cull, Asli Demirguc-Kunt and Jonathan Morduch, "Microfinance Meets the Market," *Journal of Economic Perspectives*, January 2009.

16. Gokhale, *op. cit.*, Dec. 15, 2009.

17. Rosenberg, *op. cit.*

18. *Ibid.*

19. Jonathan C. Lewis, "Microloan Sharks," *Stanford Social Innovation Review*, Summer 2008, pp. 55-59, www.mcenterprises.org/userimages/file/microloan_sharks_lewis_stanford_social_innovation_review_ 2008.pdf.

20. *Ibid.*, p. 56.

21. "Online Extra: Yunus Blasts Compartamos," *Business Week*, Dec. 13, 2007, www.businessweek.com/magazine/content/07_52/b4064045920958.htm.

22. Lewis, *op. cit.*, p. 59.

23. Alex Counts, "Reimagining Microfinance," *Stanford Social Innovation Review*, Summer 2008, pp. 46-53, p. 49, www.ssireview.org/site/printer/reimagining_microfinance/.

24. Similar estimates that worldwide demand for microfinance is about 10 times the current supply are cited in Stephen Green, "People Power," The World in 2010, *The Economist*, p. 142. See "Microfinance at a Glance-2008," *op. cit.*, for estimated loan portfolio of $44 billion worldwide.

25. Lewis, *op. cit.*

26. Email communication, March 16, 2010.

27. Christina Frank, "Stemming the Tide of Mission Drift: Microfinance Transformations and the Double Bottom Line," 2008, Women's World Banking, www.swwb.org/files/pubs/en/stemming_the_tide_of_mission_drift_microfinance_transformations_and_the_Double_Bottom_Line.pdf.

28. *Ibid.*, p. 16.

29. Connie Bruck, "A Reporter at Large: Millions for Millions," *The New Yorker*, Oct. 30, 2006, www.newyorker.com/archive/2006/10/30/061030fa_fact1.

30. Cull, *et al.*, *op. cit.*, abstract.

31. Elyssa Pachico, " 'No Pago' Confronts Microfinance in Nicaragua," Oct. 28, 2009, North American Congress on Latin America, https://nacla.org/node/6180.

32. Chuck Waterfield, "Explanation of Compartamos Interest Rates," May 19, 2008, www.microfin.com/aprcalculations.htm. This rate is the annual percentage rate (APR) — the standard used in the United States.

33. Even that 4 percent — a flat rate — is deceptive, Waterfield explains. If it were calculated on the declining balance, as American banks do, it would be twice as much. See www.mftransparency.org for explanation of the difference between flat and declining balance interest rates.

34. See "Slideshow" at www.mftransparency.org.

35. Aneel Karnani, "Regulate Microcredit to Protect Borrowers," Ross School of Business Working Paper No. 1113, September 2009, http://papers.ssrn.com/sol3/cf_dev/AbsByAuth.cfm?per_id=561150.

36. All interest rates in this paragraph are the annual percentage rate (APR) standard used in the United States.

37. Karnani, *op. cit.*

38. Wilson, *op. cit.*, p. 105.

39. Karnani, *op. cit.*, p. 6.

40. *Ibid.*, pp. 15-16.

41. See Center for Financial Inclusion at www.centerforfinancialinclusion.org.

42. Counts, *op. cit.*, p. 48. For background, see Sarah Glazer, "Fair Trade Labeling," *CQ Researcher*, May 18, 2007, pp. 433-456.

43. Karnani, *op. cit*, p. 9.

44. Beatriz Armendáriz and Jonathan Morduch, *The Economics of Microfinance* (2007), pp. 68-69.

45. Yunus, *op. cit.*, pp. 45-47.

46. *Ibid.*, pp. 47-48.

47. Armendáriz and Morduch, *op. cit.*, p. 13. According to Grameen Foundation's Alex Counts, Grameen just barred delinquent borrowers from certain premium loans — not all loans.

48. *Ibid.*, p. 13.

49. Yunus, *op. cit.*, pp. 51, 57. For most recent repayment rate, see www.grameen-info.org.

50. Anton Simanowitz, "What's Behind the Numbers?" *Microfinance Insights*, January 2010. www.microfinanceinsights.com.

51. Kim Wilson, *op. cit.*

52. Yunus, *op. cit.*, pp. 62-63.

53. *Ibid.*, pp. 62-65.

54. See Collins, *et al.*, *op. cit.*, pp. 154-158, and Yunus, *op. cit*, pp. 63-66.

55. "Fiscal Year 2009 Annual Report," *Microfinance Exchange Inc.*, July 2008-June 2009, p. 10. www.the-mix.org/sites/default/files/Annual%20Report%20 2009_0.pdf. See also, "Fact Sheet," www.themix .org/publications/microfinance-glance.

56. Blaine Stephens "Operating Efficiency: Victim to the Crisis," *The Microbanking Bulletin*, December 2009, Micro Finance Information Exchange, Inc., p. 39, www.themix.org/microbanking-bulletin/ mbb-issue-no-19-december-2009.

57. *Ibid.*

58. "Microfinance Banana Skins 2009," June 2009, Centre for the Study of Financial Innovation, p. 6, www.cgap.org/gm/document-1.9.35203/ Microfinance%20Banana%20Skins%202009.pdf.

58 *Ibid.*

59. *Ibid.*, p. 24.

60 *Ibid.*, p. 33.

61. See Simanowitz, *op. cit.*, and Xavier Reille, "The Perils of Uncontrolled Growth," Consultative Group to Assist the Poor, Jan. 11, 2010, http://microfi nance.cgap.org/2010/01/11/the-perils-of-uncon trolled-growth/.

62. Daniel Rozas and Sanjay Sinha, "Avoiding a Microfinance Bubble in India: Is Self-Regulation the Answer?" Jan. 10, 2010, Microfinance Focus, www .microfinancefocus.com/news/2010/01/10/avoid ing-a-microfinance-bubble-in-india-is-self-regula tion-the-answer/.

63. Gokhale, *op. cit.*, Aug. 13, 2009.

64. Collins, *et al.*, *op. cit.*

65. See Reuters, "U.S. Credit Card Defaults Up, Signal Consumer Stress," Sept. 15, 2009, www.reuters .com/article/idUSTRE58E6LH20090915.

66. Eric Duflos, "Governments' Responses to the Global Crisis," Nov. 26, 2009, Consultative Group to Assist the Poor, www.cgap.org. See "Governments' role in times of crisis: toward a new paradigm?" http:// microfinance.cgap.org/2009/12/10/governments'- role-in-times-of-crisis-toward-a-new-paradigm/.

67. "Microfinance Banana Skins 2009," *op. cit.*, p. 26.

68. Pachico, *op. cit.* The bill had not been passed at press time.

69. Karnani, *op. cit.*, p. 3.

70. "Strategy of Microcredit Institutions Must be Reviewed: Muhith," *The Daily Star*, March 16, 2010, www.thedailystar.net.

71. "Yunus Calls for Standardised Interest Rate," *The Daily Star*, March 18, 2010, www.thedailystar.net.

72. "Policy on Cards for Microcredit Interest," *The Daily Star*, March 15, 2010, www.thedailystar.net.

73. Green, *op. cit.*, p. 142.

74. Cull, *et al.*, *op. cit.*

75. "Microfinance Funding Continued to Grow in 2008," *op. cit.* The 2008 figures are the most recent available.

76. Bill & Melinda Gates Foundation, "Grant Signals New Movement Towards Savings Accounts for the Poor," Jan. 12, 2010, www.gatesfoundation.org/press-releases/Pages/microfinancing-institutions-helping-poor-save-money-100113.aspx. The foundation cites the financial diaries described in Daryl Collins, *et al.*

BIBLIOGRAPHY

Books

Collins, Daryl, *et al.*, *Portfolios of the Poor: How the World's Poor Live on $2 a Day*, Princeton University Press, 2009.
In this influential study of the poor in Bangladesh, India and South Africa, economists suggest that savings and loans to help the poor survive through a month of uneven earnings may be just as important as the widely heralded microloans for business.

Dichter, Thomas, and Malcolm Harper, eds., *What's Wrong with Microfinance?* Practical Action Publishing, Warwickshire England, 2008.
In this collection of essays, experts discuss problems with microfinance, including abusive behavior toward debtors who can't pay, and Tufts University lecturer Kim Wilson explains why Catholic Relief Services stopped its micro-credit program in 2005.

Yunus, Muhammad, *Creating a World Without Poverty*, Public Affairs, 2007.
The Nobel Peace-prize-winning pioneer in modern microfinance describes why he started making loans to

the poor and why he sees a future for businesses that care about social benefits, not just profit.

Articles

Bruck, Connie, "A Reporter at Large: Millions for Millions," *The New Yorker*, Oct. 30, 2006.
Bruck describes the debate between free-market entrepreneurs like eBay founder Pierre Omidyar and philanthropic groups over whether microfinance can be a fully commercial profit-making industry.

Harford, Tim, "The Undercover Economist: Perhaps Microfinance isn't Such a Big Deal After All," *Financial Times Weekend Magazine*, Dec. 5/6, 2009.
Pointing to recent studies, Harford writes that the claims that a financial product like microcredit would create millions of entrepreneurs and emancipate women "were always going to be difficult to justify — even if donors tend to lap them up in the search for the next development panacea."

Gokhale, Ketaki, "As Microfinance Grows in India, So Do Its Rivals," *The Wall Street Journal*, Dec. 16, 2009, http://online.wsj.com/article/SB126055117322287513.html.
Moneylenders charging high-interest have multiplied as microfinance has grown, perhaps because the poor use them to pay off their microcredit loans, this article suggests.

Karnani, Aneel, "Regulate Microcredit to Protect Borrowers," Sept 2009, Ross School of Business Working Paper No. 1133, http://ssrn.com/abstract=1476957.
An associate professor at the University of Michigan's Ross School of Business argues for government mandates to protect poor borrowers: placing interest rate ceilings on microfinance loans, outlawing abusive debt collection and requiring lenders to disclose annual interest rates to borrowers in a standardized fashion.

Kristof, Nicholas, "The Role of Microfinance," Kristof's *New York Times Blog*, Dec. 28, 2009, http://kristof.blogs.nytime.com/2009/12/29/the-role-of-microfinance.
In a guest piece posted on Kristof's blog, authors of recent MIT and Yale studies say that though they found

no impact for microloans on poverty, the borrowers were able to pay for things they previously couldn't afford — like a home TV or a cart for their business.

Reports and Blogs

"Microfinance Banana Skins 2009," Centre for the Study of Financial Innovation, 2009, www.csfi.org.uk.
A survey 430 microlenders, investors and experts finds that fear borrowers won't be able to repay their loans tops their list of worries in the wake of the financial crisis.

"Stemming the Tide of Mission Drift: Microfinance Transformations and the Double Bottom Line," Women's World Banking, 2008, www.swwb.org/stemming-the-tide-of-mission-drift.
When nonprofit microfinance groups convert to profit-making banks, the percentage of women borrowers drops, but the total numbers go up as the bank expands its lending.

Karlan, Dean, and Jonathan Zinman, "Expanding Micro-enterprise Credit Access: Using Randomized Supply Decisions to Estimate the Impacts in Manila," July 2009, www.financialaccess.org.
The first research to compare groups randomly to receive microfinance loans — or not — found little effect on poverty among borrowers in the Philippines.

Roodman, David, "David Roodman's Microfinance Open Book Blog," http://blogs.cgdev.org/open_book/.
A research fellow at the Center for Global Development, a think tank in Washington, posts on his blog a critical book he is writing on microfinance, along with reactions. Roodman's blog is one of the best places to follow the microfinance debate.

Rosenberg, Richard, "Does Microcredit Really Help Poor People?" Focus Note No. 59, January 2010, Consultative Group to Assist the Poor, www.cgap.org.
An adviser to a group of international agencies housed at the World Bank offers a balanced summary of recent research.

For More Information

Center for Financial Inclusion, 1401 New York Ave., N.W., Suite 500, Washington, DC 20005; (202) 393-5113; www.centerforfinancialinclusion.org. An initiative launched by microfinance lender Accion International that has initiated a consumer protection pledge for the industry known as the Smart Campaign.

Consultative Group to Assist the Poor (CGAP), 900 19th St., N.W., Suite 300, Washington, DC 20006; (202) 473-9594; www.cgap.org. A coalition of development agencies and private foundations promoting microfinance, housed at the World Bank.

David Roodman's Microfinance Open Book blog, http://blogs.cgdev.org/open_book/2010. One of the best sources of information about ongoing debates in microfinance, written by a fellow at the Center for Global Development, a Washington think tank, who posts chapters of a book he is writing on microfinance and seeks comments.

Grameen Foundation, 50 F St., N.W., 8th Floor, Washington, DC 20001; (202) 628-3560; www.grameenfoundation.org. Supports microlenders worldwide and promotes the philosophy of the first microfinance bank, Grameen Bank, founded by economist Muhammad Yunus in Bangladesh.

MFTransparency, 325 N. West End Ave., Lancaster, PA 17603; (717) 475-6733; www.mftransparency.org. A new industry-led effort to disclose the true cost of loans by posting interest rates, country by country.

Microcredit Summit Campaign, Results Educational Fund, 750 First St., N.E., Suite 1040, Washington, DC 20002; (202) 637-9600; www.microcreditsummit.org. A coalition of microfinance practitioners, donors and advocates seeking to provide microcredit to 175 million of the world's poorest families.

Microfinance Information Exchange (MIX), 1901 Pennsylvania Ave., N.W., Suite 307, Washington, DC 20006; (202) 659-9094; www.themix.org. A nonprofit founded by CGAP that receives data from over 1,400 microfinance lenders.

Microfinance Insights, 512, Palm Spring, Link Road, Malad West, Mumbai 400064, India; +91-22-4035 9222; www.microfinanceinsights.com. A widely read trade publication that focuses on the latest trends in microfinance and offers expert opinions and global viewpoints.

10

Fixing Capitalism

Peter Behr

Angelo R. Mozilo, the former CEO of Countrywide Financial Corp., testifies in March 2008 before a House committee investigating the U.S. mortgage crisis. Once the nation's largest mortgage lender, Countrywide has been widely blamed with helping to fuel the global economic meltdown. Mozilo is currently on trial in Los Angeles, charged with fraud and insider trading.

From *CQ Researcher*, July 2009.

T he head of Britain's Communist Party, Welshman Robert Griffiths, couldn't resist an "I told you so" this spring, amid the worst economic calamity in memory.[1]

"We're not given to predicting the imminent collapse of capitalism," he told *The Sunday Times* in London. "But our message for some time has been that [capitalism] is a system based on crisis and instability, and we're finding there is a very receptive audience."

Capitalism's days may not be numbered, but its reputation certainly has been battered during the current recession and credit collapse, with strikes in France and Ireland, food lines in Eastern Europe, foreclosures in the United States, rising unemployment worldwide — and a breathtaking fall in wealth and housing values.

"This is not simply a financial or banking crisis; it is a crisis of capitalism, of civilization," said Pierre-Francois Grond, a spokesman for the New Anticapitalist Party, a coalition created in February from smaller French parties.[2] Former U.S. Federal Reserve Chairman Paul A. Volcker says simply, the financial system failed.[3] As Australian Prime Minister Kevin Rudd put it, the time has come to repudiate the "wild, corporate cowboy behavior" that defined capitalism over the past two decades.[4]

The 2008 crash appears to be a defining moment for Western-led capitalism, said former Deputy U.S. Treasury Secretary Roger Altman, "Much of the world is turning a historic corner and heading into a period in which the role of the state will be larger and that of the private sector will be smaller. As it does, the United States' global power, as well as the appeal of U.S.-style democracy, is eroding."[5]

World Stock Values Declined by $17 Trillion

The total market value (capitalization*) of the 1,500 global companies in the MSCI World index** plummeted about $17 trillion since October 2007 — a 56 percent drop.

Market Capitalization of Companies in MSCI World Index
(October 2007-March 2009)

* The value of all the outstanding shares of a company.

** An index of 1,500 global stocks from 23 developed countries often used as a benchmark for global stock funds.

Source: Thomson Reuters

Many experts agree that, for the foreseeable future, the global economy will face higher government indebtedness, slower growth, stubbornly higher unemployment, greater protectionism and more volatile interest rates and currency values.[6]

The United States, especially, has intervened massively in its economy, pouring trillions of dollars into wounded banks, taking over failed mortgage institutions and bailing out its largest auto manufacturer, General Motors. Although the Obama administration says it wants to quickly shed responsibility for the firms it has aided, it will undoubtedly be stuck with the quasi-nationalization role indefinitely.[7]

The recent economic intervention by the bastion of free-market capitalism symbolizes a broader turn toward state capitalism over the past decade, say many commentators.[8] "Capitalism in the post credit-crunch era is going to look much more like the state-dominated, oligarchic but fiercely competitive and dynamic systems of the rising 'BRIC' economies" of Brazil, Russia, India and China, wrote British journalist Matthew Lynn.[9]

Like a pandemic, the financial crisis has infected every nation. More than $17 trillion in global stock market investments was wiped out between October 2007 and

March 2009, when markets turned upward, based on the MSCI World index of international stocks.[10] (*See graph, at left.*)

Production everywhere "is declining more rapidly than anything I've seen in my lifetime," said Volcker, chairman of the Board of Trustees of the Group of Thirty — a committee of international bankers, financiers and former government leaders who studied the causes of the meltdown.[11] The 81-year-old Volcker was born two years before the 1929 stock market crash.[12]

The crisis has had repercussions around the globe, including:

- Unemployment in Europe topped 9 percent in June, reaching nearly 14 percent in Latvia, a reflection of the heavy economic toll the crisis is taking on the newly capitalist nations of Eastern Europe and the former Soviet bloc.[13]
- Worldwide trade is projected to fall 9 percent in volume in 2009, the steepest drop since World War II.[14]
- Financial institutions across the globe are projected to lose $4 trillion, according to the International Monetary Fund (IMF) — double the institution's projection of six months earlier.
- The U.S. share of the losses is $2.7 trillion. The 16 nations using the euro currency were estimated to face banking losses of $1.2 trillion, while Japan's losses were expected to be $149 billion.[15]

Leaders of the Group of 20 (G20) nations — the world's largest economies — met in London in April to endorse a blueprint for banking and finance reforms that could help restore economic confidence now and protect against future crises.[16] The suggestions focused on establishing new bank and financial market oversight and regulatory systems.[17] Europe has already taken the first steps, but the United States and Britain must overcome political challenges before their reform proposals can be implemented.

Among other things, the reform agendas promise to regulate hedge funds and other unregulated financial instruments, establish higher requirements for banking reserves, crack down on international tax havens and set new performance standards for the accounting and credit-rating agencies whose lax oversight abetted the spread of high-risk investments.[18]

In the past, financial crises were almost entirely managed by the United States, Europe and the IMF. This time around, China and other emerging nations have claimed a seat at the world's policymaking table, making consensus even harder to reach and raising the stakes in the event of failure.

The G20 countries were united, however, in acknowledging their mutual interdependence with regard to cross-border commerce and finance. Until these flows are restored, commentators say, unemployment, business losses, debt and political tensions will continue to rise. And the poorest nations of Africa, Asia and Latin America, which rely vitally on commodities exports and outside funding, are perhaps the most vulnerable, according to World Bank President Robert Zoellick.

"The global economic crisis threatens to become a human crisis in many developing countries unless they can take targeted measures to protect vulnerable people in their communities," he said.[19] The recession in the developing world could force from 105 million to 143 million more people into poverty by the end of this year, according to the U.N.[20]

Finance ministers from the eight largest economies — the Group of 8 — meeting in Rome in mid-June saw "signs of stabilization" in the wounded global economy and spoke hopefully of "exit strategies" for Western governments to withdraw from deep involvement in their banking systems.[21]

But at the same time, IMF Managing Director Dominique Strauss-Kahn warned that the banking sector had not recovered fully and predicted unemployment would continue to climb this year.[22] IMF Chief Economist Olivier Blanchard predicts the global recession could end by early 2010 but that economic activity and job growth will take longer to recover.

"We can expect unemployment to crest at more than 10 percent in a fairly large number of countries," he said. Jobless rates may not return to normal levels until 2012 or 2013.[23]

As lawmakers, regulators, bankers and investors try to figure out how to fix the globe's battered capitalist system, here are some of the questions being asked:

Using groceries they didn't pay for, anti-capitalist protesters stage a free-for-all picnic inside a Paris supermarket on March 28, 2009. Similar protests held throughout France sought to eat into grocers' profits at a time when many consumers can't pay for food.

Does the financial crisis threaten capitalism?

The global banking and credit crisis is the gravest threat to market capitalism since the Great Depression, according to financier George Soros, who has made billions speculating in capital markets. He and others say the meltdown has destroyed faith in markets' abilities to police themselves and ended U.S. dominance in international commerce. He predicts "a period of great uncertainty and destruction of financial wealth before a new order emerges."[24]

Other commentators see the crisis as an indictment of capitalism's 21st-century excesses. Politicians, economists, historians and consumers everywhere are still trying to come to grips with the freewheeling version of capitalism that evolved over the past two decades. On one hand, it spurred a dramatic expansion of global trade, profoundly changing the world's economies, social conditions and political relationships. It also fed a worldwide wave of speculation.

"The past decade has seen an explosion in the dimensionality, and thus complexity, of the financial web," said Andrew G. Haldane, the Bank of England's executive director for financial stability.[25]

Stock Indices Plummeted

Three of the world's top stock indices — Britain's Financial Times Stock Exchange (FTSE), the U.S. Dow Jones Industrial Average (DJIA) and Japan's Nikkei 225 — have declined significantly since the economic crisis began in mid-2007. The Nikkei has declined the most — nearly 50 percent.

Stock Index Values
(June 2007-May 2009)

Index value: 20,000 / 15,000 / 10,000 / 5,000

June 11, 2007 — Dec. 31, 2007 — June 30, 2008 — Dec. 29, 2008 — May 26, 2009

Legend: FTSE, DJIA, Nikkei 225

Source: Yahoo! Finance

Between 2000 and 2008, the market value of over-the-counter "derivative" products soared from $2.8 trillion to $33.9 trillion.[26] (*See graph, p. 247.*) Derivatives are products whose value is derived from other financial assets or indexes, such as interest rates, currencies and commodities. The 2008 total was nearly two-thirds of the combined value of the world's economic output in 2007 ($55 trillion).[27] The investments in derivatives were so overwhelming — and the risks so unfathomable — that when the bubble finally burst, investor panic spread throughout the world's financial markets.

Now, the financial crisis is threatening the economic gains of the world's middle class, leading to a new skepticism about the viability of capitalism. Throughout the world the middle class "has lost huge wealth in the recent global financial crisis," said Raghuram Rajan, an economic advisor to the Indian government and a defender of market capitalism. "Their attitude is now against the free-market economy."[28]

The crisis has given critics of both capitalism and globalization plenty of new fodder. "As Wall Street's house of cards tumbles down, we would do well to remember that this now-discredited model has already been exported around the world," wrote Sameer Dossani, who heads 50 Years Is Enough: U.S. Network for Global Economic Justice, a U.S.-based advocacy group opposed to globalization.[29]

"We have to go back to the plan we had for the growth of Africa," says Nigerian socialist and political opposition leader Abayomi Ferreira. "We have to devise something original."[30]

But capitalism was feeling pressure even before the market's collapse, as evidenced by the dramatic rise in government control over strategic resources.[31] "Governments, not private shareholders, already own the world's largest oil companies and control three-quarters of the world's energy reserves," noted Ian Bremmer, president of the Eurasia Group, a global political risk research and consulting firm.[32]

Sovereign wealth funds, or state-owned investment portfolios, account for one-eighth of global investment, and that figure is rising, Bremmer said. "These trends are reshaping international politics and the global economy by transferring increasingly large levers of economic power and influence to the central authority of the state. They are fueling the large and complex phenomenon of state capitalism."[33]

Leaders of the industrialized countries still speak of fixing capitalism, not replacing it. "Recent events have proven that the current system of global economic governance is not adequate to today's challenges," said U.N. Secretary-General Ban Ki-moon. "Our institutions and governance structures must become more representative, credible, accountable and effective."[34]

The repair agenda centers on imposing tighter scrutiny and control of trillion-dollar capital flows through new regulations and centralized oversight of banking and finance. Populists also want the extravagance of the financial elites reined in. "The violence of the crisis, its depth, call for really profound changes," French President Nicolas Sarkozy said after paralyzing labor strikes in February protested his handling of the crisis. "We have to start capitalism again from scratch, make it more moral."[35]

"I do not believe capitalism has exhausted itself," said Czech President Vaclav Klaus. "Capitalism has been strangled, restricted and disturbed in a fundamental way by un-capitalist interventions into the functioning of the entire system." But it can recover, he added.[36]

Former Vice Chairman of the U.S. Federal Reserve Alice Rivlin agrees capitalism is not dead. "Pundits and journalists have been asking apocalyptic questions: 'Is this the end of market capitalism? Are we headed down the road to socialism?' " she told a congressional panel. "Of course not." Market capitalism is far too powerful a tool for increasing human economic well-being to be given away because we used it carelessly.

"Besides," she continued. "There's no viable alternative. . . . But market capitalism is a dangerous tool, like a machine gun or a chainsaw or nuclear reactor. It has to be inspected frequently to see if it is working properly and used with caution, according to carefully thought out rules."[37]

For his part, Chinese Prime Minister Wen Jiabao criticized the United States and Western financial institutions for spawning the crisis with an "an unsustainable model" of low savings and high consumption and a "blind pursuit of profit."[38] China remains on the capitalist road, however, barring some greater crisis. Wen said China "would rather speed up reforms" and would promote the private sector and "give full play to market forces in allocating resources."[39]

However, leftist criticism of capitalism is on the rise in China, particularly among the young, says the *South China Post*, noting the popularity of the online forum *wuyouzhixiang* (or "utopia"), among under-30 bloggers. "The debate about the role of the market and government will go on for a while. And as long as the economic crisis does not stop, people will continue the criticisms," said Zhou Ruijin, a former deputy chief editor of *People's Daily*. "But nationalisation is not socialism. . . . The base of the [market] system has not changed."[40]

"The lesson is not that capitalism is dead," says Dani Rodrik, a Turkish-born economist and Harvard University professor. "It is that we have to reinvent it for a new century in which the forces of globalization are much more powerful than before."[41]

Can global leaders agree on financial regulation?

Since the crisis began, a key reform goal has focused on the oversight of private hedge funds, whose enormous investment actions occur substantially out of regulators' eyesight.* Although studies have not implicated hedge funds as directly causing the 2008 banking crisis, they

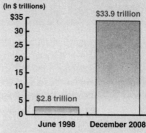

Derivatives Trade Skyrocketed

The value of high-risk over-the-counter derivatives contracts worldwide soared more than 10-fold over the past decade.

Gross Market Value of Global Derivatives Contracts*

(In $ trillions)

$33.9 trillion

$2.8 trillion

June 1998   December 2008

* Measures the cost of replacing all existing contracts for over-the-counter derivatives

Source: Bank for International Settlements, www.bis.org/ statistics/otcder/dt1920a.pdf

symbolize the "shadow" banking world that governments have determined to penetrate.

But instead of reaching agreement, the major economic powers have drawn swords over the issue. The confrontation, principally pitting France against Britain and the United States, illustrates how national interests can raise high barriers to collaborative action.

The European Union (EU) proposed requiring foreign-owned hedge funds doing business inside the EU to be based there. Critics quickly called the rule an attempt to snatch the hedge fund business from Britain and the United States.[42] In the City — the financial center of London and Europe for three centuries — the move was viewed almost as a declaration of war.

"This is a blatant attack on the U.K. and U.S. financial systems by continental countries that neither have a

---

* A hedge fund is an investment fund open to a limited range of investors that is allowed to undertake a wider range of investment and trading activities than other investment funds. The minimum investment is often $1 million.

Leaders of the world's top emerging economic powers — Brazil, Russia, India and China (BRIC) — held their first summit in June in Yekaterinburg, Russia, to develop a response to the global economic meltdown. Some commentators say capitalism in the future will look more like the flourishing, state-dominated BRIC economies. From left: Presidents Luiz Inacio Lula da Silva of Brazil; Dmitry Medvedev, Russia, Hu Jintao, China and Indian Prime Minister Manmohan Singh.

tradition of alternative investments nor a proper understanding of them," said Antonio Borges, chairman of the Hedge Fund Standards Board, in London.[43]

Today, 80 percent of Europe's hedge funds are based in Britain, supporting 40,000 jobs, according to the London-based Alternative Investment Management Association. "A whole galaxy of hedge fund strategies would be impossible under this law, and it is not necessary. The Financial Services Authority, or FSA, Britain's chief financial market regulator, tracks the top 40 funds and knows the level of systemic risk, and it keeps the cowboys out," said association communications director Christen Thomson.[44]

"This is an extremely serious crisis," said David Heathcoat-Amory, a Conservative House of Commons member. "Once we lose control over the City of London, we will never get it back, and the consequences could be catastrophic.... If the City was in Paris, you could be pretty sure [the] French would fight like tigers to save it."[45]

FSA head Adair Turner said, "If one was absolutely confident that European supervision was going to be completely politics-free . . . we would be more relaxed."[46]

European advocates for tighter regulation aren't in a trusting mood about hedge funds, which show signs of

returning to business. *The Daily Telegraph* reported in June that a former Deutsche Bank trader has raised more than $1 billion for a new hedge fund, with a substantial part of it reportedly coming from the German investment firm he worked for previously. "This suggests that despite a difficult couple of years, it is still possible to raise large sums of money for new hedge funds from investors — including banks. This is the largest hedge fund start-up this year, but at least eight others are expected to raise more than $250 million," the newspaper reported.[47]

France's Sarkozy says stronger regulation is needed to maintain order. "Either we have reason or we will have revolt," he said. "Either we have justice or we will have violence. Either we have reasonable protection or we will have protectionism. Regulation of globalisation is the central issue."[48]

Proposed EU regulations also would limit the debt level employed by hedge funds, and debt has been a key to multiplying investors' returns.

Officials of Brevan Howard, Europe's largest hedge fund, with £14 billion in assets, said the firm would leave Britain if the EU hedge fund regulations take effect, according to *The Sunday Times*. "The directive envisages setting leverage [borrowing] limits, and that wouldn't just make it difficult for us to run our business, it would make it impossible," said James Vernon, the firm's chief operating officer. "We are actively looking at non-EU locations. Singapore, Hong Kong, New York and the Middle East are all possibilities."[49]

Jochen Sanio, president of Germany's financial market watchdog, BaFin, predicted a turf battle. "Will the hedge funds . . . be put under regulatory control? Would the United States and London . . . lose a major competitive advantage? This would be a real test," he said.[50]

The EU demand that all European governments end banking secrecy by 2014 is another sore point. French socialist legislator Benoit Hamon castigated Austria, Belgium and Luxembourg for refusing to give foreign tax authorities information on their citizens' savings accounts. A resolution he sponsored calling for such disclosure passed the EU parliament in April.[51]

Sarkozy is so passionate on tax havens he threatened to renounce his title as co-prince of Andorra because of the principality's financial-secrecy laws, said French cabinet minister Nadine Morano.[52]

But Sarkozy's determination to "name and shame" major tax havens provoked Chinese ire at the London summit in April. Sarkozy's government complains that the Chinese territories Macau and Hong Kong are tax havens — *paradis fiscaux* — that don't meet financial disclosure rules established by the Paris-based Organisation for Economic Co-operation and Development (OECD).[53] A face-saving compromise at the London meeting calmed the dispute for now.

Several contested issues at the EU have yet to be resolved, and more negotiations — and ultimatums — lie ahead. "It is a race that has a long way to run," said *The Sunday Times*.[54]

Will the IMF become a global financial watchdog?

The financial crisis caught many red-faced government officials and financial authorities by surprise, among them Britain's Prime Minister Gordon Brown, who served as finance minister when the storm was brewing. Brown responded by calling for a new, international financial-oversight organization and nominated the Washington-based International Monetary Fund for the job.

The IMF "should be at the heart of an early-warning system for financial turbulence affecting the global economy," Brown said in 2008, during a meeting with Indian and British business leaders in New Delhi.[55] A year later, as world leaders prepared for the G20 summit in London, he was still touting the idea, noting that neither the Bank for International Settlements nor the Financial Stability Forum — both in Switzerland — have meaningful authority.[56]

"We have never given anybody sufficient teeth so that their views are treated so seriously that people will immediately have to act when that early warning is given," he said. The IMF "must have a surveillance role that is effective."[57]

However, the IMF's main mission over the past two decades — expanding global trade by stabilizing exchange rates and payments between buyers and sellers — has been controversial. The fund was sharply criticized by the political left during previous financial crises in Asia, Russia and Latin America, largely because it demanded austerity measures in return for emergency assistance.

Critics say the IMF embodies the so-called Washington Consensus, the view that prosperity would follow if governments would balance their budgets and pursue open trade, allowing businesses and markets to do the rest. "Stabilize, privatize and liberalize" was the reigning mantra, writes Harvard economist Rodrik.[58]

IMF defenders say granting support in crises without reforms amounts to throwing good money after bad.

During the economic boom preceding the current recession, the IMF struggled with budget cuts and questions about its purpose.[59] It "seemed to have lost its mojo," said London's *Observer*. "Before the credit crunch, during the calm years that became known as the 'great moderation,' the IMF's twin jobs of emergency lender to hard-pressed countries and guardian of the global system were both in abeyance. And as lending declined, its key source of income, from interest payments, fell away."[60]

"The IMF periodically issued warnings about the risks of the 'global imbalances' in the international economy — live-now-pay-later consumption in the U.S. and oversized trade surpluses and vast foreign currency reserves in rapidly expanding emerging countries such as China," continued the *Observer*. "But . . . governments — including Britain's — felt free to disregard its advice."

The Financial Services Authority's Turner said the IMF sometimes "simply got it wrong, and when they did get it right . . . were largely ignored."[61]

An example of how the IMF "got it wrong," said Turner, was its 2006 "Global Financial Stability Report." While noting concerns about the growth of unregulated derivatives investments by banks, the report concluded that, on balance, these investments spread market risk much more widely and "helped to make the banking and overall financial system more resilient" and "less vulnerable to shocks."[62] But, as regulators learned after the crash, banks had kept a perilous amount of the risk.

The G20 leaders pledged $750 billion in increased funding for the IMF to help developing nations get through the recession.[63] The IMF didn't expect to have all those funds in hand before the end of 2009.[64] And Brown's IMF proposal was not the top priority for world leaders at the April summit. China, which has chaffed at IMF lectures on its undervalued currency, pointedly did not embrace Brown's plan.[65]

How to Fix the Global Financial System

Two groups of international financial experts who studied last year's financial meltdown made a variety of recommendations on how to strengthen the global financial system. Some of the recommendations have been adopted by various countries, but others are still being debated.

Recommendations from the European Union panel headed by former International Monetary Fund Managing Director Jacques de Larosière include:[1]

- Requiring banks to retain 5 percent of the securitized products they originate and sell, to make sure they keep "skin in the game" — or have a vested interest in making sure the products are properly managed.
- Strengthening individual nations' investigative and enforcement agencies throughout the EU so they can detect and punish crimes.
- Creating a well-funded EU-wide clearinghouse for over-the-counter investments and complex investments, like credit default swaps — the investment insurance products that fueled the credit crisis.
- Authorizing the Financial Stability Forum — an international banking organization based in Switzerland — to set global banking standards.
- Establishing a global watchdog role for the International Monetary Fund in Washington to spot violations of financial standards and sound an alarm.

The reform plan suggested by the Group of Thirty, headed by former U.S. Federal Reserve Chairman Paul A. Volcker, called for:

- Restricting indebtedness levels and investment riskiness at banks and financial firms that are so big their failure could threaten the entire financial system.[2]
- Requiring strict disclosures by banks to prevent them from concealing debt and risk in off-book, non-bank entities.[3]
- Centralizing government oversight of financial markets, particularly in the United States, where responsibility is spread among many different federal and state regulators.
- Regulating hedge funds and other large private-capital pools if their size poses a systemwide risk.

---

[1] "Report of the High-Level Group on Financial Supervision in the European Union," European Commission, February 2009, http://ec.europa.eu/commission_barroso/president/pdf/statement_20090225_en.pdf.

[2] Eight very large, non-bank financial firms in the United States should have been closely scrutinized by regulators but were not, the report said: five investment banks; AIG, the world's largest insurance company; and the two government-backed mortgage companies, Fannie Mae and Freddie Mac. See Group of Thirty, "Financial Reform: A Framework for Financial Stability," January 2009, p. 24, www.group30.org/pubs/pub_1460.htm.

[3] Brad Keoun, "Citi Agrees to Acquire SIV Assets for $17.4 Billion," Bloomberg News, Nov. 19, 2008, www.bloomberg.com/apps/news?pid=20601087&sid=a4yl_7w1N9co&refer=home.

"It is hard to imagine that any research institutions could monitor every happening around each corner of the world," Zhou Xiaochuan, governor of the People's Bank of China (PBOC), said after the summit. Regional banks might do a better job, he added.[66]

The biggest stumbling block is whether China and other developing countries will have a larger voice in IMF decisions. The G20 asked Brown to develop a new plan to make the IMF more democratic. Developing countries also insist that before the institution gets new supervisory powers, a new global consensus must exist on its direction and management.[67]

Traditionally, a European heads the IMF, while the presidency of the World Bank goes to an American. Moreover, the 185-member IMF Executive Board favors the largest donors — the United States, Europe and Japan — and major actions must be supported by 85

percent of the board. The United States — with 17 percent of the voting power — has an effective veto, and the European members have 32 percent of the vote. Together, China, India, Brazil and Mexico have only about 10 percent.

Reformers want the IMF's power allotment to reflect the rising economic clout of China, India and Brazil and to give more representation on the board to populous nations like Pakistan and poor nations that receive IMF aid.

Vijaya Ramachandran and Enrique Rueda-Sabater, researchers at the Center for Global Development think tank in Washington, D.C., have proposed apportioning IMF seats to reflect both wealth and population. Voting shares would go to countries with either 2 percent or more of the world's people or 2 percent or more of global gross domestic product.[68]

IMF leadership says it is responding to the calls for change. IMF Managing Director Strauss-Kahn has taken a more flexible approach during the current recession. The IMF has created a new emergency credit line for countries with good economic track records, without the usual stringent loan conditions. Mexico has been offered $47 billion and Poland $20.5 billion. Hungary, Latvia, Ukraine, Serbia and Romania — whose financial markets have been hit hard by the crisis in European banking — are benefiting from more lenient IMF loans.[69]

Although the IMF has increased support for Africa as well, African Development Bank President Donald Kaberuka called the IMF moves "timid." IMF actions are "debt-creating, not adequate or not likely to be effective within the time frame that's needed," he said.[70]

It will be difficult to restructure the board, analysts agree. For instance, it took a dozen years and many crises before the world created the World Trade Organization to establish new rules for settling trade disputes.[71]

The European Union has vested oversight responsibilities in the new European Systemic Risk Board, not the IMF.[72] Commentators say the world's leaders pay lip service to creating an international financial watchdog but are not eager for an outside body to have supervisory authority over their monetary, currency or economic policies.

"We believe it is highly unlikely that an international financial-sector regulator with power over markets and institutions will emerge in the foreseeable future," professors at New York University's Stern School of Business concluded last year. "Countries are simply not willing to surrender authority."[73]

BACKGROUND

Lessons Ignored

A dress rehearsal for the 2008 credit meltdown occurred 10 years earlier, when Long-Term Capital Management (LTCM) — a Greenwich, Conn., hedge fund — collapsed. Its investment strategy was based on the theories of U.S. economists Robert C. Merton and Myron S. Scholes, who shared the 1997 Nobel Prize in economics nine months before the firm disintegrated.[74] Their complex mathematical models about markets' behavior

gave bankers and brokers confidence that riskier investments could be handled safely, generating bigger profits. The result has been an outpouring of "new types of financial instruments," the Nobel committee prophetically observed.

The firm's initial results were gold-plated, producing annual returns of more than 44 percent initially. But success bred recklessness, and LTCM turned "to outright gambling on currencies and stocks," wrote Frank Partnoy, a University of San Diego law professor.[75] When a global financial crisis erupted in the late 1990s, the firm lost $4.6 billion in less than four months, exposing fatal flaws in its market models. As the crisis peaked, the firm's indebtedness shot up to 100 times the value of its assets. The Federal Reserve intervened, fearing that because the firm had so many deals with financial partners around the world, its demise could cause a cascading financial collapse. The Fed arranged a takeover by other financial firms, and the crisis passed.

Many experts say the scare illustrated the fatal ingredients of the global crisis that would explode a decade later: a reckless plunge into highly leveraged investments in the quest for extraordinary profits; reliance on complex — and flawed — computer models to assess risk and regulators' indifference.

The late-1990s Asian financial crisis was another precursor to the 2008 crisis, say two top economists at the Monetary Authority of Singapore.[76] Thailand, Indonesia and South Korea boasted hot economies during the early 1990s, capitalizing on their strong export growth. Western banks fed huge investments into the region, hoping to ride the wave.

But the loans expanded too fast. Just as happened 10 years later with the U.S. housing bubble, lending reached a tipping point. Confidence turned into doubt, then panic. Western lenders dumped their holdings in Asian currencies and demanded immediate payment on short-term loans owed by Asians. The three nations' economies plunged, requiring a costly IMF bailout. While a full-fledged global crisis was averted, "the policymaking wizards of Washington and other capitals found themselves overwhelmed and chastened by the forces unleashed in today's world of globalized finance," wrote *The Washington Post*'s Paul Blustein.[77] The same patterns brought down Argentina's financial sector in the 1990s.[78]

But the lessons from these emergencies went unheeded. Roger M. Kubarych, a senior economist with UniCredit,

Nations at Odds Over Regulating Banking System

Current approaches represent "a remarkable biodiversity."

European financial centers were stunned in 2008 when they learned that a rogue trader from Société Générale, France's third-largest bank, had lost €5 billion — about $7.2 billion — through massive, unauthorized derivatives trades using the firm's accounts.[1]

But before making the announcement, SocGen, as it is called, had spent three days quietly selling off, or "unwinding," a big chunk of the illegal investments trader Jérôme Kerviel had made over many months, helping to insulate the bank from a shareholder run after the disclosure.[2]

"Thanks to good fortune, it was possible to liquidate the positions within three days," bank chief executive Daniel Bouton said as he revealed the bank's actions. "It would have been impossible to unwind them if they were disclosed earlier."[3]

SocGen's decision to leave markets in the dark while it acted to protect itself drew praise, not condemnation, from French authorities. Michel Prada, then-director of the Autorité des Marchés Financiers (AMF), a market watchdog, told a French Senate hearing a week later that his government department authorized Bouton to clear out the unauthorized transactions. Bouton "acted well," Prada said.[4]

But the bank's decision illustrates a fundamental conflict of interest confronting regulators as they consider how to tighten supervision of a banking system that careened out of control in the run-up to the 2008 global credit crisis. Should

SocGen have been required to let markets in on what it knew before it traded out of Kerviel's investments? Or was the overriding priority getting the bank's finances in line before the news broke?

Whether regulators should first ensure the security of the financial institution or have banks disclose critical information to investors and shareholders has become a central issue in the financial-reform debate. Some experts say responsibilities for the two functions should be lodged in separate agencies. On the other hand, divided oversight creates gaps that market innovators can exploit.

So far, there is no global consensus on how to regulate financial institutions. "There is a remarkable biodiversity in the arrangements of financial regulation at the global level," said David Green, head of international policy at Britain's Financial Services Authority (FSA).[5]

The Group of Thirty (G30) — a panel of international bankers, financiers and former government leaders who studied the causes of last year's global financial meltdown — reviewed 17 different financial regulatory structures used in various markets around the world and found four categories of oversight agencies, each with its own advantages and challenges:[6]

- **The Institutional Approach** — used by China, Hong Kong and Mexico — is the older, traditional strategy.

---

an Italian banking firm, sees several causes of the current financial firestorm:

- Reckless borrowers,
- Complicit loan originators (primarily U.S. mortgage brokers),
- Conflicted rating agencies (that approved worthless securities),
- Lazy investors, who did not adequately examine what they were buying, and
- Money that was too readily available for too long.

"Everybody was taking on too much leverage," Kubarych noted. "The Fed closed its eyes, while the SEC

[Securities and Exchange Commission] had given a nearly blank check to the entire investment-banking industry to go to extremes."[79]

Finance Ascends

The late 1980s marked the "ascendancy of finance," in the words of Nobel Prize-winning economist Joseph E. Stiglitz. Financial deregulation was in vogue in the United States and Europe, spurring a phenomenal expansion of new types of investments.[80] Global financial assets soared from $94 trillion in 2000 to $196 trillion in 2007, according to the McKinsey Global Institute, evidence of what former Federal Reserve

Different regulators are responsible for overseeing the soundness and conduct of banks, insurance companies and brokers. The approach appears under the most strain, the G30 study said, because financial markets have evolved so rapidly, blurring distinctions between the different industries.

- **The Functional Approach** — followed in Brazil, France, Italy and Spain — focuses on the type of business that each institution engages in, regardless of the legal description of the business. This can work if regulators maintain close communication and coordination, the G30 said.
- **The Integrated Approach** — used in Canada, Germany, Japan, Qatar, Singapore, Switzerland and Great Britain — concentrates oversight and consumer protection within a single regulator across all industries.
- **The "Twin Peaks" Approach** — followed in Australia and the Netherlands — lodges responsibility in two separate agencies, one to assure the safety and soundness of financial institutions and the other to provide consumer protection.

The U.S. regulatory system is a hybrid of the functional and institutional approaches, according to the G30, further complicated by divisions of authority between the federal and state governments. In response to the recent economic crisis, the Obama administration and the U.S. Congress are considering adopting the Twin Peaks model, with the Federal Reserve overseeing banks and large private funds and other agencies protecting consumers.[7]

Congress is now considering the Obama administration proposal, which faces resistance from lawmakers who believe that the Federal Reserve failed its banking oversight

Leaders of the 20 richest nations meet in London in April to discuss the crisis-wracked global economy.

responsibilities as the crisis developed. (*See "Current Situation," p. 258.*)

---

[1] "Société Générale moves quickly to halt fraud impact, cost 4.9 bln eur," Thompson Financial News, Jan. 24, 2008.

[2] Nicola Clark, "Former Société Générale trader had big bets as early as July," *The New York Times*, Nov. 9, 2008, www.nytimes .com/2008/02/19/business/worldbusiness/19iht-socgen.5.10203247 .html?pagewanted=1&_r=1.

[3] "Société Générale moves quickly to halt fraud impact," *op. cit.*

[4] "Market regulator says bank CEO acted 'well' in handling trading problems," Agence France-Presse, Jan. 30, 2008.

[5] "Hearing on Financial Regulatory Lessons from Abroad," Senate Committee on Homeland Security and Governmental Affairs, *CQ Transcripts*, May 22, 2009.

[6] "The Structure of Financial Supervision," The Group of Thirty, October 2008, www.group30.org/pubs/pub_1428.htm.

[7] "Financial Regulatory Reform: A New Foundation," U.S. Treasury, 2009, www.financialstability.gov/roadtostability/regulatoryreform.html.

Chairman Volcker calls the "modern alchemy of financial engineering."[81]

A quarter-century ago, banks typically kept their loans on their own books and had to grow either by attracting new deposits or through mergers, notes British scholar Nicholas Bayne.[82] Then the "securitization" revolution of the 1980s brought a new way to accelerate home mortgage lending. Securitization allowed banks and mortgage firms to bundle together thousands of mortgages and sell shares of the "pooled" mortgages as securities that promised investors a piece of the monthly mortgage payments coming from homebuyers.

The practice supported the goal of home ownership, which political leaders championed as a fulfillment of the "American dream." The two U.S. government-backed mortgage-buying firms, Fannie Mae and Freddie Mac, led the way in securitizing mortgages. By the mid-1990s, half of all U.S. mortgages were securitized.[83]

In the United States, two-thirds of families own their homes, which are Americans' most important asset. The equity or net worth of Americans' homes (the value minus mortgages and other home loans) approached $10 trillion before the 2008 crash.[84]

But American homeowners took on increasing household debt during the last decade, often using home-equity

CHRONOLOGY

18th-19th Centuries *Heavy war-related debts lead to financial defaults in Britain, France, Prussia and Spain.*

1825-26 Financial crisis hits Britain, Europe. Trade and financial flows to Latin America plummet, triggering continentwide defaults on government debt.

1873 German and Austrian stock markets collapse; international capital flows fall sharply, creating a global crisis.

1900-1940s *Two world wars and the Great Depression lead to new agreements to support a growing global economy.*

1907 New York bank panic is averted when financier J. Pierpont Morgan organizes healthy banks to calm the storm.

1913 Congress creates Federal Reserve, a central bank for the United States.

1929 U.S. stock market crash ignites global depression.

1930 Congress passes Smoot-Hawley law, raising tariffs on imports across the board. Other countries retaliate; global trade collapses.

1931 Britain abandons gold standard, hoping to inflate its weakened economy.

1933 President Franklin D. Roosevelt orders banks closed for a temporary "holiday" to stop epidemic of bank failures. Congress passes law insuring bank deposits, halting panic.

1944 World War II allies meet at Bretton Woods resort in New Hampshire to craft postwar global economic blueprint, with the World Bank and International Monetary Fund as cornerstones.

1960-1990s *Postwar era produces "miracle" economies, expanding global trade — and new crises.*

1982 Debt crisis pushes Mexico toward insolvency. The United States and the International Monetary Fund come to the rescue.

1997 Speculative investment bubble bursts in Asia, triggering crisis in the region's "miracle" economies.

2000s *A freewheeling "age of finance" takes hold, as deregulation invites growing speculation and an inevitable crash.*

2000 U.S. Congress bars federal regulation of derivatives contracts, enabling dramatic increase in risky "shadow" banking arrangements.

2001 China joins World Trade Organization, unleashing extraordinary trade expansion.

2007 Subprime mortgage broker New Century Financial files for bankruptcy (March). . . . Two Bear Sterns hedge funds go bankrupt (July). . . . British mortgage lender Northern Rock suffers a bank run (September). . . . U.S. government takes over mortgage lenders Fannie Mae and Freddie Mac. . . . Federal Reserve creates $20 billion fund to support banking system and joins European Central Bank and Swiss National Bank to support currency prices (December).

2008 U.S. Congress provides $100 billion in tax rebates (February). Bear Sterns investment bank is taken over by JPMorgan Chase (March). Lehman Brothers goes bankrupt. . . . Bank of America buys Merrill Lynch. . . . Federal Reserve bails out AIG insurance group (September). . . . Credit crisis goes global (October): Iceland takes over two of its largest banks; U.S. and Britain inject capital into faltering banks; stock markets sink. British and European central banks drop interest rates. . . . Federal Reserve cuts federal funds rate to lowest in history (December).

2009 Dow Jones Industrial Average drops to 6440, a greater percentage fall than in the Great Depression. Rally begins lifting stocks (March). . . . Group of 20 leaders meet in London, pledge extra $1.1 trillion to help developing countries weather crisis. . . . IMF predicts world economic growth will shrink by 1.3 percent in 2009 (April). General Motors and Chrysler go bankrupt. . . . Federal government commits $50 billion to GM (June). European Union enacts new reforms (June).

loans to borrow against the value of their homes to make consumer purchases. Loans and other credit outstanding for U.S. households and non-banking firms more than doubled between 1997 and 2007, to $38 trillion — nearly three times the nation's gross domestic product.[85]

Democratic and Republican presidents over the past two decades supported an expansion of home ownership by lower-income families, saying it would spread the "American dream." Instead, home ownership became a nightmare for millions. Banks and non-bank lending companies pushed lower-income families to buy homes that were beyond their means, offering "subprime" mortgages with higher than average interest rates. Brokers used deceptive and fraudulent tactics to boost their mortgage transaction fees, creating what one expert called "a wasteland of unethical lending practices."[86] Home sales and mortgage lending accelerated in the 2000s until the bubble burst in early 2006.

Mortgage foreclosures doubled between 2006 and 2007, setting off a devastating chain reaction of losses as the value of mortgage-backed securities plummeted, financial company stock prices plunged and commercial lending dried up.[87]

Regulators, including the U.S. Federal Reserve, had dismissed the possible threat to the financial system posed by the mortgage-lending expansion. But in fact, major international banks, investment houses and insurance companies — especially in the United States and Europe — had invested heavily in mortgage securitization and were dangerously vulnerable, according to a critique by the Stern School at New York University.[88]

As the global economy expanded rapidly, bankers sought ways to increase lending without having to set aside more cash reserves, as banking regulations require. Leading banks accomplished this by transferring mortgage-backed securities to supposedly independent investment funds called "special purpose vehicles," which they established for just this purpose. These transactions generated lucrative fees for brokers and lenders and greatly expanded a "shadow" banking system in which growing debt and risk went undetected by regulators. The game of hide-and-seek indebtedness that resulted was the product of "greed, hypocrisy and sheer folly," says American financial editor and author David M. Smick.[89]

Reckless financial transactions were also fueled by financial-industry salaries, which depend heavily on multimillion-dollar bonuses based on the annual volume of transactions rather than on long-term profitability. "Highly aggressive compensation practices encouraged risk taking in the face of misunderstood and sometimes almost incomprehensible debt instruments," former Fed Chairman Volcker said.[90]

A kind of "Ponzi" scheme resulted, in which new debt must be issued constantly to repay older debt, two British academics have concluded.[91] "In the United States, subprime lending was justified by the belief that the rising values of property would suffice to repay the loans and, like in any Ponzi scheme, this belief proved to be self-fulfilling," they wrote.

Banks or investors dealing with the securitized loans had almost no way to assess the risks attached to them, and independent U.S. credit-rating agencies — paid by the companies issuing the securitized assets — had vouched for the lucrative new financial instruments. But as events would show, those agencies — led by Standard and Poor's, Moody's and Fitch Ratings — grossly misjudged the risks to investors.

Hands Off

Despite the pressure building in global financial markets, U.S. and European regulators maintained a hands-off approach. The world's most important central banker, U.S. Federal Reserve Chairman Alan Greenspan, believed deeply that markets would regulate themselves far more efficiently than government agencies could. He and top Clinton administration officials opposed the regulation of "derivative" financial products, which derive their value from other underlying securities, commodities or financial benchmarks.

"There is nothing involved in federal regulation per se which makes it superior to market regulation," Greenspan said.[92]

Sen. Phil Gramm, a Texas Republican, led the push for Congress to exempt derivatives from federal regulation. "It will keep our markets modern, efficient and innovative," he said, "and it guarantees that the United States will maintain its global dominance of financial markets."[93]

But as debt and risk expanded, officials could not track the growing threat.[94] "No one, including regulators, could get an accurate picture of this market," said the University of San Diego's Partnoy. "It left us in the dark for the last eight years." And, "Bad things happen when it's dark."[95]

Powerful Central Banks Remain 'Last Resort' Lenders

Should the Federal Reserve have more authority?

During the global banking crisis of 2008, Western governments turned to their central banks — the powerful but little-understood reservoirs of credit in modern economies often called the "lenders of last resort."

"Central banks are mysterious institutions, the full details of their inner workings so arcane that very few outsiders, even economists, fully understand them," writes Liaquat Ahamed, author of *Lord of Finance*.[1] "A government grants a central bank a monopoly over the issuance of currency," he adds. "This power gives it the ability to regulate the price of credit — interest rates — and hence to determine how much money flows through the economy."

The wealthy Medici family served as the unofficial bank of Renaissance Italy, creating a model that the English, Dutch and Swedes soon would follow, according to historian Niall Ferguson, author of the best-selling new book *The Ascent of Money*. Britain established the Bank of England in 1694 to help finance its wars. The Banque de France was created in 1800; Germany's Reichsbank in 1875, followed by the Bank of Japan (1882) and the Swiss National Bank (1907).[2]

In the United States a highly fragmented banking industry evolved, with states insisting on supervisory powers over banks based inside their borders. In 1922, as the nation's greatest banking crisis approached, there were 30,000 national and state banks in the United States.

Only after the financial panic of 1907 — one in a series of crises that battered the U.S. economy in the 20th century — did Congress create a central bank. The panic grew out of the need for a rapidly expanding supply of money and credit to support the industrializing United States, Europe and Japan. But the supply of money was tied to the world's gold supply, and there was not enough of the precious metal to go around.

When sophisticated investors began to sell their stocks and hoard gold, stock prices from New York to Egypt to Tokyo began a long, steep slide. When Wall Street's stock market crashed in August 1907, U.S. banks suddenly faced the prospect of failure.

A massive run on banks by depositors loomed, but New York banker and financier J. Pierpont Morgan intervened, averting a collapse of the banking system. Morgan pressured a consortium of still-healthy banks to come to the nation's rescue.

Although other titans of America's "Gilded Age" — notably industrialist Andrew Carnegie and oilman John D. Rockefeller — were far richer, Morgan was the era's unrivaled financial power, held in awe by the business world but pilloried by populist critics.

Morgan and the bankers he pulled together became the unofficial lenders of last resort when financial emergencies struck. At the crisis point in 1907, when a banker fretted that his contribution to the rescue was pulling his bank's reserves below the regulatory limit, Morgan berated him, "You ought to be ashamed of yourself to be anywhere near your legal reserve. What is your reserve for at a time like this except to use?"[3]

The near-collapse of the banking system persuaded many in Congress and Wall Street that the nation could not continue to rely on the aging Morgan to keep the banks solvent. In 1913, Congress created the Federal Reserve System.[4]

As the crisis began in 2007, it appeared initially to European and Asian officials as a well-earned comeuppance for the high-flying risk-takers on Wall Street and in London's City financial center. Then, suddenly, the Europeans realized the crisis would hit them, too.[96]

Wall Street had persuaded European financial markets to trust the new, complex debt securities, and by early 2007 European securities markets were expanding three times faster than U.S. markets. And although the debt boom attracted some financial institutions in Asia and other emerging markets, it was fundamentally "a North Atlantic phenomenon."[97]

Many economists conclude, however, that China's official banking sector and other Asian and Middle

The Fed gave the United States — like most European nations — a central bank with authority to intervene in financial crises.[5] For example, when the 1929 stock market crash triggered the Great Depression, the Federal Reserve slashed interest rates and injected $500 million into the banking system.[6] But internal divisions kept the Fed largely on the sidelines as a series of bank runs forced President Franklin D. Roosevelt — the day after his inauguration in 1933 — to declare a national bank "holiday," closing the banks for four days while Congress passed emergency legislation that stemmed the panic.[7]

Fast-forward to the U.S. stock market crash in October 1987: The Federal Reserve quickly intervened to halt financial panic, pouring hundreds of billions of dollars into the economy by buying Treasury securities on the open market and committing more to support banks and currency markets.

The governance plan for the Fed that Congress created has buttressed its political independence. While the U.S. president appoints the chairman and vice chairman, Federal Reserve board members serve staggered 14-year terms and cannot be removed based on their policy actions.[8]

As the current crisis approached, the Fed's prior and current chairmen, Alan Greenspan and Ben Bernanke, underestimated the threat posed by the U.S. housing bubble.[9] But when the crisis struck, Bernanke — an expert on the Great Depression — led an unprecedented intervention by the Fed to pump trillions of dollars into the banking system, buy bad loans from banks, support foreign currency trading and deal with failing financial institutions.

Asked in March 2009 whether the Fed had battled the crisis by "printing money," Bernanke responded, "Well, effectively. And we need to do that, because our economy is very weak and inflation is very low."[10]

The Fed's next great challenge — once the crisis has eased — will be to absorb excess capital in the economy, he said. "When the economy begins to recover, that will be the time that we need to unwind those programs, raise interest rates, reduce the money supply and make sure that we have a recovery that does not involve inflation."[11]

National Portrait Gallery, Smithsonian Institution

New York financier J. Pierpont Morgan pressured healthy banks to rescue the nation's banking system in 1907.

[1] Liaquat Ahamed, *Lords of Finance* (2009), pp. 363-369.

[2] Niall Ferguson, *The Ascent of Money: A Financial History of the World* (2009), pp. 49-56.

[3] *Ibid.*, p. 582.

[4] Eric Hughson and Marc Weidenmier, "Financial markets and a lender of last resort," www.voxeu, Nov. 28, 2008, www.voxeu.org/index.php?q=node/2625, and http://mpra.ub.uni-muenchen.de/13604/2/MPRA_paper_13604.pdf.

[5] For background, see David Masci, "The Federal Reserve," *CQ Researcher*, Sept. 1, 2000, pp. 673-688.

[6] For background, see "The Federal Reserve System and Stock Speculation," in *Editorial Research Reports*, June 8, 1929, available at *CQ Researcher Plus Archive*, www.cqpress.com.

[7] Ahamed, *op. cit.*, p. 11.

[8] The Federal Reserve, "About the Fed," www.federalreserve.gov/.

[9] Peter S. Goodman, "The Reckoning: Taking Hard New Look at a Greenspan Legacy," *The New York Times*, Oct. 9, 2009, www.nytimes.com/2008/10/09/business/economy/09greenspan.html.

[10] Steven K. Beckner, "Bernanke: When Econ Begins to Recover Will Be Time to Tighten," *The Main Wire*, March 15, 2009.

[11] *Ibid.*

Eastern sovereign banking institutions played a critical role in sustaining the U.S. housing bubble. About one-tenth of all U.S. mortgages were held by overseas institutions and governments, according to British academics Ronen Palan and Anastasia Nesvetailova. That included one-fifth of the $1.5 trillion in securities issued by Fannie Mae and Freddie Mac and a handful of smaller quasi-governmental agencies. In fact, China and Japan held more than $600 billion worth of those instruments at the end of 2008, the British academics conclude.[98]

While the crisis was made in America, it quickly spread around the globe because of huge dollar surpluses that China and other exporters had earned selling consumer goods to Americans. The reinvestment of those surpluses back in the United States helped keep the bubble growing.

Emergency Actions

Over the past six months, governments — led by the United States — have injected massive amounts of government credits and loans into the world's financial markets. By April 2009, the U.S. Treasury and Federal Reserve had committed $12.8 trillion worth of loans and guarantees — nearly equal to the entire annual output of the U.S. economy. Some $2.5 trillion of that has been spent, including the $700 billion in bailout funds provided by the Troubled Asset Relief Program, or TARP.[99]

In return for the funds, the Treasury now owns stock in hundreds of banks, General Motors (GM), Chrysler and the giant insurer AIG. Since then, the Obama administration has injected another $30 billion into GM but hopes to quickly sell the government's share to private investors.[100] Meanwhile, to prevent the collapse of Britain's banking sector, Prime Minister Brown allowed the Lloyds Banking Group to take over the failing Halifax Bank of Scotland.[101]

Europe's lack of a central banking authority has frustrated attempts to create a unified strategy, and the crisis underscored the differences among European economic philosophies, with Germany resisting heavy government-stimulus spending.[102]

"Germany behaved itself during the boom," wrote British economic journalist Jeremy Warner. "It didn't have a credit bubble, it shunned the irrational exuberance of Anglo-Saxon capital markets, it invested in its manufacturing industries and it was prudent in its management of the public finances. Yet it has ended up more badly damaged than Britain and America, the countries widely blamed for causing the collapse."[103]

"European banks have suffered dearly from [the] turmoil, especially since many had liabilities supported by less capital than some of their U.S. counterparts," Brussels-based reporter Leigh Thomas reported. "EU governments have struggled to coordinate their support for struggling banks, with no pan-European authority really in charge of overseeing the sector."[104]

In December, China joined the economic-stimulus club, pledging to inject 4 trillion yuan ($586 billion) into its economy and announcing early in 2009 it was increasing spending in 10 major industries.[105]

China and East Asia are expected to lead the rest of the world out of the recession. An updated U.N. forecast in May predicted that worldwide growth would most likely rebound to 1.6 percent in 2010, from a 2.6 percent drop in 2009. The U.S. economy would grow by just 1 percent, after a projected 3.5 percent decline in 2009, while Japan, whose economy was estimated to fall 7.1 percent in 2009, could manage 1.5 percent growth. The European Union's economy was expected to be flat in 2010 after a 3.5 percent drop in output in 2009. East Asian nations, including China, were expected to grow 5.6 percent, topping a projected 3.2 percent growth in 2009.[106]

However, East Asia's rosier outlook largely depends on U.S. consumer spending and Europe recovering enough to buy Asia's exports.

CURRENT SITUATION

Obama's Plan

Within two months of the April economic summit in London, the United States, Britain and the European Union had defined their financial-reform agendas.

The Obama administration presented its plan to Congress in June. It would make the Federal Reserve responsible for regulating all banks and non-bank funds that were big enough to threaten the nation's financial stability if they were to founder. Those firms will have to maintain adequate capital reserves and meet conduct requirements.[107]

The Treasury Department would lead a new oversight council to spot large firms whose financial condition warranted close supervision, and to look for gaps in regulatory coverage that need to be filled. The currently unregulated over-the-counter derivatives trading would be moved to regulated exchanges and clearing houses.

The new plan combines the federal Office of Thrift Supervision with the Office of the Comptroller of the Currency, which regulates national banks, into a single National Bank Supervisor. But the Federal Reserve and Federal Deposit Insurance Corp. (FDIC), which takes over failed banks, would have expanded powers to seize troubled banks before they trigger a potential crisis.

The arrangement did not satisfy some experts, who say the historic division of banking supervision has encouraged "regulator shopping" by banks and funds that sought the most compliant overseer.[108] "It doesn't eliminate this lack of accountability and supervision for a major banking organization," New York attorney Ernest Patrikis, former general counsel of the influential New York Federal Reserve Bank, told Bloomberg News. "Those issues are still there. The industry probably loves being able to play between the two."[109]

The administration may have gone as far as it could, politically, analysts said. The plan already has encountered a hornet's nest of opposition from both the financial industry and leading lawmakers. The American Bankers Association said Obama's plan "needlessly rips apart the existing regulatory agencies."[110]

Europe's Plan

European Union leaders meeting in Brussels on June 19 agreed to create three new agencies — the European Banking Authority, the European Insurance and Occupational Pensions Authority and the European Securities and Markets Authority — to regulate banks, insurers and securities firms, respectively.[111] A fourth new agency, the European Systemic Risk Board, would monitor financial markets and provide early warnings of future crises.[112]

French President Sarkozy called the new regime a sea change from previous light-handed, "Anglo-Saxon" financial regulatory policy. "My objective was to get a Europe-wide regulator," he said. "We have just given birth to a new European body with binding powers. [But] it's just a starting point."[113]

But the "binding rules" are not absolute. Prime Minister Brown insisted on — and won — a provision barring EU regulators from requiring that national governments take over failing financial institutions within their borders in an emergency. Brown, joined by German Chancellor Angela Merkel, argued the new agencies should not dictate actions that affect national budgets.[114] "I have ensured that British taxpayers will be fully protected," Brown said after the Brussels meeting.

The European Commission is expected to take several months to finalize details, with the goal of instituting the program next year.

Britain Responds

The U.K. has opted for what reformers call a central "macroprudential" regulator to correct the confusion created by the three-way division of oversight responsibilities among the Bank of England, the Treasury and the Financial Services Authority (FSA). A House of Lords report in June concluded that none of Britain's financial regulators had clear responsibility for dealing with the crisis when it struck in 2008.[115]

But a struggle has ensued between Brown's government and the Bank of England. As chancellor of the exchequer, Brown had pushed in 2000 to establish the FSA as Britain's independent and top financial monitor, and he wants it to remain the dominant regulator.[116] However, the Bank of England, still smarting over the emergence of the FSA, is resisting giving it greater powers. Bank Governor Mervyn King says the best way to keep very large banks from threatening the financial system is to keep them from getting too big, implying a need to break up the current banking industry into smaller pieces. But that would threaten Brown's plans to sell troubled assets now held by major banks.[117]

The House of Lords supported the bank's position, saying, "Without a clear executive role, the bank can do no more than talk about financial stability. This exposes it to reputational risk without generating any clear benefit."[118] The outcome has been clouded by Brown's weakened political position in the wake of a recent financial scandal within his party.[119]

The only global action taken to date was the agreement by the Group of 20 in April to create a central financial market monitor, the Financial Stability Board (FSB) — an expanded version of the Financial Stability Forum, a financial oversight advisory group of banking experts formed by major nations in 1999 and based at the Bank for International Settlements in Switzerland. As a result of the recent action, the FSB will now include the entire G20 membership, but it has only an advisory role, with no power to compel countries to follow its advice.[120]

Green Shoots

This spring, the first "green shoots" of economic recovery could be seen in the major industrial countries, said a cautiously optimistic Federal Reserve Chairman Bernanke. Many others agreed.[121] U.S. financier Warren Buffett remained a skeptic. "I had a cataract operation on my left eye about a month ago, and I thought maybe now I'll be able to see green shoots. We're not seeing them."[122]

"The economic situation is extremely bad, but there are the first signs of hope," said Wolfgang Franz, president of ZEW, the Germany-based Centre for European Economic Research. "They should not be played down."[123]

As spring turned into summer, the worst predictions of a continuing banking collapse and an economic pandemic seemed less likely, and stock markets in the United States and Europe were above their 2008 lows.

The most upbeat news was coming out of China, India and other developing countries. China's immense cash reserves are helping it weather the storm. And developing nations' banks in general did not invest heavily in the derivative products that rocked U.S. and European banks. China, India and other more insulated economies have suffered less and are rebounding sooner.[124] In Singapore, the *Business Times* reported in June: "The recovery in the stock market in the last three months has been nothing short of phenomenal. The *Straits Times* index (STI) has rebounded 63 per cent. The Hong Kong Hang Seng index, meanwhile, is now up 67 per cent from its low last October."[125]

Meanwhile, the National Stock Exchange of India (the Nifty index) rose 64 percent between March and the end of May, while China's CSI 300 index was up 37 percent. Brazil's Bovespa index had climbed 41 percent. By comparison, the U.S. Standard & Poor's 500 stock index rose 28 percent.

But government officials and analysts worldwide are warning it's too soon to say a solid recovery is at hand, or that there is no risk of relapse. Indeed, global trade has withered, badly hurting economies that depend on exports to drive growth, including the wealthy Germans and striving Asians.[126] And U.S., European and Japanese banks must resolve bad loans on their books before lending can return to normal.[127]

British financier Neil Woodford said in early June that despite the rally by Britain's stocks, "no tangible sign of improvement in profitability" was evident for the nation's businesses, indicating that more cost-cutting and layoffs lie ahead.[128] Some 19 million people are jobless in Europe and 14 million in the United States, twice the number at the start of the recession in December 2007.[129]

'Zombie' Banks

While credit conditions have improved somewhat in recent months, banks' "toxic" — or significantly devalued — assets continue to restrain lending, experts say.

The IMF estimated in April that the world's banks may lose more than $2.5 trillion this year and next because of bad loans that cannot be repaid or investments that have lost value.[130]

But, in fact, no one knows how much bad debt the global banking system is holding, largely because the losses won't be fully determined until private and federal banking officials have gotten rid of or written off the value of the financial sludge.

Every major financial center is haunted by "zombie" banks, notes Willem Buiter, former chief economist of the European Bank for Reconstruction and Development, in London. "They have indeterminate but possibly large remaining stocks of toxic assets — hard or impossible to value — on their balance sheets, which they cannot or will not come clean on," wrote Buiter.[131]

Buiter, whose "maverecon" blog provides a running commentary on the credit crisis, described the Royal Bank of Scotland in April as "a dead bank walking." Its publicly traded stock amounted to only 0.3 percent of its assets — much less than the £45 billion ($74 billion) it had received from the British government and the £325 billion ($533 billion) in bad debt it has unloaded on the government.[132]

Western Europe's banks have been even less willing than the United States and Britain to acknowledge bad debt, and must somehow raise $500 billion ($700 billion) in new capital before they can resume normal lending. That is a particularly harsh prospect for Eastern Europe, where growth was heavily dependent on outside financing. "No help will come anytime soon, with the members of the old EU barely capable of keeping their own trousers up," Buiter writes.[133]

"There is going to be very little credit growth (if any) to support the economic recovery, and therefore the odds of a sustained recovery are low," Bank of Israel advisor on financial stability Michael Pomerleano said in May.[134]

Developing countries did not binge heavily on the risky, U.S.-designed financial products that swelled world debt, nor did their banking systems suffer the meltdowns that hit the United States, Europe and Japan. Nonetheless, the steep drop in world trade and capital flows has pushed developing nations into recession, too, the IMF reported in April.

"Indeed, the withdrawal of foreign investors and banks, together with the collapse of export markets, create funding pressure in emerging-market economies that require urgent attention," said the IMF.[135] Emerging markets that have relied on foreign capital to finance economic expansion could see the availability of credit contract by 15 percent a year over the next few years, the fund predicted.[136]

Furthermore, although derivatives and other new financial products have wreaked havoc on financial markets, their disappearance could prolong the worldwide recession because the shadow system of hedge funds, off-book "conduits" and structured investment vehicles was about the same size as the official banking system. With those transactions reduced to a shadow of their former dominance, they can offer little help in restoring lending.

The recovery of the U.S. and other major economies will probably be disappointing and drawn out, says Brazilian economist André Lara Resende, resembling Japan's "lost decade" during the 1990s after its real estate bubble burst. "In Japan, the government avoided the bankruptcy of the financial system," he said.[137] Interest rates were pushed to nearly zero, and the government spent freely to try to stimulate growth. But the economy "remained virtually stagnant for more than a decade" because much of the increase in public spending was saved by businesses and consumers in order to bring down debt.

Political Repercussions

Popular anger has been growing around the globe as workers cope with rising unemployment, hiring freezes, pay cuts, declining home values and shrinking personal wealth while their governments focus on rescuing failing banks in the hope that a pickup in lending will eventually trickle down to create jobs and growth.

This spring, the possibility of a long recession stirred fears of potential political backlash. "As people lose confidence in the ability of governments to restore stability, protests look increasingly likely," the *Economist* said in March. "A spate of incidents in recent months shows that the global economic downturn is already having political repercussions. This is being seen as a harbinger of worse to come. There is growing concern about a possible global pandemic of unrest," the report continued.[138]

Adm. Dennis C. Blair, the Obama administration's director of national intelligence, surprised U.S. senators in February by warning that the global economic crisis was the nation's most important immediate security concern. "The financial crisis and global recession are

The global economic crisis could push an additional 105 million to 143 million people in developing countries into poverty in 2009, according to the U.N. Above, a young scavenger in Jakarta, Indonesia.

likely to produce a wave of economic crises in emerging-market nations over the next year," he said. "The longer a recovery is delayed, the greater the risk of destructive defensive moves by desperate nations hoping to gain a competitive edge, such as competitive currency devaluations aimed at making a country's exports more competitive; import restrictions or export subsidies," he said.[139]

Michael T. Klare, a political science professor at Hampshire College, Amherst, Mass., said the crisis is only beginning to affect the developing world. "As the wealthier nations cease investing in the developing world or acquiring its exports, the crisis is hitting them with a vengeance," he said.[140]

However, the political fallout has been mixed, so far. In India's national elections this spring the National Congress Party alliance won on a platform of delivering a better standard of living for the middle class. Congress

Is a global consensus on financial reforms needed?

YES
Stuart P. M. MacKintosh
Executive Director,
The Group of Thirty

Written for *CQ Researcher*, July 2009

Ministers of finance, central bankers and supervisors are rightly concerned during this financial crisis with finding ways to immediately stabilize their national economies and repair their financial supervision systems. Their long-term goal: to strengthen the economic shock absorbers so we can better weather future downturns. However, this is not enough. A broad consensus has formed — led by former Fed Chairman Paul A. Volcker, former IMF Director Jacques de Larosière, the Group of Thirty and others — on what else needs to be done.

Today our economies are truly interconnected, with shocks in one location transmitted worldwide within hours. Many of our largest financial institutions are global in scope, and the collapse of such systemically important firms has shaken the world financial system. G20 leaders understand this and the urgent need to strengthen global banking and financial regulation. They seek to go beyond coordinated rulemaking and standard-setting to identify and modify significant national differences in the application of those rules.

Under this broad goal, particular objectives are ambitious but understood by all policy makers. The G20 is committed to strengthening international capital, liquidity and accounting standards; reinforcing crisis management coordination and improving surveillance of global and regional trends that may mutate into future crises.

We should not be naïve: Reform will not be easy. International negotiations of this sort never are. But we must act. We should learn the lessons of the current financial crisis and fashion broadly understood national and international standards that are applied in a consistent manner from country to country, with supervisors cooperating to ensure crises are recognized promptly as they build.

Does this mean countries with weak or inadequate regulation and supervision will be put under significant pressure to clean up their acts and apply the new standards, once agreed upon? Yes, absolutely. But today, no one cries any tears for the jurisdictions that permitted questionable behavior or for the Bernie Madoffs or Allen Stanfords who took advantage of lax national and international standards.

A key lesson has been internalized: Robust, common, international standards of supervision and financial regulation are required to ensure that the free market functions properly.

NO
Mark A. Calabria
Director, Financial Regulation Studies,
Cato Institute

Written for *CQ Researcher*, July 2009

The value of reaching consensus on any issue, particularly financial regulatory reform, must be weighed against the cost of building that consensus and whether it actually corrects the flaws. It is worth remembering that the international consensus that embraced a radical change in how much capital banks need to keep on hand significantly contributed to the fragility of our financial system. The change moved banks away from maintaining minimum capital ratios and toward a reliance on measures of risk determined by banks and regulators. That failure should caution against the rush toward a new international consensus.

Indeed, it was this international consensus that pushed the U.S. Securities and Exchange Commission to adopt its Consolidated Supervised Entity program, which disastrously lowered capital ratios for investment banks. In addition, it was the international consensus of regulators and bankers — not politicians — that devised the Basel capital rules known as Basel II. Had it not been for the efforts of many in Congress, particularly Sen. Richard Shelby, R-Ala., and former Sen. Paul Sarbanes, D-Md., to resist the consensus behind Basel II, our largest banks today would have even less capital.

The degree to which the world's economies have declined in unison is one of the worst features of the current crisis. To prevent that in the future, some argue for uniform international rules. Yet greater coordination could trigger more contagion rather than less. If all financial institutions are subject to the same rules, they will react similarly to external shocks, increasing the potential for shocks to significantly impact the real economy. Diversification, a basic tenet of finance, was ignored by far too many market participants in recent years. Diversification is equally valuable when choosing regulatory systems, because no one can know ahead of time how different regulatory systems will perform.

Nevertheless, consensus should be accepted when it's based on solid analysis. For instance, the Group of Thirty's recommendations that the hybrid structure of Fannie Mae and Freddie Mac be ended and that sophisticated creditors take losses should be at the top of any regulatory reform list.

Congress must carefully examine any financial reform proposals, because too much of the reaction to the crisis has been driven by panic. Lawmakers also have a responsibility to restructure our financial system's basic rules rather than delegating that task to international regulators.

Party Prime Minister Manmohan Singh was returned to office — the first time an Indian prime minister has been returned for a second term in nearly half a century.[141]

But Iceland's government fell, and Hungarian Prime Minister Ferenc Gyurcsany and his Latvian counterpart Ivars Godmanis were forced to resign early in 2009, giving way to public anger over the crisis.[142] British Prime Minister Brown was battling for his political life at home as both Labor and Conservative politicians duck public anger over lawmakers' expense fraud and abuses, while the recession continues.[143]

OUTLOOK

'Chimerica' Rules

A key to a lasting economic recovery depends critically on what is now called the G2 — China and the United States. The two nations created a framework for a long global expansion of capital, trade and debt that overheated and crashed in 2008. Their ability to adapt that relationship to a post-crisis world requires a shifting of roles, with China spending more to stimulate global growth and the United States increasing its savings to restrain government deficits and support the dollar, economists say.

"For a time it seemed like a marriage made in heaven," wrote historian Ferguson, who calls the two nations "Chimerica." "The East Chimericans did the saving. The West Chimericans did the spending." Chinese imports kept down U.S. inflation. Chinese savings kept down U.S. interest rates. Chinese labor kept down U.S. wage costs. As a result, it was remarkably cheap to borrow money.[144]

In fact, he continued, the cozy mutual dependence between China and the United States helped lead to the economic meltdown of 2008 by feeding speculative U.S. housing investment. "The more China was willing to lend to the United States," he continued, "the more Americans were willing to borrow. [It's] the underlying reason why the U.S. mortgage market was so awash with cash in 2006 that you could get a 100 percent mortgage with no income, no job or assets."[145]

Now the crisis is raising tensions between the United States — the world's richest nation and a proponent of globalization — and China, the leading example of state-directed capitalism.

Washington's stimulus spending and financial-rescue measures have pushed the projected U.S. federal budget deficit this year to $1.8 trillion — 13 percent of America's gross domestic product — up significantly from the 2006-2007 level of less than 2 percent.[146] The quantum increase makes the United States even more dependent upon China and other governments to invest in U.S. Treasury securities to balance the nation's federal account. The aging American population's demands for government-funded Social Security and medical care will compound future budget-balancing challenges.

Some Chinese officials are angered by the losses China has suffered on U.S. investments, making them wary of buying more Treasury bonds and other U.S. investments. If global confidence in the dollar shrinks, so would the value of China's dollar holdings and investments.

As of March, China held $768 billion in U.S. Treasury bonds, and Beijing's dollar-denominated government and corporate paper investments could well be twice that amount. Economists warn that if China begins to shift away from holding dollars and other countries follow suit, the Federal Reserve could be forced to raise interest rates to keep the dollar attractive to investors. That would harm U.S. consumers as well as countries that sell to the United States.[147] On the other hand, a drop in the dollar would be most painful for China, the largest foreign holder of dollar-backed investments.

China is expressing its concerns about the dollar's stability more loudly and frequently.[148] At an Asian conference in May, Chinese economists advocated increased use of the yuan as a common currency for Asian trade, while criticizing the region's excessive dependence on export sales to U.S. consumers.

"Asia is heavily dependent on U.S. markets, partly because of the U.S. dollar's role as an international currency," Fan Gang, a leading Chinese economist, said at the forum. "America's attitude in the past has always been: 'This is our currency, but it is your problem.' Asia, however, is now in a position to raise demands and choose its foreign-exchange reserve currencies."[149]

The threat was real enough to bring U.S. Treasury Secretary Timothy Geithner to Beijing in June to reassure President Hu and Premier Wen about the soundness of the U.S. financial-recovery plan.

"The American thunder of old was replaced by a willingness to please," said a *South China Post* editorial.

Geithner's "main goal was to assure Beijing that his country's monetary policy and ballooning deficit would not undermine the value of the U.S. dollar and paper bonds. . . . Beijing, not Washington, now holds the cards."[150]

China's gross domestic product will surpass Germany's and Japan's by 2015 and match the U.S. GDP by 2035, barring some upheaval, according to a 2003 Goldman Sachs forecast.[151] India's economic growth is on a similar path. "In terms of size, speed and directional flow, the global shift in relative wealth and economic power now under way — roughly from West to East — is without precedent in modern history," according to an unclassified analysis by the U.S. National Intelligence Council.[152]

Because of the dollars and other foreign currencies bulging in its treasury, "Beijing will be in a position to assist other nations financially and make key investments in, for example, natural resources at a time when the West cannot," writes former U.S. Deputy Treasury Secretary Altman. "China's global influence will thus increase, and Beijing will be able to undertake political and economic initiatives to increase it further."[153]

Vyacheslav Nikonov, president of Russia's pro-government Politika Foundation, observed that China forms the key cornerstone of the so-called BRIC nations — Brazil, Russia, India and China — whose economic and political fortunes are rising amidst the global recession. BRIC, not the West, "brings together all typical notions of the world, world problems and ways of their solution. BRIC is a compact model of the modern world."[154]

As the *South China Post* reported recently, the U.S.-China relationship remains more dependent than competitive: "Beijing has realized that China and the U.S. have to support each other instead of being preoccupied with their own calculations, as their economies have become too intertwined to be considered separately."[155]

A model for "a new, world financial architecture," in the words of Brazilian President Luiz Inacio Lula da Silva, has not been found, as the ongoing struggle over international banking and financial regulation shows.[156]

Many experts predict governments will play a much larger role in the world's economy than in the "hands-off" period that preceded the crisis. China's position will grow as the United States is obliged to share global economic leadership. But it will still take decades for China's economy to catch up with the United States — assuming the Chinese people continue to accept one-party political rule.[157]

The risks of future crises remain unless the world's economies can balance the powerful economic forces surging among them, according to C. Fred Bergsten, director of the Peterson Institute for International Economics in Washington.

"The risks range from moderate to catastrophic," he wrote. Because of the damage already done, "The room for maneuver in managing the next crisis might be considerably smaller."[158]

NOTES

1. Matthew Lynn, "The State Strikes Back," *The Sunday Times* (London), May 24, 2008, pp. 8-9, http://business.timesonline.co.uk/tol/business/economics/article6349889.ece.

2. Michael Deibert, "World crisis spurs protest from the French," *The Washington Times*, May 11, 2009, p. B1, www.washingtontimes.com/news/2009/may/11/world-crisis-spurs-protest-from-french-workers/.

3. Alison Fitzgerald, "Volcker group targets banks, hedge funds for crackdown; Bid to curtail risk-taking," *Financial Post* (Canada) via Bloomberg News, Jan. 16, 2009, p. FP10.

4. Phillip Coorey, "Time for a war on greed, tax havens — and blame," *Sydney Morning Herald* (Australia), April 6, 2009, www.smh.com.au/opinion/time-for-a-war-on-greed-tax-havens-and-blame-20090405-9t6m.html?page=1.

5. Roger C. Altman, "The Great Crash, 2008: A Geopolitical Setback for the West," *Foreign Affairs*, January-February 2009, www.foreignaffairs.com/articles/63714/roger-c-altman/the-great-crash-2008.

6. Mathew J. Burrows and Jennifer Harris, "Revisiting the Future: Geopolitical Effects of the Financial Crisis," *Washington Quarterly*, April 2009, www.twq.com/09april/docs/09apr_Burrows.pdf.

7. Steven Mufson, "U.S. in Control: Its Goal To Fix, Not Run Firms," *The Washington Post*, April 23, 2009, p. A1, www.washingtonpost.com/wp-dyn/content/article/2009/04/28/AR2009042803842.html.

8. Altman, *op. cit.*

9. Lynn, *op. cit.*

10. The MSCI World index tracks prices of 1,500 international stocks. See www.mscibarra.com/products/indices/stdindex/performance.html.

11. Barry Wood, "Former US Fed Chief Volcker Calls for Stronger Market Regulation," *Voice of America News*, Feb. 26, 2009, www.voanews.com/english/archive/2009-02/2009-02-26-voa62.cfm?moddate=2009-02-26.

12. "The Structure of Financial Supervision — Approaches and Challenges in a Global Marketplace," The Group of Thirty, January 2009, www.G30.org.

13. Nina Kolyako, "Experts: unemployment level in Latvia to surge again in coming months, putting pressure on budget," *The Baltic Course*, June 5, 2009, www.baltic-course.com/eng/analytics/?doc=14573.

14. "WTO sees 9% global trade decline in 2009 as recession strikes," statement, World Trade Organization, March 23, 2009, www.wto.org/english/news_e/pres09_e/pr554_e.htm.

15. Martin Crutsinger, "IMF: Losses from global credit crisis mounting," The Associated Press, April 21, 2009.

16. The Group of 20 finance ministers and central bank governors is an informal organization created in 1999 to coordinate global financial policies. Its members are Argentina, Australia, Brazil, Canada, China, France, Germany, India, Indonesia, Italy, Japan, Mexico, Russia, Saudi Arabia, South Africa, South Korea, Turkey, United Kingdom, United States and the European Union. The G20 was designed to represent not only major economies but also all major regions of the world; www.g20.org/about_what_is_g20.aspx.

17. "Outcomes," The London Summit 2009, www.londonsummit.gov.uk/en/summit-aims/timeline-events/summit-outcomes.

18. *Ibid.*

19. "World Bank wants G7 to address rising poverty in crisis," *Sydney Morning Herald* (Australia), via Agence France-Presse, Feb. 13, 2009, http://business.smh.com.au/business/world-business/world-bank-wants-g7-to-address-rising-poverty-in-crisis-20090213-86dt.html.

20. "Not just straw men; Brics, emerging markets and the world economy," *The Economist*, U.S. Edition, June 20, 2009, www.economist.com/displayStory.cfm?story_id=13871969.

21. "G8 note of hope on world economy," *The Sunday Times* (London), June 14, 2009, p. 1. The Group of 8 nations are Canada, France, Germany, Italy, Japan, Russia, the U.K. and the United States. The European Union also participates in group meetings.

22. Sean O'Grady, "IMF warns on recovery as jobs disappear; banks, unemployment and credit concerns continue," *The Independent* (London), June 16, 2009, p. 40.

23. Amanda Ruggeri, "IMF's Top Economist: Recession and High Unemployment Likely to Persist," *U.S. News & World Report*, April 30, 2009, www.usnews.com/articles/news/stimulus/2009/04/30/imfs-top-economist-recession-and-high-unemployment-likely-to-persist.html.

24. George Soros, *The Credit Crisis of 2008 and What it Means: The New Paradigm for Financial Markets*, Public Affairs (2008), pp. vii, 125.

25. Andrew G Haldane, speech, Financial Student Association, Amsterdam, April 28, 2009, www.bis.org/review/r090505e.pdf.

26. Bank for International Settlements, "Semi-annual OTC derivatives statistics," June 2008, www.bis.org/statistics/otcder/dt1920a.pdf; and Niall Ferguson, *The Ascent of Money* (2009), pp. 1-2. The face value or notional amount of derivative products is much larger than the market value, the amount that could actually change hands in transactions.

27. IMF, www.imf.org/external/pubs/ft/weo/2009/01/weodata/weorept.aspx?sy=2008&ey=2008&scsm=1&ssd=1&sort=country&ds=.&br=1&c=001%2C998&s=NGDPD&grp=1&a=1&pr.x=27&pr.y=8.

28. "Free Enterprise still relevant, unavoidable: Raghuram Rajan," Indo-Asian News Service, Dec. 19, 2008, www.indiaprwire.com/businessnews/20081219/36083.htm.

29. Sameer Dossani, "Ideological Failure," *Foreign Policy in Focus*, Oct. 15, 2008, www.fpif.org/fpiftxt/5595, and see www.counterpunch.org/dossani07052005.html.

30. "Nigeria; Raising Fresh Debate On Liberal Democracy," *Daily Independent*, Oct. 22, 2008, http://allafrica.com/stories/printable/2008102208 65.html.

31. For background, see Peter Behr, "Energy Nationalism," *CQ Global Researcher*, July 2007, pp. 151-180.

32. Eurasia Group, www.eurasiagroup.net/about-eur asia-group/who-is/ian-bremmer.

33. Ian Bremmer, "State Capitalism Comes of Age: The End of the Free Market?" *Foreign Affairs*, Vol. 88, No. 3, May/June 2009.

34. Ban Ki-moon, speech to a United Nations conference, April 27, 2009, www.care2.com/c2c/groups/disc.html?gpp=3479&pst=1161591.

35. Richard Carter, "European economies 'agree need for greater regulation,'" Agence France-Presse, Feb. 22, 2009; Angelique Chrisafis, "French workers down tools in general strike over handling of financial crisis," *The Guardian* (London), Jan. 29, 2009, www.guardian.co.uk/world/2009/jan/29/france-general-strike-global-recession.

36. Viliam Buchert, interview with Czech President Vaclav Klaus, *Mlada fronta Dnes*, April 16, 2009; via BBC Worldwide Monitoring, April 27, 2009, www.upi.com/Business_News/2009/02/22/EU-leaders-call-for-deep-financial-reforms/UPI-89201235341566/.

37. Alice Rivlin, testimony, "House Committee on Financial Services Holds a Hearing on Financial Services Regulation," *Political Transcript Wire*, Oct. 21, 2008, www.house.gov/financialservices/hearing110/rivlin102108.pdf.

38. "Russia, China give U.S. veiled criticism," *The Canadian Press*, Jan. 29, 2009, p. 32.

39. "A time for muscle-flexing; China and the West," *The Economist*, March 21, 2009, www.economist.com/displayStory.cfm?story_id=13326082.

40. Zhuang Pinghui and Ivan Zhai, "Leftists make comeback, blaming crisis on free-market liberalism," *South China Morning Post*, March 17, 2009, p. 6.

41. Dani Rodrik, "Reinventing Capitalism," *The International Economy*, winter 2009, p. 78.

42. Anthony Faiola, "Early On, Europe Is Out Front in Overhaul of Global Financial System," *The Washington Post*, June 13, 2009, p. 11, www.washingtonpost.com/wp-dyn/content/article/2009/06/12/AR2009061203830.html.

43. Louise Armistead, "UK and Europe headed for a rift over regulation," *The Daily Telegraph* (London), April 30, 2009, p. 1, www.telegraph.co.uk/finance/newsbysector/banksandfinance/5246128/UK-and-Europe-heading-for-rift-over-regulation.html.

44. Ambrose Evans-Pritchard, "Government can't fudge EU assault on the City," *The Daily Telegraph*, June 12, 2009.

45. *Ibid.*

46. "Gov't 'lacks interest' in EU regulation debate," *Financial Adviser*, June 18, 2009, www.ftadviser.com/FinancialAdviser/Regulation/Regulators/Treasury/News/article/20090618/de9cbbfa-5a7a-11de-b342-0015171400aa/Govt-lacks-interest-in-EU-regulation-debate.jsp, and www.reuters.com/article/companyNews/idUKLB65915520090611.

47. Tracy Corrigan, "So soon? Six signs it's already back to business as usual in the City," *The Daily Telegraph* (London), June 19, 2009, p. 5, www.telegraph.co.uk/finance/comment/tracycorrigan/5570313/Financial-crisis-Six-signs-its-already-back-to-business-as-usual-for-City-bankers.html.

48. "Not just straw men; Brics, emerging markets and the world economy," *op. cit.*

49. Kate Walsh, "Hedge funds to take on Europe," *The Sunday Times* (London), June 21, 2009, p. 1.

50. Klaus C. Engelen, "New Rules of the Road," *The International Economy*, winter 2009, www.international-economy.com/TIE_W09_Engelen.pdf.

51. "European Lawmakers Urge End to EU Tax Havens by 2014," Agence France-Presse, April 24, 2009; for background, see www.europarl.europa.eu/news/expert/infopress_page/044-54273-111-04-17-907-20090422IPR54272-21-04-2009-2009-false/default_en.htm.

52. Dragana Ignjatovia, "Tensions Increase Between France and Andorra over Tax-Haven Differences," *Global Insight*, March 27, 2009.

53. Patrick Wintour, Nicholas Watt and Julian Borger, "G20: The summit: Late night hotel peace talks that rescued deal," *The Guardian* (London), April 3,

2009, www.guardian.co.uk/politics/2009/feb/16/gordon-brown-imf1.

54. Dominic Rushe, Iain Dey and David Smith, "King puts spotlight on banks too big to fail; A new era of regulation is dawning in Europe and America," *The Sunday Times*, June 21, 2009, p. 8, http://business.timesonline.co.uk/tol/business/industry_sectors/banking_and_finance/article6543882.ece.

55. "Brown wants IMF to give early warning on financial turbulence," Press Trust of India, Jan. 21, 2008.

56. Ian Traynor, "Financial: EU leaders agree new regulatory regime to cover financial sector," *The Guardian* (London), June 20, 2009, p. 39, http://m.guardian.co.uk/ms/p/gmg/op/view.m?id=108441&tid=34&cat=Credit-Crunch.

57. Patrick Wintour, "National: Brown seeks sweeping reforms to give IMF global 'surveillance role,' " *The Guardian* (London), Feb. 17, 2009, p. 16. For background, see Bank for International Settlements, www.bis.org/ and Financial Stability Board, www.financialstabilityboard.org.

58. Dani Rodrik, "Goodbye Washington Consensus, Hello Washington Confusion?" Harvard University, January 2006, http://ksghome.harvard.edu/~drodrik/Lessons%20of%20the%201990s%20review%20_JEL_.pdf.

59. "Report on IMF internal documents," IFIWatchnet, www.ifiwatchnet.org/sites/ifiwatchnet.org/files/IMFbudgetcuts.pdf.

60. "Can the IMF Now Feed the World?" *The Observer* (England), April 26, 2009, www.guardian.co.uk/business/2009/apr/26/imf-g20-lending-global.

61. Adair Turner, speech, *The Economist*'s "Inaugural City Lecture," Jan. 21, 2009, www.fsa.gov.uk/pages/Library/Communication/Speeches/2009/0121_at.shtml.

62. "Global Financial Stability Report: Market Developments and Issues," International Monetary Fund, April 2006, p. 51, www.imf.org/External/Pubs/FT/GFSR/2006/01/index.htm.

63. "G20 leaders seal $1tn global deal," BBC News, April 2, 2009, http://news.bbc.co.uk/2/hi/business/7979483.stm.

64. "IMF Asked to Aid G-8 With Exit Strategies For Crisis Policies," International Monetary Fund, www.imf.org/external/pubs/ft/survey/so/2009/new061309a.htm.

65. Martin Crutsinger, "IMF: Losses from global credit crisis mounting," The Associated Press, April 21, 2009.

66. "China's central bank governor says IMF needs improvement," Xinhua General News Service, April 18, 2009.

67. "Governance Reforms Urged for Bretton Woods Institutions," *Voice of America News*, April 22, 2009.

68. *Ibid.*; also see William Eagle, "Activists Propose Governance Reforms for the IMF and World Bank," *Voice of America News*, April 22, 2009, www.voanews.com/english/archive/2009-04/2009-04-22-voa47.cfm?CFID=243593762&CFTOKEN=46760838&jsessionid=0030ef9b89f66368815017c2b1a10313c3a1.

69. "Governance Reforms," *op. cit.*

70. "Impact of the Global Financial Crisis on Sub-Saharan Africa," International Monetary Fund, 2009, www.imf.org/external/pubs/ft/books/2009/afrglobfin/ssaglobalfin.pdf.

71. "The Uruguay Round," World Trade Organization, www.wto.org/english/thewto_e/whatis_e/tif_e/fact5_e.htm.

72. "European Systemic Risk Board," *The Independent*, www.independent.ie/topics/European+Systemic+Risk+Board.

73. Viral V. Acharya, Paul Wachtel and Ingo Walter, "International Alignment of Financial Sector Regulation," *Restoring Financial Stability: How to Repair a Failed System*, Chapter 18, New York University Stern School of Business, p. 41, http://whitepapers.stern.nyu.edu/summaries/ch18.html.

74. Roger Lowenstein, *When Genius Failed: The Rise and Fall of Long-Term Capital Management* (2000), p. 65.

75. Frank Partnoy, *Infectious Greed, How Deceit and Greed Corrupted Financial Markets* (2003), p. 255.

76. Hoe Ee Khor and Rui Xiong Kee, "Asia: A Perspective on the Subprime Crisis," Monetary Authority of Singapore, Feb. 15, 2008, http://mpra.ub.uni-muenchen.de/9995/1/MPRA_paper_9995.pdf.

77. Paul Blustein, *The Chastening, Inside the Crisis that Rocked the Global Financial System and Humbled the IMF* (2001), pp. 3-13.

78. Paul Blustein, "Argentina Didn't Fall on Its Own: Wall Street Pushed Debt Till the Last," *The Washington Post*, Aug. 3, 2003, p. A1.

79. Roger M. Kubarych, blog comment on VoxEU, May 4, 2009, www.voxeu.org/index.php?q=node/3509.

80. Joesph E. Stiglitz, *The Roaring Nineties — A New History of the World's Most Prosperous Decade* (2003), p. xiv; William D. Nordhaus, "The Story of a Bubble," *New York Review of Books*, Jan. 15, 2004, www.nybooks.com/articles/16878.

81. The McKinsey survey includes the value of equities on stock exchanges, private debt, government debt securities and bank deposits. McKinsey Global Institute, "Mapping global capital markets: Fifth annual report," October 2008, p. 9, www.mckinsey.com/mgi/publications/fifth_annual_report_Executive_Summary.asp. Also see "BIS Papers No. 44, Financial Globalization and Emerging Market Capital Flows," Bank for International Settlements, December 2008, www.bis.org/publ/bppdf/bispap44.pdf.

82. Nicholas Bayne, "Financial Diplomacy and the Credit Crunch: The Rise of Central Banks," *Journal of International Affairs*, fall 2008.

83. Mark Zandi, *Financial Shock* (2008), pp. 41-42.

84. "Equity in Americans' homes falls to historic low," The Associated Press, June 5, 2009, www.msnbc.msn.com/id/24988315/.

85. "The U.S. Housing Bubble and the Global Financial Crisis: Vulnerabilities of the Alternative Financial System," U.S. Joint Economic Committee of Congress, June 2008.

86. Martin Eakes, chief executive, Center for Responsible Lending, testimony to the Senate Banking, Housing and Urban Affairs Committee hearing, Nov. 13, 2008.

87. For background, see the following *CQ Researchers*: Marcia Clemmitt, "Mortgage Crisis," Nov. 2, 2007, pp. 913-936; Kenneth Jost, "Financial Crisis," May 9, 2008, pp. 409-432; Thomas J. Billitteri, "Financial Bailout," Oct. 24, 2008, pp. 865-888.

88. Acharya, *et al.*, *op. cit.*

89. David M. Smick, *The World Is Curved* (2008), p. 246.

90. Paul A. Volcker, testimony to the Joint Economic Committee, Feb. 26, 2009, www.house.gov/jec/news/2009/Volcker%20testimony%202-26-09%20(2).pdf.

91. For explanation of a Ponzi scheme, see "Money Terms," http://moneyterms.co.uk/ponzi-scheme/; Ronen Palan and Anastasia Nesvetailova, "A Very North Atlantic Credit Crunch: Geopolitical Implications of the Global Liquidity Crisis," *Journal of International Affairs*, fall 2008.

92. Alan Greenspan, *The Age of Turbulence: Adventures in a New World* (2007).

93. Eric Lipton and Stephen Labaton, "The Reckoning: Deregulator Looks Back, Unswayed," *The New York Times*, Nov. 16, 2008, www.nytimes.com/2008/11/17/business/economy/17gramm.html?pagewanted=all.

94. "Special Report on Financial Reform," Congressional Oversight Panel, January 2009, p. 2, http://cop.senate.gov/documents/cop-012909-report-regulatoryreform.pdf.

95. Lipton and Labaton, *op. cit.*

96. Leslie Bennetts, "Greed and Doom on Wall Street," *Conde-Nast Portfolio.com*, December 2008, www.portfolio.com/news-markets/national-news/portfolio/2008/11/19/Greed-and-Doom-on-Wall-Street.

97. Palan and Nesvetailova, *op. cit.*

98. *Ibid.*

99. "Adding Up the Government's Total Bailout Tab," *The New York Times*, Feb. 4, 2009, www.nytimes.com/interactive/2009/02/04/business/20090205-bailout-totals-graphic.html.

100. Stephen Ohlemacher, "GM has future tax break worth billion," The Associated Press, May 29, 2009, www.google.com/hostednews/ap/article/ALeqM5gdlX9pgsPyvHa5miLf-VuY4l5WcgD98G3F6G1.

101. Simon Duke, "Lloyds Shares Plunge 30% after EU Threat to Wreck Rescue Deal," *Daily Mail* (London), May 21, 2009.

102. Xavier Vives, "Europe's Regulatory Chaos," *www.voxus.com*, April 1, 2009, www.voxeu.org/index.php?q=node/3388.

103. Jeremy Warner, "Germany's noble objectives ill-suited to coping with meltdown," *The Independent* (London), May 16, 2009, p. 46.

104. Leigh Thomas, "After US, EU to stress test banks: officials," Agence France-Presse, May 12, 2009, www.timesoftheinternet.com/73294.html. Also see Angel Gurría, OECD secretary-general, "Remarks at the China Development Forum, Beijing," OECD, March 21, 2009, www.oecd.org/document/5/0,3343,en_26 49_34487_42415877_1_1_1_1,00.html.

105. "Minister: More Stimulus Plans in the Pipelines," *Business Daily Update*, March 4, 2009.

106. "World Economic Situations and Prospects 2009, Update as of mid-2009," United Nations, May 2009, www.un.org/esa/policy/wess/wesp2009 files/wesp09update.pdf.

107. "President Obama to Announce Comprehensive Plan for Regulatory Reform," Treasury Department, June 17, 2009, www.ustreas.gov/press/releases/tg175.htm.

108. "Better broth, still too many cooks; Reforming financial regulations in America," *The Economist*, U.S. Edition, June 20, 2009.

109. Bradley Keoun and Jonathan D. Salant, "Obama Plan Gets Wary Reception From Banks, Lawmakers," Bloomberg News, June 18, 2009, www.bloomberg.com/apps/news?pid=20601070&sid=aatqQt9XStqc.

110. *Ibid.*

111. "EU pushes ahead with finance oversight shake-up," Agence France-Presse, June 19, 2009, www.eubusiness.com/news-eu/1245425522.19.

112. Gemma Westacott, "European Commission Outlines Overhaul of Financial Regulation," *FT Adviser*, May 27,2009, www.ftadviser.com/FT Adviser/Regulation/Regulators/News/article/20090527/4d632b72-4adc-11de-b2d4-0015171 400aa/European-Commission-outlines-overhaul-of-financial-regulation.jsp.

113. Traynor, *op. cit.*

114. *Ibid.*

115. Russell Lynch, "Government Should Overhaul System for Managing Bank Crises," Press Association Newsfile, June 2, 2009. Reporting by *The Telegraph*

116. "Essential Facts About the Financial Services Authority," Financial Services Authority, www.fsa.gov.uk/pubs/other/essential_facts.pdf.

117. Richard Northedge, "Darling vs King: Blood on the tablecloth," *The Independent on Sunday*, June 21, 2009, p. 80.

118. Lynch, *op. cit.*

119. "Turf wars in black tie; reforming bank regulation," *The Economist*, U.S. Edition, June 20, 2009, www.economist.com/displaystory.cfm?story_id=1388 1022.

120. Elena Mora, "Financial Stability Board: How it will work," *The Guardian* (London), April 4, 2009, www.guardian.co.uk/world/2009/apr/04/financial-stability-board-g20.

121. "60 Minutes," Interview with Federal Reserve Chairman Ben Bernanke, CBS, Federal News Service, March 15, 2009.

122. "Warren Buffett: I've Had Cataract Surgery And I Still Can't See Any Green Shoots (CNBC Clip)," *The Daily Bail*, June 26, 2009, http://dailybail.com/home/warren-buffett-ive-had-cataract-surgery-and-i-still-cant-see.html.

123. "US, German 'green shoots' spark cautious recovery hopes," Agence France-Presse, March 17, 2009, www.google.com/hostednews/afp/article/ALeqM5hoBIlXnGbSmY8WoQgVwzoevgKs7Q.

124. "60 Minutes", *op. cit.*

125. "Not out of the woods yet," *The Business Times* (Singapore), June 5, 2009.

126. Michael Stutchbury, "Exports key to real recovery," *Weekend Australian*, June 6, 2009, p. 17.

127. "East Asians Hardest Hit in World Crisis," *Forbes*, June 8, 2009, p. 19.

128. Larry Elliott and Patrick Collinson, "Financial Services growth raises hopes of an early end to downturn," *The Guardian* (London), June 4, 2009, p. 23, www.guardian.co.uk/business/2009/jun/03/hopes-early-economic-recovery-britain.

129. Emilie Melvin, "European Council: Euro chambers want focus on economic recovery and unemployment," Europolitics, June 17, 2009; "The

on the expense scandal is available at www.telegraph.co.uk/news/newstopics/mps-expenses/.

Employment Situation — June 2009," U.S. Bureau of Labor Statistics, www.bls.gov/news.release/empsit .nr0.htm.

130. *Ibid.*, p. xi.

131. Willem Buiter, "Good Bank vs Bad Bank: Don't touch the unsecured creditors! Clobber the tax payer instead. Not," *Vox*, March 14, 2009, www .voxeu.org/index.php?q=node/3264.

132. Exchange value as of July 2, 2009.

133. Buiter, *op. cit.*

134. Michael Pomerleano, "Credit growth in the aftermath of a crisis," *Vox*, May 20, 2009, *www.voxus .com*, www.voxeu.org/index.php?q=node/3591.

135. "Responding to the Financial Crisis and Measuring Systemic Risks," International Monetary Fund, April 2009, p. xi, www.imf.org/external/pubs/ft/gfsr/ 2009/01/pdf/text.pdf.

136. *Ibid.*, p. 16.

137. http://blogs.ft.com/maverecon/2009/06/after-the-crisis-macro-imbalance-credibility-and-reserve-currency/.

138. "Governments under pressure: How sustained economic upheaval could put political regimes at risk," EIU ViewsWire Select, Economist Intelligence Unit, March 19, 2009, http://views wire.eiu.com/site_info.asp?info_name=manning_ the_barricades& page=noads&rf=0.

139. Dennis C. Blair, "Annual Threat Assessment of the Intelligence Community for the Senate Select Committee on Intelligence," Feb. 12, 2009, www .dni.gov/testimonies/20090212_testimony.pdf.

140. Michael T. Klare, remarks posted March 20, 2009 at www.alternet.org/story/132523/.

141. Harmeet Shah Singh, "Indian prime minister looks set for second term," CNN, May 23, 2009, www.cnn .com/2009/WORLD/asiapcf/05/16/india.elections/.

142. Polya Lesova, "Mired in recession, Hungary looks for a way out," *Market Watch*, June 19, 2009, www .marketwatch.com/story/mired-in-recession-hunga ry-looks-for-a-way-out; "Up to 120,000 protest in recession-hit Ireland," Agence France-Presse, Feb 21, 2009, www.google.com/hostednews/afp/article/ ALeqM5h-2YAiEAC9OSrsNnMxYl0Z bagLrw.

143. Francis Elliott, "Gordon Brown faces more trouble this week after four stormy days," *The Times* (London), June 4, 2009, www.timesonline.co.uk/ tol/news/politics/article6426849.ece, and Tim Shipman and Andy Dolan, "Brown Blames the Tories in Letter to Thousands of Homes," *Daily Mail* (London), May 30, 2009.

144. Ferguson, *op. cit.*, pp. 335-336.

145. *Ibid.*

146. Lori Montgomery, "Deficit Projected to Swell Beyond Earlier Estimates," *The Washington Post*, March 21, 2009, p. A1, www.washingtonpost.com/ wp-dyn/content/article/2009/03/20/AR200 903200 1820.html. Also see "U.S. Government Spending as a Percentage of Gross Domestic Product," www .usgovernmentspending.com/federal_deficit_chart .html.

147. "Beijing, not Washington, holds economic cards," *South China Morning Post*, June 3, 2009, p. 10.

148. Zhou Xiaochuan, "Reform the international Monetary System," The People's Bank of China, March 24, 2009. For background, see Peter Behr, "The Troubled Dollar," *CQ Global Researcher*, October 2008, pp. 271-294.

149. Antoaneta Bezlova, "The global financial crisis is proving a boon for a resurgent China," *IPS* (Latin America), May 4, 2009.

150. "Beijing, not Washington, holds economic cards," *op. cit.*

151. "Global Trends 2025: A Transformed World," National Intelligence Council, November 2009. www.dni.gov/nic/PDF_2025/2025_Global_Trends_ Final_Report.pdf.

152. *Ibid.*

153. Roger C. Altman, "The Great Crash, 2008: A Geopolitical Setback for the West," *Foreign Affairs*, January-February 2009.

154. Vyacheslav Nikonov, "Birth of Multipolar World," Izvestiya, June 17, 2009, from BBC Worldwide Monitoring.

155. Cary Huang and Martin Zhou, "China sees fortunes tied to U.S. economy," *South China Morning Post*, June 4, 2009, p. 12.

156. Rob Lever, "Emerging economies press for seat at table in crisis talks," Agence France-Presse, Nov. 8, 2008.

157. "Global Trends 2025," *op. cit.*

158. C. Fred Bergsten, "The Global Crisis and the International Economic Position of the United States," Peterson Institute for International Economics, 2009, p. 7, www.piie.com/publica tions/chapters_preview/4327/01iie4327.pdf.

BIBLIOGRAPHY

Books

Ahamed, Liaquat, *Lords of Finance: The Bankers Who Broke the World*, Penguin Books, 2009.
A hedge fund manager examines the history of central bankers whose policies paved the way for the Great Depression.

Ferguson, Niall, *The Ascent of Money*, Penguin Books, 2009.
A British historian chronicles the role of money and banking in history, leading up to the current banking meltdown.

Mason, Paul, *Meltdown: The End of the Age of Greed*, Verso, 2009.
A BBC reporter argues that capitalism requires tight regulation to survive.

Shiller, Robert J., *The Subprime Solution: How Today's Global Financial Crisis Happened, and What To Do About It*, Princeton University Press, 2008.
An economist who predicted the housing bubble explains why it happened.

Tett, Gillian, *Fool's Gold: How Unrestrained Greed Corrupted a Dream, Shattered Global Markets and Unleashed a Catastrophe*, Little, Brown, 2009.
A British anthropologist turned financial reporter explores the shadow banking world.

Articles and Speeches

Bremmer, Ian, "State Capitalism Comes of Age: The End of the Free Market?" *Foreign Affairs*, Vol. 88, No. 3, May/June 2009, pp. 40-55.
A political scientist, author and economics consultant examines the impact of the financial crisis on capitalism's future.

Palan, Ronen, and Anastasia Nesvetailova, "A Very North Atlantic Credit Crunch: Geopolitical Implications of the Global Liquidity Crisis," *Journal of International Affairs*, Columbia University School of International Public Affairs, fall, 2008.
A senior lecturer in international relations at the University of Sussex, U.K. (Palan), and a lecturer in international political economics at the City University of London look at American and European links in the financial crisis.

Turner, Adair, speech, "The Economist's Inaugural City Lecture," Jan. 21, 2009, www.fsa.gov.uk/pages/Library/ Communication/Speeches/2009/0121_at.shtml.
The chairman of Britain's Financial Services Authority describes causes of the global economic crisis.

Xiaochuan, Zhou, "Reform the international monetary system," Bank for International Settlements, 2009, www.bis.org/review/r090402c.pdf.
The governor of China's central bank, the People's Bank of China, offers prescriptions for worldwide financial regulatory reform.

Reports and Studies

Acharya, Viral, and Matthew Richardson, eds., "Restoring Financial Stability: How to Repair a Failed System," Stern School of Business, New York University, March 2009, http://whitepapers.stern.nyu.edu/home .html.
Two members of the NYU business school faculty examine the causes and remedies for the financial crisis.

"Blueprint of a Modernized Financial Regulatory Structure," U.S. Treasury, March 2008, www.treas.gov/ press/releases/reports/Blueprint.pdf.
Officials from the George W. Bush administration look at what happened and why.

"Financial Reform: A Framework for Financial Stability," Group of Thirty, January 2009, www .group30.org/pubs/pub_1460.htm.
An international organization headed by the former chairman of the U.S. Federal Reserve, Paul A. Volcker, reviews financial oversight strategies.

Reinhart, Carmen M., and Kenneth S. Rogoff, "This Time is Different: A Panoramic View of Eight Centuries of Financial Crises," Harvard University, April 2008, www.economics.harvard.edu/files/faculty/51_This_Time_Is_Different.pdf.
Economics professors at the University of Maryland (Reinhart) and Harvard review the causes of eight centuries of financial calamities.

"Report of the High-Level Group on Financial Supervision in the European Union," European Commission, February 2009, http://ec.europa.eu/commission_barroso/president/pdf/statement_20090225_en.pdf.
European finance leaders, led by former IMF director Jacques de Larosière, propose comprehensive reforms in the wake of the global financial crisis.

"Semi-annual OTC derivatives statistics," Bank for International Settlements, June 2008, www.bis.org/statistics/otcder/dt1920a.pdf.
An international banking group reports on the growth of the financial derivatives trade.

For More Information

African Development Bank Group, African Development Bank Group, 15 Ave. du Ghana, P.O. Box 323-1002, Tunis-Belvédère, Tunisia; (216) 71 103 450; www.afdb.org. Provides loans for African countries.

African Economic Research Consortium, Nairobi, Kenya, 3rd Floor-Middle East Bank Towers Building, Milimani Road, P. O. Box 62882 00200, Nairobi, Kenya; (254) 20 2734150; www.aercafrica.org. Publishes economic research on sub-Saharan Africa.

Asian Development Bank, 6 ADB Avenue, Mandaluyong City 1550, Metro Manila, Philippines; (632) 632-4444; www.adb.org. Provides funds for Asian countries.

Bank for International Settlements, Centralbahnplatz 2, Basel, CH-4002 Basel, Switzerland; (41) 61 280 8080; www.bis.org. International organization of central bankers that provides economic and monetary research and facilitates financial transactions among central banks.

Cato Institute, 1000 Massachusetts Ave., N.W., Washington, DC 20001-5403; (202) 842-0200; www.cato.org. Libertarian think tank that supports limited government and free markets.

Federal Reserve Board of Governors, 20th St. and Constitution Ave., N.W., Washington, DC 20551; (202) 452-3000; www.federalreserve.gov. Presidentially appointed, independent panel sets U.S. interest-rate policies.

Financial Services Authority, 25 The North Colonnade, Canary Wharf, London E14 5HS; (44) 20 7066 1000; www.fsa.gov.uk. Regulates Britain's financial sector.

Financial Stability Board, located at the Bank for International Settlements (above), www.financialstabilityboard.org. Represents central banks and treasury departments; received authority from the Group of 20 leaders in 2009 to recommend reforms to the global financial system.

German Development Institute, Tulpenfeld 6, 53113 Bonn; (49) (0)228 94927-0; www.die-gdi.de/. Think tank focusing on economic and development issues.

Group of Thirty, 1726 M St., N.W., Suite 200, Washington, DC 20036; (202) 331-2472; www.group30.org. Nonprofit, international organization that studies global finance and banking issues.

International Monetary Fund, 700 19th St., N.W., Washington, DC 20431; (202) 623-7000; www.imf.org. Provides financial and technical assistance to countries facing economic or foreign-exchange emergencies.

Peterson Institute for International Economics, 1750 Massachusetts Ave., N.W., Washington, DC 20036; (202) 328-9000; www.iie.com. Nonprofit think tank that studies international economic policy.

Progressive Policy Institute, 1301 Connecticut Ave., N.W., Suite 450, Washington, DC 20036; (202) 525-3926; www.ppionline.org. A research and advocacy group with a liberal perspective.

Web Sites

www.eastasiaforum.org/tag/global-financial-crisis/. Australia-based forum reflects East Asian perspectives on the financial crisis.

www.nakedcapitalism.com. U.S.-based Web site providing economic analysis and criticism.

www.voxeu.org. Provides analysis from leading economists on global financial issues, with a European focus.

11

Future of Globalization

Reed Karaim

Vietnamese workers in Vietnam's Mekong Delta region process shrimp bound for American dinner plates. International trade has tumbled dramatically since the current recession began, declining by margins not seen since the Great Depression. Some economists suggest international trade is entering an era of "deglobalization" — a sustained retreat from global trade and economic integration fed by increasingly nationalistic policies and rising protectionism.

From *CQ Researcher*, September, 2009.

In a two-bedroom Mumbai apartment in 1982, young entrepreneurs Ashank Desai and two partners launched Mastek, one of India's first software companies. Today, its nearly 4,000 employees handle information-technology operations for firms around the world, many in the United States and the United Kingdom.

If Mastek is a symbol of the outsourcing phenomenon sweeping the global workplace, Caterpillar embodies the traditional, heavy manufacturing that first made America an economic powerhouse. Catepillar's big, yellow "Cats" — backhoes, bulldozers and loaders — are still ubiquitous in the United States, but these days two-thirds of Caterpillar's business comes from foreign sales.

Mastek and Caterpillar, in fact, are both examples of modern, highly globalized firms. And both companies are dealing with a world economy that looks far different than it did two years ago.

In the wake of the global recession, international trade has fallen off a cliff, tumbling by margins not seen since the Great Depression. The falloff, combined with other factors, has led some economists and historians to suggest international trade is entering an era of "deglobalization" — a sustained retreat from global trade and economic integration fed by increasingly nationalistic policies and rising protectionism. The result, they say, will increase not only economic stress but also political tensions around the world. International sales and profits have tumbled at both Mastek and Caterpillar in the last year. But as officials at the two firms contemplate the future, they see two scenarios. From India, where the economy has continued growing despite the downturn, Desai is optimistic the "Great Recession," will end within a year.

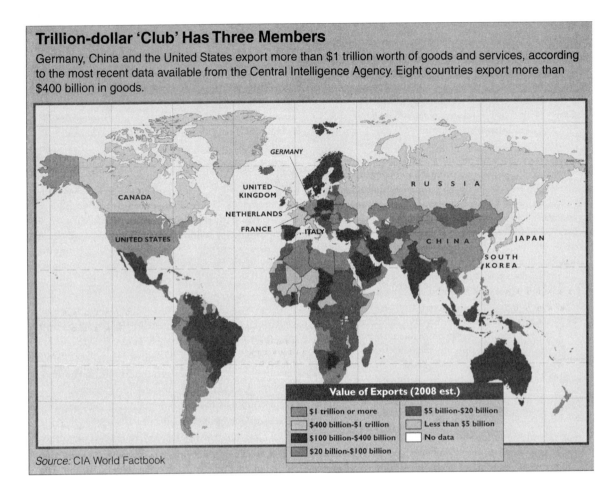

Trillion-dollar 'Club' Has Three Members

Germany, China and the United States export more than $1 trillion worth of goods and services, according to the most recent data available from the Central Intelligence Agency. Eight countries export more than $400 billion in goods.

Value of Exports (2008 est.)

- $1 trillion or more
- $400 billion–$1 trillion
- $100 billion–$400 billion
- $20 billion–$100 billion
- $5 billion–$20 billion
- Less than $5 billion
- No data

Source: CIA World Factbook

"If that happens," he says, "I don't think things will change much. We'll get back to where we were."

But from his office in Washington, Bill Lane, Caterpillar's director of governmental affairs, sees more cause for concern. "There's increasing evidence that the world could be turning inward," Lane says, "and where you will see that first is in countries embracing protectionist measures. Some of that's already happening."

Analysts who believe deglobalization lies ahead say it is being driven by more than just the recession. "Two phenomena are overlapping," says Harold James, a British professor of history and international affairs at Princeton University. "One is a crisis in the financial system that drove global integration over the past four decades; the other is worry about the character of globalization itself and a backlash against it. I think the

financial crisis is the tipping point that moved things in the direction of deglobalization, but there were already substantial pressures pushing in that direction."

In a recent article James became one of the first scholars to suggest the trade collapse heralds something more lasting.[1] Other economic analysts support his view, as do many longtime critics of globalization, but for different reasons.

James' theory — also laid out in his soon-to-be published book *The Creation and Destruction of Value: The Globalization Cycle* — has its skeptics. "If you see globalization as primarily a matter of trade flows, then, yes, it has slowed down," says Moisés Naím, editor of *Foreign Policy* magazine. "But it's really a web of interactions between institutions and individuals in a whole variety of arenas. I see it as a political and technological revolution that's essentially irreversible."

Deglobalization undoubtedly would represent a sea change in the course of history. Since World War II, global trade has grown steadily, spurred by a Western political consensus that trade promotes both peace and prosperity. In the last two decades, this process has accelerated dramatically, with China, India and other emerging economies becoming aggressive players in global markets.

But the World Trade Organization (WTO), which monitors world trade, is now predicting global trade will contract by 10 percent in 2009. [2] Other forecasts are even bleaker. The Organisation for Economic Co-operation and Development (OECD), a group of 30 nations working to promote democracy and open markets, predicts a 16 percent falloff in world trade this year.[3] (*See graph, p. 276.*)

Global trade is declining faster than at the beginning of the Great Depression, according to Kevin O'Rourke, a professor of economics at Trinity College in Dublin, Ireland, and Barry Eichengreen, a professor of economics and political science at the University of California, Berkeley.

They examined a host of factors, such as industrial output and stock market levels, and concluded that the downturn is, in fact, another depression.[4] Of all the indicators, "the one that really stands out is the world trade index. It is clearly falling more rapidly than world trade in the Great Depression," says O'Rourke. "It's really the most alarming aspect of the day."

The Depression was the last great era of deglobalization, with disastrous worldwide economic and political consequences. But while O'Rourke sees many similarities between the Great Depression and today's collapse, he is careful to point out that the current governmental responses have been very different.

In the 1930s, countries around the world retreated behind tariffs and other trade barriers, led by the protectionist Smoot-Hawley Tariff Act of 1930 in the United States. (*See "Background," p. 282.*) "There have been some protectionist actions here and there, but there's nothing dramatic like what happened in the '30s," says O'Rourke, who considers it an "open question" whether a period of deglobalization is coming.

Economists are perhaps most alarmed by the fact that world trade has fallen more precipitously than the overall global economy has contracted, suggesting

Rank	Country	Exports
		In $billions (2008 est.)
1	Germany	$1,500.0
2	People's Republic of China	$1,400.0
3	United States	$1,300.0
4	Japan	$776.8
5	France	$761.0
6	Italy	$566.1
7	Netherlands	$537.5
8	Russia	$476.0
9	United Kingdom	$468.7
10	Canada	$461.8
11	South Korea	$419.0
12	Belgium	$372.9
—	Hong Kong*	$362.1
13	Saudi Arabia	$311.1
14	Mexico	$294.0
15	Spain	$292.8
16	Republic of China (Taiwan)	$255.7
17	Singapore	$235.8
18	United Arab Emirates	$207.7
19	Brazil	$200.0
20	Malaysia	$195.7

The World's Top 20 Exporters

Listed separately from mainland China

Source: CIA World Factbook

strongly that something more fundamental is occurring.

However, an analysis by Joseph Francois, an economics professor at Johannes Kepler University in Linz, Austria, indicates the decline is not as out of line as it appears. Rather, Francois says, trade has fallen off most sharply in those sectors that have been hardest hit by the recession, such as automobiles, machinery and tools.[5]

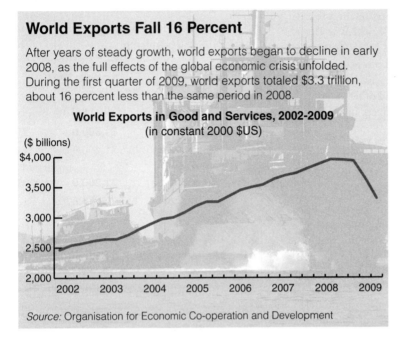

World Exports Fall 16 Percent

After years of steady growth, world exports began to decline in early 2008, as the full effects of the global economic crisis unfolded. During the first quarter of 2009, world exports totaled $3.3 trillion, about 16 percent less than the same period in 2008.

World Exports in Good and Services, 2002-2009
(in constant 2000 $US)

Source: Organisation for Economic Co-operation and Development

Leaders of the industrialized nations, known as the G-20, met in Washington in November and vowed not to repeat the protectionist mistakes made during the Great Depression. [6] By February, however, a World Bank study found that between October 2008 and February 2009 at least 17 of the G-20 nations had implemented 47 protectionist measures at the expense of other countries, and more were proposed. [7] (*See graph, above.*)

Still, protectionist impulses have been largely contained so far, most economists note. "Even if you look at the 'surge' in trade remedies, they don't really cover a lot of trade," says Francois. "These actions are like steam valves, allowing governments to blow off some of the protectionist pressure they're feeling, while still maintaining the basic system."

But to globalization's longtime critics, the world economic order is collapsing from the weight of its own excesses and inequities. "The whole idea that we've got a free market is a misnomer, because it's actually bound by rules that protect corporate power and not the rights of people," says David Korten, author of the new book *Agenda for a New Economy: From Phantom Wealth to Real Wealth.*

Until now the anti-globalization movement — a loose coalition of disparate groups, ranging from anarchists to union members seeking labor protections in international trade agreements — has been unable to derail the political consensus favoring expanded trade. Now, however, those who see deglobalization on the horizon worry that anti-globalization sentiment and other political pressures could usher in a new world order characterized by greater international tension and conflict.

"I'm absolutely convinced that eras of deglobalization are much more destructive and difficult for people living in them than periods of globalization," says Princeton's James. He doesn't see the world economy getting back to normal anytime soon.

As analysts study the global economy, here are some of the questions they are trying to answer:

Does rising protectionism threaten global economic recovery?

Some analysts worry that recently adopted protectionist measures may signal that more protectionism is on the way.

James says last November's G-20 meeting reminded him of the World Economic Conference organized by the League of Nations in 1927, in which the major industrial nations pledged to reduce tariffs — a proclamation that proved empty after the global economy crashed. He sees a similar hollowness to the G-20 declaration.

The G-20 "vowed to stand by free trade, and within a day or so Russia imposed a whole series of tariffs on automobiles, and India imposed a whole set of protectionist regulations," he says. "It was a kind of political verbiage that was disconnected from what immediately happened."

But Douglas Irwin, a Dartmouth College professor specializing in trade history, believes international structures now in place will prevent a tariff war like the one that broke out in the 1930s. "We have the World Trade Organization," he says, "and in previous times, most notably the Depression, there wasn't such an organization, and it wasn't clear you'd be retaliated against if you took protectionist action. Today, it's very clear that if you violate a rule, you are going to be penalized."

Jaime Daremblum, a Costa Rican author of several works on economics and former ambassador to the United States, notes that much of world trade nowadays is governed through regional pacts, such as the North American Free Trade Agreement (NAFTA).[8] Although trade issues can still flare up, he says, larger trading blocs created through regional agreements like the European Union or NAFTA have "taken a lot of trade off the table," when it comes to retaliatory battles.

But other analysts see a threat from so-called soft, or indirect, protectionism. "It's protectionism with a smile," says Caterpillar's Lane. "In today's world, no one will give a speech openly promoting protectionism and isolationism, but they will support policies that have the same effect." Soft protectionism includes industrial policies that favor domestic companies or shield them from larger economic forces, such as the original "Buy American" provisions in the U.S. stimulus package, which mandated that U.S. materials be used for any public-works projects funded by the act.[9]

Nearly all of the stimulus packages passed by Western industrial nations in response to the recession included some protectionist measures, notes Austin Hughes, chief economist for KBC Bank Ireland. He considers indirect protectionism one of the threats to economic recovery. "It's almost inevitable, really," Hughes says, "that as governments get more involved in bailing out sectors of their economy, they become more susceptible to this sort of thing."

The German stimulus plan, for example, is "designed to primarily benefit the German auto industry," according to *Der Spiegel*, the leading German newspaper. [10] And French President Nicolas Sarkozy caused a furor when he announced his country's stimulus benefits would include nationalist requirements at odds with European Union principles of economic integration.

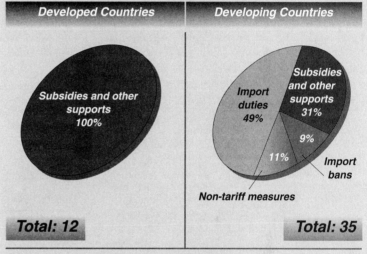

Crisis Triggers Protectionist Measures

Developed and developing nations implemented 47 protectionist measures during the height of the global economic crisis last winter. Developed countries adopted subsidies totaling $48 billion worldwide. Developing countries adopted a variety of measures, including import duties and subsidies. Russia raised tariffs on used autos, and Argentina used non-tariff measures, such as imposing licensing requirements on textiles, TVs, toys and shoes.

Types of Trade Protections Implemented
(October 2008-February 2009)

Developed Countries

Subsidies and other supports
100%

Total: 12

Developing Countries

Import duties
49%

Subsidies and other supports
31%

9%

11%

Import bans

Non-tariff measures

Total: 35

Source: "Trade Protection: Incipient but Worrisome Trends," The World Bank, March 2, 2009

"We want to stop moving factories abroad, and perhaps we will bring them back," Sarkozy said, specifically citing French auto companies that have moved production to the Czech Republic, a fellow EU member.[11]

But Irwin believes most world leaders recognize that trade inequities did not cause the Great Recession. "It's not a problem of too many imports," he says. "Cracking down on trade is not going to solve the problem."

If the global economy begins to turn around within the next year or so, Irwin predicts that protectionist impulses will quickly fade. But Lane is not so sure, noting that political leaders are becoming reluctant to actively champion free trade. "Normally, during an economic downturn, the reaction from policy makers is to promote exports by opening foreign markets, and one of the easiest ways to do that is to negotiate trade barriers

Does a 'Level Playing Field' Exist in Global Trade?

Critics say rules often favor competitors.

American critics of free-trade policies often say they only want to establish "a level playing field" so U.S. and foreign businesses all compete under the same rules.

When American companies compete with Chinese manufacturers, for instance, the Chinese companies have an advantage because of exploitative government labor policies, argues Sen. Byron Dorgan, D-N.D. In his book *Take this Job and Ship It: How Corporate Greed and Brain Dead Politics are Selling Out America*, Dorgan writes that government policies in China allow "for children to work, or for workers to be put in unsafe workplaces, or for companies to pollute the air and water, or jail [for] those who try to start a union. Manufacturing is less expensive in China precisely because workers are exploited.[1]

But what constitutes a "level" playing field in trade, and are U.S. companies really being forced to compete at a disadvantage? The answers aren't as simple as they may seem.

Free-trade policies today are based on the classical economic theory of "comparative advantage," developed by 19th-century English political economist David Ricardo. The theory states that each nation has natural advantages and disadvantages when it comes to producing different crops and goods. Prosperity, Ricardo argued, is achieved if each nation concentrates on its strengths by producing crops and products it can create the most efficiently (cheaply) and selling them in the international marketplace.

For example, Ricardo noted, England's lush, cool landscape was perfect for raising sheep, while Portugal enjoyed other natural advantages for growing grapes. While wine could be made in England and sheep raised in Portugal, the economic efficiency and thus the wealth of both nations

would increase if each nation played to its strength and traded its key product for the other's country's specialty.

Trade today is vastly more complicated than exchanging wine and wool, encompassing services and complex manufactured goods made from raw materials that can come from dozens of countries. But Ricardo's theory remains at the heart of free-trade ideology, particularly the idea that

Cotton farmers in Burkina Faso gather cotton bolls for market. Farmers in the West African nation and other developing countries say they can't compete with cotton farmers in industrialized countries, particularly those in the United States, who receive hefty government subsidies.

free trade allows a country to concentrate on areas in which the field is tilted decidedly in its favor. The concept of a level playing field is largely irrelevant under Ricardo's theory, say some economists.

away," he says. "That's not going on right now. The bilateral free-trade agreements before Congress aren't moving forward, and the WTO talks are stalled."[12]

In India, Mastek's Desai believes globalization will prevail, since he's seen the difference it has made in his country's burgeoning IT industry. "Maybe there was a time when globalization's benefits just went one way, to the wealthier nations," he says. "But now the benefits are

spread across so many countries. There's so much more diversity, I don't think protectionism will really take hold unless the recession lasts three or four years."

Some economists see a shorter window of opportunity. If global economic conditions continue to deteriorate for another year, says Irish economist O'Rourke, "not only would protectionism be likely, it would be almost inevitable. I don't think you could expect

"The idea of competitive or uncompetitive applied to a country is problematic," says Arvind Panagariya, a former economist at the World Bank, the Asian Development Bank and the World Trade Organization.[2] "In an industry, you can be competitive or uncompetitive, but as a nation you can't be." Nations can always find areas where a trading partner seems to have an unfair advantage, he says. For instance, while U.S. free-trade critics cite a lack of safety and labor standards in competing nations, "If you are India or China, you could say, 'There's no level playing field because America has so much money to invest in new technology, and we've got such limited capital, it's not fair.'"

Likewise, cotton farmers in a developing country who don't receive government subsidies say it's unfair for them to have to compete with cotton farmers in industrialized countries, particularly the United States, who get hefty government subsidies.

But critics of globalization believe the theory of comparative advantage isn't working. As proof, critics like Dorgan cite the $673 billion U.S. trade deficit, the result of U.S. imports exceeding exports.[3] "Yes, they can create an economic advantage," Dorgan writes. "But it is not a *natural* competitive advantage."[4]

However, Jaime Daremblum, former Costa Rican ambassador to the United States, says trade agreements can help reduce such disparities. "Free-trade agreements like CAFTA [Central American Free Trade Agreement] are not just about trade," Daremblum says. "They're also plans for governance, in terms of improving the judiciary, improving the enforcement of labor laws and labor standards, improving transparency and accountability. The field is being leveled as we speak."

But many free-trade critics see such trade rules as unfair intrusions into national policies. If CAFTA, NAFTA (North American Free Trade Agreement) and other trade pacts are leveling the playing field, they are doing so by encouraging a "race to the bottom," forcing wages and standards in the wealthier nations down to those in the poorest

Farmers halt traffic in Zagreb, Croatia, on June 10, 2009, to protest plummeting milk and wheat prices. Such well-organized resistance from farm groups in developed countries prevents officials from lowering agricultural subsidies that harm Third World farmers.

nations, according to Lori Wallach, head of Global Trade Watch for Public Citizen, a U.S. advocacy group.

Wallach claims advocates of free trade cite the wrong statistic to prove it's working. "They look at the volume of trade flows between countries, but that is not the measure of the success of a trade agreement," she says. Instead, the question should be: "Did it raise incomes?" U.S. median wages have now declined to 1972 levels, and income inequality has drastically increased since NAFTA and the World Trade Organization accords were adopted, she says.

To Wallach and other critics of current trade policy, the increase in income inequality helps prove the playing field remains far from level.

---

[1] Byron Dorgan, *Take this Job and Ship It: How Corporate Greed and Brain Dead Politics are Selling Out America* (2006), pp. 42-43.

[2] Panagariya is now an economics professor at Columbia University.

[3] Christopher Rugaber, "U.S. Trade Deficit Fell Sharply in 2008," The Associated Press, March 18, 2009.

[4] Dorgan, *op. cit.*

political leaders not to succumb to the pressure that would ensue."

Are some protectionist measures appropriate in today's economy?

Arvind Panagariya, an Indian economist at Columbia University who has worked for both the World Bank and the World Trade Organization, notes that WTO rules

allow "countries, in certain situations, to safeguard domestic companies from foreign competition" during times of economic distress.

The so-called safeguard provisions allow restrictions on certain imports if they threaten serious injury to a domestic industry. But the restrictions must be temporary, providing the domestic industry time to adjust to new conditions. Countries also may restrict imports if they believe a foreign company is "dumping" goods into their market at subsidized or unfairly low prices.[13]

In 2002 when the U.S. steel industry sought protection from foreign imports, President George W. Bush used the safeguard provisions to impose temporary tariffs on imports.[14] Some critics said the action betrayed the administration's free-trade principles.[15] But Kevin Dempsey, senior vice president for public policy and general counsel for the American Iron and Steel Institute, says Bush made the right choice. "The U.S. industry worked hard during that period to become more competitive," he says, "It gave us time to restructure."

In the current recession, the U.S. automobile tire industry has applied for similar relief from Chinese imports. Manufacturers of several different steel products also have brought dumping charges against Chinese competitors, which the Commerce Department is reviewing.[16]

Dempsey believes such actions are necessary and legitimate, particularly in today's economic climate. "Unfortunately, when companies invoke their rights under WTO law to insure that other countries' actions don't harm them, a lot of people refer to this as protectionism," he says. "But bringing an anti-dumping case or a safeguard case can be an important way to make sure we have fair competition."

Panagariya is skeptical, noting "a big surge in anti-dumping actions" since the economic crisis began. "There are signs people may be abusing the privilege." Even if these actions meet the WTO definition of a legal action, he believes they are usually counterproductive. "In the end, two can play the same game," he says. "You're simply inviting retaliation, and it's ultimately detrimental to everyone."

The Obama administration moved aggressively early in its term to back the U.S. auto industry, believing its survival was essential to the nation's economic health. The industry's troubles were, in part, the result of the financial crisis, which dried up credit, and not of the industry's making, Dempsey notes. "We support the efforts to help the U.S. auto industry to restructure," he says. "It's critical to give them breathing room to adjust, and under these circumstances, it's warranted."

But Panagariya believes subsidized loans and other aid provided to domestic auto industries by the United States, Germany, France, Australia and Brazil were protectionist,

discriminating against foreign manufacturers selling cars in those countries. The actions "will almost certainly be challenged and found to break WTO rules," he predicted.[17]

Other analysts, however, think even stronger measures are needed to protect domestic industries. The Trade Reform, Accountability, Development and Employment (TRADE) Act, supported by organized labor and other U.S. interest groups, would require the president to renegotiate NAFTA and other trade agreements with more stringent environmental, labor and safety standards for nations exporting goods into the United States. The legislation, which has more than 100 House cosponsors, also sets out what could not be included in trade agreements, such as requirements that economic sectors be privatized or deregulated.

Lori Wallach, director of Global Trade Watch for Public Citizen, a U.S. consumer advocacy organization that has lobbied for legislation to dramatically revamp U.S. trade law, rejects the notion that such measures will hurt global commerce.

"The question isn't whether there's going to be trade," she says. "The question is 'Under what rules?' The TRADE Act is about taking a different approach, fixing the rules to get agreements that are consistent with the goals and values of the American people."

But Boris Kozolchyk — director of the National Law Center for Inter-American Free Trade at the University of Arizona in Tucson — believes the effort is protectionist and will fail.

"In today's global economy, there's always going to be a replacement buyer or seller to take your place," he says. "It would be a loss economically for whoever tries it."

Will globalization survive the world economic crisis?

The recession, by numerous measures, is the worst economic crisis since the Great Depression. But economists disagree over what impact the recession will have and whether globalization will be one of its casualties. Those who believe deglobalization could worsen see political and economic conditions combining to create a fundamental breakdown in the existing order.

"It is now clear that the global economic crisis will be deep and prolonged and that it will have far-reaching geopolitical consequences," former U.S. Deputy Treasury Secretary Roger Altman wrote recently. "The long movement toward market liberalization has stopped, and a new period of state intervention, re-regulation and creeping protectionism has begun. Indeed, globalization itself is reversing. The long-standing wisdom that everyone wins in a single world market has been undermined."[18]

Altman and others see deglobalization as the start of a new geopolitical era that will be accompanied by escalating conflicts over key natural resources and the ascendancy of China to a position of greater worldwide influence. In effect, they say, the world's economic problems and geopolitical tensions will create a feedback loop of growing distrust and disagreement, pushing the world into the deglobalized era. In this scenario, countries with a smaller economic base, particularly developing nations, will be especially hard hit. (*See "Outlook," p. 291.*)

In Honduras, however, former trade minister Norman García sees nothing so severe in his crystal ball. Despite the severity of the recession, he says, "We haven't really felt that much effect in our trade with the United States. We're still maintaining the same levels." Honduras' primary exports are clothing and agricultural goods, and its primary markets are the United States and Europe, he says.

Indeed, García says that while trade is down overall, "No trading partner has enacted any protectionist measures that have had any effect on us," thanks mostly to the Central American Free Trade Agreement (CAFTA). The pact includes the United States, Honduras and five other countries.[19] The Honduran government was determined to sign CAFTA for that very reason, García says.

"What we were doing is guaranteeing that that market was here to stay for good," he says. Because of such agreements, including the WTO, he says, "I don't think this so-called deglobalization will get any momentum."

But David Smick, an economic policy strategist and author of the 2008 book *The World Is Curved: Hidden Dangers to the Global Economy*, has less faith. "The whole economic model under which the world has operated in the last two decades is crash landing," he says. "The global emerging-market export model is in real trouble."

In that model, he explains, less developed nations such as China promoted rapid growth by setting up their economy "as an export platform, heavily dependent on the U.S. consumer." The model depended on several factors, including a favorable rate of currency exchange with

Farmers — Both Rich and Poor — Demand Protection

European milk producers seeking protection from falling milk prices clash with police outside European Commission headquarters in Brussels, Belgium, on July 22, 2009 (top). As economic stress increases, farmers in poor countries are also flexing their political muscle. In New Delhi, thousands of protesting Indian farmers on Dec. 16, 2008, demand help in competing in global markets (bottom). Among other things, they were seeking higher subsidies, lower diesel prices and interest-free agricultural loans.

the dollar to keep exports relatively inexpensive. [20] But most critically, it depended on Americans' voracious consuming habits and their willingness to pile up debt as they kept buying. The debt habit was fed by easy credit, underwritten by ever-appreciating home equity.

But the housing bubble has burst, and Americans appear to have changed their buying habits, at least for the moment. "There are surveys showing Americans are pulling back, and they're finding pleasure in pulling back," Smick says. "A large part of the world is in denial about this. They think the U.S. consumer is coming back. Well, the U.S. consumer is never coming back in the same way because U.S. regulators are never going to allow that kind of over-leveraging again."

The contraction of that export market, he believes, will significantly strain export-dependent countries such as China, Germany and Korea, along with many smaller developing nations. "I really think we are entering a period of deglobalization," Smick says. "The question is just how fast and to what extent."

But Alan Winters, an economist at the University of Sussex in the United Kingdom, is more optimistic about the future, citing the G-20's April pledge of additional aid to help developing nations weather the crisis. [21] "There's certainly room to do more, but we have avoided a meltdown," he says.

Moreover, he says, the world's two rising economic powers, China and India, have tremendous incentives to avoid a retreat from globalization. "When people ask me, 'Is this the end of capitalism as we know it?' I say, 'No, capitalism is safe in the hands of the Chinese. They know they've done incredibly well out of the global markets, and the Indians know that, too.'"

But after considerable time in China, Smick believes China's ability to adjust to the changing trade picture is complicated by an authoritarian political structure, an aging population and a bureaucratic culture that can still discourage individual innovation.

The United States remains the engine of the global economy, he says, and American political leaders are losing their determination to resist Americans' rising protectionist sentiment. But without U.S. leadership, he warns, the global consensus in favor of free trade could splinter.

"Today there are just so many parallels to where we were in the '30s, when every country paid attention to their own bilateral priorities," Smick says. "I'm afraid that's the world we're moving in again."

BACKGROUND

Ancient Traders

Globalization is either a modern phenomenon or nearly as old as civilization itself — depending on one's viewpoint.

Many economists see globalization as the unprecedented level of worldwide economic and financial integration, fueled by technological advances, witnessed in the last 30 years. Others view globalization as the age-old exchanging of goods and ideas by people from different parts of the world. As financial historian William J. Bernstein puts it: Globalization "is a process that has been slowly evolving for a very, very long time."[22]

In his 2008 book *A Splendid Exchange, How Trade Shaped the World*, Bernstein traces the role of trade in world affairs since the dawn of recorded history, depicting a surprising range and diversity of trading in the ancient world.

Bronze-age Mesopotamians actively traded grain, metals and goods across southern Arabia. The Roman Empire traded across Europe, much of Africa and as far away as India and China. In 30 B.C., "Rome was flooded with pepper, exotic animals and precious jewels from the Orient," Bernstein writes. "Chinese silk was the most famous and coveted of these commodities."[23]

In more recent times, the disruptive impacts of international trade were felt long before modern treaties like the North American Free Trade Agreement sought to promote open trade between nations. More than 200 years ago, for example, a flood of cheaper tanned hides from the Americas undercut Europe's leather industry. "If *The New York Times* columnist Thomas Friedman had been writing in 1800, he would have had little trouble explaining the flattening of world commerce to European tanners," Bernstein observes.[24] (Friedman, *The New York Times* columnist and author of *The World Is Flat, A Brief History of the Twenty-first Century*, embraces globalization as a nearly unstoppable revolution brought forth by a convergence of new technologies and an emerging world order.)

"Globalization is such a diverse, broad-based, and potent force that not even today's massive economic crash will dramatically slow it down," writes *Foreign Policy* editor Naím. "Love it or hate it, globalization is here to stay."[25]

But historians such as Bernstein and Princeton's James believe the longer view reveals many eras of globalization, usually followed by periods in which trade and other contacts declined significantly. In the period around 30 B.C., for example, trade expanded within the Roman Empire, followed by a period in which it slowed to a trickle, Bernstein notes, as Rome fell into decline following

CHRONOLOGY

1920s *Trade flourishes until Great Depression hits.*

October 1929 U.S. stock market crashes.

1930s *Protectionism worsens the Depression.*

1930 Smoot-Hawley Tariff Act in U.S. raises more than 900 import duties; other nations later follow suit.

1929-1934 World trade drops 66 percent.

1940s *Nations seek to build postwar international economic relationships.*

1944 Allied nations meet in Bretton Woods, N.H., to create international monetary and financial structure.

1947 General Agreement on Tariffs and Trade (GATT) encourages free trade by reducing tariffs.

1950s-1960s *Growing economic and political cooperation expands ties among Western nations.*

1951 Six countries form European Coal and Steel Community, the precursor of the Common Market.

1957 European Economic Community, or Common Market, expands economic cooperation and cross-border trade.

1962 Trade Expansion Act empowers President John F. Kennedy to negotiate major tariff reductions. . . . European Union gives members joint control over food production and prices.

1967 Kennedy round of trade talks, honoring the slain president, conclude.

1970s-1980s *Open markets and political changes in West appear to reverse economic stagnation, while dramatic reforms unleash China's economy. Soviet Union and former satellite nations embrace free markets, open trade.*

1973 Arab oil embargo causes gas shortages and worsens economic malaise known as "stagflation."

1978 China initiates free-market reforms.

1985 Soviet leader Mikhail Gorbachev initiates reforms that lead to the USSR's collapse in 1991.

1989 U.S. and 11 Pacific nations form Asia Pacific Economic Cooperation forum to discuss free trade.

1990s *Global trade grows, but backlash develops.*

1992 A European Union treaty moves toward a common currency. Union eventually grows to 27 nations.

1994 North American Free Trade Agreement eliminates most trade barriers between U.S., Canada and Mexico.

1995 The 123-member World Trade Organization (WTO) replaces GATT.

1999 Anti-globalization protesters shut down WTO Seattle meeting.

2000s *Recession undercuts global trade.*

2001 Trade talks begin in Doha, Qatar, to lower remaining trade barriers.

2007 U.S. housing prices begin to collapse, rattling U.S. financial institutions.

2008 Worst recession in nearly 80 years hits world economy. Banking institutions worldwide face insolvency. . . . Doha round talks collapse.

2009 Global trade plummets in the first two quarters and is expected to drop 10 percent or more for the year. . . . China and Western nations initiate massive stimulus spending to revive their econo-mies. By mid-summer signs of recovery are mixed with economic difficulties, prompting some experts to predict deglobalization will fracture the global status quo.

Rejecting Globalization Produces Winners and Losers

Developing nations could suffer economically and politically.

For two decades, Ireland flourished as "the poster child for globalization," in the words of Irish economist Austin Hughes. Today, the country's battered economy reflects the sharp reversal of fortune that can come with a collapse in world trade.

Ireland's embrace of policies that opened the island to global markets and international investment had turned its economy into the "Celtic Tiger." But the global economic downturn sent Ireland's property values plummeting, its banks required a government bailout and unemployment has soared to close to 12 percent.

"There was a sense that we had discovered the crock of gold at the end of the rainbow," Hughes says. "Now there's this fatalism that says it was just a crock."

Some desperate economies that once embraced globalization are now beginning to turn inward, in a trend called deglobalization, in which they adopt restrictive tariffs and other protective policies. If the trend continues, experts say, there will be winners and losers on both the global and national stages. The losers will far outnumber the winners, according to many mainstream economists, but in anything

as vast and complicated as the global economy, some industries and even nations will find themselves with a relative advantage in the new status quo.

Ireland is hardly the only nation that will face a significant economic adjustment if the recession triggers an era of deglobalization. Several smaller Western nations, including Iceland and Latvia, are in similar straits, and many of the world's successful economies are highly export dependent, notes David Smick, an international economic strategist. Exports provide more than 40 percent of the gross domestic product (GDP) in China, Germany and Korea, among other nations, he says.

Boris Kozolchyk, director of the National Law Center for Inter-American Free Trade in Tucson, Ariz., believes developing countries would be big losers in an era of deglobalization. Many Latin American countries, for example, have staked their economic and political development on free trade.

Kozolchyk says the banking crisis that sparked the recession illustrates intertwined global relationships. "There was a chain of finance: you had Wells Fargo Bank

---

the death of Emperor Marcus Aurelius. [26] And other periods of robust globalization — including the era of trade expansion that occurred during the Renaissance and the emergence of French and English colonial empires in the 18th century — also eventually slowed or ended dramatically, James observes.

"All of these previous globalization episodes came to an end, almost always with wars . . . accompanied by highly disruptive and contagious financial crises," he writes.[27]

Depression and Protection

Whether globalization is an old story or uniquely modern, the contemporary chapter clearly begins about 80 years ago, with a worldwide economic disaster.

Contrary to popular belief, the Great Depression of the 1930s wasn't started by protectionist tariffs and other trade barriers rising around the globe. The economic debacle was well under way when President Herbert Hoover signed the 1930 Smoot-Hawley act, which increased nearly 900 different import tariffs on foreign goods.

Authors Rep. Willis Hawley, R-Ore., and Sen. Reed Smoot, R-Utah, reaped political infamy for their efforts, but the measure reflected lawmakers' widespread protectionist sentiments. Thomas Hall, a professor of economics at Miami University in Ohio and co-author of *The Great Depression: An International Disaster of Perverse Economic Policies*, believes it was more the Depression that caused Smoot-Hawley, rather than the reverse. "Smoot-Hawley

providing financing to Banco Atlántida in Honduras, which was financing local businesses," he says. "Now it's all come to a halt."

Kozolchyk also fears developing nations could lose politically, as their economic struggles lead them to turn away from democracy in search of other solutions. "This has already started happening," he says, citing the influence of Venezuelan President Hugo Chávez. "You definitely have a return to demagoguery and authoritarian government, all in the name of false economic development."

Large and economically diverse nations will be hurt less. Only 11 percent of the U.S. GDP is tied to exports, according to Smick. "We will be hurt," he says, "but we will be less vulnerable than most of the rest of the world."

Within the U.S. economy, however, certain industries would be disproportionately affected by deglobalization. Exports in medical equipment, industrial engines and aircraft engines all grew significantly last year. [1] Other industries, however, were already heavily export driven. For example, nearly 40 percent of the computer and electronics-industry jobs in the United States are dependent upon exports, according to government statistics. Heavy manufacturing, the chemical industry and the U.S. leather goods trade also count on exports for a substantial share of their business.[2]

Even distinctly American industries are global enterprises these days and could suffer if the world deglobalizes. Hollywood made nearly twice as much money on its movies overseas as it did in the United States.[3] If deglobalization triggers a rise in economic and cultural nationalism, the entertainment industry could be a big loser.

The winners? It depends on your perspective on globalization. David C. Korten — a longtime critic of "corporate globalization" and author of *Agenda for a New Economy: From Phantom Wealth to Real Wealth* — sees a retreat from international markets sparking a more sustainable lifestyle in the United States and abroad. The trend would embrace smaller-scale, local agriculture and green technologies, including alternative-energy production and more efficient building practices. In the view of anti-globalists like Korten, the final winners would include Americans, who would enjoy better-quality lives.

Others take a more cynical view of how winners would be determined. "It really depends on which industries have the political clout to get the best protectionism," says Douglas Irwin, a specialist in trade policy at Dartmouth College.

---

[1] "U.S. Export Fact Sheet," International Trade Administration, U.S. Department of Commerce, Feb. 11, 2009, http://trade.gov/press/press_releases/2009/export-factsheet_021109.pdf.

[2] "Total Jobs Supported by Manufactured Exports, 2006," Office of Industry and Trade Information, U.S. Department of Commerce, www.trade.gov/td/industry/otea/jobs/Reports/2006/jobs_by_industry.html.

[3] "Entertainment Industry Market Statistics 2007," Motion Picture Association of America, p. 3, www.mpaa.org/USEntertainment IndustryMarketStats.pdf.

had been kicking around in Congress for some years," he says. "What the Depression did was align the political forces to get it passed."

The measure became law despite desperate opposition from financial and economic circles, remarkably including 1,028 economists who signed an open letter calling on Hoover not to sign the bill. Thomas Lamont, a partner at J. P. Morgan and an economic adviser to the president, recalled: "I almost went down on my knees" to beg Hoover to veto the bill. [28]

Hoover, however, had long harbored protectionist sentiments and signed the bill into law. As opponents had predicted, the act led to a trade war, with nations around the world raising their own import barriers in retaliation.

Economists differ on how much responsibility Smoot-Hawley bears for the calamitous collapse in world trade in the 1930s. U.S. imports from Europe declined from a 1929 high of $1.3 billion to just $390 million in 1932 — a precipitous 69 percent drop. U.S. exports to Europe declined 65 percent — from $2.3 billion to $784 million — over the same period. Overall, world trade fell a breathtaking 66 percent from 1929 to 1934. [29]

But many historians have noted that the real impact of Smoot-Hawley was to turn nations inward at a time of international political and economic crisis. In its 1941 obituary for Hawley, *Time* went so far as to call Smoot-Hawley "one of the most enormous acts of isolationism in U.S. history." The magazine even suggested that the act set the world on course for the worst war in history. "Economic nationalism, forced into full flower by the Smoot-Hawley Tariff, became the physical basis for the ideology of fascism," *Time* intoned. "The lines were written, the stage was set for World War II."[30]

Whether that verdict was too harsh — and most historians would argue the conditions that gave birth to fascism ranged beyond isolationist trade policies — it reflects postwar convictions. The democracies of the West, led by the United States, emerged from World War II convinced that protectionist tariffs had not only exacerbated the worst economic collapse in modern history but also helped lead to a catastrophic war.

For the rest of the 20th century, trade policy would be seen through the lens of the negative impact of protectionism. With only occasional demurrals, the Free World agreed that trade must be kept open to maintain peace and prosperity. In the aftermath of the war, the West would go about setting up the international structures to make that happen.

From GATT to WTO

The years immediately after World War II produced watershed events in international integration. The United Nations held its first General Assembly in 1946.[31] The North Atlantic Treaty Organization (NATO) set up its collective defense agreement in 1949. And the forerunner of the European Economic Community was formed in 1951.

But before the war had even ended, representatives of the 44 Allied nations met in tiny Bretton Woods, N.H., in July 1944, to hammer out the postwar economic order, establishing the International Monetary Fund (IMF) and the International Bank for Reconstruction and Development (the World Bank).

The delegates also established a new global monetary system. Because the United States had become far and away the world's most powerful economy and also held most of the world's gold reserves, Bretton Woods tied the world's currencies to the dollar, which the delegates agreed should be convertible into gold at $35 per ounce. The goal was to prevent the wild currency fluctuations that had contributed to instability in the 1930s. The IMF was charged with maintaining the system of exchange rates.[32]

Guiding all these efforts was the belief that a stable global economic system, allowing a free exchange of goods and services, was essential to world order. "Unhampered trade dovetailed with peace. High tariffs, trade barriers and unfair economic competition with war," U.S. Secretary of State Cordell Hull later wrote in his autobiography.[33]

Three years after Bretton Woods, 23 nations met in Geneva, Switzerland, to finalize work on a General Agreement on Tariffs and Trade (GATT). It established basic trade rules and included 45,000 tariff concessions, eliminating or reducing duties on $10 billion worth of products being traded at the time — about one-fifth of the worldwide total.[34]

GATT membership would grow dramatically through the years, as would its scope, which was expanded in a series of negotiations known as "trade rounds," named after the cities in which they were convened. For nearly half a century, GATT would provide the basic framework for world trade.

Dartmouth trade historian Irwin notes that GATT didn't always succeed in boosting trade. For instance, its inability to eliminate agricultural subsidies, still widely protected around the globe, is considered one of the treaty's largest failings. And its provisions are often ignored by some countries during economic stress, such as in the late 1970s and early '80s, when sluggish growth again led to a rise in protectionism.[35]

But overall the picture has been positive. "There's been a demonstrable lowering of trade barriers over the last 60 or so years, and GATT was largely responsible," says Irwin. World trade has expanded dramatically in the 60 years since GATT was first signed, growing 8 percent a year through the 1950s and '60s.[36]

"It added stability to the system," he notes, making people "more willing to make investments in other countries, which has helped the developing world, in particular."

But GATT was only meant to be a stop-gap measure. The architects of the postwar world order envisioned an International Trade Organization (ITO), operating as a U.N. agency, which would serve as a third pillar of the world economy alongside the IMF and the World Bank. The draft charter for the ITO included rules on employment, business practices, international investment and services.[37] Eventually, ITO negotiations foundered on the sheer magnitude of the concept. However, nearly half a century later, the international community would return to the idea, creating the World Trade Organization in 1995 as the successor to GATT.

The WTO represented the culmination of the original postwar vision of a new level of international commerce. But at the end of the millennium the world was a much different place than in the years immediately after World War II. And since its inception, the WTO has attracted ardent critics and supporters.

But on one thing they all agree: the WTO in the 21st century faces a series of challenges that reflect the stresses of the global economic and political order.

Governing Trade Today

In recent years, countries have focused more on crafting regional and bilateral trade agreements, while international trade talks have languished. In fact, regional free-trade agreements have proliferated so rapidly they've become an alphabet soup of acronyms: NAFTA, CAFTA, SAFTA (the South Asia Free Trade Agreement) and more.

Bilateral free-trade agreements have also proliferated. The United States, for example, now has trade agreements — both bilateral and multilateral — with 17 countries, and three more are pending in Congress.[38] Many other countries have similar agreements with neighboring countries or important trading partners.

As the number of trade agreements has multiplied, the size of global markets has grown dramatically. Before the collapse of the Soviet Union in 1991 and the opening up of the Chinese and Indian economies, a large share of the world's population was essentially shut off from international trade. As a result of political changes in those countries, however, more than 1.5 billion people joined the competitive global work force.[39] Many smaller, developing nations also turned to low-cost global exports in an attempt to raise living standards.

Simultaneously, the World Trade Organization has expanded its reach into areas such as the trade in services and intellectual-property rights. The expanded authority, however, required new rules that reach much farther into the internal practices and regulation of national economies.

"Until the mid-1990s, trade rules were about trade. They set tariffs, that sort of thing," says Wallach at Global Trade Watch. "Now you have a whole bunch of policies that have nothing to do with how goods move between countries. They have to do with domestic policies."

WTO rules on intellectual property, for instance, have been particularly controversial because they can involve patents for lifesaving drugs and can restrict or increase the cost of medicine in many parts of the world. Proponents view the WTO's intellectual-property-rights provisions as essential to boosting trade, encouraging innovation and promoting the adoption of best practices around the globe. Opponents see them as a form of exploitation by multinational corporations.

Trade agreements and other WTO policies have caused job losses in certain economic sectors in participating countries, such as the U.S. textile industry, and have contributed to downward pressure on wages, particularly in developed nations.

Not surprisingly, a backlash developed against the WTO and the whole idea of globalization. The scope of the anti-globalization movement and the depth of its frustration became apparent during the 1999 WTO meeting in Seattle, where a massive, largely peaceful protest was marked by violent outbursts that so rattled officials they ended the conference early.[40]

Globalization's critics cite the economic crisis that hit in 2007 and '08 as proof of its failure, while supporters urged that eight-year-long trade negotiations, known as the Doha round, be concluded to help lift the world out of the recession.

Although these debates reflect modern tensions, Bernstein points out that anti-globalization protests have occurred for centuries. "Today's debates over globalization repeat, nearly word for word in some cases, those of earlier eras," he writes. "Wherever trade arrives, resentment, protectionism and their constant companions — smuggling, disrespect for authority and occasionally war — will follow."

Yet Bernstein also notes, "The instinct to truck and barter is part of human nature; any effort to stifle it is doomed to fail in the long run."[41]

CURRENT SITUATION

Clouded Forecast

Several analysts say evidence suggests the recession in the United States, China and other nations could be coming to an end. In early August, the U.S. government said the nation's economic output shrank only 1 percent in the second quarter of the year, a dramatic improvement over the 6.4 percent contraction in the previous quarter.[42]

AP Photo/Dolores Ochoa

In one of the most protectionist responses to the global economic crisis, Ecuador's government in February imposed restrictions on most imported items. Now many imports — like this hair conditioner and deodorant being sold in a store in Quito — are more expensive.

Moreover, the U.S. stock market recorded its best July in 20 years, and home prices appeared to be creeping upward.[43] A number of major banks also have recorded profits, leading some to predict the financial system has stabilized. Since the United States is the largest driver of the global economy, these signs indicate a recovery may be in the cards for the last half of 2009 or early 2010.

Two of the world's emerging economic powerhouses, India and China, also offer reason for optimism. In June, the World Bank raised its 2009 growth forecast for China from 6.5 percent to 7.2 percent.[44] In July, Chinese manufacturing expanded at its fastest rate in a year, according to a survey.[45] Also in July, the IMF revised its projection for India's economic growth for 2009 upward to 5.4 percent while forecasting an overall global contraction of 1.4 percent.[46]

"My take is that the U.S. will come out of this in another six months to a year, and the large majority of nations will start pulling out once the U.S. economy does," says Panagariya, the former World Bank and WTO economist.

But for every patch of blue sky visible on the economic horizon there remains a cloud. U.S. consumer spending, which comprises 70 percent of economic activity, has continued to fall. And with U.S. unemployment not expected to peak until later this year or early in 2010, a consumer-driven recovery will be delayed. The Obama administration's $787 billion stimulus package now accounts for 20 percent of U.S. output, but federal officials acknowledge that the current level of deficit spending is unsustainable in future years.[47]

Meanwhile, credit markets remain tight, both globally and in the United States, limiting money for new investments, particularly in riskier economies. Conditions continue to look bleak in many leading Western industrial nations. The IMF predicts continued contraction of 4 percent or more this year in Germany, Japan, the United Kingdom, Russia and Italy — among other nations — with negative or only negligible growth seen in 2010.[48]

"There's all this talk right now about 'green shoots' [signs of economic recovery] and the end of the recession, and I understand why people feel this way: They hope they can get back to normal very quickly," says James, the Princeton University economic historian, "but I just don't think they're going to be able to do that."

Indeed, the overall world economy looks remarkably grim by any historical measure. As of June, the declines in world industrial output and other key indicators were slightly worse than during the Great Depression at the same point in its history, according to one analysis.[49] In a late June assessment, the World Bank noted that "unemployment continues to rise throughout the world, housing prices in many countries are still falling . . . bank balance sheets are fragile."[50]

Several factors could derail the beginnings of a recovery, analysts say, especially rising energy costs. In early August, Fatih Birol, chief economist for the International Energy Agency, warned that rising oil prices — which had reached $73 a barrel — threaten economic recovery. Sustained oil prices above $70 a barrel could strangle a recovery, he says.[51]

Even if the recession is ending, the recovery is widely expected to be feeble, barely relieving public suffering or discontent. "While the global economy is likely to begin expanding again in the second half of 2009, the recovery is expected to be subdued as global demand remains depressed, unemployment remains high and recession-like conditions continue until 2011," Hans Timmer, director of the World Bank's Development Prospects Group, said recently.[52]

In this environment, the determination of the world's political leaders to maintain global trade could be critical. But the latest signals can be read both ways.

Will a period of deglobalization disrupt world trade?

YES

Harold James
*Professor of History and International Af
Author, The Creation and Destruction of
Value: The Globalization Cycle*

Written for *CQ Researcher*, September 2009

Globalization is a very old phenomenon. It has also produced tremendous benefits in terms of poverty reduction in many countries. But historically, globalization is also vulnerable to terrible and costly backlashes, as in the late 18th century, when it was interrupted by wars and revolutions, or in the early 20th century, when the very integrated world of the late 19th century was pulled apart by the First World War and by the Great Depression. We might think of the globalization phenomenon as cyclical.

Because so much recent globalization was driven by financial flows, the financial meltdown is a very serious setback. The most immediate impact of the financial collapse of September 2008 was on world trade, with a 30 percent decline in the last quarter of 2008, and only very fragile signs of recovery in 2009. The World Trade Organization estimates that global trade will be 10 percent lower in 2009 than in 2008.

The measures that governments take against the crisis are likely to produce a longer-term deglobalization trend. State rescues of entire banking systems will tend to produce a different financial system, in which large parts of finance are renationalized. Italian and French taxpayers will not want to see their money used to bail out remote East European debtors. Banks rescued by governments are under substantial pressure to cut back foreign lending and increase domestic loans.

Fiscal stimulus packages have a similar effect, in that they are intended to benefit domestic producers and involve the assumption of additional debt, which constitutes a long-term liability of domestic taxpayers. In consequence, many of the large stimulus packages are accompanied by more or less explicit provisions ("Buy America" or "Buy China") that attempt to ensure domestic, not foreign, producers are stimulated.

The reactions against globalization are as much driven by a new psychology as by economic reality or a precise weighing of the costs and benefits of globalization. Crises give rise to conspiracy theories, often directed against foreigners or foreign countries. Many Americans argue that the mess is the fault of Chinese surpluses. Many people in other countries already argue that they are being hit by a U.S. crisis made in America. We will see trade protectionism and massive and powerful xenophobic sentiment. Perhaps many former so-called "globalization critics" will see just how good the integration was when it starts to fall apart.

NO

Moisés Naím
*Editor in Chief, Foreign Policy Author, Illicit: How
Smugglers, Traffickers and Copycats Are
Hijacking the Global Economy*

Excerpted with permission from *Foreign
Policy* #171 (March/April 2009) www.foreignpolicy.com

Rumors of globalization's demise — such as Princeton economic historian Harold James' recent obituary for "The Late, Great Globalization" — have been greatly exaggerated. . . .

All kinds of groups are still connecting, and the economic crisis will not slow their international activities. . . . It might even bolster them. Global charities, for instance, will face soaring demand for their services. . . . At a time when cash is king and jobs are scarce, globalized criminals will be one of the few . . . sources of credit, investment and employment in some places. . . .

It's true that private flows of credit and investment across borders have temporarily plummeted. . . . But as private economic activity falls, the international movement of public funds is booming. Last fall, the U.S. Federal Reserve and the central banks of Brazil, Mexico, Singapore and South Korea launched $30 billion worth of currency arrangements for each country designed to stabilize their financial markets. Similar reciprocal deals now tie together central banks throughout Asia, Europe and the Middle East.

Yes, some governments might be tempted to respond to the crisis by adopting trade-impairing policies, imposing rules that inhibit global financial integration or taking measures to curb immigration. The costs of doing so, however, are enormous and hard to sustain in the long run. What's more, the ability of any government to shield its economy and society from outside influences and dangers has steadily evaporated in the past two decades. . . .

Globalization is such a diverse, broad-based and potent force that not even today's massive economic crash will dramatically slow it down or permanently reverse it. . . .

But claims about the return of strong governments and nationalism are equally overstated. Yes, China might team up with Russia to counterbalance the United States in relation to Iran, but meanwhile the Chinese and U.S. economies will be joined at the hip (China holds more than a trillion dollars of U.S. debt, and the United States is the main destination for its exports). . . .

The bottom line: Nationalism never disappeared. Globalization did not lessen national identities; it just rendered them more complex. . . . Globalization and geopolitics coexist, and neither is going anywhere.

Chinese factory workers in Huaibei manufacture clothes for export to the United States. China's rapid growth has been based on an export-driven economy that heavily depended on Americans' voracious consuming habits. U.S. demand for Chinese products declined during the recession, however, prompting China to protect its textile and other labor-intensive industries with tax rebates.

Trade Policy Pressure

In July, U.S. Trade Representative Ron Kirk addressed workers at a steel plant outside Pittsburgh, Pa. The steel industry continues to be hit hard by foreign imports and has been pushing the administration to act against what it considers unfair competition from China. Kirk's language was as combative as any heard from a White House trade official in some time.

The United States will get tough on foreign governments that ignore trade rules, he said, and would no longer wait for a complaint to be filed but would proactively identify and investigate potential violations of labor rules in countries with free-trade agreements with the United States.

"We will take new steps to protect the rights of American farmers and small-business owners. We will hold our trading partners to their word on labor standards," Kirk said. "And we will use work we're already doing to fight even harder for the men and women who fuel our economy and support their families."[53]

Kirk's speech could be read as a tilt toward the wing of the Democratic Party that has pushed for more aggressive action to level the playing field in trade. Even before Kirk spoke, some free-trade supporters worried the Obama administration was less committed to the idea of free trade than its predecessors.

"I do not believe the current administration is at all protectionist," says Lane, the governmental affairs director for Caterpillar. "But by the same token, there's been a reluctance to engage their core constituencies on these measures. What's missing so far is advocacy. So far, they haven't made it a priority."

Yet some observers saw the speech as an attempt to reassure labor unions and other Democratic Party interest groups before a push by the administration for ratification of bilateral trade agreements with Panama, Colombia and South Korea.[54] The deals, signed by the Bush administration, are pending in Congress but have been put on hold by a wary Democratic leadership.

The G-20 will meet again later this month in Pittsburgh, where President Obama is expected to discuss his administration's trade agenda.

Doha Stalls

More than eight years after negotiators began working on the latest international trade agreement, known as the Doha round, the adjective most commonly attached to the negotiations is "stalled."

In mid-summer, WTO Director-General Pascal Lamy laid out what he described as a road map for negotiations to be completed in 2010. But his plan was met with only muted responses from the world's leading industrial nations.

Yet finishing Doha is critical in helping the world economy recover and preventing deglobalization, says Winters, the economist at Sussex University in the U.K., who studies the problems of developing nations. "If the Doha round fails, it's not clear that we can maintain the status quo," he says. "Doha helps us head off a big increase in protectionism that could occur if we don't get it."

The Doha impasse centers on disagreements between developed and developing nations, which believe they were promised certain concessions in return for opening up their economies in the last round. Perhaps the most highly publicized dispute is over EU and U.S. agricultural price supports. Many developed nations use price supports, import quotas and other programs to protect producers of some farm commodities from cheaper foreign imports.

For example, government programs in the United States subsidize politically powerful cotton producers, helping to depress the world price for cotton and hurting producers in Africa and India. The African nations, in particular, have been pushing for reduced cotton price supports in the developed nations. A 2007 study by Oxfam, a London-based nongovernmental organization dedicated to fighting global poverty, estimated that if the United States — the world's largest cotton-exporting nation — eliminated its cotton subsidies, the price for West African cotton would increase by 5 to 12 percent, dramatically improving the lives of the region's cotton farmers.[55]

Winters believes the disagreement over agricultural policy in developed countries has come to carry more weight than it should. Rather than pressing the developed nations to make politically difficult reforms, Winters thinks developing nations should concentrate on getting rid of quotas, tariffs and other more traditional agricultural trade barriers. "Most African nations are net food importers," he says. "For a good part of the developing world, it's really far more important that the West open up its markets than it is that they lower their agricultural subsidies."

While most analysts are pessimistic that Doha will move forward anytime soon, others remain hopeful. Jagdish Bhagwati, a professor at Columbia University who has been an adviser for both GATT and the WTO, notes that no trade round has ever failed.

"They often break down, are often thought to be in intensive care where the pessimists predict that they will expire," he wrote with Panagariya, "and they come back like the proverbial cat and are concluded. Doha will be no exception."[56]

But others see a watershed moment. Smick, the author and global economic policy strategist, sees the economic crisis combining with existing tensions to splinter the international political consensus in favor of continuing trade liberalization, even though globalization has lifted millions of people around the world out of poverty.

"You're seeing the collapse of world trade authority with Doha, unless there's a miracle," Smick says, "and it doesn't look like that's going to happen."

OUTLOOK

Era of Deglobalization?

Experts who fear the world is headed into a period of deglobalization paint a gloomy picture of increased international tensions, conflict and nationalist fervor. Great

Power politics — specifically the United States and China — will predominate, and governments will aggressively intervene in their national economies as state power grows.

Princeton professor James says a drop in international commerce combined with growing demand for limited resources such as oil is a recipe for increased international hostility. "Issues like the fuel supply or the supply of food — countries have and may again go to war about exactly this," says James.

Developing countries will be hit particularly hard, according to former Clinton deputy Treasury secretary Altman. "Already unstable nations, such as Pakistan, could disintegrate. And poverty will rise sharply in a number of African nations," he wrote in a recent issue of *Foreign Affairs*.[57]

Like James, Altman sees one nation in particular emerging in a more powerful position. "The one clear winner is China, whose unique political-economic model has come through unscathed," he wrote.

A recent report of the U.S. National Intelligence Council considers it a "relative certainty" that the global tensions predicted by James and Altman lie ahead. The report, "Global Trends 2025: A Transformed World," concludes that world population — expected to increase by 1.2 billion people by 2025 — will put increasing pressure on energy, food and water resources. But the council is less certain that the world will retreat from global markets, calling it one of the "key uncertainties" of the next 16 years.[58]

Deglobalization would be a welcome development for globalization's longtime critics. Walden Bello, a sociology professor at the University of the Philippines and a leading critic of globalization, called the current crisis proof that globalization has "ended in massive failure." The crisis is an opportunity for developing nations to build regional relationships that go beyond trade to shared economic and social goals, promoting greater equity and justice, he says, citing recent efforts by Venezuelan President Hugo Chávez to build regional economic relationships.[59]

Other globalization critics see the crisis as the end of an unsustainable system of corporate economic domination and excessive consumption. Korten, the author and longtime critic of "corporate globalization," thinks the world will eventually embrace a radically different approach. "Food sources would be primarily local," he says.

People would rely more on renewable energy, including solar and wind. "It would mean much more energy-efficient buildings and a far greater attention to . . . sustainable development."

In Korten's vision, global prosperity would depend not on what a country sells abroad but what it produces close to home. "The economy would be much more based on what our real needs are," he says.

But other experts predict a less calamitous or revolutionary future. Panagariya, the Columbia University economist, says under the most pessimistic scenario the U.S. economy would follow the route of the Japanese in the 1990s, with a lost decade of little or no economic growth. But he considers that unlikely.

"The U.S. is a lot more proactive policywise," Panagariya says. "It's willing to take a lot more risks, and the U.S. markets are a lot more flexible."

He also doesn't expect any significant changes in habits, among nations or individuals. "If housing prices go up," he says, "I think we'll go on a spending spree again."

Ireland did as well as any nation under globalization, but its crash has been as severe as any in Europe. Looking ahead, Irish economist Hughes hopes the future is found in the middle ground.

"I don't think the question is whether globalization is the right thing or not, but whether you can have a trajectory that's more sustainable and deals with the downsides of globalization," he says. "I'm suggesting that wise counsel prevails and people realize they have to learn to move it forward at a walking pace, rather than just rocket forward."

NOTES

1. Harold James, "The Late Great Deglobalization," *Current History*, January 2009.

2. Jonathan Lynn and Kazunori Takada, "World trade to shrink 10 pct, Asia leads recovery: WTO," Reuters, July 22, 2009, www.reuters.com/article/businessNews/idUSSP48113720090722.

3. Angel Gurría and Jørgen Elmeskov, "Economic Outlook No. 85," Organisation for Economic Co-operation and Development, June 24, 2009, www.oecd.org/dataoecd/36/57/43117724.pdf.

4. Barry Eichengreen and Kevin O'Rourke, "A Tale of Two Depressions," at VoxEU.org, Centre for Economic Policy Research, June 4, 2009, www.voxeu.org/index.php?q=node/3421.

5. Joseph Francois, "The Big Drop: Trade and the Great Recession," *The Random Economist*, May 2, 2009, www.intereconomics.com/blogs/jff/2009/05/big-drop-trade-and-great-recession.html.

6. "Statement from G-20 Summit," Nov. 15, 2008. The complete text can be found at www.cfr.org/publication/17778/.

7. Elisa Gamberoni and Richard Newfarmer, "Trade Protection: Incipient but Worrisome Trends," *Tradenotes*, No. 37, The World Bank, March 2, 2009, www.voxeu.org/index.php?q=node/3183.

8. For background, see Mary H. Cooper, "Rethinking NAFTA," *CQ Researcher*, June 7, 1996, pp. 481-504.

9. Those provisions were subsequently modified, at the insistence of the Obama administration, to include a stipulation that they must comply with WTO rules.

10. Wolfgang Münchau, "Europe and the Protectionism Trap," Spiegel Online International, Feb. 13, 2009, www.spiegel.de/international/europe/0,1518,607457,00.html.

11. *Ibid.*

12. The latest round of WTO-sponsored trade talks, known as the Doha round, have been stalled over disagreements between developing and developed countries.

13. "Anti-dumping, subsidies, safeguards: contingencies, etc," "Understanding the WTO: the Agreements," www.wto.org/english/theWTO_e/whatis_e/tif_e/agrm8_e.htm.

14. "President Announces Temporary Safeguards for Steel Industry," White House press release, March 5, 2002, http://georgewbush-whitehouse.archives.gov/news/releases/2002/03/20020305-6.html.

15. Daniel J. Ikenson, "Sordid Steel Shenanigans," Fox News Online, Sept. 18, 2002, www.cato.org/pub_display.php?pub_id=3608.

16. Daniel Lovering, "Steel Product Makers Claim China Dumping Goods," *Manufacturing.net*, June 9, 2009.

17. Jagdish Bhagwati and Arvind Panagariya, "Legal Trade Barriers Must Be Kept in Check," *The Financial Times*, June 11, 2009, www.ft.com/cms/s/0/bcdf98c8-56b2-11de-9a1c-00144feabdc0.html.

18. Roger Altman, "Globalization in Retreat, Further Geopolitical Consequences of the Financial Crisis," *Foreign Affairs*, July/August 2009, p. 2.

19. The agreement is formally known as the CAFTA-DR, and the other signatories are Costa Rica, El Salvador, Guatemala, Nicaragua and the Dominican Republic.

20. For background, see Peter Behr, "The Troubled Dollar," *CQ Global Researcher*, October 2008, pp. 271-294.

21. For background, see Peter Behr, "Fixing Capitalism," *CQ Global Researcher*, July 2009, pp. 177-204.

22. William Bernstein, *A Splendid Exchange, How Trade Shaped the World* (2008), p. 14.

23. *Ibid.*, p. 8.

24. *Ibid.*, pp. 13-14.

25. Moisés Naím, "Think Again: Globalization," *Foreign Policy*, March/April 2009, www.foreign policy.com/story/cms.php?story_id=4678.

26. Bernstein, *op. cit.*, p. 8.

27. James, *op. cit.*, p. 21.

28. "The Battle of Smoot-Hawley," *The Economist*, Dec. 18, 2009, www.economist.com/displayStory.cfm?story_id=12798595.

29. Statistical information on U.S. and international trade volumes from the U.S. Department of State Historical Timeline, http://future.state.gov/when/timeline/1921_timeline/smoot_tariff.html.

30. "The Congress: Death of a Woodcutter," *Time*, Aug. 4, 1941.

31. "Milestones in United Nations History, a Selective Chronology," www.un.org/Overview/milesto4.htm.

32. "The Bretton Woods Conference," from the U.S. Department of State Timeline of U.S. Diplomatic History, www.state.gov/r/pa/ho/time/wwii/98681.htm. For background, see Behr, "The Troubled Dollar," *op. cit.*

33. Cordell Hull, "The Memoirs of Cordell Hull: Vol. 1" (1948), p. 81.

34. "The GATT Years: From Havana to Marrakesh," Understanding the WTO, World Trade Organization, www.wto.org/english/thewto_e/whatis_e/tif_e/fact4_e.htm.

35. Douglas Irwin, "GATT Turns 60," *The Wall Street Journal*, April 9, 2007, http://online.wsj.com/article/SB117607482355263550.html.

36. "The GATT Years: From Havana to Marrakesh," *op. cit.*

37. *Ibid.*

38. For a list see Office of the United States Trade Representative, www.ustr.gov/trade-agreements/free-trade-agreements.

39. Tom Friedman, *The World Is Flat: A Brief History of the Twenty-first Century* (2007), p. 212.

40. For background, see Brian Hansen, "Globalization Backlash," *CQ Researcher*, Sept. 28, 2001, pp. 761-784.

41. Bernstein, *op. cit.*, p. 367.

42. Catherine Rampell and Jack Healy, "In Hopeful Sign, Output Declines at Slower Pace," *The New York Times*, Aug. 1, 2009, p. A1, www.nytimes.com/2009/08/01/business/economy/01econ.html.

43. Nick Timraos and Kelly Evans, "Home Prices Rise Across U.S.," *The Wall Street Journal*, July 29, 2009, p. A1.

44. *China Quarterly Update*, The World Bank, June 2009, http://go.worldbank.org/9FV11IHMF0.

45. Joe McDonald, "Survey: China manufacturing improved in July," The Associated Press, Aug. 3, 2009.

46. "World Economic Outlook Update," International Monetary Fund, July 8, 2009, www.imf.org/external/pubs/ft/weo/2009/update/02/pdf/0709.pdf.

47. Rampell and Healy, *op. cit.* U.S. Treasury Secretary Timothy Geithner, speaking on ABC's "This Week," Aug. 2, 2009.

48. "World Economic Outlook Update," *op. cit.*

49. Eichengreen and O'Rourke, *op. cit.*

50. "Global Development Finance 2009: Outlook Summary," The World Bank, June 22, 2009, http://go.worldbank.org/HCR2ABQPX0.

51. Kate Mackenzie, "Global economy at risk from oil price rise," *The Financial Times*, Aug. 3, 2009, www.ft.com/

cms/s/0/1281aad6-8049-11de-bf04-00144feabdc0
.html.

52. "The Financial Crisis: Charting a Global Recovery," The World Bank, June 22, 2009, http://go.world-bank.org/KUG53HWZY0.

53. A complete text of Kirk's speech can be found at www.ustr.gov/about-us/press-office/speeches/transcripts/ 2009/july/ambassador-kirk-announces-new-initiatives-trade.

54. Ian Swanson, "Kirk Sooths on Trade," *The Hill*, July 16, 2009, http://thehill.com/the-executive/kirk-soothes-on-trade-2009-07-16.html.

55. Julian M. Alston, Daniel A. Sumner and Henrich Brunke, "Impacts of Reductions in US Cotton Subsidies on West African Cotton Producers," Oxfam America, 2007.

56. Jagdish Bhagwati and Arvind Panagariya, "Doha: The Last Mile," *The New York Sun*, Aug. 21, 2008, www .nysun.com/opinion/doha-the-last-mile/84314/.

57. Altman, *op. cit.*

58. "Global Trends 2025: A Transformed World," National Intelligence Council, www.dni.gov/nic/PDF_2025/2025_Global_Trends_Final_Report.pdf.

59. Walden Bello, "Challenges of Regional Integration," presented July 21, 2009, to the Universidad de Deportes, Asunción, Paraguay, reprinted by Focus on the Global South, http://focusweb.org/index.php.

BIBLIOGRAPHY

Books

Bernstein, William, *A Splendid Exchange, How Trade Shaped the World*, Grove Press, 2008.
An American financial theorist comprehensively examines how trade has influenced world events throughout history.

Dorgan, Byron, *Take This Job and Ship It: How Corporate Greed and Brain-dead Politics are Selling Out America*, Thomas Dunn Books, St. Martin's Press, 2006.
The populist Democratic senator from North Dakota takes on what he considers the misguided political choices and false perceptions about world trade that have cost Americans jobs and income.

Ferguson, David, and Thomas Hall, *The Depression: An International Disaster of Perverse Economic Policies*, University of Michigan Press, 1998.
Two economists examine policy decisions that helped to create the Great Depression and then make it worse.

Friedman, Thomas, *The World Is Flat: A Brief History of the Twenty-first Century*, Picador, 2007.
The New York Times columnist's international best-seller presents a largely optimistic take on the globalization phenomenon.

James, Harold, *The Creation and Destruction of Value, The Globalization Cycle*, Harvard University Press, forthcoming, September 2009.
The British professor of history and international affairs at Princeton University who started the current debate about deglobalization puts the current crisis into historical context.

Korten, David, *Agenda for a New Economy: From Phantom Wealth to Real Wealth*, Berrett-Koehler, 2009.
An intellectual leader of the opposition to what he terms "corporate globalization" offers a radically different view of economic prosperity, focused not on corporate profits but on quality of life.

Smick, David, *The World Is Curved, Hidden Dangers to the Global Economy*, Portfolio, 2008.
In what amounts to a response to Friedman's book, a global economic policy strategist and free-trade proponent presents reasons to worry about globalization's future.

Articles

"The Battle of Smoot-Hawley," *The Economist*, Dec. 18, 2009.
The article examines how Congress passed and President Herbert Hoover signed one of the world's most disastrous anti-trade measures.

Altman, Roger, "Globalization in Retreat: Further Geopolitical Consequences of the Financial Crisis," *Foreign Affairs*, July/August 2009.
A former deputy U.S. Treasury secretary under President Bill Clinton sees a "new period of state intervention, re-regulation and creeping protectionism" under way.

Irwin, Douglas, "GATT Turns 60," *The Wall Street Journal*, April 9, 2009.
A Dartmouth College professor who specializes in trade history traces the beginnings of modern globalization from the GATT negotiations after World War II.

James, Harold, "The Late, Great Globalization," *Current History*, January 2009.
A Princeton history professor suggests a period of deglobalization is beginning in which trade will decline and tensions between nations will rise as they compete for critical resources.

Naím, Moisés, "Think Again: Globalization," *Foreign Policy*, March/April, 2009.
The magazine's editor, a former minister of trade and industry in Venezuela, argues that globalization is more than an economic phenomenon but an unstoppable cultural and technological transformation.

Reports and Studies

Eichengreen, Barry, and Kevin O'Rourke, "A Tale of Two Depressions," VoxEU.org, June 4, 2009.
Irish and American economists examine a series of key economic indicators that reveal how closely the current economic downturn tracks the first years of the Great Depression.

Gameroni, Elisa, and Richard Newfarmer, "Trade Protection: Incipient but Worrisome Trends," *Tradenotes, No. 37,* The World Bank, March 2, 2009.
The authors examine protectionist measures taken since the economic downturn started.

Gurría, Angel, and Jørgen Elmeskov, "Economic Outlook No. 85," *Organisation for Economic* Co-operation and Development, June 24, 2009.
The OECD's secretary general (Gurría) and the head of its Economics Department examine major trends in the world economy.

Mattoo, Aaditva, and Arvind Subramian, "Multilateralism Beyond Doha," "Working Paper No. 153," Center for Global Development, October 2008.
The authors contend the international trading system has failed to adapt to changing world economic conditions and suggest what should be done.

For More Information

Focus on the Global South, http://focusweb.org. An anti-globalization research and activist group with offices in Thailand, the Philippines and India, which aims to transform the global economy "from one centered around the needs of transnational corporations to one that focuses on the needs of people, communities and nations."

Organisation for Economic Co-operation and Development, 2, rue André Pascal F 75775 Paris Cedex 16, France; 33 1 45 24 82 00; www.oecd.org. Organization made up of 30 industrialized countries that provides economic research and advises governments on handling the economic, social and governance challenges associated with a globalized economy.

Peterson Institute for International Economics, 1750 Massachusetts Ave., N.W., Washington, DC 20036-1903; (202) 328-9000; www.iie.com. A private, nonpartisan research institution devoted to the study of international economic policy; advocates expanded global trade.

Public Citizen's Global Trade Watch, 1600 20th St., N.W., Washington, DC 20009; (202) 588-1000; www.citizen.org/trade. Nongovernmental organization that promotes democracy "by challenging corporate globalization, arguing that the current globalization model is neither a random inevitability nor 'free trade.' "

World Trade Organization, Centre William Rappard, Rue de Lausanne 154, CH-1211 Geneva 21, Switzerland; (41-22) 739 51 11; www.wto.org. A 153-member international organization established to set global trade rules and manage disputes.

12

U.S.-China Relations

Roland Flamini

Bustling Shanghai — with twice the number of high rises as Manhattan — reflects China's phenomenal growth. Some economists worry that China holds nearly $900 billion in U.S. Treasury securities, refuses to fairly value its currency and maintains an annual trade advantage over the U.S. of more than $230 billion.

From *CQ Researcher*,
May 7, 2010.

President Bill Clinton's trip to China in July 1998 was a splashy, 10-day display of America's power and prestige. Clinton arrived in Beijing with an entourage that included his wife, Hillary, and daughter Chelsea, five Cabinet secretaries, more than 500 White House staffers, members of Congress and security personnel, plus a swarm of journalists. His meetings with China's leaders turned into vigorous and lively debates. At Beijing University, Clinton delivered a forthright speech on human rights and answered questions from Chinese students, all of which was televised live nationwide. The authorities released a number of dissidents, and as the American visitors toured China's landmarks large crowds turned out to greet them.[1]

But that was then. President Obama's China visit in November 2009 was a low-key, four-day affair, part of a swing through Southeast Asia. Wife Michelle and daughters Malia and Sasha remained at home in Washington. His one direct contact with the Chinese public, a town meeting with 500 Chinese students in Shanghai, was deemed a local event and not broadcast nationwide. Throughout his stay, Obama made no public statement on human rights — although he did criticize China's Internet censorship, without mentioning China by name. In Beijing, his joint press appearance with his Chinese host, President Hu Jintao, was limited to a statement from each leader, with no press questions taken. Like Clinton, Obama visited the Forbidden City, but only after it was emptied of tourists.

In the years between the two presidential visits, China has emerged as the world's third-largest economy after the United States and Japan, and a force to be reckoned with in global affairs. And

Trigger Points in the East and the West

China shares a western border with Pakistan, which buys 36 percent of all China's arms exports — the largest share. Security experts worry that some of those arms may end up in the hands of anti-American insurgents in Afghanistan. In the east, concern focuses on the buildup of China's naval fleets and its bellicose comments about U.S.-supported Taiwan.

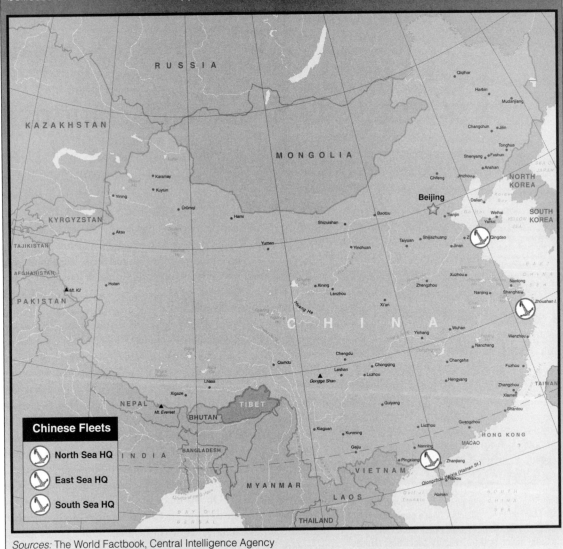

Sources: The World Factbook, Central Intelligence Agency

while the United States and Europe continue their uphill struggle to recover from the world recession, China is back on track, posting a phenomenal 11.9 percent growth rate for the first quarter of 2010 — well above the annual 8 percent its leaders consider crucial to keeping unemployment and social unrest at bay.[2]

Last year, China overtook Germany as the world's top exporter. China is now America's second-biggest trading partner after Canada, with $62.3 billion in trade to date in 2010 (up from $52.5 billion during the same period in 2009).[3] But China is also the leading trading partner of the European Union, Japan, Brazil and India, reflecting the global reach of its burgeoning commercial activity. It is second only to the United States in energy consumption, has overtaken the U.S. as the biggest producer of greenhouse gasses on the planet and is also the No. 1 market for automobile sales.

The string of accomplishments has tilted the balance of the world's most important bilateral relationship in favor of the Chinese. With America's economy weakened, its military mired in two long and costly wars and its trade imbalance with China heavily in the red (-$238 billion) Obama's trip was fashioned to Beijing's specifications — brief and businesslike. Because China holds more than $877 billion of U.S. Treasury securities, commentators likened the visit to a debtor meeting with his bank manager.

Persuading the Chinese to increase the value of their currency was high on Obama's talks agenda. Concerned American manufacturers and unions say China deliberately keeps the renminbi (also referred to as the yuan) low against the dollar, giving China's goods an unfair advantage in U.S. and other foreign markets. China's refusal to adopt a floating currency system, according to experts, leads to so-called goods "dumping" by Chinese exporters — making their goods cheaper and undercutting foreign manufacturers.

The dispute over pricing has led to a tit-for-tat tariff battle. The United States currently imposes special tariffs and duties on 95 categories of goods imported from China — the highest for any country.[4]

When — shortly before Obama's visit — the United States announced stiff penalties on $3.2 billion in steel pipe from China for use in oil and gas fields, the Ministry of Commerce denounced the move as "protectionist"

China at a Glance		
Area: 9.6 million sq. km. (slightly smaller than the U.S.)		
Population: 1.34 billion (July 2009 est.); U.S.: 308 million		
Birth rate: 14 births/1,000 population (2009 est.); United States: 13.82 births/1,000 population (2009 est.)		
Ethnic groups: Han Chinese 91.5%; Zhuang, Manchu, Hui, Miao, Uyghur, Tujia, Yi, Mongol, Tibetan, Buyi, Dong, Yao, Korean, and other nationalities 8.5% (2000 census)		
Religions: Mainly Daoist (Taoist) and Buddhist; Christian 3%-4%, Muslim 1%-2%		
Languages: Standard Chinese or Mandarin (Putonghua, based on the Beijing dialect) about 70%; Yue (Cantonese), Wu (Shanghainese), Minbei (Fuzhou), Minnan (Hokkien-Taiwanese), Xiang, Gan, Hakka dialects, minority languages		
Government: Communist state. President and vice president elected by National People's Congress for five-year terms. Unicameral National People's Congress with 2,987 seats; members elected by municipal, regional and provincial people's congresses and People's Liberation Army to five-year terms.		
Economy: GDP: $8.8 trillion (2009 est.); United States: $14.43 trillion (2009 est.)		
Exports: mining and ore processing, iron, steel, aluminum, other metals, coal; machine building; armaments; textiles and apparel; petroleum; cement; chemicals; fertilizers; consumer products, including footwear, toys, electronics; food processing; transportation equipment, including automobiles, rail cars and locomotives, ships and aircraft; telecommunications equipment, commercial space launch vehicles, satellites.		
Unemployment rate: 4.3% (Sept. 2009 est.); United States: 9.3% (2009 est.)		
Military expenditures: 4.3% of GDP (2006); United States: 4.06% of GDP (2005 est.)		

Sources: The World Factbook, Central Intelligence Agency

and said it was looking into whether American sedans and big sport utility vehicles on sale in China were subsidized by the United States government. "By not recognizing China as a market economy, the U.S. is acting in a discriminatory manner," stated ministry spokesman Yao Jian.[5]

Not so, said U.S. Steelworkers Union president Leo Gerard. "We're fed up with [the Chinese] cheating on our trade laws. Penalties for these transgressions are long overdue."[6]

On the foreign-policy front, the Obama administration needs China's help in containing Iran's nuclear ambitions. The next planned step in Washington's high-priority attempt to stymie the ruling ayatollahs' efforts to produce nuclear weapons is tight U.N. sanctions to block Iran from acquiring any more of the technology it still needs. As one of the five veto-wielding, permanent members of the U.N. Security Council, China possesses an indispensable vote needed to pass any U.N. sanctions resolution. (The other members are the United States, Russia, Britain and France.)

But Iran is China's third-largest crude oil supplier, shipping 460,000 barrels a day in 2009 and about the same this year. China's National Petroleum Corp. also has sizable investments in Iranian oil production. [7] In Beijing, the Chinese shared Obama's concern that Iran should become a nuclear power but resisted his pressure to cooperate. Since then they have agreed to help in drafting a U.N. resolution — but have said nothing about voting for it. The president also raised U.S. concern over China's lack of respect for copyright laws and patent rights — a perennial Western complaint. Despite some new legislation to protect intellectual property, the production of knock-offs of famous brand names and the piracy of music, films and electronic game software remains a full-blown industry.[8]

In China's latest copyright scandal, the embarrassed organizers of Shanghai's $40 billion Expo 2010, which opened on May 1, recently withdrew the trade fair's promotional theme song after being deluged with protests that it had been plagiarized from a Japanese pop song.[9]

Such controversies are hardly new, but as China's economy and military have become more robust, so has its belief that it is operating from a position of strength, and the United States from growing weakness. "I think it is a common perception in the region that U.S. influence has been on the decline in the last decade, while Chinese influence has been increasing," Jeffrey Bader, director of Asian affairs at the National Security Council, declared prior to Obama's Asian trip. "And one of the messages that the president will be sending in his visit is that we are an Asia-Pacific nation and we're there for the long haul." Coming from a senior White House adviser the admission was revealing.[10]

In the end there was very little give by the Chinese leadership on either trade or Iran. Obama also made a pitch to the Chinese for what he described as "a positive, constructive and comprehensive relationship that opens the door to partnership on the big global issues of our time: economic recovery, development of clean air energy, stopping the spread of nuclear weapons and the surge of climate change, the promotion of peace in Asia and around the globe."[11]

Zbigniew Brzezinski, a former U.S. national security adviser who advised the Obama election campaign, described Obama's proposal more succinctly as a Washington-Beijing G-2 partnership. But the Chinese seemed lukewarm to Obama's power-sharing offer. "China fundamentally has not promoted the idea that China and the U.S. will form the two major powers," says Feng Zhongping, the head of the European section of the Beijing-based Chinese Institute of Contemporary International Relations. "China believes that the idea that [China and the United States] could undertake the responsibility of administering the world is incorrect."[12]

As experts try to read the tea leaves on the future of U.S.-China relations, here are some of the questions being asked:

Is a U.S.-China partnership actually possible?

Until the early 1970s, when President Richard M. Nixon made his historic trip to China, the two countries were virtual enemies — militarily and ideologically. Today, as China becomes a global powerhouse and a challenge to U.S. commercial and political interests, the relationship is deeply complex.

"It may be a cliché, but there are issues on which the United States and China have a common interest, and other issues with divergent interests, and difficulties are going to persist for some time, and occasionally there will be some friction," says China specialist Bonnie Glaser at Washington's Center for Strategic and International Studies. "But China does not want to have an unstable, unhealthy relationship with the United States. It's extremely important to the Chinese to have good relations."

To underline this, Chinese officials pointed out to the author that in Beijing Obama signed 11 bilateral agreements, including those on nuclear proliferation, economic cooperation, climate change, participation in multinational anti-pirate patrols in the Horn of Africa, visits between U.S. and Chinese forces (the U.S. carrier *USS Nimitz* visited Hong Kong in February), plus a joint commitment to strengthen people-to-people exchanges. As part of an enlarged U.S. academic-exchange program, Obama has promised to send 100,000 American students to China — roughly the same number of Chinese currently studying in the United States.[13]

The Chinese leadership's determination to avoid even the impression of giving in to pressure is almost a conditioned reflex because this would mean a dreaded loss of face.

Thus when Obama in Beijing held out the prospect of a closer partnership to tackle the major global issues, the response was noncommittal. Four months later, President Hu came to Washington to attend the Nuclear Security Summit. In a one-on-one with Obama, according to the official Xinhua news agency, he put forward a five-point proposal "to establish a partnership to jointly deal with common challenges."

Hu's overture covered much the same ground as Obama's, but only up to a point: The second of his five points stressed that each country "would respect the other's core interests and major concerns," a point not specifically made by Obama, and one that left wide latitude for divergence. Two of these interests were Tibet and Taiwan, which "concern China's sovereignty and territorial integrity and its interests," Xinhua stated, and which the United States should "handle with caution."[14]

This balance-of-interests approach by the Chinese is typically — and almost cryptically — expressed by Kaiser Kuo, an associate researcher at Beijing's World Politics Institute. "Sino-American competition and cooperation are increasingly intertwined," Kaiser says. "There is cooperation within competition, and competition within cooperation. There is no absolute cooperation or competition. Therefore, we should not completely reject competition — and we should strengthen cooperation."[15]

In Washington, President Hu also hinted that China might be considering a revaluation of its currency, "based on its own economic and social-development needs." In other words, not because Washington is pressing for it.[16]

Hu also agreed that Beijing should cooperate on the wording of an Iran sanctions resolution. But in Beijing, Chinese Foreign Ministry spokeswoman Jiang Yu repeated China's position that "dialogue and negotiations are the best way."[17]

But some analysts think U.S.-Chinese relations may be less about cooperation and more about an ascendant China challenging the United States in areas once firmly in America's sphere of influence. "Obama and his policy makers are required to face up to a new reality," commented the Seoul-based English-language *Korean Times*, "in which China is jockeying for the world's No. 2

A February meeting between the Dalai Lama — Tibet's exiled leader — and President Obama miffed the Chinese government, which maintains that Tibet is an inherent part of China and refuses to recognize Tibetan independence.

AFP/Getty Images/STR

position while the U.S., the world's sole superpower, is waning, especially in the aftermath of the global financial and economic crisis."[18]

Unlike U.S.-Soviet relations during the Cold War, the challenge is not ideological. Still, according to the Congressional Research Service, "China's growing 'soft power' — primarily diplomatic and economic influence in the developing world — has become a concern among many U.S. policy leaders, including members of Congress."[19]

Because of its voracious demand for raw materials, Chinese trade with Latin America — the United States' back yard — grew tenfold between 2002 and 2007. In 2008, Chinese trade with Latin America ($142 billion) was a sixth of U.S. trade with the region — but growing at a faster rate. China's footprint in Africa is even larger in terms of both financial aid and investments.[20] But more significant from Washington's point of view is Beijing's increasing involvement in the Middle East.

In 2009, exports of Saudi Arabian crude to China were higher than to the United States, as Beijing courted the world's largest oil producer — and longtime U.S. ally.

"Saudi Arabia used to be very much an American story, but those days are over," said Brad Bourland, head researcher at Jadwa Investment in Riyadh, Saudi Arabia. The Saudis "now see their relationship with China as very strategic, and very long term."[21]

China Sells Most Arms to Pakistan

Pakistan purchased more than a third of all Chinese conventional arms from 2003-2007 — by far the largest share. The second-largest buyer was Sudan, followed by Iran, Saudi Arabia and Egypt.

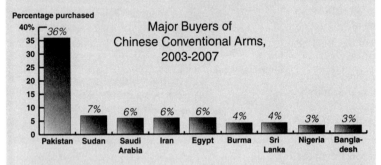

Percentage purchased

Major Buyers of Chinese Conventional Arms, 2003-2007

Source: "Military Power of the People's Republic of China, 2009," Office of the Secretary of Defense

In a recent interview, Xu Xueguan, director of North American affairs at the Chinese Foreign Ministry's huge headquarters in Beijing, told the author he couldn't understand why China had not been included in the so-called Quartet, the coalition of the United Nations, European Union, United States and Russia that is seeking a peaceful solution to the Israel-Palestine confrontation. When the Quartet was set up eight years ago, China did not yet have the clout to insist on being included. More recently, Beijing has expressed interest in becoming the fifth member of the U.N.-sponsored peace effort, without success — at least so far.

Is a confrontation with China inevitable, as some predict?

The Chinese leadership is "gunning for a paradigm shift in geopolitics. In particular, Beijing has served notice that it won't be shy about playing hardball to safeguard what it claims to be 'core national interests,' " writes Willy Lam, a China specialist at the Washington-based Jamestown Foundation think tank. [22] At the top of those national interests is Taiwan which, *The Economist* magazine said recently, "has been where the simmering distrust between China and America most risks boiling over."[23]

The chance of a war between China and the United States is generally regarded as remote. The Chinese threat to the United States is indirect — for example, if China should decide to use force to annex Taiwan, and

America intercedes — as it is committed to do even though the United States does not recognize the island as an independent state.

China hands like Elizabeth Economy, director of Asia Studies at the Council on Foreign Relations think tank in Washington, downplay the new "Red Scare." Economy argues that the West — particularly the United States — has "completely lost perspective on what constitutes reality in China today." Economy concedes that "there is a lot that is incredible about China's economic story, but there is a lot that is not working well on both the political and economic fronts," distorting the real picture.

In other words, China has enough problems without provoking the challenge of an international nemesis. The Chinese leadership appears to worry about a fragile society: A persistent nightmare is that a sudden significant spike in unemployment, officially kept at 4 percent (but possibly higher because of the huge, hard-to-track migrant-worker population) could lead to widespread unrest.[24]

Still, looking at the Chinese as the potential aggressors, does China have the capacity for a military confrontation with the United States?

In the past five years China has spent hundreds of billions of dollars modernizing its armed forces, with special emphasis on the navy. China's 1.7 million Chinese under arms is considerably more than the 1.4 million in the U.S. armed forces, but in 2009 the U.S. defense budget was $738 billion and China's estimated at between $69.5 billion and $150 billion.[25]

The government insists it seeks a peaceful solution to the issue of uniting Taiwan to the mainland, but the Chinese have built up a formidable fleet of submarines and developed anti-ship missiles to counter a possible U.S. defense of the Taiwan Strait. The Americans will be ready for them. In its annual report to Congress on China's military power, the Pentagon said it was "maintaining the capacity to defend against Beijing's use of force or coercion against Taiwan."

Beyond the strait, the Pentagon reported, "China's ability to sustain military power . . . remains limited."[26] The Pentagon's annual report is a source of irritation to the Chinese, who routinely denounce it. This year, the Xinhua news agency dismissed the assessment as "a largely subjective report with distorted facts and groundless speculation."[27]

Less hypothetical is the threat to the U.S. government's computer system. The Pentagon's 2009 report said U.S. government computers had been the target of "intrusions that appear to have originated" in China, although not necessarily from the military.[28] And in his annual "Threat Assessment" to the Senate Select Committee on Intelligence, Director of National Intelligence Dennis C. Blair warned in February that "malicious cyber activity is occurring on an unprecedented scale with extraordinary sophistication."

As a result, Blair added, the United States "cannot be certain that our cyberspace infrastructure will remain available and reliable during a time of crisis." Blair did not refer to China directly at that point. However, later in his assessment he called "China's aggressive cyber activities" a major concern.[29]

In January, after Google reported that hackers in China had targeted the computers of more than 30 U.S. corporations, including its own, and that the e-mail accounts of human rights activists had also been hacked, Secretary of State Hillary Rodham Clinton called on the Chinese government to investigate and to make its findings public.[30] (*See sidebar, p. 308.*)

U.S. officials and business executives warn that a trade war could also erupt if the Chinese don't yield to international pressure and raise the aggressive undervaluation of the renminbi, kept artificially low to favor Chinese exports. China's cheap currency is a serious problem for the global economy by undercutting exports throughout the industrial world, including the United States, and contributing to the trade imbalance. (President Obama has contended that if China lets the renminbi appreciate, U.S. exports would increase.)

The Obama administration has so far avoided picking a public fight with China over its currency — even

to the extent of postponing indefinitely a Treasury Department report on worldwide currencies originally due out on April 15. Without any movement by Beijing on the currency front, the report could well label China a "currency manipulator." If that happens, Sen. Charles E. Schumer, D-N.Y., is ready with draft legislation that would place more tariffs on Chinese goods.

Chinese Commerce Minister Chen Deming recently told *The Washington Post* that the United States would lose a trade war with China. "If the United States uses the exchange rate to start a new trade war," he said, "China will be hurt. But the American people and U.S. companies will be hurt even more."[31]

One way for America to increase its exports, said Chen, would be to remove the restrictions on high-tech goods with possible military applications, which the United States imposed following Beijing's repressive crackdown on student demonstrations in 1989 in Tiananmen Square — something the Obama administration shows no signs of doing.

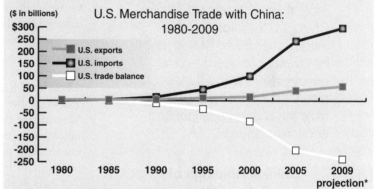

U.S. Trade Deficit With China Has Surged

The United States imports far more from China than it exports, causing a significant and growing trade gap. U.S-China trade rose rapidly after the two nations reestablished diplomatic relations and signed a bilateral trade agreement in 1979 and provided mutual most-favored-nation treatment beginning in 1980. In recent years, China has been one of the fast-growing U.S. export markets, and it is expected to grow even further as living standards continue to improve and a sizable Chinese middle class emerges.

* Based on actual data for January-April 2009

Source: Wayne M. Morrison, "China-U.S. Trade Issues," Congressional Research Service, June 23, 2009

China's U.S. Holdings Greatly Increased

Since the early 2000s, China's holdings of U.S. securities — including U.S. Treasury securities and corporate stocks and bonds — have risen above $1.2 trillion — an increase of more than 500 percent. While China's U.S. holdings have helped the United States meet its investment needs, some policymakers worry they could give China increased leverage over the U.S. on political and economic issues.

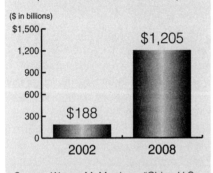

China's Holdings of U.S. Securities
(June 2002-June 2008)

Source: Wayne M. Morrison, "China-U.S. Trade Issues," Congressional Research Service, June 23, 2009

Has China's "market authoritarian" model of government emerged as an alternative to Western democracy?

Despite predictions, China's emergence from isolation and its spectacular economic growth have not led to democratization. Instead, China has developed what Stefan Halper, director of the Atlantic Studies Program at Cambridge University, calls "a market authoritarian

form of government, in which the free market is allowed to operate, but the government holds a very firm hand on political activity in the country."

In so doing, says Halper, author of the recent book *The Beijing Consensus,* the Chinese have produced an alternative to the Western democratic system that is thought to go hand in hand with a free-market economy. Non-democratic countries around the world like Egypt, Indonesia, Myanmar and Malaysia must find much to envy in a country that has achieved a 9 percent growth rate yet "managed to control its media, the legislature and the dissident voices, and has achieved global prominence," Halper adds.

The Chinese system "offers a seductive model that is eagerly taken up by the leaders of countries that have not yet settled on democratic structures," writes Australian China hand Rowan Callick in *The American,* the magazine of the American Enterprise Institute, a conservative Washington think tank. The Chinese model attracts autocrats because "their broader populations become content and probably supportive because their living standards are leaping ahead."[32]

China, however, has no interest in exporting its form of government. Its dealings with the rest of the world are dominated by the single-minded pursuit of one objective: economic development. As a ubiquitous lender and financial aid donor, China finds the door open in developing countries because Beijing's money comes with no strings attached about human rights and democracy — which is hardly the case with financial assistance from either the United States or the European Union.

Chinese money "is made available relatively easily and quickly without the political, economic, social and environmental conditions . . . that U.S. and European donors typically impose," says the Congressional Research Service report on China's foreign trade.[33]

But envious autocratic leaders should take note: Authoritarian capitalism may only work up to a point, writes Thomas P.M. Barnett, author of the recent book *Great Powers: America and the World after Bush.* He argues that when an economy starts to mature and needs to become more efficient, productive and innovative-based —"then we're talking intensive growth . . . something that nobody ever has been able to plan, because it lives and breathes on fierce competition, which only a true free market, accompanied by democracy, can supply."[34]

1970s-1980s *After Mao's death Deng institutes sweeping reforms, including relations with the United States.*

1972 President Richard M. Nixon makes historic trip to China, meets Mao Zedong and signs Shanghai Joint Communiqué declaring Taiwan part of mainland China.

1975 President Gerald R. Ford visits China, meets the ailing Mao, who dies the next year.

1978 Deng Xiaoping emerges as new leader, launches economic and social reforms.

1979 U.S. and China establish diplomatic relations. . . . Congress passes Taiwan Relations Act pledging to continue to supply Taiwan with weapons. . . . Deng visits United States.

1982 In joint U.S.-Chinese communiqué, United States pledges to gradually reduce arms sales to Taiwan.

1984 President Ronald Reagan visits China and meets Deng, who says that Taiwan remains a crucial problem in bilateral relations.

1989 President George H. W. Bush visits Beijing, invites dissidents to dinner. . . . People's Liberation Army crushes student-led pro-democracy demonstration in Beijing's Tiananmen Square, killing hundreds of protesters. . . . White House National Security Adviser Brent Scowcroft holds secret meeting in Beijing with Chinese leaders following the Tiananmen Square massacre.

1990s-2000s *China's economy welcomes Western investors; U.S.-China relations continue to warm.*

1992 Reversing a decade of U.S. policy, President George H. W. Bush decides to sell Taiwan F-16 combat planes, infuriating the Chinese.

1993 Newly elected President Bill Clinton establishes policy of "constructive engagement" with China, meets President Jiang Zemin in Seattle.

1996 China tests missiles off Taiwan to discourage vote for separatist Lee Teng-hui in the presidential election; U.S.

sends two aircraft carrier battle groups to area to support Taiwan.

1997 Britain hands Hong Kong back to China after 156 years. . . . Clinton is first U.S. president to visit China in a decade; criticizes Tiananmen massacre but strengthens U.S. commitment not to support Taiwan independence.

2000 U.S. Senate passes Permanent Normal Trade Relations bill (PNTR) giving China the same low-tariff access to the American market as other trading partners.

2001 China seizes U.S. spy plane after midair collision with Chinese fighter, hands over 24 American crewmembers after President George W. Bush apologizes for the Chinese pilot's death. . . . Bush makes first trip to China. . . . China joins World Trade Organization.

2002 Bush makes second visit to China to mark the 30th anniversary of Nixon's historic trip. . . . Future leader Hu Jintao visits White House for talks. . . . President Jiang Zemin visits Bush at his Texas ranch; they agree to cooperate on crisis following North Korea's announcement that it has nuclear weapons.

2003 With U.S. participation, Beijing hosts six-party talks on a unified approach to North Korea's nuclear weapons program.

2006 China's Great Firewall, or Golden Shield, Internet censorship system goes into service.

2008 China closes down Twitter, YouTube to block discussion on 20th anniversary of Tiananmen massacre.

2009 President Obama visits Shanghai and Beijing, makes no headway in persuading Chinese to raise value of their currency or to back sanctions against Iran.

2010 President Hu attends summit on nuclear security in Washington, despite tense U.S.-China relations over Iran sanctions, currency issues and imminent American weapons sale to Taiwan. . . . Expo 2010 opens in Shanghai. . . . Annual "strategic dialogue" between U.S. and China set for late May. . . . U.S. and China to attend G20 summit in Seoul, South Korea, in late June.

Is China Less Welcoming to U.S. Investors?

As Chinese know-how grows, opportunities diminish for foreigners.

It's one of the ironies of the U.S. trade deficit with China that a sizable portion of the goods exported to America are made by Chinese workers for U.S. firms. Earlier this year, the state-run Xinhua news agency reported that of the 200 top exporting firms last year, 153 were "foreign funded firms" — up from 141 in 2008.[1]

It's estimated that at least a third of those companies are U.S.-owned. For example, Shanghai alone has about 3,600 American expatriate business executives — although it was around 4,000 before the 2008 economic downturn. Chongqinq, China's largest city, with a population of 32 million, lists 41 foreign firms operating there, including Lear, Du Pont, Delphi Packard and Pepsi. General Motors, the largest auto maker in China, expects to sell 3 million vehicles in the Asian market by 2015 from its Chinese plants. In 2009, the 665,000 foreign firms in China accounted for 28 percent of the nation's industrial output, 56 percent of its exports and 45 million of its workers. In the first quarter of this year, foreign investment rose 12.1 percent, to $9.4 billion, according to Business Week.[2]

Even so, Google's recent difficulties with hackers in China may be an indication that as the Chinese economy matures the investment climate may no longer be as welcoming as it once was. One American executive doing business in Beijing says industrial espionage is rife and that the Chinese are experts at copying products. A foreign firm has at most a two-year window to establish itself on the Chinese market before it is challenged by an emerging local competitor.

As Chinese industrial know-how grows, the opportunities for foreign investors continue to diminish, according to business executives in Shanghai and Beijing. Recently, the Chinese authorities issued a directive encouraging government agencies to buy Chinese goods.

In a country where the state is still a major customer, this is a disturbing measure. But investors remain attracted by China, argues writer Zachary Karabell, author of the 2009 book Superfusion: How China and America Became One Economy and Why the World's Prosperity Depends on It. Says Karabell, "There's really nowhere else to go where you have 10 percent growth, 300-600 million emerging middle class Chinese who want to buy stuff and an environment where the rule of law is increasingly at least adequate in enforcement of contracts and getting your investments out of the country."

Google quit China after its servers were hacked, adds Karabell, partly because it wasn't doing very well in the Chinese market, and because it could afford not to do business with China.

The continued uncertain global environment has focused the Chinese government's attention on generating a domestic consumer market, so far with mixed results. Parting older-generation Chinese with their money means

Moreover, under closer scrutiny, China's economic success has fragile underpinnings, with some doubting its long-term sustainability. For example, for all its progress, China's per capita income is still $6,546, compared to $40,208 in the United States. China's gross domestic product barely reaches $9 trillion, whereas allowing for the recent volatility of exchange rates, U.S. GDP exceeds $14 trillion.

Because China's economic development is export driven, the world recession caused 23 million Chinese workers to be laid off as Chinese exports dropped by 15-18 percent, says Stephen Green, chief economist at the Sun Trust Bank in Shanghai. By the end of 2009, however, 98 percent of those had found other work, as the Chinese economy bounced back quicker than Western economies, boosted by a 4 trillion renminbi

($586 billion) stimulus package. (The U.S. economic stimulus was $874 billion.)

But the lesson to Beijing was that China can't export itself to growth. Though exports have picked up, the Chinese have turned their attention to trying to develop a domestic market. For example, to stimulate sales of domestic appliances in rural areas, the government offered 13 percent rebates to farmers who buy refrigerators, TV sets and even mobile phones. In 2009, Beijing also spent $755 million to push car sales, cutting the purchase tax from around 15 percent to 5 percent. The result was a record 770,000 sales in March alone, a 27 percent jump over the previous month. Banks had instructions to increase mortgage lending, but the government reined them in again when they started granting loans for third homes.[35]

reversing a culture of saving, but the younger generations are avid shoppers. In the modern high rise that houses the Standard Chartered Bank in Shanghai — one of the thousands that crowd the city's skyline — Stephen Green, head of research, says older Chinese stubbornly stick to the "rainy day" syndrome — but "anyone born after 1980 behaves like an American."

In the past decade, for example, Starbucks has opened more than 350 coffee shops in China, where it is flourishing at the same time its U.S. business has been hammered by recession. Starbucks' success is puzzling because the Chinese really don't drink coffee; China produces about 30,000 tons of beans a year but exports most of it.

Caren Li, Starbucks' spokeswoman at the company's downtown Chinese headquarters in Shanghai, says Green Tea Frappuccino is a predictably steady seller, but "we're promoting a coffee culture, offering the Chinese more choices besides tea." Even so, it's not really about coffee: The coffee houses with the round green logo have become trendy meeting venues (there's even one in Beijing's Forbidden City), the chic place to be seen.

In 2009, a former Starbucks executive in China, Eden Woon, launched Toys R Us in China (locally called Toy LiFung), and today the American retailer has 15 stores in the country. China may be the world's leading toy manufacturer, but its citizens buy mainly for very young children. "There's no toy culture in China because parents think toys distract children from their studies," Woon says over breakfast in a bustling hotel restaurant offering acres of dishes ranging from American pancakes and waffles to wonton soup. So Woon launched a campaign in this nation

Chinese flock to the 350 Starbucks coffee shops in China, including this one in Shanghai, but customers come for tea, not coffee, and because Starbucks is considered cool.

of overachievers with the message: "Toys are an important part of growing up."

Mary Kay Inc., the Texas-based home-sales cosmetics firm, began operating in China in 1995. Headquartered in Shanghai, it marshals about 200,000 independent beauty "consultants," thanks to a skin-care line tailored to the local market, including a four-week "whitening cream" treatment that sells for the equivalent of $120.

— *Roland Flamini*

1 Xinhua news agency, http://news.xinhuanet.com/english2010/business/2010-04/20/c_13260044.htm.

2 "Foreign Investment in China Jumped in First Quarter," Business Week/Bloomberg, April 14, 2010, www.businessweek.com/news/2010-04-14/foreign-investment-in-china-jumps-in-first-quarter-update1-.html.

Though officials in China say 250 million Chinese were lifted out of poverty between 1980 and 2005, about 70 percent of China's population of 1.3 billion still lives in rural areas, often in villages with few paved roads and frequent water and power shortages. An ambitious and costly urbanization program is trying to shift people to the cities.

State-controlled media limit reports about unrest, but "bottom-up pressures for change in China are intense, spontaneous and multifaceted," according to a report by Ying Ma, a visiting fellow at the Hoover Institution at Stanford University. "Every day, Chinese leaders worry about the challenge to regime stability, but they have responded by continuing to exert brutal and sophisticated top-down control."[36]

"Riots take place in China every day," Ying says. The Chinese authorities reported 10,000 protests throughout the country in 1994, and 87,000 in 2005. Mobile phones and the Internet have given protesters and activists effective new weapons, which the regime is battling tooth and nail. Using the new technology the Chinese people clamor for the government to address their grievances on the local level in increasing numbers: 10 million petitions in 2004 jumped to 30 million the following year.[37]

BACKGROUND
Presidential Challenges

Shortly after Mao Zedong's death in 1976, Chinese leaders took a hard look at their country and didn't like what

'Harmonizing' the Internet in China

China's love affair with the Net is increasing along with censorship.

When a website is censored in China, the screen usually doesn't reveal that the government has blocked it. Instead, either a fake error message appears or an announcement about the site being unavailable, with an invitation to "Please try again."

By now, most of China's estimated 384 million "netizens" (nearly a quarter of the world's Internet users) are not taken in: They know the site has been "harmonized."[1]

In China, Internet censorship is often ironically called "harmonizing" because "harmony" — the absence of public dissent — is a key phrase in the government's propaganda. So as China's love affair with the Internet increases so does the Communist regime's censorship effort intensify — possibly because there is so much more material online for the government to worry about.

"China's blocking of overseas websites — including Facebook, Twitter and thousands of other sites is more extensive and technically more sophisticated than ever," Rebecca MacKinnon, a Hong Kong-based university journalism professor and China Internet expert, tells me via e-mail from Princeton's Center for Information Technology Policy, where she is currently a visiting fellow. "Controls over domestic content have also been tightening."

The Chinese authorities use a filtering system nicknamed The Great Firewall of China, but officially referred to as Golden Shield, to scan Internet content for specific key words and then block, or try to block, Web pages in which such words are used.

A list of blacklisted terms compiled by ConceptDoppler, a tool developed for the purpose by the universities of California, Davis, and New Mexico includes triggers such as "eighty-nine" and "June 4", the year and date of the Tiananmen Square protests, "massacre," "political dissident," "Voice of America," "Playboy magazine" and "Xinjiang independence" — a reference to the restive, predominantly Muslim province in northwestern China. Any one of these terms sends a series of three reset commands to both the source and the destination, effectively breaking the connection, says Jed Crandall, a professor of computer science at the University of New Mexico and one of the developers of ConceptDoppler, in an e-mail message.

A more recent addition to the list is "Charter 08," a lengthy manifesto calling on the Communist regime to relinquish its monopoly of power and introduce democratic reforms. Originally, Charter 08 was signed by 300 intellectuals and activists. After the document appeared briefly on the Internet — and before Chinese censors banned it — some 10,000 other signatures were added.

U.S. computer giants like Google entered the market knowing that they would have to comply with the regime's policy and exercise content censorship. Ultimately, Google found the controls too constricting to live with and earlier this year shifted its operations to less restrictive Hong Kong, at the same time complaining of Chinese hacking into the e-mail accounts of human rights activists and U.S. corporations.

Other U.S. Internet companies still operating in China, including Microsoft and Yahoo!, now face even tougher censorship restrictions. A new law, adopted on April 29 and set to take effect Oct. 1, requires them to stop the transmission of "state secrets" over the Internet, if they "discover" them — effectively requiring them to act as police informers.[2]

Some analysts maintain that while flowers were placed outside Google's Beijing office by users sorry to see it go, the impact of Google's departure is limited because the majority of China's netizens prefer to use homegrown Internet servers that exercise self-censorship rather than jeopardize their access.

Besides, the analysts point out, even with the constraints that grow daily the Internet has given Chinese citizens an unprecedented voice in the country's affairs.

"We should measure protest in China not by protests on the streets or availability of news on protests, but by the involvement of the Chinese citizens in policy decisions," says Yasheng Huang, a China expert at MIT's Sloan School.

they saw. China was just emerging from the Cultural Revolution, a decade of mob-led extremism started by Mao himself that had kept the country in chaos. China was desperately poor, deliberately isolated from the world economy and aloof from or opposed to nearly every international institution, including — until 1971 — the United Nations. Under Deng Xiaoping, China's leaders reversed course and embraced globalization.

"By the latter yardstick, China had made huge progress, thanks largely to the Internet."[3]

In recent years, Internet-based campaigns have pressured the Chinese government to release political prisoners, launch investigations into scandals, such as kidnapping boys for slave labor in mines, and convict corrupt officials.[4] China's version of Facebook, called Douban, and YouTube, called YouKu, as well as thousands of Internet bulletin boards teem with debate on current events.

Still, the censorship is not well-defined, and some well-known dissident bloggers don't know when they have crossed the line until there is a knock at the door.

But mainly, it works by suggestion: "Many Internet users only have access to public computers at Internet cafes or universities, and just the existence of censorship might cause them to avoid topics they know they're not supposed to access, changing their online behavior," says Crandall.

The government maintains that censorship is partly a security measure and partly a responsibility to protect the public from what it sees as the negative side of the Internet's rapid growth.

Qian Xiaoqian, vice minister at the Chinese State Council information office, whose functions include deciding what gets blocked, says that while the government intervenes when a site is seen as plotting to overthrow the state, on another level it is also responding to public worry about the addictive nature of the Net.

"There is a discussion going on in this country about the potential negative influences of the Internet," Qian said last December over cups of tea, invariably served to visitors to any Chinese office. "Chinese parents are worried about the pornography; but not just the pornography." The government blames "Internet addiction" for youthful alienation.

A recently published survey by the Chinese National People's Congress found that 10 percent of Chinese youth were addicted to the Internet, Qian says. Many Chinese parents are sending their children to "boot camp" to cure them of "internetitis" — a solution which the government first encouraged but later seemed to back away from, warning against too much brutality in rehab methods.[5]

Critics of Chinese Internet censorship, including MacKinnon, say the regime uses such arguments to justify tightening control over the Net.

Mounting concerns over security and censorship by the government led Google to leave mainland China in March and relocate in Hong Kong.

But Qian claims "the Chinese government assumes a very important responsibility in managing the Internet. America is a mature society. At this stage Chinese society is still not — and besides, different people have different interpretations of freedom."

For those who prefer the Internet censor-free, the United States is leading the effort to produce circumvention software that connects to blocked websites via proxy computers outside the country. Programs like Psiphon, Tor and the Global Internet Freedom Consortium have been increasingly successful at breaching the wall.[6]

— *Roland Flamini*

---

[1] David Talbot, "China's Internet Paradox," *MIT Technology Review*, May/June 2010, www.technologyreview.com/web/25032/page1/.

[2] Mike Elgan, "New Chinese law may force Microsoft, Yahoo, to follow Google," *ITWorld*, April 29, 2010, www.itworld.com/internet/106191/new-chinese-law-may-force-microsoft-yahoo-follow-google-out, and Jonathan Ansfield, "Amendment Tightens Law on State Secrets in China," *The New York Times*, April 30, 2010, p. A9.

[3] Quoted in Talbot, *op. cit.*

[4] *Ibid.*

[5] The information is from a Chinese television news "magazine" show, with a translation provided to the author.

[6] For example, www.FreeGate.com, the Freedom Consortium's software developed by a group of Chinese expatriates in the United States.

Since then successive U.S. presidents have wrestled with the challenge of how to deal with China's rapid rise. The Clinton administration fashioned a policy of "constructive engagement," calling for close bilateral economic and political cooperation, at the same time urging democratization and human rights.

"Seeking to isolate China is clearly unthinkable," President Bill Clinton declared in July 1998, defending his approach. "We would succeed instead in isolating ourselves and our own policy."[38]

The George W. Bush administration used the catch-phrase "responsible stakeholder," pressing China to become a responsible member of the international community and to embrace democracy. Prior to President Obama's November China trip, Deputy Secretary of State James B. Steinberg mapped out a policy of "strategic reassurance" towards Beijing, and the phrase — as intended — has stuck.

"Just as we are prepared to accept China's arrival as a prosperous and successful power," Steinberg explained, the Chinese must "reassure the rest of the world that its development and growing global role will not come at the expense of the security and well-being of others."[39]

Whatever the label, the fundamental underpinning of American policy toward China has been economic engagement. In 2000, for example, Congress granted China permanent normal trade relations (PNTR) with the United States. In 2001, the United States backed China's entry into the World Trade Organization, thus placing the Chinese under international business rules, which was reassuring for would-be foreign investors.

All Business

In his inaugural address last year, Obama echoed Clinton's 1997 statement that communist China stood "on the wrong side of history." The conventional wisdom about China was that the market forces unleashed by global trade and investment would inevitably give more people a stake in the economy and open up China politically, leading to the creation of political parties and more democracy and respect for human rights.

Only it hasn't happened. In China, the party's far from over. China calls its authoritarian capitalism a "socialist market system," and the ruling Chinese Communist Party (CPC) appears more entrenched than ever — helped by a large, efficient and pervasive police organization.

In 2009, the party celebrated its 60th anniversary, and the state-controlled media took care to trumpet the regime's economic and political achievements.

Yet how much is left of communist ideology is open to question: As the author discovered during a reporting trip to China last November, the huge portrait of Mao still looks out over Tiananmen Square, and Marxist theory is still taught at the party school for senior officials. But the old party slogans praising the proletariat class and condemning capitalism have disappeared from the walls and factories.

The party has opened membership to entrepreneurs and business people, and the state-held shares of the country's 1,300 companies, many of which are listed on the Beijing stock exchange, are publicly traded.

Challenged to explain exactly how Marxism-Leninism fits into the "socialist market system," Chinese officials quote Deng Xiaoping's famous observation that it doesn't matter whether the cat is black or white as long as it kills the mouse.

Officials today will even quote Confucius without first cautiously looking over their shoulder. The great Chinese sage has had his ups and downs. In the Cultural Revolution he was reviled as an imperial lackey because of his position as adviser to the emperor.

But Confucius has been rehabilitated as a symbol of China's glorious past. The Chinese have set up hundreds of Confucius institutes worldwide, including 25 in the United States. The institutes promote Chinese language and culture, just as the Goethe institutes promote German culture, and the Dante Alighieri institutes do the same for Italy.

Even so, "China did not take a missionary approach to world affairs, seeking to spread an ideology or a system of government," writes Robert D. Kaplan, a senior fellow at the Center for a New American Security. "Moral progress in international affairs is an American goal, not a Chinese one. China's actions abroad are propelled by its need to secure energy, metals and strategic materials in order to support the living standards of its immense population."

In Kaplan's view, Beijing "cares little about the type of regime with which it is engaged. It requires stability, not virtue as the West conceives it."[40]

As early as 2005, when China for the first time was included in the annual economic survey of the Organization for Economic Cooperation and Development (OECD), it noted, "Well over half of China's GDP is produced by privately controlled enterprises."[41] But while the trend has continued, communications, transport, infrastructure, banking and energy remain under tight state supervision.

In late November 2009, Xu Kuangdi, a senior adviser to the Chinese Communist Party, told this reporter and other visiting U.S. journalists that it would be dangerous to hold free elections because China was "not ready," and some demagogue might win by promising to take the money from the new rich and give it to the poor! "The ultimate goal is common prosperity," he said, "but we have to let a group of people get rich first."

In 2003, looking for places to put its growing export revenue, China began buying U.S. Treasury bills on a large scale. By 2005, China had acquired $243 billion worth of the U.S. debt, second only to Japan. In 2006, China overtook Japan when its holdings climbed to $618 billion. In 2009, possibly fearing that the global recession would undermine the dollar, China sold some $34 billion of its Treasuries — but was soon back on a buying spree. By February 2010, China held a whopping $877.5 billion in Treasuries.[42] Meanwhile, a well-heeled middle class has emerged in China. Cars create traffic jams in Chinese cities, and the once ubiquitous bicycles are now kept by many Chinese for week-end country excursions.

In Beijing, a five-star hotel is flanked by two glass-fronted dealerships, one for Maseratis, the other for Lamborghinis. Four years ago, the China branch of HSBC Bank launched a credit card: It now boasts 11 million cardholders, said D.G. "Dicky" Yip, of the Bank of Communications in Shanghai last November.

China's new rich have acquired a taste for art as well as luxury cars. First it was contemporary art by artists who a decade earlier had been suppressed or even jailed because of their avant garde works. More recently, classic traditional paintings and Chinese calligraphy have been sold at auction for millions of RMB. In a crowded auction hall in Beijing filled with Chinese bidders in November, a scroll painting by the Ming Dynasty landscape master Wu Bin sold for the equivalent of $24.7 million to a Chinese bidder.

The bad news for the government has been the widening gap between the urban prosperous and the rural impoverished. China's poor are a restive majority running into the hundreds of millions. In 2008, the average income of a rural worker was $690, compared to a city average of $2,290 — and higher in Shanghai and Beijing. [43] But the annual salary of a chief executive in China is around $100,000, a fraction of corporate salaries in the United States but still astronomical in Chinese terms.

To make matters worse for the poor, the government has been slow to reform a social system that cuts off the medical and other benefits of China's millions of internal migrant workers once they quit their hometowns. As things now stand many immigrants are left to fend for themselves — even when they find employment.

The social system also needs to catch up with the aging Chinese population, which is getting older faster than in the United States. The problem is exacerbated by a relatively high life expectancy — about 73 — versus 77 in the United States. By 2040 demographers say that each Chinese worker will be forced to support two parents and four grandparents.

An 'Edgy' Game

With the economic boom unfolding against a background of frequent unrest, "The No. 1 challenge for China is to maintain domestic stability and at the same time sustainable economic development," says Yang Jiemian, director of the Shanghai Institute of International Studies.

The Internet, which has gone from 620,000 users in China in 1997 to 370 million users today — more people than the entire U.S. population — has become a forum for online dissent. The authorities crack down on the deluge of cyber-dissent using a (patchy at best) online censorship, ironically known as the Great Firewall of China — which also tries to block pornographic sites. (*See sidebar, p. 308.*) Persistent blogging about subjects deemed subversive can lead to imprisonment. (There are 20 million bloggers in China.) For example, Chinese writer Liu Xiaobo was jailed for 11 years on Dec. 25 after co-drafting and posting "Charter '09," a lengthy manifesto calling on the government to introduce democratic reforms.

The regime's biggest nightmare remains large-scale unemployment. To keep it at the current 4 percent level China needs to ensure continued growth generating 24 million new jobs every year.[44] Hence the need to buttress its current dependence on exports by boosting consumer demand at home. But the Chinese are not only great savers but also traditionally have an aversion to being in debt. For example, no doubt to the chagrin of HSBC officials, 80 percent of the bank's credit card holders avoid interest charges by paying their whole bill every month — compared to the national U.S. average of 20 percent.

More than 150 nations and 50 international organizations have registered for the Shanghai World Expo, and 70 million visitors are anticipated, making the six-month-long world's fair the largest ever. The Expo's theme — "Better City — Better Life" — is intended to showcase Shanghai as the next great world city in the 21st century.

Commenting on the government's combination of a market economy and tight control, Halper at Cambridge University says, "This is an edgy game, and things could go seriously wrong. Just trying to control the Internet is really tough work. The glue that holds the whole thing together is a ferociously powerful security service."

CURRENT SITUATION

Tense Beginning

This is a period of waiting for the other shoe to drop in U.S.-China relations following a tense first quarter of 2010.

There is unresolved business on the currency front, on Iran sanctions, on the issue of U.S. weapons sales to Taiwan and on the broader question of how the two countries should engage in the future.

The Obama administration has put a lot of effort into trying to convince the Chinese government that it is in both sides' interest to move toward what Obama calls "a more market-oriented exchange rate" for the renminbi. Following a meeting between President Obama and President Hu Jintao in Washington in April, during the Nuclear Security Summit, it seemed clear that the Chinese had not budged on revaluing their currency. Any change would not come from U.S. pressure, Hu said.[45]

In New York, the five permanent members of the U.N. Security Council are working on an Iran-sanctions resolution. "The Chinese were very clear they share our concern about the Iranian nuclear program," said Bader at the National Security Council. [46] Still, the Chinese government has not said that it will vote for a U.N. resolution and still insists publicly that diplomacy and negotiation are the way to go.

Cooperation on climate control seems at a stalemate after Hu told the December Copenhagen summit that China's own emissions control program would not be subject to U.N. supervision. For its part, the United States rejected a Chinese request that developing countries should be compensated for cutting carbon emissions.

Yu Qintgou, the official responsible for climate change at China's Ministry of Foreign Affairs, explained the familiar Chinese position in an interview in Beijing on Dec. 1. Simply put, Yu said, the world's climate change problem was not the making of China or India but of the developed countries. The United States and the other industrialized nations should "acknowledge their historic responsibility" as emitters of greenhouse gases and not put so great a burden on the emerging nations that it would set back their development, he said.

The latest tension had its origins in November, when Obama's Chinese hosts insisted on a low-key visit that minimized his contact with the public.

"It's a mystery," David Shamburgh, a professor of Chinese studies at Georgetown University, told *The Wall Street Journal* during the presidential visit. "[Obama is] a populist politician, but he's not getting any interaction with Chinese people."[47] It's not such a mystery, perhaps, when one considers Obama's popularity worldwide, in contrast to a Chinese leadership with limited contact with its own people.

Indeed, on the morning following Obama's arrival in Shanghai, the city's government-controlled English-language paper carried a large front-page photo of Hu with the prime minister of Canada, who was in China at the time. A one-column photo of Obama appeared below the fold. In a country where much importance is attached to not losing face, such signals matter.

The tension had escalated two months later when Obama made two moves calculated to anger the Chinese. First, in February the president received Tibet's exiled spiritual leader, the Dalai Lama, after Beijing had expressly asked him not to do so.

AT ISSUE

Is today's China a communist country?

YES

Xu Kuangdi
President, Chinese Academy of Engineering in Beijing, former Shanghai mayor

Written for *CQ Researcher*, May 2010

The Chinese Communist Party (CPC) has never done things by the book. In the early days, some party members, following the lead of the Soviet Union, launched the workers' movement in the cities. But the party shifted its focus to the rural areas where government control was relatively weak. We mobilized the peasants; we developed land reform.

Today, we don't do things according to what Karl Marx wrote or Vladimir Lenin said 80 years ago. We're doing things to advance the development of productive forces, and we are doing things to serve the interests of the vast majority of people.

Marx is still widely respected by the party. He is a great mind and a very great thinker on the development of civilization. His theories on capitalism inspired us on how to overcome the current financial crisis. But Marx lived 100 years ago; he couldn't predict how science and technology would develop. That is why our new ideology is to keep pace with the times. That doesn't mean we have forgotten Marx. Marxism is still our long-term goal.

The CPC is committed to building a society in which property and well-being can be enjoyed by all, a society of harmony between rich and poor. Today, we have a problem of a widening gap between rich and poor, which we are trying our best to narrow. But it will not be solved by dividing the property of the rich among the poor.

Our previous lessons showed us that the division of property is not the answer. Nor is Western democracy the answer. If we introduced Western democracy, we may have turbulence in the society.

A Western friend told me that he would only go to church three times in his lifetime. The first time is to be baptized, the second for his marriage and the third for his funeral. It doesn't follow that he doesn't have God in his heart. It's the same for us with Communism.

To live up to our beliefs we sometimes have to take different paths. As [former CPC leader] Deng Xiaoping has put it: The ultimate goal is common prosperity, but we have to let some people get rich first.

NO

Stefan Halper
Director, Atlantic Studies Program, Cambridge University'
Author, The Beijing Consensus: How China's Authoritarian Model Will Dominate the Twenty-First Century

Written for *CQ Researcher*, April 2010

There's a wonderful comment by the legendary U.S. diplomat and Russia expert George F. Kennan, who said, "Let's not ask what communism has done to Russia, but rather what Russia has done to communism." Much the same didactic is applicable to today's China.

Mao and Stalin would be spinning in their graves if they saw what was happening in China in the name of communism. China has shed any remnants of Marxist ideology, even to the point of directly addressing the question of who owns the land, a serious point of contention in the recent People's Congress. It is now accepted that land can be privately owned and houses built on it.

China is not expansionist, it does not seek to undermine the Western system: instead, its market-authoritarian system provides an example for the world beyond the West where growing numbers of leaders admire China, see China as a Third World nation at the pinnacle of world power and wish to emulate China's progress.

So while China may continue to call itself communist, it certainly isn't communism as we know it, but more of a form of state capitalism; the role of state is market authoritarian, not Marxist-Leninism. A Marxist economy is the polar opposite of the dynamic market economy China is developing today.

The Chinese leadership is highly practical, opportunistic and focused on economic growth and stability. The only remnants of communism are the single party rule of the party, a general embrace of socialist principles and the various structures that the party employs to govern the country: a politburo, a people's congress and a central committee.

Of course, it still calls itself communist, but it's just as much a corporatist state, even a form of fascism in its classical, Mussolini-type form, which is to say a process that coordinates the interest of the state and large corporations. Put another way, the business of China is business.

China spends more than 4 percent of its gross domestic product (GDP) on its military, about the same ratio as the United States. The country's rising military spending, including the beefing up of key naval bases near Taiwan, has caused concern in Washington.

The meeting drew a protest from Beijing even though the White House kept the visit private and carefully avoided showing pictures of Obama and the Dalai Lama together.

In a second affront, Obama approved a long-delayed $6.4 billion weapons sale to Taiwan, which China continues to threaten with hundreds of missiles while at the same time insisting that it wants a peaceful solution to the island's claims of independence. The package includes 114 Patriot missiles worth $2.2 billion, and 60 Blackhawk helicopters worth $3.1 billion.

Beijing promptly ratcheted up its rhetoric, and U.S.-Chinese relations took "a nosedive," *The Washington Post* said.[48] A senior Chinese Defense Ministry official, Huang Xueping, said China was resolved to punish the United States if the weapons were delivered and that the U.S. could expect even greater consequences if Washington added advanced F-16 jet fighters to the sale.[49]

The Chinese went still further. Beijing threatened to sanction U.S. firms involved in the deal. And then it showed off its military prowess by successfully testing — without warning — an advanced missile interception system. The timing also seemed a further demonstration of Beijing's ire. "The people who tied the knot should untie the knot," said Chinese Foreign Ministry spokesman Qin Gang.[50]

Commentators attributed China's new tough and uncompromising attitude to more than one factor. They said China's seemingly quick recovery from the global financial crisis while the West continues to struggle has vindicated the Chinese development model in Chinese eyes and the weakness of the less-disciplined Western approach.

A second explanation, though, was the jostling for position in the leadership in advance of the 2012 Communist Party Congress, an event that spurs aspiring candidates to display their nationalist credentials. Behind the united front China's leadership shows to the world, deep divisions exist between the hard-line "realists" and those who favor openness in China's international dealings — and the hard-liners currently have the upper hand. According to another explanation, the regime's aggressiveness toward the outside world stems from the government's desire to find a distraction from socio-economic problems at home.

After all, this is the Year of the Tiger — always turbulent and often unpredictable.[51]

OUTLOOK
The Taiwan Question

It remains to be seen how the Chinese will react, if or when the United States begins delivery of the weapons sold to Taiwan.

Analysts say the recently proposed (but not finalized) additional sale of F-16s would raise the level of China's objections even further. Although the original weapons deal drew protests, it had initially been negotiated by the Bush administration and was well-known to the Chinese. But Jean-Pierre Cabestan, a professor of international studies at Hong Kong Baptist University, predicts that "if an F-16 sale moves forward, we can expect another wave of difficulties between the U.S. and China."

The outlook is hard to forecast with any accuracy because of the ongoing cooperation-competition dance between China and the U.S. For example, despite its protests over Taiwan, Beijing at the same time is committed to working with Washington and other governments in securing vital sea lanes and enforcing regional stability. Early in 2010, China agreed to take a lead role in anti-piracy patrols off Somalia. Chinese navy units had not strayed outside Chinese waters for centuries, but today 80 percent of China's oil imports are shipped through the narrow Straits of Malacca that connect the Indian Ocean and the South China Sea.

> *Despite its protests over Taiwan, Beijing at the same time is committed to working with Washington and other governments in securing vital sea lanes and enforcing regional stability.*

There is no indication that China would actually support sanctions against Iran. In the past, China had signed on to three previous U.N. sanctions resolutions — and the Chinese eventually delayed and weakened every one of them, said Iran expert Flynt Leverett, a senior fellow at the centrist New America Foundation think tank.[52]

Also casting a shadow over the next few months is the thorny question of China's undervalued renminbi. Foreign-policy issues are rarely prominent in U.S. elections, but at a time of high unemployment and economic uncertainty, some analysts believe China's currency seems set to become a thorny question in November's mid-term elections, possibly creating anti-Chinese public sentiment.

Given the upcoming elections, some analysts say a slight currency revaluation designed to take the dispute out of the campaign is in the offing. But, says Glaser at the Center for Strategic and International Studies, "The Chinese are not going to revalue their currency because we tell them to. They will choose their own time."

One reason: Chinese leaders cannot afford seeming to act in response to pressure from the "foreign devils" (*qwai lo*) — which to the Chinese is just about everybody including the United States — without serious loss of face in the eyes of their own people.

The United States has a risky card of sorts to play in the shape of the annual U.S. Treasury analysis (mandated by the 1988 Omnibus Trade and Competitiveness Act) of the currencies of foreign countries to determine whether they are manipulating the currency to gain unfair trade advantage. To Congress' exasperation, the Treasury has so far not labeled China a "currency manipulator."

If and when it does, New York's Sen. Schumer has a draft bill waiting that would impose stiff penalties on countries that manipulate their currencies, including possible tariffs. "China's currency manipulation would be unacceptable even in good economic times," Schumer said in a recent statement. "At a time of 10 percent unemployment, we simply will not stand for it."

There is an obvious political edge to Schumer's bill: The senator is up for re-election. But others also feel the time has come to confront the Chinese. The Obama administration "needs to draw a line in the sand, and say to the Chinese: 'You're exporting unemployment by undervaluing your currency by 20 percent to 40 percent,' " says Cambridge University's Halper. If the Chinese don't revalue, "we should impose similar tariffs."

It was out of consideration for Hu's visit in April that Treasury Secretary Timothy Geithner postponed publication of the Treasury report, which is normally released on April 15. No new date has been announced, but analysts say the delay is strategic, giving the Chinese more time for further reflection.

Two important dates are coming up for possible further discussion — the U.S.-China yearly "strategic dialogue" in late May, and the broader forum of the G20 summit in Seoul, South Korea, in late June.

The Chinese, however, are focused on another event they hope will boost their prestige, much as the 2008 Summer Olympics had done: The Shanghai Expo 2010, which the city expects will attract over 70 million visitors. Its theme reflects China's hopes and aspirations — "Better city, better life."

NOTES

1. "Clinton in China," BBC Special Report, July 3, 1998, http://news.bbc.co.uk/2/hi/special_report/1998/06/98/clinton_in_china/118430.stm. Also Lin Kim, "Sino-American Relations: a new stage?" *New Zealand International Review*, Vol. 23, 1998, www.questia.com/googleScholar.qst;jsessionid= LY2JTpnRvl29qyD1Byf HwVQxJtmVQQ7bcyJ6RW47LJJnw6WmnYwg!555 708061!-1331918248?docId= 5001372599.

2. "China's economy grew 11.9 pct y/y in Q1 — sources," *The Guardian*, April 14, 2010. www.guardian.co.uk/business/feedarticle/9031081.

3. U.S. Census Bureau, www.census.gov/foreign-trade/balance/c5700.html#2010.

4. Howard Schneider, "U.S. sets tariff of up to 90 percent on imports of Chinese oilfield pipes," *The Washington Post*, April 10, 2010.

5. Wang Yanlin and Jin Jing, "Trade dispute heats up while Obama visit nears," *ShanghaiDaily.com*, Nov. 7,

2009, www.shanghaidaily.com/sp/article/2009/200911/20091107/article_418781.htm.

6. Schneider, *op. cit.*

7. "China, India, Japan Iran's Top Partners in Crude Oil Trade," Moinews.com, April 14, 2010, www.mojnews.com/en/Miscellaneous/ViewContents.aspx?Contract=cms_Contents_I_News&r=485205.

8. For background see Alan Greenblatt, "Attacking Piracy," *CQ Global Researcher*, August 2009, pp. 205-232.

9. "China Must Protect Intellectual Property," *Korea Herald*, April 22, 2010, www.koreaherald.co.kr/national/Detail.jsp?newsMLId=20100422000363.

10. White House transcript, Nov. 9. 2009, www.whitehouse.gov/the-press-office/briefing-conference-call-presidents-trip-asia.

11. "Commentary: China, U.S. sail in one boat amid global issues," Xinhua news service, Nov. 16, 2009; http://news.xinhuanet.com/english/2009-11/16/content_12463881.htm.

12. Martin Walker, "Walker's World: Haiku Herman's G2," United Press International, Dec 7, 2009, www.spacewar.com/reports/Walkers_World_Haiku_Hermans_G2_999.html.

13. U.S.-China Joint Statement, U.S. Embassy, Beijing, http://beijing.usembassy-china.org.cn/111709.html.

14. "Hu presents 5-point proposal for boosting China-U.S. ties," Xinhua, April 13, 2010, http://english.cctv.com/20100413/102277.shtml.

15. Kaiser Kuo, "The Intertwining of Sino-American Cooperation and Competition," China Geeks Translation and Analysis of Modern China, February 2010, http://chinageeks.org/2010/02/the-intertwining-of-sino-american-competition-and-cooperation/.

16. Edwin Chen and Rob Delaney, "Hu Tells Obama China Will Follow Its Own Path on Yuan," Bloomberg, April 13, 2010, www.bloomberg.com/apps/news?pid=20601070&sid=a07psM9uKD6g.

17. "China-U.S. agreement sends warning to Iran," *The National*, April 13, 2010, www.thenational.ae/apps/pbcs.dll/article?AID=/20100413/FOREIGN/704139996/1014.

18. "Obama's Asia Visit," editorial, *Korea Times*, Nov. 10, 2009, www.koreatimes.co.kr/www/news/opinon/2010/04/202_55210.html.

19. Thomas Lunn, *et al.*, China's Foreign Aid Activities in Africa, Latin America, and Southeast Asia, Feb. 25, 2009, www.fas.org/sgp/crs/row/R40361.pdf. Report is based largely on research by New York University's Robert F. Wagner Graduate School of Public Service.

20. *Ibid.*

21. Jad Mouawad, "China's Growth Shifts the Geopolitics of Oil," *The New York Times*, March 19, 2010, www.nytimes.com/2010/03/20/business/energy-environment/20saudi.html.

22. Willy Lam, "Beijing Seeks Paradigm Shift in Geopolitics, "The Jamestown Foundation, March 5, 2010, www.jamestown.org/programs/chinabrief/single/?tx_ttnews%5Btt_news%5D=36120&tx_ttnews%5BbackPid%5D=25&cHash=a9b9a1117e.

23. "Facing up to China," *The Economist*, Feb. 4, 2010, www.economist.com/PrinterFriendly.cfm?story_id=15452821.

24. Nicholas D. Kristof, "China, Concubines, and Google," *The New York Times*, March 31, 2010, www.nytimes.com/2010/04/01/opinion/01kristof.html.

25. Drew Thompson, "Think Again: China's Military," *Foreign Policy*, March/April 2010, www.foreignpolicy.com/articles/2010/02/22/think_again_chinas_military.

26. "Annual Report to Congress: Military Power of the People's Republic of China, 2009," Department of Defense, www.defense.gov/pubs/pdfs/China_Military_Power_Report_2009.pdf.

27. "Pentagon issues annual report on China's military power," Xinhuanet, March 26, 2009, www.news.xinhuanet.com/english/2009-08/26/content_11079173.htm.

28. Pentagon report to Congress, *op. cit.*

29. Dennis Blair, "Annual Threat Assessment of the U.S. Intelligence Community for the Senate Select Committee on Intelligence," February 2010, www.dni.gov/testimonies/20100202_testimony.pdf.

30. Cecilia Kang, "Hillary Clinton calls for Web freedom, demands China investigate Google attack," *The Washington Post*, Jan. 22, 2010, www.washingtonpost

.com/wp-dyn/content/article/2010/01/21/AR2010012101699.html.

31. John Pomfret, "China's Commerce Minister: U.S. has most to lose in a trade war," *The Washington Post*, March 22, 2010, www.washingtonpost.com/wp-dyn/content/article/2010/03/21/AR2010032101111.html.

32. Rowan Callick, "The China Model," *The American*, November/December 2007, www.american.com/archive/2007/november-december-magazine-contents/the-china-model.

33. Lunn, *et al.*, *op. cit.*

34. Thomas P.M. Barnett, "The New Rules: Why China Will Not Bury America," *World Politics Review*, Feb. 1, 2010, www.worldpoliticsreview.com/articles/5031/the-new-rules-why-china-will-not-bury-america.

35. Wieland Wagne, "How China is battling global economic crisis," *San Francisco Sentinel*, May 23, 2009, www.sanfranciscosentinel.com/?p=28287.

36. Ma Ying, "China's Stubborn Anti-Democracy," Hoover Institution Policy Review, February/March 2007, www.hoover.org/publications/policyreview/5513661.html.

37. *Ibid.*

38. Brian Knowlton, "Citing 'Constructive Engagement,' He Acts to Counter Critics in Congress: Clinton Widens Defense of China Visit," *The New York Times*, July 12, 1998, www.nytimes.com/1998/06/12/news/12iht-prexy.t.html?pagewanted=1.

39. Evan Osnos, "Despatches from Evan Osnos: Strategic Reassurance," *The New Yorker Online*, Oct 6, 2009, www.newyorker.com/online/blogs/evanosnos/2009/ 10/strategic-reassurance.html.

40. Robert D. Kaplan, "The Geography of Chinese Power," *Foreign Affairs*, May/June 2010.

41. "China could become World's largest exporter by 2010," Organization for Economic Cooperation and Development, Sept. 16, 2005, www.oecd.org/document/29/0,3343,en_2649_201185_35363023_1_1_1_1,00.html.

42. U.S. Department of Treasury, www.ustreas.gov/tic/mfh.txt.

43. http://news.bbc.co.uk/2/hi/asia-pacific/7833779.stm.

44. Li Beodong, head of China's delegation to the United Nations in Geneva, official transcript of speech in 2009.

45. The Associated Press, "China's Hu rebuffs Obama on yuan," *Minneapolis Star Tribune*, April 13, 2010, www.startribune.com/business/90728804.html.

46. Transcript of White House press briefing, April 12, 2010, www.whitehouse.gov/the-press-office/press-briefing-jeff-bader-nsc-senior-director-asian-affairs.

47. Ian Johnson and Jonathan Wiseman, "Beijing limits Obama's exposure," *The Wall Street Journal* Online, Nov. 17, 2009, http://online.wsj.com/article/SB125835068967050099.html.

48. John Pomfret and Jon Cohen, "Many Americans see U.S. influence waning as that of China grows," *The Washington Post*, Feb. 25, 2010, p. A11.

49. Andrew Jacobs, "China Warns U.S. Against Selling F-16s to Taiwan,"

50. *Ibid.*

51. David Shambaugh, "The Year China Showed its Claws," *Financial Times*, Feb. 16, 2010, www.ft.com/cms/s/0/7503a600-1b30-11df-953f-00144feab49a.html.

52. Corey Flintoff, "Will China Help Sanction Iran's Nuke Program?" NPR, April 14, 2010, www.npr.org/templates/story/story.php?storyId=125991589&ft=1&f=1004.

BIBLIOGRAPHY

Books

Halper, Stefan, *The Beijing Consensus*, Basic Books, 2010.
A Cambridge University professor analyzes the economic and strategic sides of U.S.-China relations.

Jacques, Martin, *When China Rules the World: The Rise of the Middle Kingdom and the End of the Western World*, Penguin, 2010.
A British commentator predicts that history is about to restore China to its ancient position of global power.

Karabell, Zachary, *Superfusion: How China and America Became One Economy and Why the World's Prosperity Depends on It*, Simon & Schuster, 2009.

An economist and historian writes that despite an increasingly less hospitable business environment, foreign investors keep flocking to China.

Mann, James, *The China Fantasy: How Our Leaders Explain Away Chinese Repression*, Viking, 2007.
A veteran China reporter files a passionate complaint that U.S. elites are misleading the American public to boost trade with a hostile regime.

Shirk, Susan, *China: Fragile Superpower: How China's Internal Politics Could Derail Its Peaceful Rise*, Oxford University Press, 2007.
A former top State Department official says understanding the fears that drive China's leadership is essential to managing the U.S.-China relationship without military confrontation.

Tyler, Patrick, *A Great Wall: Six Presidents and China*, Public Affairs, 1999.
An investigative reporter describes the struggles of six presidential administrations in shaping a sustainable China policy.

Articles

Mufson, Stephen, and John Pomfret, "There's a New Red Scare, but is China Really So Scary?" *The Washington Post*, Feb. 28, 2010, www.washingtonpost. com/wp-dyn/content/article/2010/02/26/AR2010022 602601.html.
Two *Post* correspondents argue that America's reading of China is an insight into America's collective psyche.

Talbot, David, "China's Internet Paradox," *MIT Technology Review*, May-June 2010, www.technologyreview.com/web/25032/.
China's Internet usage is not as restricted as the regime would wish despite intense censorship efforts.

Wong, Edward, "Chinese Military to Extend its Naval Power," *The New York Times*, April 23, 2010, www. nytimes.com/2010/04/24/world/asia/24navy.html.
The Chinese military is building a deepwater navy to protect its oil tankers.

Xue, Litai, and Jiang Wenran, "Debate Sino-U.S. Ties," *China Daily*, April 20, 2010, www.chinadaily.net/ opinion/2010-04-26/content_9772895_2.htm.

Two U.S.-based Chinese scholars debate the state of the U.S.-China relationship.

Ying, Ma, "China's Stubborn Anti-Democracy," *Hoover Institution Policy Review*, February-March 2007, www. hoover.org/publications/policyreview/5513661.html.
An American Enterprise Institute fellow examines why China's economic development hasn't led to democratization.

Reports and Studies

"Annual Report to Congress: Military Power of the People's Republic of China — 2009," Office of the Secretary of State, 2009, www.defense.gov/pubs/pdfs/ China_Military_Power_Report_2009.pdf.
The Pentagon's annual assessment of the People's Liberation Army invariably draws criticism from Beijing.

Godement, Francois, *et al.*, "No Rush to Marriage: China's Response to the G2," China Analysis, European Council on Foreign Relations and the Asia Center of the Sciences Po, June 2009, ecfr.3cdn.net/d40ce525f765f 638c4_bfm6ivg3l.pdf.
An East Asian historian and analyst says that while Europeans worry about an emerging U.S.-Chinese global duopoly, the Chinese are still examining their options.

Green, Michael J., "U.S.-China Relations Under President Obama," July 14-15, 2009, Brookings Institution, iir.nccu.edu.tw/attachments/news/modify/ Green.pdf.
A scholar at the centrist think tank examines whether the administration's cooperative China policy will work.

Huang, Ping, *et al.*, "China-U.S. Relations Tending Towards Maturity," Institute of American Studies, Chinese Academy of Social Sciences, June 2009, ias.cass. cn/en/show_project_ls.asp?id=1012.
Four analysts offer a Chinese perspective on relations between the United States and their country.

Lunn, Thomas, "Human Rights in China: Trends and Policy Implications," Congressional Research Service, Jan. 25, 2010, www.fas.org/sgp/crs/row/RL34729.pdf.
The nonpartisan research agency offers the most current periodic report to Congress on human rights in China.

For More Information

American Enterprise Institute, 1150 17th St., N.W., Washington, DC 20036; (202) 862-5800; www.aei.org. A nonpartisan think tank dedicated to research and education on government, politics, economics and social welfare.

Brookings Institution, 1775 Massachusetts Ave., N.W., Washington, DC 20036; (202) 797-6000; www.brookings. edu. Non-profit public policy institution working for a more cooperative international system.

Center for a New American Security, 1301 Pennsylvania Ave., N.W., Suite 403, Washington, DC 20004; (202) 457-9400; www.cnas.org. An independent, nonpartisan think tank established in 2007 dedicated to developing strong, pragmatic and principled national security and defense policies that promote and protect American interests and values.

Center for Strategic and International Studies, 1800 K St., N.W., Washington, DC 20006; (202) 887-0200; www.csis. org. A nonpartisan think tank that provides strategic insights and policy solutions to decision-makers in government, international institutions, the private sector and civil society.

Center for U.S.-China Relations, Tsinghua University, Beijing, China 100084; (86-10) 62794360; www.chinausa.org .cn. First research institute specializing in U.S.-China relations established by a Chinese institute of higher education.

China Institute, 125 E. 65th St., New York, NY 10065; (212) 744-8181; www.chinainstitute.org. Promoting a better understanding of China through programs in education, culture and business.

China Institute of International Studies, 3 Toutiao, Taijichang, Beijing, China 100005; (86-10) 85119547; www. ciis.org.cn. Think tank and research institution arm of the Chinese Ministry of Foreign Affairs.

China-United States Exchange Foundation, 15/f Shun Ho Tower, 24-30 Ice House Street, Hong Kong; (852) 25232083; www.cusf.hk. Fostering dialogue between Chinese and U.S. individuals from the media, academic, think tank and business environments.

Confucius Institute, 0134 Holzapfel Hall, University of Maryland, College Park, MD 20742; (301) 405-0213; www .international.umd.edu/cim. One of more than 60 Chinese cultural institutes established on U.S. campuses by the Chinese government, offering language courses and cultural programs.

National Security Council, www.whitehouse.gov/administration/eop/nsc. The NSC is the president's principal forum for considering national security and foreign policy matters with his senior national security advisors and Cabinet officials.

Nottingham University China Policy Institute, International House, Jubilee Campus, Nottingham NG8 1B8, England, United Kingdom; (44-115) 8467769; www.nottingham.ac.uk/cpi. Think tank aimed at expanding knowledge and understanding of contemporary China.

Shanghai Institutes for International Studies, 195-15 Tianlin Rd., Shanghai, China 200233; (86-21) 54614900; www.siis.org.cn. Research organization focusing on international politics, economy, security strategy and China's international relations.

U.S.-China Policy Foundation, 316 Pennsylvania Ave., S.E., Suites 201-203, Washington, DC 20003; (202) 547-8615; www.uscpf.org. Works to broaden awareness of China and U.S.-China relations within the Washington policy community.

13

Women's Rights

Karen Foerstel

Iraqi teenager Du'a Khalil Aswad lies mortally wounded after her "honor killing" by a mob in the Kurdish region of Iraq. No one has been prosecuted for the April 2007 murder, even though a cell-phone video of the incident was posted on the Internet. Aswad's male relatives are believed to have arranged her ritualistic execution because she had dated a boy from outside her religious sect. The United Nations estimates that 5,000 women and girls are murdered in honor killings around the globe each year.

AFP/Getty Images

From *CQ Researcher*,
May 1, 2008.

S he was 17 years old. The blurry video shows her lying in a dusty road, blood streaming down her face, as several men kick and throw rocks at her. At one point she struggles to sit up, but a man kicks her in the face forcing her back to the ground. Another slams a large, concrete block down onto her head. Scores of onlookers cheer as the blood streams from her battered head.[1]

The April 7, 2007, video was taken in the Kurdish area of northern Iraq on a mobile phone. It shows what appear to be several uniformed police officers standing on the edge of the crowd, watching while others film the violent assault on their phones.

The brutal, public murder of Du'a Khalil Aswad reportedly was organized as an "honor killing" by members of her family — and her uncles and a brother allegedly were among those in the mob who beat her to death. Her crime? She offended her community by falling in love with a man outside her religious sect.[2]

According to the United Nations, an estimated 5,000 women and girls are murdered in honor killings each year, but it was only when the video of Aswad's murder was posted on the Internet that the global media took notice.[3]

Such killings don't only happen in remote villages in developing countries. Police in the United Kingdom estimate that up to 17,000 women are subjected to some kind of "honor"-related violence each year, ranging from forced marriages and physical attacks to murder.[4]

But honor killings are only one type of what the international community calls "gender based violence" (GBV). "It is universal," says Taina Bien-Aimé, executive director of the New York-based women's-rights group Equality Now. "There is not one country in the world where violence against women doesn't exist."

Only Four Countries Offer Total Equality for Women

Costa Rica, Cuba, Sweden and Norway receive the highest score (9 points) in an annual survey of women's economic, political and social rights. Out of the world's 193 countries, only 26 score 7 points or better, while 28 — predominantly Islamic or Pacific Island countries — score 3 or less. The United States rates 7 points: a perfect 3 on economic rights but only 2 each for political and social rights. To receive 3 points for political rights, women must hold at least 30 percent of the seats in the national legislature. Women hold only 16.6 percent of the seats in the U.S. Congress. The U.S. score of 2 on social rights reflects what the report's authors call "high societal discrimination against women's reproductive rights."

Status of Women's Rights Around the Globe

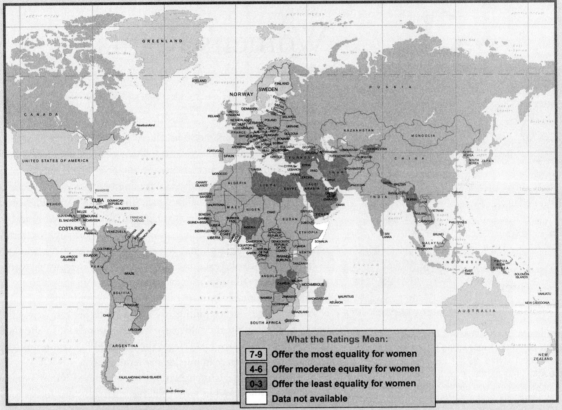

What the Ratings Mean:
- **7-9** Offer the most equality for women
- **4-6** Offer moderate equality for women
- **0-3** Offer the least equality for women
- Data not available

Source: Cingranelli-Richards Human Rights Dataset, http://ciri.binghamton.edu/, based on Amnesty International's annual reports and U.S. State Department annual Country Reports on Human Rights. The database is co-directed by David Louis Cingranelli, a political science professor at Binghamton University, SUNY, and David L. Richards, an assistant political science professor at the University of Memphis.

Thousands of women are murdered or attacked around the world each day, frequently with impunity. In Guatemala, where an estimated 3,000 women have been killed over the past seven years, most involving some kind of misogynistic violence, only 1 percent of the perpetrators were convicted.[5] In India, the United Nations estimates that five women are burned to death each day by husbands upset that they did not receive sufficient dowries from their brides.[6] In Asia, nearly 163 million females are "missing" from the population — the result of sex-selective abortions, infanticide or neglect.

And since the 1990s some African countries have seen dramatic upsurges in rapes of very young girls by men who believe having sex with a virgin will protect or cure them from HIV-AIDS. After a 70-year-old man allegedly raped a 3-year-old girl in northern Nigeria's commercial hub city of Kano, Deputy Police Chief Suleiman Abba told reporters in January, "Child rape is becoming rampant in Kano." In the last six months of 2007, he said, 54 cases of child rape had been reported. "In some cases the victims are gang-raped."[7]

Epidemics of sexual violence commonly break out in countries torn apart by war, when perpetrators appear to have no fear of prosecution. Today, in Africa, for instance, UNICEF says there is now a "license to rape" in eastern regions of the Democratic Republic of the Congo, where some human-rights experts estimate that up to a quarter of a million women have been raped and often sexually mutilated with knives, branches or machetes.[8] Several of the Congolese rapists remorselessly bragged to an American filmmaker recently about how many women they had gang-raped.[9]

"The sexual violence in Congo is the worst in the world," said John Holmes, the United Nations under secretary general for humanitarian affairs. "The sheer numbers, the wholesale brutality, the culture of impunity — it's appalling."[10]

In some cultures, the female victims themselves are punished. A report by the Human Rights Commission of Pakistan found that a woman is gang-raped every eight hours in that country. Yet, until recently, rape cases could not be prosecuted in Pakistan unless four Muslim men "all of a pious and trustworthy nature" were willing to testify that they witnessed the attack. Without their

Women's Suffering Is Widespread

More than two decades after the U.N. Decade for Women and 29 years after the U.N. adopted the Convention on the Elimination of All Forms of Discrimination against Women (CEDAW), gender discrimination remains pervasive throughout the world, with widespread negative consequences for society.

According to recent studies on the status of women today:

- Violence against women is pervasive. It impoverishes women, their families, communities and nations by lowering economic productivity and draining resources. It also harms families across generations and reinforces other violence in societies.
- Domestic violence is the most common form of violence against women, with rates ranging from 8 percent in Albania to 49 percent in Ethiopia and Zambia. Domestic violence and rape account for 5 percent of the disease burden for women ages 15 to 44 in developing countries and 19 percent in developed countries.
- Femicide — the murder of women — often involves sexual violence. From 40 to 70 percent of women murdered in Australia, Canada, Israel, South Africa and the United States are killed by husbands or boyfriends. Hundreds of women were abducted, raped and murdered in and around Juárez, Mexico, over the past 15 years, but the crimes have never been solved.
- At least 160 million females, mostly in India and China, are "missing" from the population — the result of sex-selective abortions.
- Rape is being used as a genocidal tool. Hundreds of thousands of women have been raped and sexually mutilated in the ongoing conflict in Eastern Congo. An estimated 250,000 to 500,000 women were raped during the 1994 genocide in Rwanda; up to 50,000 women were raped during the Bosnian conflict in the 1990s. Victims are often left unable to have children and are deserted by their husbands and shunned by their families, plunging the women and their children into poverty.
- Some 130 million girls have been genitally mutilated, mostly in Africa and Yemen, but also in immigrant communities in the West.
- Child rape has been on the increase in the past decade in some African countries, where some men believe having sex with a virgin will protect or cure them from HIV-AIDS. A study at the Red Cross children's hospital in Cape Town, South Africa, found that 3-year-old girls were more likely to be raped than any other age group.
- Two million girls between the ages of 5 and 15 are forced into the commercial sex market each year, many of them trafficked across international borders.
- Sexual harassment is pervasive. From 40 to 50 percent of women in the European Union reported some form of sexual harassment at work; 50 percent of schoolgirls surveyed in Malawi reported sexual harassment at school.
- Women and girls constitute 70 percent of those living on less than a dollar a day and 64 percent of the world's illiterate.
- Women work two-thirds of the total hours worked by men and women but earn only 10 percent of the income.
- Half of the world's food is produced by women, but women own only 1 percent of the world's land.
- More than 1,300 women die each day during pregnancy and childbirth — 99 percent of them in developing countries.

Sources: "Ending violence against women: From words to action," United Nations, October, 2006, www.un.org/womenwatch/daw/public/VAW_Study/VAW studyE.pdf; www.womankind.org.uk; www.unfp.org; www.oxfam.org.uk; www.ipu.org; www.unicef.org; www.infant-trust.org.uk; "State of the World Population 2000;" http://npr.org; http://asiapacific.amnesty.org; http://news.bbc. co.uk

Negative Attitudes Toward Women Are Pervasive

Negative attitudes about women are widespread around the globe, among women as well as men. Rural women are more likely than city women to condone domestic abuse if they think it was provoked by a wife's behavior.

Location	Percentage of women in selected countries who agree that a man has good reason to beat his wife if:						Women who agree with:	
	Wife does not complete housework	Wife disobeys her husband	Wife refuses sex	Wife asks about other women	Husband suspects infidelity	Wife is unfaithful	One or more of the reasons mentioned	None of the reasons mentioned
Bangladesh city	13.8	23.3	9.0	6.6	10.6	51.5	53.3	46.7
Bangladesh province	25.1	38.7	23.3	14.9	24.6	77.6	79.3	20.7
Brazil city	0.8	1.4	0.3	0.3	2.0	8.8	9.4	90.6
Brazil province	4.5	10.9	4.7	2.9	14.1	29.1	33.7	66.3
Ethiopia province	65.8	77.7	45.6	32.2	43.8	79.5	91.1	8.9
Japan city	1.3	1.5	0.4	0.9	2.8	18.5	19.0	81.0
Namibia city	9.7	12.5	3.5	4.3	6.1	9.2	20.5	79.5
Peru city	4.9	7.5	1.7	2.3	13.5	29.7	33.7	66.3
Peru province	43.6	46.2	25.8	26.7	37.9	71.3	78.4	21.6
Samoa	12.1	19.6	7.4	10.1	26.0	69.8	73.3	26.7
Serbia and Montenegro city	0.6	0.97	0.6	0.3	0.9	5.7	6.2	93.8
Thailand city	2.0	0.8	2.8	1.8	5.6	42.9	44.7	55.3
Thailand province	11.9	25.3	7.3	4.4	12.5	64.5	69.5	30.5
Tanzania city	24.1	45.6	31.1	13.8	22.9	51.5	62.5	37.5
Tanzania province	29.1	49.7	41.7	19.8	27.2	55.5	68.2	31.8

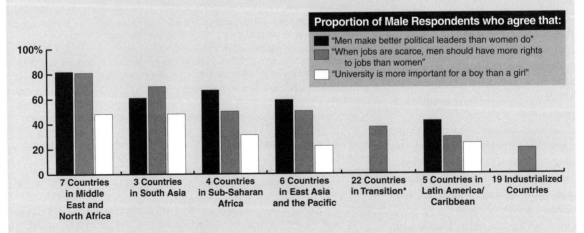

Proportion of Male Respondents who agree that:
- ■ "Men make better political leaders than women do"
- ■ "When jobs are scarce, men should have more rights to jobs than women"
- □ "University is more important for a boy than a girl"

7 Countries in Middle East and North Africa · 3 Countries in South Asia · 4 Countries in Sub-Saharan Africa · 6 Countries in East Asia and the Pacific · 22 Countries in Transition* · 5 Countries in Latin America/Caribbean · 19 Industrialized Countries

* Countries in transition are generally those that were once part of the Soviet Union.

Sources: World Heath Organization, www.who.int/gender/violence/who_multicountry_study/Chapter3-Chapter4.pdf; "World Values Survey," www.worldvaluessurvey.org

testimony the victim could be prosecuted for fornication and alleging a false crime, punishable by stoning, lashings or prison.[11] When the law was softened in 2006 to allow judges to decide whether to try rape cases in Islamic courts or criminal courts, where such witnesses are not required, thousands took to the streets to protest the change.[12]

Honor killings are up 400 percent in Pakistan over the last two years, and Pakistani women also live in fear of being blinded or disfigured by "acid attacks" — a common practice in Pakistan and a handful of other countries — in which attackers, usually spurned suitors, throw acid on a woman's face and body.

But statistics on murder and violence are only a part of the disturbing figures on the status of women around the globe. Others include:

- Some 130 million women have undergone female genital mutilation, and another 2 million are at risk every year, primarily in Africa and Yemen.
- Women and girls make up 70 percent of the world's poor and two-thirds of its illiterate.
- Women work two-thirds of the total hours worked by men but earn only 10 percent of the income.
- Women produce more than half of the world's food but own less than 1 percent of the world's property.
- More than 500,000 women die during pregnancy and childbirth every year — 99 percent of them in developing countries.
- Two million girls between the ages of 5 and 15 are forced into the commercial sex market each year.[13]
- Globally, 10 million more girls than boys do not attend school.[14]

Despite these alarming numbers, women have made historic progress in some areas. The number of girls receiving an education has increased in the past decade. Today 57 percent of children not attending school are girls, compared to two-thirds in the 1990s.[15]

And women have made significant gains in the political arena. As of March, 2008, 14 women are serving as elected heads of state or government, and women now hold 17.8 percent of the world's parliamentary seats — more than ever before[16] And just three months after the brutal killing of Aswad in Iraq, India swore in its first female president, Pratibha Patil, who vows to eliminate that country's practice of aborting female fetuses because girls are not as valued as boys in India. (See "At Issue," p. 343.)[17]

Spain's visibly pregnant new Defense minister, Carme Chacón, reviews troops in Madrid on April 14, 2008. She is the first woman ever to head Spain's armed forces. Women hold nine out of 17 cabinet posts in Spain's socialist government, a reflection of women's entrance into the halls of power around the world.

AP Photo/Bernat Armangue

Last October, Argentina elected its first female president, Cristina Fernández de Kirchner,* the second woman in two years to be elected president in South America. Michelle Bachelet, a single mother, won the presidency in Chile in 2006.[18] During her inaugural speech Kirchner admitted, "Perhaps it'll be harder for me, because I'm a woman. It will always be harder for us."[19]

Indeed, while more women than ever now lead national governments, they hold only 4.4 percent of the world's 342 presidential and prime ministerial positions. And in no country do they hold 50 percent or more of the national legislative seats.[20]

"Women make up half the world's population, but they are not represented" at that level, says Swanee Hunt, former U.S. ambassador to Austria and founding director of the Women and Public Policy Program at Harvard's Kennedy School of Government.

While this is "obviously a fairness issue," she says it also affects the kinds of public policies governments pursue. When women comprise higher percentages of officeholders, studies show "distinct differences in legislative outputs," Hunt explains. "There's less funding of bombs and bullets and more on human security — not just how to defend territory but also on hospitals and general well-being."

---

* Isabel Martínez Perón assumed the presidency of Argentina on the death of her husband, Juan Perón, in 1974 and served until she was deposed in a coup d'etat in 1976; but she was never elected.

Female Peacekeepers Fill Vital Roles

Women bring a different approach to conflict resolution.

The first all-female United Nations peacekeeping force left Liberia in January after a year's mission in the West African country, which is rebuilding itself after 14 years of civil war. Comprised of more than 100 women from India, the force was immediately replaced by a second female team.

"If anyone questioned the ability of women to do tough jobs, then those doubters have been [proven] wrong," said U.N. Special Representative for Liberia Ellen Margrethe Løj, adding that the female peacekeepers inspired many Liberian women to join the national police force.[1]

Women make up half of the world's refugees and have systematically been targeted for rape and sexual abuse during times of war, from the 200,000 "comfort women" who were kept as sex slaves for Japanese soldiers during World War II[2] to the estimated quarter-million women reportedly raped and sexually assaulted during the current conflict in the Democratic Republic of the Congo.[3] But women account for only 5 percent of the world's security-sector jobs, and in many countries they are excluded altogether.[4]

In 2000, the U.N. Security Council unanimously adopted Resolution 1325 calling on governments — and the U.N. itself — to include women in peace building by adopting a variety of measures, including appointing more women as special envoys, involving women in peace negotiations, integrating gender-based policies in peacekeeping missions and increasing the number of women at all decision-making levels.[5]

But while Resolution 1325 was a critical step in bringing women into the peace process, women's groups say more women should be sent on field missions and more data collected on how conflict affects women around the world.[6]

"Women are often viewed as victims, but another way to view them is as the maintainers of society," says Carla Koppell, director of the Cambridge, Mass.-based Initiative for Inclusive Security, which promotes greater numbers of women in peacekeeping and conflict resolution. "There must be a conscious decision to include women. It's a detriment to promote peace without including women."

Women often comprise the majority of post-conflict survivor populations, especially when large numbers of men have either fled or been killed. In the wake of the 1994 Rwandan genocide, for example, women made up 70 percent of the remaining population.

And female peacekeepers and security forces can fill vital roles men often cannot, such as searching Islamic women wearing burkas or working with rape victims who may be reluctant to report the crimes to male soldiers.

"Women bring different experiences and issues to the table," says Koppell. "I've seen it personally in the Darfur

Today's historic numbers of women parliamentarians have resulted partly from gender quotas imposed in nearly 100 countries, which require a certain percentage of women candidates or officeholders.[21]

During the U.N.'s historic Fourth World Conference on Women — held in Beijing in 1995 — 189 governments adopted, among other things, a goal of 30 percent female representation in national legislatures around the world.[22] But today, only 20 countries have reached that goal, and quotas are often attacked as limiting voters' choices and giving women unfair advantages.[23]

Along with increasing female political participation, the 5,000 government representatives at the Beijing conference — one of the largest gatherings in U.N. history — called for improved health care for women, an end to violence against women, equal access to education for girls, promotion of economic independence and other steps to improve the condition of women around the world.[24]

"Let Beijing be the platform from which our global crusade will be carried forward," Gertrude Mongella, U.N. secretary general for the conference, said during closing ceremonies. "The world will hold us accountable for the implementation of the good intentions and decisions arrived at in Beijing."[25]

But more than 10 years later, much of the Beijing Platform still has not been achieved. And many question whether women are any better off today than they were in 1995.

"The picture's mixed," says June Zeitlin, executive director of the Women's Environment & Development

and Uganda peace negotiations. Their priorities were quite different. Men were concerned about power- and wealth-sharing. Those are valid, but you get an entirely different dimension from women. Women talked about security on the ground, security of families, security of communities."

In war-torn countries, women have been found to draw on their experiences as mothers to find nonviolent and flexible ways to solve conflict.[7] During peace negotiations in Northern Ireland, for example, male negotiators repeatedly walked out of sessions, leaving a small number of women at the table. The women, left to their own, found areas of common ground and were able to keep discussions moving forward.[8]

"The most important thing is introducing the definition of security from a woman's perspective," said Orzala Ashraf, founder of Kabul-based Humanitarian Assistance for the Women and Children of Afghanistan. "It is not a man in a uniform standing next to a tank armed with a gun. Women have a broader term — human security — the ability to go to school, receive health care, work and have access to justice. Only by improving these areas can threats from insurgents, Taliban, drug lords and warlords be countered."[9]

The first all-female United Nations peacekeeping force practices martial arts in New Delhi as it prepares to be deployed to Liberia in 2006.

[1] "Liberia: UN envoy welcomes new batch of female Indian police officers," U.N. News Centre, Feb. 8, 2008, www.un.org/apps/news/story.asp?News ID=25557&Cr=liberia&Cr1=.

[2] "Japan: Comfort Women," European Speaking Tour press release, Amnesty International, Oct. 31, 2007.

[3] "Film Documents Rape of Women in Congo," "All Things Considered," National Public Radio, April 8, 2008, www.npr.org/templates/story/story.php? storyId=89476111.

[4] "Ninth Annual Colloquium and Policy Forum," Hunt Alternatives Fund, Jan. 22, 2008, www.huntalternatives.org/pages/7650_ninth _annual_colloquium_and_policy_forum.cfm. Also see Elizabeth Eldridge, "Women cite utility in peace efforts," *The Washington Times*, Jan. 25, 2008, p. A1.

[5] "Inclusive Security, Sustainable Peace: A Toolkit for Advocacy and Action," International Alert and Women Waging Peace, 2004, p. 15, www.huntalternatives.org/download/35_introduction.pdf.

[6] *Ibid.*, p. 17.

[7] Jolynn Shoemaker and Camille Pampell Conaway, "Conflict Prevention and Transformation: Women's Vital Contributions," Inclusive Security: Women Waging Peace and the United Nations Foundation, Feb. 23, 2005, p. 7.

[8] The Initiative for Inclusive Security, www.huntalternatives.org /pages/460_the_vital_role_of_women_in_peace_building.cfm.

[9] Eldridge, *op. cit.*

Organization (WEDO). "In terms of violence against women, there is far more recognition of what is going on today. There has been some progress with education and girls. But the impact of globalization has exacerbated differences between men and women. The poor have gotten poorer — and they are mostly women."

Liberalized international trade has been a two-edged sword in other ways as well. Corporations have been able to expand their global reach, opening new businesses and factories in developing countries and offering women unprecedented employment and economic opportunities. But the jobs often pay low wages and involve work in dangerous conditions because poor countries anxious to attract foreign investors often are willing to ignore safety and labor protections.[26] And increasingly porous

international borders have led to growing numbers of women and girls being forced or sold into prostitution or sexual slavery abroad, often under the pretense that they will be given legitimate jobs overseas.[27]

Numerous international agreements in recent years have pledged to provide women with the same opportunities and protections as men, including the U.N.'s Millennium Development Goals (MDGs) and the Convention on the Elimination of All Forms of Discrimination Against Women (CEDAW). But the MDGs' deadlines for improving the conditions for women have either been missed already or are on track to fail in the coming years.[28] And more than 70 of the 185 countries that ratified CEDAW have filed "reservations," meaning they exempt themselves from certain parts.[29] In fact,

Few Women Head World Governments

Fourteen women currently serve as elected heads of state or government including five who serve as both. Mary McAleese, elected president of Ireland in 1997, is the world's longest-serving head of state. Helen Clark of New Zealand has served as prime minister since 1999, making her the longest-serving female head of government. The world's first elected female head of state was Sirimavo Bandaranaike of Sri Lanka, in 1960.

Current Female Elected Heads of State and Government

Heads of both state and government:

 Gloria Macapagal-Arroyo — President, the Philippines, since 2001; former secretary of Defense (2002) and secretary of Foreign Affairs (2003 and 2006-2007).

 Ellen Johnson-Sirleaf — President, Liberia, since 2006; held finance positions with the government and World Bank.

 Michelle Bachelet Jeria — President, Chile, since 2006; former minister of Health (2000-2002) and minister of Defense (2002-2004).

Cristina E. Fernández — President, Argentina, since 2007; succeeded her husband, Nestor de Kirchner, as president; former president, Senate Committee on Constitutional Affairs.

 Rosa Zafferani — Captain Regent, San Marino, since April 2008; secretary of State of Public Education, University and Cultural Institutions (2004 to 2008); served as captain regent in 1999; San Marino elects two captains regent every six months, who serve as co-heads of both state and government.

Heads of Government:

 **Helen Clark** — Prime Minister, New Zealand, since 1999; held government posts in foreign affairs, defense, housing and labor.

Luísa Días Diogo — Prime Minister, Mozambique, since 2004; held several finance posts in Mozambique and the World Bank.

Angela Merkel — Chancellor, Germany, since 2005; parliamentary leader of Christian Democratic Union Party (2002-2005).

 Yuliya Tymoshenko — Prime Minister, Ukraine, since 2007; chief of government (2005) and designate prime minister (2006).

Zinaida Grecianîi — Prime Minister, Moldova, since March 2008; vice prime minister (2005-2008).

Heads of State:

 Mary McAleese — President, Ireland, since 1997; former director of a television station and Northern Ireland Electricity.

Tarja Halonen — President, Finland, since 2000; former minister of foreign affairs (1995-2000).

Pratibha Patil — President, India, since 2007; former governor of Rajasthan state (2004-2007).

Borjana Kristo — President, Bosnia and Herzegovina, since 2007; minister of Justice of Bosniak-Croat Federation, an entity in Bosnia and Herzegovina (2003-2007).

Source: www.guide2womenleaders.com

there are more reservations against CEDAW than against any other international human-rights treaty in history. [30] The United States remains the only developed country in the world not to have ratified it. [31]

"There has certainly been progress in terms of the rhetoric. But there are still challenges in the disparities in education, disparities in income, disparities in health," says Carla Koppell, director of the Cambridge, Mass.-based Initiative for Inclusive Security, which advocates for greater numbers of women in peace negotiations.

"But women are not just victims," she continues. "They have a very unique and important role to play in solving the problems of the developing world. We need to charge policy makers to match the rhetoric and make it a reality. There is a really wonderful opportunity to use the momentum that does exist. I really think we can."

Amidst the successes and failures surrounding women's issues, here are some of the questions analysts are beginning to ask:

Has globalization been good for women?

Over the last 20 years, trade liberalization has led to a massive increase of goods being produced and exported from developing countries, creating millions of manufacturing jobs and bringing many women into the paid workforce for the first time.

"Women employed in export-oriented manufacturing typically earn more than they would have in traditional sectors," according to a World Bank report. "Further, cash income earned by women may improve their status and bargaining power in the family."[32] The report cited a study of 50 families in Mexico that found "a significant proportion of the women reported an improvement in their 'quality of life,' due mainly to their income from working outside their homes, including in (export-oriented) factory jobs."

But because women in developing nations are generally less educated than men and have little bargaining power, most of these jobs are temporary or part-time, offering no health-care benefits, overtime or sick leave.

Women comprise 85 percent of the factory jobs in the garment industry in Bangladesh and 90 percent in Cambodia. In the cut flower industry, women hold 65 percent of the jobs in Colombia and 87 percent in Zimbabwe. In the fruit industry, women constitute 69 percent of temporary and seasonal workers in South Africa and 52 percent in Chile.[33]

Frequently, women in these jobs have no formal contract with their employers, making them even more vulnerable to poor safety conditions and abuse. One study found that only 46 percent of women garment workers in Bangladesh had an official letter of employment.[34]

"Women are a workforce vital to the global economy, but the jobs women are in often aren't covered by labor protections," says Thalia Kidder, a policy adviser on gender and sustainable livelihoods with U.K.-based Oxfam, a confederation of 12 international aid organizations. Women lack protection because they mostly work as domestics, in home-based businesses and as part-time workers. "In the global economy, many companies look to hire the most powerless people because they cannot demand high wages. There are not a lot of trade treaties that address labor rights."

Women Still Far from Reaching Political Parity

Although they have made strides in the past decade, women hold only a small minority of the world's leadership and legislative posts (right). Nordic parliaments have the highest rates of female representation — 41.4 percent — compared with only 9 percent in Arab countries (below). However, Arab legislatures have nearly tripled their female representation since 1997, and some countries in Africa have dramatically increased theirs as well: Rwanda, at 48.8 percent, now has the world's highest percentage of women in parliament of any country. The U.S. Congress ranks 70th in the world, with 89 women serving in the 535-member body — or 16.6 percent.

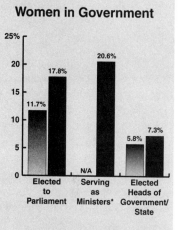

Women in Government

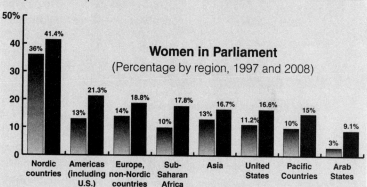

Women in Parliament
(Percentage by region, 1997 and 2008)

* Includes deputy prime ministers, ministers and prime ministers who hold ministerial portfolios.

Sources: Interparliamentarian Union, www.ipu.org/wmn-e/world.htm; *State of the World's Children 2007*, UNICEF, www.unicef.org/sowc07/; "Worldwide Guide to Women in Leadership" database, www.un.org/womenwatch/daw/csw/41sess.htm.

In addition to recommending that countries embrace free trade, Western institutions like the International Monetary Fund and the World Bank during the 1990s recommended that developing countries adopt so-called structural adjustment economic reforms in order to qualify for certain loans and financial support. Besides

National Geographic/Getty Images/Melvyn Goldstein

AP Photo/Rajesh Kumar Singh

Women's Work: From Hauling and Churning . . .

Women's work is often back-breaking and monotonous, such as hauling firewood in the western Indian state of Maharashtra (top) and churning yogurt into butter beside Lake Motsobunnyi in Tibet (bottom). Women labor two-thirds of the total hours worked around the globe each year but earn only 10 percent of the income.

opening borders to free trade, the neo-liberal economic regime known as the Washington Consensus advocated privatizing state-owned businesses, balancing budgets and attracting foreign investment.

But according to some studies, those reforms ended up adversely affecting women. For instance, companies in Ecuador were encouraged to make jobs more "flexible" by replacing long-term contracts with temporary, seasonal and hourly positions — while restricting collective

bargaining rights.[35] And countries streamlined and privatized government programs such as health care and education, services women depend on most.

Globalization also has led to a shift toward cash crops grown for export, which hurts women farmers, who produce 60 to 80 percent of the food for household consumption in developing countries.[36] Small women farmers are being pushed off their land so crops for exports can be grown, limiting their abilities to produce food for themselves and their families.

While economic globalization has yet to create the economic support needed to help women out of poverty, women's advocates say females have benefited from the broadening of communications between countries prompted by globalization. "It has certainly improved access to communications and helped human-rights campaigns," says Zeitlin of WEDO. "Less can be done in secret. If there is a woman who is condemned to be stoned to death somewhere, you can almost immediately mobilize a global campaign against it."

Homa Hoodfar, a professor of social anthropology at Concordia University in Montreal, Canada, and a founder of the group Women Living Under Muslim Laws, says women in some of the world's most remote towns and villages regularly e-mail her organization. "Globalization has made the world much smaller," she says. "Women are getting information on TV and the Internet. The fact that domestic violence has become a global issue [shows globalization] provides resources for those objecting locally."

But open borders also have enabled the trafficking of millions of women around the world. An estimated 800,000 people are trafficked across international borders each year — 80 percent of them women and girls — and most are forced into the commercial sex trade. Millions more are trafficked within their own countries.[37] Globalization has sparked a massive migration of women in search of better jobs and lives. About 90 million women — half of the world's migrants and more than ever in history — reside outside their home countries. These migrant women — often unable to speak the local language and without any family connections — are especially susceptible to traffickers who lure them with promises of jobs abroad.[38]

And those who do not get trapped in the sex trade often end up in low-paying or abusive jobs in foreign factories or as domestic maids working under slave-like conditions.

But some experts say the real problem is not migration and globalization but the lack of labor protection. "Nothing is black and white," says Marianne Mollmann, advocacy director for the Women's Rights Division of Human Rights Watch. "Globalization has created different employment opportunities for women. Migration flows have made women vulnerable. But it's a knee-jerk reaction to say that women shouldn't migrate. You can't prevent migration. So where do we need to go?" She suggests including these workers in general labor-law protections that cover all workers.

Mollmann said countries can and should hammer out agreements providing labor and wage protections for domestic workers migrating across borders. With such protections, she said, women could benefit from the jobs and incomes promised by increased migration and globalization.

Should governments impose electoral quotas for women?

In 2003, as Rwanda struggled to rebuild itself after the genocide that killed at least 800,000 Hutus and Tutsis, the country adopted an historic new constitution that, among other things, required that women hold at least 30 percent of posts "in all decision-making organs."[39]

Today — ironically, just across Lake Kivu from the horrors occurring in Eastern Congo — Rwanda's lower house of parliament now leads the world in female representation, with 48.8 percent of the seats held by women.[40]

Before the civil war, Rwandan women never held more than 18 percent of parliament. But after the genocide, the country's population was 70 percent female. Women immediately stepped in to fill the vacuum, becoming the heads of households, community leaders and business owners. Their increased presence in leadership positions eventually led to the new constitutional quotas.[41]

"We see so many post-conflict countries going from military regimes to democracy that are starting from scratch with new constitutions," says Drude Dahlerup, a

. . . to Gathering and Herding

While many women have gotten factory jobs thanks to globalization of trade, women still comprise 70 percent of the planet's inhabitants living on less than a dollar a day. Women perform a variety of tasks around the world, ranging from gathering flax in Belarus (top) to shepherding goats in central Argentina (bottom).

professor of political science at Sweden's Stockholm University who studies the use of gender quotas. "Today, starting from scratch means including women. It's seen as a sign of modernization and democratization."

Both Iraq and Afghanistan included electoral quotas for women in their new constitutions, and the number of women in political office in sub-Saharan Africa has increased faster than in any other region of the world, primarily through the use of quotas.[42]

But many point out that simply increasing the numbers of women in elected office will not necessarily expand women's rights. "It depends on which women and which positions they represent," says Wendy Harcourt, chair of Women in Development Europe (WIDE), a feminist network in Europe, and editor of *Development*, the journal of the Society for International Development, a global network of individuals and institutions working on development issues. "It's positive, but I don't see yet what it means [in terms of addressing] broader gender issues."

While Afghanistan has mandated that women hold at least 27 percent of the government's lower house seats and at least 17 percent of the upper house, their increased representation appears to have done little to improve women's rights.[43] Earlier this year, a student journalist was condemned to die under Afghanistan's strict Islamic sharia law after he distributed articles from the Internet on women's rights.[44] And nongovernmental groups in Afghanistan report that Afghan women and girls have begun killing themselves in record numbers, burning themselves alive in order to escape widespread domestic abuse or forced marriages.[45]

Having gender quotas alone doesn't necessarily ensure that women's rights will be broadened, says Hoodfar of Concordia University. It depends on the type of quota a government implements, she argues, pointing out that in Jordan, for example, the government has set aside parliamentary seats for the six women who garner the most votes of any other female candidates in their districts — even if they do not win more votes than male candidates.[46] Many small, conservative tribes that cannot garner enough votes for a male in a countrywide victory are now nominating their sisters and wives in the hope that the lower number of votes needed to elect a woman will get them one of the reserved seats. As a result, many of the women moving into the reserved seats are extremely conservative and actively oppose providing women greater rights and freedoms.

And another kind of quota has been used against women in her home country of Iran, Hoodfar points out. Currently, 64 percent of university students in Iran are women. But the government recently mandated that at least 40 percent of university enrollees be male,

forcing many female students out of school, Hoodfar said.

"Before, women didn't want to use quotas for politics because of concern the government may try to use it against women," she says. "But women are beginning to look into it and talk about maybe developing a good system."

Quotas can be enacted by constitutional requirements, such as those enacted in Rwanda, by statute or voluntarily by political parties. Quotas also can vary in their requirements: They can mandate the number of women each party must nominate, how many women must appear on the ballot (and the order in which they appear, so women are not relegated to the bottom of the list), or the number of women who must hold government office. About 40 countries now use gender quotas in national parliamentary elections, while another 50 have major political parties that voluntarily use quotas to determine candidates.

Aside from questions about the effectiveness of quotas, others worry about the fairness of establishing quotas based on gender. "That's something feminists have traditionally opposed," says Harcourt.

"It's true, but it's also not fair the way it is now," says former Ambassador Hunt. "We are where we are today through all kinds of social structures that are not fair. Quotas are the lesser of two evils."

Stockholm University's Dahlerup says quotas are not "discrimination against men but compensation for discrimination against women." Yet quotas are not a panacea for women in politics, she contends. "It's a mistake to think this is a kind of tool that will solve all problems. It doesn't solve problems about financing campaigns, caring for families while being in politics or removing patriarchal attitudes. It would be nice if it wasn't necessary, and hopefully sometime in the future it won't be."

Until that time, however, quotas are a "necessary evil," she says.

Do international treaties improve women's rights?

In recent decades, a variety of international agreements have been signed by countries pledging to improve women's lives, from the 1979 Convention for the Elimination of All Forms of Discrimination Against Women to the Beijing Platform of 1995 to the Millennium Development Goals (MDGs) adopted in 2000. The agreements aimed to provide women with greater access to health, political representation, economic stability and social status. They also focused attention on some of the biggest obstacles facing women.

But despite the fanfare surrounding the launch of those agreements, many experts on women's issues say on-the-ground action has yet to match the rhetoric. "The report is mixed," says Haleh Afshar, a professor of politics and women's studies at the University of York in the United Kingdom and a nonpartisan, appointed member of the House of Lords, known as a crossbench peer. "The biggest problem with Beijing is all these things were stated, but none were funded. Unfortunately, I don't see any money. You don't get the pay, you don't get the job done."

The Beijing Platform for Action, among other things, called on governments to "adjust budgets to ensure equality of access to public sector expenditures" and even to "reduce, as appropriate, excessive military expenditure" in order to achieve the Platform goals.

But adequate funding has yet to be provided, say women's groups. [47] In a report entitled "Beijing Betrayed," the Women's Environment & Development Organization says female HIV cases outnumber male cases in many parts of the world, gender-related violence remains a pandemic and women still make up the majority of the world's poor — despite pledges in Beijing to reverse these trends.[48]

And funding is not the only obstacle. A 2004 U.N. survey revealed that while many countries have enacted laws in recent years to help protect women from violence and discrimination, long-standing social and cultural traditions block progress. "While constitutions provided for equality between women and men on the one hand, [several countries] recognized and gave precedent to customary law and practice in a number of areas . . . resulting in discrimination against women," the report said. "Several countries noted that statutory, customary and religious law coexist, especially in regard to family, personal status and inheritance and land rights. This perpetuated discrimination against women."[49]

While she worries about the lack of progress on the Beijing Platform, WEDO Executive Director Zeitlin says international agreements are nevertheless critical in raising global awareness on women's issues. "They have a major impact on setting norms and standards," she says. "In many countries, norms and standards are very important in setting goals for women to advocate for. We complain about lack of implementation, but if we didn't have the norms and standards we couldn't complain about a lack of implementation."

Indian women harvest wheat near Bhopal. Women produce half of the food used domestically worldwide and 60 to 80 percent of the household food grown in developing countries.

Like the Beijing Platform, the MDGs have been criticized for not achieving more. While the U.N. says promoting women's rights is essential to achieving the millenium goals — which aim to improve the lives of all the world's populations by 2015 — only two of the eight specifically address women's issues.[50]

One of the goals calls for countries to "Promote gender equality and empower women." But it sets only one measurable target: "Eliminate gender disparity in primary and secondary education, preferably by 2005, and in all levels of education" by 2015.[51] Some 62 countries failed to reach the 2005 deadline, and many are likely to miss the 2015 deadline as well.[52]

Another MDG calls for a 75 percent reduction in maternal mortality compared to 1990 levels. But according to the human-rights group ActionAid, this goal is the "most off track of all the MDGs." Rates are declining at less than 1 percent a year, and in some countries — such as Sierra Leone, Pakistan and Guatemala — maternal mortality has increased since 1990. If that trend continues, no region in the developing world is expected to reach the goal by 2015.[53]

Activist Peggy Antrobus of Development Alternatives with Women for a New Era (DAWN) — a network of feminists from the Southern Hemisphere, based currently in Calabar, Cross River State, Nigeria — has lambasted the MDGs, quipping that the acronym stands for the "Most Distracting Gimmick."[54] Many feminists

CHRONOLOGY

1700s-1800s *Age of Enlightenment and Industrial Revolution lead to greater freedoms for women.*

1792 Mary Wollstonecraft publishes *A Vindication of the Rights of Women*, later hailed as "the feminist declaration of independence."

1893 New Zealand becomes first nation to grant women full suffrage.

1920 Tennessee is the 36th state to ratify the 19th Amendment, giving American women the right to vote.

1940s-1980s *International conventions endorse equal rights for women. Global conferences highlight need to improve women's rights.*

1946 U.N. creates Commission on the Status of Women.

1951 U.N. International Labor Organization adopts convention promoting equal pay for equal work, which has been ratified by 164 countries; the United States is not among them.

1952 U.N. adopts convention calling for full women's suffrage.

1960 Sri Lanka elects the world's first female prime minister.

1974 Maria Estela Martínez de Perón of Argentina becomes the world's first woman president, replacing her ailing husband.

1975 U.N. holds first World Conference on Women, in Mexico City, followed by similar conferences every five years. U.N. launches the Decade for Women.

1979 U.N. adopts Convention on the Elimination of All Forms of Discrimination against Women (CEDAW), dubbed the "international bill of rights for women."

1981 CEDAW is ratified — faster than any other human-rights convention.

1990s *Women's rights win historic legal recognition.*

1993 U.N. World Conference on Human Rights in Vienna, Austria, calls for ending all violence, sexual harassment and trafficking of women.

1995 Fourth World Conference on Women in Beijing draws 30,000 people, making it the largest in U.N. history. Beijing Platform outlining steps to grant women equal rights is signed by 189 governments.

1996 International Criminal Tribunal convicts eight Bosnian Serb police and military officers for rape during the Bosnian conflict — the first time sexual assault is prosecuted as a war crime.

1998 International Criminal Tribunal for Rwanda recognizes rape and other forms of sexual violence as genocide.

2000s *Women make political gains, but sexual violence against women increases.*

2000 U.N. calls on governments to include women in peace negotiations.

2006 Ellen Johnson Sirleaf of Liberia, Michelle Bachelet of Chile and Portia Simpson Miller of Jamaica become their countries' first elected female heads of state. . . . Women in Kuwait are allowed to run for parliament, winning two seats.

2007 A woman in Saudi Arabia who was sentenced to 200 lashes after being gang-raped by seven men is pardoned by King Abdullah. Her rapists received sentences ranging from 10 months to five years in prison, and 80 to 1,000 lashes. . . . After failing to recognize any gender-based crimes in its first case involving the Democratic Republic of the Congo, the International Criminal Court hands down charges of "sexual slavery" in its second case involving war crimes in Congo. More than 250,000 women are estimated to have been raped and sexually abused during the country's war.

2008 Turkey lifts 80-year-old ban on women's head-scarves in public universities, signaling a drift toward religious fundamentalism. . . . Former housing minister Carme Chacón — 37 and pregnant — is named defense minister of Spain, bringing to nine the number of female cabinet ministers in the Socialist government. . . . Sen. Hillary Rodham Clinton becomes the first U.S. woman to be in a tight race for a major party's presidential nomination.

argue that the goals are too broad to have any real impact and that the MDGs should have given more attention to women's issues.

But other women say international agreements — and the public debate surrounding them — are vital in promoting gender equality. "It's easy to get disheartened, but Beijing is still the blueprint of where we need to be," says Mollmann of Human Rights Watch. "They are part of a political process, the creation of an international culture. If systematically everyone says [discrimination against women] is a bad thing, states don't want to be hauled out as systematic violators."

In particular, Mollmann said, CEDAW has made real progress in overcoming discrimination against women. Unlike the Beijing Platform and the MDGs, CEDAW legally obliges countries to comply. Each of the 185 ratifying countries must submit regular reports to the U.N. outlining their progress under the convention. Several countries — including Brazil, Uganda, South Africa and Australia — also have incorporated CEDAW provisions into their constitutions and legal systems.[55]

Still, dozens of ratifying countries have filed official "reservations" against the convention, including Bahrain, Egypt, Kuwait, Morocco and the United Arab Emirates, all of whom say they will comply only within the bounds of Islamic sharia law.[56] And the United States has refused to ratify CEDAW, with or without reservations, largely because of conservatives who say it would, among other things, promote abortion and require the government to pay for such things as child care and maternity leave.

BACKGROUND

'Structural Defects'

Numerous prehistoric relics suggest that at one time matriarchal societies existed on Earth in which women were in the upper echelons of power. Because early societies did not understand the connection between sexual relations and conception, they believed women were solely responsible for reproduction — which led to the worship of female goddesses.[57]

In more modern times, however, women have generally faced prejudice and discrimination at the hands of a patriarchal society. In about the eighth century B.C.

creation stories emerged describing the fall of man due to the weakness of women. The Greeks recounted the story of Pandora who, through her opening of a sealed jar, unleashed death and pain on all of mankind. Meanwhile, similar tales in Judea eventually were recounted in Genesis, with Eve as the culprit.[58]

In ancient Greece, women were treated as children and denied basic rights. They could not leave their houses un-chaperoned, were prohibited from being educated or buying or selling land. A father could sell his unmarried daughter into slavery if she lost her virginity before marriage. If a woman was raped, she was outcast and forbidden from participating in public ceremonies or wearing jewelry.[59]

The status of women in early Rome was not much better, although over time women began to assert their voices and slowly gained greater freedoms. Eventually, they were able to own property and divorce their husbands. But early Christian leaders later denounced the legal and social freedom enjoyed by Roman women as a sign of moral decay. In the view of the early church, women were dependent on and subordinate to men.

In the 13th century, the Catholic priest and theologian St. Thomas Aquinas helped set the tone for the subjugation of women in Western society. He said women were created solely to be "man's helpmate" and advocated that men should make use of "a necessary object, woman, who is needed to preserve the species or to provide food and drink."[60]

From the 14th to 17th centuries, misogyny and oppression of women took a step further. As European societies struggled against the Black Plague, the 100 Years War and turmoil between Catholics and Reformers, religious leaders began to blame tragedies, illnesses and other problems on witches. As witch hysteria spread across Europe — instituted by both the religious and non-religious — an estimated 30,000 to 60,000 people were executed for allegedly practicing witchcraft. About 80 percent were females, some as young as 8 years old.[61]

"All wickedness is but little to the wickedness of a woman," Catholic inquisitors wrote in the 1480s. "What else is woman but a foe to friendship, an unescapable punishment, a necessary evil, a natural temptation, a desirable

Women Suffer Most in Natural Disasters

Climate change will make matters worse.

In natural disasters, women suffer death, disease and hunger at higher rates then men. During the devastating 2004 tsunami in Asia, 70 to 80 percent of the dead were women [1] During cyclone-triggered flooding in Bangladesh that killed 140,000 people in 1991, nearly five times more women between the ages of 20 and 44 died than men.[2]

Gender discrimination, cultural biases and lack of awareness of women's needs are part of the problem. For instance, during the 1991 cyclone, Bangladeshi women and their children died in higher numbers because they waited at home for their husbands to return and make evacuation decisions.[3] In addition, flood warnings were conveyed by men to men in public spaces but were rarely communicated to women and children at home [4]

And during the tsunami, many Indonesian women died because they stayed behind to look for children and other family members. Women clinging to children in floodwaters also tired more quickly and drowned, since most women in the region were never taught to swim or climb trees.[5] In Sri Lanka, many women died because the tsunami hit early on a Sunday morning when they were inside preparing breakfast for their families. Men were generally outside where they had earlier warning of the oncoming floods so they were better able to escape.[6]

Experts now predict global climate change — which is expected to increase the number of natural disasters around the world — will put women in far greater danger than men because natural disasters generally have a disproportionate impact on the world's poor. Since women comprise 70 percent of those living on less than $1 a day, they will be hardest hit by climate changes, according to the Intergovernmental Panel on Climate Change.[7]

"Climate change is not gender-neutral," said Gro Harlem Brundtland, former prime minister of Norway and now special envoy to the U.N. secretary-general on climate change. "[Women are] more dependent for their livelihood on natural resources that are threatened by climate change. . . . With changes in climate, traditional food sources become more unpredictable and scarce. This exposes women to loss of harvests, often their sole sources of food and income."[8]

Women produce 60 to 80 percent of the food for household consumption in developing countries.[9] As drought, flooding and desertification increase, experts say women and their families will be pushed further into poverty and famine.

Women also suffer more hardship in the aftermath of natural disasters, and their needs are often ignored during relief efforts.

In many Third World countries, for instance, women have no property rights, so when a husband dies during a natural disaster his family frequently confiscates the land from his widow, leaving her homeless and destitute.[10] And because men usually dominate emergency relief and response agencies, women's specific needs, such as contraceptives and sanitary napkins, are often overlooked. After floods in Bangladesh in 1998, adolescent girls reported high rates of rashes and urinary tract infections because they had no clean water, could not wash their menstrual rags properly in private and had no place to hang them to dry.[11]

"In terms of reconstruction, people are not talking about women's needs versus men's needs," says June Zeitlin, executive

calamity. . . . Women are . . . instruments of Satan, . . . a structural defect rooted in the original creation."[62]

Push for Protections

The Age of Enlightenment and the Industrial Revolution in the 18th and 19th centuries opened up job opportunities for women, released them from domestic confines and provided them with new social freedoms.

In 1792 Mary Wollstonecraft published *A Vindication of the Rights of Women*, which has been hailed as "the feminist declaration of independence." Although the book had been heavily influenced by the French Revolution's notions of equality and universal brotherhood, French revolutionary leaders, ironically, were not sympathetic to feminist causes. [63] In 1789 they had refused to accept a Declaration of the Rights of Women when it was presented at the National Assembly. And Jean Jacques Rousseau, one of the philosophical founders of the revolution, had written in 1762:

director of the Women's Environment and Development Organization, a New York City-based international organization that works for women's equality in global policy. "There is a lack of attention to health care after disasters, issues about bearing children, contraception, rape and vulnerability, menstrual needs — things a male programmer is not thinking about. There is broad recognition that disasters have a disproportionate impact on women. But it stops there. They see women as victims, but they don't see women as agents of change."

Women must be brought into discussions on climate change and emergency relief, say Zeitlin and others. Interestingly, she points out, while women are disproportionately affected by environmental changes, they do more than men to protect the environment. Studies show women emit less climate-changing carbon dioxide than men because they recycle more, use resources more efficiently and drive less than men.[12]

"Women's involvement in climate-change decision-making is a human right," said Gerd Johnson-Latham, deputy director of the Swedish Ministry for Foreign Affairs. "If we get more women in decision-making positions, we will have different priorities, and less risk of climate change."[13]

AP Photo

The smell of death hangs over Banda Aceh, Indonesia, which was virtually destroyed by a tsunami on Dec. 28, 2004. 70 to 80 percent of the victims were women.

[1] "Tsunami death toll," CNN, Feb. 22, 2005. Also see "Report of High-level Roundtable: How a Changing Climate Impacts Women," Council of Women World Leaders, Women's Environment and Development Organization and Heinrich Boll Foundation, Sept. 21, 2007, p. 21, www.wedo.org/files/Round table%20Final%20Report%206%20Nov .pdf.

[2] *Ibid.*

[3] "Cyclone Jelawat bears down on Japan's Okinawa island," CNN.com, Aug. 7, 2000, http://archives.cnn.com/ 2000/ASIANOW/east/08/07/ asia .weather/index.html.

[4] "Gender and Health in Disasters," World Health Organization, July 2002, www.who.int/gender/other_health/en /genderdisasters.pdf.

[5] "The tsunami's impact on women," Oxfam briefing note, March 5, 2005, p. 2, www.oxfam.org/en/files /bn050326_tsunami_women/ download.

[6] "Report of High-level Roundtable," *op. cit.*, p. 5.

[7] "Gender Equality" fact sheet, Oxfam, www.oxfam.org.uk/resources / issues/gender/introduction.html. Also see *ibid.*

[8] *Ibid.*, p. 4.

[9] "Five years down the road from Beijing: Assessing progress," *News and Highlights*, Food and Agriculture Organization, June 2, 2000, www.fao. org/News/2000/000602-e.htm.

[10] "Gender and Health in Disasters," *op. cit.*

[11] *Ibid.*

[12] "Women and the Environment," U.N. Environment Program, 2004, p. 17, www.unep.org/Documents.Multilingual/Default.asp?Document ID=468&ArticleID=4488&l=en. Also see "Report of High-level Roundtable," *op. cit.*, p. 7.

[13] *Ibid.*

"The whole education of women ought to be relative to men. To please them, to be useful to them, to make themselves loved and honored by them, to educate them when young, to care for them when grown, to counsel them, to make life sweet and agreeable to them — these are the duties of women at all times, and what should be taught them from their infancy."[64]

As more and more women began taking jobs outside the home during the 19th century, governments began to pass laws to "protect" them in the workforce and expand their legal rights. The British Mines Act of 1842, for instance, prohibited women from working underground. [65] In 1867, John Stuart Mill, a supporter of women's rights and author of the book *Subjection of Women*, introduced language in the British House of Commons calling for women to be granted the right to vote. It failed.[66]

But by that time governments around the globe had begun enacting laws giving women rights they had been denied for centuries. As a result of the Married Women's

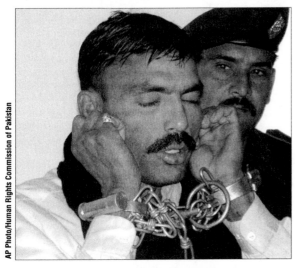

Honor Killings on the Rise

Women in Multan, Pakistan, demonstrate against "honor killings" in 2003 (top). Although Pakistan outlawed such killings years ago, its Human Rights Commission says 1,205 women were killed in the name of family honor in 2007 — a fourfold jump in two years. Nazir Ahmed Sheikh, a Punjabi laborer (bottom), unrepentantly told police in December 2005 how he slit the throats of his four daughters one night as they slept in order to salvage the family's honor. The eldest had married a man of her choice, and Ahmed feared the younger daughters would follow her example.

Property Act of 1870 and a series of other measures, wives in Britain were finally allowed to own property. In 1893, New Zealand became the first nation to grant full

suffrage rights to women, followed over the next two decades by Finland, Norway, Denmark and Iceland. The United States granted women suffrage in 1920.[67]

One of the first international labor conventions, formulated at Berne, Switzerland, in 1906, applied exclusively to women — prohibiting night work for women in industrial occupations. Twelve nations signed on to it. During the second Berne conference in 1913, language was proposed limiting the number of hours women and children could work in industrial jobs, but the outbreak of World War I prevented it from being enacted.[68] In 1924 the U.S. Supreme Court upheld a night-work law for women.[69]

In 1946, public attention to women's issues received a major boost when the United Nations created the Commission on the Status of Women to address urgent problems facing women around the world.[70] During the 1950s, the U.N. adopted several conventions aimed at improving women's lives, including the Convention on the Political Rights of Women, adopted in 1952 to ensure women the right to vote, which has been ratified by 120 countries, and the Convention on the Nationality of Married Women, approved in 1957 to ensure that marriage to an alien does not automatically affect the nationality of the woman.[71] That convention has been ratified by only 73 countries; the United States is not among them.[72]

In 1951 The International Labor Organization (ILO), an agency of the United Nations, adopted the Convention on Equal Remuneration for Men and Women Workers for Work of Equal Value, to promote equal pay for equal work. It has since been ratified by 164 countries, but again, not by the United States.[73] Seven years later, the ILO adopted the Convention on Discrimination in Employment and Occupation to ensure equal opportunity and treatment in employment. It is currently ratified by 166 countries, but not the United States.[74] U.S. opponents to the conventions claim there is no real pay gap between men and women performing the same jobs and that the conventions would impose "comparable worth" requirements, forcing companies to pay equal wages to men and women even if the jobs they performed were different.[75]

In 1965, the Commission on the Status of Women began drafting international standards articulating equal rights for men and women. Two years later, the panel completed the Declaration on the Elimination of Discrimination Against Women, which was adopted by the General Assembly but carried no enforcement power.

The commission later began to discuss language that would hold countries responsible for enforcing the declaration. At the U.N.'s first World Conference on Women in Mexico City in 1975, women from around the world called for creation of such a treaty, and the commission soon began drafting the text.[76]

Women's 'Bill of Rights'

Finally in 1979, after many years of often rancorous debate, the Convention on the Elimination of All Forms of Discrimination Against Women (CEDAW) was adopted by the General Assembly — 130 to none, with 10 abstentions. After the vote, however, several countries said their "yes" votes did not commit the support of their governments. Brazil's U.N. representative told the assembly, "The signatures and ratifications necessary to make this effective will not come easily."[77]

Despite the prediction, it took less than two years for CEDAW to receive the required number of ratifications to enter it into force — faster than any human-rights convention had ever done before.[78]

Often described as an international bill of rights for women, CEDAW defines discrimination against women as "any distinction, exclusion or restriction made on the basis of sex which has the effect or purpose of impairing or nullifying the recognition, enjoyment or exercise by women, irrespective of their marital status, on a basis of equality of men and women, of human rights and fundamental freedoms in the political, economic, social, cultural, civil or any other field."

Ratifying countries are legally bound to end discrimination against women by incorporating sexual equality into their legal systems, abolishing discriminatory laws against women, taking steps to end trafficking of women and ensuring women equal access to political and public life. Countries must also submit reports at least every four years outlining the steps they have taken to comply with the convention.[79]

CEDAW also grants women reproductive choice — one of the main reasons the United States has not ratified it. The convention requires signatories to guarantee women's rights "to decide freely and responsibly on the number and spacing of their children and to have access to the information, education and means to enable them to exercise these rights."[80]

While CEDAW is seen as a significant tool to stop violence against women, it actually does not directly mention violence. To rectify this, the CEDAW committee charged with monitoring countries' compliance in 1992 specified gender-based violence as a form of discrimination prohibited under the convention.[81]

In 1993 the U.N. took further steps to combat violence against women during the World Conference on Human Rights in Vienna, Austria. The conference called on countries to stop all forms of violence, sexual harassment, exploitation and trafficking of women. It also declared that "violations of the human rights of women in situations of armed conflicts are violations of the fundamental principles of international human rights and humanitarian law."[82]

Shortly afterwards, as fighting broke out in the former Yugoslavia and Rwanda, new legal precedents were set to protect women against violence — and particularly rape — during war. In 1996, the International Criminal Tribunal in the Hague, Netherlands, indicted eight Bosnian Serb police officers in connection with the mass rape of Muslim women during the Bosnian war, marking the first time sexual assault had ever been prosecuted as a war crime.[83]

Two years later, the U.N.'s International Criminal Tribunal for Rwanda convicted a former Rwandan mayor for genocide, crimes against humanity, rape and sexual violence — the first time rape and sexual violence were recognized as acts of genocide.[84]

"Rape is a serious war crime like any other," said Regan Ralph, then executive director of Human Rights Watch's Women's Rights Division, shortly after the conviction. "That's always been true on paper, but now international courts are finally acting on it."[85]

Today, the International Criminal Court has filed charges against several Sudanese officials for rape and other crimes committed in the Darfur region.[86] But others are demanding that the court also prosecute those responsible for the rapes in the Eastern Congo, where women are being targeted as a means of destroying communities in the war-torn country.[87]

Getty Images/Paula Bronstein

Pakistani acid attack survivors Saira Liaqat, right, and Sabra Sultana are among hundreds, and perhaps thousands, of women who are blinded and disfigured after being attacked with acid each year in Pakistan, Bangladesh, India, Cambodia, Malaysia, Uganda and other areas of Africa. Liaqat was attacked at age 18 during an argument over an arranged marriage. Sabra was 15 when she was burned after being married off to an older man who became unsatisfied with the relationship. Only a small percentage of the attacks — often perpetrated by spurned suitors while the women are asleep in their own beds — are prosecuted.

Beijing and Beyond

The U.N. World Conference on Women in Mexico City in 1975 produced a 44-page plan of action calling for a decade of special measures to give women equal status and opportunities in law, education, employment, politics and society.[88] The conference also kicked off the U.N.'s Decade for Women and led to creation of the U.N. Development Fund for Women (UNIFEM).[89]

Five years later, the U.N. held its second World Conference on Women in Copenhagen and then celebrated the end of the Decade for Women with the third World Conference in Nairobi in 1985. More than 10,000 representatives from government agencies and NGOs attended the Nairobi event, believed to be the largest gathering on women's issues at the time.[90]

Upon reviewing the progress made on women's issues during the previous 10 years, the U.N. representatives in Nairobi concluded that advances had been extremely limited due to failing economies in developing countries, particularly those in Africa struggling against drought, famine and crippling debt. The conference developed a set of steps needed to improve the status of women during the final 15 years of the 20th century.[91]

Ten years later, women gathered in Beijing in 1995 for the Fourth World Conference, vowing to turn the rhetoric of the earlier women's conferences into action. Delegates from 189 governments and 2,600 NGOs attended. More than 30,000 women and men gathered at a parallel forum organized by NGOs, also in Beijing.[92]

The so-called Beijing Platform that emerged from the conference addressed 12 critical areas facing women, from poverty to inequality in education to inadequate health care to violence. It brought unprecedented attention to women's issues and is still considered by many as the blueprint for true gender equality.

The Beijing Conference also came at the center of a decade that produced historic political gains for women around the world — gains that have continued, albeit at a slow pace, into the new century. The 1990s saw more women entering top political positions than ever before. A record 10 countries elected or appointed women as presidents between 1990 and 2000, including Haiti, Nicaragua, Switzerland and Latvia. Another 17 countries chose women prime ministers.[93]

In 2006 Ellen Johnson Sirleaf of Liberia became Africa's first elected woman president.[94] That same year, Chile elected its first female president, Michelle Bachelet, and Jamaica elected Portia Simpson Miller as its first female prime minister.[95] Also that year, women ran for election in Kuwait for the first time. In Bahrain, a woman was elected to the lower house of parliament for the first time.[96] And in 2007, Fernández de Kirchner became the first woman to be elected president of Argentina.

Earlier, a World Bank report had found that government corruption declines as more women are elected into office. The report also cited numerous studies that found women are more likely to exhibit "helping" behavior, vote based on social issues, score higher on "integrity tests," take stronger stances on ethical behavior and behave more generously when faced with economic decisions.[97]

"Increasing the presence of women in government may be valued for its own sake, for reasons of gender equality," the report concluded. "However, our results suggest that there may be extremely important spinoffs stemming from increasing female representation: If women are less likely than men to behave opportunistically, then bringing more women into government may have significant benefits for society in general."[98]

CURRENT SITUATION

Rise of Fundamentalism

Despite landmark political gains by women since the late 1990s, violence and repression of women continue to be daily occurrences — often linked to the global growth of religious fundamentalism.

In 2007, a 21-year-old woman in Saudi Arabia was sentenced to 200 lashes and ordered jailed for six months after being raped 14 times by a gang of seven men. The Saudi court sentenced the woman — who was 19 at the time of the attack — because she was alone in a car with her former boyfriend when the attack occurred. Under Saudi Arabia's strict Islamic law, it is a crime for a woman to meet in private with a man who is not her husband or relative.[99]

After public outcry from around the world, King Abdullah pardoned the woman in December. A government spokesperson, however, said the king fully supported the verdict but issued the pardon in the "interests of the people."[100]

Another Saudi woman still faces beheading after she was condemned to death for "witchcraft." Among her accusers is a man who claimed she rendered him impotent with her sorcery. Despite international protest, the king has yet to say if he will pardon her.[101]

In Iraq, the rise of religious fundamentalism since the U.S. invasion has led to a jump in the number of women being killed or beaten in so-called honor crimes. Honor killings typically occur when a woman is suspected of unsanctioned sexual behavior — which can range from flirting to "allowing" herself to be raped. Her relatives believe they must murder her to end the family's shame. In the Kurdish region of Iraq, the stoning death of 17-year-old Aswad is not an anomaly. A U.N. mission in October 2007 found that 255 women had been killed in Iraqi Kurdistan in the first six months of 2007 alone — most thought to have been murdered by their communities or families for allegedly committing adultery or entering into a relationship not sanctioned by their families.[102]

The rise of fundamentalism is also sparking a growing debate on the issue of women wearing head scarves, both in Iraq and across the Muslim world. Last August Turkey elected a conservative Muslim president whose wife wears a head scarf, signaling the emergence of a new ruling elite that is more willing to publicly display religious beliefs.[103] Then in February, Turkey's parliament voted to ease an 80-year ban on women wearing head scarves in universities, although a ban on head scarves in other public buildings remains in effect.

"This decision will bring further pressure on women," Nesrin Baytok, a member of parliament, said during debate over the ban. "It will ultimately bring us Hezbollah terror, al Qaeda terror and fundamentalism."[104]

But others said lifting the ban was actually a victory for women. Fatma Benli, a Turkish women's-rights activist and lawyer, said the ban on head scarves in public buildings has forced her to send law partners to argue her cases because she is prohibited from entering court wearing her head scarf. It also discourages religiously conservative women from becoming doctors, lawyers or teachers, she says.[105]

Many women activists are quick to say that it is unfair to condemn Islam for the growing abuse against women. "The problem women have with religion is not the religion but the ways men have interpreted it," says Afshar of the University of York. "What is highly negative is sharia law, which is made by men. Because it's human-made, women can unmake it. The battle now is fighting against unjust laws such as stoning."

She says abuses such as forced marriages and honor killings — usually linked in the Western media to Islamic law — actually go directly against the teachings of the *Koran*. And while the United Nations estimates that some 5,000 women and girls are victims of honor killings each year, millions more are abused and killed in violence unrelated to Islam. Between 10 and 50 percent of all women around the world have been physically abused by an intimate partner in their lifetime, studies show.[106]

"What about the rate of spousal or partner killings in the U.K. or the U.S. that are not called 'honor killings'?" asks Concordia University's Hoodfar. "Then it's only occasional 'crazy people' [committing violence]. But when it's present in Pakistan, Iran or Senegal, these are uncivilized people doing 'honor killings.' "

And Islamic fundamentalism is not the only brand of fundamentalism on the rise. Christian fundamentalism is also growing rapidly. A 2006 Pew Forum on Religion and Public Life poll found that nearly one-third of all Americans feel the Bible should be the basis of law across the United States.[107] Many women's-rights activists say Christian fundamentalism threatens women's rights, particularly with regard to reproductive issues. They also

Female farmworkers in Nova Lima, Brazil, protest against the impact of big corporations on the poor in March 2006, reflecting the increasing political activism of women around the globe.

condemn the Vatican's opposition to the use of condoms, pointing out that it prevents women from protecting themselves against HIV.

"If you look at all your religions, none will say it's a good thing to beat up or kill someone. They are all based on human dignity," says Mollmann of Human Rights Watch. "[Bad things] are carried out in the name of religion, but the actual belief system is not killing and maiming women."

In response to the growing number of honor-based killings, attacks and forced marriages in the U.K., Britain's Association of Chief Police Officers has created an honor-based violence unit, and the U.K.'s Home Office is drafting an action plan to improve the response of police and other agencies to such violence. Legislation going into effect later this year will also give U.K. courts greater guidance on dealing with forced marriages.[108]

Evolving Gender Policies

This past February, the U.N. Convention on the Elimination of All Forms of Discrimination Against Women issued a report criticizing Saudi Arabia for its repression of women. Among other things, the report attacked Saudi Arabia's ban on women drivers and its system of male guardianship that denies women equal inheritance, child custody and divorce rights.[109] The criticism came during the panel's regular review of countries that have ratified CEDAW. Each government must submit reports every four years outlining steps taken to comply with the convention.

The United States is one of only eight countries — among them Iran, Sudan and Somalia — that have refused to ratify CEDAW.[110] Last year, 108 members of the U.S. House of Representatives signed on to a resolution calling for the Senate to ratify CEDAW, but it still has not voted on the measure.[111] During a U.N. vote last November on a resolution encouraging governments to meet their obligations under CEDAW, the United States was the lone nay vote against 173 yea votes.[112]

American opponents of CEDAW — largely pro-life Christians and Republicans — say it would enshrine the right to abortion in *Roe v. Wade* and be prohibitively expensive, potentially requiring the U.S. government to provide paid maternity leave and other child-care services to all women.[113] They also oppose requirements that the government modify "social and cultural patterns" to eliminate sexual prejudice and to delete any traces of gender stereotypes in textbooks — such as references to women's lives being primarily in the domestic sector.[114] Many Republicans in Congress also have argued that CEDAW would give too much control over U.S. laws to the United Nations and that it could even require the legalization of prostitution and the abolition of Mother's Day.[115]

The last time the Senate took action on CEDAW was in 2002, when the Senate Foreign Relations Committee, chaired by Democratic Sen. Joseph Biden of Delaware, voted to send the convention to the Senate floor for ratification. The full Senate, however, never took action. A Biden spokesperson says the senator "remains committed" to the treaty and is "looking for an opportune time" to bring it forward again. But Senate ratification requires 67 votes, and there do not appear to be that many votes for approval.

CEDAW proponents say the failure to ratify not only hurts women but also harms the U.S. image abroad. On this issue, "the United States is in the company of Sudan and the Vatican," says Bien-Aimé of Equality Now.

Meanwhile, several countries are enacting laws to comply with CEDAW and improve the status of women. In December, Turkmenistan passed its first national law guaranteeing women equal rights, even though its constitution had addressed women's equality.[116] A royal decree in Saudi Arabia in January ordered an end to a long-time ban on women checking into hotels or renting apartments without male guardians. Hotels can now book rooms to women who show identification, but the hotels must register the women's details with the police.[117] The

Should sex-selective abortions be outlawed?

YES
Nicholas Eberstadt
Henry Wendt Chair in Political Economy,
American Enterprise Institute; Member,
President's Council on Bioethics

Written for *CQ Researcher*, April 2008

The practice of sex-selective abortion to permit parents to destroy unwanted female fetuses has become so widespread in the modern world that it is disfiguring the profile of entire countries — transforming (and indeed deforming) the whole human species.

This abomination is now rampant in China, where the latest census reports six boys for every five girls. But it is also prevalent in the Far East, South Korea, Hong Kong, Taiwan and Vietnam, all of which report biologically impossible "sex ratios at birth" (well above the 103-106 baby boys for every 100 girls ordinarily observed in human populations). In the Caucasus, gruesome imbalances exist now in Armenia, Georgia and Azerbaijan; and in India, the state of Punjab tallies 126 little boys for every 100 girls. Even in the United States, the boy-girl sex ratio at birth for Asian-Americans is now several unnatural percentage points above the national average. So sex-selective abortion is taking place under America's nose.

How can we rid the world of this barbaric form of sexism? Simply outlawing sex-selective abortions will be little more than a symbolic gesture, as South Korea's experience has shown: Its sex ratio at birth continued a steady climb for a full decade after just such a national law was passed. As long as abortion is basically available on demand, any legislation to abolish sex-selective abortion will have no impact.

What about more general restrictions on abortion, then? Poll data consistently demonstrate that most Americans do not favor the post-*Roe* regimen of unconditional abortion. But a return to the pre-*Roe* status quo, where each state made its own abortion laws, would probably have very little effect on sex-selective abortion in our country. After all, the ethnic communities most tempted by it are concentrated in states where abortion rights would likely be strongest, such as California and New York.

In the final analysis, the extirpation of this scourge will require nothing less than a struggle for the conscience of nations. Here again, South Korea may be illustrative: Its gender imbalances began to decline when the public was shocked into facing this stain on their society by a spontaneous, homegrown civil rights movement.

To eradicate sex-selective abortion, we must convince the world that destrtroying female fetuses is horribly wrong. We need something akin to the abolitionist movement: a moral campaign waged globally, with victories declared one conscience at a time.

NO
Marianne Mollmann
Advocacy Director, Women's Rights Division,
Human Rights Watch

Written for *CQ Researcher*, April 2008

Medical technology today allows parents to test early in pregnancy for fetal abnormalities, hereditary illnesses and even the sex of the fetus, raising horrifying questions about eugenics and population control. In some countries, a growing number of women apparently are terminating pregnancies when they learn the fetus is female. The resulting sex imbalance in countries like China and India is not only disturbing but also leads to further injustices, such as the abduction of girls for forced marriages.

One response has been to criminalize sex-selective abortions. While it is tempting to hope that this could safeguard the gender balance of future generations, criminalization of abortion for whatever reason has led in the past only to underground and unsafe practices. Thus, the criminalization of sex-selective abortion would put the full burden of righting a fundamental wrong — the devaluing of women's lives — on women.

Many women who choose to abort a female fetus face violence and exclusion if they don't produce a boy. Some see the financial burden of raising a girl as detrimental to the survival of the rest of their family. These considerations will not be lessened by banning sex-selective abortion. Unless one addresses the motivation for the practice, it will continue — underground.

So what is the motivation for aborting female fetuses? At the most basic level, it is a financial decision. In no country in the world does women's earning power equal men's. In marginalized communities in developing countries, this is directly linked to survival: Boys may provide more income than girls.

Severe gaps between women's and men's earning power are generally accompanied by severe forms of gender-based discrimination and rigid gender roles. For example, in China, boys are expected to stay in their parental home as they grow up, adding their manpower (and that of a later wife) to the family home. Girls, on the other hand, are expected to join the husbands' parental home. Thus, raising a girl is a net loss, especially if you are only allowed one child.

The solution is to remove the motivation behind sex-selective abortion by advancing women's rights and their economic and social equality. Choosing the blunt instrument of criminal law over promoting the value of women's lives and rights will only serve to place further burdens on marginalized and often vulnerable women.

Saudi government has also said it will lift the ban on women driving by the end of the year.[118]

And in an effort to improve relations with women in Afghanistan, the Canadian military, which has troops stationed in the region, has begun studying the role women play in Afghan society, how they are affected by military operations and how they can assist peacekeeping efforts. "Behind all of these men are women who can help eradicate the problems of the population," said Capt. Michel Larocque, who is working with the study. "Illiteracy, poverty, these things can be improved through women."[119]

In February, during the 52nd session of the Commission on the Status of Women, the United Nations kicked off a new seven-year campaign aimed at ending violence against women. The campaign will work with international agencies, governments and individuals to increase funding for anti-violence campaigns and pressure policy makers around the world to enact legislation to eliminate violence against women.[120]

But women's groups want increased U.N. spending on women's programs and the creation of a single unified agency addressing women's issues, led by an under-secretary general.[121] Currently, four different U.N. agencies address women's issues: the United Nations Development Fund for Women, the International Research and Training Institute for the Advancement of Women (INSTRAW), the Secretary-General's Special Advisor on Gender Issues (OSAGI) and the Division for the Advancement of Women. In 2006, the four agencies received only $65 million — a fraction of the more than $2 billion budget that the U.N.'s children's fund (UNICEF) received that year.[122]

"The four entities that focus on women's rights at the U.N. are greatly under-resourced," says Zeitlin of the Women's Environment & Development Organization. "If the rhetoric everyone is using is true — that investing in women is investing in development — it's a matter of putting your money where your mouth is."

Political Prospects

While the number of women leading world governments is still miniscule compared to their male counterparts, women are achieving political gains that just a few years ago would have been unthinkable.

While for the first time in U.S. history a woman is in a tight race for a major party's nomination as its candidate for president, South America — with two sitting female heads of state — leads the world in woman-led governments. In Brazil, Dilma Rousseff, the female chief of staff to President Luiz Inacio Lula da Silva, is the top contender to take over the presidency when da Silva's term ends in 2010.[123] In Paraguay, Blanca Ovelar was this year's presidential nominee for the country's ruling conservative Colorado Party, but she was defeated on April 20.[124]

And in Europe, Carme Chacón was named defense minister of Spain this past April. She was not only the first woman ever to head the country's armed forces but also was pregnant at the time of her appointment. In all, nine of Spain's 17 cabinet ministers are women.

In March, Pakistan's National Assembly overwhelmingly elected its first female speaker, Fahmida Mirza.[125] And in India, where Patil has become the first woman president, the two major political parties this year pledged to set aside one-third of their parliamentary nominations for women. But many fear the parties will either not keep their pledges or will run women only in contests they are unlikely to win.[126]

There was also disappointment in Iran, where nearly 600 of the 7,000 candidates running for parliament in March were women.[127] Only three won seats in the 290-member house, and they were conservatives who are not expected to promote women's rights. Several of the tallies are being contested. Twelve other women won enough votes to face run-off elections on April 25; five won.[128]

But in some countries, women running for office face more than just tough campaigns. They are specifically targeted for violence. In Kenya, the greatest campaign expense for female candidates is the round-the-clock security required to protect them against rape, according to Phoebe Asiyo, who served in the Kenyan parliament for more than two decades.[129] During the three months before Kenya's elections last December, an emergency helpdesk established by the Education Centre for Women in Democracy, a non-governmental organization (NGO) in Nairobi, received 258 reports of attacks against female candidates.[130]

The helpdesk reported the attacks to police, worked with the press to ensure the cases were documented and helped victims obtain medical and emotional support. Attacks included rape, stabbings, threats and physical assaults.[131]

"Women are being attacked because they are women and because it is seen as though they are not fit to bear flags of the popular parties," according to the center's

Web site. "Women are also viewed as guilty for invading 'the male territory' and without a license to do so!"[132]

"All women candidates feel threatened," said Nazlin Umar, the sole female presidential candidate last year. "When a case of violence against a woman is reported, we women on the ground think we are next. I think if the government assigned all women candidates with guns . . . we will at least have an item to protect ourselves when we face danger."[133]

Impunity for Violence

Some African feminists blame women themselves, as well as men, for not doing enough to end traditional attitudes that perpetuate violence against women.

"Women are also to blame for the violence because they are the gatekeepers of patriarchy, because whether educated or not they have different standards for their sons and husbands [than for] their daughters," said Njoki Wainaina, founder of the African Women Development Communication Network (FEMNET). "How do you start telling a boy whose mother trained him only disrespect for girls to honor women in adulthood?"[134]

Indeed, violence against women is widely accepted in many regions of the world and often goes unpunished. A study by the World Health Organization found that 80 percent of women surveyed in rural Egypt believe that a man is justified in beating a woman if she refuses to have sex with him. In Ghana, more women than men — 50 percent compared to 43 percent — felt that a man was justified in beating his wife if she used contraception without his consent.[135] (*See survey results, p. 324.*)

Such attitudes have led to many crimes against women going unpunished, and not just violence committed during wartime. In Guatemala, no one knows why an estimated 3,000 women have been killed over the past seven years — many of them beheaded, sexually mutilated or raped — but theories range from domestic violence to gang activity.[136] Meanwhile, the government in 2006 overturned a law allowing rapists to escape charges if they offered to marry their victims. But Guatemalan law still does not prescribe prison sentences for domestic abuse and prohibits abusers from being charged with assault unless the bruises are still visible after 10 days.[137]

In the Mexican cities of Chihuahua and Juárez, more than 400 women have been murdered over the past 14 years, with many of the bodies mutilated and dumped in

Seaweed farmer Asia Mohammed Makungu in Zanzibar, Tanzania, grows the sea plants for export to European companies that produce food and cosmetics. Globalized trade has helped women entrepreneurs in many developing countries improve their lives, but critics say it also has created many low-wage, dangerous jobs for women in poor countries that ignore safety and labor protections in order to attract foreign investors.

AP Photo/Karel Prinsloo

the desert. But the crimes are still unsolved, and many human-rights groups, including Amnesty International, blame indifference by Mexican authorities. Now the country's 14-year statute of limitations on murder is forcing prosecutors to close many of the unsolved cases.[138]

Feminists around the world have been working to end dismissive cultural attitudes about domestic violence and other forms of violence against women, such as forced marriage, dowry-related violence, marital rape, sexual harassment and forced abortion, sterilization and prostitution. But it's often an uphill battle.

After a Kenyan police officer beat his wife so badly she was paralyzed and brain damaged — and eventually died — media coverage of the murder spurred a nationwide debate on domestic violence. But it took five years of protests, demonstrations and lobbying by both women's advocates and outraged men to get a family protection bill enacted criminalizing domestic violence. And the bill passed only after legislators removed a provision outlawing marital rape. Similar laws have languished for decades in other African legislatures.[139]

But in Rwanda, where nearly 49 percent of the elected representatives in the lower house are female, gender desks have been established at local police stations, staffed mostly by women trained to help victims of sexual and other violence. In 2006, as a result of improved reporting, investigation and response to rape cases, police referred 1,777 cases for prosecution and convicted 803 men. "What we need now is to expand this approach to more countries," said UNIFEM's director for Central Africa Josephine Odera.[140]

Besides criticizing governments for failing to prosecute gender-based violence, many women's groups also criticize the International Criminal Court (ICC) for not doing enough to bring abusers to justice.

"We have yet to see the investigative approach needed to ensure the prosecution of gender-based crimes," said Brigid Inder, executive director of Women's Initiatives for Gender Justice, a Hague-based group that promotes and monitors women's rights in the international court.[141] Inder's group released a study last November showing that of the 500 victims seeking to participate in ICC proceedings, only 38 percent were women. When the court handed down its first indictments for war crimes in the Democratic Republic of the Congo last year, no charges involving gender-based crimes were brought despite estimates that more than 250,000 women have been raped and sexually abused in the country. After an outcry from women's groups around the world, the ICC included "sexual slavery" among the charges handed down in its second case involving war crimes in Congo.[142]

The Gender Justice report also criticized the court for failing to reach out to female victims. It said the ICC has held only one consultation with women in the last four years (focusing on the Darfur conflict in Sudan) and has failed to develop any strategies to reach out to women victims in Congo[143]

OUTLOOK

Economic Integration

Women's organizations do not expect — or want — another international conference on the scale of Beijing. Instead, they say, the resources needed to launch such a conference would be better used to improve U.N. oversight of women's issues and to implement the promises made at Beijing.

They also fear that the growth of religious fundamentalism and neo-liberal economic policies around the globe have created a political atmosphere that could actually set back women's progress.

"If a Beijing conference happened now, we would not get the type of language or the scope we got 10 years ago," says Bien-Aimé of Equity Now. "There is a conservative movement, a growth in fundamentalists governments — and not just in Muslim countries. We would be very concerned about opening up debate on the principles that have already been established."

Dahlerup of Stockholm University agrees. "It was easier in the 1990s. Many people are afraid of having big conferences now, because there may be a backlash because fundamentalism is so strong," she says. "Neo-liberal trends are also moving the discourse about women toward economics — women have to benefit for the sake of the economic good. That could be very good, but it's a more narrow discourse when every issue needs to be adapted into the economic discourse of a cost-benefit analysis."

For women to continue making gains, most groups say, gender can no longer be treated separately from broader economic, environmental, health or other political issues. While efforts to improve the status of women have historically been addressed in gender-specific legislation or international treaties, women's groups now say women's well-being must now be considered an integral part of all policies.

Women's groups are working to ensure that gender is incorporated into two major international conferences coming up this fall. In September, the Third High-Level Forum on Aid Effectiveness will be hosted in Accra, Ghana, bringing together governments, financial institutions, civil society organizations and others to assess whether assistance provided to poor nations is being put to good use. World leaders will also gather in November in Doha, Qatar, for the International Conference on Financing for Development to discuss how trade, debt relief and financial aid can promote global development.

"Women's groups are pushing for gender to be on the agenda for both conferences," says Zeitlin of WEDO. "It's important because . . . world leaders need to realize that it really does make a difference to invest in women. When it comes to women's rights it's all micro, but the big decisions are made on the macro level."

Despite decades of economic-development strategies promoted by Western nations and global financial institutions such as the World Bank, women in many regions are getting poorer. In Malawi, for example, the percentage of women living in poverty increased by 5 percent between 1995 and 2003.[144] Women and girls make up 70 percent of the world's poorest people, and their wages rise more slowly than men's. They also have fewer property rights around the world.[145] With the growing global food shortage, women — who are the primary family caregivers and produce the majority of crops for home consumption in developing countries — will be especially hard hit.

To help women escape poverty, gain legal rights and improve their social status, developed nations must rethink their broader strategies of engagement with developing countries. And, conversely, female activists say, any efforts aimed at eradicating poverty around the world must specifically address women's issues.

In Africa, for instance, activists have successfully demanded that women's economic and security concerns be addressed as part of the continent-wide development plan known as the New Partnership for Africa's Development (NEPAD). As a result, countries participating in NEPAD's peer review process must now show they are taking measures to promote and protect women's rights. But, according to Augustin Wambo, an agricultural specialist at the NEPAD secretariat, lawmakers now need to back up their pledges with "resources from national budgets" and the "necessary policies and means to support women."[146]

"We have made a lot of progress and will continue making progress," says Zeitlin. "But women's progress doesn't happen in isolation to what's happening in the rest of the world. The environment, the global economy, war, peace — they will all have a major impact on women. Women all over world will not stop making demands and fighting for their rights."

NOTES

1. http://ballyblog.wordpress.com/2007/05/04/warning-uncensored-video-iraqis-stone-girl-to-death-over-loving-wrong-boy/.

2. Abdulhamid Zebari, "Video of Iraqi girl's stoning shown on Internet," Agence France Presse, May 5, 2007.

3. *State of the World Population 2000*, United Nations Population Fund, Sept. 20, 2000, Chapter 3, "Ending Violence against Women and Girls," www.unfpa.org/swp/2000/english/ch03.html.

4. Brian Brady, "A Question of Honour," *The Independent on Sunday*, Feb. 10, 2008, p. 8, www.independent.co.uk/news/uk/home-news/a-question-of-honour-police-say-17000-women-are-victims-every-year-780522.html.

5. Correspondance with Karen Musalo, Clinical Professor of Law and Director of the Center for Gender & Refugee Studies at the University of California Hastings School of Law, April 11, 2008.

6. "Broken Bodies, Broken Dreams: Violence Against Women Exposed," United Nations, July 2006, http://brokendreams.wordpress.om/2006/12/17/dowry-crimes-and-bride-price-abuse/.

7. Various sources: www.womankind.org.uk, www.unfpa.org/gender/docs/studies/summaries/reg_exe_summary.pdf, www.oxfam.org.uk. Also see "Child rape in Kano on the increase," IRIN Humanitarian News and Analysis, United Nations, www.irinnews.org/report.aspx?ReportId=76087.

8. "UNICEF slams 'licence to rape' in African crisis," Agence France-Press, Feb. 12, 2008.

9. "Film Documents Rape of Women in Congo," "All Things Considered," National Public Radio, April 8, 2008, www.npr.org/templates/story/story.php?storyId=89476111.

10. Jeffrey Gettleman, "Rape Epidemic Raises Trauma Of Congo War," *The New York Times*, Oct. 7, 2007, p. A1.

11. Dan McDougall, "Fareeda's fate: rape, prison and 25 lashes," *The Observer*, Sept. 17, 2006, www.guardian.co.uk/world/2006/sep/17/pakistan.theobserver.

12. Zarar Khan, "Thousands rally in Pakistan to demand government withdraw rape law changes," The Associated Press, Dec. 10, 2006.

13. *State of the World Population 2000, op. cit.*

14. Laura Turquet, Patrick Watt, Tom Sharman, "Hit or Miss?" ActionAid, March 7, 2008, p. 10.

15. *Ibid.*, p. 12.

16. "Women in Politics: 2008" map, International Parliamentary Union and United Nations Division for the Advancement of Women, February 2008, www.ipu.org/pdf/publications/wmnmap08_en.pdf.

17. Gavin Rabinowitz, "India's first female president sworn in, promises to empower women," The Associated Press, July 25, 2007. Note: India's first female prime minister was Indira Ghandi in 1966.

18. Monte Reel, "South America Ushers In The Era of La Presidenta; Women Could Soon Lead a Majority of Continent's Population," *The Washington Post*, Oct. 31, 2007, p. A12. For background, see Roland Flamini, "The New Latin America," *CQ Global Researcher*, March 2008, pp. 57-84.

19. Marcela Valente, "Cristina Fernandes Dons Presidential Sash," Inter Press Service, Dec. 10, 2007.

20. "Women in Politics: 2008" map, *op. cit.*

21. *Ibid.*; Global Database of Quotas for Women, International Institute for Democracy and Electoral Assistance and Stockholm University, www.quotaproject.org/country.cfm?SortOrder=Country.

22. "Beijing Betrayed," Women's Environment and Development Organization, March 2005, p. 10, www.wedo.org/files/gmr_pdfs/gmr2005.pdf.

23. "Women in Politics: 2008" map, *op. cit.*

24. Gertrude Mongella, address by the Secretary-General of the 4th World Conference on Women, Sept. 4, 1995, www.un.org/esa/gopher-data/conf/fwcw/conf/una/950904201423.txt. Also see Steven Mufson, "Women's Forum Sets Accord; Dispute on Sexual Freedom Resolved," *The Washington Post*, Sept. 15, 1995, p. A1.

25. "Closing statement," Gertrude Mongella, U.N. Division for the Advancement of Women, Fourth World Conference on Women, www.un.org/esa/gopher-data/conf/fwcw/conf/una/closing.txt.

26. "Trading Away Our Rights," Oxfam International, 2004, p. 9, www.oxfam.org.uk/resources/policy/trade/downloads/trading_rights.pdf.

27. "Trafficking in Persons Report," U.S. Department of State, June 2007, p. 7, www.state.gov/g/tip/rls/tiprpt/2007/.

28. Turquet, *et al.*, *op. cit.*, p. 4.

29. United Nations Division for the Advancement of Women, www.un.org/womenwatch/daw/cedaw/.

30. Geraldine Terry, *Women's Rights* (2007), p. 30.

31. United Nations Division for the Advancement of Women, www.un.org/womenwatch/daw/cedaw/.

32. "The impact of international trade on gender equality," The World Bank PREM notes, May 2004, http://siteresources.worldbank.org/INTGENDER/Resources/premnote86.pdf.

33. Thalia Kidder and Kate Raworth, " 'Good Jobs' and hidden costs: women workers documenting the price of precarious employment," *Gender and Development*, July 2004, p. 13.

34. "Trading Away Our Rights," *op. cit.*

35. Martha Chen, *et al.*, "Progress of the World's Women 2005: Women, Work and Poverty," UNIFEM, p. 17, www.unifem.org/attachments/products/PoWW2005_eng.pdf.

36. Eric Neumayer and Indra de Soys, "Globalization, Women's Economic Rights and Forced Labor," London School of Economics and Norwegian University of Science and Technology, February 2007, p. 8, http://papers.ssrn.com/sol3/papers.cfm?abstract_id=813831. Also see "Five years down the road from Beijing — assessing progress," *News and Highlights*, Food and Agriculture Organization, June 2, 2000, www.fao.org/News/2000/000602-e.htm.

37. "Trafficking in Persons Report," *op. cit.*, p. 13.

38. "World Survey on the Role of Women in Development," United Nations, 2006, p. 1, www.un.org/womenwatch/daw/public/WorldSurvey2004-Women&Migration.pdf.

39. Julie Ballington and Azza Karam, eds., "Women in Parliament: Beyond the Numbers," International Institute for Democracy and Electoral Assistance, 2005, p. 155, www.idea.int/publications/wip2/upload/WiP_inlay.pdf.

40. "Women in Politics: 2008," *op. cit.*

41. Ballington and Karam, *op. cit.*, p. 158.

42. *Ibid.*, p. 161.

43. Global Database of Quotas for Women, *op. cit.*

44. Jerome Starkey, "Afghan government official says that student will not be executed," *The Independent*, Feb. 6, 2008, www.independent.co.uk/news/world/asia/afghan-government-official-says-that-student-will-not-be-executed-778686.html?r=RSS.

45. "Afghan women seek death by fire," BBC, Nov. 15, 2006, http://news.bbc.co.uk/1/hi/world/south_asia/6149144.stm.

46. Global Database for Quotas for Women, *op. cit.*

47. "Beijing Declaration," Fourth World Conference on Women, www.un.org/womenwatch/daw/beijing/beijingdeclaration.html.

48. "Beijing Betrayed," *op. cit.*, pp. 28, 15, 18.

49. "Review of the implementation of the Beijing Platform for Action and the outcome documents of the special session of the General Assembly entitled 'Women 2000: gender equality, development and peace for the twenty-first century,' " United Nations, Dec. 6, 2004, p. 74.

50. "Gender Equality and the Millennium Development Goals," fact sheet, www.mdgender.net/upload/tools/MDGender_leaflet.pdf.

51. *Ibid.*

52. Turquet, *et al.*, *op. cit.*, p. 16.

53. *Ibid.*, pp. 22-24.

54. Terry, *op. cit.*, p. 6.

55. "Inclusive Security, Sustainable Peace: A Toolkit for Advocacy and Action," International Alert and Women Waging Peace, 2004, p. 12, www.huntalternatives.org/download/35_introduction.pdf.

56. "Declarations, Reservations and Objections to CEDAW," www.un.org/womenwatch/daw/cedaw/reservations-country.htm.

57. Merlin Stone, *When God Was a Woman* (1976), pp. 18, 11.

58. Jack Holland, *Misogyny* (2006), p. 12.

59. *Ibid.*, pp. 21-23.

60. Holland, *op. cit.*, p. 112.

61. "Dispelling the myths about so-called witches" press release, Johns Hopkins University, Oct. 7, 2002, www.jhu.edu/news_info/news/home02/oct02/witch.html.

62. The quote is from the *Malleus maleficarum* (*The Hammer of Witches*), and was cited in "Case Study: The European Witch Hunts, c. 1450-1750," *Gendercide Watch*, www.gendercide.org/case_witch-hunts.html.

63. Holland, *op. cit.*, p. 179.

64. Cathy J. Cohen, Kathleen B. Jones and Joan C. Tronto, *Women Transforming Politics: An Alternative Reader* (1997), p. 530.

65. *Ibid.*

66. Holland, *op. cit.*, p. 201.

67. "Men and Women in Politics: Democracy Still in the Making," IPU Study No. 28, 1997, http://archive.idea.int/women/parl/ch6_table8.htm.

68. "Sex, Equality and Protective Laws," *CQ Researcher*, July 13, 1926.

69. The case was *Radice v. People of State of New York*, 264 U. S. 292. For background, see F. Brewer, "Equal Rights Amendment," *Editorial Research Reports*, April 4, 1946, available at *CQ Researcher Plus Archive*, www.cqpress.com.

70. "Short History of the CEDAW Convention," U.N. Division for the Advancement of Women, www.un.org/womenwatch/daw/cedaw/history.htm.

71. U.N. Women's Watch, www.un.org/womenwatch/asp/user/list.asp-ParentID=11047.htm.

72. United Nations, http://untreaty.un.org/ENGLISH/bible/englishinternetbible/partI/chapterXVI/treaty2.asp.

73. International Labor Organization, www.ilo.org/public/english/support/lib/resource/subject/gender.htm.

74. *Ibid.*

75. For background, see "Gender Pay Gap," *CQ Researcher*, March 14, 2008, pp. 241-264.

76. "Short History of the CEDAW Convention" *op. cit.*

77. "International News," The Associated Press, Dec. 19, 1979.

78. "Short History of the CEDAW Convention" *op. cit.*

79. "Text of the Convention," U.N. Division for the Advancement of Women, www.un.org/womenwatch/daw/cedaw/cedaw.htm.

80. Convention on the Elimination of All Forms of Discrimination against Women, Article 16, www.un.org/womenwatch/daw/cedaw/text/econvention.htm.

81. General Recommendation made by the Committee on the Elimination of Discrimination against Women No. 19, 11th session, 1992, www.un.org/womenwatch/daw/cedaw/recommendations/recomm.htm#recom19.

82. See www.unhchr.ch/huridocda/huridoca.nsf/(Symbol)/A.CONF.157.23.En.

83. Marlise Simons, "For First Time, Court Defines Rape as War Crime," *The New York Times*, June 28, 1996, www.nytimes.com/specials/bosnia/context /0628warcrimes-tribunal.html.

84. Ann Simmons, "U.N. Tribunal Convicts Rwandan Ex-Mayor of Genocide in Slaughter," *Los Angeles Times*, Sept. 3, 1998, p. 20.

85. "Human Rights Watch Applauds Rwanda Rape Verdict," press release, Human Rights Watch, Sept. 2, 1998, http://hrw.org/english/docs/1998/09/02/ rwanda1311.htm.

86. Frederic Bichon, "ICC vows to bring Darfur war criminals to justice," Agence France-Presse, Feb. 24, 2008.

87. Rebecca Feeley and Colin Thomas-Jensen, "Getting Serious about Ending Conflict and Sexual Violence in Congo," Enough Project, www.enoughproject .org/reports/congoserious.

88. "Women; Deceived Again?" *The Economist*, July 5, 1975.

89. "International Women's Day — March 8: Points of Interest and Links with UNIFEM," UNIFEM New Zealand Web site, www.unifem.org.nz/IWDPoints ofinterest.htm.

90. Joseph Gambardello, "Reporter's Notebook: Women's Conference in Kenya," United Press International, July 13, 1985.

91. "Report of the World Conference to Review and Appraise the Achievements of the United Nations Decade for Women: Equality Development and Peace," United Nations, 1986, paragraph 8, www.un.org/wom enwatch/confer/nfls/Nairobi1985report.txt.

92. U.N. Division for the Advancement of Women, www .un.org/womenwatch/daw/followup/background.htm.

93. "Women in Politics," Inter-Parliamentary Union, 2005, pp. 16-17, www.ipu.org/PDF/publications/ wmn45-05_en.pdf.

94. "Liberian becomes Africa's first female president," Associated Press, Jan. 16, 2006, www.msnbc.msn .com/id/10865705/.

95. "Women in the Americas: Paths to Political Power," *op. cit.*, p. 2.

96. "The Millennium Development Goals Report 2007," United Nations, 2007, p. 12, www.un.org/ millenniumgoals/pdf/mdg2007.pdf.

97. David Dollar, Raymond Fisman, Roberta Gatti, "Are Women Really the 'Fairer' Sex? Corruption and Women in Government," The World Bank, October 1999, p. 1, http://siteresources.world-bank.org/INTGENDER/Resources/wp4.pdf.

98. *Ibid.*

99. Vicky Baker, "Rape victim sentenced to 200 lashes and six months in jail; Saudi woman punished for being alone with a man," *The Guardian*, Nov. 17, 2007, www.guardian.co.uk/world/2007/nov/17/ saudiarabia.international.

100. Katherine Zoepf, "Saudi King Pardons Rape Victim Sentenced to Be Lashed, Saudi Paper Reports," *The New York Times*, Dec. 18, 2007, www.nytimes .com/2007/12/18/world/middleeast/18saudi.html.

101. Sonia Verma, "King Abdullah urged to spare Saudi 'witchcraft' woman's life," *The Times* (Of London), Feb. 16, 2008.

102. Mark Lattimer, "Freedom lost," *The Guardian*, Dec. 13, 2007, p. 6.

103. For background, see Brian Beary, "Future of Turkey," *CQ Global Researcher*, December, 2007, pp. 295-322.

104. Tracy Clark-Flory, "Does freedom to veil hurt women?" *Salon.com*, Feb. 11, 2008.

105. Sabrina Tavernise, "Under a Scarf, a Turkish Lawyer Fighting to Wear It," *The New York Times*, Feb. 9, 2008, www.nytimes.com/2008/02/09/ world/europe/09benli.html?pagewanted=1&sq=w omen&st=nyt&scp=96.

106. Terry, *op. cit.*, p. 122.

107. "Many Americans Uneasy with Mix of Religion and Politics," The Pew Forum on Religion and Public Life, Aug. 24, 2006, http://pewforum.org/ docs/index.php?DocID=153.

108. Brady, *op. cit.*

109. "Concluding Observations of the Committee on the Elimination of Discrimination against Women: Saudi Arabia," Committee on the Elimination of Discrimination against Women, 40th Session, Jan. 14-Feb. 1, 2008, p. 3, www2 .ohchr.org/english/ bodies/cedaw/docs/co/CEDAW.C.SAU.CO.2.pdf.

110. Kambiz Fattahi, "Women's bill 'unites' Iran and US," BBC, July 31, 2007, http://news.bbc.co.uk/2/ hi/middle_east/6922749.stm.

111. H. Res. 101, Rep. Lynn Woolsey, http://thomas .loc.gov/cgi-bin/bdquery/z?d110:h.res.00101.

112. "General Assembly Adopts Landmark Text Calling for Moratorium on Death Penalty," States News Service, Dec. 18, 2007, www.un.org/News /Press/ docs//2007/ga10678.doc.htm.

113. Mary H. Cooper, "Women and Human Rights," *CQ Researcher*, April 30, 1999, p. 356.

114. Christina Hoff Sommers, "The Case against Ratifying the United Nations Convention on the Elimination of All Forms of Discrimination against Women," testimony before the Senate Foreign Relations Committee, June 13, 2002, www.aei .org/publications/filter.all,pubID.15557/pub_ detail.asp.

115. "CEDAW: Pro-United Nations, Not Pro-Woman" press release, U.S. Senate Republican Policy Committee, Sept. 16, 2002, http://rpc.senate .gov/_files/FOREIGNje091602.pdf.

116. "Turkmenistan adopts gender equality law," BBC Worldwide Monitoring, Dec. 19, 2007.

117. Faiza Saleh Ambah, "Saudi Women See a Brighter Road on Rights," *The Washington Post*, Jan. 31, 2008, p. A15, www.washingtonpost.com/wp-dyn/ content/article/2008/01/30/AR2008013003805. html.

118. Damien McElroy, "Saudi Arabia to lift ban on women drivers," *The Telegraph*, Jan. 1, 2008.

119. Stephanie Levitz, "Lifting the veils of Afghan women," *The Hamilton Spectator* (Ontario, Canada), Feb. 28, 2008, p. A11.

120. "U.N. Secretary-General Ban Ki-moon Launches Campaign to End Violence against Women," U.N. press release, Feb. 25, 2008, http://endviolence .un.org/press.shtml.

121. "Gender Equality Architecture and U.N. Reforms," the Center for Women's Global Leadership and the Women's Environment and Development Organization, July 17, 2006, www.wedo.org/files/ Gender%20Equality%20Architecture%20 and%20UN%20Reform0606.pdf.

122. Bojana Stoparic, "New-Improved Women's Agency Vies for U.N. Priority," Women's eNews, March 6, 2008, www.womensenews.org/article.cfm?aid=3517.

123. Reel, *op. cit.*

124. Eliana Raszewski and Bill Faries, "Lugo, Ex Bishop, Wins Paraguay Presidential Election," Bloomberg, April 20, 2008.

125. Zahid Hussain, "Pakistan gets its first woman Speaker," *The Times* (of London), March 20, p. 52.

126. Bhaskar Roy, "Finally, women set to get 33% quota," *Times of India*, Jan. 29, 2008.

127. Massoumeh Torfeh, "Iranian women crucial in Majlis election," BBC, Jan. 30, 2008, http://news .bbc.co.uk/1/hi/world/middle_east/7215272.stm.

128. "Iran women win few seats in parliament," Agence-France Presse, March 18, 2008.

129. Swanee Hunt, "Let Women Rule," *Foreign Affairs*, May-June 2007, p. 109.

130. Kwamboka Oyaro, "A Call to Arm Women Candidates With More Than Speeches," Inter Press Service, Dec. 21, 2007, http://ipsnews.net/ news.asp?idnews=40569.

131. Education Centre for Women in Democracy, www.ecwd.org.

132. *Ibid.*

133. Oyaro, *op. cit.*

134. *Ibid.*

135. Mary Kimani, "Taking on violence against women in Africa," *AfricaRenewal*, U.N. Dept. of Public Information, July 2007, p. 4, www.un.org/eco-socdev/geninfo/afrec/vol21no2/212-violence-aganist-women.html.

136. Correspondence with Karen Musalo, Clinical Professor of Law and Director of the Center for Gender & Refugee Studies, University of California Hastings School of Law, April 11, 2008.

137. "Mexico and Guatemala: Stop the Killings of Women," Amnesty International USA Issue Brief, January 2007, www.amnestyusa.org/document .php?lang=e&id=engusa20070130001.

138. Manuel Roig-Franzia, "Waning Hopes in Juarez," *The Washington Post*, May 14, 2007, p. A10.

139. Kimani, *op. cit.*

140. *Ibid.*

141. "Justice slow for female war victims," *The Toronto Star*, March 3, 2008, www.thestar.com/News/ GlobalVoices/article/308784p.

142. Speech by Brigid Inder on the Launch of the "Gender Report Card on the International Criminal Court," Dec. 12, 2007, www.iccwomen .org/news/docs/Launch_GRC_2007.pdf

143. "Gender Report Card on the International Criminal Court," Women's Initiatives for Gender Justic, November 2007, p. 32, www.iccwomen .org/publications/resources/docs/GENDER_04-01- 2008_FINAL_TO_PRINT.pdf.

144. Turquet, *et al.*, *op. cit.*, p. 8.

145. Oxfam Gender Equality Fact Sheet, www.oxfam .org.uk/resources/issues/gender/introduction.html.

146. Itai Madamombe, "Women push onto Africa's agenda," *AfricaRenewal*, U.N. Dept. of Public Information, July 2007, pp. 8-9.

BIBLIOGRAPHY

Books

Holland, Jack, *Misogyny: The World's Oldest Prejudice*, Constable & Robinson, 2006.
The late Irish journalist provides vivid details and anecdotes about women's oppression throughout history.

Stone, Merlin, *When God Was a Woman*, Harcourt Brace Jovanovich, 1976.
The book contends that before the rise of Judeo-Christian patriarchies women headed the first societies and religions.

Terry, Geraldine, *Women's Rights*, Pluto Press, 2007.
A feminist who has worked for Oxfam and other nongovernmental organizations outlines major issues facing women today — from violence to globalization to AIDS.

Women and the Environment, UNEP, 2004.
The United Nations Environment Programme shows the integral link between women in the developing world and the changing environment.

Articles

Brady, Brian, "A Question of Honour," The Independent on Sunday, Feb. 10, 2008, p. 8.
"Honor killings" and related violence against women are on the rise in the United Kingdom.

Kidder, Thalia, and Kate Raworth, " 'Good Jobs' and hidden costs: women workers documenting the price of precarious employment," Gender and Development, Vol. 12, No. 2, p. 12, July 2004.
Two trade and gender experts describe the precarious working conditions and job security experienced by food and garment workers.

Reports and Studies

"Beijing Betrayed," Women's Environment and Development Organization, March 2005, www.wedo . org/files/gmr_pdfs/gmr2005.pdf.
A women's-rights organization reviews the progress and shortcomings of governments in implementing the commitments made during the Fifth World Congress on Women in Beijing in 1995.

"The Millennium Development Goals Report 2007," United Nations, 2007, www.un.org/millenniumgoals/ pdf/mdg2007.pdf.
International organizations demonstrate the progress governments have made — or not — in reaching the Millennium Development Goals.

"Trafficking in Persons Report," U.S. Department of State, June 2007, www.state.gov/documents/organi zation/82902.pdf.
This seventh annual report discusses the growing problems of human trafficking around the world.

"The tsunami's impact on women," Oxfam briefing note, March 5, 2005, www.oxfam.org/en/files/bn05 0326_tsunami_women/download.
Looking at how the 2004 tsunami affected women in Indonesia, India and Sri Lanka, Oxfam International suggests how governments can better address women's issues during future natural disasters.

"Women in Politics," Inter-Parliamentary Union, 2005, www.ipu.org/PDF/publications/wmn45-05_en.pdf.
The report provides detailed databases of the history of female political representation in governments around the world.

Ballington, Julie, and Azza Karam, "Women in Parliament: Beyond the Numbers," International Institute for Democracy and Electoral Assistance, 2005, www.idea.int /publications/ wip2/upload/WiP_inlay.pdf.

The handbook provides female politicians and candidates information and case studies on how women have overcome obstacles to elected office.

Chen, Martha, Joann Vanek, Francie Lund, James Heintz, Renana Jhabvala and Christine Bonner, "Women, Work and Poverty," UNIFEM, 2005, www .unifem.org/attachments/products/PoWW2005_eng.pdf.
The report argues that greater work protection and security is needed to promote women's rights and reduce global poverty.

Larserud, Stina, and Rita Taphorn, "Designing for Equality," International Institute for Democracy and Electoral Assistance, 2007, www.idea.int/publications/ designing_for_equality/upload/Idea_Design_low.pdf.

The report describes the impact that gender quota systems have on women's representation in elected office.

Raworth, Kate, and Claire Harvey, "Trading Away Our Rights," Oxfam International, 2004, www .oxfam.org. uk/resources/policy/trade/downloads/trading_rights .pdf.
Through exhaustive statistics, case studies and interviews, the report paints a grim picture of how trade globalization is affecting women.

Turquet, Laura, Patrick Watt and Tom Sharman, "Hit or Miss?" ActionAid, March 7, 2008.
The report reviews how governments are doing in achieving the U.N.'s Millennium Development Goals.

For More Information

Equality Now, P.O. Box 20646, Columbus Circle Station, New York, NY 10023; (212) 586-1611; www.equalitynow .org. An international organization working to protect women against violence and promote women's human rights.

Global Database of Quotas for Women; www.quotaproj ect.org. A joint project of the International Institute for Democracy and Electoral Assistance and Stockholm University providing country-by-country data on electoral quotas for women.

Human Rights Watch, 350 Fifth Ave., 34th floor, New York, NY 10118-3299; (212) 290-4700; www.hrw.org. Investigates and exposes human-rights abuses around the world.

Hunt Alternatives Fund, 625 Mount Auburn St., Cambridge, MA 02138; (617) 995-1900; www.huntalternatives.org. A private foundation that provides grants and technical assistance to promote positive social change; its Initiative for Inclusive Security promotes women in peacekeeping.

Inter-Parliamentary Union, 5, Chemin du Pommier, Case Postale 330, CH-1218 Le Grand-Saconnex, Geneva, Switzerland; +(4122) 919 41 50; www.ipu.org. An organization of parliaments of sovereign states that maintains an extensive database on women serving in parliaments.

Oxfam International, 226 Causeway St., 5th Floor, Boston, MA 02114; (617) 482-1211; www.oxfam.org. Confederation of 13 independent nongovernmental organizations working to fight poverty and related social injustice.

U.N. Development Fund for Women (UNIFEM), 304 East 45th St., 15th Floor, New York, NY 10017; (212) 906-6400; www.unifem.org. Provides financial aid and technical support for empowering women and promoting gender equality.

U.N. Division for the Advancement of Women (DAW), 2 UN Plaza, DC2-12th Floor, New York, NY 10017; www .un.org/womenwatch/daw. Formulates policy on gender equality, implements international agreements on women's issues and promotes gender mainstreaming in government activities.

Women's Environment & Development Organization (WEDO), 355 Lexington Ave., 3rd Floor, New York, NY 10017; (212) 973-0325; www.wedo.org. An international organization that works to promote women's equality in global policy.

14

Aiding Refugees

John Felton

Residents struggle to maintain normalcy in Kenya's Eldoret camp, home to 14,000 Kenyans who fled their homes during post-election rioting in December 2007. But they are the lucky ones. Many of the world's 26 million internally displaced people (IDPs) receive no aid at all or live in crude huts made of sticks and plastic sheeting, without reliable access to food or clean water. The U.N. High Commissioner for Refugees provided aid to some 13.7 million IDPs in 2007.

From *CQ Researcher*,
March, 2009.

For more than two decades, the guerrilla group known as the Lord's Resistance Army (LRA) has been terrorizing villagers in Uganda — forcibly recruiting child soldiers and brutally attacking civilians. In recent years, the dreaded group has crossed the border into the Democratic Republic of Congo.

Last October, LRA marauders attacked Tambohe's village in northeastern Congo. They shot and killed her brother-in-law and two others, then torched the houses, even those with people inside.

Tambohe and her surviving family members — five adults and 10 children — fled into the forest, briefly returning five days later to bury the bodies after the raiders had left. The family then walked north for three days until they found safety in a village just across the border in southern Sudan, living with several hundred other Congolese displaced by the LRA.

"We have built a hut, and we live there," the 38-year-old Tambohe later told the medical aid group Doctors Without Borders. "The children sleep badly due to the mosquitoes and because we sleep on the ground. I sleep badly because I dream of the stench of burnt flesh. I dream they [the LRA] come and . . . take us to their camp."[1]

LRA violence is only one aspect of ongoing conflict in Congo that has killed 5 million people in the past decade and forced millions from their homes — including more than 400,000 last year, according to Human Rights Watch.[2]

Many, like Tambohe, fled their homes and crossed into another country, making them legally refugees. Under international law, she and her family should be able to remain in Sudan and receive humanitarian aid, shelter and protection because they have a "well-founded fear" of persecution if they return home.[3]

Most Displaced People Are in Africa and the Middle East

The U.N. High Commissioner for Refugees (UNHCR) monitors nearly 32 million people around the world who have been uprooted for a variety of reasons, including 25 million who fled their homes to escape war or conflict, mostly in Africa and the Middle East. Among those are 11 million refugees — those who have crossed borders and thus are protected by international law — and nearly 14 million internally displaced people (IDPs) who remain in their home countries. Some critics want the UNHCR to monitor and assist the world's other 12.3 million IDPs now being aided by other agencies.

Displaced Populations Monitored by the UNHCR

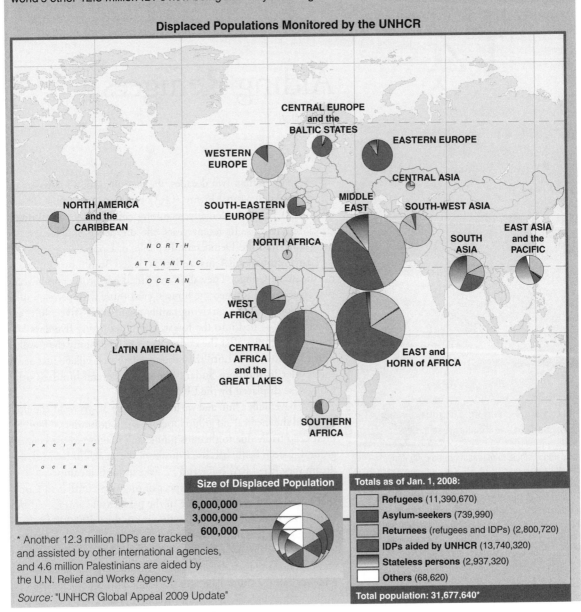

Size of Displaced Population

6,000,000
3,000,000
600,000

Totals as of Jan. 1, 2008:

Refugees (11,390,670)
Asylum-seekers (739,990)
Returnees (refugees and IDPs) (2,800,720)
IDPs aided by UNHCR (13,740,320)
Stateless persons (2,937,320)
Others (68,620)

Total population: 31,677,640*

* Another 12.3 million IDPs are tracked and assisted by other international agencies, and 4.6 million Palestinians are aided by the U.N. Relief and Works Agency.

Source: "UNHCR Global Appeal 2009 Update"

If Tambohe had fled her home but remained in Congo, she would have been considered an "internally displaced person" (IDP), and the Congolese government would be legally responsible for aiding and protecting her. But in the Democratic Republic of the Congo and many other countries, international law is little more than a theory. The Kinshasa government is weak, and the army itself has been accused of abusing civilians.[4] So helping the Tambohes of the world falls primarily to the United Nations (U.N.) and nongovernmental aid agencies.

Today, there are more than 90 million refugees, displaced persons and disaster victims around the world. More than 40 million have fled conflict or violence, according to Antonio Guterres, U.N. High Commissioner for Refugees (UNHCR), who leads international efforts to aid the displaced.[5] Of those, about 16 million are refugees (including 4.6 million Palestinians) and 26 million are IDPs. (*See map, p. 356.*) Up to 50 million more people are victims of natural disaster, according to the U.N.'s Office for the Coordination of Humanitarian Affairs. In China's Sichuan Province, for example, many of the 5 million people who lost their

homes last May in an earthquake remain homeless, and thousands of Americans are still displaced from Hurricane Katrina, which struck New Orleans in 2005.[6]

Millions of displaced people overseas live in sprawling camps or settlements established by governments or the United Nations, often in harsh desert or jungle environments. A large but unknown number of others, like Tambohe, find their own temporary shelter — sometimes living with friends or relatives but more often building makeshift tents and huts or moving into crowded rental housing in urban slums.

Food insecurity — or even starvation — rank among the most serious consequences of displacement. In

U.N. Serves About Half the World's Displaced

The U.N. High Commissioner for Refugees (UNHCR) has provided aid to an average of about 5.7 million of the globe's 11 million refugees each year — mostly in developing countries — over the past decade (blue lines). Meanwhile, the world's population of internally displaced persons (IDPs) has risen from 19 million in 1998 to 26 million in 2007. Individual governments are responsible for IDPs. But since 2005 the UNHCR has more than doubled the number of IDPs it serves each year — from 6.6 million in 2005 to 13.7 million in 2007 (orange lines).

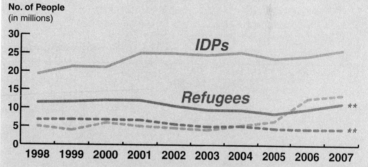

Total Refugees and IDPs vs. Those Receiving UNHCR Aid (1998-2007)

* Does not include 4.6 million Palestinians assisted by the U.N. Relief and Works Agency in 2007.

** 2007 figures include people "in refugee-like situations" who were not included in previous years and excludes some 822,000 resettled refugees previously included in refugee statistics. Thus the 2007 data is not comparable with previous years.

Sources: 2007 U.N. High Commissioner for Refugees, Statistical Yearbook; "Global IDP Estimates (1990-2007)," Internal Displacement Monitoring Centre

Kenya, for example, last year's post-election bloodshed caused so many farmers from key food-producing areas to flee their homes — leaving crops unplanted or unharvested — that an estimated 10 million Kenyans now face starvation.[7]

Some experts predict the world increasingly will be forced to deal with massive displacements — potentially involving hundreds of millions of people — caused by natural disasters intensified by climate change. Elisabeth Rasmusson, secretary general of the Norwegian Refugee Council, which aids and advocates for the displaced, warned last December that the world faces a potential vicious cycle: As climate change degrades the

Sudan Hosts Most Displaced People

Of the millions of refugees and internally displaced persons (IDPs) monitored by the U.N. High Commissioner for Refugees, Sudan houses nearly 4 million — more than any other country. Four of the top 10 host countries are in Africa. Most refugees and IDPs come from Iraq, Afghanistan, Colombia and five African countries.

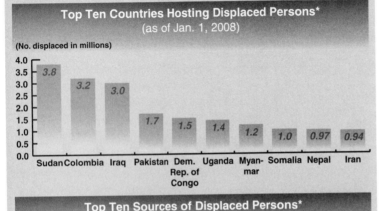

Top Ten Countries Hosting Displaced Persons*
(as of Jan. 1, 2008)

(No. displaced in millions)

Sudan 3.8; Colombia 3.2; Iraq 3.0; Pakistan 1.7; Dem. Rep. of Congo 1.5; Uganda 1.4; Myanmar 1.2; Somalia 1.0; Nepal 0.97; Iran 0.94

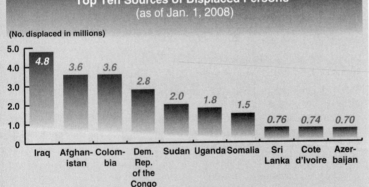

Top Ten Sources of Displaced Persons*
(as of Jan. 1, 2008)

(No. displaced in millions)

Iraq 4.8; Afghanistan 3.6; Colombia 3.6; Dem. Rep. of the Congo 2.8; Sudan 2.0; Uganda 1.8; Somalia 1.5; Sri Lanka 0.76; Cote d'Ivoire 0.74; Azerbaijan 0.70

* Does not include 4.6 million Palestinians assisted by the U.N. Relief and Works Agency.

Source: "UNHCR Global Appeal, 2009 Update," U.N. High Commissioner for Refugees, January 2009

under $1 billion to $1.8 billion this year — the agency struggles to protect and care for refugees and IDPs in 116 countries around the world. As of Jan. 1, 2008, the agency was aiding 4.5 million of the world's 11.4 million refugees and 13.7 million of the world's 26 million IDPs. (*See graph, p. 357.*) Because the UNHCR and other aid agencies often operate in or near conflict zones, the delivery of humanitarian relief can be dangerous and, at times, impossible. In the Darfur region of western Sudan, for example, aid groups repeatedly have been forced to halt aid shipments because of attacks on relief convoys.[10]

But the lack of security is only one of a daunting litany of challenges faced by the UNHCR and its dozens of partner agencies, including chronic shortages of funds and reliance on "emergency" appeals to wealthy countries, the hostility of local governments, bureaucratic turf battles and indifference among world leaders.

And, despite promises to the contrary, the U.N. Security Council often has been unable or unwilling to take effective action — such as in Rwanda in 1994 and in Darfur since 2003 — to halt horrific death and displacement tolls. In both situations, ill-equipped and undermanned U.N. peacekeepers were unable to prevent what some have called the genocidal slaughter of hundreds of thousands of people. Yet some critics question whether the U.N. is trying to do either too much or too little, and others say international refugee law needs to be updated to take into account recent trends, such as the rapid increase in IDPs.

Those living in refugee and IDP camps have more immediate concerns, including overcrowded conditions; inadequate housing, food and medical care; and the refusal of local governments to allow them to work (or even to leave the camps). Negash, an Ethiopian who has

environment, it triggers more civil conflicts as people fight for access to water and other resources, further damaging the environment — displacing more people at each stage.[8]

Long before concern about climate change, however, international agencies were overwhelmed by the magnitude of conflict-caused displacements, which have been rising dramatically over the past decade.[9] And while the UNHCR's budget has nearly doubled since 2000 — from

Refugees Fall into Eight Categories

When people flee their homes and seek aid, they can be assigned to one of eight classifications, each of which conveys unique legal rights or restrictions. For instance, some are entitled under international law to receive humanitarian aid, shelter and protection because they have a "well-founded fear" of persecution if they return home. Here are the key definitions under international law and commonly accepted practice of the various categories of people who are seeking, or in need of, assistance:

Asylum-seeker: A person who has applied (either individually or as part of a group) for legal refugee status under national and international laws. If refugee status is denied, the asylum-seeker must leave the country (and could face expulsion) unless he or she is given permission to stay on humanitarian grounds.

Internally displaced person (IDP): Someone who has been forced to flee his home due to armed conflict, generalized violence, human-rights violations or natural or man-made disasters but has not crossed an international border.

Migrants: In the absence of a universally accepted definition of a migrant, the International Organization on Migration says the term is "usually understood" to cover all cases in which "the decision to migrate is taken freely by the individual concerned for reasons of 'personal convenience' and without intervention of an external compelling factor. An "economic migrant" is someone who leaves his home country in search of better economic opportunities elsewhere.

Persons in "IDP-like" situations: This relatively new term developed by the U.N. High Commissioner for Refugees (UNHCR) describes "groups of persons who are inside their country of nationality or habitual residence and who face protection risks similar to those of IDPs, but who, for practical or other reasons, could not be reported as such." For example, the UNHCR has used the term to describe displaced people in Georgia (including former residents of the breakaway provinces of Abkhazia and South Ossetia) and Russia.

Persons in "refugee-like" situations: Another relatively recent term used by the UNHCR to describe people who are outside their country or territory of origin "who face protection risks similar to those of refugees, but for whom refugee status has, for practical or other reasons, not been ascertained." In many cases, these are refugees who have settled more or less permanently in another country on an informal basis. The largest single population in this group is the estimated 1.1 million Afghans living outside formal refugee camps in Pakistan.

Refugee: Under the 1951 Refugee Convention (as amended in 1967), a refugee is someone who, due to a "well-founded fear of being persecuted for reasons of race, religion, nationality, membership of a particular social group or political opinions," has left his home country and is unable or, owing to fear, "unwilling to avail himself of the protection of that country." A person becomes a refugee by meeting the standards of the Refugee Convention, even before being granted asylum (*see above*), which legally confirms his or her refugee status.

Returnee: A refugee or IDP who has returned to his home — or home country or region.

Stateless person: Anyone who is not recognized as a citizen of any country. Stateless persons lack national or international legal protections and cannot legally cross international borders because they don't have and cannot obtain a valid passport or other identity papers. Between 3 million and 12 million people worldwide are stateless; the wide range results from a lack of information in some countries and conflicting assessments about which groups actually are stateless.

Sources: "Glossary on Migration," International Migration Law, International Organization for Migration, Geneva, Switzerland, www.iom.int/jahia/webdav/site/myjahiasite/shared/shared/mainsite/published_docs/serial_publications/Glossary_eng.pdf; and "Glossary," U.N. High Commissioner for Refugees, Geneva, Switzerland, www.unhcr.org/publ/PUBL/4922d4390.pdf.

lived in Kenya's sprawling Kakuma refugee camp for nearly four years, says aid officials often don't understand how their decisions affect the camp's 50,000 residents every day. "There are people who work for agencies here that don't know what is happening in the camp," he says. "They live in their own compounds and don't really communicate with the refugees to find out what is happening to them."

The United Nations began reforming its humanitarian system in 2005, partly to address concerns about its inability to deliver timely and effective aid to internally displaced people. Jeff Crisp, director of policy and evaluations for UNHCR, says the U.N.'s reforms are having "a solid and positive impact" on the lives of displaced people even though revamping such a large-scale system of delivering aid "clearly is a work in progress."

The rise in refugees and IDPs is the direct result of dozens of small wars between rebels and government soldiers during the last 50 years, particularly in Africa and Asia. Some have dragged on for decades, creating generations of displaced families. For instance, Sudan's 20-year-long civil war displaced 400,000 people, but at least 130,000 remain in neighboring countries, according to the U.N. [11] Colombia's ongoing civil conflict has displaced nearly 10 percent of the country's population. [12]

Even when the wars end, civilians often remain displaced because they fear returning home, their homes have been destroyed or they have become settled elsewhere. In Afghanistan, for example, more than 5 million Afghan refugees have returned home since the United States ousted the Taliban regime seven years ago, but some 3 million remain in neighboring Pakistan and Iran — a large number of whom probably never will go back. [13]

The Afghan refugees represent what experts call a "protracted situation," which is defined as when at least 25,000 people are displaced from their homes for five years or more. (*See sidebar, p. 370.*) More than 30 protracted situations exist around the world, according to Elizabeth Ferris, director of the Brookings-Bern Project on Internal Displacement, run by the Brookings Institution in Washington, D.C., and the University of Bern (Switzerland) School of Law.

As governments, international agencies and specialists in the field seek better ways to protect and aid refugees and internally displaced people, here are some of the questions being debated:

Is the U.N. meeting refugees' needs?

Since its founding in 1951, the UNHCR has been the world's frontline agency for aiding and protecting refugees. Working with other U.N. agencies and nongovernmental agencies — such as CARE and the International Federation of Red Cross and Red Crescent Societies — the Geneva, Switzerland-based agency is spending $1.8 billion this year to provide housing, food, medical care and protection for millions of refugees and displaced

persons in 116 countries. [14] The agency also decides the legal status of refugees in 75 countries that can't, or won't, make those determinations themselves. In 2007, the UNHCR determined the status of 48,745 people. [15]

Both critics and its defenders, however, say the agency often falls short of its official mandate to safeguard "the rights and well-being of refugees." [16] Barbara Harrell-Bond, the founder and former director of the Refugee Studies Center at Oxford University and a harsh critic of the UNHCR, says one of her biggest concerns is how aid programs are funded.

"The funds . . . always come from emergency budgets and are allocated to UNHCR by governments at their discretion," she says. As a result, agency programs are "at the mercy of the whims of international politics."

If world leaders become fixated on a particular crisis that is making headlines in Western countries — such as the situation in Sudan's Darfur region — refugees elsewhere suffer, Harrell-Bond says. In addition, education and job training programs designed to help refugees lead dignified lives once they leave the camps are considered "development" programs, she says, which "come from a completely different budget . . . and never the twain shall meet."

Moreover, local governments rarely receive international aid for hosting refugees and usually are anxious for refugees to go home, she says, so they have little incentive to improve camp conditions. As a consequence, refugees are "just warehoused" in camps for years and years. Furthermore, she adds, the UNHCR and its partner agencies routinely deny refugees' basic rights, including the right to leave the camps. Most host governments want refugees to be contained in camps, and the U.N. complies "by putting them in what amounts to gigantic cages," Harrell-Bond says.

In her 2005 book, *Rights in Exile: Janus Faced Humanitarianism*, Harrell-Bond and a co-author argue that "the rights of refugees cannot be protected in camps and settlements." They harshly criticize the UNHCR for not protecting refugees' rights, based on extensive research into the treatment of Kenyan and Ugandan refugees during the late 1990s — treatment the authors say continues today in many refugee camps.

For instance, refugees usually are not allowed to leave the camps and are not allowed to work. Harrell-Bond says the UNCHR should push governments harder to accept refugees into the local community. "Refugees can contribute to the societies where they have taken refuge and not simply live on handouts from the U.N.," she says, citing examples in Uganda and Zambia where so-called "local integration" has worked.

UNHCR Policy Director Crisp acknowledges the agency sometimes fails to meet refugees' needs but says decisions to "warehouse" refugees are made by the host countries. "In many cases, refugees are admitted to countries on strict condition that they be accommodated in camps and provided with their basic needs by UNHCR and other agencies," he says. UNHCR tries to get governments to improve refugees' situations, "but this is not always possible."

Despite such constraints, Crisp says the UNHCR is trying new approaches, particularly for those trapped in protracted situations. For instance, in 2008 the high commissioner set deadlines for getting people out of five specific protracted situations:

- Afghan refugees in Iran and Pakistan;
- Bosnian and Croatian refugees in Serbia;
- Eritrean refugees in eastern Sudan;
- Burundians in Tanzania; and
- Members of Myanmar's Rohingya minority who fled to Bangladesh.[17]

More broadly, as part of its 2005 reform program, the U.N. established clear guidelines for which U.N. agency should provide services in specific situations.[18] The so-called cluster approach made the UNHCR responsible for managing camps for IDPs displaced by natural disasters and providing emergency shelter and protection for IDPs displaced by conflict.[19]

A 2007 evaluation found the new approach had improved humanitarian responses in Chad, the Democratic Republic of the Congo, Somalia and Uganda.[20] Ramesh Rajasingham, head of the Displacement and Protection Support Section for the U.N.'s humanitarian affairs office, says giving UNHCR a "clear leadership" role in managing displacement camps and emergency shelters has fostered "an improved IDP response."

But some non-U.N. experts say the bureaucratic changes have produced only modest benefits. Implementation has been "half-hearted," especially in protecting IDPs, says Roberta Cohen, a senior fellow at the Brookings Institution and prominent IDP advocate.

IRN/Manoocher Deghati (both)

Camp Life

Tents patched together from scraps of cloth house Afghans living in a camp near Kabul, Afghanistan (top). The government helps Afghans uprooted by decades of war, but many face overcrowded conditions and inadequate housing, food and medical care. Typically, internally displaced persons cannot work for wages in order to preserve jobs for local residents, so some set up their own small businesses inside the camps, such as a Kenyan seamstress at the Eldoret camp in Kenya (bottom).

The UNHCR is not "playing the robust leadership role" she had hoped for in protecting IDPs.

Likewise, Joel Charny, vice president for policy at Refugees International, says the UNHCR's protection of IDPs remains "problematic." Ferris, Cohen's successor at the Brookings-Bern Project on Displacement, recommends a rewards structure that would give agencies and individuals an incentive to better aid and protect displaced persons.

Most Refugees Flee to Neighboring Countries

Contrary to the perception that refugees are flooding into developed countries in Europe and other regions, most find asylum in neighboring countries and remain there. Only between 10 percent and 17 percent leave the countries where they were granted asylum.

Refugees Remaining in or Leaving Their Asylum Regions
(As of December 2007)

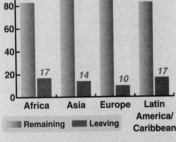

Source: "2007 Global Trends: Refugees, Asylum-seekers, Returnees, Internally Displaced and Stateless Persons," U.N. High Commissioner for Refugees, June 2008

"Agencies need to internalize their work with IDPs and not see it as something separate from their missions or a burden they have to carry," she says.

James Milner, a refugee policy analyst at Carleton University in Ottawa, Ontario, Canada, and former UNHCR consultant, says the agency "does a good job in some places and a bad job in some places." While it has saved millions of lives during civil wars, the agency also ends up "warehousing" refugees for long periods, he says, causing them to abandon hope for better lives and become totally dependent on aid.

Like Harrell-Bond, Milner — who coauthored a 2008 book sympathetic to the agency's successes and failures — traces most of UNHCR's problems to its funding procedures. In effect, he says, industrialized countries that provide the bulk of UNHCR's money "earmark" where they want the money to go.[21]

"The United States, for example, gives funding to emergencies it considers important" but gives less to other situations, Milner says. "When I worked in Cameroon, each October we simply ran out of funding to provide health care for nursing mothers, because that was not a priority for the people in Washington. You can criticize UNHCR for not being more aggressive in some of these situations, but when you recognize the constraints placed on UNHCR, it places the challenges in a broader context."

Should the Refugee Convention be updated?

The 1951 Convention Relating to the Status of Refugees — known as the Refugee Convention — is the basic underpinning of refugee law. Created to protect European refugees during and after World War II, the treaty was amended in 1967 to apply worldwide.

The treaty grants "asylum" to refugees, or groups of them, who can demonstrate a "well-founded fear of being persecuted" because of race, nationality, religion or political beliefs. Those who flee their country because of such a fear are considered refugees. The process of demonstrating that fear and seeking permission to stay in the country of refuge is called seeking asylum. However, in many places — including the United States — asylum seekers may be imprisoned for months or even years while their cases are reviewed. Once asylum is granted, refugees can stay in the host country until it is safe to return home. Refugees who are denied asylum often are deported, usually back to their home countries.

Even with the 1967 amendment, the convention does not apply to the vast majority of people who flee from their homes. For example, IDPs do not have legal protection because they do not cross international borders, nor do those who flee across borders to escape natural disasters.[22] Being covered by the treaty might have little significance for people forced from their homes by violent groups like the Lord's Resistance Army. Even so, some advocates say applying the treaty to IDPs might, in some cases, pressure the governments involved to take better care of their citizens.

The treaty has critics across the ideological spectrum. Some refugee advocates, including Harrell-Bond, complain that it lacks universal standards for granting asylum, so Western countries, in particular, "are free to turn away asylum-seekers on no basis whatsoever."

Some Western officials say the treaty is being misused by "economic migrants" — would-be immigrants from poor countries simply seeking a better life — who claim to be refugees but do not qualify for asylum on the basis of a fear of persecution.

The treaty "is no longer working as its framers intended," then British Home Secretary Jack Straw said in 2001, citing the large increase in displaced people worldwide. "Too much effort and resources are being expended on dealing with unfounded claims for asylum, and not enough on helping those in need of protection."[23] He called for "radical thinking" on a better way to determine who is a refugee and who is not.

Despite such concerns, many experts say the convention will not be amended or updated any time soon. The U.N. treaty-making process is cumbersome and takes years to complete. Moreover, global interest in new treaties has dwindled in recent years, and even IDP advocates aren't willing to risk having the treaty watered down instead of strengthened.

Carleton University's Milner notes the current treaty was negotiated shortly after World War II, "when notions of human justice were quite powerful because of what happened during the war, particularly in Nazi Germany." Nearly six decades later, Western countries — the desired destination for many refugees — are increasingly reluctant to open their borders. "If we reopened the Refugee Convention, we likely would see a race to the lowest common denominator — protecting borders — rather than refugees," Milner says. "That's a risk I'm not willing to take."

Khalid Koser, an analyst specializing in refugee affairs at the Geneva Center for Security Policy, agrees. "At least

Most Funds Go to Africa, Come From U.S.

More than one-third of U.N. refugee aid in 2009 will go to programs in Africa, more than any other region. In 2007, the United States contributed nearly one-third of the funds for the Office of the U.N. High Commissioner for Refugees (UNHCR) — four times more than No. 2-donor Japan.

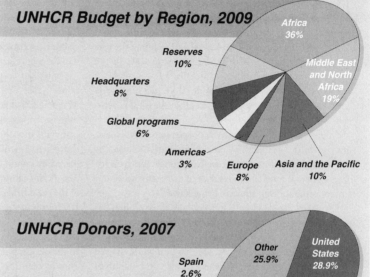

UNHCR Budget by Region, 2009

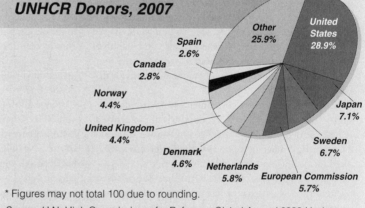

UNHCR Donors, 2007

* Figures may not total 100 due to rounding.

Source: U.N. High Commissioner for Refugees Global Appeal 2009 Update

the current convention has 150-odd signatories, most of whom abide by it," Koser says.

The UNHCR has expressed similar concerns. In a recent paper exploring whether those fleeing natural disasters should be given legal status under the treaty, the agency warned that any attempt to modify the convention could lower refugee-protection standards "and even undermine the international refugee-protection regime altogether."[24]

Meanwhile, Europe is engaged in a spirited debate over implementation of the treaty; since 2001 the European

Chaos in Somalia Puts Nation at Risk

Humanitarian aid feeds nearly half the population.

Mohamed Abdi, his wife, and five children fled the never-ending violence in Somalia's capital city of Mogadishu last October, finding safety — but not much more — in the breakaway region of Somaliland to the north. The trip took nine days, and all along the way they feared being attacked by the opposing sides in the most recent round of conflict in Somalia.

Once they reached Somaliland, Abdi and his family found very little in the way of services, but the local government welcomed them as refugees. "We don't have much, and we depend on the kindness of these people; some days we eat, some we don't," he told the United Nations' IRIN news service in October. "But at least we have peace and security. That is what we want and the chance to make a living for our families without being afraid of being killed."[1]

Displaced people like Abdi never have it easy, often living in crude shelters and on starvation rations. But the situation is especially grave in Somalia — the only country in the world that for nearly two decades has been without even a functioning government — where a fatal combination of internal conflict and natural disaster has generated hundreds of thousands of refugees, migrants and internally displaced people (IDPs).

Ever since the last real government — a harsh dictatorship — was overthrown in 1991, hundreds of thousands of refugees settled in Kenya and other neighboring countries. Thousands of others have crossed the dangerous Gulf of Aden to equally impoverished Yemen.

Meanwhile, an estimated 1.3 million Somalis have become IDPs — displaced but living within their own country.[2] Most had fled Mogadishu, decimated by years of fighting among warlords, rebel groups, failed temporary governments and the Ethiopian army, which invaded in late 2006 and withdrew in January.

But IDPs escaping violence are not the only Somalis suffering. The U.N. Food and Agriculture Organization

reported in October 2008 that 3.2 million people — 43 percent of the population — regularly need humanitarian assistance to survive.[3] While armed conflict has created most of the dislocations among Somalis, frequent droughts and floods have also caused recurrent famines that sent rural families fleeing to urban areas, often to be displaced by fighting.

Waves of conflict and displacement have swept over Somalia ever since the military dictatorship of Major General Mohamed Siad Barre was pushed from power in 1991. The most severe recent displacement occurred in August 2007, just eight months after Ethiopia invaded Somalia to oust a short-lived Islamist regime. Some 400,000 people were displaced by fighting in Mogadishu; most of them ended up in one of 200 camps that cropped up along a nine-mile stretch of the main road outside of the capital — "the most congested IDP nexus in the world," according to a refugee official.[4]

The U.N. High Commissioner for Refugees (UNHCR) and other aid groups provide limited food and medical aid to the camps, but little in the way of shelter. Patrick Duplat, an advocate for Refugees International who visited the camps twice in 2008, describes them as "mostly a sprawl of makeshift shelters — twigs and cloth, and sometimes plastic sheeting, whatever people are able to find."

Since Ethiopia withdrew its army in January, some 40,000 IDPs have returned to several Mogadishu neighborhoods, apparently with the intention of staying, according to the UNHCR.[5] Even so, continued fighting in the city has displaced an unknown number of others. The UNHCR said on Feb. 27 it is still discouraging IDPs from returning to what would be "ruined homes and livelihoods."[6]

In recent years nearly 500,000 people have fled Somalia to neighboring countries, but they have encountered daunting hazards along the way, including bandits, security forces demanding bribes and even possible death on the high seas.[7] Those who avoid violence and persecution may be eligible for refugee status and entitled to return home someday;

Union (EU) has been developing a common system for granting asylum among its 27 member countries. The European Pact on Immigration and Asylum, adopted by EU leaders on Oct. 16, 2008, promises that EU countries will speed up asylum determinations, eliminating delays that often stretch into months or years.[25] Refugee rights

advocates, however, worry the EU is trying to close its doors to legitimate refugees, not just economic migrants who are not entitled to asylum under the treaty.

At Human Rights Watch, refugee policy Director Bill Frelick says the new European pact also does little to relieve unequal burden-sharing. Most migrants and

others probably would be considered migrants because they are searching for economic opportunities overseas.

Thousands of Somalis have risked crossing the Gulf of Aden or the Red Sea by boat to reach Yemen. On Feb. 28, 45 Somalis drowned when their boat capsized as they were crossing the gulf. Those who arrive safely generally are given *de jure* refugee status, even though many might be considered migrants because they never plan to return to their homes. About 82,000 Somalis were registered as refugees in Yemen in late 2008, but the UNHCR said the total could be closer to 150,000.[8]

Most Somali refugees, however, have fled into neighboring Kenya, even though it closed its borders to Somalis in 2007. According to the U.N., some 250,000 Somali refugees are in Kenya, including at least 45,000 who entered in 2008.[9]

At the border, would-be refugees often set out on foot to the U.N.'s official transit camps at Dadaab, 50 miles inside Kenya, frequently traveling at night to evade Kenyan police. As of late January the camps held 244,127 people — nearly triple their capacity. "Trying to squeeze 200,000-plus people into an area intended for 90,000 is inviting trouble," said Craig Johnstone, deputy U.N. high commissioner for refugees, after visiting on Feb. 5.[10] The UNHCR has been trying to raise $92 million from international donors to build two new camps for 60,000 more refugees.[11]

Human Rights Watch researcher Gerry Simpson, who visited the camps in late 2008, said many people told him they had tried to register as refugees but had given up because of the lack of space in the camps. "After risking their lives to flee appalling violence in Somalia and make it to the relative safety of Kenya, they end up with nothing: no food, no shelter, and incredibly difficult access to water and health care," Simpson said.[12]

An estimated 1.3 million people have been uprooted by the ongoing conflict in Somalia but are still living inside the country. Persistent violence, drought and flooding have created one of the world's longest ongoing humanitarian crises.

AFP/Getty Images/Radu Sigheti

[4] "Somalia: To Move Beyond the Failed State," International Crisis Group, Dec. 23, 2008, pp. 12, 18.

[5] "Thousands of Somalis Return to Mogadishu Despite Renewed Fighting," U.N. High Commissioner for Refugees, Feb. 27, 2009, www.unhcr.org/news/ NEWS/49a7d8bb2.html.

[6] *Ibid.*

[7] "Somalia Complex Emergency: Situation Report," Jan. 15, 2009, U.S. Agency for International Development, www.usaid.gov/our_work/humanitarian_assistance/disaster_assistance/countries/somalia/template/fs_sr/fy2009/somalia _ce_sr04_01-15-2009.pdf.

[8] "2009 Global Update for Yemen," U.N. High Commissioner for Refugees, p. 1, www.unhcr.org/publ/PUBL/4922d4240.pdf.

[9] "Displaced Populations Report," *op. cit.*, p. 6.

[10] "Camp resources stretched by influx of Somali refugees," IRIN news service, Feb. 6, 2009, www.irinnews.org/Report.aspx?ReportId=82792.

[11] "Somali refugees suffer as Dadaab camp populations swell to 230,000," UNHCR, www.unhcr.org/news/NEWS/4950ef401.html.

[12] "Kenya: Protect Somali Refugees. Government and Donors Should Urgently Address Refugee Crisis," Human Rights Watch, Nov. 13, 2008, www.hrw.org/en/news/2008/11/13/kenya-protect-somali-refugees.

[1] "Fleeing from the frying pan into the fire," IRIN news service, Oct. 29, 2008, www.irinnews.org/Report.aspx?ReportId=81164.

[2] "Displaced Populations Report," U.N. Office for the Coordination of Humanitarian Affairs, Regional Office for Central and East Africa, July-December 2008, p. 5.

[3] "Poor rains intensify human suffering and deprivation — report," IRIN news service, Oct. 17, 2008, www.irinnews.org/Report.aspx?ReportId=80971.

refugees from Africa and the Middle East enter Europe through the poorest countries in southeastern Europe, which have been rejecting refugees at very high rates. For instance, since 2004 Greece has granted asylum to fewer than 1 percent of the refugees from Iraq, Afghanistan and other countries, according to the European Council on Refugees and Exiles, a coalition of 69 nongovernmental organizations.[26] By contrast, some other European countries, particularly in Scandinavia, accept upwards of 90 percent of asylum-seekers, Frelick notes.

"There has been an utter failure to share the refugee burdens," Frelick says. "The richer countries have done

More than 250,000 Sri Lankans have been forced from their homes, often repeatedly, in the latest — and possibly final — round of the 26-year war between government forces and separatist Tamil Tiger guerrillas. Above, internally displaced Tamil civilians wait to enter a government shelter near Colombo.

an effective job of deflecting the burden off onto the poor countries, which are responding by turning people away, even those who are legitimate refugees."

Should the United States admit more Iraqi refugees?

Fearing that some could be terrorists, the United States has been slow to accept Iraqis who have fled to neighboring countries — notably Syria and Jordan — since the U.S. invasion in 2003.

Through the middle of 2008, the Bush administration accepted only about 10,000 Iraqi refugees out of the 1-2 million who have fled, according to Refugees International and other nongovernmental organizations.[27] But under pressure from Congress and advocacy groups, it stepped up Iraqi admissions last year and admitted more than 13,800 Iraqis as permanent residents — slightly more than the administration's 12,000 annual goal for fiscal 2008, which ended on Oct. 1. The administration's 2009 goal is 17,000 Iraqi admissions.[28]

Several major refugee and human-rights groups want the U.S. quota raised to 105,000 Iraqis in 2009. Among the Iraqi refugees in Syria and Jordan are thousands who worked directly with the U.S. military and other government agencies, American contractors and the news media. Some served as translators or even intelligence

operatives, while others filled jobs such as drivers and cooks.

"Their stay in neighboring states remains extremely precarious, and many live in fear of being forcibly returned to Iraq, where they face death threats and further persecution," said a joint statement by Refugees International and a dozen other organizations on July 31, 2008. Helping these Iraqis resettle in the United States "will demonstrate America's dedication to protecting the most vulnerable and our commitment to peace and security in the region."[29]

The U.S. Department of Homeland Security said in September it was "committed to streamlining the process for admitting Iraqi refugees to the U.S. while ensuring the highest level of security."[30] However, the Obama administration has not announced plans for a dramatic increase in admissions. A State Department spokesman said in early February a decision was pending.

A report released in January by the Center for American Progress, a liberal think tank in Washington, D.C., said 30,000 to 100,000 Iraqis have been "affiliated" with the United States in one way or another during the war, and many would be "in imminent danger" of assassination if they returned home.[31]

The group advocates bringing up to 25,000 of those Iraqis and their families to the United States over the next five years. Natalie Ondiak, lead author of the proposal, says the United States "has a moral obligation to the Iraqis who have worked for the government, were loyal to us and now fear for their lives because of the stigma of having been associated with the United States."

However, Ann Corcoran — a Maryland blogger who runs the Refugee Resettlement Watch blog — is a vocal critic of such proposals. She cites cases in which church groups and other agencies bring refugees to the United States but fail to help them adjust to their new lives.

"These organizations are not taking very good care of the refugees who are already here, and they say they don't have the resources to do the job," she says. "So, if we are talking about another 25,000 or 100,000 refugees, where do they think these people will be cared for? Who is going to make sure they have housing and jobs and education for their children? It's just insane."[32]

A better alternative, she says "is to keep them in the region, to keep them comfortable and proceeding with their lives in the Middle East until the situation in Iraq is safe enough for them to return."

Congress in 2006 created a program to speed up admissions for up to 500 Iraqi and Afghan translators per year. In 2008 Congress added another program allowing up to 5,000 Iraqis who worked in various capacities for the U.S. government or contractors to enter the United States in each of the five fiscal years, beginning in 2008. However, Ondiak says only about 600 translators gained admission in 2008.

BACKGROUND

Refugee Rights and Needs

Although the forced displacement of people from their homes is as old as human history, the idea that society has a moral obligation to come to their aid is relatively new.

After World War I, the newly formed League of Nations created the post of High Commissioner for Refugees but gave the office little authority and few resources. The league (the forerunner of the U.N.) also adopted two treaties in the 1930s offering limited legal protection to refugees, but only a handful of countries ratified them.[33]

The displacement of millions of people during World War II finally brought significant action on refugees. As the war was winding down, the United States and its allies created the United Nations Relief and Rehabilitation Agency, which gave emergency aid to 7 million displaced people. After the war, a successor organization, the International Refugee Organization, helped some 1 million dislocated Europeans find new homes.[34]

The modern era of international aid to refugees began in 1950-51, when the United Nations created the office of the U.N. High Commissioner for Refugees and held a special conference in Geneva to draft the treaty that became known as the Refugee Convention. Both the UNHCR and the treaty were aimed at aiding European war refugees or those who fled Eastern Europe after the Soviet Union imposed communist rule across the region. In fact, the treaty applied only to those who had become refugees before Jan. 1, 1951, and the text made clear the drafters had Europeans in mind. Moreover, the U.N. General Assembly gave the UNHCR only a three-year mandate, assuming the refugee problem would be quickly solved.[35]

In 1949, before the UNHCR started work, the U.N. Relief and Works Agency for Palestine Refugees in the Near East (known as UNRWA) was created to assist the 700,000 Palestinians who fled or were driven from their homes in what is now Israel during the 1948 Arab-Israeli war.[36] The UNRWA also was considered short-lived. But nearly 60 years later the ultimate status of the Palestinians remains unresolved, and the UNRWA is still providing food, medical care and other aid to a Palestinian population that has grown to 4.6 million. About 1.4 million Palestinians live in UNRWA camps in Jordan, Lebanon, Syria, the West Bank and Gaza Strip; the rest live on their own.[37]

Conflicts continued across the globe after World War II, some of them widely seen as proxy wars among governments and rebel groups backed by the two Cold War superpowers, the Soviet Union and the United States. In each case, dislocated civilians crossed international borders and created a new generation of refugees.

The U.N. General Assembly officially recognized the new refugee trend in 1967, adopting an amendment, or protocol, to the refugee convention. The Protocol Relating to the Status of Refugees dropped the pre-1951 limitation, giving legal protection to refugees worldwide, not just in Europe.[38] The convention and its protocol are now among the most widely adopted U.N. treaties; each has been ratified by 144 countries.[39]

The collapse of the Soviet Union in 1991 brought new hope for peace. But bloody sectarian conflicts in the Balkans and Africa's Great Lakes region shattered such dreams. Some conflicts dislocated enormous populations, but many people, for one reason or another, stayed in their own countries, where as IDPs they were not covered by the international refugee treaties.

In the 1990s international agencies and human-rights advocates began demanding aid and legal protections for these large groups. In 1992, U.N. Secretary-General Boutros Boutros-Ghali appointed Francis Deng, a former Sudanese diplomat, as the U.N.'s first special representative on internally displaced people.

Deng, who held the post until 2004, was largely responsible for drafting the Guiding Principles on Internal Displacement.[40] Although the document has never been put into international law, U.N. agencies and a dozen countries have incorporated its principles into their laws and policies. (*See box, p. 378.*)

CHRONOLOGY

1940s-1950s *Newly created United Nations (U.N.) aids refugees after World War II ends.*

1949 U.N. Relief and Works Agency is established to aid Palestinians pushed from their homes during the 1949 Arab-Israeli war.

1950 Office of U.N. High Commissioner for Refugees (UNHCR) is created.

1951 Special U.N. conference adopts Convention Relating to the Status of Refugees (the Refugee Convention) to protect those who fled their countries before Jan. 1, 1951, to escape persecution due to "race, religion, nationality or membership of a particular social group." Generally viewed as applying only to Europeans, the treaty goes into effect in 1954.

1960s-1980s *Cold War conflicts and upheavals create waves of new refugees.*

1967 U.N expands Refugee Convention to cover all refugees fleeing persecution as described in the treaty, not just Europeans who left their home countries before 1951.

1969 Organization of African Unity broadly defines a refugee in Africa as anyone who flees his country because of "external aggression, occupation, foreign domination or events seriously disturbing public order in either part or the whole of his country of origin."

1984 The Colloquium on the International Protection of Refugees in Central America, Mexico and Panama adopts the Cartagena Declaration, defining refugees as anyone fleeing their country because their "lives, safety or freedom" are threatened by "generalized violence, foreign aggression, internal conflicts, massive violation of human rights or other circumstances." Although not official policy, many regional governments adopt the declaration.

1990s-2000s *New wave of civil conflicts forces policy makers to pay more attention to the needs of people displaced within their own borders.*

1992-1995 Civil conflicts in the former Yugoslavia displace several hundred thousand people.

1994 Genocidal rampage in Rwanda kills 800,000 Hutus and Tutsis; hundreds of thousands of others flee their homes, many into neighboring countries.

1997 Government-backed rebels oust longtime dictator Mobutu Sese Seko of Zaire (later the Democratic Republic of the Congo), triggering years of civil war in Africa's Great Lakes region; an estimated 5 million people die, and thousands are displaced during fighting that continues today.

1998 The Guiding Principles on Internal Displacement establish rules for aiding and protecting internally displaced persons (IDPs); the guidelines eventually are incorporated into U.N procedures but are not legally binding.

2002 About 2 million Afghan refugees return home (mostly from Pakistan and Iran) after a U.S.-led invasion topples the Taliban government. Some 6 million had fled during three decades of war — the largest number of refugees generated by any conflict since World War II.

2004 In a landmark decision, Colombia's Constitutional Court orders the government to increase aid to about 2 million people displaced by conflict.

2005 U.N. adopts "responsibility to protect" doctrine, which holds every government responsible for protecting the rights of its citizens and says the international community has a responsibility to intervene if a government abuses its own citizens. . . . U.N. gives UNHCR more responsibility for helping IDPs.

2008 U.N. launches a year-long publicity campaign to focus international attention on the needs of IDPs. . . . UNHCR starts a campaign to help end long-term displacements of those forced from their homes in Afghanistan, the Balkans, Burundi, Eritrea and Myanmar.

2009 African Union is scheduled in April to adopt a treaty recognizing the rights of internally displaced people, based on the 1998 Guiding Principles.

However, says refugee specialist Koser at the Geneva Center for Security Policy, "there is very little political will to formalize [the principles] into a binding convention, and few states would ratify it."

Rising Displacements

U.N. officials and policy experts count more than four dozen countries — most in Africa and Asia — with significant populations displaced by civil wars or other violence. When the consequences of natural disasters are considered, however, the displacement problem becomes nearly universal. Thousands of Gulf Coast residents in the United States remain displaced by Hurricane Katrina in 2006, and millions in China's Sichuan Province are homeless nearly a year after a major earthquake.

Colombia has one of the world's largest IDP populations, and hundreds of thousands of people are still displaced in Chechnya and Georgia in the Caucuses and in Bosnia, Croatia, Kosovo and Serbia as a result of the Balkan wars. Thousands more have been displaced by ongoing conflict and instability in Somalia. (*See sidebar, p. 364.*)

Here are some of the displacements that are high on the international agenda:

Afghanistan — At least 6 million Afghans fled — mostly to Pakistan and Iran — between the Soviet Union's December 1979 invasion and the U.S. ousting of the Taliban government in late 2001. During periods of relative calm in the 1980s and '90s, hundreds of thousands of Afghan refugees returned home, but many fled again when fighting resumed.[41]

Shortly after a new Western-backed government took office in Kabul at the end of 2001, refugees began returning home in large numbers. Between 2002 and late 2008, about 5.6 million refugees returned, of whom nearly 4.4 million received UNHCR aid (the rest returned on their own).[42] Since 2007, thousands of refugees have returned because Pakistan closed some refugee camps, and Iran deported thousands of mostly undocumented Afghan men seeking work.[43]

By late 2008, the UNHCR estimated that about 2 million Afghan refugees were still in Pakistan and nearly 1 million in Iran.[44] Worried about its inability to provide housing, jobs and other services for returning refugees, the Afghan government in 2008 began discouraging large-scale returns. "We don't have the means to provide an encouraging environment for refugees to repatriate," Shir Mohammad Etibari, minister of refugees and returnees, said in September. The U.N. and other international agencies "only make promises but do little."[45]

Another 235,000 Afghans are displaced but still in Afghanistan. Some were forced to return to Afghanistan against their will, only to find that they had no place to live and could find no jobs. Among the most vulnerable are several thousand returnees who were forced out of Pakistan and now live at a camp in the Chemtala desert, about 15 miles west of Jalalabad. Last winter they struggled to survive in mud huts and tents provided by the UNHCR and the Norwegian Refugee Council. "I wish we hadn't left Pakistan," said elderly returnee Golam Shah. "Life was much better there."[46]

A similar complaint came from 18-year-old Wali, who grew up in Pakistan's Jalozai refugee village. Forced out last May, he now lives in a tent in Balkh Province in northern Afghanistan. "I didn't expect to face such problems or to end up in such a place," he said. "There is nothing here — no shelter, not enough water, no trees for firewood, no electricity and no work."[47]

Colombia — A long-running rebel insurgency and the government's aggressive, U.S.-backed war against narcotics cartels have created what the U.N. calls the worst humanitarian crisis in the Western Hemisphere. Up to half a million Colombians have fled to neighboring countries, and thousands have emigrated to the United States. At least 2.8 million mostly rural people are internally displaced in the nation of 45 million.[48]

Since the 1960s the military has brutally suppressed two leftist guerrilla groups claiming to be fighting for land reform and other social causes — the Revolutionary Armed Forces of Colombia (FARC) and the National Liberation Army (ELN). Right-wing paramilitary armies formed by major landowners and elements of the military aided the anti-insurgency campaign.

Both the guerrillas and paramilitaries eventually became deeply involved in the drug trade, turning an ideological war over land reform and other social issues into a battle for control of illegal cocaine production. The government's war against cocaine — most of which is consumed in the United States — has been funded largely by Washington.

Colombia is now the hemisphere's major source of refugees, most of whom have fled to Ecuador and Venezuela; others sought refuge in Brazil, Panama and

Millions Remain in Exile for Decades

"Whole generations of kids grow up in refugee camps."

Miljo and Milica Miljic grabbed their two children and fled Tuzla, Bosnia, in 1992, at the beginning of a nearly four-year civil war that tore their country apart. "We didn't take anything with us because we didn't have time," Miljo told a representative of the U.N. High Commissioner on Refugees (UNHCR) this past January. "We had to run for our lives. The only thing that comes to mind in such a situation is to save your children and your own life. You don't think about the photographs, about personal documents, clothes, whatever."[1]

The Miljacs are among nearly 97,000 refugees from Bosnia and Croatia who have not returned to their homes, even though the war ended in late 1995. They are still in Serbia, where the refugee population has slowly dwindled down from more than 500,000 in 1996.[2]

The words "refugees" and "displaced persons" conjure up images of short-term emergencies: people fleeing their homes temporarily because of wars, hurricanes or earthquakes, only to return home a few weeks, or at most a few months, later. While many do return home once a crisis has passed, most refugees and internally displaced persons (IDPs) remain displaced long after the emergency is over.

In fact, refugees fleeing conflict end up staying away from their homes an average of 18 years, and many IDPs are displaced for comparable periods. James Milner, a refugee expert at Carleton University in Ottawa, Canada, says some situations last even longer: The Palestinians who fled Israel during the 1948-49 Arab-Israeli war have been in exile ever since.

In recent years experts have begun focusing on "protracted situations" involving refugees and IDPs displaced for at least five years, and numerous conferences have been held to discuss the problem of long-term displacements. U.N. High Commissioner Antonio Guterres said more than 30 situations around the world involve a total of about 6 million refugees who have been living in long-term exile.

"Many are effectively trapped in the camps and communities where they are accommodated," Guterres said. "Their home countries are caught in endless conflict or afflicted by political stalemate or human-rights violations, and most are not allowed to hold jobs, work the land where they live or integrate into the local communities."[3]

Most of the long-term displaced are children and youth, says Elizabeth Ferris, director of the Brookings-Bern Project on Internal Displacement. "You have whole generations of kids who grow up and live in refugee camps, where typically you have a breakdown of normal social institutions," she says.

From 11 million to 17 million people have been displaced for at least five years but are still living inside their own countries, Ferris says. "Unfortunately, the world has paid very little attention to these situations, which are allowed to fester for years and years," she says.

Aside from the Palestinians, perhaps the best-known protracted refugee situation involves the estimated 6 million people who have fled their homes during three decades of warfare in Afghanistan, which began with the Soviet Union's invasion in 1979. Most went to neighboring Iran or Pakistan, where they settled in formal camps or moved into cities. Millions of Afghan refugees returned home after the U.S. invasion in 2001, but nearly 3 million are still refugees.[4]

Many scholars and aid officials worry that another long-term refugee situation is developing among the 2 million or more Iraqis who have fled their homeland. Although the Baghdad government has encouraged some to return, the U.N. and private aid groups say it is still too unsafe, especially for Sunni Muslims or members of other minority groups.[5]

Other protracted refugee situations prioritized by the UNHCR include:

- **Myanmar/Bangladesh.** Some 200,000 Rohingya, a Muslim ethnic group in North Rakhine state in Myanmar, fled to neighboring Bangladesh in 1991 to escape persecution by the military junta in Myanmar. Thousands have since returned to Myanmar, but the majority remain in Bangladesh and are classified by the U.N. as "stateless" persons because Myanmar no longer considers them as citizens.[6]
- **Eritrea/Sudan.** Some 90,000 Eritreans are long-term refugees in eastern Sudan, many since the late 1960s when Eritrean rebels launched a 30-year-long war against Ethiopia. (Eritrea gained its independence in 1993, but the two countries fought another bloody war from 1998 until 2000.) Additional Eritrean refugees continue to arrive in Sudan, joined by refugees from Ethiopia and Somalia. Most live in camps and lack any rights or protections but have increasingly begun to move into Khartoum and other Sudanese cities, over the government's objection.[7]
- **The Balkans.** Like the Miljics, hundreds of thousands of people dislocated by war in the former Yugoslavia during the 1990s have not returned to their home regions. Some 200,000 refugees, mostly ethnic Serbs, became naturalized citizens in Serbia rather than return to Bosnia or Croatia, where Serbs are in the minority.[8]
- **Burundi/Tanzania.** Violent civil conflict in Burundi in 1972 forced thousands to flee into neighboring Tanzania, where the government created three settlements in central and western Tanzania and provided land and other services for them. In 2007, about 218,000 refugees were still in the settlements. Under an agreement that many experts consider historic,

Burundi and Tanzania decided in 2008 to resolve the status of these so-called "old settlement" refugees from 1972. Tanzania agreed to grant citizenship to, and fully integrate into local communities, some 176,000 of the remaining refugees. Those wanting to return to Burundi were to be allowed to do so by September 2009.[9]

Protracted IDP Situations

Globally, about half of the estimated 26 million IDPs displaced by violence are stuck in protracted situations, according to Neill Wright, the UNHCR's senior coordinator for IDPs. And some who were forced from their homes by natural disasters also remain displaced after five years.

Both types of protracted situations exist in Kenya, where about 350,000 people have been displaced long-term by conflict, unresolved land disputes and natural disasters.[10] Post-election violence displaced another 500,000 Kenyans in late 2007 and early 2008, but about half of those had returned home by late 2008.[11]

Ferris, of the Brookings-Bern project, says at least three-dozen countries have long-term displacement situations, and people are still being displaced in about a dozen others, such as Colombia, the Democratic Republic of the Congo and Somalia. In most other countries, the fighting has ended, but thousands remain displaced because peace agreements were never negotiated or the IDPs there are afraid, or unwilling, to return to their homes for other reasons.

Experts say no single solution will solve the protracted-displacement problem. Even negotiating peace agreements does not guarantee that displaced people can or will return home.

But policy makers have identified several essential elements that would help create "durable solutions" for protracted situations. One element, they say, is recognizing that forcing or encouraging people to return to their original homes may not always be the best solution, particularly when people have been displaced for many years, and they no longer have reasons for returning home.

An alternative to repatriation is "local integration" — allowing displaced people to become part of the local communities where they have taken refuge. This route is often politically difficult because local communities usually don't want to absorb large numbers of outsiders. Milner says he hopes Tanzania's willingness to accept Burundians displaced for nearly four decades as citizens will become a model for other countries.

"This creates a significant strategic opportunity for the international community to demonstrate that local integration can work," he says. "Now, the next step is for the donor community to meet its responsibilities to help countries, like Tanzania, that might be willing to resolve these situations."

The UNHCR also acknowledged in November 2008 that its policy of providing only short-term humanitarian aid to refugees in camps had failed to help them develop personal independence and job skills that would allow them to live on their own. Too often, a UNHCR report said, "refugees were left to live in camps indefinitely, often with restrictions placed on their rights, as well as their ability to support themselves by means of agriculture, trade or employment."[12]

AFP/Getty Images/Mohammed Abed

The U.N. Relief and Works Agency, which for 60 years has aided Palestinian refugees, was stretched thin during prolonged Israeli military strikes earlier this year. More than 1,000 Palestinians were killed and many homes were destroyed, such as this woman's house in the Jabalia refugee camp in northern Gaza.

Under the U.N.'s "humanitarian reform" program adopted in late 2005, the agency is changing its approach, says Jeff Crisp, director of UNHCR's policy and evaluation service.

[1] "The continuing struggle of Europe's forgotten refugees," U.N. High Commissioner for Refugees, Jan. 12, 2009, www.unhcr.org/news/ NEWS/496b6ad12.html..

[2] *Ibid.*

[3] "Protracted Refugee Situations: High Commissioner's Initiative," U.N. High Commissioner for Refugees, December 2008, p. 2, www.unhcr.org/ protect/ PROTECTION/4937de6f2.pdf.

[4] "Protracted Refugee Situations: Revisiting The Problem," U.N. High Commissioner for Refugees, June 2, 2008, pp. 5-6, www.unhcr.org/excom/ EXCOM/ 484514c12.pdf.

[5] "NGOs warn against encouraging large-scale refugee returns," IRIN news service, Nov. 3, 2008, www.irinnews.org/Report.aspx?ReportId=81258.

[6] "Protracted Refugee Situations: The High Commissioner's Initiative," *op. cit.*, pp. 9-11.

[7] *Ibid.*, p. 14.

[8] *Ibid.*, p. 32.

[9] *Ibid.*, pp. 25-29.

[10] "Frequently Asked Questions on IDPs," U.N. Office for the Coordination of Humanitarian Affairs, Dec. 4, 2008, p. 4.

[11] *Ibid.*, p. 2.

[12] "Protracted Refugee Situations: A discussion paper prepared for the High Commissioner's Dialogue on Protection Challenges," Nov. 20, 2008, p. 13, www.unhcr.org/protect/PROTECTION/492ad3782.pdf.

AFP/Getty Images/Alejandra Vega

Colombia's long-running rebel insurgency and the government's aggressive, U.S.-backed war against narcotics cartels have created the worst humanitarian crisis in the Western Hemisphere, according to the U.N. This family living in a tent in a Bogotá park is among at least 2.8 million displaced Colombians.

Costa Rica.[49] About 460,000 Colombians are in "refugee-like situations" — they've fled Colombia but are not officially considered refugees and receive little if any official aid.[50] The flow of refugees has worsened Colombia's relations with left-leaning Ecuador and Venezuela.

Colombia estimates it has 2.8 million registered IDPs — among the world's highest for an individual country.[51] But nongovernmental agencies say the real number is much higher. The Catholic Church-affiliated Consultancy for Human Rights and Displacement puts the number at more than 4.3 million.[52] Many displaced people do not register for fear of retaliation or being forced to return to unsafe areas. The displacement rate has escalated in recent years, according to both the government and private agencies: About 300,000 people were displaced in 2007, but 270,000 were displaced in just the first six months of 2008.[53]

Colombia's IDPs have received serious attention since the country's Constitutional Court in 2004 ordered the government to provide aid — one of the few instances where an activist court has significantly helped IDPs.

Andrea Lari, a senior advocate at Refugees International, says the government helps IDPs survive on a daily basis but does virtually nothing to enable them to escape from urban shantytowns. The government provides "too much social welfare and not enough . . . job training or education beyond primary schools — the help needed to sustain

themselves where they now live," he says. Going home "is not a serious option" for most because they have lost their land and are afraid to return.

Democratic Republic of the Congo — Hundreds of thousands of civilians continue to suffer from fighting in the eastern provinces of Africa's second-largest country — a war that officially ended more than five years ago. At least 400,000 Congolese were displaced in 2008 and early this year by continuing violence, bringing the total displaced to about 1.25 million.[54]

Two major wars — involving five other African countries at one point — raged in Congo from 1997 until peace agreements hammered out in 2002-03 ended most of the fighting and led to elections in 2006. More than 5 million people may have died during the wars — the largest toll by far of any post-World War II conflict, according to the International Rescue Committee.[55]

Lingering conflicts still plague several areas, including North Kivu Province on the borders with Rwanda and Uganda. There, remnants of the Hutu extremist forces responsible for Rwanda's genocide in 1994 have battled a rebel force claiming to support the Congolese Tutsis, members of the same ethnic group targeted by the Hutus in the Rwandan genocide. Until recently, the Congolese army had not curbed either faction.

In January, however, the Congolese and Rwandan armies launched an unusual joint military operation targeting both the Hutu and Tutsi forces in North Kivu. And in a potential step toward peace, the Rwandan army on Jan. 22 arrested the self-styled Tutsi general Laurent Nkunda, whose rebels had wreaked havoc in the region.[56] The arrest — coming on the heels of a related international campaign against the Lord's Resistance Army — offered the first tangible hope in many years that the region's troubles might some day come to an end.[57]

Iraq — The 1991 Persian Gulf War and sectarian violence following the 2003 U.S. invasion of Iraq have swelled the ranks of displaced Iraqis to between 3 million and 5 million — out of a total population of around 28 million. Most have remained in the country but fled their home regions, usually to escape sectarian violence.[58]

Many of the Iraqi IDPs live with friends or relatives and receive government food rations. For those who cannot get rations, the World Food Program on Jan. 3 announced a one-year program to aid about 750,000 Iraqis inside Iraq and 360,000 in Syria.[59]

Online Newspaper Fights for Refugees in Kenya

'We need to be able to help ourselves.'

Problems with the water supply, inadequate health inspections of food suppliers, indifferent officials. Such issues would be the meat-and-potatoes of any local newspaper. But who draws attention to such concerns in a refugee camp as big as a mid-size city?

Most refugee camps have community organizations that present residents' concerns to camp officials, but they rarely receive wide attention locally. Since last December, however, the problems faced by the 50,000 refugees at the Kakuma camp in northwest Kenya have been exposed not only to local resident but to people around the world via the camp's Internet newspaper, *Kanere* (KAkuma NEws REflector).

The paper (http://kakuma.wordpress.com) is run by staff of volunteer journalists aided by Bethany Ojalehto, a 2008 Cornell University graduate who is studying the rights of refugees at the camp on a Fulbright research scholarship. She says several refugees interested in starting a newspaper approached her for help when she arrived at the camp last October, and she agreed because their interests and her research "blended seamlessly and have now been channeled into this project."

So far *Kanere* is published only in English, which is a common language for many of the camp's residents, who can read it at computer stations in several locations. The paper's editors say they hope to expand into other languages once they get more help.

Twenty-four-year-old Qabaata, one of the paper's editors, says he fled Ethiopia in 2003 after being targeted by government security forces for writing an article supporting a student strike. A journalism student at the time, he went with other students to Kakuma after being arrested and released by authorities in Addis Ababa, Ethiopia's capital. He is seeking asylum status from the UNHCR because he says he cannot return to Ethiopia. "It is not safe for me there," he says. He hopes to win a scholarship to finish his journalism studies but has no immediate prospects for attaining that goal.

Kakuma has one of the most diverse camp populations in Africa. Opened in 1992 to aid refugees from the long civil war in southern Sudan, Kakuma now houses about 25,000 Sudanese, 18,000 Somalis, 4,500 Ethiopians and 1,800 other Africans.[1] Since mid-2008 the U.N. High Commissioner for Refugees (UNHCR) has transferred thousands of Somali refugees to Kakuma from three overcrowded camps at Dadaab, Kenya, about 700 miles to the east. (*See Somalia box, p. 364.*)

Qabaata says *Kanere* provides a unique opportunity to share concerns across the camp's different ethnic and national communities and to voice grievances to camp officials. "The refugees here don't have access to the people who are governing them," he says. "They only have access through their community leaders, but even their leaders do not always have access."

Negash, another Ethiopian refugee who works on *Kanere*, notes that one crucial issue is water. All water for the camp comes from underground aquifers and is rationed at about 20 liters per refugee per day. And some refugees have to walk long distances to get it. The paper's first issue, in December 2008, pointed out that refugees in one section of the camp had recently gone without adequate water for three days while a broken pump was being fixed. Why is water rationed for refugees, the paper asked, while U.N. and other aid agencies' staff members living nearby "are given unlimited water?"

Kanere also deals with UNHCR budget cutbacks, long food-distribution lines, the lack of job opportunities, low pay for refugees compared to local Kenyans and the "poor performance" of the camp's 14 primary and two secondary schools.

Above all, say Qabaata and Negash, *Kanere* advocates on behalf of refugees' basic human rights. "As refugees, we are told we have rights, but in reality we have no rights here in the camp," Negash says. "We hope *Kanere* will empower the refugee community, help it to be self-reliant. As it is, the humanitarian community is just making us dependent, reliant on them. We need to be able to help ourselves."

---

[1] "Kenya: Population of Concern to UNHCR," November 2008, p. 6, www.unhcr.org/partners/PARTNERS/4951ef9d2.pdf.

Permanent Solutions Sought for the Displaced

Aid agencies turning away from short-term solutions.

In the past, the U.N. High Commissioner for Refugees (UNHCR) and other aid agencies have focused primarily on short-term fixes — such as providing emergency food, medical care and other aid — for those displaced by war, conflict or natural disaster. They also generally assumed that displaced people wanted to return to their homes, and encouraging them to do so was easier than resettling them elsewhere.

But in recent years aid agencies have begun paying more attention to moving displaced people out of camps and makeshift shelters and back into normal lives.

Three so-called durable solutions have been proposed for refugees as well as internally displaced persons (IDPs), or those still living in their own countries:

- **Return or repatriation** — Returning either to their past residence or to their home neighborhood or region;
- **Local integration** — Settling permanently in the locality or country where the person has sought temporary refuge.
- **Resettlement elsewhere** — For refugees, moving to a willing third country; for IDPs, moving to a different part or region of their home countries.

In the absence of universally accepted standards for deciding when an IDP is no longer displaced, the Brookings-Bern Project on Internal Displacement in 2007 created a "Framework for Durable Solutions" for IDPs, which has been officially "welcomed" by the U.N.[1] It says IDPs' displacement should be considered ended when one of the three durable solutions occurs, and they "no longer have needs specifically related to their displacement." Although former IDPs may still have humanitarian needs, at this point "their needs are basically the same as other people in the local population, and it's the government's responsibility to help them," says project director Elizabeth Ferris.

In 2007, about 2 million IDPs and 731,000 refugees returned to their home countries, their actual homes or to their home regions, according to the UNHCR.[2] About half were in the Democratic Republic of the Congo, although conflict displaced another 500,000 Congolese that same year.[3] More than half of the returning refugees — some 374,000 — were Afghans.[4]

Barbara Harrell-Bond, a veteran advocate for refugees and leading critic of the UNHCR, faults the agency for continuing to focus on repatriation for refugees, because she says integration in asylum countries "often is the only solution." UNHCR officials, however, say local integration and resettlement are difficult because host countries are not inclined to accept refugees and displaced people on a permanent basis.

But resettlement efforts are occurring, albeit on a small scale, say the UNHCR and refugee advocacy groups. In 2007, the UNHCR recommended 99,000 refugees for resettlement in third countries, nearly double the previous year, but only 70,000 were able to resettle — less than 1 percent of the total refugees.[5] Historically, the United States has accepted more refugees than any other country; in 2006, the last year for which comparative figures are available, the United States accepted 41,300 refugees — more than half of the 71,700 resettlements that occurred that year.[6]

Many IDPs live in informal camps inside Iraq. The Iraqi government early in 2008 had announced an ambitious plan to build IDP housing, but falling oil prices have forced budget cuts that endanger the effort.[60] Then in late 2008 the government moved to close some of the camps by giving families one-time $4,250 stipends to return to their homes or find new places to live.[61] The UNHCR plans to help about 400,000 Iraqi IDPs this year.[62]

Some 300,000 displaced Iraqis have returned home, and nearly two-thirds of those still displaced want to return to their original home regions, according to a survey released on Feb. 22 by the International Organization for Migration.[63]

Since 2003 at least 2 million Iraqis have fled to several neighboring countries: Syria (1.2 million), Jordan (450,000), the Gulf states (150,000), Iran (58,000), Lebanon (50,000) and Egypt (40,000).[64]

Some experts question the government estimates. Amelia Templeton, an analyst at Human Rights First, suggests only about 1 million Iraqi refugees are living in

Local integration sometimes occurs informally, particularly when displaced people are not confined to official camps or settlements. For instance, in Pakistan, many of the estimated 1.8 million remaining Afghan refugees have established new lives in Peshawar, Quetta and other cities. Many had been refugees for more than 20 years, and more than half were born outside Afghanistan; a substantial number were ethnic Pashtuns, which also is the dominant ethnic group in the border areas of Pakistan. As a result, remaining in Pakistan has been a natural solution for them.[7]

In contrast, official agreements allowing large numbers of refugees or IDPs to move permanently from camps into local communities are rare. An exception is Tanzania, where more than 200,000 Burundians have been refugees since 1972. Seeking to resolve a situation that had dragged on so long, and with U.N. help that included limited financial aid, Burundi and Tanzania agreed in 2007 that 172,000 refugees could remain in Tanzania as citizens, while 46,000 would return to Burundi. The agreement is expected to be implemented by late 2009.[8]

James Milner, of Canada's Carleton University, says Tanzania's willingness to accept long-term refugees as permanent refugees "creates a strategic opportunity for the international community to show that there are alternatives to warehousing refugees forever in camps."

The only missing element, he says, is a willingness by the major donor nations to put their money and diplomatic leverage to work to encourage other countries to follow Tanzania's example. "The United States is the hegemon in the global refugee regime," he says. "If the United States were to support more of this kind of action, eventually we could see real solutions for refugees."

Afghan refugees who have just returned from Pakistan wait to register at a transition center in Kabul in June 2008. Aid agencies have begun focusing on moving displaced people out of camps and back into normal lives, often by returning them to their home countries.

IRIN/Manoocher Deghati

[1] "When Displacement Ends: A Framework for Durable Solutions," Brookings-Bern Project on Internal Displacement, June 2007, www.brookings.edu/reports/2007/09displacementends.aspx.

[2] "Note on International Protection," U.N. High Commissioner for Refugees, June 2008, p. 2, www.unhcr.org/publ/PUBL/484807202.pdf.

[3] *Ibid.*, p. 15.

[4] *Ibid.*

[5] *Ibid.*, p. 17.

[6] "Global Trends for 2006: Refugees, Asylum-seekers, Returnees, Internally Displaced and Stateless Persons," U.N. High Commissioner for Refugees, June 2007, p. 8, www.unhcr.org/statistics/STATISTICS/4676a71d4.pdf.

[7] "Afghanistan — The Challenges of Sustaining Returns," U.N. High Commissioner for Refugees, www.unhcr.org/cgi-bin/texis/vtx/afghan?page=intro.

[8] "Protracted Refugee Situations: The High Commissioner's Initiative," U.N. High Commissioner for Refugees, December 2008, pp. 25-29, www.unhcr.org/protect/PROTECTION/4937de6f2.pdf.

neighboring countries, based on school registrations and the number of refugees receiving UNHCR aid.

In contrast to many other refugee situations, nearly all of the Iraqi refugees live in or near major cities, such as Damascus, Syria, and Amman, Jordan, because Iraq's neighbors don't permit refugee camps. A high proportion of Iraqi refugees are lawyers, doctors, professors and other well-educated professionals.

National Public Radio journalist Deborah Amos tells the stories of Iraqi refugees in Syria and Lebanon in a soon-to-be-published book. She says many of the professionals belonged to the Sunni elite or Christian minority groups (such as Chaldeans), who for centuries were tolerated in Iraq but suddenly were targeted with violence. Many have spent their life savings during the years in exile and now rely on U.N. handouts. As in much of the world, local governments will not allow the refugees to work, forcing some female refugees in Damascus to turn to prostitution to support their families, Amos writes.

Myanmar — Cyclone Nargis struck on May 2, 2008, killing 140,000 people — mostly by drowning — and forcing up to 800,000 from their homes.[65] Humanitarian agencies pressed the government to allow international aid workers into the vast Irrawaddy Delta, but the secretive generals who run Myanmar resisted the appeals for several weeks until U.N. Secretary-General Ban Ki-moon finally persuaded the top general, Thwan Shwe, to accept outside aid.

Aid agencies and foreign governments donated emergency relief supplies and began helping rebuild homes and communities. But about 500,000 people remained displaced at year's end.[66] Many of those displaced by cyclone-caused floods have faced severe water shortages in recent months due to the recent onset of the dry season and water contamination caused by the cyclone.[67] Full recovery from the cyclone could take three to four years, a senior U.N. aid official said in January.[68]

Meanwhile, members of the Muslim Rohingya minority, from the northern state of Rakhine, are officially stateless. According to Amnesty International, thousands of Rohingyas flee Myanmar each year because of land confiscation, arbitrary taxation, forced eviction and denial of citizenship.[69] Since 1991, more than 250,000 have fled, mostly to neighboring Bangladesh, where the UNHCR runs two camps housing 28,000 refugees; another 200,000 unregistered Rohingyas live outside the camps.[70]

In early 2009, the Thai navy reportedly intercepted boats carrying hundreds of Rohingya trying to cross the Andaman Sea. The action generated international outrage after CNN published a photo purportedly showing armed forces towing refugee boats out to sea and leaving the occupants to die, but the Thai government denied the reports. Some were later rescued off the coasts of India and Indonesia, but many went missing.[71]

In early February actress and U.N. goodwill ambassador Angelina Jolie visited refugee camps in Thailand housing 110,000 Karen and Kareni ethnic refugees from Myanmar. She called on the Thai government to lift its ban on refugees working outside the camps and asked the government to extend hospitality to the Rohingyas.[72]

Prime Minister Abhisit Vejjajiva had said earlier that Thailand would not build a camp for the Rohingyas and will continue to expel them. "They are not refugees," he said. "Our policy is to push them out of the country because they are illegal migrants."[73]

Leaders of the Association of Southeast Asian Nations agreed on March 2 to discuss the status of the Rohingyas at a mid-April summit in Bali. Malaysian Prime Minister, Abdullah Ahmad Badawi said the Ronhingya problem "is a regional issue that needs to be resolved regionally."[74]

Sudan — Two major internal conflicts plus other conflicts in central and eastern Africa have displaced millions of Sudanese in the past three decades. At the beginning of 2009, more than 3.5 million were still displaced, including about 130,000 in neighboring countries. Sudan hosts more than 250,000 refugees from nearby countries.[75]

Sudan's two-decade civil war between the government in Khartoum and a separatist army in south Sudan ended with an uneasy peace in January 2005. More than 300,000 refugees who had fled the violence have returned to their home regions, but UNHCR has estimated that about 130,000 remain in Egypt, Ethiopia, Kenya and Uganda.[76] And more conflict could erupt if, as expected, the southerners vote in 2011 for full independence.

Elsewhere in Sudan, a series of inter-related conflicts between the Khartoum government and rebel groups in western Darfur have displaced about 2.7 million people and killed an estimated 300,000.[77] Although Darfur has generally faded from world headlines, the conflict continues, with about 1,000 people fleeing their homes every day.[78] Complicating the refugee crisis, 243,000 Darfuris have fled into Chad, while some 45,000 Chadians have crossed into Darfur to escape a related conflict.[79]

More than 200,000 other refugees also are in Sudan, mostly from Eritrea, having fled the long war between Eritrea and Ethiopia.[80]

CURRENT SITUATION

'Responsibility to Protect'

Since last fall, 26-year-old Kandiah and his family have moved eight times to avoid the long-running civil war between the Sri Lankan army and rebels known as the Tamil Tigers. By late February they had joined several dozen people sleeping on a classroom floor in Vavuniya, in northern Sri Lanka.

At one point, Kandiah (not his real name) and his family stayed in an area that was supposed to be safe for civilians. For more than a week, he said, "We stayed in the open air with scores of other families . . . but the

Should the U.N. High Commissioner for Refugees help more displaced people?

YES
Joel R. Charny
Vice President for Policy
Refugees International

NO
Guglielmo Verdirame
Professor, International Human Rights and
Refugee Law
Cambridge University
Co-author, Rights in Exile: Janus-Faced
Humanitarianism

Written for *CQ Researcher*, February 2009

Current efforts to help displaced populations do not reflect the fact that twice as many people displaced by conflict remain inside their own borders rather than crossing an international one, thus failing to become refugees protected under international law. With the U.N. High Commissioner for Refugees (UNHCR) focusing primarily on legal protection for refugees, the current system is outmoded. A bold solution is needed to prevent further unnecessary suffering.

Internally displaced people (IDPs) suffer when their governments don't aid and protect their own citizens. They also suffer from the lack of a dedicated international agency mandated to respond to their needs when their states fail. With IDP numbers growing, expanding the UNHCR's mandate to include IDPs is the best option available to fill this gap.

A dedicated agency would be more effective than the current system, characterized by the "cluster leadership" approach, under which international agencies provide help by sectors, such as health, water and sanitation and shelter. For example, in the 1990s the U.N. secretary-general mandated that UNHCR respond to the needs of IDPs displaced by the civil war in Sri Lanka. Over the years, the agency effectively fulfilled this responsibility with donor support, and the entire U.N. country team — as well as the Sri Lankan government — benefited from the clarity of knowing that the agency was in charge. Moreover, carrying out this exceptional mandate did not undermine either the UNHCR's work with refugees in the region or the right of Tamil Sri Lankans to seek asylum in southern India.

Giving one agency responsibility for an especially vulnerable population is more effective than patching together a response system with multiple independent agencies. Because the circumstances and needs of IDPs are so similar to those of refugees, and because UNHCR has a proven capacity to respond holistically to displacement, it is best suited to take on this responsibility.

Having a formal mandate for IDPs would triple UNHCR's caseload and pose an immense challenge. The agency already has difficulty fulfilling its current mandate and perpetually lacks sufficient funds. Taking the lead on internal displacement would require new thinking, more advocacy work with governments and flexible approaches to programming outside of camp settings. But the alternative is worse: Maintain the status quo and perpetuate the gap in protection and assistance for some of the world's most vulnerable people.

Written for *CQ Researcher*, February 2009

Forced displacement is a human tragedy even when it occurs within the boundaries of a state. But the test for deciding whether it would be appropriate for the U.N. High Commissioner for Refugees (UNHCR) to add internally displaced people (IDPs) to its current mandate on a permanent basis is not one of comparability of suffering. Rather, the proper test is whether UNHCR is the right institution for dealing with this problem. I think it is not, for several reasons.

First, crossing an international boundary continues to make a difference in today's world. By virtue of being outside their country of nationality, refugees are in a different position than the internally displaced.

Second, the international legal regime for refugees was established as an exception to the sovereign prerogatives enjoyed by states over admission and expulsion of aliens in their territory. While most refugees were the victims of a human-rights violation in their home country, the focus of the refugee legal regime is not on the responsibility of the country of nationality but on the obligations of the country where they take refuge. Because internally displaced persons are still inside their home countries, protecting their rights will require different strategies and methods.

Third, human-rights bodies, including the office of the U.N. High Commissioner for Refugees, are better-placed to deal with what are, in essence, violations of human rights against citizens.

Finally, the rationale for getting the UNHCR involved with IDPs is premised on a distinctly problematic view of the organization as a provider of humanitarian relief rather than as the international protector of refugees. UNHCR's work with refugees has already greatly suffered from the sidelining of the agency's role as legal protector: The warehousing of refugees in camps is just one example. It would not help the internally displaced if the UNHCR's involvement resulted in their being warehoused in camps, as refugees already are.

In a world where asylum is under serious threat, the real challenge for UNHCR is to rediscover its protection mandate, to act as the advocate of refugees and as the institutional overseer of the obligations of states under the 1951 Refugee Convention. It is a difficult enough task as it is.

Legal Protections for Displaced Populations

A 1951 treaty gives refugees the most protection.

International law protects some — but not all — refugees who cross international borders, while the non-binding Guiding Principles on Internal Displacement cover internally displaced people (IDPs), or those forcibly displaced within their home countries.

Here are the main laws protecting refugees and IDPs:

1951 Refugee Convention

The Convention Relating to the Status of Refugees — the basic international treaty concerning refugees — was adopted by a United Nations conference on July 28, 1951, and became effective on April 22, 1954. It defines a refugee as someone who, "owing to well-founded fear of being persecuted for reasons of race, religion, nationality, membership of a particular social group or political opinion, is outside the country of his nationality and is unable or, owing to such fear, is unwilling to avail himself of the protection of that country; or who, not having a nationality and being outside the country of his former habitual residence as a result of such events, is unable or, owing to such fear, is unwilling to return to it."

Excluded are those who flee their countries because of generalized violence (such as a civil war) in which they are not specifically targeted, or those who flee because of natural disasters or for economic reasons, such as a collapsing economy. The convention also prohibits a host country from expelling or returning refugees against their will to a territory where they have a "well-founded" fear of persecution.

The 1967 Protocol

Because the 1951 convention applied only to people who became refugees before Jan. 1, 1951, it was widely considered to apply only to European refugees from World War II. To aid those displaced by subsequent events, the United Nations adopted a new treaty, known as a Protocol, which eliminated the pre-1951 limitation. It took effect on Oct. 4, 1967.[1]

As of October 2008, 144 countries were parties to both the convention and the Protocol, though the two groups are not identical.[2]

Regional Treaties

Two regional documents expanded refugee protections of the convention and Protocol to Africa, Mexico and Central America. The 1969 Convention Governing the Specific Aspects of Refugee Problems in Africa — adopted

shelling was intense. There was shelling every day. We barely escaped with our lives."[81]

Kandiah and his family are among more than 250,000 people forced from their homes, often repeatedly, in the latest — and possibly final — round of the 26-year war. Claiming to represent the ethnic Tamil minority, the Tigers have been fighting for independence in the eastern and northern portions of the island.

Although the conflict has been among the world's most violent, international pressure to end it has been modest, at best. The U.N. Security Council, for example, considered it an "internal" affair to be resolved by Sri Lankans themselves, not by the international community and has never even adopted a resolution about it. Norway took the most significant action, mediating a cease-fire in 2002 that lasted nearly three years.

The plight of people like Kandiah illustrates the international community's failure to follow through on

promises world leaders made in September 2005. At a summit marking the U.N.'s 60th anniversary, world leaders adopted the "responsibility to protect" philosophy, which holds every government responsible for protecting its own citizens.[82] Moreover, if a government fails to protect its citizens, it cannot prevent the international community from intervening on their behalf. World leaders at the summit declared the U.N.'s right to take "collective action, in a decisive and timely manner," when governments failed to protect their own citizens.[83]

The U.N. has not followed through on that ringing declaration, however, usually because of dissension within the Security Council — the only U.N. body authorized to take forceful action. In addition, major countries with large, well-equipped armies — notably the United States and many European countries — have been unwilling to contribute sufficient troops to U.N. peacekeeping forces. The U.N.'s inability to protect displaced

by what is now the African Union — defined refugees in Africa, while the 1984 Cartagena Declaration on Refugees is an informal statement of principles drafted by legal experts from Mexico and Central America.[3]

Guiding Principles on Internal Displacement

The U.N. has never adopted a treaty specifically aimed at establishing legal rights for IDPs. However, in 1998 the organization endorsed a set of 30 nonbinding guidelines intended to heighten international awareness of the internally displaced and offer them more legal protection. Known as the Guiding Principles on Internal Displacement, they have been presented to the various U.N. bodies but never formally adopted.

Based on the Universal Declaration of Human Rights and other treaties and agreements, the principles provide legal and practical standards for aiding and protecting displaced people. For example, the first principle states that displaced persons should enjoy "the same rights and freedoms under international and domestic law as do other persons in their country. They shall not be discriminated against . . . on the ground that they are internally displaced."

Regional bodies (including the European Union and the Organization of American States) and numerous nongovernmental organizations have endorsed the principles, and the UNHCR has treated them as official policy since world leaders — meeting at the U.N. in September 2005 —

endorsed them. Nearly a dozen countries also have incorporated all or some of the principles into national legislation. In one case, the Colombian Constitutional Court in 2001 placed them into the country's "constitutional block," effectively making them a binding part of national law. Other countries that have adopted the principles into national laws or policies include the Maldives, Mozambique, Turkey and Uganda.

IDP advocates say the most significant potential use of the Guiding Principles is in Africa, where the African Union since 2006 has been working on a plan to incorporate a version of them into a binding regional treaty. This treaty — to be called the Convention for the Prevention of Internal Displacement and the Protection of and Assistance to Internally Displaced Persons in Africa — is expected to be adopted by African leaders at a summit meeting in Kampala, Uganda, in April.[4]

---

[1] Text of the Convention and Protocol is at www.unhcr.org/protect/PROTECTION/3b66c2aa10.pdf.

[2] "States Parties to the Refugee Convention," U.N. High Commissioner for Refugees, www.unhcr.org/protect/PROTECTION/3b73b0d63.pdf.

[3] Text of Refugee Convention in Africa is at www.unhcr.org/basics/BASICS/45dc1a682.pdf; Text of the Cartagene Declaration is at www.unhcr.org/basics/BASICS/45dc19084.pdf.

[4] Text of the Guiding Principles is at www3.brookings.edu/fp/projects/idp/resources/GPEnglish.pdf.

---

people has been most evident in eastern Congo and Darfur, where peacekeeping forces, mainly from African Union countries, are ill-equipped and undermanned.[84]

Early in February, for example, Doctors Without Borders bitterly denounced the U.N. peacekeeping mission in Congo for its "inaction" in response to the recent LRA attacks. Laurence Gaubert, head of mission in Congo for the group, said the U.N. peacekeepers "are just based in their camp, they don't go out of their camp, they don't know what is happening in the area."[85] Gaubert noted that the Security Council last Dec. 22 adopted Resolution 1856 demanding protection for civilians in Congo.[86] "This is something they have signed," she said, "but is not something you can see in the field that they have put in place."[87]

U.N. Under-Secretary-General for Humanitarian Affairs John Holmes acknowledged that the peacekeepers could do more to protect civilians but said the harsh criticism of them was "unreasonable and unjustified."

Only 250-300 troops were in the area at the time, he said, and most were engineers, not combat forces.[88]

The U.N. has faced similar hurdles in trying to protect the millions of civilians displaced in Darfur since 2003. African Union peacekeepers began limited operations in Sudan in 2004 but lacked either the mandate or the resources to prevent government-backed militias or rebel groups from attacking civilians in camps and settlements. The Sudanese government agreed in 2006 and 2007 to allow beefed up U.N. peacekeeping missions, but — as in Congo — the U.N. has been unable to deploy adequate forces over such an enormous area. In Sudan, the government dragged its feet in following through on its agreement, and other countries have failed to provide the necessary money and manpower. The UNHCR operates in seven displaced-persons camps in Darfur (and in six camps in eastern Chad) but must rely on the peacekeeping mission for security.[89]

Serb refugees stage a demonstration along the Kosovo border in April 2007 to urge the U.N. to return them to their home provinces. Hundreds of thousands of people dislocated by war in the former Yugoslavia during the 1990s have not yet returned to their home regions.

U.N. officials have repeatedly called for more forceful action to protect Darfuri civilians, only to be stymied by the Security Council — largely because of resistance from China, which has economic interests in Sudan — and delaying tactics by Sudan. The Khartoum government on Feb. 17 signed an agreement with the largest Darfur rebel group, the Justice and Equality Movement, calling for negotiation of a formal peace accord within three months.[90] The hurdles to such an accord were evident the very next day, when government forces reportedly bombed some of the rebel group's positions. The future of the peace agreement was further complicated by the International Criminal Court's (ICC) landmark decision on March 4 to issue an arrest warrant for Sudanese President Omar al-Bashir, charging him with directing the mass murder of tens of thousands of Darfuri civilians and "forcibly transferring large numbers of civilians, and pillaging their

property." It was the first time the Hague-based court has accused a sitting head of state of war crimes. Unless he leaves Sudan, there is no international mechanism for arresting Bashir, who denies the accusations and does not recognize the court's jurisdiction. Some aid organizations fear the ICC ruling could trigger more violence — and thus more displacements.[91]

Focusing on IDPs

The number of people displaced by violence who remain within their own countries has been averaging more than 20 million per year, according to the Internal Displacement Monitoring Center, an arm of the Norwegian Refugee Council. More than a third of them are in just three countries: Colombia (up to 4.3 million), Sudan (3.5 million) and Iraq (up to 2.8 million).[92] Tens of millions more have been driven from their homes by natural disasters.

In December 2008, to give IDPs more international attention, the U.N.'s Office for the Coordination of Humanitarian Affairs launched a series of events focusing on IDPs, including workshops, panel discussions, a Web site and high-level conferences.

The agency is particularly concerned about displaced people who languish for years without help from their governments. "For millions of IDPs around the world, an end to their years of displacement, discrimination and poverty seems to be of little concern for those in power," said the U.N.'s Holmes. The U.N. also is encouraging governments to adopt the Guiding Principles on Internal Displacement for dealing with IDPs. And, it is pressing for "more predictable, timely and principled funding" for programs that help IDPs return home or find new homes, he said.[93]

In recent years, displaced people, usually from rural areas, have tended to head for cities. Experts say it is difficult to calculate the number of urban IDPs, but the monitoring center put the 2007 figure at 4 million, and the UNHCR estimated in 2008 that about half of the 11.4 million refugees were in cities.[94]

Urban IDPs and refugees pose logistical problems for local and international agencies charged with helping them. "In a camp, you have all these tents lined up in a row, and so it's easy to know how many people are there, and how much food and medicine you need every day," says Patrick Duplat, an advocate for Refugees International.

"In an urban setting, it's much more complicated to reach people. Who is a refugee, who is an IDP and how are they different from the local population?"

U.N. High Commissioner Guterres acknowledged in a speech last October that global efforts to aid and protect urban refugees and IDPs have been "weak."[95] The approximately 2 million Iraqi refugees living in Damascus and Amman represent "a completely new and different challenge in relation to our usual activities in encampment situations," he told a conference in Norway.[96]

Last year the UNHCR tried handing out cash coupons and ATM cards to several thousand Iraqi refugees in Damascus, enabling them to buy food and other goods at local markets. The UNHCR and the World Food Program also gave food baskets or rice, vegetable oil and lentils to Iraqi refugees considered most in need, aiding about 177,000 Iraqis in 2008.[97] But some refugees reportedly were selling their rations to pay for housing and other needs.[98]

A major step toward legally protecting African IDPs could come in April at a planned special African Union (AU) summit meeting in Uganda. Experts have been working for nearly three years on a Convention for the Protection and Assistance of Internally Displaced Persons in Africa. This treaty would incorporate some, but not all, of the 1998 Guiding Principles on Internal Displacement, which sets nonbinding standards for protecting IDPs.[99]

If a treaty is produced, ratified and implemented, it could be an important step in protecting IDPs, because so many are in Africa, says Cohen from Brookings. But she is concerned that the final treaty, which already has been revised several times, might not be as strong in protecting human rights as the voluntary Guiding Principles. "We'll have to wait and see what the leaders agree to, and even if they adopt it," she says.

Guterres strongly endorses the AU's plan for a binding treaty. He also says that because the treaty has been developed by Africans, not imposed by outsiders, it "will not be subject to questions about the legitimacy of its objectives."[100]

OUTLOOK

Environmental Refugees

Environmental deterioration caused by climate change could force up to 1 billion people from their homes in coming decades, according to a paper presented to a high-level U.N. meeting last October.[101] Small island nations, notably the Maldives in the Indian Ocean and Kiribati and Tuvalu in the Pacific, could be inundated — causing mass evacuations — if sea levels rise to the extent predicted by many scientists.[102]

Rising seas also endanger several hundred million people in low-lying coastal regions. Many of these areas are in developing countries — such as Bangladesh and the Philippines — that already are prone to cyclones, floods, earthquakes or volcanic eruptions.[103] Many scientists believe that climate change will increase the severity and frequency of weather-linked disasters, particularly cyclones and floods, thus displacing even more people in the future.

L. Craig Johnstone, deputy U.N. High Commissioner for Refugees, said "conservative" estimates predict that up to 250 million people could be displaced by the middle of the 21st century due to climate change. The minority of scientists who doubt the impact of climate change dismiss such estimates as overblown.[104] But aid officials at the U.N. and other international agencies say they have no choice but to prepare for the worst.

Regardless of the impact of climate change on displacements, experts across the spectrum say it is becoming increasingly important for the international community to decide how long to provide humanitarian aid for displaced people. Decades-long displacements are difficult for both the IDPs and refugees as well as the aid groups and host countries involved. (*See sidebar, p. 370.*)

"When can they stop being vulnerable as a result of their displacement and simply be compared to any other poor person in their country?" asks Koser, at the Geneva Center for Security Policy. He cites the 4.6 million Palestinians still being aided by the United Nations six decades after their original displacement.

UNHCR officials acknowledge that international aid programs are not always equitable but say addressing the vulnerability of the world's poor and ending the causes of displacement depend on the political will of global leaders. In his annual remarks to the Security Council on Jan. 8, High Commissioner Guterres said global displacement issues won't be solved until the conflicts that force people from their homes are ended.

"While it is absolutely vital that the victims of armed conflict be provided with essential protection and assistance, we must also acknowledge the limitations of humanitarian action and its inability to resolve deep-rooted conflicts within and between states," he said. "The solution, as always, can only be political."[105]

NOTES

1. "Only after five days we dared to bury the bodies," Doctors Without Borders, Jan. 19, 2009, www.condition-critical.org/.

2. "Congo Crisis" fact sheet, International Rescue Committee, p. 1, www.theirc.org/resources/2007/congo_onesheet.pdf; also see "World Report 2009," Human Rights Watch, www.hrw.org/en/world-report/2009/democratic-republic-congo-drc.

3. "Convention and Protocol Relating to the Status of Refugees," U.N. High Commissioner for Refugees, www.unhcr.org/protect/PROTECTION/3b66c2aa10.pdf.

4. "World Report 2009," *op. cit.*

5. "Statement by Mr. Antonio Guterres, United Nations High Commissioner for Refugees, to the Security Council, New York," U.N. High Commissioner for Refugees, Jan. 8, 2009, www.unhcr.org/admin/ADMIN/496625484.html.

6. "Internally Displaced People: Exiled in their Homeland," U.N. Office for the Coordination of Humanitarian Affairs, http://ochaonline. un.org/News/InFocus/InternallyDisplacedPeopleIDPs/tabid/5132/language/en-US/Default. aspx; also see "China Earthquake: Facts and Figures," International Federation of Red Cross and Red Crescent Societies, Oct. 31, 2008, www.ifrc.org/Docs/pubs/disasters/sichuan-earthquake/ff311008.pdf.

7. Jeffrey Gettleman, "Starvation And Strife Menace Torn Kenya," *The New York Times*, March 1, 2009, p. 6.

8. "Top UNHCR official warns about displacement from climate change," U.N. High Commissioner for Refugees, Dec. 9, 2008, www.unhcr.org/news/NEWS/493e9bd94.html.

9. "2007 Statistical Yearbook," U.N. High Commissioner for Refugees, p. 23, www.unhcr.org/cgi-bin/texis/vtx/home/opendoc.pdf?id=4981c32

52&tbl=STATISTICS; "Statement by Mr. Antonio Guterres," *op. cit.*

10. For background, see Karen Foerstel, "Crisis in Darfur," *CQ Global Researcher*, September 2008, pp. 243-270.

11. "2009 Global Update: Sudan," U.N. High Commissioner for Refugees, pp. 1-3, www.unhcr.org/publ/PUBL/4922d4130.pdf.

12. "Millions of Hectares of Land Secured for Internally Displaced," International Organization for Migration, Jan. 9, 2009, www.iom.int/jahia/Jahia/pbnAM/cache/offonce;jsessionid= 29AD6E92A35FDE971CDA-B26007A67DB2.worker01? entryId=21044.

13. "Afghanistan — The Challenges of Sustaining Returns," U.N. High Commissioner for Refugees, www.unhcr.org/cgi-bin/texis/vtx/afghan?page=home.

14. See "UNHCR Global Appeal, 2009"; "2009 Global Update, Mission Statement," U.N. High Commissioner for Refugees, www.unhcr.org/ publ/PUBL/4922d43f11.pdf; "Statement by Mr. Antonio Guterres," *op. cit.*; "2009 Global Update, Working with the Internally Displaced," U.N. High Commissioner for Refugees, www.unhcr.org/publ/PUBL/4922d44c0.pdf.

15. The Refugee Status Determination (RSD) Unit, U.N. High Commissioner for Refugees, www.unhcr.org/protect/3d3d26004.html.

16. "2009 Global Update, Mission Statement," *op. cit.*

17. "Protracted Refugee Situations: High Commissioner's Initiative," U.N. High Commissioner for Refugees, December 2008, www.unhcr.org/protect/PROTECTION/4937de6f2.pdf.

18. "Humanitarian Reform," United Nations, www.humanitarianreform.org.

19. "The Global Cluster Leads," U.N. Office for the Coordination of Humanitarian Affairs, http://ocha.unog.ch/humanitarianreform/Default.aspx? tabid=217.

20. "Cluster Approach Evaluation 2007," United Nations, www.humanitarianreform.org/Default.aspx? tabid=457.

21. The book Milner co-authored is *The United Nation's High Commissioner for Refugees (UNHCR):*

The Politics and Practice of Refugee Protection into the 21st Century (2008).

22. "Convention and Protocol Relating to the Status of Refugees," *op. cit.*

23. "Full Text of Jack Straw's Speech," *The Guardian*, Feb. 6, 2001, www.guardian.co.uk/ uk/2001/feb/06/ immigration.immigrationandpublicservices3.

24. "Climate change, natural disasters and human displacement: a UNHCR perspective," www.unhcr .org/protect/PROTECTION/4901e81a4.pdf.

25. "European Pact on Immigration and Asylum," www.immigration.gouv.fr/IMG/pdf/Plaquette_ EN.pdf.

26. "ECRE calls for suspension of Dublin transfers to Greece," European Council on Refugees and Exiles, April 3, 2008, www.ecre.org/resources/Press_ releases/1065.

27. "NGO Statement Addressing the Iraqi Humanitarian Challenge," July 31, 2008, www .refugeesinternational.org/policy/letter/ngo-state ment-addressing-iraqi-humanitarian-challenge.

28. "Fact Sheet: USCIS Makes Major Strides During 2008," U.S. Citizenship and Immigration Services, Nov. 6, 2008, www.uscis.gov/ portal/site/uscis/ menuitem.5af9bb95919f35e66f614176543f6d1a/ ?vgnextoid=2526ad6f16d6d110VgnVCM100000 4718190aRCRD&vgnextchannel=68439c7755cb 9010VgnVCM10000045f3d6a1RCRD.

29. "NGO Statement: Addressing the Iraqi Humanitarian Challenge," *op. cit.*

30. "Fact Sheet: Iraqi Refugee Processing," U.S. Citizenship and Immigration Services, Sept. 12, 2008, www.dhs.gov/xnews/releases/pr_12212 49274808.shtm.

31. "Operation Safe Haven Iraq 2009," Center for American Progress, www.americanprogress.org/ issues/2009/01/iraqi_airlift.html.

32. Her blog site is http://refugeeresettlementwatch .wordpress.com/.

33. "The 1951 Refugee Convention," U.N. High Commissioner for Refugees, www.unhcr.org/ 1951convention/dev-protect.html.

34. *Ibid.*

35. *Ibid.*

36. "Establishment of UNRWA," www.un.org/unrwa/ overview/index.html.

37. "UNRWA Statistics," www.un.org/unrwa/publica tions/index.html.

38. "A 'Timeless' Treaty Under Attack: A New Phase," U.N. High Commissioner for Refugees, www .unhcr.org/1951convention/new-phase.html.

39. "States Parties to the Convention and the Protocol," U.N. High Commissioner for Refugees, www .unhcr.org/protect/PROTECTION/3b73b0d63 .pdf.

40. "Guiding Principles on Internal Displacement," www3.brookings.edu/fp/projects/idp/resources/ GPEnglish.pdf.

41. "FMO Research Guide: Afghanistan," Teresa Poppelwell, July 2007, pp. 17-19, www.forcedmi gration.org/guides/fmo006/.

42. "Afghanistan — The Challenges of Sustaining Returns," U.N. High Commissioner for Refugees, www.unhcr.org/cgi-bin/texis/vtx/afghan? page=home.

43. "Jalozai camp closed, returnees face difficulties at home," IRIN news service, June 2, 2008, www .irinnews.org/Report.aspx?ReportId=78506; also see "Iran called upon to halt winter deportations," IRIN news service, Dec. 18, 2008, www.irinnews .org/PrintReport.aspx?ReportId=82007.

44. "Afghanistan — The Challenges of Sustaining Returns," *op. cit.*

45. "Minister disputes call to boost refugee returns," IRIN news service, Sept. 10, 2008, www.irinnews .org/Report.aspx?ReportId=80218.

46. "Cold tents for returnees in east," IRIN news service, Jan. 15, 2009, www.irinnews.org/Report .aspx?ReportId=82373.

47. "Afghanistan at the crossroads: Young Afghans return to a homeland they never knew," U.N. High Commissioner for Refugees, Nov. 14, 2008, www .unhcr.org/cgi-bin/texis/vtx/afghan?page= news&id=491d84c64.

48. "2009 Global Update, Colombia situation," U.N. High Commissioner for Refugees, www.unhcr.org/ publ/PUBL/4922d43411.pdf.

49. "Colombia Situation," U.N. High Commissioner for Refugees 2008-09 Global Appeal for Colombia, p. 2, www.unhcr.org/home/PUBL/474ac8e814 .pdf.

50. *Ibid.*

51. "Millions of Hectares of Land Secured for Internally Displaced," International Organization for Migration, Jan. 9, 2009, www.iom.

52. *Ibid.*

53. *Ibid.*

54. "2009 Global Update," Democratic Republic of the Congo, U.N. High Commissioner for Refugees, www.unhcr.org/publ/ PUBL/4922d4100.pdf.

55. "Congo Crisis" fact sheet, *op. cit.*

56. "A Congolese Rebel Leader Who Once Seemed Untouchable Is Caught," *The New York Times*, Jan. 24, 2009, www.nytimes.com/2009/01/24/world/ africa/24congo.html?_r=1.

57. "An arresting and hopeful surprise," *The Economist*, Jan. 29, 2009, www.economist.com/displayStory .cfm?story_id=13022113. For background, see David Masci, "Aiding Africa," *CQ Researcher*, Aug. 29, 2003, pp. 697-720; John Felton, "Child Soldiers," *CQ Global Researcher*, July 2008.

58. "2009 Global Update: Iraq," U.N. High Commissioner for Refugees, p. 2, www.unhcr.org/ publ/PUBL/4922d4230.pdf.

59. "WFP to help feed one million displaced Iraqis," World Food Program, Jan. 3, 2009, www.wfp.org/ English/?ModuleID=137&Key=2732.

60. "Budget cuts threaten IDP housing projects," IRIN news service, Jan. 6, 2009, www.irinnews.org/ Report.aspx?ReportId=82209.

61. "IDPs enticed to vacate southern camp," IRIN news service, Dec. 15, 2008, www.irinnews.org/ Report.aspx?ReportId=81963.

62. "2009 Global Update: Iraq," *op. cit.*, p. 2.

63. "Three Years of Post-Samarra Displacement in Iraq," International Organization for Migration, Feb. 22, 2009, p. 1, www.iom.int/jahia/webdav/ shared/shared/mainsite/published_docs/studies_ and_reports/iom_displacement_report_post_ samarra.pdf.

64. *Ibid.*

65. "Post-Nargis Periodic Review I," Tripartite Core Group, December 2008, p. 4, www.aseansec .org/22119.pdf.

66. "2009 Global Update: Myanmar," U.N. High Commissioner for Refugees, p. 2, www.unhcr.org/ publ/PUBL/4922d42b0.pdf.

67. "Cyclone survivors face water shortages," IRIN news service, Dec. 29, 2008, www.irinnews.org/ Report.aspx?ReportId=82129.

68. "Cyclone recovery 'will take up to four years,' " IRIN news service, Jan. 15, 2009, www.IRINnews .org/Report.aspx?ReportId=82383.

69. Michael Heath, "Angelina Jolie, U.N. Envoy, Asks Thailand to Aid Myanmar Refugees," Bloomberg News, www.bloomberg.com/apps/news?pid=2060 1080&sid=aL5VlfM46aAc&refer=asia#.

70. "2009 Global Update: Bangladesh," U.N. High Commissioner for Refugees, p. 1, www.unhcr.org/ publ/PUBL/4922d42818.pdf.

71. "Myanmar Refugees Rescued at Sea," *The New York Times*, Feb. 3, 2009, www.nytimes. com/2009/02/04/ world/asia/04indo.html?ref=world.

72. "Angelina Jolie voices support for Myanmar refugees in northern Thailand camps," U.N. High Commissioner for Refugees, Feb. 5, 2009, www .unhcr.org/news/NEWS/498ab65c2. html.

73. *Ibid.*

74. "ASIA: Regional approach to Rohingya boat people," IRIN news service, March 2, 2009, www.irinnews.org/Report.aspx?ReportId=83232.

75. "2009 Global Update: Sudan," U.N. High Commissioner for Refugees, pp. 1-3, www.unhcr .org/publ/PUBL/4922d4130.pdf.

76. "Number of returnees to South Sudan passes the 300,000 mark," U.N. High Commissioner for Refugees, Feb. 10, 2009, www.unhcr.org/news/ NEWS/4991a8de2.html; "2009 Global Update," *op. cit.*, p. 1.

77. "Darfur remains tense after recent eruption of fighting, U.N. reports," IRIN news service, Jan. 28, 2009, www.un.org/apps/news/story.asp?News ID=29699&Cr=darfur&Cr1=.

78. "Report of the Secretary-General on the deployment of the African Union-United Nations Hybrid Operation in Darfur," United Nations, Oct. 17, 2008, p. 11, http://daccessdds.un.org/doc/UNDOC/GEN/N08/553/95/PDF/N0855395.pdf?OpenElement.

79. "2009 Global Update: Sudan," *op. cit.*; "2009 Global Update: Chad," U.N. High Commissioner for Refugees, www.unhcr.org/publ/PUBL/4922d41214.pdf.

80. "2009 Global Update: Sudan," *op. cit.*, p. 3; "World Refugee Survey, 2008," Sudan chapter, U.S. Committee for Refugees and Immigrants, www.refugees.org/countryreports.aspx?id=2171.

81. "Kandiah: 'There was shelling every day. We barely escaped with our lives,' " IRIN news service, Feb. 19, 2009, www.IRINnews.org/Report.aspx?ReportId=83015.

82. For background, see Lee Michael Katz, "World Peacekeeping," *CQ Global Researcher*, April 2007, pp. 75-100.

83. "World Summit Outcome 2005," U.N. General Assembly, Resolution A/RES/60/1, paragraphs 138-139, September 2005, www.un.org/summit2005/documents.html.

84. See Foerstel, *op. cit.*

85. "DRC: MSF denounces the lack of protection for victims of LRA violence in Haut-Uélé," Doctors Without Borders, Feb. 4, 2009, www.msf.org.

86. Security Council Resolution 1856, Dec. 22, 2006, http://daccessdds.un.org/doc/UNDOC/GEN/N08/666/94/PDF/N0866694.pdf?OpenElement.

87. *Ibid.*

88. "Press Conference by Humanitarian Affairs Head on Recent Trip to Democratic Republic of Congo," U.N. Department of Public Information, Feb. 13, 2009, www.un.org/News/briefings/docs/2009/090213_DRC.doc.htm.

89. "2009 Global Update: Sudan," *op. cit.*

90. "Sudan and Darfur Rebel Group Agree to Peace Talks," *The New York Times*, Feb. 18, 2009, www.nytimes.com/2009/02/18/world/africa/18sudan.html?_r=1&ref=todayspaper.

91. "Sudan bombs rebels day after Darfur deal: rebels," Agence France-Presse, Feb. 18, 2009. See Mike Corder, "International court issues warrant for Sudan president on charges of war crimes in Darfur," The Associated Press, March 4, 2009.

92. "2009 Global Update," *op. cit.*; "Global Overview of Trends and Developments: 2007," Internal Displacement Monitoring Centre, Norwegian Refugee Council, p. 12, April 2008, www.internal-displacement.org/idmc/website/resources.nsf/(httpPublications)/0F926CFAF1EADE5EC125742E003B7067?OpenDocument.

93. "UN launches year-long campaign to highlight, and solve, plight of displaced," IRIN news service, Dec. 18, 2009, www.un.org/apps/news/story.asp?NewsID=29358&Cr=IDPs&Cr1.

94. "Addressing Urban Displacement: A Project Description," Internal Displacement Monitoring Centre, Norwegian Refugee Council, 2007, p. 2; also see "2007 Global Trends," U.N. High Commissioner for Refugees, June 2008, p. 2, www.unhcr.org/statistics/STATISTICS/4852366f2.pdf.

95. "Ten years of Guiding Principles on Internal Displacement: Achievements and Future Challenges," statement by Antonio Guterres, Oslo, Oct. 16, 2008, www.unhcr.org/admin/ADMIN/48ff45e12.html.

96. *Ibid.*

97. "WFP to help feed one million displaced Iraqis," World Food Program, Jan. 3, 2008, www.wfp.org/English/?ModuleID=137&Key=2732.

98. "Iraqi refugees selling some of their food rations," IRIN news service, Jan. 28, 2009, http://one.wfp.org/english/?ModuleID=137&Key=2732.

99. "From Voluntary Principles to Binding Standards," *IDP Action*, Jan. 9, 2009, www.idpaction.org/index.php/en/news/16-principles2 standards.

100. "Ten Years of Guiding Principles on Internal Displacement," *op. cit.*

101. "Climate Change, Migration and Displacement: Who will be affected?" Working paper submitted by the informal group on Migration/Displacement and Climate Change of the U.N. Inter-Agency Standing Committee, Oct. 31, 2008, http://unfccc.int/resource/docs/2008/smsn/igo/022.pdf.

102. "Climate Change and Displacement," *Forced Migration Review*, p. 20, October 2008, www.fmreview.org/climatechange.htm; for background see Colin Woodard, "Curbing Climate Change," *CQ Global Researcher*, February 2007, pp. 27-50, and Marcia Clemmitt, "Climate Change," *CQ Researcher*, Jan. 27, 2006, pp. 73-96.

103. "Climate Resilient Cities: A Primer on Reducing Vulnerabilities to Disasters," World Bank, 2009, pp. 5-6.

104. "Top UNHCR official warns about displacement from climate change," *op. cit.*

105. "Statement by Mr. Antonio Guterres," *op. cit.*

BIBLIOGRAPHY

Books

Evans, Gareth, *The Responsibility to Protect: Ending Mass Atrocity Crimes Once and For All*, Brookings Institution Press, 2008.
A former Australian foreign minister and current head of the International Crisis Group offers an impassioned plea for world leaders to follow through on their promises to protect civilians, even those abused by their own governments.

Loescher, Gil, Alexander Betts and James Milner, *The United Nations High Commissioner for Refugees (UNHCR): The Politics and Practice of Refugee Protection Into the 21st Century*, Routledge, 2008.
Academic experts on refugee issues offer a generally sympathetic but often critical assessment of the UNHCR's performance as the world's main protector of refugees.

Verdirame, Guglielmo, and Barbara Harrell-Bond, with Zachary Lomo and Hannah Garry, *Rights in Exile: Janus-Faced Humanitarianism*, Berghahn Books, 2005.
A former director of the Refugee Studies Center at Oxford University (Harrell-Bond) and an expert on refugee rights at Cambridge University offer a blistering critique of the U.N. and nongovernment agencies that protect refugees.

Articles

"Managing the Right of Return," *The Economist*, Aug. 4, 2008.

The practical implications of refugees' legal right to return to their home countries are examined.

Cohen, Roberta, and Francis Deng, "The Genesis and the Challenges," *Forced Migration Review*, December 2008.
This is the keystone article in an issue devoted to the Guiding Principles on Internal Displacement 10 years after their creation. Cohen and Deng were prime movers of the document.

Feyissa, Abebe, with Rebecca Horn, "Traveling Souls: Life in a Refugee Camp, Where Hearts Wander as Minds Deteriorate," *Utne Reader*, September-October 2008, www.utne.com/2008-09-01/GreatWriting/Traveling-Souls.aspx.
An Ethiopian who has lived in northwestern Kenya's Kakuma refugee camp for 16 years writes about life in the camp.

Guterres, Antonio, "Millions Uprooted: Saving Refugees and the Displaced," *Foreign Affairs*, September/October 2008.
The U.N. High Commissioner for Refugees lays out an ambitious agenda of action to aid and protect the displaced.

Harr, Jonathan, "Lives of the Saints: International Hardship Duty in Chad," *The New Yorker*, Jan. 5, 2009, www.newyorker.com/reporting/2009/01/05/090105fa_fact_harr.
A frequent *New Yorker* contributor offers a sympathetic portrait of idealistic aid workers at refugee camps in Chad.

Stevens, Jacob, "Prison of the Stateless: The Derelictions of UNHCR," *New Left Review*, November-December 2006, www.newleftreview.rg/?page=article&view=2644.
A review of the memoirs of former High Commissioner Sadako Ogata becomes a strongly worded critique of the U.N. refugee agency. A rebuttal by former UNHCR special envoy Nicholas Morris is at www.unhcr.org/research/RESEARCH/ 460d131d2.pdf.

Reports and Studies

"2009 Global Update," U.N. High Commissioner for Refugees, November 2008, www.unhcr.org/ga09/index.html.
Published in November, this is the most recent summary from the UNHCR of its operations, plans and budget for 2009.

"**Future Floods of Refugees: A comment on climate change, conflict and forced migration,**" Norwegian Refugee Council, April 2008, www.nrc.no/arch/_img/9268480.pdf.
The refugee council surveys the debate over whether climate change will worsen natural disasters and force untold millions of people from their homes.

"**Protracted Refugee Situations: High Commissioner's Initiative,**" U.N. High Commissioner for Refugees, December 2008, www.unhcr.org/protect/PROTECTION/4937de6f2.pdf.
The UNHCR offers a plan of action for resolving several long-term situations in which refugees have been trapped in camps or settlements for decades.

"**When Displacement Ends: A Framework for Durable Solutions,**" Brookings-Bern Project on Internal Displacement, June 2007, www.brookings.edu/reports/2007/09displacementends.aspx.
This detailed blueprint for how international agencies can help IDPs find "durable solutions" to their displacements is the product of conferences and other studies.

Cohen, Roberta, "**Listening to the Voices of the Displaced: Lessons Learned,**" Brookings-Bern Project on Internal Displacement, September 2008, www.brookings.edu/reports/2008/09_internal_displacement_cohen.aspx.
The author recommends better ways to aid and protect displaced people around the world, based on interviews with dozens of IDPs.

For More Information

Brookings-Bern Project on Internal Displacement, The Brookings Institution, 1775 Massachusetts Avenue, N.W., Washington, DC, 20036; (202) 797-6168; www.brookings.edu/projects/idp.aspx. A joint project of the Brookings Institution and the University of Bern (Switzerland) School of Law; conducts research and issues reports on policy questions related to internally displaced people (IDPs).

Institute for the Study of International Migration, Georgetown University, Harris Building, Third Floor, 3300 Whitehaven St., N.W., Washington, DC, 20007; (202) 687-2258; www12.georgetown.edu/sfs/isim/index.html. An academic research center focusing on all aspects of international migration, including refugees.

Internal Displacement Monitoring Centre, Chemin de Balexert, 7-9 1219 Chatelaine Geneva, Switzerland; 41-22-799-07 00; www.internal-displacement.org. Provides regular reports on IDPs globally; the major source of information about the numbers of people displaced by conflict.

International Organization for Migration, 17 Route des Morillons, CH-1211, Geneva 19, Switzerland; 41-22-717-9111; www.iom.int. A U.N. partner (not officially within the U.N. system) that aids refugees and migrants and studies migration trends.

Norwegian Refugee Council, P.O. Box 6758, St. Olavs Plass, 0130 Oslo, Norway; 47-23-10 9800; www.nrc.no. A

prominent nongovernmental organization that provides aid programs for displaced persons and advocates on their behalf.

Refugee Studies Centre, Queen Elizabeth House, University of Oxford, 3 Mansfield Road, Oxford OX1 3TB, United Kingdom; 44-1865-281720; www.rsc.ox.ac.uk/index.html?main. A prominent research center on refugees and the displaced. Publishes the *Forced Migration Review*, a quarterly journal written by experts in the field.

Refugees International, 2001 S St., N.W., Suite 700, Washington, DC, 20009; (202) 828-0110; www.refugeesinternational.org. Advocates on behalf of refugees and IDPs and publishes regular reports based on site visits to key countries.

U.N. High Commissioner for Refugees, Case Postale 2500, CH-1211, Geneva 2 Depot, Switzerland; 41-22-739-8111; www.unhcr.org/home.html. The U.N. agency with prime responsibility for aiding and protecting refugees; increasingly has taken on a similar role in regard to IDPs.

U.S. Committee for Refugees and Immigrants, 2231 Crystal Dr., Suite 350, Arlington, VA 22202-3711; (703) 310-1130; www.refugees.org. An advocacy group that publishes reports focusing on human-rights abuses and other problems encountered by refugees and immigrants.

15

Armenian demonstrators in Tel Aviv, Israel, mark the 94th anniversary last April of what historians say was genocide by the Ottoman Empire, Turkey's predecessor, during World War I. Armenians say Turkish soldiers killed hundreds of thousands of Armenians; Turkey, which outlaws calling the deaths "genocide," claims Armenians killed thousands of Turks. The two countries recently agreed to set up a joint historical commission to look into the deaths.

From *CQ Researcher*,
December, 2009.

Rewriting History

Alan Greenblatt

In a move hailed as a diplomatic breakthrough, Turkey and Armenia on Oct. 10 agreed to establish diplomatic relations and reopen their borders, sealed by the Turks in 1993. But the new protocols have been highly controversial, particularly among members of the Armenian diaspora.

The protocols call for the two nations to set up a joint historical commission to look into the deaths of hundreds of thousands of Armenians — more than 90 years ago. Lingering questions about the deaths are a testament to the lasting passion and anger generated by disagreements over interpretations of historical events.

"History is written by the victors," former British Prime Minister Winston Churchill famously said. Perhaps nowhere is that more true than in the long-festering debate over what the Ottoman Turks, who were Muslims, did or did not do to the Christian ethnic Armenians during World War I. The Armenians, along with smaller numbers of Assyrians and Greeks, say they were killed by Ottoman Turks through massacres and forced marches through deserts, without food or water — marches the Armenians say were designed to kill the marchers.

Armenians insist it was the first genocide of the 20th century, but the Turkish Republic, which was established after the postwar collapse of the Ottoman Empire, has always denied that it was genocide, and in fact has outlawed such discussions as treasonous insults to the nation of Turkey.

For Armenians, the denial is an open wound. Imagine, they say, if the Germans denied the Holocaust. "This denial of the genocide has become the central organizing principle among Armenians in

389

Some Countries Deny Past Wrongs, Others Apologize

Nations around the world are embroiled in controversies over interpretations of historical events. In several nations, influential interest groups or the government itself either deny certain events occurred or limit access to information about them. Some countries have tried to address painful past events by apologizing to affected parties.

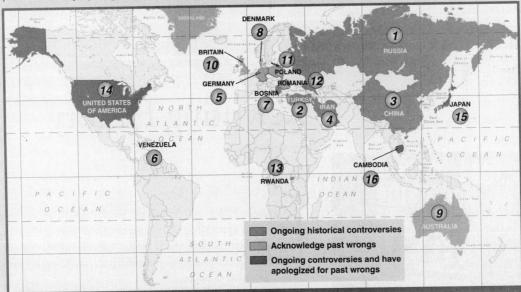

Ongoing historical controversies
Acknowledge past wrongs
Ongoing controversies and have apologized for past wrongs

How Selected Countries Have Dealt With Historical Controversies

1 *Russia* — Soviet leader Joseph Stalin had certain events such as his own mass murders and executions of political opposition figures erased from Soviet history books, a policy many say has been continued by Russian President Dmitri A. Medvedev, who recently authorized the prosecution of anyone equating Stalin and Hitler.

2 *Turkey* — Referring to Armenian deaths in World War I as genocide is a crime (treason) in Turkey that can be punishable by death.

3 *China* — Media discussion of the 1989 Tiananmen Square massacre is prohibited, resulting in a generation of students who don't know about the incident; "Great Firewall" limits Internet access.

4 *Iran* — Government blocks Internet and cell phone access to prevent people from discussing fraud that occurred during the June 2009 elections. President Mahmoud Amadinejad denies the Holocaust occurred.

5 *Germany* — Beginning in the 1950s, Germany began apologizing for the Holocaust and anti-Semitism, building memorials and requiring that the Holocaust be included in school curricula.

6 *Venezuela* — President Hugo Chávez has appointed a special commission to investigate whether the Latin American revolutionary leader Simón Bolívar was poisoned by Colombian oligarchs.

How Selected Countries Have Dealt With Historical Controversies (Cont.)

7 **Bosnia** — International courts have found that a 1995 massacre in Srebrenica constituted genocide in the former Yugoslavia but that the broader Serb campaign of ethnic cleansing in Bosnia did not. Bosnian Muslims and Bosnian Serbs continue to debate whether the conflict as a whole amounted to genocide.

8 **Denmark** — Denmark apologized to Ireland in 2007 for rape and pillage committed by the Vikings.

9 **Australia** — In February 2008, Australia apologized for forcibly removing Aboriginal children from their families as part of a state-sanctioned assimilation program during the 20th century. In November 2009, Australia apologized for emotional, physical and sexual abuse of children transported from Britain to Australia to populate the colony.

10 **Britain** — In November 2009, Britain apologized for transporting poor children from the U.K. to Australia and other colonies.

11 **Poland** — In July 2001, Poland formally apologized for the suffering and deaths of Jews during World War II.

12 **Romania** — In June 2008, the government apologized for deporting the Roma, or Gypsies, to Nazi death camps during World War II.

13 **Rwanda** — The government has acknowledged the genocidal rampage that occurred over a three-month period in 1994, when Hutus murdered nearly 900,000 Tutsis and moderate Hutus.

14 **United States** — Controversies periodically erupt, especially in the South, over textbook descriptions of historical events and trends. Recent controversies have involved attempts to deny the effectiveness of New Deal programs in lifting the country out of the Great Depression and the extent of the negative impact of slavery. In 1988 the government formally apologized — and paid $1.6 billion in reparations — to Japanese-Americans interned during WWII. The U.S. House of Representatives has approved legislation to formally apologize for slavery, and the Senate has approved a resolution apologizing for mistreatment of Native Americans.

15 **Japan** — Some textbooks have downplayed Japan's aggression during WWII and the scope of Japanese atrocities during the so-called Rape of Nanking in China. Japan has, however, apologized repeatedly for its aggression against neighbors, including China and Korea, leading up to and during World War II, for the sexual enslavement of "comfort women" during that war and for its treatment of British prisoners of war.

16 **Cambodia** — After years of silence about atrocities committed by the Khmer Rouge regime of Pol Pot from 1975 to 1979, Cambodia is coming to terms with its bloody past. The first U.N.-backed trial of a leading figure in the torture and killings of nearly 2 million people concluded on Nov. 27, with a verdict expected in early 2010; four other Khmer officials will be tried later. A new textbook describing the regime's excesses is also being released.

Source: Research by CQ Global Researcher

the diaspora," says Ronald Grigor Suny, a professor of Armenian and Russian history at the University of Michigan.

The Turks insist the Armenians were not targeted for extermination and that ethnic massacres were committed by both sides. They also say the Ottomans feared that Armenians in their midst might form a fifth column in support of invading Russians. Most scholars dismiss this argument, but Turkey is adamant that the killings did not amount to genocide. It has funded academic positions, research and publications to make its point and has lobbied hard against resolutions that would condemn the killings as genocide. (*See "At Issue," p. 407.*)

Turkish President Abdullah Gul said in April that Turkey was willing to open its archives. "It is not a political but an historic issue," he said. "That's why we should let historians discuss the matter."[1]

But Armenian protesters in France, Lebanon and the United States have shown up by the thousands in recent months when Armenian President Serzh Sargsyan has visited their countries and tried, unsuccessfully, to get diaspora leaders to support the new accord with Turkey.

Author and historian Peter Balakian, who had many ancestors killed by the Turks, says the commission idea itself is a "political gimmick." Scholars ask, he points out, "how can a society that has criminalized for 90 years reporting of a genocide be part of its scholarship?"

But the Turks and Armenians are not the only ones arguing about the past. International historical debates remain very much part of the politics of the present. Despite Japan's numerous apologies for its aggression and atrocities in World War II, its neighbors continue to criticize Japan's portrayals of that period in textbooks. International tribunals and truth and reconciliation commissions are unearthing secrets and seeking to create a consensus about what happened in bloody periods in recent years in countries such as Liberia, Sudan, Yugoslavia and Sierra Leone.

Russia and its neighbors are engaged in a heated debate about whether the Soviets rescued the Eastern bloc countries from Hitler or invaded and occupied those countries. And Russia is having its own internal argument about the historical legacy left by Stalin's atrocities. (*See sidebar, p. 402.*)

Being aware that a shared sense of the past is a powerful force, leaders seek to curate the national history with nearly the same care they give to their present-day image management. Sometimes the effort is overt, as in Stalinist Russia, when "history was not what the archives said but what the (Communist) Party decreed," as Stalin biographer Simon Sebag Montefiore writes.[2]

There's an old adage that history is written by the winners. But all political leaders seek to show themselves as emblematic of the national character and to suggest that they embody its best characteristics. Nations also seek to find glory in their own pasts and to trumpet their founding fathers. This is why so many 19th-century American home displayed a portrait of George Washington and why nearly every Turkish shopkeeper sits in front of a picture of Ataturk.

All nations seek to identify the core values and traditions that help to unify them as a culture. And the process of creating a sense of what the Germans call *Wir-Gefühl*, or unity or "us-ness," leads to exclusion, a sense that others are not like "us."

"One nation's defining victories — the defeat of the Armada, Trafalgar — may be defeats that another would prefer to forget," writes Geoffrey Cubitt, a senior lecturer in history at the University of York. Conversely, "two nations may compete for 'ownership' of the same heroic ancestors (Greece and Macedonia for Alexander the Great, France and Germany for Charlemagne)."[3]

In "What Is a Nation?" — his famous 1882 lecture — French philosopher Ernst Renan put shared memory at the core of nationality, positing that a given people are animated by virtue of "possession in common of a rich legacy of memories" and their determination to develop that legacy in the present.[4]

The idea that a sense of history — or at least a mythology constructed out of historical events and figures — is central to national identity has become increasingly influential among historians, particularly since the 1983 publication of Cornell University historian Benedict Anderson's book *Imagined Communities*. "Nations are created in people's minds," says Charles W. Ingrao, a specialist in German and Eastern European history at Purdue University. "When nations are created, they have to construct a history that justifies the separate existence of this state. It's not genetic. It's not based on anything but the choice individuals make to be part of a given group, which means that there are others who aren't part of this group."

"Nation-making is never a fixed process," the University of Michigan's Suny says. Groups of people come together to form nations because they have some idea about themselves, he adds. A century ago, nations were thought to be defined by ethnicity, language or culture. But in more recent years, many historians have become convinced that what truly binds a people together is a shared sense of the past.

"Scholars and historians would say that we live in the era of remembrance," says Alon Confino, a historian at the University of Virginia, "in the sense that societies attribute great importance to the past, the construction of the past and struggles over who defines the past."

"What we're talking about here is not academic history but public history and the way that forms a sense of who we are," says Peter Catterall, a lecturer in history at the University of London and founding editor of the journal *National Identities.*

"The nation shouldn't be confused with the state," says M. Lane Bruner, a communications professor at Georgia State University. "The state and its institutions are concrete things, while the nation is something that's more of a fantasy. Not complete fantasy, but a politically consequential fiction. Once people believe it, it becomes real."

Many nations engage in heated arguments over how history — or even what history — is included in school textbooks. German and Polish scholars have negotiated questions for 30 years about what to include about World War II in a set of joint textbooks.

Traditionally, states have shirked from owning up to their own atrocities. There are countless stories of unflattering documentaries being blocked from airing on television or playing at film festivals. Short of outright censorship, most national leaders simply prefer not to dwell on past disgraces.

"Countries try to protect the narrative that justified their creation and avoid the criticism that would lower their national self-esteem," Ingrao says.

Turkey's denial of the Armenian genocide does not sit well with many Europeans, especially the French, where the parliament in 2006 passed a law making it a crime to deny that Armenians suffered "genocide" at the hands of the Turks, infuriating Turkey.[5]

Although it took a generation for Germany to reconcile with its Nazi past, in today's world countries are expected to formally apologize for their most embarrassing historic sins. Australia, for example, has apologized recently for both its treatment of its Aboriginal population and its role in the forced migration of children, while Britain has apologized for its part in the Irish potato famine.

Apologies and other official acknowledgements of past wrongdoing are important because they "draw a line between how we acted in the past and how we'll act in the future," says Laura Hein, who teaches Japanese history at Northwestern University. "No, we will not lynch you any more. No, we will not massacre any more."

Truth and reconciliation commissions, such as the one set up a decade ago in post-apartheid South Africa, have become almost the expected end to internal conflicts.[6] An accord signed on Oct. 30 between the deposed and current presidents of Honduras, for instance, calls for a truth commission to investigate the June coup that ousted President Manuel Zelaya.[7]

Often, it takes a regime change for the historical record to be fully explored. As has happened often in the past, ongoing — and potential — war-crimes trials involving figures such as Bosnian Serb leader Radovan Karadzic, former Liberian President Charles Taylor and Sudanese President Omar al-Bashir will shed important light on recent atrocities in their countries.

"I don't know about history being written by the winners," says Eric Gordy, a senior lecturer at University College London, "but the winners never put one another on trial."

As scholars and citizens ponder how nations construct — or reconstruct — their own pasts, here are some of the questions they're debating:

Can nations cover up atrocities?

The identity of the Chinese man who stopped a column of tanks during the Tiananmen Square protests of 1989 remains unknown, but a photograph of his act has become iconic. In 1998, *Time* named the "unknown rebel" one of the 100 most important people of the 20th century.[8]

In the 2006 "Frontline" documentary "The Tank Man," four students from Beijing University are shown the famous photograph. Although an earlier generation of students from their own university had been at the

A Chinese protester blocks tanks in Beijing's Tiananmen Square in June 1989 during the government's violent crackdown on pro-democracy demonstrations. But few Chinese students today have read about the protests, in which hundreds of unarmed protesters were killed, because Chinese textbooks are not allowed to discuss the event. Some historians say that China — which wants Japan to acknowledge its wartime atrocities, particularly in Nanjing — should admit its own human rights violations, including those during the 1989 protests.

forefront of the protests — which resulted in the massacre of at least hundreds and possibly thousands of people — the four well-educated young people were baffled by the image, complaining it had "no context."[9]

This kind of amnesia "was the effect of a complete ban that the government slapped on discussion of the events, one that exists to this day," *The Globe and Mail of Toronto* reported in May. "The events of 1989 are never mentioned on state-controlled media, and those who try and speak out about the crackdown usually find themselves in prison or under house arrest."[10]

China's so-called Great Firewall, which blocks Chinese Internet users from visiting Web sites critical of the government, has been the subject of international protest. And there have been many past examples of nations destroying documents and shuttering archives to try to "delete" memory of embarrassing or politically damaging incidents. It took at least a couple of years, for example, for the first photographs of the harsh conditions under the Khmer Rouge regime to emerge out of Cambodia back in 1977, and even those did not yet depict the magnitude of the genocidal killings that had occurred.[11]

But it seems incredible, in this age of instant access to global sources of information, that any regime can still block its citizens — and the world — from learning about important events and decisions, no matter how horrific.

"It's nearly impossible for a regime or a country to cover up an atrocity outside of its own borders," says Balakian, the poet and historian at Colgate University. But, he adds, "Regimes that are genuinely authoritarian can brainwash a good segment of their population for a good period of time."

"Clearly, in closed societies where you don't have a history of free inquiry and freedom of expression and thought, it's much easier just to try to deny something and try to erase it," says Stephen Vaughn, a communications professor at the University of Wisconsin.

In the aftermath of the Iranian presidential election in June, the regime sought to block Internet and cell phone access — both to cut off information to the outside world and to take away protesters' organizing tools. For a time, protesters were able to upload accounts and photographs of the government's violent crackdown through Twitter. The U.S. State Department even asked the Web site to delay a scheduled upgrade that would have temporarily blocked Iranians from posting.[12]

During a Nov. 16 town hall meeting with Chinese students in Shanghai, U.S. President Barack Obama was asked about the nation's Internet firewall and about whether Twitter use should be unrestricted. "I'm a big supporter of not restricting Internet use, Internet access, other information technologies like Twitter," Obama said. "The more open we are, the more we can communicate. And it also helps to draw the world together."[13] Chinese television, however, did not show the exchange, and accounts of it were quickly deleted from news Web sites.[14]

William A. Schabas, director of the Irish Centre for Human Rights at the National University of Ireland, Galway, says while it's still possible for nations to hide their dirtiest laundry, it has become increasingly difficult — and not just because of the Internet. "Today, you have people monitoring human rights, you have a very sophisticated NGO [non-governmental organization] culture, you have the U.N. structure," he says. "It's a lot harder today to keep anything secret."

"Basically, it's impossible," says Confino, the University of Virginia historian. "There will always be someone with some connections to some electronic device that will tell other people about an event."

The important question, he and others argue, is not whether nations can cover up or completely censor terrible events, which they say is a relatively rare occurrence. The key question is how people respond to information that they do have.

"The cases where there is active censorship is a subset of a larger issue," says Hein, the co-editor of *Censoring History*, a collection that examines how history is presented in Japan, Germany and the United States. The larger issue, she says, is where atrocities are not secret, but reaction remains muted.

"You can certainly talk about a large number of atrocities in the world that are not well-known by most people," says Catterall, the British historian. "The fact that you've got 24-hour news coverage does not of course mean that things get picked up."

"Most of the time somebody knows, and a lot of the time everybody knows," Hein says. "But we don't do anything about it, for a variety of reasons."

Both Hein and Confino cite the case of Congo during the late 19th and early 20th centuries. Under the reign of King Leopold II of Belgium, the Congolese were forced into labor, slow workers were maimed and millions died — an atrocity that took decades to emerge into European consciousness due in part to the remoteness of the African colony.

In recent years, more people have died in a series of wars in the Democratic Republic of the Congo than in any war since World War II. The deaths have not been a secret, and the United Nations has called Congo the rape capital of the world. U.S. Secretary of State Hillary Rodham Clinton addressed the issue during her visit to the country in August, announcing a $17 million plan to help address the "rape epidemic," which often involves the military and which Clinton called "evil in its basest form."[15]

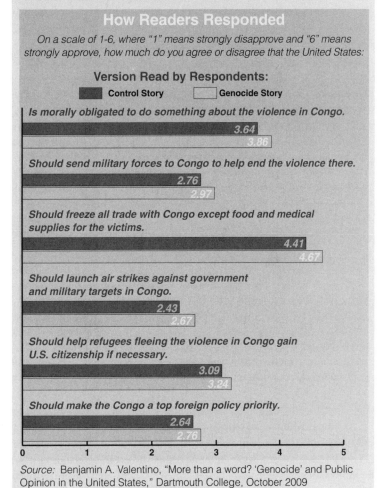

'Genocide' Label Has Little Impact on Public

Governments often go to great lengths to avoid being labeled as having committed "genocide." But if a U.S. study is an indication, the distinction is lost on the average citizen. Researchers presented readers with two mock news stories — one using the word "genocide" to describe the ongoing violence in the Democratic Republic of the Congo and one (the "control" story) that only referred to "the intentional killing of civilians" in Congo. Readers who read the "genocide" story were only slightly more likely to call for intervention in Congo than those who read the story that didn't use the term.

How Readers Responded

On a scale of 1-6, where "1" means strongly disapprove and "6" means strongly approve, how much do you agree or disagree that the United States:

Version Read by Respondents:
█ Control Story ▢ Genocide Story

Is morally obligated to do something about the violence in Congo.
Control: 3.64
Genocide: 3.86

Should send military forces to Congo to help end the violence there.
Control: 2.76
Genocide: 2.97

Should freeze all trade with Congo except food and medical supplies for the victims.
Control: 4.41
Genocide: 4.67

Should launch air strikes against government and military targets in Congo.
Control: 2.43
Genocide: 2.67

Should help refugees fleeing the violence in Congo gain U.S. citizenship if necessary.
Control: 3.09
Genocide: 3.24

Should make the Congo a top foreign policy priority.
Control: 2.64
Genocide: 2.76

0   1   2   3   4   5

Source: Benjamin A. Valentino, "More than a word? 'Genocide' and Public Opinion in the United States," Dartmouth College, October 2009

When Is Mass Murder 'Genocide'?

Using the G-word can stymie action and reconciliation.

The term genocide was coined during World War II to denote a crime so terrible that it must not be confused with any other. But some people are wondering whether, in this sense, the word has worked too well.

Numerous mass killings of particular populations have occurred throughout history — from the destruction of Carthage during the Third Punic War in 146 BC to the Anglo-Zulu War of 1879. But, until World War II, genocide was a "crime without a name," as British Prime Minister Winston Churchill, put it.[1]

The term was coined by Raphael Lemkin, a Polish Jew who had evaded capture by the Germans and eventually resettled in the United States, in his 1944 book *Axis Rule in Occupied Europe.* Lemkin combined the Greek word *genos,* meaning race or tribe, with the Latin suffix *-cide,* derived from *caedare,* which means killing. Genocide was distinguished from mass murder — wrote Lemkin, who served as an advisor to the prosecutor at the Nuremberg trials — in that it is "directed against the national group as an entity, and the actions involved are directed against individuals, not in their individual capacity, but as members of the national group."[2]

Lemkin's neologism quickly found its way into international law with the 1948 adoption of the United Nations Convention on Genocide.[3] The convention defines genocide as the attempt to destroy, in whole or in part, a national, ethnic, racial or religious group by killing its members or creating other disruptive and destructive acts such as attempting to prevent births within the targeted group or separating children from it. Member states can call on the United Nations to try to prevent genocide and are bound by the treaty to stop genocide from taking place within their own borders.

To Lemkin's dismay, however, the document did not define mass murder for political reasons as genocide. That has turned out to be an enormous loophole. In Indonesia, for example, an anti-communist purge in 1965-1966 by the army resulted in the deaths of an estimated 500,000 people. Yet, because of their political nature, the massacres have not been considered genocide. In other cases — to get around the political loophole when outside observers have considered large-scale killings to be genocide — the perpetrator regimes have argued that their intent was based on self-defense or military necessity, not to target members of a particular ethnic or religious group.

The word's association with Nazi Germany and the Holocaust has, in fact, presented a barrier to defining mass killings as genocide because it "set the bar for concern so high" that people assumed contemporary genocides "were not measuring up," writes Samantha Power, a public policy professor at Harvard University and author of *A Problem from Hell: America and the Age of Genocide.*

"Lemkin's hybrid term would cause endless confusion for policy makers and ordinary people who assumed that genocide occurred only where the perpetrator of atrocity could be shown, like Hitler, to possess an intent to exterminate every last member of an ethnic, national or religious group."[4]

In some contemporary cases, the debate among wealthy nations has seemed to turn more on the semantic question

"In Congo, millions of innocent civilians have died in civil wars and in wars with neighbors. We know about it, it's not a secret, but to people in the West, has it become an important place of remembrance? No," says Confino. "The important thing is not whether we know about an event but whether we choose to remember and make it an example and care about it."

Daqing Yang, a George Washington University historian, argues that the very tools that make it easier for information to travel, including Web sites such as YouTube, may make it more difficult for bad news to penetrate deeply into a national or international consciousness. With so much information hurled at us on a minute-by-minute basis, it becomes challenging to gather a sense of the importance of events that may seem remote.

"The market mechanism may work against focusing on events in parts of the world that otherwise do not hold the huge interest of people living in the advanced part of the world," Yang says.

of whether events technically qualify as "genocide" than on formulating any response. "As in Rwanda, discussions about the dreaded 'G-word' dominate policy discussions about Darfur rather than the initiation of concrete measures to stop the . . . murderous excesses," writes Stanford University historian Norman M. Naimark.[5]

Such linguistic debates and the ramifications imposed by the international convention once an atrocity is called a genocide have made use of the term "deleterious to understanding, analysis and ultimately doing anything" about mass killings, says Daniel Jonah Goldhagen, author of a new book about genocide, *Worse Than War.*

"There's a legal structure out there that makes the word very powerful. It can trigger certain actions. That's why there's so much debate about whether something is genocide or isn't," Goldhagen says. "The reality is that the term is a great hindrance, because fixating on the term hinders our understanding of what both happens and should happen."

Although policy makers may be hung up on the ramifications of using the word, the public apparently is not. Dartmouth College historian Benjamin Valentino concocted two fake news stories about a Darfur-like slaughter in the Democratic Republic of the Congo in order to gauge Americans' reaction to the word genocide. The responses were essentially the same whether the article had labeled the events as genocide or not. "The bottom line is that people are not fixated on the term genocide," he says. "Instead, they care about what is actually happening."

Purdue University historian Charles W. Ingrao notes that former combatants can sometimes agree on the facts — including mass murder and mass rape — but the aggressor will still not accept the opprobrium of the genocide label. "The use of the term genocide throws a monkey wrench into what could be the smoothly working machinery of inter-ethnic reconciliation," he says. "It has a political dimension that makes it counterproductive."

Because the word has such power — both in deciding whether to intervene in present conflicts and in determining whether past slaughters should be considered genocide — some genocide scholars, including Goldhagen, have proposed alternative terms. They argue that fixating on the label is less productive than addressing mass killings or their underlying politics.

The relatively narrow legal definition of genocide remains important, however. "In order to prosecute people . . . , it's important to have a legal description," says Alon Confino, a University of Virginia historian. "You can prosecute people only if there's a law. It's not enough to have some kind of description."

But the political and public arguments about whether to embrace or deny the term have become largely symbolic. Calling something genocide rather than "murder between foreigners" may make citizens more likely to lobby Congress or the European Union. It may not make it any more likely, however, that political leaders will choose to intervene.

"Quite obviously, the system is broken," Goldhagen says. "The central term has not been helpful in doing much of anything to save people's lives. The simple fact is that since the Holocaust, it has never once been invoked to save people's lives."

— Alan Greenblatt

---

[1] Adam Jones, *Genocide: A Comprehensive Introduction* (2006), p. 8.

[2] "Coining a Word and Championing a Cause," *Holocaust Encyclopedia*, U.S. Holocaust Memorial Museum, www.ushmm.org/wlc/article.php?lang=en&ModuleId=10007500.

[3] For background, see Sarah Glazer, "Stopping Genocide," *CQ Researcher*, Aug. 27, 2004, pp. 685-708.

[4] Samantha Power, *A Problem from Hell: America and the Age of Genocide* (2003), p. 43.

[5] Norman M. Naimark, "Srebrenica in the History of Genocide," in Nanci Adler, *et al.*, eds., *Memories of Mass Repression* (2009), p. 11.

And a kind of mass awareness may be as important in formulating a response as whether information is available to begin with. "If a determined citizen in China wants to get the information, he or she can circumvent the firewalls set up by government," Yang says, "but not at levels significant enough to make a difference."

Is historical accountability a human right?

After a broad-scale atrocity, societies demand some kind of reckoning for several reasons, most importantly to recognize the suffering that the survivors and the dead experienced.

"It has been said that denial is the final phase of genocide," writes Richard G. Hovannisian, an Armenian history expert at the University of California-Los Angeles. "Following the physical destruction of a people and their material culture, memory is all that's left and is targeted as the last victim."[16]

"If you talk to survivors, and I've talked to survivors of many genocides and assaults, they all say the same thing: They want the truth to be known," says Daniel Jonah Goldhagen, author of a new book on genocide called *Worse Than War.* "A wound that is denied and sometimes turned against them is a source of ongoing pain for them."

The second reason for pursuing the truth, as with any crime, is to bring the perpetrators to justice, rather than offering them easy rehabilitation. "Nothing encourages lawlessness more than the sight of villains getting away with it, living off their spoils and laughing in the public's face," writes *Washington Post* columnist Anne Applebaum in her history of the Soviet gulag.[17]

The third is the hope that, by owning up to past sins through a thorough airing of the facts and their meanings, the affected society can move forward without leaving these wounds open to fester. "Some countries simply forget the past and attempt to induce a national amnesia in its people," writes South African Judge Richard J. Goldstone, who served as a prosecutor at the international tribunals on genocides in Rwanda and Yugoslavia and recently issued a controversial report on allegations of excessive violence during last winter's Israeli-Hamas conflict in Gaza.

"Wiser leaders recognized that in order to lay a foundation for an enduring peace, measures had to be taken to manage the past," Goldstone continues. "It was acknowledged that history has to be recorded, calls for justice have to be heeded and perpetrators have to be called to account."[18]

The import of this line of thinking is that we live in an "era of remembrance," as the University of Virginia's Confino says. Governments and other official institutions such as the Catholic Church apologize for historical wrongdoings with some regularity, there are occasional arguments about cash reparations for victims of past crimes and there are now nearly continual truth and reconciliation commissions meant to help an injured society sort though, understand and begin to move past recent conflicts.

Borrowing from religious traditions, the belief that truth can set nations free — or at least on a path toward repentance and reconciliation — has become a major new norm in international relations. "Perpetrators and victims can come to some kind of peaceful accommodation only when the past is explored openly and honestly, with full participation of survivors and scholars alike,"

writes Stanford University historian Norman M. Naimark.[19]

But since so many modern conflicts have been fought within states, rather than between them, getting countries to cope with a difficult past has become seemingly more imperative. If a nation can't find peace with itself until owning up to its dark past, has the need for historic accountability become akin to a human right?

"For me, it is a human rights matter," Colgate's Balakian says. "It's a continuation of the process. The denial of genocide is the final stage of genocide because it seeks to demonize the victims and rehabilitate the offenders."

Schabas — at the Irish Centre for Human Rights, who served on the international tribunal for war crimes in Sierra Leone — agrees. "I can't point you to an article in the Universal Declaration of Human Rights that says there's a right to have history clarified, but there's a growing feeling that it is a part of human rights," Schabas says. "There's considerable authority in the human rights literature for what's known as the right to truth, the right to know the truth."

But even if the United Nations adopts a right to historical truth, as Schabas predicts it will, guaranteeing the truth will be deeply problematic. Historians are already wary of laws demanding fealty to certain versions of events — from the Turkish law that makes it an insult against the state to describe the deaths of Armenians during World War I as genocide, to the French law that makes Holocaust denial a crime.

Aside from criminalizing accounts of history, historians are also wary of the inevitable politicization of the past that an official, sanctioned version necessarily would create. "With most of these events, there's actually pretty much agreement on the facts. The fight is then over what symbolic meaning it has for the society as a whole," says Hein of Northwestern. "When governments create commissions to look into things, they're often quite politicized — there's an agenda."

"One cannot be certain that official historians . . . will always serve the best interests of the public," writes the University of Wisconsin's Vaughn. "When historians are in the service of the government, and the public policy of that government rests on a certain set of historical precedents, it is difficult for men to place truth above public advantage, when public advantage might mean the winning of a war, the covering of a reputation or even an improvement in general welfare."[20]

Vaughn cites regimes seeking to use history to justify their present policies. But the claims on truth that survivors of atrocities make can also, it should be remembered, be subject to their own kinds of distortion, from vengeance-seeking to engaging in identity politics as victims.

While insisting that acknowledgement of the Holocaust has become central to European identity, historian Tony Judt of New York University, the author of a standard history of postwar Europe, notes that the extermination of the Jews was not the central project of the European nations involved in the war — even Germany. "In retrospect, 'Auschwitz' is the most important thing to know about World War II," he writes. "But that is not how things seemed at the time."[21]

Capturing "the totality of the truth" is difficult, suggests British historian Catterall, because such debates typically take place after there has been a change in regime. "While it's very important to acknowledge the faults of the past, I think it's also important to put them in perspective, not to try to use them to serve as political grievances for the present," he says. "There's always a risk that you end up creating a binary division in which there are many white hats and many black hats," he says.

Japanese history expert Yang suggests that historians "at least establish a perimeter around what is commonly accepted and acceptable. As historians, the best we can do is establish what happened and how it happened, and let others pass judgment."

Are national identities defined by shared history?

At a Nov. 12 ceremony honoring victims of the German occupation, French President Nicolas Sarkozy harkened back to the values of France's past. "National identity concerns us all," he said. "What is at stake . . . is not only economic. It is also the disappearance of a form of civilization, of a heritage of values, of a culture of work."[22]

Sarkozy's remarks were in keeping with a months-long "grand debate" he has begun about France's national identity. Sarkozy — whose father was a Hungarian immigrant and whose mother was of mixed Catholic and Jewish descent — launched a Web site on Nov. 2 to solicit ideas from citizens about what it means, exactly, to be French.[23]

Government officials described the effort as a chance to restore a sense of national pride and celebrate France's unifying values. "We must reaffirm the values of national identity and pride in being French," said Éric Besson, France's minister of Immigration and National Identity. "This debate doesn't scare me. I even find it passionate."[24]

But as the public and the popular press debate the relative virtues and importance of cheeses, proper French grammar and the national anthem — *La Marseillaise* — many see the effort as a political distraction and worry that it will lead to an attack on immigrants leading up to national elections next year. Traditionally white and Catholic France is home to more than 6 million Muslims and rapidly increasing populations of immigrants from Africa and Eastern Europe.

French national culture, based on the revolutionary ideals of *liberté, égalité, fraternité*, offers no official recognition of ethnicity. Yet the country has engaged in heated debates in recent years about the performance of immigrants in schools and economically. The French public school ban on religious symbols, notably the *hijab*, or Muslim headscarf, has also caused considerable tension.

"It is an important debate," said Karim Emile Bitar, an associate fellow at the International Institute of Strategic Relations in Paris. "France needs to find a way to preserve its universalist model, which is remarkable on philosophical grounds, with new realities that make the model seem hypocritical because of the giant gap between . . . proclamations of equality . . . [and] the reality on the ground . . . discrimination and unequal opportunities."[25]

Rosamond McKitterick, a medieval historian at Cambridge University, argues that "an idea can hold a people together and sustain it."[26] The creation of historical memory, she says, is a collective act; that is, as nations construct their histories, they're simultaneously constructing a national identity by coming to agreement about what is fundamental from their past.

"It's not just one individual's conception," she says. "To have some kind of impact, it has to have some resonance with memories of people whose identities it's shaping."

Clearly, a shared sense of the past is a major binding agent in holding a nation together, says Colgate's Balakian. "The historical discourse that any culture embraces is certainly part of its national identity," he says.

CHRONOLOGY

1940s-1980s *Many countries begin reexamining their roles in World War II.*

1948 United Nations adopts Convention on Genocide, outlawing mass killings motivated by race, religion or other factors.

1958 In a secret speech, Soviet Premier Nikita Khrushchev denounces the atrocities of his predecessor, Joseph Stalin.

1965 Saburo Ienaga, a prominent Japanese historian whose textbook had been rejected for containing "too many illustrations of the 'dark side' of the war," challenges the nation's textbook-screening process in court.

1986 U.S. Senate ratifies the genocide convention after years of near-daily floor speeches — 3,211 in all — by Sen. William Proxmire, R-Wis., calling for passage.

1989 China massacres several hundred pro-democracy protesters in Tiananmen Square and imposes a blackout on discussion of the incident.

1990s *Most countries have atoned for their World War II-era sins, but some continue to deny them.*

1991 A Korean "comfort woman" testifies in court that the Japanese government forced her and thousands of others to provide sex to Japanese soldiers in World War II.

1994 A Smithsonian Institution exhibit about the *Enola Gay*, the plane that dropped an atomic bomb on Hiroshima in 1945, stirs controversy as U.S. veterans' groups complain it focuses too much attention on Japanese casualties.

1995 South Africa establishes a Truth and Reconciliation Commission charged with exploring and determining the effects of the nation's former apartheid policy.

1998 U.N. adopts Rome Statute establishing International Criminal Court to prosecute genocide, crimes against humanity and war crimes. . . . British Prime Minister Tony Blair establishes a parliamentary inquiry into Bloody Sunday, the 1972 shooting by a British parachute regiment of 27 civil protesters in

Northern Ireland; the report is scheduled for publication in March 2010.

2000-Present *Arguments about history continue to rage across the globe, but a clear trend toward repentance leads to numerous official apologies and truth and reconciliation commissions.*

2000 Pope John Paul II apologizes for past sins committed by the "children" of the Roman Catholic Church during the Counter-Reformation and World War II.

2004 Poland officially recognizes the suffering of Polish Jews during World War II; Romania soon follows suit.

2005 Turkish authorities arrest Nobel Prize-winning Turkish novelist Orhan Pamuk for discussing the genocide of Armenians by the Turks under the Ottoman Empire. . . . Germany opens Memorial to the Murdered Jews of Europe near Brandenburg Gate in Berlin. . . . Publication of a revisionist textbook in Japan downplaying the country's war crimes triggers rioting across China, notably in Shanghai, where protesters damaged the Japanese consulate, broke windows of Japanese restaurants and businesses and overturned Japanese model vehicles.

2008 U.S. House of Representatives adopts resolution apologizing for slavery.

2009 Russian president Dmitri Medvedev creates historical commission to counter "anti-Russian propaganda" in former Soviet republics; Russian Duma criminalizes the rehabilitation of Nazism (May 19). . . . U.S. Senate approves measure apologizing to American Indians for misdeeds by the federal government and "many instances of violence, maltreatment and neglect" by U.S. citizens (Oct. 8). . . . Turkey and Armenia begin normalizing relations by opening their border and calling for a joint commission to examine Turkey's slaughter of Armenians during World War I, triggering protests in the Armenian diaspora (Oct. 10). . . . France launches Web site soliciting citizens' ideas for a "grand debate" on what constitutes national identity. . . . India's parliament tables a report on the 1992 demolition of the Babri Masjid mosque by Hindu fundamentalists, concluding senior members of the opposition Bharatiya Janata Party fueled the anti-Muslim violence (Nov. 24).

U.S. nation-building exercises in Iraq and Afghanistan have been frustrated in part because ethnic and tribal loyalties in both countries are stronger than a sense of national identity and a shared past.

"In Iraq, you had a strong sense of Islamic identity and Arabic identity, but there really wasn't a national identity because it was carved out artificially" from the Ottoman Empire after World War I, says Prasenjit Duara, a humanities professor at the National University of Singapore. "Someone like Saddam Hussein kept them all together by force, rather than by creating a sense of national identity."

By contrast, consider Switzerland. "The Swiss may speak four different languages and still act as one people," wrote the late Czech historian Karl W. Deutsch, "for each of them has enough learned habits, preferences, symbols, memories, patterns of landholding and social stratification, events in history and personal associations, all of which together permit [him] to communicate more effectively with other Swiss than with the speakers of his own language who belong to other peoples."[27]

But national identity consists of more than simply history. Even historians concede that there's more going on within a nation's sense of itself than just memories of the past. Language, ethnicity and culture are all inextricably linked with history in defining a nation. "You can't really separate them, particularly history and ethnicity — and language is often seen as expressive of ethnicity," says Donald Bloxham, a professor of modern history at the University of Edinburgh.

"History is culture, language and ethnicity," says Hein at Northwestern. "These are all narratives of belonging to a group and don't really exist separately from each other. The issue is: What is interpreted as being central, rather than peripheral?

"In some places language is at the center of identity," she continues. "But all societies have people who speak more than one language. It's how you think about it that matters, and religion is the same way. It's how you define which aspects of the culture are the most important ones."

George Washington University's Yang, a Japanese history expert, agrees that while history is "definitely one of the building blocks" of national identity, it may not be the most important one.

History can help construct national identities, Yang argues, precisely because it is the element that is most subject to change. "It's the most malleable, compared to purely ethnic or linguistic boundaries, which are somewhat more fixed. Whoever is intent on building the identity can reshape historical memory or discourse in the ways that they prefer, by including certain people and ethnic groups (as central) or excluding them."

BACKGROUND
History and Nationhood

Throughout much of the 19th century, historians concerned themselves largely with recording facts as presented in official documents. But the "cult of facts" — parodied by Charles Dickens with the character of Gradgrind in *Hard Times*, who was "a veritable idiot for Facts" — gave way early in the 20th century.

The old notion that history was about "kings and battles" began to merge with studies of everyday life, in part because war had come to involve the entirety of society, not just mercenaries and other soldiers.[28] Soon after World War I, the noted British biographer Lytton Strachey wrote that history is "not an accumulation of facts but a relation of them."[29]

By 1925, the French philosopher and sociologist Maurice Halbwachs was writing about history as a collective social project, arguing that groups construct their own images of the world by establishing an agreed-upon version of the past.[30] As the age of small principalities and enormous empires gave way to nation-states and the global economic competition between them, a new type of nationalism emerged.

The creation of symbols of national identity, including flags and anthems, became more important, while religious and linguistic cleavages were minimized. "Modern nationalism, especially, hinges on the presentation of the nation as a community whose members are bound together by powerful ties of common interest, common background and common destiny," writes British historian Cubitt.[31]

"For a variety of political, economic and social reasons, nations needed much more identification with the nation itself, rather than kinship, communities and other groups," says Duara, the National University of Singapore historian. "At the same time, they're claiming it's for the people itself, that the people are the basis of the nation."

Stalin Left Behind a Distorted History

Russia and its neighbors are taking a new look at the past.

Joseph Stalin loved history. He often fell asleep on the couch with a history book in his hand. But the man who ruled the Soviet Union from 1922 until his death in 1953 was also, ironically, one of the greatest revisionists of Soviet history.

Stalin insisted on versions of the past that bore little resemblance to what had actually happened, literally erasing the names and images of his political opponents — and his own mass murders and executions — from the pages of Soviet history books.

Stalin's historical dissembling has helped make his legacy enormously complicated for Russia and its neighbors, including the former Soviet republics. In the West, Stalin is largely remembered as one of the bloodiest despots in modern history, responsible for the deaths of millions through arrests, executions and a famine in Ukraine caused by Stalin's agricultural policies that killed up to 8 million people. But in Russia, his reign is remembered as well for its glory and sacrifice, given the nation's central role — and losses of an estimated 20 million soldiers and civilians — in defeating Adolf Hitler during what Russians call the Great Patriotic War. And in recent years, state-sponsored accounts have portrayed Stalin as an effective manager.

Russia is now actively arguing with its neighbors about Stalin's legacy. Ukraine wants the international community to acknowledge that the famine of 1932-1933 was genocide because it was deliberate — the result of Stalin's forced collectivization of agriculture. Ukraine became "a vast death camp," according to Ukrainian President Vicktor Yuschenko, when millions of landed peasants known as *kulaks* — who had rebelled against Stalin's agricultural policies — died. Last year, however, the lower house of the Russian parliament, the Duma, passed a resolution saying that "there is no historical proof that the famine was organized along ethnic lines."[1]

In Poland, contemporary Poles have met only resistance to their requests for Russian declassification of documents relating to the infamous Katyn massacre, in which as many as 22,000 Poles — largely military officers — were slaughtered

by Soviet soldiers during World War II. And Poland and the Baltic states want Russia to denounce the Molotov-Ribbentrop Pact Stalin made with Hitler, which led to the Soviet and German invasions of their neighbors before World War II. The Russians say they were "liberating" the countries from Hitler.

In response, Russian Prime Minister Vladimir Putin published an article in August calling the pact immoral, but Russian ministers and state-sponsored media have suggested that Poland was complicit in causing the war by provoking Hitler.

"The rows Russia is having with its neighbors are like scenes from a divorce. Everyone is throwing dishes and breaking furniture," said Mikhail Margelov, chairman of the Committee for Foreign Affairs in the Federation Council of Russia, parliament's upper house.[2]

The current Russian regime, while widely criticized in the international press for its rehabilitation of Stalinist symbols, such as the restoration of a prominent quote from Stalin himself at the Kremlin metro station, is still not as shuttered about its past as the Soviets were.

"Stalin was not the first leader to enforce a myth of history, only the most successful," writes *New Yorker* editor David Remnick, a former *Washington Post* Moscow correspondent and author of the best-selling *Lenin's Tomb: The Last Days of the Soviet Empire.*[3]

For decades after his death, Stalin was barely mentioned in the Soviet Union, with public discussion of his rule strictly forbidden. His successor, Nikita Khrushchev, denounced Stalin's crimes in a 1956 "secret speech" that was meant only for the ears of top officials in the Soviet bloc. But the text was leaked to the West almost immediately.

Remarkably, however, the Russian Education Ministry announced in September that excerpts from Aleksandr Solzhenitsyn's *The Gulag Archipelago* would be required reading in schools. The 1973 history of the Stalinist system of prisons and slave labor camps had been banned and the author exiled during Soviet times. In October, Russian

The question of what makes a people a people — and how that is shaped by history and memory — has become a central preoccupation in historical studies in recent years. "The treatment of the past through remembering and

forgetting crucially shapes the present and future for individuals and entire societies," writes Martha Minow, dean of Harvard Law School and a noted human rights scholar.[32]

Soviet leader Joseph Stalin routinely altered historical photographs and documents to suit his political aims. In the photo at left, a former ally, Nikolai Yezhov, stands at Stalin's left. After Stalin had the man executed, his image was removed from the official photo, at right.

President Dmitri A. Medvedev called for construction of museums and memorial centers devoted to Stalin's atrocities.

"If the Russian people and the Russian elite remembered — viscerally, emotionally remembered — what Stalin did to the Chechens, they could not have invaded Chechnya in the 1990s, not once and not twice," writes *Washington Post* columnist Anne Applebaum in her history of the Stalinist gulags. "To do so was the moral equivalent of postwar Germany invading Poland."[4]

Ironically, Medvedev earlier had established an historical commission to put an official stamp on the Russian version of the early days of World War II. In it the Soviet Union "liberated" some of its neighbors from Hitler — rather than invaded them. Russia now needs to "liberate" historians in Ukraine, Latvia, Estonia, Georgia and Poland — as one commissioner put it —"from the pressure of state dictatorship applied upon them."[5]

The law creating the commission also stated that "anyone who 'falsifies' the Kremlin's version of history, for example by equating Hitler and Stalin . . . may be prosecuted. Suggesting that 1945 brought not liberation but new occupation for Eastern Europe is also banned."[6]

Russians today are aware of Stalin's political crimes, but current leaders clearly find more value in restoring patriotism and selectively celebrating the glories of the past than in talking about war crimes and mass killings.

The nation's near-neighbors, meanwhile, are seeking to reestablish their own national identities following the transnational ideology and imperialism of the Soviet regime. The breakup of the Soviet Union has led to a "surge of attempts at national identity construction," says M. Lane Bruner, a communications professor at Georgia State University.

"This is all being rehabilitated because this is now a very lively issue for Russia," said Moscow-based military analyst Pavel Felgenhauer. "This is not about history at all."[7]

— *Alan Greenblatt*

[1] Peter Finn, "Aftermath of a Soviet Famine," *The Washington Post*, April 27, 2008, p. A14, www.washingtonpost.com/wp-dyn/content/article/2008/04/26/AR2008042602039.html.

[2] Owen Matthews and Anna Nemtsova, "The World According to Russia," *Newsweek International*, Sept. 7, 2009, www.newsweek.com/id/214243.

[3] David Remnick, *Lenin's Tomb* (1993), p. 37.

[4] Anne Applebaum, *Gulag: A History* (2003), p. 572.

[5] Masha Lipman, "Russia, Again Evading History," *The Washington Post*, June 20, 2009, p. A17, www.washingtonpost.com/wp-dyn/content/article/2009/06/19/AR2009061902062.html.

[6] "The Unhistory Man," *The Economist*, Sept. 5, 2009, www.economist.com/opinion/displaystory.cfm?story_id=14363315.

[7] "Russia Defends Pact With Hitler 70 Years Later," The Associated Press, Aug. 21, 2009; www.foxnews.com/story/0,2933,541602,00.html?test=latestnews.

And, just as war and other great events began to involve more of the populace, the study of those events came to rely on a wider variety of sources, including eyewitness accounts. Written records were insufficient for reconstructing mass events — particularly genocide and other atrocities — so survivor testimonies that might once have been avoided as overly emotional or subjective have become paramount. "After years of extensive academic debate, there is consensus among most researchers that accounts of survivors form an important basis for the study of genocide and mass violence," write the editors of a recent book.[33]

In recent decades, arguing about history and its meanings has become a central project among nations, prompted in large part by the enduring resonance of atrocities committed during World War II. "Historical remembrance is not some abstract issue that historians conceived," says Confino, of the University of Virginia. "This is an issue with political, economic, moral and legal implications."

The German Model

Remembrance of the Holocaust — the extermination of millions of people, including 6 million Jews, for their perceived "racial inferiority" by Nazi Germany during World War II — has become the defining event in both historical studies and contemporary European identity.

Confino points out that the debates about the Holocaust and its dynamics are shaping the thinking and work of historians writing about entirely different events dating well before the 20th century. And New York University's Judt points out that "Holocaust recognition is our contemporary European entry ticket," noting that in 2004 Poland's president officially recognized the suffering of Polish Jews during the war, "seeking to close a painful chapter in his nation's past and bring Poland into line with its EU partners." The following year, Romania's president made a similar concession for similar reasons.[34]

Germany is widely hailed as a model of a "guilty" nation grappling with the sins of its past, offering official apologies, constructing a massive memorial to Holocaust victims at the center of its capital and making school instruction about the atrocities mandatory. Even during last month's 20th-anniversary celebrations of the fall of the Berlin Wall, German Chancellor Angela Merkel went out of her way to point out that Nov. 9 is also the anniversary of *Kristallnacht*, the 1938 pogrom against the Jews that was an early indication of the coming terror.[35]

But the Holocaust was not always at the center of German consciousness. It took a generation or more for the country to begin to own up to its past. The German preoccupation with the Holocaust was much broader and deeper in 1990 than in 1945, points out Cynthia Miller-Idriss, a professor of international education and sociology at New York University, in her 2009 book about

contemporary German identity, *Blood and Culture*.[36] West German schools after the war had even stopped teaching history beyond the empire of Kaiser Wilhelm II, which ended with World War I.

"Germans rejected the Nuremberg trials" — the immediate postwar trials of top Nazi officials for crimes against humanity, says Bloxham, the Edinburgh historian. "They claimed that it only involved a small number of people, that Germans were killed in the war, too, and that most Germans knew nothing about the Holocaust."

A later series of trials in Germany and Israel began bringing the Holocaust to the forefront of German consciousness. The trials, held between 1958 and 1965, presented an opportunity for Holocaust survivors to publicly testify about their experiences. After a wave of anti-Semitic violence and a growing recognition that young Germans knew next to nothing about their nation's fascist past, 10 West German states began requiring that schools teach about the nation's policies during 1933 to 1945, including the extermination of the Jews, Gypsies, homosexuals and others.[37]

German young people rebelled against authority and their parents' generation during the 1960s. For them, "the Holocaust becomes a useful weapon," as Bloxham says. They were able to portray themselves as untainted by the sins of their fathers and mothers. "Faced with the silence of their parents' generation about their actions during the war and well aware of the Nazis' manipulation of national sentiments, the 68ers simultaneously called their parents' generation to account for their actions and rejected the nation and anything national," writes Miller-Idriss.[38]

Further events, including German Chancellor Willy Brandt famously dropping to his knees at the Warsaw Ghetto memorial in 1970, the murder of Israeli athletes at the 1972 Munich Olympic Games and the West German telecast of the American miniseries "Holocaust" in 1979 — watched by more than half the nation's adult population — "combined to place Jews and their sufferings at the head of the German public agenda," Judt writes.[39] In 1968 only 471 German school groups visited Dachau, the Nazi concentration camp just outside Munich; by the end of the 1970s more than 5,000 such groups were visiting annually, he points out.

Germany dealt with its *Schuldfrage*, or guilt issue, in a much more systematic way than other countries that had collaborated with or were implicated in Nazi crimes. "The Germans should be the model," says genocide scholar Goldhagen. "They've said, 'Yes, our country, our government at the time committed a terrible genocide, and we look back on it with horror.' It only brings credit and honor to them. It's how they actually say we're not like [our predecessors.] As long as you deny that something happened or try to deny that something happened, you make yourself suspect."

The Germans, in fact, engaged in "a kind of righteous self-hate," as the German novelist Peter Schneider once put it. In 1988, Philipp Jenninger, president of Germany's national parliament, the Bundestag, gave an address on the 50th anniversary of *Kristallnacht* that attempted to explain why the German people were drawn to Nazism. Although he stressed the notion of responsibility, he was heckled and accused of attempting to "justify" Hitler. Jenninger had to resign the following day.[40] Even as late as 2001, German President Johannes Rau publicly stated that German pride was impossible. But by 2006, when Germany hosted the World Cup, Merkel said the waving of German flags in the states was a display of a relaxed pride in the nation.

"In a short span of years, it seemed," Miller-Idriss writes, "Germans had set aside the automatic association of flag-waving with negative associations of nationalism and displayed what one newspaper reporter called 'a sort of unembarrassed patriotism.' "[41]

Asian Arguments

If Germany is now hailed as a model of a national remembrance and reconciliation with a horrific past,

'History Is Written by the Victors'

Through the ages, politicians, philosophers and writers from Plato to Mark Twain to Winston Churchill have commented on the validity of historical facts — some with more skepticism than others.

"What is history but a fable agreed upon?"
— Napoleon Bonaparte, 19th-century French emperor

"History will be kind to me, for I intend to write it."
— Winston Churchill, former British prime minister

"The very ink with which history is written is merely fluid prejudice."
— Mark Twain, American author and humorist

"Poetry is nearer to vital truth than history." — Plato, Greek philosopher

"History is a pack of lies about events that never happened told by people who weren't there."
— George Santayana, Spanish philosopher

"History is an account, mostly false, of events, mostly unimportant, which are brought about by rulers, mostly knaves, and soldiers, mostly fools."
— Ambrose Bierce, American writer and satirist

"The past is malleable and flexible, changing as our recollection interprets and re-explains what has happened."
— Peter Berger, Austrian-born American sociologist

"History is written by the victors."
— Winston Churchill, former British prime minister

"So very difficult a matter it is to trace and find out the truth of anything by history."
— Plutarch, Greek historian and essayist

"Those who cannot remember the past are condemned to repeat it."
— George Santayana, Spanish philosopher

"I have issued the command — and I'll have anybody who utters but one word of criticism executed by a firing squad — that our war aim does not consist in reaching certain lines, but in the physical destruction of the enemy . . . with orders . . . to send to death mercilessly and without compassion, men, women and children of Polish derivation and language. . . . Who, after all, speaks today of the annihilation of the Armenians?"
— Adolf Hitler, former fuhrer of Germany and leader of the Nazi party

"You speak about history. But one must sometimes correct history."
— Joseph Stalin, former leader of the Soviet Union

"He who controls the present controls the past. He who controls the past controls the future."
— George Orwell, British satirical novelist

"For governments, patriotic history is the only legitimate kind of history."
— Keith Wilson, Australian politician

Sources: "History Quotes," Brainy Quote, 2009www.brainyquote.com/quotes/keywords/history. html; "History," Bartlett's Quotations, 2009, www.bartleby.com/cgibin/texis/webinator/sitesearch? FILTER=col100&query= history&x=9&y=9; author's research

American soldiers survey rows of corpses at the Nazi concentration camp at Nordhausen, Germany, on April 17, 1945. More than 3,000 unburied bodies were found when the camp was liberated. Hailed as a model of a "guilty" nation grappling with the sins of its past, Germany has constructed in Berlin a massive memorial to the millions of people killed during the Holocaust and makes school instruction about the atrocities mandatory.

Japan — Germany's fellow Axis power in World War II — has had a more contentious relationship with its history of that period. Even though the Japanese government has adopted a strict pacifist stance in foreign affairs and repeatedly apologized to neighboring countries for the suffering it caused them during the war, it has also argued about the war — both internally and with its neighbors.

Since new textbooks could not be printed immediately after Japan's surrender to the United States, Japanese students were instructed to ink out all passages considered nationalistic, militaristic or undemocratic.[42]

But while later Japanese history textbooks abandoned the doctrines of the defeated imperial regime, they also did not contain detailed accounts of Japanese wartime atrocities.[43] In fact, a textbook written by prominent historian Saburo Ienaga was rejected for containing "too many illustrations of the 'dark side' of the war." Beginning in 1965, he began filing a series of lawsuits challenging the Ministry of Education's book-screening process, and in 1997 Japan's Supreme Court ordered that he be paid modest damages, but it upheld the ministry's right to screen textbooks.[44]

By that time, Ienaga and thousands of his supporters had won a de facto if not de jure victory. The most widely used Japanese textbooks by then contained references to the Rape of Nanking — the six-week-long massacre and rape of tens of thousands of Chinese soldiers and civilians in 1937 by members of Japan's imperial army. The books also described Unit 731, which conducted gruesome medical experiments on prisoners of war, and the plight of the "comfort women" — the more than 100,000 women and girls, mostly from Korea, forced to have sex with Japanese soldiers.

But debate surrounding all these issues has remained contentious. In 2007, the ministry instructed publishers to delete a passage stating that the Japanese military "forced" residents of Okinawa to commit mass suicide in 1945. More than 100,000 Okinawans staged a protest to complain that Japan's role in the suicides should not be forgotten. The government then allowed publishers to correct their texts.[45]

Japanese nationalists continued to chafe at the attention given to war crimes. In 2001, a group called the Japanese Society for History Textbook Reform published a revisionist textbook that whitewashed war crimes during World War II and earlier conflicts. Although it was adopted by fewer than 20 schools, the book sold widely to the general public. The Ministry of Education's continuing approval of the work has triggered protests overseas, notably widespread anti-Japanese rioting in China in 2005.

The Japanese parliament also launched an inquiry into the training given to military officers to determine whether it subverts official policy expressing regret for the nation's wartime aggression. Toshio Tamogami was removed from his post as air force chief last year after winning an essay contest in which he said that Japan had been trapped into bombing Pearl Harbor and that "many Asian countries take a positive view" of Japan's wartime role. "I was fired after saying Japan is a good country," Tamogami told parliament. "It seems a bit strange."[46]

Despite Japan's official contrition, its version of the past continues to stir up anger among its neighbors. The Chinese have protested repeatedly in recent years whenever Japanese prime ministers visit the Yasukuni Shrine in Tokyo, which honors convicted war criminals among millions of the nation's war dead. "As seen by the Japanese themselves, there's a lack of perspective about whether Japan was an aggressor or a victimized nation," says Yang, the professor of modern Japanese history at George Washington University.

AT ISSUE

Should a Turkish-Armenian historical commission be established?

YES
David Cuthell
Executive Director
Institute of Turkish Studies

NO
Helen Fein, Board Chairman
Institute for the Study of Genocide,
John Jay College of Criminal Justice,
And six other former presidents of the
International Association of Genocide Scholars

Written for *CQ Researcher*, November 2009

From an open letter to Turkish Prime Minister Recep Tayyip Erdogan, Nov. 3, 2009

The question of whether there was an Armenian Genocide is not debatable for the majority of scholars in the field. They maintain it was a genocide. Case closed.

Those who reject the term genocide to describe the slaughter of innocent human beings in eastern Anatolia in 1915 are pilloried in academic circles and elsewhere. To disagree with the narrative of the event is to be labeled the equivalent of a Holocaust denier. The fact that Raphael Lemkin — who coined the term — labeled the Armenian massacres as genocide effectively closes the book on the subject for most scholars.

This is precisely why the subject must be revisited and resolved by a joint commission of Armenian, Turkish and international scholars. Unlike the pronouncements of those who have never set foot in the Turkish archives or gone through Armenian archives, a mutually agreed upon commission starting with no preconditions or conclusions would have the best chance of getting to the bottom of the destruction of Armenian civilization in eastern Anatolia during the First World War. Removing this process from the realm of political lobbies can only serve to set the stage for reconciliation and resolution.

Sadly, this has not been the case to date. Instead, the environment has been toxic, marked by violence and vitriol. It has also been almost entirely one-sided in Western Europe and the United States. The late Ottoman historian Stanford Shaw even had his house bombed by some with whom he disagreed.

Fortunately, the current environment is slightly better. Turkish-Armenian relations are showing some early signs of a thaw. Contrary to what many scholars believe, the Turkish archives are largely accessible, and there is a growing movement within Turkey itself to examine the tragedies of the past. There is also a growing body of scholarship about the social, political and economic situation in eastern Anatolia during the late 19th and early 20th centuries that provides a better backdrop to the events of 1915.

Lastly, there is growing confidence in Turkey that, whatever an Armenian-Turkish historical commission finds, Turkey will emerge with a better understanding of the past and a more confident sense of the future.

It is hoped that the same would apply to the citizens of Armenia. For scholars, it should raise the question of why this process of real debate did not take place decades ago.

The recent signing of protocols by the governments of Armenia and Turkey . . . marks the beginning of a process that would lead to establishing diplomatic relations between the two countries. Constituencies in both countries find some or all of the protocols problematic. We, the former presidents of the International Association of Genocide Scholars, write to you to express our concern about one of them: the establishment of a historical commission to study the fate of the Armenian people in the Ottoman Empire in 1915.

We reiterate our objection to your insistence that there be a historical commission in which Turkey would be involved. Because Turkey has denied the Armenian Genocide for the past nine decades — and currently under Article 301 of the Turkish penal code public affirmation of the genocide is a crime — it would seem impossible for Turkey to be part of a process that would assess whether or not Turkey committed genocide against the Armenians.

[It] is not just Armenians who are affirming the Armenian Genocide, but it is the overwhelming conclusion of scholars who study genocide: hundreds of independent scholars, who have no affiliations with governments, and whose work spans many countries and nationalities and the course of decades. Outside of your government, there is no doubt about the facts of the Armenian Genocide; therefore our concern is that your demand for a historical commission is political sleight of hand designed to deny those facts.

Turkey has, in fact, shown no willingness to accept impartial judgments made by outside commissions. Five years ago, the Turkish members of the Turkish Armenian Reconciliation Commission pulled out of the commission after the arbitrator, the International Center for Transitional Justice, rendered an assessment that the events of 1915 were genocide. And, Prime Minister Erdogan, you have repeatedly stated that even if a historical commission found that the Armenian case is genocide, Turkey would ignore the finding. As William Schabas, the current president of the International Association of Genocide Scholars, said in his letter to you and [Armenian] President [Sargsyan], "acknowledgment of the Armenian Genocide must be the starting point of any 'impartial historical commission,' not one of its possible conclusions."

We believe the integrity of scholarship and the ethics of historical memory are at stake.

Japan suffered not just from the two atomic bombs but fire-bombing and the period of U.S. occupation.

"Within Japan, there's a yearning for recognition of Japanese suffering, although many leaders and ordinary people recognize that Japan has done a great deal of harm," he says.

And some historians note that China's government has used anti-Japanese feelings to stir Chinese nationalism, particularly after China's isolationist period during the Maoist era. Japan, at the same moment, was feeling insecure due to the long recession that dogged the country in the 1990s and was particularly concerned about criticism coming from a neighbor that was a rising economic and military power.

"The idea was if you teach the younger generation these negative legacies, it's masochistic," Yang says. "It will make it even more difficult for the younger generation to be proud to be Japanese at a time when we need them to rebuild the economy and build a sense of confidence."

These conflicts have emerged so late, suggests Northwestern historian Hein, because in Japan, "the benefits for self-criticism were not as clear" as in Germany. "There was no future for Germany if it did not develop a better relationship with Europe, and the only way they could get there was to repudiate the past," she says. "The U.S., for its own Cold War reasons, protected Japan from Asian criticism very deliberately."

Yasuo Fukuda, Japan's prime minister in 2007 and 2008, wanting better relations with the country's neighbors, did not visit Yasukuni and distanced himself from the efforts of his predecessor, Shinzo Abe, to downplay the role of the Japanese military in the recruitment and rape of "comfort women." Fukuda's efforts paid off with a "warm spring" in relations between the countries, as Chinese President Hu Jintao said during a visit to Japan last year that played down such disputes.

"This unfortunate history not only caused tremendous suffering to the Chinese people but also gravely hurt the Japanese people," Hu said. "It's important for us to remember history, but this does not mean we should hold grudges."[47]

CURRENT SITUATION

Endless Debates

Debates about the past remain a constant in contemporary politics. The dispute between Armenians and Turks about the mass slaughter of the former during World War I is a prominent example.

Author and historian Balakian argues that genocide must be seen not as a national issue but a universal issue that leaves scars across the globe. "This should not be framed as an Armenian-Turkish issue," he says. "It's an international human rights issue."

That may be, but both the Turks and Armenians — particularly the Armenian diaspora — have been willing at times to put their insistence on their version of the past ahead of their present self-interest. Turkey has talked of scuttling defense deals — such as the use of NATO bases in Turkey for the war in Iraq — if the United States were to condemn the deaths of the Armenians as genocide. A resolution to do just that nearly passed Congress in 2007 but was blocked by leaders concerned about the foreign-policy fallout. Armenians have been disappointed that President Obama has not kept a campaign promise to term the genocide as such.

Armenians living outside of Armenia seem to take a harder line on these issues than those still living in the country. "The government of Armenia is not going to push this issue as much as they might have," says Suny, of the University of Michigan. "They want to make some realistic state-to-state agreements with the Turks."

For the Armenian diaspora — like expatriate Cubans in South Florida and American Jews regarding Israel — their sense of national identity is inextricably tied to a vision of their home country that does not change as much as it must for those still living there. "People who see themselves as slightly dissipated from the homeland want some point of identity," says Bloxham, the genocide scholar at Edinburgh. "This negotiation is about what's good for the people living in the region, here and now. . . . The Armenian diaspora has other priorities."

"The diaspora is relatively shielded and protected" from the effects of growing or continuing hostility with Turkey, says Duara, the Singapore scholar. "Their identity, what their home was when they left, is something that freezes, and they cannot afford to let go."

Official Regrets

Of course, Armenians have a hard time letting go of the need for international recognition of the Armenian killings, precisely because the Turks have never admitted their culpability. Armenians argue it would be better for the Turks, not just for them, if Turkey were to concede its wrongdoing and apologize for it. This almost psychoanalytical reading of nations — that they have cannot move forward until they have admitted past mistakes and reconciled with their guilt — has become a powerful idea in recent years.

Setting up truth and reconciliation commissions has become almost an automatic and predictable end to contemporary conflicts. And many nations have issued formal apologies for atrocities deeper into their pasts. In November, both British Prime Minister Gordon Brown and Australian Prime Minister Kevin Rudd apologized for the forced migration and institutionalization of 150,000 British children from the 1930s to the 1970s.

Rudd apologized to Australia's mistreated Aborigines as soon as he took office in 2008, while Brown's predecessor, Tony Blair, apologized in 2006 for his nation's part in slavery and the slave trade. Blair also apologized in 1997 for Britain's role in the Irish potato famine.

Pope John Paul II in 2000 issued an apology for sins committed by the "children" of the Catholic Church over the previous two millennia, including violence that occurred during the Counter-Reformation and a partial apology for the church's role in World War II. Since the 1950s, Japanese leaders have issued dozens of apologies for its aggression and atrocities it committed during World War II.

"When people commit injustices and do bad things, they ought to apologize and ask for forgiveness," said Rep. Steve Cohen, D-Tenn., who sponsored a U.S. House resolution apologizing for slavery, which passed in 2008. "Countries should operate in the same manner. Slavery is abhorrent."[48]

The House action followed apologies from half a dozen states in the old Confederacy for their role in slavery. Three years earlier the Senate apologized for not passing an anti-lynching law decades earlier, marking the first time that chamber had apologized for the nation's treatment of African-Americans.

"At the end of the day, we said three words: 'I am sorry,'" said state Sen. Anthony C. Hill Sr., a Florida Democrat, after the state legislature formally apologized in March 2008 for the state's "shameful" history of slavery. "I think now we can begin the healing process of reconciliation."[49]

Some have criticized such resolutions and statements as being politically motivated — a way for political leaders to distance themselves conveniently from the actions of past leaders. "Trading apologies and forgiveness on behalf of dead

AFP/Getty Images/Chhin Sothy

The grisly Choeung Ek memorial in Phnom Penh is dedicated to the nearly 2 million Cambodians murdered by the Khmer Rouge regime of Pol Pot between 1975 and 1979. After decades of relative silence, Cambodia is engaging in public discourse about its genocidal past. Meanwhile, the first U.N.-backed trial of a Khmer official who oversaw the torture and killings concluded on Nov. 27; a verdict is expected in 2010, with other trials to follow. A new textbook about the regime's excesses is also being released.

people sounds phony," editorialized *The Economist* in 2008, "especially when the issue is centuries old (such as Viking rape and pillage in Ireland, which Denmark's culture minister Brian Mikkelson bemoaned in 2007)."[50]

Even Adam Hochschild, the liberal author of a widely praised book about the abolition of the slave trade, *Bury the Chains*, is concerned that focusing too much on atoning for past sins ignores "clear, glaring injustices of the present."

"To feel outrage at a dreadful crime in history is natural and right," Hochschild wrote in 2006. "But does it make sense to extend the principle of guilt and responsibility backward in time over generations? Two centuries ago, scholars estimate, about three-quarters of the people on Earth were slaves, indentured servants, laborers in debt bondage, serfs or in servitude of one sort or another. Add to that grim tally the wars, colonial conquests, genocides, concentration camps and other barbarities human beings have inflicted on each other since then. If we were to take responsibility for everything done by our ancestors, few of us — anywhere in the world — would have clean hands. Few of us, also, would be without victims among our forebears. The entire world would be awash in apologies."[51]

OUTLOOK

Globalizing Forces

All declining cultures cling to rituals and traditions that can provide a sense of place and belonging in a rapidly changing world.

That appears to be a major motivation behind French President Sarkozy's project in search of a national identity. "Globalization erases a little more of every nation's characteristics every day," said Frédéric Lefebvre, spokesman for Sarkozy's ruling Union for a Popular Majority Party, calling for a defense of France's "cultural model."[52]

Some historians predict that similar outbreaks of nationalistic feeling are likely to pop up elsewhere as the world economy continues to globalize. "Memory is, in a globalizing world, if anything more important to people," says Catterall of the University of London. "It's something to hold onto, it becomes a more crucial part of identity."

Bruner, the Georgia State communications professor, suggests there will be continuing tension between the transnational cosmopolitan culture and local traditions. "In most major cities in the world, whether Hong Kong or London, they could care less about whether they're dancing the local dance. They want to know how their stock portfolios look," he says. But there is a countervailing force in the "desire for community and belonging. There's a point where people say they need to hold onto their culture in order to have meaning in life."

Many scholars agree the recent trends toward greater historical accountability through formal apologies and truth commissions will continue. "As the world becomes more and more aware of the horrors of eliminationist genocide, and regimes talk about what they've done, there's likely to be more openness," predicts author Goldhagen.

And the University of Virginia's Confino notes that, in contrast to earlier eras when people may have been ashamed to talk about their suffering, "the idea of victimhood has become very important."

"There is a phenomenon we can call 'Holocaust envy.' The Holocaust has given us the language to talk about mass killing, witnessing, trauma and survivors," he continues. "People want to have the legitimacy that comes with being identified as being like Holocaust [victims] — it means you really suffered a lot."

The generation that witnessed atrocities may never feel comfortable. That's why certain disputes — between the Israelis and the Palestinians, between India and Pakistan — never seem to get resolved. The cycle of conflict continues with such limited interruption that the wounds are always afflicted anew," says Duara, the historian at the National University of Singapore. "You don't get a generation that passes without wounds."

"You get into this game, who did the first bad thing," says Bloxham, the Edinburgh historian. "The thing is that it's impossible to get a neutral history that everyone can buy into. There's inevitable self-serving, with people picking into the past for the purposes that suit them."

As Catterall points out, historical disputes are frequently based upon differences in memory that don't necessarily produce reconciliation. But some nations may be getting closer to putting difficult pasts behind them. It's a tough trick for national leaders to pull off, balancing the need to honor even the difficult parts of the past while not becoming unduly burdened by them.

Yang of George Washington University, while agreeing that historical commemoration will remain a potent force, says there's a growing "awareness that bilateral relations have many facets. The past is important, but it's only one of them."

In his area of expertise — Japan and China —Yang notes that in the last three years there's been a decline in official animosity. "Leaders in Japan and China are putting greater emphasis on areas of cooperation, education and economic management," he says. "They are not ignoring the contentious issues of the past, but leaders can shift the tone of their rhetoric."

"It's very important not only to remember the past but also to remember it responsibly and to reject any claim of the past over our life's present," says Confino. "If you become a slave of the past, it's as bad as forgetting the past."

NOTES

1. Christie Parsons and Laura King, "Obama Avoids 'Genocide' Term," *Los Angeles Times*, April 7, 2009, p. A22; http://articles.latimes.com/2009/apr/07/world/fg-obama-armenia7.

2. Simon Sebag Montefiore, *Stalin: The Court of the Red Tsar* (2003), p. 139.

3. Geoffrey Cubitt, *History and Memory* (2008), p. 225.

4. *Ibid.*

5. See "French in Armenia 'genocide' row," BBC News, Oct. 12, 2006, http://news.bbc.co.uk/2/hi/6043730.stm.

6. For background, see "Truth and Reconciliation Commissions," *CQ Global Researcher*, January 2010 (forthcoming).

7. Zelaya's Scrap of Paper," *The Economist*, Nov. 7, 2009, p. 37; www.economist.com/displayStory.cfm?story_id=14802313.

8. Pico Iyer, "The Unknown Rebel," *Time*, April 13, 1998, p. 192; www.time.com/time/time100/leaders/profile/rebel.html.

9. The documentary is available online at www.pbs.org/wgbh/pages/frontline/tankman/.

10. Mark McKinnon, "The Tiananmen Dream: Lost in One Generation," *The Globe and Mail*, May 30, 2009, p. A14; www.theglobeandmail.com/news/world/tiananmen-dream-dead-in-one-generation/article1160927/.

11. Samantha Power, *A Problem From Hell: America and the Age of Genocide* (2003), p. 121.

12. Sue Pleming, "U.S. State Department Speaks to Twitter About Iran," Reuters, June 16, 2009; www.reuters.com/article/rbssTechMediaTelecomNews/idUSWBT01137420090616.

13. Christina Bellantoni, "In China Obama Touts Freedom Through Twitter," Talking Points Memo DC, Nov. 16, 2009; http://tpmdc.talkingpointsmemo.com/2009/11/obama-in-china-touts-freedom-basketball-stars-and-making-history-as-first-black-president.php?ref=fpa.

14. Keith B. Richburg, "Obama Backs Non-Censorship; China, Apparently, Does Not," *Washingtonpost.com*, Nov. 16, 2009; www.washingtonpost.com/wp-dyn/content/article/2009/11/16/AR2009111601512.html?hpid=topnews.

15. Jeffrey Gettleman, "Clinton Presents Plan to Fight Sexual Violence in Congo," *The New York Times*, Aug. 12, 2009, p. A8; www.nytimes.com/2009/08/12/world/africa/12diplo.html.

16. Richard G. Hovannisian, ed., *Remembrance and Denial: The Case of the Armenian Genocide* (1998), p. 202.

17. Anne Applebaum, *Gulag: A History* (2003), p. 572.

18. Martha Minow, *Between Vengeance and Forgiveness: History After Genocide and Mass Violence* (1998), p. x.

19. Norman M. Naimark, "Srebrenica in the History of Genocide," in Nanci Adler, *et al.*, eds., *Memories of Mass Repression: Narrating Life Stories in the Aftermath of Atrocity* (2009), p. 15.

20. Stephen Vaughn, *The Vital Past: Writings on the Uses of History* (1985), p. 357.

21. Tony Judt, *Postwar: A History of Europe Since 1945* (2005), p. 821.

22. Edward Coty, "French Town Cannot Let Bookstore Die," *The Washington Post*, Nov. 16, 2009, p. A13; www.washingtonpost.com/wp-dyn/content/article/2009/11/15/AR2009111502519.html.

23. www.debatidentitenationale.fr/.

24. Ruadhan McCormaic, "Identity Debate Rouses Passion of French Public," *The Irish Times*, Nov. 13, 2009; www.irishtimes.com/newspaper/opinion/2009/1113/1224258726047.html.

25. Robert Marquand, "France's Sarkozy Launches Controversial National Identity Debate," *The Christian Science Monitor*, Nov. 2, 2009, p. 6; www.csmonitor.com/2009/1103/p06s04-woeu.html.

26. Rosamond McKitterick, *History and Memory in the Carolingian World* (2004), p. 120.

27. Karl W. Deutsch, *Nationalism and Social Communication*, 2nd edition (1953), p. 97.

28. John Vincent, *History* (1995), p. 61.

29. John Lukacs, *Historical Consciousness; or, The Remembered Past* (1968), p. 101.

30. McKitterick, *op. cit.*, p. 85.

31. Cubitt, *op. cit.*, p. 225.

32. Minow, *op. cit.*, p. 119.

33. Adler, *op. cit.*, p. ix.

34. Judt, *op. cit.*, p. 803.

35. Craig Whitlock, "In Germany, an Ode to Joy," *The Washington Post*, Nov. 10, 2009, p. A6; www.washingtonpost.com/wp-dyn/content/article/2009/11/09/AR2009110900450.html.

36. Cynthia Miller-Idriss, *Blood and Culture: Youth, Right-wing Extremism and National Belonging in Contemporary Germany* (2009), p. 51.

37. Judt, *op. cit.*, p. 810.

38. Miller-Idriss, *op. cit.*, p. 51.

39. Judt, *op. cit.*, p. 811.

40. M. Lane Bruner, *Strategies of Remembrance: The Rhetorical Dimensions of National Identity Construction* (2002), p. 13.

41. Miller-Idriss, *op. cit.*, p. ix.

42. John Dower, *Embracing Defeat: Japan in the Wake of World War II* (1999), p. 247.

43. Kathleen Woods Masalski, "Examining the Japanese History Textbook Controversies," *Japan Digest*, November 2001; available at http://iis-db.stanford .edu/docs/134/textbook.pdf.

44. Jonathan Watts, "Saburo Ienaga," *The Guardian*, Dec. 3, 2002, p. 22; www.guardian.co.uk/news/ 2002/dec/03/guardianobituaries.japan.

45. "Don't Allow Interference in Textbook Screening," *The Daily Yomiuri* (Tokyo), Nov. 2, 2007, p. 4; www. japannewsreview.com/editorials/editorials/2007 1103page_id=2821.

46. Blaine Harden, "Japanese General Defends Revised Version of WWII," *The Washington Post*, Nov. 12, 2008, p. A12; www.washingtonpost.com/wp-dyn/ conent/article/2008/11/11/AR2008111100952.html.

47. Blaine Harden, "On Visit to Japan, China's Hu Has No Time for Old Grudges," *The Washington Post*, May 10, 2008, p. A9; www.washingtonpost.com/wp-dyn/con tent/article/2008/05/09/AR20080 50902724.html.

48. Darryl Fears, "Slavery Apology: A Sincere Step or Mere Politics?" *The Washington Post*, Aug. 2, 2008, p. C1; www.washingtonpost.com/wp-dyn/content/ article/2008/08/01/AR2008080103460.html? nav =emailpage&utm_source=feedburner&utm_ medium=feed&utm_campaign=Feed%3A+wp-dyn %2Frss%2Fprint%2Fstyle%2Findex_ xml+%28washingtonpost.com+-+Style%29.

49. Damien Cave and Christine Jordan Sexton, "Florida Legislature Apologizes for State's History of Slavery," *The New York Times*, March 27, 2008, p. A18; www .nytimes.com/2008/03/27/us/27florida.html.

50. "Who's Sorry Now?", *The Economist*, Oct. 4, 2008; www.economist.com/world/international/display- story.cfm?story_id=E1_TNPPJVNS.

51. Adam Hochschild, "The False Justice of Reparations," *Los Angeles Times*, Dec. 9, 2006, p. A31.

52. Bruce Crumley, "Berets and Baguettes? France Rethinks Its Identity," *Time.com*, Nov. 4, 2009; www.time.com/time/world/article/0,8599,19341 93,00.html?iid=tsmodule#ixzz0WzEVaVUg.

BIBLIOGRAPHY

Books

Adler, Nancy, *et al.*, eds., *Memories of Mass Repression: Narrating Life Stories in the Aftermath of Atrocity*, Transaction Publishers, 2009.
Historians and scholars explore the memories of ordinary people subjected to horrific events in Yugoslavia, Algeria, Turkey and other war zones.

Cubitt, Geoffrey, *History and Memory*, Manchester University Press, 2008.
A University of York historian explores memory and how it is shaped both by individuals and groups.

Hochschild, Adam, *The Unquiet Ghost: Russians Remember Stalin*, Viking, 1994.
An American author and journalist traveled through the former Soviet Union talking to people about their experiences under Stalin, finding both memories of horrific experiences and widespread amnesia about Stalin's atrocities.

Judt, Tony, *Postwar: A History of Europe Since 1945*, Penguin Press, 2005.
A British-born historian, now at New York University, closes his epic history with an examination of the

Holocaust and how its memory is central to European identity.

Miller-Idriss, Cynthia, *Blood and Culture: Youth, Right-Wing Extremism and National Belonging in Contemporary Germany*, Duke University Press, 2009.
A New York University education professor examines Germany's relationship to its troubled 20th-century past.

Paris, Erna, *Long Shadows: Truth, Lies and History*, Bloomsbury, 2001.
A Canadian author traveled to four continents to witness and record arguments about history as old as slavery in the United States and as recent as ethnic cleansing in the former Yugoslavia.

Articles

Harden, Blaine, "Japanese General Defends Revised Version of WWII," *The Washington Post*, Nov. 12, 2008, p. A12.
A Japanese air force chief was removed from his post for writing a revisionist essay about Pearl Harbor and Asian views toward Japan's role in World War II.

Harden, Blaine, "On Visit to Japan, China's Hu Has No Time for Old Grudges," *The Washington Post*, May 10, 2008; www.washingtonpost.com/wp-dyn/content/article/2008/05/09/AR2008050902724.html.
A state visit from Chinese President Hu Jintao has leaders of both China and Japan hoping they can begin to put painful World War II memories behind them.

Levy, Clifford J., "At Turkish Border, Armenians Are Wary of a Thaw," *The New York Times*, May 22, 2009, p. A8; www.nytimes.com/2009/05/22/world/europe/22armenia.html.
Armenians who live near the Turkish border welcome a thaw in relations but still want Turkey to admit that it committed genocide during World War I.

Marquand, Robert, "France's Sarkozy Launches Controversial National Identity Debate," *The Christian Science Monitor*, Nov. 2, 2009, p. 6; www.csmonitor.com/2009/1103/p06s04-woeu.html.
The French president believes his country can recapture its former glory by examining its own past and rediscovering its own best values.

Masalski, Kathleen Woods, "Examining the Japanese History Textbook Controversies," *Japan Digest*, November 2001; http://iis-db.stanford.edu/docs/134/textbook.pdf.
The author examines controversies surrounding Japan's view of its wartime past as seen through its textbook-adoption process.

Matthews, Owen, "The History Wars," *Newsweek International*, July 20, 2009; www.newsweek.com/id/205373.
Russia is coming closer to criminalizing alternative versions of history as President Dmitri Medvedev sets up an historical commission to put forward the Russian version of the Stalinist era to counter the more negative accounts of its neighbors.

McKinnon, Mark, "The Tiananmen Dream: Lost in One Generation," *The Globe and Mail*, May 30, 2009, p. A14; www.theglobeandmail.com/news/world/tiananmen-dream-dead-in-one-generation/article1160927/.
Twenty years after the Tiananmen Square protests, students in Beijing are much more interested in economic questions than political debates.

Reports and Studies

Cole, Elizabeth A., and Judy Barsalou, "Unite or Divide? The Challenge of Teaching History in Societies Emerging from Violent Conflict," *Special Report 163*, United States Institute of Peace, June 2006; www.usip.org/files/resources/sr163.pdf.
The authors look at how nations begin to construct or reconstruct their histories following traumatic events, noting how pedagogy is complicated by disagreements about how to frame what happened.

For More Information

Center for Holocaust and Genocidal Studies, Herengracht 380, Amsterdam, The Netherlands 1016 CJ; +31 (0) 20-5233808; www.chgs.nl/. Organization devoted to university teaching, public lectures and research in Holocaust and genocidal studies.

Eva and Marc Besen Institute for the Study of Historical Consciousness, School of Historical Studies, Tel Aviv University, Tel Aviv, Israel 69978; 972-3-6409326; www.tau.ac.il/humanities/besen/. Publishes *History and Memory*, a twice-yearly journal devoted to the formulation of historical consciousness.

Facing History and Ourselves, 16 Hurd Rd., Brookline, MA 02445; (617) 232-1595; www.facinghistory.org. Utilizes the Internet and school systems worldwide to educate children about taking responsibility for their world.

Georg Eckert Institute for International Textbook Research, Celler Strasse 3, Braunschweig, Germany D-38114; 49 (0) 531-590-99-0; www.gei.de/. Accredited and internationally connected reference center, primarily for social studies research; also studies how textbooks interpret history.

International Association of Genocide Scholars, www.genocidescholars.org/. A global, interdisciplinary organization that seeks to further research and teaching about the nature, causes and consequences of genocide.

International Coalition of Sites of Conscience, 333 7th Ave., 14th Floor, New York, NY 10001; (646) 755-6180; www.sitesofconscience.org/about-us/contact/en/. A global network of historic sites dedicated to past struggles for justice.

Memory and Reconciliation in the Asia-Pacific, Sigur Center for Asian Studies, 1957 E St., N.W., Suite 503, Washington, DC 20052; www.gwu.edu/~memory/. A research program dedicated to lasting reconciliation between China, Japan and Korea, specifically with regard to past wrongs related to colonialism and World War II.

United Nations, 760 United Nations Plaza, New York, NY 10017; (212) 963-1234; www.un.org/en/. An international organization committed to global peace.

U.S. Institute of Peace, 1200 17th St., N.W., Washington, DC 20036; (202) 457-1700; www.usip.org. Provides analysis, training and tools aimed at helping to end and prevent conflicts, promote stability and build peace.

16

Climate Change

Reed Karaim

Erosion is washing away beachfront land in the Maldives. The island nation in the Indian Ocean faces possible submersion as early as 2100, according to some climate change predictions. President Mohamed Nasheed said the voluntary emission cuts goal reached in Copenhagen last December was a good step, but at that rate "my country would not survive."

From *CQ Researcher*,
February, 2010.

It was the global gathering many hoped would save the world. For two weeks in December, delegates from 194 nations came together in Copenhagen, Denmark, to hammer out an international agreement to limit global warming. Failure to do so, most scientists have concluded, threatens hundreds of millions of people and uncounted species of plants and animals.

Diplomatic preparations had been under way for years but intensified in the months leading up to the conference. Shortly before the sessions began, Yvo de Boer, executive secretary of the United Nations Framework Convention on Climate Change — the governing body for negotiations — promised they would "launch action, action and more action," and proclaimed, "I am more confident than ever before that [Copenhagen] will be the turning point in the fight to prevent climate disaster."[1]

But delegates found themselves bitterly divided. Developing nations demanded more financial aid for coping with climate change. Emerging economic powers like China balked at being asked to do more to limit their emissions of the greenhouse gases (GHGs) — created by burning carbon-based fuels — blamed for warming up the planet. The United States submitted proposed emissions cuts that many countries felt fell far short of its responsibility as the world's dominant economy. As negotiations stalled, frustration boiled over inside the hall and on the streets outside, where tens of thousands of activists had gathered to call world leaders to action. A historic opportunity — a chance to reach a global commitment to battle climate change — seemed to be slipping away.

Then, on Dec. 18 — the final night of the conference — leaders from China, India, Brazil, South Africa and the United States emerged

Major Flooding, Drought Predicted at Century's End

Significant increases in runoff — from rain or melting snow and ice — are projected with a high degree of confidence for vast areas of the Earth, mainly in northern regions. Up to 20 percent of the world's population lives in areas where river flood potential is likely to increase by the 2080s. Rainfall and runoff are expected to be very low in Europe, the Middle East, northern and southern Africa and the western United States.

Projected Changes in Annual Runoff (Water Availability), 2090-2099
(by percentage, relative to 1980-1999)

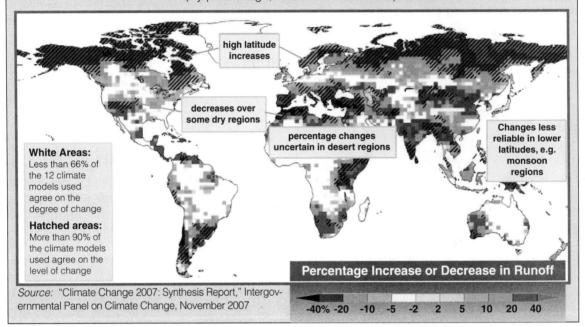

Source: "Climate Change 2007: Synthesis Report," Intergovernmental Panel on Climate Change, November 2007

from a private negotiating session with a three-page, non-binding accord that rescued the meeting from being judged an abject failure.

But the accord left as much confusion as clarity in its wake. It was a deal, yes, but one that fell far short of the hopes of those attending the conference, and one largely lacking in specifics. The accord vowed to limit global warming to 2 degrees Celsius (3.6 Fahrenheit) above pre-Industrial Revolution levels, provide $30 billion in short-term aid to help developing countries cope with the effects of climate change — with more promised longer-term — and included significant reporting and transparency standards for participants, including emerging economic powers such as China and India.

The accord did not, however:

- Include earlier language calling for halving global greenhouse gas emissions by 2050;
- Set a peak year by which greenhouse gases should begin to decline;
- Include country-specific targets for emission reductions (signatories began filling in the numbers by the end of January) (*See Current Situation, p. 430*);
- Include a timetable for reaching a legally binding international treaty, or
- Specify where future financial help for the developing world to cope with climate change will come from.[2]

Called back into session in the early morning hours, delegates from much of the developing world reacted with dismay to a deal they felt left their countries vulnerable to catastrophic global warming.

"[This] is asking Africa to sign a suicide pact — an incineration pact — in order to maintain the economic dependence [on a high-carbon economy] of a few countries," said Lumumba Di-Aping, the Sudanese chair of the G77 group of 130 poor countries.[3]

British Prime Minister Gordon Brown, however, hailed the deal as a "vital first step" toward "a green and low-carbon future for the world."[4] A total of 55 countries, including the major developed nations, eventually signed onto the deal.

But at the Copenhagen conference, delegates agreed only to "take note" of the accord, without formally adopting it.

Since then, debate has raged over whether the accord represents a step backward or a realistic new beginning. "You had the U.S., China and India closing ranks and saying it's too hard right now to have a binding agreement," says Malini Mehra, an Indian political scientist with 20 years of involvement in the climate change debate. "It's really worse than where we started off."

Others are more upbeat. Michael Eckhart, president of the American Council on Renewable Energy, points out that the convention had revealed how unworkable the larger effort — with 194 participants — had become. "The accord actually sets things in motion in a direction that is realistic," he says. "To have these major nations signed up is fantastic."

Copenhagen clearly demonstrated how extremely difficult and complex global climate negotiations can be. Getting most of the world's nations to

Carbon Emissions Rising; Most Come from China

Global emissions of carbon dioxide (CO_2) — the most common greenhouse gas (GHG) blamed for raising the planet's temperature — have grown steadily for more than 150 years. Since 1950, however, the increases have accelerated and are projected to rise 44 percent between 2010 and 2030 (top graph). While China emits more CO_2 than any other country, Australians produce the most carbon emissions per person (bottom left). Most manmade GHG comes from energy production and transportation (pie chart).

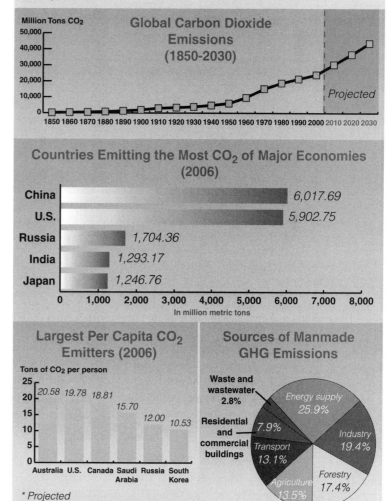

Global Carbon Dioxide Emissions (1850-2030)

Million Tons CO_2

Projected

Countries Emitting the Most CO_2 of Major Economies (2006)

China	6,017.69
U.S.	5,902.75
Russia	1,704.36
India	1,293.17
Japan	1,246.76

In million metric tons

Largest Per Capita CO_2 Emitters (2006)

Tons of CO_2 per person

Australia 20.58, U.S. 19.78, Canada 18.81, Saudi Arabia 15.70, Russia 12.00, South Korea 10.53

* Projected

Sources of Manmade GHG Emissions

Waste and wastewater 2.8%
Residential and commercial buildings 7.9%
Transport 13.1%
Energy supply 25.9%
Industry 19.4%
Forestry 17.4%
Agriculture 13.5%

Sources: "Climate Change 101: International Action," Pew Center on Global Climate Change, undated; "Climate Change 2007: Synthesis Report," Intergovernmental Panel on Climate Change, November 2007; Union of Concerned Scientists

Warming Trends Continue to Accelerate

During the last 25 years the Earth's average temperature steadily increased — and at increasingly higher increments — compared to the average temperature from 1880-1910. From 2004-2008, the increase was about 1.4 degrees F., or nearly double the increase from 1984 to 1988.

Average Temperature Increases in Five-year Periods, Relative to the Average Temperature in 1880-1910

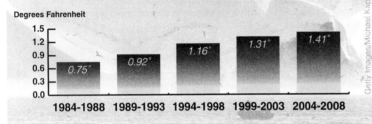

Degrees Fahrenheit

1984-1988	0.75°
1989-1993	0.92°
1994-1998	1.16°
1999-2003	1.31°
2004-2008	1.41°

Source: "Realities vs. Misconceptions About the Science of Climate Change," Pew Center on Global Climate Change, August 2009

agree on anything is no easy task, but climate change straddles the biggest geopolitical fault lines of our age: the vast economic disparity between the developed and developing worlds, questions of national sovereignty versus global responsibility and differences in political process between democratic and nondemocratic societies.

Climate change also involves a classic example of displaced hardship — some of the worst effects of global warming are likely to be felt thousands of miles from those nations that are most responsible for the higher temperatures and rising seas, making it easier for responsible parties to delay action. Finally, tackling the problem is likely to take hundreds of billions of dollars.

None of this is comforting to those already suffering from climate change, such as Moses Mopel Kisosion, a Maasai herdsman who journeyed from Kenya to tell anyone who would listen how increasingly severe droughts are destroying his country's traditional way of life. (*See story on climate refugees, p. 424.*) But it does explain why reactions to the Copenhagen Accord — which even President Barack Obama acknowledged is simply a "beginning" — have varied so widely.[5]

For some U.S. environmental groups, the significance of the accord was in the commitment Obama secured from emerging economies to provide greater transparency

and accountability, addressing one of the U.S. Senate's objections to earlier climate change proposals. The Senate never ratified the previous international climate agreement, known as the Kyoto Protocol.

Carl Pope, executive director of the Sierra Club, called the accord "historic — if incomplete," but said, "Now that the rest of the world — including countries like China and India — has made it clear that it is willing to take action, the Senate must pass domestic legislation as soon as possible."[6]

But to nongovernmental organizations focused on global poverty and economic justice, the accord represented an abdication of responsibility by the United States and other developed countries. Tim Jones, chief climate officer for the United Kingdom-based anti-poverty group World Development Movement, called the accord "a shameful and monumental failure that has condemned millions of people around the world to untold suffering."[7]

Easily lost in the heated rhetoric, however, is another part of the Copenhagen story: The conference illustrated how a consensus now unites most of the globe about the threat climate change poses. And although skeptics continue to speak out (*see p. 425*), the scientific community has overwhelmingly concluded that average global temperatures are rising and that manmade emissions — particularly carbon dioxide from burning coal, oil and other fossil fuels — are largely to blame. According to a comprehensive assessment released in June 2009 by the U.S. Global Change Research Program, "Observations show that warming of the climate is unequivocal."[8] The conclusion echoes earlier findings by the U.N.'s Intergovernmental Panel on Climate Change (IPCC).[9]

The costs of climate change, both economic and in human lives, already appear significant. Disasters tied to climate change kill around 300,000 people a year and cause roughly $125 billion in economic losses, according to the Global Humanitarian Forum, a Geneva-based think tank led by former U.N. Secretary General Kofi Annan.[10] Evidence widely cited during the conference strengthens the conclusion the world is heating up. The World Meteorological Organization (WMO) reported that the last decade appeared to be the warmest on record, continuing a trend. The years 2000 through 2009 were "warmer than the 1990s, which were warmer than the 1980s, and so on," said Michel Jarraud, the secretary general of the WMO, as Copenhagen got under way.[11] Other reports noted that sea levels appeared likely to rise higher than previously estimated by 2100, with one estimating seas could rise more than six feet by then. The Antarctic ice shelves and the Greenland ice sheet are also melting faster than the U.N. scientific body previously found.[12]

Copenhagen also provided evidence of a growing international political consensus about climate change. About 120 heads of state attended the final days of the conference, hoping to sign their names to an agreement, an indication of the seriousness with which the global community now views the issue.

"It was remarkable the degree to which Copenhagen galvanized the public," says David Waskow, Oxfam America's climate change policy adviser, who attended the conference. "That's true with the literally millions who came out to show their support for strong action on climate change around the world. It's true with the number of heads of state who showed up, and even in terms of the number of developing countries making substantial offers to tackle their emissions."

As observers try to determine where the world is headed on climate change and how the Copenhagen Accord helps or hinders that effort, here are some of the questions they are considering:

Is the Copenhagen Accord a meaningful step forward in the fight against global warming?

No one claims that a three-page accord that leaves out hard emission-reduction targets or a firm timetable is the final answer to global climate change. But does it bring the world closer to adequately addressing the problem?

Accord supporters range from the dutiful to the enthusiastic. But the unifying thread is a feeling that the accord is better than no deal at all, which is where the conference seemed to be headed until the 11th-hour negotiations.

"If the standard is — were we going to get a blueprint to save the world? The fact is, we were never going to

Protesters outside the U.N. Climate Change Conference in Copenhagen on Dec. 10, 2009, call for rich countries to take responsibility for their disproportionate share in global warming. Greenhouse gas emissions by industrial countries are causing climate changes in poor countries thousands of miles away. The nonbinding Copenhagen Accord calls for $10 billion a year for the next three years to help them deal with climate change.

Reuters/Christian Charisius

meet it. None of the documents circulating were a feasible basis for agreement among the major players," says Michael A. Levi, director of the Program on Energy Security and Climate Change for the U.S. Council on Foreign Relations. "What we ended up with is something that can be useful if we use it the right way. It has pieces that empower all sorts of other efforts, like increased transparency, some measure of monitoring and reporting. It sets a political benchmark for financing. It can be a meaningful step forward."

Levi also notes that countries signing the accord agreed to fill in their targets for emissions cuts (as the major signatories and other nations did at the end of January), addressing one of the main criticisms of the deal.

But the Indian political scientist Mehra says even if countries abide by their commitments to cut emissions, the accord will not meet its target of holding global warming to 2 degrees Celsius (3.6-degrees Fahrenheit), which U.N. scientists consider the maximum increase that could avoid the worst effects of climate change, including a catastrophic rise in sea levels and severe damage to world food production.

She cites an IPCC conclusion that says in order to meet the 2-degree goal industrialized countries must reduce their emissions to 25-40 percent of 1990 levels by 2020 and by 50 percent by 2050. "What we actually got in the various announcements from the developed nations are far below that, coming in at around 18 percent," Mehra says.

Indeed, research by Climate Interactive — a joint effort by academic, nonprofit and business entities to assess climate policy options — found that the countries' commitments would allow temperatures to rise about 3.9 degrees Celsius (7 degrees Fahrenheit) by 2100 — nearly twice the stated goal.[13] "If you're looking at an average of 3 to 4 degrees, you're going to have much higher rises in significant parts of the world. That's why so many of the African negotiators were so alarmed by this," says Mehra. "It's worse than where we started because it effectively sets in stone the lowest possible expectations."

But other analysts point out that President Obama and other leaders who backed the accord have acknowledged more must be done.[14] They add that focusing on the initial emissions goals ignores the areas where the deal breaks important ground. "A much bigger part of the story, I think, is the actual money the developed world is putting on the table, funds for mitigation and adaptation," says Mike Hulme, a professor at the University of East Anglia in Great Britain who has been studying the intersection between climate and culture. "This is as much part of the game as nominal reduction targets."

The accord calls for $10 billion a year to help poorer, more vulnerable countries cope with climate change over the next three years, rising to $100 billion a year by 2020. The money will come from "a wide variety of sources, public and private, bilateral and multilateral, including alternative sources of finance," according to the agreement.[15]

Equally important, say analysts, is the fact that the agreement sets new standards of participation and accountability for developing economies in the global warming fight. "The developing countries, particularly China, made a step forward and agreed not only to undertake some actions to reduce emissions, but to monitor and report those. I think that's significant," says Stephen Eule, a U.S. Chamber of Commerce climate expert and former George W. Bush administration climate official.

However, to many of the accord's critics, the accord mostly represents a failure of political leadership. "It was hugely disappointing. Watching world leaders lower expectations for three months coming into this, and then actually having them undershoot those expectations was unbelievable," says Jason Blackstock, a research scholar at the International Institute for Applied Systems Analysis in Austria, who studies the intersection of science and international affairs. He places some of the blame at the feet of President Obama: "This is clearly not one of his top issues, and that's disappointing."

But Thomas Homer-Dixon, who holds an international governance chair at the Balsillie School of International Affairs in Waterloo, Canada, and studies climate policy, believes critics are underestimating the importance of leaders from around the globe sitting down face-to-face to tackle the problem. "Symbolically, that photograph of the leaders of those countries sitting around the table with their sleeves rolled up was enormous," he says. "All of a sudden we're having a direct conversation among the actors that matter, both in the developed and developing world."

He also credits the conference for tackling difficult questions such as how much money developed countries need to transfer to the developing world to fight climate change and how much countries have to open themselves up to international inspection. "There's been sort of an agreement not to talk about the hard stuff," he says, "and now, at Copenhagen, it was finally front and center."

But to those who believe that the time for talk is running out, the dialogue meant nothing without concrete results. "This [deal], as they themselves say, will not avert catastrophic climate change," said Kumi Naidoo, Greenpeace International's executive director. "That's the only thing on which we agree with them. Everything else is a fudge; everything else is a fraud, and it must be called as such."[16]

Is the U.N.'s climate change negotiating framework outdated?

Although delegations from most of the world's nations came to Copenhagen, the final deal was hammered out by the leaders of only five countries. Those nations — the United States, China, India, Brazil and South Africa — provide a snapshot of the changing nature of geopolitical power.

Although they had been involved in larger group discussions of about 30 nations, the traditional European powers and Japan were not involved in the final deal. The five key players represented the world's largest economy (the United States), the largest emitter of greenhouse gases and second-biggest economy (China) and significant emerging economies in South America (Brazil), Africa (South Africa) and India, with the world's second-largest population.

The five-nation gathering could be seen as an effort to fashion a thin cross-section of the global community. But the U.N.-sponsored Copenhagen conference was supposed to embody the entire world community. To some observers, the fact that the accord was fashioned outside the official sessions appeared to be an attempt to undermine the U.N. effort.

Anne Petermann, co-director of the Global Justice Ecology Project, an international grassroots organization, notes the Bush administration also worked outside the U.N., setting up a smaller meeting of major economies to discuss climate change. "It wasn't particularly surprising the U.S. negotiated an accord that was completely outside the process," she says. "This wasn't the first time that the U.S. had come in with a strategy of undermining the U.N. Framework Convention."

To other analysts, however, the ability of the small group of leaders to come together where the larger conference had failed shows that the U.N. effort no longer fits the crisis. "The Framework Convention is actually now an obstacle to doing sensible things on climate change," says East Anglia's Hulme. "Climate change is such a multi-faceted problem that we need to find sub-groups, multiple frameworks and initiatives to address it."

To others, the U.N. effort remains both the best chance for the world to reach a binding climate change agreement and essential to proceeding. "Because you've really got to have a global solution to this problem, it's essential that all the interested parties, including the most vulnerable countries, be around the table," says Oxfam's Waskow. "There's no question the U.N. Framework Convention, which has been working on this for many years, is the right place for that."

But Homer-Dixon, of the Balsillie School of International Affairs, believes the U.N. Framework process "has too many parties." He expects that on the negotiating side "we're going to migrate to something like the G-20 [economic forum], which includes all the major emitters. It would make sense to have the G-20 responsible."

However, Kassie Siegel, the climate law expert for the Center for Biological Diversity, a U.S. environmental group, thinks critics underestimate the U.N. effort. "Both the U.N. Framework Convention and the Intergovernmental Panel on Climate Change have been building capacity since 1992," she says. "There's not any other institution that came close to their experience on this issue. The U.N. Framework process is the best and fastest way forward."

Supporters also note that the United States and other signatories to the Copenhagen Accord have called for efforts to continue toward reaching a binding agreement at the next U.N. climate gathering in Mexico City at the end of this year. "I don't think the U.N. negotiations are irrelevant because the U.S. is still engaged in the Framework Convention," says Nicola Bullard, a climate change analyst and activist with Focus on the Global South, a nongovernmental group in Bangkok, Thailand.

But Eckhart believes the results in Copenhagen mean that key countries will now focus most of their efforts outside the U.N. framework. "I doubt Mexico City is still relevant," he says. "What can they get done in Mexico City that they couldn't get done in Copenhagen?"

The relationship between the Copenhagen Accord and the U.N. Framework Convention is somewhat ambiguous. Jacob Werksman, a lawyer specializing in international environmental and economics law at the World Resources Institute, concludes the conference's decision to only "take note" of the accord means that some provisions, including the call for setting up a Copenhagen Green Climate Fund to manage billions of dollars in aid through the U.N. mechanism, cannot occur without a conference decision to accept the accord.

U.N. Secretary General Ban Ki-moon has called on all U.N. countries to back the accord.[17] (*See "At Issue," p. 432.*) But some analysts believe the U.N. Framework Convention can't legally adopt it until the Mexico City conference, which would push the Climate Fund and possibly other accord provisions down the road another year — a delay climate change activists say the world can't afford.

Would a carbon tax reduce emissions more effectively?

Obscured by the immediate furor over Copenhagen is a longer-term debate over whether the developed world

AFP/Getty Images/Ahmad Zamroni

Residents grin and bear flooding in Jakarta, Indonesia, in December 2007. Similar scenes would be played out in coastal cities and communities around the world if climate change causes glaciers and polar ice caps to melt, which many researchers predict. Analysts say the worst effects of climate change are expected to be felt in Asia.

is taking the right tack in its approach to reducing emissions.

The most popular approach so far has been the so-called cap-and-trade programs.[18] Progressively lower caps on overall emissions allow power companies and other entities to trade their emission quotas, creating a market-based approach to cutting greenhouse gases. Several European nations have embraced "cap-and-trade," and the climate change legislation that passed the U.S. House last June takes such an approach. But the system has been criticized for its complexity and susceptibility to manipulation and abuse.

Some analysts believe a carbon tax — a levy on carbon-emitting fuels, coupled with a system to rebate most of the tax back to consumers, is a more straightforward and effective way to control emissions. Robert Shapiro, former undersecretary of commerce during the Clinton administration and chair of the U.S. Climate Task Force, advocates such a program and works to educate the public on the need for action on climate change.

Shapiro's plan would use 90 percent of the carbon tax revenue to cut payroll taxes paid by workers and businesses, with the remaining 10 percent going to fund research and development of clean energy technology. The tax would provide a price incentive for discouraging the use of carbon emitting fuels and encouraging the use of green energy, while the tax cut would keep the

approach from unduly burdening lower-income Americans. "A carbon tax would both directly reduce greenhouse gas emissions and provide powerful incentives for technological progress in this area," Shapiro wrote. "It offers the best way forward in both the national and global debate over climate change."[19]

However, carbon tax opponents argue it would be no more effective than cap-and-trade and would lead to a huge expansion of government. Analysts at the Heritage Foundation, a conservative U.S. think tank, wrote that a carbon tax "would cause significant economic damage and would do very little to reduce global temperatures." Even coupling it with a payroll tax cut, they continue, "would do little to offset the high energy prices that fall particularly hard on low-income households." The real agenda of a carbon tax, they charge, is "about raising massive amounts of revenue to fund a huge expansion in government."[20]

Several Scandinavian countries have adopted carbon taxes, with mixed results. Norway has seen its per capita CO_2 emissions rise significantly. But Denmark's 2005 emissions were 15 percent below what they were in 1990, and the economy still remained strong.[21]

But to Bullard, at Focus on the Global South, a carbon tax is the approach most likely to spur changes in personal behavior. "Reducing consumption is really important, reducing our own dependence on fossil fuels," she says. "I think it's very important to have a redistributive element so that working people and elderly people don't end up with a huge heating bill. But it's really a simpler and more effective route than a complicated solution like cap-and-trade."

However, Bill McKibben — an American environmentalist and the founder of 350.org, an international campaign dedicated to scaling back GHG emissions — says a carbon tax faces an almost insurmountable political hurdle in the United States. "Even I can't convince myself that America is going to sit very long with something called a carbon tax," he says.

McKibben thinks "cap and rebate" legislation recently introduced by Sens. Maria Cantwell, D-Wash., and Susan Collins, R-Maine, would be more palatable to voters. It would cap total emissions — a limit that would be tightened over time — with the government auctioning off available carbon credits. The money raised would be rebated to consumers to offset any higher energy bills.[22]

Congressional efforts, however, have focused on cap-and-trade. But as wariness grows in the U.S. Senate toward the ramifications of cap-and-trade, Shapiro believes a carbon tax could prove a more appealing option. "A real public discussion and debate about a carbon tax tied to offsetting cuts in payroll or other taxes," he said, "could be the best news for the climate in a very long time."[23]

BACKGROUND

Road to Copenhagen

The road to Copenhagen was a long one. In one sense, it began with the Industrial Revolution in the 18th and 19th century, which brought with it the increased burning of coal and the beginning of large-scale carbon dioxide emissions in Europe and America. It also started with scientific speculation in the 1930s that manmade emissions could be changing the planet's climate.

Those first studies were widely discounted, a reflection of the difficulty humanity has had coming to grips with the idea it could be changing the global climate. But by the mid-1980s, thanks in large part to the work of David Keeling at the Mauna Loa Observatory in Hawaii, the world had a nearly three-decade record of rising carbon dioxide levels in the atmosphere.[24] Scientists were also reporting an overall warming trend in the atmosphere over the last 100 years, which they considered evidence of a "greenhouse effect" tied to CO_2 and other manmade emissions.

Humankind began a slow, often painful struggle to understand and deal with a global challenge. From the beginning, there were doubters, some well-intentioned, some with a vested interest in making sure that the world continued to burn fossil fuels. Even as the scientific consensus on climate change has grown stronger, and many nations have committed themselves to tackling global warming, the issue continues to provoke and perplex.

Climate and Culture

In her book *Field Notes from a Catastrophe, Man, Nature and Climate Change*, American writer Elizabeth Kolbert visits, among other spots, Greenland's ice fields, a native village in Alaska and the countryside in northern England, surveying how global warming is changing the Earth. In the opening section, she admits her choices about where to go to find the impact of climate change were multitudinous.

"Such is the impact of global warming that I could have gone to hundreds if not thousands of other places," Kolbert writes, "From Siberia to the Austrian Alps to the Great Barrier Reef to the South African *fynbos* (shrub lands)."[25]

Despite mounting evidence, however, climate change remains more a concept than a reality for huge parts of the globe, where the visible impacts are still slight or nonexistent. Research scholar Blackstock, whose work focuses on the intersection between science and international affairs, points out that for many people this makes the issue as much a matter of belief as of fact.

"It really strikes to fundamental questions on how we see the human-nature interface," he says. "It has cultural undertones, religious undertones, political undertones." Blackstock thinks many climate scientists have missed this multifaceted dimension to the public dialogue. "Pretending this is just a scientific debate won't work," he says. "That's important, but we can't have that alone."

The heart of the matter, he suggests, is how willing we are to take responsibility for changes in the climate and how we balance that with other values. This helps to explain the varying reactions in the United States, which has been reluctant to embrace limits on carbon emissions, and Europe, which has been more willing to impose measures. "You're seeing the cultural difference between Europe and America," Blackstock says, "the American values of individualism and personal success versus the communal and collective good, which Europe has more of a sense of being important."

Other analysts see attitudes about climate deeply woven into human culture. The University of East Anglia's Hulme, author of *Why We Disagree About Climate Change*, notes that climate and weather have been critical to humanity for most of its history. The seasons, rains and hot or cold temperatures have been so essential to life — to the ability to obtain food and build stable communities — that they have been attributed to deities and formed the basis for religious ceremonies. Even in the modern age, Hulme says, "People have an instinctive sense that weather and climate are natural phenomena, that they work at such scales and complexity that humans could not possibly influence them."

He points out that weather was once the realm of prophets, "and part of our population is still resistant to the idea that science is able to predict what the weather

Climate Change Could Force Millions to Relocate

"Climate Refugees" from Africa to the Arctic could be affected.

Maasi herdsman Moses Mopel Kisosion had never been outside Kenya before. He'd never ridden on a plane. But he flew across parts of two continents to deliver a message to anyone who would listen at the Copenhagen climate conference in December.

Climate change, he believes, is destroying the ability of his people, the Kajiado Maasi, to make a living. "I am a pastoralist, looking after cattles, walking from one place to another looking for grass and pastures," Kisosion said. "And now, for four years, we have a lack of rain, so our animals have died because there's no water and no grass. . . . We are wondering how our life will be because we depend on them."[1]

The Maasi are hardly alone in worrying if they will be able to continue living where they are. From small South Pacific island nations to the Arctic, hundreds of millions of people might have to relocate to survive as a result of climate change. If global warming predictions prove accurate, some researchers believe the world could soon find itself dealing with a tidal wave of "climate refugees."

A study by the U.N. Office for the Coordination of Humanitarian Affairs and the Internal Displacement Monitoring Centre found that "climate-related disasters — that is, those resulting from hazards that are already being or are likely to be modified by the effects of climate change — were responsible for displacing approximately 20 million people in 2008."[2]

Norman Myers, a British environmentalist, sees the situation worsening as the effects of climate change grow. In a 2005 study, he concluded that up to 200 million people could become climate refugees.[3] But he recently revised his estimate significantly. "We looked at the best prognosis for the spread of desertification and sea level rise, including the associated tsunamis and hurricanes, and we meshed those figures with the number of people impoverished or inhabiting coastal zones," says Myers. "We believe we could see half a billion climate refugees in the second half of the century."

The human displacement is likely to take place over several decades, experts say, and determining who is a climate refugee and who is simply a political or economic refugee could be difficult. International organizations have just begun the discussion about their status and what kind of assistance they might require.

The European Commission is funding a two-year research project, "Environmental Change and Forced Migration Scenarios," based on case studies in 24 vulnerable countries.[4] An African Union Summit in Kampala, Uganda, also met last October to consider how it would address the growing number of displaced Africans.[5]

Wahu Kaara, a Kenyan political activist, says the need for action is pressing. Kenya has recorded four major droughts in the last decade, significantly higher than the average over the previous century. "Very many people are dislocated and have to move to where they can salvage their lives," she says. "We have seen people die as they walk from one place to another. It's not a hardship; it's a catastrophe. They not only have lost their animals, they have lost their lives, and the framework of their lives for those who survive."

While Africa already may be suffering population movement due to climate change, the worst consequences are

will be. This deep cultural history makes climate change a categorically different phenomenon than other scientifically observed data."

Climate is also often confused with weather. England, for example, has a temperate, damp climate, but can have dry, hot years. The human inclination is to believe what's before our eyes, so every cold winter becomes a reason to discount global warming.

Sander van der Leeuw, director of the School of Human Evolution and Social Change at Arizona State University in Tempe, Ariz., notes that facing climate change also means contemplating the costs of consumerism. "Those of us in the developed world have the most invested in this particular lifestyle," he says. "If that lifestyle has to change, we'll be facing the most wrenching dislocations."

likely to be felt in Asia, analysts say. Rising sea levels threaten low-lying coastal areas, which constitute only 2 percent of the land surface of the Earth but shelter 10 percent of its population. About 75 percent of the people living in those areas are in Asia.[6]

The Maldives, a nation of low-lying islands in the Indian Ocean that could be submerged if predictions prove accurate, has taken the lead in trying to organize smaller island nations in the global warming debate. President Mohamed Nasheed initially supported the Copenhagen Accord and its 2-degree Celsius target for limiting global warming as a beginning. But before the deal was struck, he declared, "At 2 degrees, my country would not survive."[7]

Rising sea levels threaten every continent, including the Americas. Until recently, Kivalina Island, an eight-mile long barrier island in northern Alaska, had survived the punishing storms that blew in from the ocean because of ice that formed and piled up on the island.[8]

Inupiat hunters from the island's small village began noticing changes in the ice years ago, says the island's tribal administrator, Colleen Swan, but the change has accelerated in recent years. "In early September and October, the ice used to start forming, but now it doesn't form anymore until January and it's not building up," she says. "When that happened, we lost our barrier from fall sea storms, and our island just started falling apart. We started losing a lot of land beginning in 2004."

The U.S. Army Corps of Engineers is building a seawall to protect what's left of Kivalina, but Swan says it is expected to buy only 10 or 15 years. "People in the United States are still debating whether climate change is happening. The U.N. is focusing on the long-term problem of emissions," Swan says, "but we're in the 11th hour here. The bottom line is we need someplace to go."

— *Reed Karaim*

A house tumbles into the Chukchi Sea in Shishmaref, Alaska. Like other victims of climate change, residents may have to abandon the tiny community due to unprecedented erosion caused by intense storms.

AP Photo/Diana Haecker

official conference. It is available online at http://en.cop15.dk/blogs/view+blog?blogid=2929.

[2] "Monitoring disaster displacement in the context of climate change," the U.N. Office for the Coordination of Humanitarian Affairs and The Internal Displacement Monitoring Centre, September 2009, p. 12.

[3] Norman Myers, "Environmental Refugees, an Emergent Security Issue," presented at the 13th Economic Forum, Prague, May 2005.

[4] "GLOBAL: Nowhere to run from nature," IRIN, Nov. 9, 2009, www.irinnews.org/report.aspx?ReportId=78387.

[5] "AFRICA: Climate change could worsen displacement — UN," IRIN, Nov. 9, 2009, www.irinnews.org/report.aspx?ReportId=86716.

[6] Anthony Oliver-Smith, "Sea Level Rise and the Vulnerability of Coastal Peoples," U.N. University Institute for Environment and Human Security, 2009, p. 5, www.ehs.unu.edu/file.php?id=652.

[7] "Address by His Excellency Mohamed Nasheed, President of the Republic of Maldives, at the Climate Vulnerable Forum," Nov. 9, 2009, www.actforclimatejustice.org/2009/11/address-by-his-excellency-mohamed-nasheed-president-of-the-republic-of-maldives-at-the-climate-vulnerable-forum/.

[8] See John Schwartz, "Courts As Battlefields in Climate Fights," *The New York Times*, Jan. 26, 2010.

[1] Moses Mopel Kisosion spoke in a video blog from Kilmaforum09, the "people's forum" on climate change held in Copenhagen during the

---

Van der Leeuw, who worked for the European Union on climate change issues in the 1990s, is actually optimistic about the progress the world has made on climate change in the face of these challenges. "It's a very long process," he says, "but I'm encouraged by my students. It's wonderful to see how engaged they are, how open to thinking differently on these issues. I know we have very little time, but history is full of moments where we've reacted in the nick of time."

However, there are still those who doubt the basic science of climate change.

The Doubters

To enter the world of the climate change skeptics is to enter a mirror reflection of the scientific consensus on the issue. Everything is backwards: The Earth isn't warming; it may be cooling. If it is warming, it's part of the

CHRONOLOGY

1900-1950s *Early research indicates the Earth is warming.*

1938 British engineer Guy Stewart Callendar concludes that higher global temperatures and rising carbon dioxide levels are probably related.

1938 Soviet researchers confirm that the planet is warming.

1957 U.S. oceanographer Roger Revelle and Austrian physicist Hans Suess find that the oceans cannot absorb carbon dioxide as easily as thought, indicating that manmade emissions could create a "greenhouse effect," trapping heat in the atmosphere.

1958 U.S. scientist David Keeling begins monitoring atmospheric carbon dioxide levels, creating a groundbreaking record of their increase.

1960s *Climate science raises the possibility of global disaster.*

1966 U.S. geologist Cesare Emiliani says ice ages were created by tiny shifts in Earth's orbit, backing earlier theories that climate reacts to small changes.

1967 Leading nations launch 15-year program to study the world's weather.

1968 Studies show Antarctica's huge ice sheets could melt, raising sea levels.

1970s-1980s *Research into climate change intensifies, and calls for action mount.*

1975 A National Aeronautics and Space Administration (NASA) researcher warns that fluorocarbons in aerosol sprays could help create a greenhouse effect.

1979 The National Academy of Sciences finds that burning fossil fuels could raise global temperatures 6 degrees Fahrenheit in 50 years.

1981 U.S. scientists report a warming trend since 1880, evidence of a greenhouse effect.

1985 Scientists from 29 nations urge governments to plan for warmer globe.

1988 NASA scientist James Hansen says global warming has begun; he's 99 percent sure it's manmade.

1988 Thirty-five nations form a global panel to evaluate climate change and develop a response.

1990s *As the world responds to global warming, industry groups fight back.*

1990 The carbon industry-supported Global Climate Coalition forms to argue that climate change science is too uncertain to take action.

1995 The year is the hottest since the mid-19th century, when records began being kept.

1997 More than 150 nations agree on the Kyoto Protocol, a landmark accord to reduce greenhouse gases. The U.S. signs but never ratifies it.

2000s *The political battle over climate change action escalates worldwide.*

2000 Organization of Petroleum Exporting Countries (OPEC) demands compensation if global warming remedies reduce oil consumption.

2006 National Academy of Sciences reports the Earth's temperature is the highest in 12,000 years, since the last Ice Age.

2007 A U.N. report concludes that global warming is "unequivocal" and human actions are primarily responsible.

2009 The 194 nations attending the Copenhagen Climate Change Conference cannot agree on a broad treaty to battle global warming. After two weeks of contentious discussion, five nations create a nonbinding climate change accord, which 55 nations eventually sign, but which falls far short of delegates' hopes.

2010 The U.N effort to get a global, legally binding climate change treaty is scheduled to continue in November-December in Mexico City.

planet's natural, long-term climate cycles. Manmade carbon dioxide isn't the heart of the problem; it's a relatively insignificant greenhouse gas. But even if carbon dioxide is increasing, it's beneficial for the planet.

And that scientific consensus? It doesn't exist. "What I see are a relatively small number, perhaps a few hundred at most, of extremely well-funded, well-connected evangelistic scientists doing most of the lobbying on this issue," says Bob Carter, a geologist who is one of Australia's more outspoken climate change skeptics.

Many scientists who take funds from grant agencies to investigate global warming, he says, "don't speak out with their true views because if they did so, they would lose their funding and be intimidated."

It's impossible to know if people are keeping views to themselves, of course. But professional science has a method of inquiry — the scientific method — and a system of peer review intended to lead to knowledge that, as much as possible, is untainted by prejudice, false comparison or cherry-picked data. The process isn't always perfect, but it provides our best look at the physical world around us.

In December 2004, Naomi Oreske, a science historian at the University of California, San Diego, published an analysis in *Science* in which she reviewed 928 peer-reviewed climate studies published between 1993 and 2003. She did not find one that disagreed with the general consensus on climate change.[26]

The U.S. National Academy of Sciences, the Royal Society of London, the Royal Society of Canada, the American Meteorological Society, the American Association for the Advancement of Science and 2,500 scientists participating in the IPCC also have concluded the evidence that humans are changing the climate is compelling. "Politicians, economists, journalists and others may have the impression of confusion, disagreement or discord among climate scientists, but that impression is incorrect," Oreske wrote, after reviewing the literature.[27]

The debate over climate change science heated up last fall, when, shortly before the Copenhagen conference, hackers broke into the University of East Anglia's computer network and made public hundreds of e-mails from scientists at the school's climate research center — some prominent in IPCC research circles. Climate change skeptics were quick to point to the "Climategate" e-mails as evidence researchers had been squelching contrary opinions and massaging data to bolster their claims.

Reviews by *Time*, *The New York Times* and the Pew Center on Climate Change, however, found the e-mails did not provide evidence to alter the scientific consensus on climate change. "Although a small percentage of the e-mails are impolite and some express animosity toward opponents, when placed into proper context they do not appear to reveal fraud or other scientific misconduct," the Pew Center concluded.[28]

Some skeptics are scientists, but none are climate researchers. Perhaps the most respected scientific skeptic is Freeman Dyson, a legendary 86-year-old physicist and mathematician. Dyson does not dispute that atmospheric carbon-dioxide levels are rapidly rising and humans are to blame. He disagrees with those who project severe consequences. He believes rising CO_2 levels could have some benefits, and if not, humanity could bioengineer trees that consume larger amounts of carbon dioxide or find some other technological solution. He is sanguine about the ability of the Earth to adapt to change and is suspicious of the validity of computer models.

"The climate-studies people who work with models always tend to overestimate their models," Dyson has said. "They come to believe models are real and forget they are only models."[29]

Unlike Dyson, many climate change skeptics are connected to groups backed by the oil, gas and coal industries, which have worked since at least 1990 to discredit global warming theories. A 2007 study by the Union of Concerned Scientists found that between 1998 and 2005 ExxonMobil had funneled about $16 million to 43 groups that sought to manufacture uncertainty about global warming with the public.[30]

The tactics appear to be patterned after those used by the tobacco industry to discredit evidence of the hazards of smoking. According to the study, ExxonMobil and others have used ostensibly independent front groups for "information laundering," as they sought to sow doubts about the conclusions of mainstream climate science.

Several prominent climate change skeptics — including physicist S. Fred Singer and astrophysicists Willie Soon and Sallie Baliunas — have had their work published by these organizations, some of which seem to have no other purpose than to proliferate the information. "By publishing and re-publishing the non-peer-reviewed works of a small group of scientific spokespeople, ExxonMobil-funded organizations have propped up and amplified work that

Climate Scientists Thinking Outside the Box

"Geoengineering" proposes futuristic solutions that sound like science fiction.

Imagine: A massive squadron of aircraft spewing sulfur particles into the sky. An armada of oceangoing ships spraying sea mist into the air. A swarm of robotic mirrors a million miles out in space reflecting some of the sun's harmful rays away from the Earth. Thousands of giant, air-filtering towers girdling the globe.

The prospect of devastating global warming has led some scientists and policy analysts to consider the kind of planet-altering responses to climate change that were once the province of science fiction. The underlying concept, known as "geoengineering," holds that manmade changes in the climate can be offset by futuristic technological modifications.

That idea raises its own concerns, both about the possibility of unintended consequences and of technological dependence. But from an engineering perspective, analysts say the sulfur particle and sea vapor options — which would reflect sunlight away from the Earth, potentially cooling the planet — appear feasible and not even that expensive.

"Basically, any really rich guy on the planet could buy an ice age," says David Keith, a geoengineering expert at the University of Calgary, estimating that sulfur injection could cost as little as $1 billion or so a year. "Certainly, it's well within the capability of most nations."

"Technologically, it would be relatively easy to produce small particles in the atmosphere at the required rates," says Ken Caldiera, a climate scientist at the Carnegie Institution for Science's Department of Global Ecology in Stanford, Calif. "Every climate-model simulation performed so far indicates geoengineering would be able to diminish most climate change for most people most of the time."

To spread sulfur, planes, balloons or even missiles could be used.[1] For sea vapor, which would be effective at a lower altitude, special ships could vaporize seawater and shoot it skyward through a rotor system.[2]

A global program of launching reflective aerosols higher into the atmosphere would cost around $5 billion annually — still small change compared to the economic costs of significant global warming, says Caldiera. Other geoengineering options are considerably more expensive. The cost of launching the massive (60,000 miles by 4,500 miles) cloud of mirrors into space to block sunlight would cost about $5 trillion.[3] Building air-scrubbing towers would also be expensive and would require improved technology.[4]

---

has been discredited by reputable climate scientists," the study concludes.[31]

Is the world cooling? Is global warming a natural phenomenon? Is more CO_2 really good for the planet? Science and media watchdog groups have published detailed rebuttals to the claims of climate change skeptics.[32] To cite one example, assertions that the Earth is actually cooling often use 1998 as the base line — a year during the El Niño weather system, which typically produces warmer weather. The Associated Press gave temperature numbers to four statisticians without telling them what the numbers represented. The scientists found no true declines over the last 10 years. They also found a "distinct, decades-long" warming trend.[33]

James Hoggan, a Canadian public relations executive who founded DeSmogblog to take on the skeptics, feels climate scientists have done a poor job of responding to the skeptics, too often getting bogged down in the minutiae

of detail. "We need to start asking these so-called skeptics a number of basic questions," says Hoggan, the author of *Climate Cover-Up: The Crusade to Deny Global Warming.* "The first one is, 'Are you actually a climate scientist?' The second one is, 'Have you published peer-reviewed papers on whatever claims you're making?' And a third one is, 'Are you taking money directly or indirectly from industry?' "

Untangling the Threads

Since nations first began to seriously wrestle with climate change, most of the effort has gone into fashioning a legally binding international treaty to cut greenhouse gas emissions while helping poorer nations cope with the effects of global warming.

The approach has a powerful logic. Climate change is a worldwide problem and requires concerted action around the planet. Assisting those most likely to be affected — populations in Africa and Asia who are among the poorest

But cost is not what worries those studying geoengineering. "Everyone who's thinking about this has two concerns," says Thomas Homer-Dixon, a political scientist at Canada's Balsillie School of International Affairs in Waterloo, Ontario. "One is unintended consequences — because we don't understand climate systems perfectly — something bad could happen like damage to the ozone layer. The second is the moral-hazard problem: If we start to do this, are a lot of people going to think it means we can continue the carbon party?"

Keith thinks the consequences could be managed. "One of the advantages of using aerosols in the atmosphere is that you can modulate them," he says. "If you find it's not working, you can stop and turn the effect off." But he shares a concern with Caldiera and Homer-Dixon that geoengineering could be used as an excuse to avoid reducing carbon-dioxide emissions.

Geoengineering also raises geopolitical concerns, in part because it could be undertaken unilaterally. Unlike lowering greenhouse gas emissions, it doesn't require a global agreement, yet its effects would be felt around the planet — and not evenly.

That could aggravate international tensions: Any sustained bad weather in one nation could easily raise suspicion that it was the victim of climate modifications launched by another country. "If China, say, were to experience a deep drought after the deployment of a climate-intervention system," says Caldiera, "and people were starving as a result, this could cause them to lash out politically or even militarily at the country or countries that were engaged in the deployment."

Such scenarios, along with the fear of undercutting global negotiations to reduce emissions, make serious international consideration of geoengineering unlikely in the near term, says Homer-Dixon. But if the direst predictions about global warming prove accurate that could change. "You could see a political clamor worldwide to do something," he says.

Some scientists believe stepped-up geoengineering studies need to start soon. "We need a serious research program, and it needs to be international and transparent," says Keith. "It needs to start small. I don't think it needs to be a crash program, but I think there's an enormous value in doing the work. We've had enough hot air speculation. We need to do the work. If we find out it works pretty well, then we'll have a tool to help manage environmental risk."

— *Reed Karaim*

---

[1] Robert Kunzig, "A Sunshade for Planet Earth," *Scientific American*, November 2008.

[2] *Ibid.*

[3] *Ibid.*

[4] Seth Borenstein, "Wild ideas to combat global warming being seriously entertained," *The Seattle Times*, March 16, 2007, http://seattletimes.nwsource.com/html/nationworld/2003620631_warmtech16.html.

on the globe — is also a burden that is most equitably shared.

But the all-in-one-basket approach also comes with big problems. The first is the complexity of the negotiations themselves, which involve everything from intellectual-property rights to hundreds of billions of dollars in international finance to forest management. Global nations have been meeting on these issues for nearly two decades without a breakthrough deal.

Some observers believe the best chance for moving forward is untangling the threads of the problem. "We don't have to try to set the world to rights in one multilateral agreement," says East Anglia's Hulme. "It's not something we've ever achieved in human history, and I doubt we can. It seems more likely it's acting as an unrealistic, utopian distraction."

Analysts cite the 1987 Montreal Protocol, which phased out the use of chlorofluorocarbons that were damaging the ozone layer, as an example of a successful smaller-scale deal.

So far, the effort to control global warming has focused on limiting carbon-dioxide emissions from power plants and factories. But CO_2 accounts for only half of manmade greenhouse gas emissions.[34] The rest comes from a variety of sources, where they are often easier or cheaper to cut.

Black carbon, mainly produced by diesel engines and stoves that burn wood or cow dung, produces from one-eighth to a quarter of global warming.[35] Promoting cleaner engines and helping rural villagers move to cleaner-burning stoves would cut global warming gases, yet hardly requires the wrenching shift of moving from coal-fired electricity. Hydrofluorocarbons (HFCs) are more than a thousand times more potent as greenhouse gases than CO_2, but are used in comparably minuscule amounts and should be easier to limit.

Getty Images /Christopher Furlong

Ap Photo/John Stanmeyer

Hunger and Thirst

A young Turkana girl in drought-plagued northern Kenya digs for water in a dry river bed in November 2009 (top). Momina Mahammed's 8-month-old son Ali suffers from severe malnutrition in an Ethiopian refugee camp in December 2008 (bottom). Food and water shortages caused by climate changes are already affecting many countries in Africa. A sudanese delegate to the Copenhagen Climate Change Conference called the nonbinding accord reached at the convention "an incineration pact" for poor countries.

"Why are we putting all the greenhouse gases into one agreement? CO_2 is very different from black soot, or methane or HFCs," Hulme says. "Tropical forests, why do they have to be tied to the climate agenda? They sequester carbon, yes, but they're also valuable resources in other regards."

Those who support negotiating a sweeping climate change accord believe that untangling these threads could

weaken the whole cloth, robbing initiative from critical parts of the deal, such as assistance to developing countries. But Hulme believes the poorer parts of the world could benefit.

"We can tend to the adaptation needs of the developing world without having them hitched to the much greater complexity of moving the economy in the developed world away from fossil fuels," he says.

Other analysts, however, are unconvinced that climate change would be easier to deal with if its constituent issues were broken out. "There are entrenched interests on each thread," says Blackstock, at Austria's International Institute in Applied Systems Analysis. "That's the real problem at the end of the day."

CURRENT SITUATION

Next Steps

The whole world may be warming, but as has been said, all politics is local — even climate change politics. "It's still the legislatures of the nation states that will really determine the pace at which climate policies are driven through," notes the University of East Anglia's Hulme. "In the end, that's where these deals have to make sense."

Nations around the globe are determining their next steps in the wake of Copenhagen. Most greenhouse gases, however, come from a relative handful of countries. The United States and China, together, account for slightly more than 40 percent of the world's manmade CO_2 emissions.[36] If India and the European Union are added, the total tops 60 percent.[37] The post-Copenhagen climate change status is different for each of these major players.

China — China presents perhaps the most complex case of any of the countries central to climate change. It was classified as a developing country in the Kyoto Protocol, so it was not required to reduce carbon emissions.[38] But as the country's economy continued to skyrocket, China became the world's largest carbon dioxide emitter in 2006, passing the United States.[39] (*See graph, p. 417.*)

But with roughly 700 million poorer rural citizens, promoting economic growth remains the Chinese government's essential priority. Nevertheless, shortly before Copenhagen, China announced it would vow to cut CO_2 emissions by 40 to 45 percent *per unit of gross domestic product* below 2005 levels by 2020. The complicated formula meant that emissions would still rise, but at a slower rate. China subsequently committed to this reduction when confirming its Copenhagen pledge at the end of January.

U.N. climate policy chief de Boer hailed the move as a critical step. But the United States — especially skeptical members of the U.S. Congress — had hoped to see more movement from China and wanted verification standards.

Some participants say China's recalcitrance is why Copenhagen fell short. The British seemed particularly incensed. Ed Miliband, Great Britain's climate secretary, blamed the Chinese leadership for the failure to get agreement on a 50-percent reduction in global emissions by 2050 or on 80-percent reductions by developed countries. "Both were vetoed by China," he wrote, "despite the support of a coalition of developed and the vast majority of developing countries."[40]

But the Global Justice Ecology Project's Petermann places the blame elsewhere. "Why should China get involved in reducing emissions if the U.S. is unwilling to really reduce its emissions?" she asks.

Jiang Lin, director of the China Sustainable Energy Program, a nongovernmental agency with offices in Beijing and San Francisco, thinks China's leaders take the threat of climate change seriously. "There's probably a greater consensus on this issue in China than the United States," says Jiang. "The Chinese leadership are trained engineers. They understand the data."

Jiang points out that China already is seeing the effects predicted by climate change models, including the weakening of the monsoon in the nation's agricultural northwest and the melting of the Himalayan glaciers. "The Yellow River is drying up," he adds. "This is very symbolic for the Chinese. They consider this the mother river, and now almost half the year it is dry."

More Countries Agree to Emissions Cuts

The nonbinding climate agreement reached in Copenhagen, Denmark, on Dec. 18 was originally joined by 28 countries, which were to send the United Nations by the end of January their individual goals for reducing carbon emissions by 2020. But other nations also were invited to sign on by submitting their own plans to cut emissions. On Feb. 1, the U.N. reported that a total of 55 nations had submitted targets for cutting greenhouse gases. Analysts say while these countries produce 78 percent of manmade carbon emissions, more cuts are needed. The U.N. will try to use the accord as a starting point for a binding treaty at the next international climate conference in Mexico City, Nov. 29-Dec. 10.

Key provisions in the Copenhagen Accord:

- Cut global greenhouse gas emissions so global temperatures won't rise more than 2 degrees Celsius above the pre-Industrial Revolution level.
- Cooperate in achieving a peak in emissions as soon as possible.
- Provide adequate, predictable and sustainable funds and technology to developing countries to help them adapt to climate change.
- Prioritize reducing deforestation and forest degradation, which eliminate carbon-consuming trees.
- Provide $30 billion in new and additional resources from 2010 to 2012 to help developing countries mitigate climate change and protect forests; and provide $100 billion a year by 2020.
- Assess implementation of the accord by 2015.

Sources: "Copenhagen Accord," U.N. Framework Convention on Climate Change, Dec. 18, 2009; "UNFCCC Receives list of government climate pledges," press release, United Nations Framework Convention on Climate Change, Feb. 1, 2010, http://unfccc.int/files/press/news_room/press_releases_and_advisories/application/pdf/pr_accord_100201.pdf

The Copenhagen Accord is not legally binding, but Jiang believes the Chinese will honors its provisions. "When they announce they're committed to something, that's almost as significant as U.S. law," he says, "because if they don't meet that commitment, losing facing is huge for them."

While attention has focused on international negotiations, China is targeting improved energy efficiency and renewable power. In 2005, China's National People's Congress set a goal of generating 20 gigawatts of power through wind energy by 2020. The goal seemed highly ambitious, but China expected to meet it by the end of 2009 and is now aiming for 150 gigawatts by 2020. The target for solar energy has been increased more than 10-fold over the same period.[41]

Is the Copenhagen Accord a meaningful step forward in halting climate change?

YES
Ban Ki-moon
Secretary-General, United Nations

From opening remarks at press conference, U.N. Climate Change Conference, Copenhagen, Dec. 19, 2009

The Copenhagen Accord may not be everything that everyone hoped for. But this decision of the Conference of Parties is a new beginning, an essential beginning.

At the summit I convened in September, I laid out four benchmarks for success for this conference. We have achieved results on each.

- All countries have agreed to work toward a common, long-term goal to limit global temperature rise to below 2 degrees Celsius.
- Many governments have made important commitments to reduce or limit emissions.
- Countries have achieved significant progress on preserving forests.
- Countries have agreed to provide comprehensive support to the most vulnerable to cope with climate change.

The deal is backed by money and the means to deliver it. Up to $30 billion has been pledged for adaptation and mitigation. Countries have backed the goal of mobilizing $100 billion a year by 2020 for developing countries. We have convergence on transparency and an equitable global governance structure that addresses the needs of developing countries. The countries that stayed on the periphery of the Kyoto process are now at the heart of global climate action.

We have the foundation for the first truly global agreement that will limit and reduce greenhouse gas emission, support adaptation for the most vulnerable and launch a new era of green growth.

Going forward, we have three tasks. First, we need to turn this agreement into a legally binding treaty. I will work with world leaders over the coming months to make this happen. Second, we must launch the Copenhagen Green Climate Fund. The U.N. system will work to ensure that it can immediately start to deliver immediate results to people in need and jump-start clean energy growth in developing countries. Third, we need to pursue the road of higher ambition. We must turn our back on the path of least resistance.

Current mitigation commitments fail to meet the scientific bottom line.

We still face serious consequences. So, while I am satisfied that we have a deal here in Copenhagen, I am aware that it is just the beginning. It will take more than this to definitively tackle climate change.

But it is a step in the right direction.

NO
Nnimmo Bassey
Chair, Friends of the Earth International

Written for *CQ Researcher*, February 2010

The Copenhagen Accord is not a step forward in the battle to halt climate change. Few people expected the Copenhagen climate talks to yield a strong outcome. But the talks ended with a major failure that was worse than predicted: a "Copenhagen Accord" in which individual countries make no new serious commitments whatsoever.

The accord sets a too-weak goal of limiting warming to 2 degrees Celsius, but provides no means of achieving this goal. Likewise, it suggests an insufficient sum for addressing international solutions but contains no path to produce the funding. Individual countries are required to do nothing.

The accord fails the poor and the vulnerable communities most impacted by climate change. This non-agreement (it was merely "noted," not adopted, by the conference) is weak, nonbinding and allows false solutions such as carbon offsetting. It will prove completely ineffective. Providing some coins for developing countries to mitigate climate change and adapt to it does not help if the sources of the problem remain unchecked.

The peoples' demands for climate justice should be the starting point when addressing the climate crisis. Instead, in Copenhagen, voices of the people were shut out and peaceful protests met brutal suppression. Inside the Bella Center, where the conference took place, many of the poor countries were shut out of back-room negotiations. The accord is the result of this anti-democratic process.

The basic demands of the climate justice movement remain unmet. The U.N. climate process must resume, and it must accomplish these goals:

- Industrialized countries must commit to at least 40 percent cuts in emissions by 2020 by using clean energy, sustainable transport and farming and cutting energy demand.
- Emission cuts must be real. They cannot be "achieved" by carbon offsetting, such as buying carbon credits from developing countries or by buying up forests in developing countries so they won't be cut down.
- Rich countries must make concrete commitments to provide money for developing countries to grow in a clean way and to cope with the floods, droughts and famines caused by climate change. Funding must be adequate, not the minuscule amounts proposed in the accord.

Wealthy nations are most responsible for climate change. They have an obligation to lead the way in solving the problem. They have not done so with the Copenhagen Accord.

Coal still generates 80 percent of China's power, and the country continues to build coal-fired plants, but Chinese leaders clearly have their eyes on the green jobs that President Obama has promoted as key to America's future.[42] "Among the top 10 solar companies in the world, China already has three," says Jiang, "and China is now the largest wind market in the world. They see this as an industry in which China has a chance to be one of the leaders."

The United States — To much of the world, the refusal of the United States so far to embrace carbon emission limits is unconscionable. U.S. emissions are about twice Europe's levels per capita, and more than four times China's.

"The United States is the country that needs to lead on this issue," says Oxfam's Waskow. "It created a lot of problems that the U.S. wasn't able to come to Copenhagen with congressional legislation in hand."

In the Copenhagen Accord, President Obama committed the United States to reduce its carbon dioxide emissions to 17 percent below 2005 levels by 2020. That equates to about 4 percent below 1990 levels, far less stringent than the European and Japanese pledges of 20 percent and 25 percent below 1990 levels, respectively. However, Congress has not passed global warming legislation. Last year, the House of Representatives passed a bill that would establish a cap-and-trade system, which would limit greenhouse gases but let emitters trade emission allowances among themselves. The legislation faces stiff opposition in the Senate, however.

In 1997, after the Kyoto Protocol was adopted, the Senate voted 95-0 against signing any international accord unless it mandated GHG emission reductions by developing countries as well. Securing such commitments in Copenhagen — especially from China, along with improved verification — was considered critical to improving the chances a climate change bill would make it through the Senate.

Some analysts also blamed the lack of U.S. legislation for what was considered a relatively weak American proposal at Copenhagen. "Obama wasn't going to offer more than the U.S. Senate was willing to offer," says the International Institute for Applied System's Blackstock. "He could have done more and said, 'I cannot legally commit to this, but I'll go home and fight for it.' He didn't."

But Obama's negotiating effort in Copenhagen impressed some observers. "He could have stood back and worried about looking presidential," says the American Council on Renewable Energy's Eckhart. "He didn't. He rolled up his sleeves and got in there and tried to do good for the world."

Early reviews of the Copenhagen Accord were favorable among at least two key Republican senators, Lisa Murkowski of Alaska and Richard Lugar of Indiana. "Whenever you have developing countries, and certainly China and India stepping forward and indicating that they have a willingness to be a participant . . . I think that that is progress," said Murkowski.[43]

Still, analysts remain skeptical whether it will make a real difference on Capitol Hill. "I don't see Congress doing anything, even in line with the position in the Copenhagen Accord unless Obama makes it his 2010 priority," says 350.org's McKibben. "There's no question it's going to be hard because it's going to require real change."

The administration is planning to regulate some greenhouse gases through the Environmental Protection Agency (EPA). The Center for Biological Diversity has petitioned the EPA to make further use of regulation to reduce greenhouse emissions. "The president has the tools he needs. He has the Clean Air Act," says the center's Siegel. "All he has to do is use it."

However, some Senate Republicans are already calling for a resolution to undo the EPA's limited actions, and polls show a rising number of Americans skeptical about global warming, particularly Republicans.[44] Given the highly polarized nature of American politics, any significant move on climate change is likely to prove a bruising battle. President Obama has made promoting green energy jobs a priority, but with health care and joblessness still leading the administration's agenda, further action on climate change seems unlikely in the next year. Chances for major legislative action shrunk even further with the election of Republican Scott Brown, a climate change skeptic, to the Senate from Massachusetts. Brown's win ended the democrats' 60-vote, filibuster-proof majority.[45]

India — Although India's economy has grown almost as rapidly as China's in recent years, it remains a much poorer country. Moreover, its low coastline and dependence on seasonal monsoons for water also make it sensitive to the dangers of global warming. Jairam Ramesh, India's environment minister, said, "The most vulnerable country in the world to climate change is India."[46]

India's leaders announced recently they will pursue cleaner coal technology, higher emissions standards for automobiles and more energy-efficient building codes. Prior to Copenhagen, India also announced it would cut CO_2 emissions per unit of GDP from 2005 levels, but rejected legally binding targets.

After the negotiations on the accord, Ramesh told the *Hindustan Times* that India had "upheld the interest of developing nations."[47] But some analysts said India had largely followed China's lead, a position that could cost India some prestige with other developing nations, whose cause it had championed in the past.

"The worst thing India did was to align itself uncritically to China's yoke," says Indian political scientist Mehra, "because China acted purely in its own self interest."

The European Union — European leaders are calling for other countries to join them in backing the Copenhagen Accord, but they've hardly tried to hide their disappointment it wasn't more substantial. The European Union had staked out one of the stronger positions on emissions reductions beforehand, promising to cut emissions by 20 percent from 1990 levels to 2020, or 30 percent if other countries took similarly bold action. They also wanted rich nations to make 80 to 95 percent cuts in GHG emissions by 2050.[48]

Some national leaders also had expended political capital on global warming before the conference. French President Nicolas Sarkozy had announced a proposal to create a French "carbon tax" on businesses and households for use of oil, gas and coal. The proposal was blocked by the French Constitutional Council, but Sarkozy's party plans to reintroduce it this year.[49]

In the United Kingdom, Prime Minister Brown's government passed legislation committing to an 80 percent cut in U.K. greenhouse gas emissions by 2050.[50] Brown also pressed publicly for $100 billion a year in aid to the developing world to cope with climate change.

The European efforts were designed to lead by example. But analysts say the approach yielded little fruit in Copenhagen. "The European perspective that they could lead by example was the wrong strategy. This was a negotiation. Countries do not check their national interests at the door when they enter the U.N.," says the Chamber of Commerce's Eule, who worked on climate change in the Bush administration.

Although Europe's leaders finally backed the accord and formally pledged 20 percent emission reductions, they had only limited influence on the deal's final shape. "Europe finds itself now outside the driver's seat for how this is going to go forward," says Hulme at the University of East Anglia. "I think in Brussels [home of the E.U. headquarters], there must be a lot of conversations going on about where Europe goes from here." He believes Europe's stricter emissions regulations could now face a backlash.

Framework Conference chief de Boer, who is a citizen of the Netherlands, captured the resignation that seemed to envelope many European diplomats during his post-Copenhagen comments to the press. Before the climate conference kicked off, de Boer had predicted that Copenhagen would "launch action, action and more action" on climate change.

But in his December 19 press conference, when asked what he hoped could be accomplished in the year ahead, he responded, "Basically, the list I put under the Christmas tree two years ago, I can put under the Christmas tree again this year."

OUTLOOK

Too Late?

The world's long-term climate forecast can be summed up in a word: warmer. Even if the nations of the world were to miraculously agree tomorrow to reduce global greenhouse gas emissions, global warming could continue for some time because of the "lag" in how the climate system responds to GHG emission reductions.

In the last decade, researchers have poured a tremendous amount of effort into trying to foresee where climate change could take us. But the projections come with an element of uncertainty. Still, taken together, the most startling forecasts amount to an apocalyptic compendium of disaster. Climate change could:

- Lead to droughts, floods, heat waves and violent storms that displace tens of millions of people, particularly in Asia and sub-Saharan Africa (*see "Climate Refugees," p. 424*);
- Create a high risk of violent conflict in 46 countries, now home to 2.7 billion people, as the effects of

climate change exacerbate existing economic, social and political problems;[51]

- Cause the extinction of about a quarter of all land-based plant and animal species — more than a million — by 2050;[52]
- Effectively submerge some island nations by 2100,[53] and create widespread dislocation and damage to coastal areas, threatening more than $28 trillion worth of assets by 2050; and[54]
- Cause acidification of the oceans that renders them largely inhospitable to coral reefs by 2050, destroying a fragile underwater ecosystem important to the world's fisheries.[55]

If temperatures climb by an average of 3.5 to 4 degrees Celsius (6.3 to 7.2 Fahrenheit) by the end of the century, as some projections predict, it would mean "total devastation for man in parts of the world," says the Global Justice Ecology Project's Petermann. "You're talking about massive glaciers melting, the polar ice caps disappearing. It would make life on this planet completely unrecognizable."

But some analysts, while endorsing the potential dangers of climate change, still back away from the view that it's a catastrophe that trumps all others. "The prospective tipping points for the worst consequences are just that, prospective tipping points, and they're resting on the credibility of scientific models," says East Anglia University's Hulme. "We should take them seriously. But they're not the Nazis marching across Belgium. We need to weigh our response within the whole range of needs facing the human race."

The critical question likely to determine the shape of the planet's future for the rest of this century and beyond is when humans will stop pouring greenhouse gases into the atmosphere. If done soon enough, most scientists say, climate change will be serious but manageable on an international level, although billions of dollars will be needed to mitigate the effects in the most vulnerable parts of the globe.

But if emissions continue to rise, climate change could be far more catastrophic. "It is critically important that we bring about a commitment to reduce emissions effectively by 2020," said IPCC Chairman Rajendra Pachauri, shortly before Copenhagen.[56]

To accomplish Copenhagen's goal of holding warming to 2 degrees Celsius, Pachauri said emissions must peak

AFP/Getty Images STR

Getty Images/Robert Nickelsberg

Rapidly industrializing China has surpassed the United States as the world's largest emitter of carbon dioxide—one of the greenhouse gases (GHG) responsible for rising world temperatures. Although most GHGs are invisible, air pollution like this in Wuhan, China, on Dec.3, 2009 (above) often includes trapped greenhouse gases. The destruction of tropical rainforests decreases the number of trees available to absorb carbon dioxide. Palm oil trees once grew on this 250-acre plot being cleared for farming in Aceh, Indonesia (below).

by 2015. The agreement, however, sets no peaking year, and the emission-reduction pledges by individual nations fall short of that goal, according to recent analysis by Climate Interactive, a collaborative research effort sponsored by the Sustainability Institute in Hartland, Vt.[57]

World leaders acknowledge they need to do more, and some observers remain hopeful the upcoming climate conference in Mexico City could provide a breakthrough that will avert the worst, especially if pressure to act continues to grow at the grassroots level. "Right now there is a massive gulf between where the public is and where the political process is," says India's Mehra. "But I think [in 2010] you will see government positions mature. And I think you will see more politicians who have the conviction to act."

Canadian political scientist Homer-Dixon considers bold action unlikely, however, unless the world's major emitting nations, including the United States and China, start suffering clearly visible, serious climate-change consequences.

"In the absence of those really big shocks, I'm afraid we're probably achieving about as much as possible," he says. "Because of the lag in the system, if you wait until the evidence is clear, it's too late."

NOTES

1. Yvo de Boer, the United Nation's Framework Convention on Climate Change video message before the opening of the Cop15 conference, Dec. 1, 2009, www.youtube.com/climateconference#p/u/11/xUTXsdkinq0.

2. The complete text of the accord is at http://unfccc.int/resource/docs/2009/cop15/eng/l07.pdf.

3. John Vidal and Jonathan Watts, "Copenhagen closes with weak deal that poor threaten to reject," *The Guardian*, Dec. 19, 2009, www.guardian.co.uk/environment/2009/dec/19/copenhagen-closes-weak-deal.

4. *Ibid.*

5. "Remarks by the President," The White House Office of the Press Secretary, Dec. 18, 2009, www.whitehouse.gov/the-press-office/remarks-president-during-press-availability-copenhagen.

6. http://action.sierraclub.org/site/MessageViewer?em_id=150181.0.

7. See Jones' complete comments at http://wdm.gn.apc.org/copenhagen-'deal'-'shameful-and-monumental-failure'.

8. Jerry Melillo, Karl Thomas and Thomas Peterson, editors-in-chief, "Global Climate Change Impacts in the United States," U.S. Global Change Research Program, executive summary, June 16, 2009, www.education-research-services.org/files/USGCRP_Impacts_US_executive-summary.pdf.

9. Intergovernmental Panel on Climate Change staff, "Climate Change 2007: Synthesis Report," The U.N. Intergovernmental Panel on Climate Change, Nov. 17 2007, www.ipcc.ch/pdf/assessment-report/ar4/syr/ar4_syr_spm.pdf.

10. "Climate Change responsible for 300,000 deaths a year," Global Humanitarian Forum, http://ghfgeneva.org/NewsViewer/tabid/383/vw/1/ItemID/6/Default.aspx.

11. Andrew C. Revkin and James Kanter, "No Slowdown of Global Warming, Agency Says," *The New York Times*, Dec. 8, 2009, www.nytimes.com/2009/12/09/science/earth/09climate.html.

12. "Key Scientific Developments Since the IPCC Fourth Assessment Report," in Key Scientific Developments Since the IPCC Fourth Assessment Report, Pew Center on Global Climate Change, June 2009.

13. "Final Copenhagen Accord Press Release," The Sustainability Institute, Dec. 19, 2009, http://climateinteractive.org/scoreboard/copenhagen-cop15-analysis-and-press-releases.

14. "Remarks by the President," *op. cit.*

15. "Copenhagen Accord," draft proposal, United Nations Framework Convention on Climate Change, Dec. 18, 2009, p. 3. http://unfccc.int/resource/docs/2009/cop15/eng/l07.pdf.

16. Kumi Naidoo, speaking at Copenhagen in a video blog posted by Greenpeace Australia, www.facebook.com/video/video.php?v=210068211237.

17. Ban Ki-moon, remarks to the General U.N. Assembly, Dec. 21, 2009, www.un.org/News/Press/docs/2009/sgsm12684.doc.htm.

18. Jennifer Weeks, "Carbon Trading, Will it Reduce Global Warming," *CQ Global Researcher*, November 2008.

19. Robert Shapiro, "Addressing the Risks of Climate Change: The Environmental Effectiveness and Economic Efficiency of Emissions Caps and Tradable Permits, Compared to Carbon Taxes," February 2007, p. 26, http://67.23.32.13/system/files/carbon-tax-cap.pdf.

20. Nicolas Loris and Ben Lieberman, "Capping Carbon Emissions Is Bad, No Matter How You Slice the Revenue," Heritage Foundation, May 14, 2009, www.heritage.org/Research/EnergyandEnvironment/wm2443.cfm.

21. Monica Prasad, "On Carbon, Tax and Don't Spend," *The New York Times*, March 25, 2008, www.nytimes.com/2008/03/25/opinion/25prasad.html.

22. "Cantwell, Collins Introduce 'Cap and Rebate' Bill," Clean Skies, Energy and Environment Network, Dec. 11, 2009, www.cleanskies.com/articles/cantwell-collins-introduce-cap-and-rebate-bill.

23. Robert J. Shapiro, "Carbon Tax More Likely," *National Journal* expert blog, Energy and the Environment, Jan. 4, 2010, http://energy.nationaljournal.com/2010/01/whats-next-in-the-senate.php-1403156.

24. A concise history of Keeling and his work is at "The Keeling Curve Turns 50," Scripps Institution of Oceanography, http://sio.ucsd.edu/special/Keeling_50th_Anniversary/.

25. Elizabeth Kolbert, *Field Notes from a Catastrophe: Man, Nature, and Climate Change* (2006), p. 2.

26. Naomi Oreskes, "Beyond the Ivory Tower: The Scientific Consensus on Climate Change," *Science*, Dec. 3, 2004, www.sciencemag.org/cgi/content/full/306/5702/1686.

27. *Ibid.*

28. "Analysis of the Emails from the University of East Anglia's Climatic Research Unit," Pew Center on Global Climate Change, December 2009, www.pewclimate.org/science/university-east-anglia-cru-hacked-emails-analysis.

29. Quoted by Nicholas Dawidoff, "The Civil Heretic," *The New York Times Magazine*, March 23, 2009, p. 2, www.nytimes.com/2009/03/29/magazine/29Dyson-t.html?pagewanted=1&_r=1.

30. "Smoke, Mirrors & Hot Air: How ExxonMobil Uses Big Tobacco's Tactics to Manufacture Uncertainty on Climate Science," Union of Concerned Scientists, January 2007, p. 1, www.ucsusa.org/assets/documents/global_warming/exxon_report.pdf.

31. *Ibid.*

32. Many are summarized in a policy brief by the non-profit Pew Center on Global Climate Change, "Realities vs. Misconceptions about the Science of Climate Change," August 2009, www.pewclimate.org/science-impacts/realities-vs-misconceptions.

33. Seth Borenstein, "AP IMPACT: Statisticians Reject Global Cooling," The Associated Press, Oct. 26, 2009, http://abcnews.go.com/Technology/wireStory?id=8917909.

34. Unpacking the problem," *The Economist*, Dec. 5-11, 2009, p. 21, www.economist.com/specialreports/displaystory.cfm?story_id=14994848.

35. *Ibid.*

36. It is important to note that if CO_2 emissions are calculated on a per capita basis, China still ranks far below most developed nations. The highest emitter on a per capita basis is Australia, according to the U.S. Energy Information Agency, with the United States second. See www.ucsusa.org/global_warming/science_and_impacts/science/each-countrys-share-of-co2.html.

37. A chart of the top 20 CO_2 emitting countries is at www.ucsusa.org/global_warming/science_and_impacts/science/graph-showing-each-countrys.html.

38. "China ratifies global warming treaty" CNN.com, Sept. 4, 2002, http://archives.cnn.com/2002/WORLD/africa/09/03/kyoto.china.glb/index.html.

39. "China overtakes U.S. in greenhouse gas emissions," *The New York Times*, June 20, 2007, www.nytimes.com/2007/06/20/business/worldbusiness/20iht-emit.1.6227564.html.

40. Ed Miliband, "The Road from Copenhagen," *The Guardian*, Dec. 20, 2009, www.guardian.co.uk/commentisfree/2009/dec/20/copenhagen-climate-change-accord.

41. "A Long Game," *The Economist*, Dec. 5-11, 2009, p. 18.

42. *Ibid.* Keith Bradsher, "China Leading Global Race to Make Clean Energy" *The New York Times*, Jan. 31, 2010, p. A1.

43. Darren Samuelsohn, "Obama Negotiates 'Copenhagen Accord' With Senate Climate Fight in Mind," *The New York Times*, Dec. 21, 2009, www.nytimes.com/cwire/2009/12/21/21climatewire-obama-negotiates-copenhagen-accord-with-senat-6121.html.

44. Juliet Elperin, "Fewer Americans Believe in Global Warming, Poll Shows," *The Washington Post*, Nov.

25, 2009, www.washingtonpost.com/wp-dyn/content/article/2009/11/24/AR2009112402989.html.

45. Suzanne Goldenberg, "Fate of US climate change bill in doubt after Scott Brown's Senate win," *The Guardian*, Jan. 20, 2010, www.guardian.co.uk/environment/2010/jan/20/scott-brown-climate-change-bill.

46. "India promises to slow carbon emissions rise," BBC News, Dec. 3, 2009, http://news.bbc.co.uk/2/hi/8393538.stm.

47. Rie Jerichow, "World Leaders Welcome the Copenhagen Accord," Denmark.dk, Dec. 21, 2009, www.denmark.dk/en/menu/Climate-Energy/COP15-Copenhagen-2009/Selected-COP15-news/World-leaders-welcome-the-Copenhagen-Accord.htm.

48. "Where countries stand on Copenhagen," BBC News, undated, http://news.bbc.co.uk/2/hi/science/nature/8345343.stm.

49. James Kantor, "Council in France Blocks Carbon Tax as Weak on Polluters," *The New York Times*, Dec. 31, 2009, www.nytimes.com/2009/12/31/business/energy-environment/31carbon.html.

50. Andrew Neather, "Climate Change could still be Gordon Brown's great legacy," *The London Evening Standard*, Dec. 15, 2009, www.thisislondon.co.uk/standard/article-23783937-climate-change-could-still-be-gordon-browns-great-legacy.do.

51. Dan Smith and Janini Vivekananda, "A Climate of Conflict, the links between climate change, peace and war," *International Alert*, November 2007, www.international-alert.org/pdf/A_Climate_Of_Conflict.pdf.

52. Alex Kirby, "Climate Risk to a Million Species," BBC Online, Jan. 7, 2004, http://news.bbc.co.uk/2/hi/science/nature/3375447.stm.

53. Adam Hadhazy, "The Maldives, threatened by drowning due to climate change, set to go carbon-neutral," *Scientific American*, March 16, 2009, www.scientificamerican.com/blog/post.cfm?id=maldives-drowning-carbon-neutral-by-2009-03-16.

54. Peter Wilkinson, "Sea level rise could cost port cities $28 trillion," CNN, Nov. 23, 2009, www.cnn.com/2009/TECH/science/11/23/climate.report.wwf.allianz/index.html.

55. "Key Scientific Developments Since the IPCC Fourth Assessment Report," *op. cit.*

56. Richard Ingham, "Carbon emissions must peak by 2015: U.N. climate scientist," Agence France-Presse, Oct. 15, 2009, www.google.com/hostednews/afp/article/ALeqM5izYrubhpeFvOKCRrZmWSYWCkPoRg.

57. "Final Copenhagen Accord Press Release," *op. cit.*

BIBLIOGRAPHY

Books

Hoggan, James, *Climate Cover-Up: The Crusade to Deny Global Warming*, Greystone Books, 2009.
A Canadian public relations executive who founded the anti-climate-skeptic Web site DeSmogblog takes on what he considers the oil and gas industry's organized campaign to spread disinformation and confuse the public about the science of climate change.

Hulme, Mike, *Why We Disagree About Climate Change: Understanding Controversy, Inaction and Opportunity*, Cambridge University Press, 2009.
A professor of climate change at East Anglia University in Great Britain looks at the cultural, political and scientific forces that come into play when we consider climate and what that interaction means for dealing with climate change today.

Kolbert, Elizabeth, *Field Notes from a Catastrophe: Man, Nature and Climate Change*, Bloomsbury, 2006.
A *New Yorker* writer summarizes the scientific evidence on behalf of climate change and looks at the consequences for some of the world's most vulnerable locations.

Michaels, Patrick J., and Robert C. Balling, *Climate of Extremes: Global Warming Science They Don't Want You to Know*, The Cato Institute, 2009.
Writing for a libertarian U.S. think tank, the authors argue that while global warming is real, its effects have been overstated and do not represent a crisis.

Articles

"Stopping Climate Change, A 14-Page Special Report," *The Economist*, Dec. 5, 2009.
The authors provide a comprehensive review of the state of global climate change efforts, including environmental, economic and political conditions.

Broder, John and Andrew Revkin, "A Grudging Accord in Climate Talks," *The New York Times*, Dec. 19, 2009.
The Times assesses the Copenhagen Accord and reports on the final hours of the climate change convention.

Kunzig, Robert, "A Sunshade for Planet Earth," *Scientific American*, November 2008.
An award-winning scientific journalist examines the various geoengineering options that might reduce global warming, their costs and possible consequences.

Schwartz, John, "Courts as Battlefields in Climate Fights," *The New York Times*, Jan. 26, 2009.
A reporter looks at environmental groups' and other plaintiffs' efforts to hold corporations that produce greenhouse gases legally liable for the effects of climate change on vulnerable areas, including Kivalina Island off the coast of Alaska.

Walsh, Bryan, "Lessons from the Copenhagen Climate Talks," *Time*, Dec. 21, 2009.
Time's environmental columnist provides predictions about the future of the climate change battle, based on the final Copenhagen Accord.

Walsh, Bryan, "The Stolen Emails: Has 'Climategate' been Overblown," *Time Magazine online*, Dec. 7, 2007.
The stolen East Anglia University e-mails, the author concludes, "while unseemly, do little to change the overwhelming scientific consensus on the reality of man-made climate change."

Reports and Studies

"Climate Change 101: Understanding and Responding to Global Climate Change," Pew Center on Global Climate Change, January 2009.
This series of reports aims to provide an introduction to climate change science and politics for the layman.

"World Development Report 2010: World Development and Climate Change," World Bank, November 2009, http://econ.worldbank.org/WBSITE/EXTERNAL/EXTDEC/EXTRESEARCH/EXTWDRS/EXTWDR2010/0,,contentMDK:21969137~menuPK:5287816~pagePK:64167689~piPK:64167673~theSitePK:5287741,00.html.
This exhaustive, 300-page study examines the consequences of climate change for the developing world and the need for developed nations to provide financial assistance to avert disaster.

Bernstein, Lenny, *et al.*, "Climate Change 2007: Synthesis Report," The Intergovernmental Panel of Climate Change, 2007, www.ipcc.ch/pdf/assessment-report/ar4/syr/ar4_syr_spm.pdf.
The international body tasked with assessing the risk of climate change caused by human activity gathered scientific research from around the world in this widely quoted report to conclude, "warming of the climate system is unequivocal."

Thomas, Karl, Jerry Melillo and Thomas Peterson, eds., "Global Climate Change Impacts in the United States," United States Global Change Research Program, June 2009, www.globalchange.gov/publications/reports/scientific-assessments/us-impacts.
U.S. government researchers across a wide range of federal agencies study how climate change is already affecting the United States.

For More Information

Cato Institute, 1000 Massachusetts Avenue, N.W., Washington D.C. 20001; (202) 842-0200; www.cato.org/global-warming. A conservative U.S. think tank that maintains an extensive database of articles and papers challenging the scientific and political consensus on climate change.

Climate Justice Now; www.climate-justice-now.org. A network of organizations and movements from around the world committed to involving people in the fight against climate change and for social and economic justice at the grassroots level.

Climate Research Unit, University of East Anglia, Norwich, NR4 7TJ, United Kingdom; 44-1603-592722; www.cru.uea.ac.uk. Recently in the news when its e-mail accounts were hacked; dedicated to the study of natural and manmade climate change.

Greenpeace International, Ottho Heldringstraat 5, 1066 AZ Amsterdam, The Netherlands; 31 (0) 20 718200; www. greenpeace.org/international. Has made climate change one of its global priorities; has offices around the world.

Intergovernmental Panel on Climate Change, c/o World Meteorological Organization, 7bis Avenue de la Paix, C.P. 2300 CH- 1211, Geneva 2, Switzerland; 41-22-730-8208; www.ipcc.ch. U.N. body made up of 2,500 global scientists; publishes periodic reports on various facets of climate change, including a synthesis report summarizing latest findings around the globe.

Pew Center on Global Climate Change, 2101 Wilson Blvd., Suite 550, Arlington, VA, 22201; (703) 516-4146; www.pewclimate.org. Nonprofit, nonpartisan organization established in 1998 to promote research, provide education and encourage innovative solutions to climate change.

United Nations Framework Convention on Climate Change, Haus Carstanjen, Martin-Luther-King-Strasse 8 53175 Bonn, Germany; +49-228-815-1000; http://unfccc.int/2860.php. An international treaty that governs climate change negotiations.